M. TVLLI CICERONIS
DE FINIBVS BONORVM
ET MALORVM
LIBRI I, II

CAMBRIDGE
UNIVERSITY PRESS

LONDON: Fetter Lane

NEW YORK
The Macmillan Co.

BOMBAY, CALCUTTA and
MADRAS
Macmillan and Co., Ltd.

TORONTO
The Macmillan Co. of
Canada, Ltd.

TOKYO
Maruzen-Kabushiki-Kaisha

M. TVLLI CICERONIS
DE FINIBVS BONORVM
ET MALORVM
LIBRI I, II

EDITED BY

J. S. REID, Litt.D.

FELLOW OF GONVILLE AND CAIUS COLLEGE
AND FORMERLY PROFESSOR OF ANCIENT
HISTORY IN THE UNIVERSITY
OF CAMBRIDGE

CAMBRIDGE
AT THE UNIVERSITY PRESS
1925

PRINTED IN GREAT BRITAIN

PREFACE

WHEN many treasures of Latin literature were re-discovered at the opening of the Renaissance period, no Latin writer aroused so much interest and enthusiasm as Cicero. Before the end of the fifteenth century many editions of his works had appeared. The labours of the great early scholars bore more fruit for the study of Greek than of Latin literature[1]. Increased attention to Latin, and especially to the Latin of Cicero, was promoted by Erasmus. An important date in the history of Latin scholarship is 1566, when the complete edition of Cicero's works by Lambinus was published. Lambinus had perhaps a more intimate knowledge of Latin usage than any scholar who lived before Madvig. In the *Onomasticon Tullianum*, published by Orelli and Baiter in 1836, is reprinted a life of Lambinus by P. Lazzeri (a learned Jesuit who was Professor of Ecclesiastical History in Rome and was protected in that post by Cardinal Zelada when the Jesuit Order was dissolved, but resigned his Chair and accepted the post of Librarian to the Cardinal, his protector), in which are reproduced many statements of Lambinus himself concerning his own life and works. He died in 1572 at the age of 52. His death is stated to have been due to terror inspired by the massacre of St Bartholomew's day. His friend, Petrus Ramus, who was his colleague as Professor in the Collège de France, was one of the victims. Ramus had been persecuted during the preceding years for his conversion to Protestantism. Lambinus feared to share his fate, and the horror inspired by the massacre is said to have been the cause of his death.

By far the greatest exponent of Ciceronian Latinity who has appeared since the time of Lambinus is J. N. Madvig, whose *magnum opus* was his edition of the *De Finibus*. An admirable account of his life and work is given by Sir John Sandys, in his *History of Scholarship*, III, 319–323. To appreciate fully the services which Madvig rendered to Latin studies, it is necessary to understand the low estate of those studies when he began his career. Readers of his commentary on the *De Finibus* are sometimes repelled by his continual denunciations of "Goerenzius"

---

[1] See a quotation from Erasmus in Sandys' *History of Scholarship*, vol. II, p. 125.

or "Gzius," who intrudes as perpetually as King Charles' head intruded on everything that Mr Dick tried to write. This Goerenz was reputed in Germany to be the best Latin scholar of his day. He was born in 1767 at Fürstenwalde in Saxony. He studied at Meissen and at the University of Halle, in which University he was made (1792) "Adjunct" Professor. Later (1795), he was placed at the head of the Gymnasium at Plauen, the capital of the Vogtland. A little later (1800) he was made rector of the Lyceum at Zwickau, a town about 80 miles from Dresden, in the great manufacturing region of which Chemnitz is the chief place, and was called in 1817 to Schwerin as Director of the Gymnasium (afterwards styled Fredericianum) where he died in 1836, having retired in 1833 owing to ill-health. There is some evidence to show that Goerenz was really successful as a school-master. Success in teaching has often been obtained on a small modicum of scholarship, and has frequently led to an excessive estimate of the schoolmaster's learning. Herein seems to lie the secret of the reputation which Goerenz enjoyed. An article on him written by a good scholar, F. W. Döring, praises Goerenz as possessing all the highest qualities of the man of learning.

The Manuscripts on which the text of Madvig rests were all carefully described by him in his preface. He benefited much by the labours of Orelli and Baiter. A fresh and independent examination of the text was given in the Teubner edition of Cicero's works, by C. F. W. Müller. Where the two texts of Madvig (in the latest edition) and Müller agree, I have accepted their readings excepting in a few passages, which are indicated in my critical notes. Comments which I wished to make on the text have generally been incorporated with the explanatory notes, a convenient plan since general Latin usage or Ciceronian Latin usage in very many cases must be the ground of decision between various readings. Müller has accepted the views of Madvig as to the relative value of the principal sources for the text. The two "Palatine" MSS. (A and B) are of the first importance. There are corrections in A by a second hand. The effect of A^2 is usually to bring the reading nearer to that of B, but the corrections were not derived from B. A is defective, ending at the 16th section of the fourth book. The third fundamental MS. is one in the library at Erlangen (E) which is usually in close agreement with

B, and on the whole the agreement of ABE is very marked. BE are less trustworthy than A where the order of the words is concerned, and in orthography B is inferior to A; thus *his* is without exception in B written as *hys*, an indication that in the MS. from which B was copied, *hiis*, derived from *iis*, was written for *his*.

Madvig demonstrated that all known MSS. of the *De Finibus* descend from an original which was far enough removed from the age of Cicero to have become already corrupt in many places. The derivation of existing MSS. from this *archetypus* is not in one and the same line of descent.

Among MSS. other than ABE, a certain Paris MS. (n. 6331) receives some attention from Madvig. The collation of this *codex* made by Nigoles, and published in the *Revue de Philologie* for 1880, is more accurate than those previously made, and where I have had occasion to refer to P, I have followed Nigoles.

On the general character of the philosophical writings of Cicero I have written at length in the Introduction to my edition of the *Academica*, to which I will only refer, so far as this topic is concerned. The references in Cicero's letters to the writing of the *De Finibus* are also discussed in that Introduction (pp. 30, 31). I have only to add one or two remarks. The question raised about Tubulus and Scaevola in *Att.* 12, 5, 3 (written on June 11 or 12 in the year 45) has some connexion with the *De Finibus*, 2, 54.

As to the Greek sources of Books I and II there has been much debate. The most natural suggestion is the one that has been most frequently made, viz. that Cicero used a work of Antiochus of Ascalon; for whom see the passages in my edition of the *Academica* which are indicated in the Index, s. v. Antiochus. I must protest against the assumption, which has been often made, that Cicero had no first-hand knowledge of the writings of Epicurus. The hypothesis that he resorted to some Greek to give him an epitome of the Epicurean philosophy for the purposes of the *De Finibus* is in no way demonstrable, nor is it even probable. A judgment on this issue must depend mainly on a comparison of Cicero's statements with those in other ancient sources referring to the same topics, and this I have endeavoured to make in the course of my commentary. Usener in the Preface, pp. lxv *sq.*, of his great work entitled *Epicurea* (Leipzig, 1887), passes a severe judgment on Cicero's use of his Greek

originals, with the exception of those belonging to the Academic School. Of this side of Cicero's philosophical writing he writes thus: "Longe alium sibique parem Tullium in eis librorum partibus observes, ubi Academici personam induit. hic eleganter acuteque disertum, hic facetum, hic scriptorem videas scribendo delectatum sibique merito placentem. hic denique eruditio quoque emicat non volgaris."

I must defend Cicero from one attack made upon him by one of the greatest scholars of our time, whom I admire with all the world. In the Introduction to his great and most important work entitled *Doxographi Graeci*, Diels repeatedly charges Cicero with tampering with his Greek originals. But his allegations concern only some passages in which enumerations of philosophers are given with very brief references to their doctrine. The assumption of Diels that the existing catalogues found in the *Doxographi* were the only ones from which Cicero might have drawn his information seems to me to be neither provable nor probable. In *Quellenforschung*, both historical and philosophical, it has been a common error to underestimate grossly the compass of the ancient literature which has disappeared. Certain severe strictures by Diels on the Latin expressions chosen by Cicero to represent the Greek are somewhat discounted by infelicities in the Latin written by the critic himself, who presents his readers with such things as "ambaginibus" and "praestavisse."

J. S. REID.

CAMBRIDGE
18 *August*, 1923

I wish to express my sincere thanks to my friend, Dr Louis C. Purser, for the assistance he has kindly given in seeing the MS. of my edition of Cicero's *De Finibus* through the press, ill-health having prevented my doing so myself. My long association with Dr Purser in the furtherance of Ciceronian study has been a most valued experience of my life, and I feel much indebted to him for all the time and trouble which he has bestowed on the work.

I would also like to thank Mr A. D. Nock of Clare College, my friend and former pupil, for valuable help.

J. S. R.

CAMBRIDGE 1925

M. TVLLI CICERONIS
DE FINIBVS BONORVM ET MALORVM

LIBER PRIMVS

I. Non eram nescius, Brute, cum, quae summis ingeniis ex- **1**
quisitaque doctrina philosophi Graeco sermone tractavissent, ea
Latinis litteris mandaremus, fore ut hic noster labor in varias
reprehensiones incurreret. Nam quibusdam, et eis quidem non
5 admodum indoctis, totum hoc displicet philosophari. Quidam
autem non tam id reprehendunt, si remissius agatur, sed tantum

4 eis quidem: *his quidem* A; *hys q.* B ut semper; 'ne semel quidem iis' Baiter.
6 tam: *tantum* scriptum est ante Orellium.

§§ 1–12. Cic. defends his work against four classes of objectors: (1) those who hate philosophy altogether; (2) those who tolerate it only if it be carried on in a lax fashion; (3) those who prefer to read Greek literature on the subject; (4) those who prefer that Cicero should employ his pen on other themes. Similar apologies are prefixed to the *Lucullus* and the *De Natura Deorum*. Also Orator, § 140 and Acad. i, 11; see Introd. to Academica, p. 23.

1. **eram...mandaremus**: this change from sing. to plur. is not very uncommon in Cic.; so Cato m. § 5: sapientiam meam...in hoc sumus sapientes. In his n. on that passage, Allen quotes a good many parallels. The subj. *mandaremus* is Hale's 'qualitative' time-clause, as opposed to 'determinative'; i.e. it describes the *kind* of time, not merely the *point* of time. The second subjunctive, *tractavissent*, merely follows the first.

nescius: see n. on 5, 51.

summis ing.: not dependent on *tractavissent*, but qualitative.

3. **fore ut**: Cic. avoids *futurum ut* (Caec. 4 is not an ex.).

hic noster labor: De opt. d. g. 18 huic labori duo genera reprehensionum opponuntur; ib. 15 hic labor meus.

5. **totum hoc...philosophari**: so De Or. 2, 39: hoc totum diserte dicere; 2, 218: totum hoc risum movere; Tusc. 5, 33: totum hoc beate vivere; for other

exx. of infin. used as substantive see below, 2 §§ 9, 18, 19, 43, 86; 3 § 44, and Wölfflin, Archiv 3, 70 sq.

6. **non tam**: Madv. contends that *non tam* and *non ita* do not in Cic. or the older writers take on them the force of *non admodum*, but that there is always a comparison either expressed or clearly implied, excepting where *non ita* (not *non tam*) goes with an adjective or an adverb. He however (ed. 3, p. lxviii) says that in Qu. Fr. 1, 1, 16 neque tam fideles sunt, the comparison is hardly apparent. The same may be said of Scaur. 33: neque vero tam haec ipsa cotidiana res Appium Claudium illa humanitate et sapientia praeditum per se ipsa movisset, nisi hunc C. Claudi, fratris sui competitorem fore putasset. Madv., rejecting several explanations of implied comparison (with Otto) supposes anacoluthon; Cic. should have said 'non tam id (ipsam rem) reprehendunt quam nimis magnum studium,' but, changing the construction, he substituted *sed tantum* etc. for the second limb of the comparison. In Virg. Ecl. 5, 83, we have tantum...tam with verb (but there is distinct ellipse). In illustration Madvig gives Brut. 58: quae (suaviloquentia) nunc quidem non tam est in plerisque; latrant enim iam quidam oratores, non locuntur; sed est ea laus eloquentiae certe maxima ('significat non tam esse suaviloquentiam nunc in oratoribus, quam ipsam laudandam et requirendam

studium tamque multam operam ponendam in eo non arbitrantur. Erunt etiam, et hi quidem eruditi Graecis litteris, contemnentes Latinas, qui se dicant in Graecis legendis operam malle consumere. Postremo aliquos futuros suspicor qui me ad alias litteras vocent, genus hoc scribendi, etsi sit elegans, per- 5
2 sonae tamen et dignitatis esse negent. Contra quos omnis dicendum breviter existimo; quamquam philosophiae quidem vituperatoribus satis responsum est eo libro quo a nobis philosophia defensa et collaudata est, cum esset accusata et vituperata ab Hortensio. Qui liber cum et tibi probatus videretur et eis 10 quos ego posse iudicare arbitrarer, plura suscepi, veritus ne movere hominum studia viderer, retinere non posse. Qui autem, si maxime hoc placeat, moderatius tamen id volunt fieri, difficilem

---

3 contemnentes Latinas: glossema suspicor esse.   9 collaudata: *collata* P.

esse'); also § 10 below (which see); and (in ed. 3) Leg. 1, 40 (already qu. by Boeckel), non tam iudiciis...sed; add Just. 11,7,4 qu. by Allen. [The use of *tam* with verbs is not so very common, so Tac. restricts admodum to adj. and part.; there is no ex. in Caesar.] The objection brought by Madv. against the order of the words given by the inferior mss. (*non id tam*) is hardly sound. Cic. loves to interpose a monosyllable between two words closely connected by grammar.

  1. **tamque multam:** usage did not allow *tantam operam*, but Cic. might have said *tantum operae.*

  1, 2. **non arbitrantur:** the negative coalesces very closely with the verb, as in *non censere*; see Allen's note.

  erunt etiam, etc.: this view must be restricted to philosophic writing, and it is put into Varro's mouth by Cic. himself in Acad. 1, 4; cf. ib. §§ 8, 10.

  3. **contemnentes Latinas:** i.e. such Latin philosophical literature as existed before Cicero's time; see Acad. 1, 5.

  5. **litteras:** 'writings'; see n. on § 12.

  genus hoc: Hor. s. 1, 4, 24 quod sunt quos genus hoc minime iuvat, utpote plures | culpari dignos.

  6. **dignitatis:** cf. § 11 and Acad. 1, 11, where a direct answer is given to these critics.

  7. **philosophiae vituperatoribus:** i.e. those who totally reject it; cf. Tusc. 2, 4.

  8. **eo libro:** the earliest in the series of Cicero's philosophical works. The most recent and at the same time the fullest

and most accurate account of the dialogue is that by Plasberg (Leipzig, 1894).

  11. **iudicare:** the word is rarely used in such a purely absolute sense, excepting when it is applied to the *iudices*. No exact parallel in Merguet. Perhaps there is a reference here to the courts 'qualified to sit in judgment.' In favour of this is the use of *defensa...accusata* above.

  12. **movere...retinere:** so Cic. in Acad. 1, 9 says of Varro that he had written of philosophy 'ad impellendum satis, ad edocendum parum.' It is a mistake to suppose (with many scholars) that *movere* is dependent on *posse* to be supplied from *non posse*. Cic. could not leave a positive to be supplied from a coming negative verb in this fashion, though the usage is Tacitean, as in An. 12, 64; 13, 56.

  13. **si maxime:** Goerenz strangely says that *si vel maxime* is usual; that phrase does not seem to occur, in Cicero at least; *si maxime* is common enough. Augustine vit. beata c. 25 has *si minime*, 'however little.'

  hoc...id: the less emphatic pronoun *is* constantly in Cicero repeats thus the more emphatic *hic* or *ille* or *iste*; see my n. on Acad. 2, 29; Landgraf on Pro Rosc. Am. 6; add Plaut. Asin. 527 illos qui dant, eos derides; Ter. Ad. 357; Eun. 952; Haut. 591; Cic. Fam. 13, 26, 3; Quint. 10, 1, 10. Rarely is the *same* pronoun repeated, and rarely does *is* precede *hic, ille, iste*. See my n. on Acad. 2, 27 and Madv. on Fin. 5, 22; cf. below § 11; 2, 49.

quandam temperantiam postulant in eo quod semel admissum coerceri reprimique non potest, ut propemodum iustioribus utamur illis qui omnino avocent a philosophia, quam his qui rebus infinitis modum constituant in reque eo meliore quo maior 5 sit, mediocritatem desiderent. Sive enim ad sapientiam perveniri **3** potest, non paranda nobis solum ea, sed fruenda etiam est; sive

1 admissum: *iam missum* AE et multi alii.   6 inter *etiam* et *est* interponunt *sapientia* MSS. et edd. ante Madvigium, quod fort. retinendum est. Vide comm.

1. **quandam**: the indefinite pronoun has here an intensifying, but in many cases a slightening effect.

admissum: best taken (with Madvig) in a general sense, opposite to *exclusum*, 'when once accepted'; cf. Sen. De Ira 1, 7, 2 facilius est excludere perniciosa quam regere, et non admittere quam admissa moderari. But many scholars have found a metaphor in *admissum*, either from horsemanship (*admittere equum*) or from some other source. However, as Madvig objects, this metaphorical use needs support, and the general form *in eo quod* ill accords with a special metaphor, while the objectors to whom Cicero is giving an answer were far from wishing to allow the rein to philosophy. The same flaws affect *immissum*, used by Sen. De Ira 3, 6, 2 quis se regere potuit immissum? ('when he has once let himself go') and Ep. 40, 6 oratio...reprimi immissa. The reading *iam missum* (defended by Gustafsson, p. 34, and others) would easily arise from *ammissum*, a common substitute in MSS. for *admissum*. The awkwardness of *iam*, and the unsuitability of *coerceri* and *reprimi* to a metaphor derived from launching a missile, point to the falseness of the reading. [In Caes. B. C. 2, 34, 3 *equis admissis* has been changed in nearly all MSS. to *eq. amissis*.] A passage in the so-called 'Sententiae Varronis,' 79 (ed. Riese) seems to give an echo of Cicero's words here: 'odere multi philosophiam quia quum sciri multa necesse sit, non est res tanta nisi amplis contenta spatiis.'

2. **propemodum**: qualifies the whole clause 'I may almost say.'

3. **utamur**: 'find them to be'; so Fam. 1, 9, 14 usus es quibusdam...fortioribus in me restituendo quam fuerant idem in tenendo; ib. 9, 1, 2; 7, 33, 2; Mil. 34; Acad. 2, 53.

6. **etiam sapientia**: most editors from Manutius onwards have ejected *sapientia*. The *mere* fact that it occurs in the preceding line has no weight (cf. 2, 19). But

Madvig (partly following earlier scholars) brings two special objections: (1) that elsewhere a nominative in protasis is not repeated in the apodosis, if the apodosis *immediately* follows ('continuo subiecta'), excepting in certain passages which are syllogistic in form, when the repetition is intentional ('de industria'); (2) that the pronoun *ea*, referring to the nominative in the protasis, renders the repetition impossible. The rule laid down in (1) involving three conditions, viz. that the noun must be in the nominative case, that the apodosis must immediately follow, and that the passage must not be syllogistic in form, is oversubtle and artificial. If the rule accords with facts, the accord may well be accidental. It would be possible to lay down many similar refined canons, which could not be overthrown by appeal to the remnants of Latin literature now existing. Objection (2) is difficult to understand; there is nothing obviously inconsistent with Cicero's usage either in the meaning of *ea*, or in its position in the sentence. For the repetition cf. Fam. 12, 8, and 12, 30, 2; Pro Flacc. 53 hunc auctorem; Fam. 7, 30, 3; 11, 6, 1.

6. **fruenda**: Cic. generally avoids the gerundive where the corresponding verb does not govern an accusative, particularly if the nominative case be required, and substitutes the gerund with the appropriate case. There is doubtless here assimilation to *paranda*; cf. Tusc. 5, 50 beata vita glorianda et praedicanda et prae se ferenda est. So Cael. 51 vel in legatis insidiandis vel in servis ad hospitem domini necandum sollicitandis. Fam. 4, 3, 1 in bello cavendo. The verbs *utor fruor potior vescor glorior insidiari cavere* are the only verbs not governing an accusative which in the language of Cicero form gerundives; of course forms like *disserendus, respondendus* are accommodated to the transitive uses of the corresponding verbs.

hoc difficile est, tamen nec modus est ullus investigandi veri, nisi
inveneris, et quaerendi defetigatio turpis est, cum id quod
quaeritur sit pulcherrimum. Etenim si delectamur, cum scribi-
mus, quis est tam invidus qui ab eo nos abducat? sin laboramus,
quis est qui alienae modum statuat industriae? Nam ut Terenti- 5
anus Chremes non inhumanus, qui novum vicinum non volt

     Fodere aut arare aut aliquid ferre denique

2 defetigatio: sic A².   4 invidus: *timidus* E et *deducat* pro *abducat*.

1. **difficile est**: at first sight *non
potest fieri* might have been expected.
But the words in the text better represent the position of the Sceptics, who
could not consistently make a statement so dogmatic as the doctrine that
the discovery of truth is impossible.

     modus...veri: the gen. is the prevalent
construction with *modus est*, though the
dat. occasionally occurs (Ad Herenn.
2, 50). With gerunds or gerundives the
dat. is very rare, not merely after *modus
est* or *fit*, but after such phrases as
modum facere, constituere. (Below, *industriae* is probably dat.) Cf. modum
crescendi ponere in Lucan 10, 331. In
Plaut. Asin. 167 the MSS. give *qui modus
dandi?* where almost all editors have
wrongly changed *dandi* to *dando*.

     nisi inveneris: Acad. 2, 26 quaes-
tionisque finis inventio.

     2. **defetigatio**: probably this spelling
(not *defatigatio*) was alone used in the
Latin of the Republic. So in the
Ambrosian MS. of Plaut. Trin. 225 (the
only passage where any cognate is
contained in the MS.). For the phrase
cf. Aristotle 984 *a* 30 ἡττᾶσθαι ὑπὸ τῆς
ζητήσεως.

     3. **etenim**: the note of Madvig will
show that the force of this particle has
often been misconceived, from the idea
that it must needs be confirmative of
the sentence immediately preceding.
Here it has almost the force of *porro or
praeterea*. Indeed the word is rarely
(never, I think, in Cicero) a causal
particle, giving reason for words which
immediately precede; nor (like *nam* or
enim) is it ever elliptically used, so as
to refer to some consideration which
the writer has left the reader to supply
for himself. It either continues the
general argument, as here, or if it stands
in close connexion with preceding words,
merely emphasises an additional point;
e.g. Verr. 4, 15 eius legationis princeps
est Heius, etenim est primus civitatis,

not 'because he is the first man in the
community' but 'and indeed he is.'

     4. **eo**: often used, as here, without any
substantival word in the context.

     laboramus: 'trouble ourselves over
it'; so below, 3, 8 and often.

     5. **ut...non inhumanus...sic isti curi-
osi**: the omission of the verb is especially
common in the Ciceronian writings, in
short clauses where great stress lies on
one word, such as a negative, pronoun,
or adverb; cf. n. on 1, 18.

     The employment of *ut* and *sic* with
clauses which are not in correspondence
but in contrast, as here, is very common;
see below, 1, 49 and 67; 2, 67 and 100.

     7. **fodere**, etc.: from Terence, Hau-
tontim. 67 ff. (Chremes addresses Menedemus): numquam tam mane egredior
neque tam vesperi | domum revortor,
quin te in fundo conspicer | fodere aut
arare aut aliquid ferre denique | nullum
remittis tempus neque te respicis. There
can be no doubt that Cicero found *ferre*
in his MSS. of Terence, and intended to
connect *denique* with the preceding
words. If this be done the sense of *aut...
denique* (as Madvig shows) must be 'or
at all events' (this use of *aut...denique*
is common enough in Cicero); and it
follows that the idea attaching to *ferre*
(if right) should be slighter than those
involved in *fodere* and *arare*, or else that
the meaning of *ferre* should *generalise*
the meanings of *fodere* and *arare*. It
has been assumed that *ferre* cannot fit
in with either of these conditions; but
it may have the sense 'to bear some
toil' in which case it may fairly be said
to be general in meaning, or 'to carry
something in the hand,' so that it would
indicate a slighter exertion than those
indicated by *fodere* and *arare*. There
seems therefore to be no necessity (even
on the assumption that Cicero is right
in connecting *denique* with what goes
before) to suppose that Terence really
wrote *facere*, not *ferre*. This supposition

(non enim illum ab industria, sed ab illiberali labore deterret), sic isti curiosi, quos offendit noster minime nobis iniucundus labor.

II. Eis igitur est difficilius satis facere, qui se Latina scripta 4 5 dicunt contemnere. In quibus hoc primum est in quo admirer, cur in gravissimis rebus non delectet eos sermo patrius, cum idem fabellas Latinas ad verbum e Graecis expressas non inviti legant.

4 Latina: *Latine* A².

was made by Bentley, relying on a quotation by the scholiast who, in a note on Phormio 121, gives the line of the Haut. with *facere* instead of *ferre*. This was probably a mere slip, caused by the occurrence of *faceret* in the line on which he was commenting at the moment. [The scholiast wrongly interprets *denique* as equivalent to *deinde* or *postremum*.] Many scholars (including Madvig and Fleckeisen) make *ferre* end a sentence and *denique* begin the next. This measure, however, does not render *ferre* any easier to explain.

2. **curiosi**: περίεργοι.

4. **igitur**: here, as often, not a particle of inference ('therefore') but merely continuative ('well, then'); so sometimes ergo (as in Tusc. Disp. 3, 55).

Latina scripta: the reading *Latine* is no doubt wrong, since we need the contrast with *Graeca*, and *Latina* is supported by *Latinas fabellas* and *Latinas litteras* below. But yet exception may be taken to the statement of Madvig that *Latine scripta* would of necessity mean 'res Latine dictae et verba recte et Latine posita,' that is to say that if *Latine* were attached to *scripta* the latter word would inevitably be participle, not noun. The neuter nouns derived from passive participles have this peculiarity, traceable to their origin, that they sometimes are linked with an adverb without ceasing to be nouns. Cf. pro Sull. 72 ecquod est huius factum aut commissum, non dicam audacius; Fam. 10, 16, 2 ut ante factum aliquod a te egregium audiamus (so MSS.); Nep. Timoth. 1, 2 multa huius sunt praeclare facta; Lucret. 5, 1224 nequod ob admissum foede dictumve superbe (so MSS.), Lachmann *nequid* ('a necessary change' says Munro, if it is joined with *admissum*). *Bene factum, recte factum* (wrongly written as compounds) afford other examples of the same usage.

5. **in quibus...in quo admirer**, etc.: the sentence is somewhat awkwardly

put together. The slight carelessness involved in the succession *in quibus...in quo*, has of course many parallels. In both cases the preposition *in* means 'in connexion with' as often, e.g. N.D. 2, 124 est admiratio in bestiis 'there is reason for astonishment in the case of animals.' The *cur*-clause is properly explanatory of *hoc*, but depends for its form on *admirer*; the indirect question being of common occurrence with this verb. Cf. Phil. 2, 49 in quo demiror cur ...; cf. also n. on 1, 39 below (*delectari in*). For a somewhat similar, but less complicated sentence, cf. N.D. 2, 124 in quo admirandum est congressune aliquo inter se an iam inde ab ortu natura ipsa congregatae sint. But for the intervention of *admirer*, the clause epexegetic of *hoc* would probably have taken its usual form of an infinitive clause.

7. **fabellas**: followed by *fabulis* below: so Cael. 64 velut haec tota fabella veteris et plurimarum fabularum poetriae quam est sine argumento!; also N.D. 1, 41; Tusc. 1, 113, 114.

e Graecis: but *de Graecis conversa* in § 6; cf. 3, 15 exprimi verbum e verbo. The Greek plays were *not* literally translated by the early Latins. See Ribbeck, Trag. 213. For different phrases used by Cicero to express literal translation see my n. on Acad. 2, 17. The use of the word *fabellas* seems to indicate that only some inferior Latin plays are alleged to have been literal translations from the Greek. In § 7 it is implied that Afranius, in borrowing from Menander, translated him literally in certain passages only. There is therefore no contradiction between the words of Cicero here and those which he applies to Roman playwrights generally in Acad. 1, 10, where he states that they conveyed the force rather than the language of the Greeks. A good deal of ingenuity has been expended in attempts to explain a supposed incongruity between the two passages.

Quis enim tam inimicus paene nomini Romano est, qui Enni
Medeam aut Antiopam Pacuvi spernat aut reiciat, quod se isdem
Euripidi fabulis delectari dicat, Latinas litteras oderit? Synephebos ego, inquit, potius Caecili aut Andriam Terenti quam
5 utramque Menandri legam? A quibus tantum dissentio ut, cum 5

5 tantum: fortasse *tamen* scripsit Tullius.

1. inimicus...nomini R.: so Nep.
Han. 7 inimicissimum nomini Romano.
The phrase *nomen Romanum* is here
hardly like *n. Latinum, n. Volscum,* etc.
(as Otto declared), but means 'the very
name of Roman'; cf. e.g. below, 5, 62
cui Tubuli nomen odio non est? Off.
2, 2 vereor ne...philosophiae nomen sit
invisum; Verr. 2, 1, 79 deficere ab nomine
nostro.

paene: as Madvig notes, this word
does not qualify *inimicus* but goes with
nomini. In Cicero's writings *paene,* and
prope with the sense of *paene,* far
oftener refer to words that follow than
to words preceding.

2. spernat aut reiciat: when Cicero
uses (as he very frequently does) two
nearly synonymous words, he generally
places between them a copulative, not
a disjunctive word. Probably *aut* for
ac is due here to the form of the sentence,
which involves a question equivalent to
a negation. See n. on 3, 70, 71.

quod...dicat: see n. on § 24.

3. Euripidi: see n. on § 14.

Latinas litteras: as has often been
pointed out, this phrase affords no
exact contrast with *Euripidi fabulis;*
hence scholars have proposed to omit
litteras, but the omission leaves the contrast still imperfect. There are other
inexactnesses in the passage. We set out
with certain persons who dislike *Latina
scripta* (when philosophy is in question)
but yet are ready to read the most
literal translations of Greek plays. Then
the question is asked 'who is so un-
patriotic as to scorn Latin renderings
of Greek plays, on the ground that he
loves the originals, but cannot bear
Latin literature?' The question implies
that there is no such man; yet immediately afterwards a speech is put into
the mouth of such an one: 'am I to read
the renderings of Menander by Caecilius
or Terence, rather than the original text
of Menander?' (Something very similar
occurs in § 8 quis non legat? etc. and
in § 11 the implied negative in the
question *quis alienum putet* etc. con-
tradicts the words in § 1, personae et
dignitatis esse negent; see also my n. on

Acad. 2 § 89 quid loquar de insanis?)
Then Cicero pleads for even bad translations of Greek plays, coming back to
the point from which he started. It is
much more probable that these irregularities are chargeable to Cicero's haste
than to any errors in the MSS. tradition.
[Jacob in Philol. vi, 480; Iwan Müller
A[11].] There is a passage in De opt. gen.
oratorum § 18 which contains arguments
similar to those of our text, but has been
corrupted by assimilation to this.

4. inquit: 'says such an one'; for the
indefiniteness of the reference see illustrations in my n. on Acad. 2, 79.

Caecili...Terenti: note the avoidance
of chiasmus.

5. quibus: transition from the (supposed) individual to the class of which
he is a specimen. Cf. 5, 94 hic si Peripateticus fuisset, qui dicunt, where see
n.

tantum dissentio: here and in pro
Font. 30 for the more usual tanto opere
dissentio (Acad. 2, 132; N.D.1, 5; cf. Acad.
2, 147 (discrepant)). As Madv. says, this
sense of *tantum* is rarely found, excepting
where the correlative *quantum* is expressed, or where the verb is such that
tantum indicates 'magis pro substantivo mensuram quam pro adverbio
gradum,' as in *tantum abesse.* Madvig
compares the not uncommon employment of *multum* in the sense of *magno
opere* or *valde,* and of *plus* for *magis.* The
assertion often made (as here by Madvig)
that *multum* with verbs has the value
of *saepe* is not precisely correct. There
is no apparent difference between *multum* in Att. 14, 13, 3 multum me litterae
consolantur, 'literature solaces me a
great deal,' and in 8, 13, 2 multum mecum municipales homines locuntur,
'people in the country-towns talk to me
a great deal'; yet in the one case Madvig interprets the word as *valde,* in the
other as *saepe.* Of course the notion of
frequency often lies close to that of
extent or degree, and the transition is
easily made from the one to the other
(as in Brut. 310 multum...saepius), yet
the two ideas are not confounded and
'multum et saepe' is a common phrase

Sophocles vel optime scripserit Electram, tamen male conversam
Atili mihi legendam putem, de quo Licinus: 'Ferreum scriptorem!' verum, opinor, scriptorem tamen, ut legendus sit. Rudem
enim esse omnino in nostris poetis aut inertissimae segnitiae est
5 aut fastidi delicatissimi. Mihi quidem nulli satis eruditi videntur,
quibus nostra ignota sunt. An

Vtinam ne in nemore...

nihilo minus legimus quam hoc idem Graecum, quae autem de
bene beateque vivendo a Platone disputata sunt, haec explicari

3 tamen: fortasse excidit aut *Latinum* aut *nostrum*.

in Cicero's writings and elsewhere, in
conjunction with verbs (e.g. Acad. 1, 4).
Tantum for *tanto opere* is avoided
altogether by some writers, as by Caesar.

2. **Atili**: apparently 'Atilius poeta
durissimus,' from whom a quotation is
made in Att. 14, 20, 3. After the
assassination of Julius Caesar, a pathetic
passage from the 'Electra,' capable of
being applied to the disaster, was sung
in the theatre (Suet. Iul. 84).

Licinus: in all probability Porcius
Licinus, versifier and literary critic of
the generation before Cicero, is meant.
All available information concerning
him will be found in the work by
Büttner, 'Porcius Licinus und der
literarische Kreis des Q. Lutatius
Catulus' (Leipzig, 1893). Büttner sees
an allusion to him in the *tonsor Licinus*
of Horace (A.P. 301).

ferreum, etc.: many scholars from
Voss onwards (including Weichert and
Büttner) have assumed the quotation
to extend from *ferreum* to *legendus sit*.
But, as Madvig urged, it is exceedingly
unlikely that Cicero would have found
in the poet words so precisely adapted
to his argument. Büttner contends,
most improbably, that Cicero's whole
argument in the context was suggested
to him by Licinus. The fact that the
words in question can be scanned as
one whole trochaic septenarius with part
of another, must be accidental. Büttner
urges that verses in this metre are
quoted from Licinus by Gellius, but this
has really no bearing on the extent of
Cicero's quotation here. Nor can any
weight be attributed to the contention
that if the words *ut legendus sit* are
Cicero's own he was guilty of tautology,
after having written *mihi legendam* just
before (Büttner, Philol. XLII, 54, after
Detlefsen). Madvig admits that the
direct quotation of two words only from

an author is unusual with Cicero, but
there are exx.

3. **scriptorem tamen**: one would have
expected *Latinum* or *nostrum* to be
added; or *poetam* instead of *scriptorem*;
but perhaps the thought is 'no one can
deny him a literary character, so that
he ought to be read.' The form of the
correction in *ferreum scriptorem, verum
scriptorem tamen* is of frequent occurrence; cf. e.g. Brut. 221 non satis acutus
orator sed tamen orator.

rudem: in contrast with *eruditi* below.

4. **inertissimae segnitiae**: not exactly pleonastic (Holstein and others);
the reference in *inertissimae* is to 'has
maximas artes quibus qui carebant,
inertes a maioribus nominabantur'
(Fin. 2, 115, where see n.).

5. **fastidi**: often used of great or excessive refinement in taste (literary or
gastronomic); cf. especially De opt.
gen. orat. 18 and Tusc. 4, 23 ad certas
res vitiosam offensionem atque fastidium.

delicatissimi: the word conveys
the notion of whimsicality or capri-
ciousness or wantonness such as that
of a spoilt child or other favourite;
deliciae has corresponding applications.

6. **an**: the change from *at* to *an* is
necessary. The form of argument, con-
sisting of a bimembral question, the one
limb comprising an admitted fact, while
the other puts a fact cognate, yet not
admitted, is exceedingly common in
Cicero. The second limb is frequently
placed side by side with the first, without any connecting link such as *autem*
provides here. Cf. below § 12.

7. **utinam ne in nemore**: these often
quoted first words of the Medea of
Ennius are substituted for the name of
the play.

9. **bene beateque vivendo**: see n. on

6 non placebit Latine? Quid si nos non interpretum fungimur munere, sed tuemur ea quae dicta sunt ab eis quos probamus, eisque nostrum iudicium et nostrum scribendi ordinem adiungimus? quid habent cur Graeca anteponant eis, quae et splendide dicta sint neque sint conversa de Graecis? Nam si dicent ab 5 illis has res esse tractatas, ne ipsos quidem Graecos est cur tam multos legant quam legendi sunt. Quid enim est a Chrysippo

2 ea quae dicta: fort. *res quae dictae.*　　　5 dicta sint: ita P; *d. sunt* AE.
6 ipsos dett. P²: *ipso* codd.　　　7 quam legendi sunt: glossema esse coniecit
Ernesti.

§ 11. The reference in the words *a Platone* appears to be quite general. If there is any allusion to a particular dialogue, it can be no other than the *Philebus*. But Plato is here typical of Greek philosophers in general; Cicero chooses the noblest representative. So below, in § 7, where Plato and Aristotle are joined together. The words *quae... haec* refer not to the actual writings of Plato, but to the ethical problems debated in those writings. *Disputare aliquid* for *de aliqua re* is of course commonly found. Below, *ea quae dicta sunt* mean actual statements.

1. **interpretum**: often used of literal translators, as in Off. 1, 6 Stoicos sequemur, non ut interpretes.

2. **tuemur**: not 'defend' (as some of the translators understand the word) but 'keep to.' Without departing from the doctrines of the chosen authors, Cicero is to choose his own language and arrangement. Cf. 2, 11 where we have the succession *tenere, tueri, defendere.*

probamus: Seyffert in his *Scholae Latinae* curiously takes this as meaning 'to quote' probably because the meaning 'approve' is not suitable to the opposing philosophers who are followed in different parts of the treatise. But Cicero may be deemed to have 'approved' all of these as representatives of their schools.

3. **iudicium**: the context shows that the word here implies literary taste, not intellectual judgment. The usage is of course familiar.

scribendi ordinem: these words are applicable only to the employment of one book as an authority, and would be entirely out of place had Cicero drawn his material from numerous books or authorities.

4. **et...neque**: see Draeger,Hist. Synt. § 323, 5 (II, 84).

5. **dicta sint**: it is difficult to decide whether *dicta sunt...conversa sunt*, should be read, or *d. sint...c. sint*. The previous sentence might suggest that Cicero had in his mind particular complete writings (the 'De Rep.,' 'De Legibus' and the 'Hortensius'), and not the *quality* of all his philosophical compositions, whether finished or contemplated. But even so, the indicative verbs might be drawn into the subjunctive in sympathy with the preceding clause. Baiter's omission of the *sint* after *dicta* can scarcely be right. Cicero would rather have dropped the *sint* before *conversa* The omission of the earlier *sint* is made very awkward by the interposition of the *neque*, and the circumstances are quite different here and in § 30 quam ob rem voluptas expetenda, fugiendus dolor sit.

Graecis: quite possibly masc. although *Graeca* precedes. Cf. *illis* in the next sentence (which may however be κατὰ σύνεσιν like *ille* in 5, 16, where see n.); and § 7 *Platonem verterem.* Just below, *in Stoicis* is rather 'in treating the Stoic system' than 'among the Stoics' (as though referring to Chrysippus).

6. **ne ipsos**: there is a small ellipse in the introduction of the apodosis, 'I give the following answer'; cf. Nägelsbach, Stilistik, § 184, 1.

7. **legendi sunt**: in a masterly note Madvig refutes the opinion of Davies that these words bear the sense of *leguntur*, and that of others, who gave them the value of *legi possunt*. His view that there is slight ellipse ('quam legendi sunt, si quis doctus et eruditus haberi vult') is unquestionably true. Madvig lays down clearly the limits within which the gerundive assumed or bordered on the idea of possibility in the Latin of Cicero. But his quotations are confined to *vix ferendus*, or *non ferendus*, with the exception of In Cat. 2, 28 *vix optandum*, where, however, the sense of

praetermissum in Stoicis? Legimus tamen Diogenen, Anti-
patrum, Mnesarchum, Panaetium, multos alios in primisque
familiarem nostrum Posidonium. Quid? Theophrastus mediocriterne delectat, cum tractat locos ab Aristotele ante tractatos?
5 quid? Epicurei num desistunt de isdem, de quibus et ab Epicuro
scriptum est et ab antiquis, ad arbitrium suum scribere? Quod

propriety clearly comes out, 'a thing
for which we scarce should pray.'
Cicero never, as M. says, adds words
which render the sense of possibility
conspicuous, as Velleius does (2, 46):
'res vix multis voluminibus enarran-
dae.' Poets and later prose writers not
only introduce such negative phrases as
nulli cernendus, but positive expressions,
like Ovid, Fast. 6, 720 continua Delphin
nocte videndus erit. Madvig also points
out that the notion of simple futurity
seems to be attached to the gerundive
in only one passage of Latin before the
time of Lactantius and Jerome, viz.
Liv. 3, 45, 3 promitto puellam sisten-
dam, 'I undertake that the girl shall be
produced'; with which he compares
voveo aedem faciendam. The two expressions are indeed strictly parallel.
Promittere puellam, 'to promise a girl,'
can stand by itself just as well as *vovere
aedem,* and the extension in both cases
is the same: 'I vow a temple, which is
to be constructed,' and 'I promise a
girl, who is to be produced'; so *habuit
aedem tuendam* and many like phrases.
It is therefore, perhaps, hardly correct
to say that even in the passage of Livy
the gerundive conveys the idea of simple
futurity.

1. **lĕgimus** or **lēgimus**? Probably the
latter.

Diogenen: see n. on 2, 24.

2. **Mnesarchum, Panaetium:** the
chronological order is here disturbed,
since Mnesarchus was pupil of Panaetius. As a rule Cicero is careful in such
enumerations to preserve the order of
time. In Tusc. 5, 107 there is a similar
disturbance, according to some of the
MSS., but recent editors have corrected
the passage.

multos alios: the asyndeton at the
end of the summation is usual but not
universal. So with *cetera* in 4, 35, where
see n. Also cf. 2, 23 his omnibus.

in primisque: Cicero does not attach
que to *ex* or *in* (apart from a few
examples of old-fashioned formulae, as
exque re publica in Phil. 3. 38 and 5, 36
and 10, 26; cf. Div. 1, 102 *inque*) unless

a demonstrative pronoun follows. He
also observes as a rule the condition
accepted by nearly all writers for all
prepositions, that *que* is only attached
when the preposition is repeated. To
many prepositions *que* is never joined;
so *ad* (hence *ad easque* in 3, 72). See
Landgraf on Rosc. Am. 114 (with
additional remarks in appendix) also
Krebs-Schmalz, Antibarbarus, s.v. *que.*

3. **familiarem:** Cicero had known P.
both at Rome and at Rhodes, and had
corresponded with him. In a fragment
of the Hortensius (44 in C. F. W.
Müller's text) he is called 'the greatest
of all Stoics.' This statement of Cicero
that, for the Stoic philosophy, he read
Posidonius more than others, is of some
importance.

quid? this little anticipative question
(like τί δέ;) is almost invariably followed by a second question.

mediocriterne: the interrogative particle is often not attached to the earliest
possible word in the sentence. Similarly
num and *nonne* often come late.

4. **locos:** Horace, who uses *loca* in
this sense (ep. 2, 1, 223), is not followed
by any good writer, though later poets
and later prose writers often use *loci* in
the sense of *loca.* See Neue, Formen-
lehre, 1², 543.

5. **Epicurei,** etc.: Diels, Doxogr. Gr.
p. 105, seems to misunderstand the
passage.

isdem: possibly neut. just as *omnibus* is used by Cic. for *omnibus rebus*; but
perhaps *locis* is to be supplied.

et ab Epicuro...et ab antiquis: the
antiqui here do not include Epicurus,
but embrace his immediate followers,
Hermarchus Metrodorus and one or two
others; just as the phrase *vetus Academia*
often includes Plato's immediate followers, while excluding Plato himself.

6. **ad arbitrium:** no more freedom of
treatment is implied here than in the
words *nostrum iudicium et nostrum
scribendi ordinem* above. Cicero often
reproaches the later Epicureans with a
parrot-like adherence to the lessons of
their founder; see n. on 2, 95.

si Graeci leguntur a Graecis isdem de rebus alia ratione compositis, quid est cur nostri a nostris non legantur?

7   III. Quamquam, si plane sic verterem Platonem aut Aristotelen, ut verterunt nostri poetae fabulas, male, credo, mererer de meis civibus, si ad eorum cognitionem divina illa ingenia 5 transferrem. Sed id neque feci adhuc nec mihi tamen ne faciam interdictum puto. Locos quidem quosdam, si videbitur, transferam, et maxime ab eis quos modo nominavi, cum inciderit ut id apte fieri possit, ut ab Homero Ennius, Afranius a Menandro

1. **isdem de rebus...compositis**: Rath proposed to eject *de*, which might well have arisen, by dittographia, from *dem* (*dē*) of *isdem*. Although I have found no parallel to the phrase *legere aliquem de aliqua re*, it does not look un-Latin.

3. **plane sic**: the *plane* qualifies the *sic*; cf. *sic prorsus*.

Platonem...Aristotelen: the context would lead an unwary reader to suppose that the material for the *De Finibus* was found in one or other of these philosophers. But (as is the case with the mention of Plato in § 5) they are merely taken as typical. Plato, Aristotle and Theophrastus are similarly put forward in Acad. 1, 10. Yet *quos modo nominavi* (below, § 7) presents a real difficulty. It may refer back to the Stoics above. Cic. of course is not necessarily referring exclusively to the De Finibus but to the whole scheme of his philosophic writings and may here be expressing intentions never carried out.

5. **si ad eorum**, etc.: the second protasis, coming after the apodosis, has the effect of giving a new aspect to the first, pressing it with more vigour. The usage is so common that it is not worth while to give instances; cf. Nägelsbach, Stilistik § 149. The same kind of repetition is found with *cum*-clauses, and other clauses also; and the principal clause does not always stand in the middle; cf. e.g. Acad. 2, 97. See n. on 2, 112; and cf. Goodwin, Moods and Tenses, § 510. [Madvig quotes Q. Fr. 2, 15 *a* (13), 2 with a doubtful reading.]

si...transferrem, etc.: the force of this passage is misunderstood by Prof. Sonnenschein in C.R. 1, 126.

6. **transferrem**: this verb is never used by Cicero *simpliciter*, in the sense of *translating*, a sense which would here fit ill with *ingenia*. The idea of close translation springs not from this verb, but from the context. So Att. 6, 2, 3, istum ego locum totidem verbis a Dicaearcho transtuli: 'I have *borrowed* the passage from D., *rendering it literally*.' Madvig lays down, somewhat arbitrarily, that *transferre locos ex aliquo* for *ab aliquo*, would not be good Latin. But what essential difference is there between *intellegere aliquid e Platone*, 'something may be understood from Plato's pages' (2 § 2), and *transferre aliquid e Platone*, 'to borrow something from Plato's pages'?

7. **interdictum**: the word was originally used of an order issued by a magistrate, and retains in its secondary applications traces of its origin. Cf. De Or. 1, 215 neque enim est interdictum aut a rerum natura, aut a lege aliqua atque more. After *nec, quominus* would have been more usual; see Riemann, Synt. Latine, § 189, 1.

transferam...cum inciderit: in such sentences Cicero often resorts to the fut. perf. tense even where (as here) the future would stand. In 1, 63 morati melius erimus cum didicerimus, the tense is of course made necessary by the sense.

8. **inciderit**: the impersonal use occurs only here and Lael. 33 in the philosophical writings of Cicero, not at all in the speeches, and is rare in his other works. It is common in Livy.

9. **ab Homero**, etc.: Cicero purposely quotes an epic writer and a dramatist, both of whom dealt with Roman subjects, and were therefore not so slavishly dependent as other writers on the Greeks. Yet Afranius in his lifetime had to defend himself against the charge of borrowing too largely from Menander (Macrob. sat. 6, 1, 4); but the story itself testifies to his comparative originality. Cic. here certainly misleads by comparing the *togatae* of Afranius and the *Annales* of Ennius with his own dialogues. The only passages which he *openly* translates in these books are from Epicurus and Metrodorus in Fin. 1, 11.

Ennius of Rudiae said he had 'tria

solet. Nec vero, ut noster Lucilius, recusabo quo minus omnes mea legant. Vtinam esset ille Persius! Scipio vero et Rutilius multo etiam magis; quorum ille iudicium reformidans Tarentinis ait se et Consentinis et Siculis scribere. Facete is quidem, sicut alia;

4 alia Ursinus: *alias* omnes ante Madvigium.

corda': cf. Gell. 17, 17, 1 Q. Ennius tria corda habere sese dicebat quod loqui Graece et Osce et Latine sciret. It is strange that Oscan is mentioned and not Messapian. Mommsen thought he did not mention it because he regarded it as a dialect of Greek. Rudiae was probably Hellenised more or less.

1. **nec recusabo**, etc.: cf. De Or. 1, 256 nec repugnabo quominus, id quod modo hortatus es, omnia legant, with a reference in the context to the same passage of Lucilius, which is quoted in 2, 25: 'Persium non curo legere, Laelium Decumum volo,' and by Plin. praef. 7: 'nec doctissimis. Manium Persium haec legere nolo, Iunium Congum volo.' As the name of Persius was Gaius, L. Müller changes *Manium* to *nam Gaium* (and is followed by Baehrens) while Marx reads *Manilium Persiumve*. As there is mention of *Congus* in the context of De Orat. 1, 256 it is clear that both he and Laelius were mentioned by Lucilius. It is natural to suppose that two others were contrasted with them, Persius being set against Laelius, and against Congus some other man, for whose name Pliny has substituted that of Persius. Munro (J. Phil. VIII, 207–210) plausibly reconstructs the passage thus:

nec doctissimis *scribuntur haec*
neque indoctissimis:
Persium non curo legere, Laelium
Decumum volo
........................Manium
[Persium] haec *ego* legere nolo,
Iunium Congum volo.

Possibly, as Marx supposes, the missing name is that of Manilius, the celebrated jurist and member of the Scipionic circle. It is evident from the words of Cicero here that Lucilius also named Scipio and Rutilius among the very learned; no doubt each of them was pitted against a specimen of the moderately learned class. The passage of Pliny to which reference is made above shows that Cicero quoted the lines of Lucilius in a lost portion of his 'De Republica.' As the interlocutors and listeners in that dialogue were the very men of the

Scipionic circle to whom Lucilius alludes, Cicero would very naturally in the prelude to his work, give a full quotation. There is reason to think, as Lachmann and L. Müller have shown, that the lines of Lucilius were introductory to his XXVIth book, and that this book was the earliest of his writings. Very nearly all the fragments which can be referred to that book are in this same trochaic metre (note the few iambic fragments at the end of Baehrens' text). If, as I believe, the whole book dealt in a popular manner with philosophic themes, there would be an especial reason why Cicero should have quoted its opening lines in the introduction to his two dialogues, De Republica and De Finibus.

2. **ille Persius**: nothing is known of him but what may be gathered from the passages quoted above, and from Brut. 99: alii a C. Persio litterato homine scriptam esse (sc. orationem) aiebant, illo quem significat valde doctum esse Lucilius.

3. **magis**: sc. *vellem esse*. I see no reason for supposing (with Madvig) that Cicero here alludes to a different passage of Lucilius.

iudicium: 'criticism.'

Tarentinis: these are specimens of bilingual people. Wesenberg (ap. Madvig.) supposes (with much probability) that Lucilius was in the passage apologising for his loose phrases and his frequent mixture of Greek with Latin. For the dative with *scribere* see my n. on Acad. 1, 9, and add the following to the references there given: De Or. 2, 341; Qu. Fr. 3, 1, 11; Ovid, Trist. 2, 245 and 303; ib. 5, 7, 27 nil equidem feci—tu scis hoc ipse—theatris (the reading has been disputed but is quite sound); Ex Pont. 3, 3, 51; Sen. suas. 2 § 19; Plin. n. h. 18 § 24; Martial, pref. to Book 1, epigrammata illis scribuntur qui solent spectare Florales; Avian. Fab. 1, 15. Cic. does not say 'scribo tibi,' meaning 'I write a letter to you,' as do Plin. ep. 1, 5, 17, Tacitus and many other authors.

4. **Consentinis**: see Budinsky, 'Die Ausbreitung der lateinischen Sprache'

sed neque tam docti tum erant ad quorum iudicium elaboraret, et sunt illius scripta leviora, ut urbanitas summa appareat, 8 doctrina mediocris. Ego autem quem timeam lectorem, cum ad te ne Graecis quidem cedentem in philosophia audeam scribere? quamquam a te ipso id quidem facio provocatus gratissimo mihi 5 libro quem ad me de virtute misisti. Sed ex eo credo quibusdam usu venire ut abhorreant a Latinis, quod inciderint in inculta quaedam et horrida, de malis Graecis Latine scripta deterius.

(Berlin, 1881). Varro called the Massilienses 'trilingues,' 'quod et Graece loquantur et Latine et Gallice' (Isid. Orig. 15, 1, 63 ed. Lindemann).

facete: in a n. on Acad. 2, 94 I have given exx. of the omission of the verb in brief clauses where emphasis is thrown on an adverb, and many others might be added, such as Fam. 9, 15, 3 (where Madvig cleverly set a passage right by the change of *urbanae* to *urbane*); Att. 5, 11, 2; Caelius ap. Fam. 8, 6, 1; Cato, agr. 110 si demptus est odor deterior, id optime (sc. fecisti); Lucan 3, 111 melius (sc. Caesar fecit) quod plura iubere erubuit quam Roma pati (a passage misunderstood by Francken and others).

sicut alia: cf. 4, 73 facete Piso...et alia multa; Off. 3, 42 scite Chrysippus ut multa; N.D. 2, 69 concinneque, ut multa, Timaeus; Lael. 90 scitum est enim illud Catonis, ut multa. There can be no reasonable doubt that Madvig is right in reading *alia*. As he says, writers before Pliny never give *alias* the sense of *alio loco* but always that of *alio tempore*. Also *alias* 'significat unum aliquod aliud tempus,' a statement which should be modified by adding that *alias* can take on a plural signification when *saepe* (very common), *non numquam* (Caes. B. C. 1, 64 and Cic. Hort. fragm. 46) or other similarly qualifying expression is attached, or when it is contrasted with a plural word, such as *plerumque* (Cato m. 51). In like manner *alias alios* in post red. in sen; 30; and *alias...alias* with imperfect of frequency in Verr. 2, 1, 120. The word occurs often in Cicero's philosophical works but only thrice in the speeches. On *alias...alias* see 2, 87 *n*.

1. **sed neque**, etc.: the argument is far from clear. It appears to be: 'the *doctissimi* of Lucilius were not sufficiently *docti* to induce him to give a fine finish to his writings, and his themes were slight, and afforded an opening for

urbanitas rather than *doctrina*.' *Tam docti...ad quorum*=*t. d. ut ad eorum*, not (as Madvig has it) *t. d. quam nunc sunt, ad quorum*.

2. **urbanitas**: in Lucilius, this consisted in the bonhomie and wit of the town-bred man rather than in ease and polish of style, to which the word is often applied (Quint. 6, 3, 107).

4. **ne...philosophia**: see my ed. of the Acad. p. 32 and n. on 1, 12. Brutus' book must have been written but a short time before, as he speaks of seeing Marcellus in exile at Mitylene (Seneca dial. 12, 9, 4).

ad te scribere...ad me misisti: both *scribere ad aliquem* and *mittere librum ad aliquem* are employed of *dedicating* books to a friend. Both expressions occur together in Varro agr. 3, 1, 9 (in 1, 1, 10 he has *mittere* with the dative in the same sense; so Censor. de die n. 1, 5). See further illustrations in my n. on Acad. 1, 2.

6. **quem...misisti**: for the position of the words *de virtute* cf. Tusc. 4, 66 eam rationem quae minime probatur de...; De Or. 2, 61 libri qui sunt fere inscripti de...; Lael. 4 in Catone maiore, qui est scriptus ad te de senectute.

ex eo: the preposition is unusual here, *eo...quod* being the ordinary form; *ex* may have arisen by dittography from *eo*. But cf. Tusc. 1, 30 ex eo est quod (where *eo* alone could hardly go with *quod*).

7. **horridus** and **incultus** are often combined as here; see Landgraf on Rosc. Am. 75.

inculta: the Latin books by Amafinius, Rabirius and Catius on Epicureanism, for which see my ed. of the Academica, p. 21 sq. Probably they were only a little older than Cicero; Catius died in 45 B.C.

8. **de malis**: probably *de* is 'after the pattern of.' This sense of *de* is however unusual in Cic. Possibly *scribere de aliquo aliquid* is like *audire de aliquo*

Quibus ego assentior, dum modo de isdem rebus ne Graecos quidem legendos putent. Res vero bonas verbis electis graviter ornateque dictas quis non legat? nisi qui se plane Graecum dici velit, ut a Scaevola est praetore salutatus Athenis Albucius.
5 Quem quidem locum cum multa venustate et omni sale idem 9 Lucilius, apud quem praeclare Scaevola:

3 dictas: *dictatas* E.   4 praetore: *praetor* AE (teste Iwan Müller).   5 venustate: fort. post hoc verbum excidit *tetigit* (cf. e.g. De Leg. 2 § 9 et De Off. 3 § 8).

aliquid, or *de* may be due to the fact that *scripta* here implies *conversa* (§ 6).

malis Graecis: Madvig's argument that *male* could not be applied to Graecus and paene Graecus Brut. 131 because that adjective is 'definitae notionis' and does not admit of degree, would seem to apply equally to Graece. But cf. *semi-Graecus* (Varro and others). *Malus Graecus* for *malus Graecus auctor* seems unparalleled.

Latine...deterius: cf. Tusc. 3, 20 male Latine videtur, sed praeclare Accius (sc. scripsisse); Brut. 210 Curio...Latine non pessime loquebatur; below, 2, 19.

1. **rebus:** Cic. always assumes that no Epicurean writes well; but Stoic literature may be read, whatever the style (3, 19). There is a slight ellipse for *Gr. qui de isdem rebus scripserunt.*

2. **res...dictas:** *scriptas* might have been expected, but cf. 3, 19 istius modi res dicere ornate velle.

3. **plane Graecum:** so 3, 5 eorum...qui se Graecos magis quam nostros haberi volunt.

4. **Scaevola:** the augur, who appears to have been praetor in 121 B.C., and became consul in 117. At the time of the interview imagined by Lucilius (or worked up from Scaevola's report) Scaevola must have been on his way to Asia. On his return he was prosecuted for maladministration by Albucius, possibly in revenge for ridicule; but he was acquitted. A. was himself afterwards exiled on a similar charge, and again took up his abode at Athens. Cicero twice quotes (De Orat. 3, 171 and Orat. 149) and once again (Brut. 274) refers to lines of Lucilius ridiculing the artificial and affected style of Albucius. Cicero also mentions speeches by him as extant (Brut. 131), calls him *perfectus Epicureus,* and 'doctus Graecis vel potius paene Graecus' (ib.). There is a curious passage of Fronto (p. 114 Nab.) in which he is connected with Lucilius and Lucretius as a poet. But the mention of Lucilius in Fronto may fit

in with the Luciliano charactere libelli of Varro r. r. 3, 2, 17 (where the author is *apprime doctus*). The *aridus* of Fronto also fits in well with the passage of Varro. Too much stress, however, must not be laid on the passage in Fronto who goes on to refer to Pacuvius, Accius, Ennius (and other poets of the Republic). Cic. in N.D. 1, 93 hints that Albucius had written on Epicureanism, and had vilified philosophers of other schools. Possibly he supported Epicureanism in verse.

praetore: there is no proof that Albucius went to Asia as *propraetor* or as *praetor.* The word *praetor* is of course often loosely used with the sense of *pro praetore.*

5. **locum:** the word indicates that the whole subject of Graecomania was dealt with by Lucilius in the poem from which the passage specifically touching Albucius is quoted. The omission of a verb with the sense of *persequitur, tractat,* is, as Madvig rightly declares in an important note, inconceivable. I suggest adding *tetigit* between *venustate* and *et,* where it would easily fall out. The insertion by A[2] of *dicit* after *Scaevola* seems to support my conjecture. For *locum tangere* cf. Leg. 2, 9; Off. 3, 8.

cum...omni: *cum* may be due to dittographia after *lo-cum.* Cicero does not as a rule insert the preposition where an epithet is attached to the noun, excepting where the phrase refers to some concrete and visible fact: so Verr. 2, 4, 54 maiorem partem diei cum tunica pulla sedere solebat et pallio; cf. below, 4, 60 (where, however, *cum* is necessary). I do not know why Madvig pronounced in his note *fide amicitiai colere* to be bad Latin. Cic. says in Quinct. 26 veritate amicitia, fide societas, pietate propinquitas colitur. Cf. Acad. 2, 1 magna cum gloria persecutus inimicitias.

The collocation is usually *summa cum* (as in Rep. 2, 56) but there are examples to the contrary. In many passages, if *cum* were not inserted the

Graecum te, Albuci, quam Romanum atque Sabinum,
Municipem Ponti, Tritani, centurionum,
Praeclarorum hominum ac primorum signiferumque
Maluisti dici. Graece ergo praetor Athenis,
Id quod maluisti, te, cum ad me accedis, saluto: 5
'Χαῖρε,' inquam, 'Tite!' lictores, turma omnis cohorsque:
'Χαῖρε, Tite!' Hinc hostis mi Albucius, hinc inimicus.

2 Tritani: *Tiranii* A[1]; *Tritannii* A[2]P; *Ponti Titi et Anni* Baehrens.   6 cohorsque: *chorus ceu* Baehrens, non bene; *chorusque* codd. et edd. ante Manutium.

ablative would be ambiguous, and might be taken for instrumental or some other kind of dative, cf. e.g. N.D. 2, 101. In some other passages there seems no such reason, as N.D. 2, 97.

A curious passage is Verr. 5, 28 erant autem convivia non illo silentio praetorum populi Romani, neque eo pudore qui in magistratuum conviviis versari solet, sed cum maximo clamore atque convicio.

Cf. ib. 5, 158 quo dolore animi dicam with e.g. Rab. Post. 45 quanto hoc dixi cum dolore.

Compare also Verr. 2, 51 Syracusis Marcellia tolluntur maximo gemitu civitatis, with 4, 76 magno cum luctu et gemitu totius civitatis multis cum lacrumis lamentationibusque virorum mulierumque omnium simulacrum Dianae tollendum locatur.

Similarly Font. 23 and Flacc. 10 (pudore); Phil. 7, 8 and Rab. Post. 5 (spe); Sull. 61 and Imp. Pomp. 69 (studio).

1. **atque**: it is hardly likely that *atque* is here substituted for *aut*. Rather *Romanum* means 'Roman citizen' and *Sabinum* is introduced because Sabines were reputed the simplest and severest of all the Roman burgesses; perhaps also Albucius may have been connected by birth with the Sabine country. See the inscription from Novaria quoted in Forcellini's Onomasticon s.v. Albucia. She was priestess of a 'diva Sabina' (C.I.L. 5, 6514).

2. **Ponti, Tritani**: proverbially strong soldiers. Pontius is no doubt the centurion T. Pontius mentioned as a mighty man of muscle in Cato m. § 33, whence Baehrens derives in part his correction of the text here to *Ponti Titi et Anni*. The centurion Tritanus is unknown, but a gladiator of that name is mentioned by Solinus 1, 75 and Vopiscus, Firm. c. 4, and Plin. n. h. 7, 81 (if in the last passage *Tritanus*, read by some edd., be a true correction of the reading of the MSS., which is *Tributanus*). The difficulties of the passage are discussed fully by Marx in his work on Lucilius, pp. 41 sq. Centurions were

partly chosen for their strong physique; cf. Veget. 2, 14 centurio eligendus est qui sit magnis viribus et procera statura; Cic. Phil. 8 §§ 9, 26 lacertosi centuriones. The 'brawny captain' often figures as typical 'Philistine'; see Pers 3, 77 and 5, 189; Juvenal 14, 194 and 16, 17. In Tusc. 4, 55 the *centurio* and the *signifer* are contrasted with the *constans vir ac sapiens*.

3. **primorum**: nothing is gained by assuming (as L. Müller does) that this is from *primores* (fighters in the front rank) rather than from *primi*. As Madvig shows *homines primi* is a not uncommon phrase. Cf. Virgil, Aen. 4, 133 and 9, 453; Ovid, Pont. 1, 4, 33 primos telluris Achivae, and Ad Herenn. 4, 19, 68 primus in civitate (for the usual *princeps*); and elsewhere. As Madvig says, the rank of centurion in country towns constituted a title to a sort of 'rustica nobilitas,' to which the line of Horace bears testimony: magni pueri magnis e centurionibus orti (sat. 1, 6, 73). For the close association of the *centurio* and the *signifer* cf. Liv. 10, 36, 10; Polybius 6, 24, 6: and for the *nobilitas* of the *centurio* cf. Cic. Att. 5, 20, 4 centurionem primi pili nobilem sui generis Asinium Dentonem (on which passage some commentators have made unnecessary difficulty). Perhaps Lucilius was thinking of those select centurions to whom the expression 'primi ordines' applied (see Marq. v, 359 sq.) and who are called 'centurionum primi' by Tacitus hist. 2, 89.

signiferumque: these were, it seems, not usually centurions but (with the *optio* = οὐραγός) sub-centurions. Marquardt has little or nothing about them. Cf. Liv. 8, 8, 18; 10, 36, 10 centuriones signiferique; and see Polyb. 6, 24, 6.

4. **maluisti**: see L. Müller, De re metr. p 299 sq. (maluisti trisyllabic, twice in Lucil., also genua, tenuia disyllabic).

5. **accedis**: for the silent *s* see L. Müller, De re metrica, pp. 427-9.

6. **lictores**: sc. eadem dicunt.

turma...cohorsque: the corruption

Sed iure Mucius. Ego autem mirari *satis* non queo unde hoc **10**
sit tam insolens domesticarum rerum fastidium. Non est omnino
hic docendi locus, sed ita sentio et saepe disserui, Latinam linguam non modo *non* inopem, ut volgo putarent, sed locupletiorem
5 etiam esse quam Graecam. Quando enim nobis, vel dicam aut

1 mirari *satis*: *satis* om. codd. omnes; supplevit Orellius post P. Manutium;
rimari Allen et Baiter: *non mirari non queo* Boeckel.   4 *non* om. ABE.

ín the MSS. points (as Ursinus said) to
the spelling *chors* for *cohors* in the archetype. The *cohors praetoria*, the special
guards of the general, included both
cavalry and infantry, but the word is
here used of the infantry portion only.
For *turma* cf. Sall. Jug. 98, 1. The same
contrast in pro Marcell. 7 nihil sibi ex
ista laude centurio, nihil praefectus,
nihil cohors, nihil turma decerpit
(the only occurrence of *turma* in the
speeches). The jest of Scipio about
turmalis in De Orat. 2, 262 seems to be
somewhat misunderstood by editors (see
Wilkins *ad loc.*). Scipio compared the
other statues to the equestrian members
of a general's suite. *Hostis* and *inimicus*
are combined in Att. 2, 19, 3.

1. **sed...autem:** the force of the *sed*
is not easy to see. It is not resumptive,
and the adversative idea is excluded.
Probably *et* should be read. Cicero
seems not to write *sed...autem*, though
sed...vero occurs, and *ast...autem* in
'Prognostica,' 160. In Comedy we have
sed quid autem, and once in Virgil (Aen.
2, 101). There are two suspicious passages of Plautus (untouched by editors)
in which *sed...autem* occurs in the MSS.,
viz. Bacch. 519 and Rud. 472, where the
true reading seems to be: sed hanc quid
autem si hinc abstulerit quispiam.

mirari satis non queo: the formula is
common in Cicero and occurs elsewhere,
as in Plin. n.h. 14 § 2; Sall. or. Lepid. § 2.
The form *non mirari non queo* is unknown; and *rimari* (conjectured here
by Allen), common in some writers,
as Quintilian, is used by Cicero once
only (De Div. 1, 130). *Queo* occurs
in ten passages of the speeches and about
twenty-eight of the phil. works, all with
negatives or in sentences equivalent to
negative. In all the passages *queo* is in
pres. indic. or subj. *Non queo* stands for
nequeo in Cicero; and other parts are
rare. He has *nequeo* only in a quotation
(Tusc. 2, 24). The verb occurs only once
in the speeches (nequeamus in Verr. 3,
21); of the eighteen exx. in the philosophical works fifteen are in present
indicative or subjunctive, two in im-

perfect subjunctive, one in pluperfect
subjunctive. Cicero avoids both *quis*
and *nequis*, both *quit* and *nequit*,
quimus and *nequimus*; *nequitis* he has
once (Rep. 6. 19). The unsuitability of
rimari is shown by Madvig.

unde: i.e. the feeling which gives rise
to distaste for home products; i.e.
Graecomania. *Mirari* is 'to express won-
derment.'

3. **disserui:** so 3, 5 saepe diximus;
but the statement is not to be found in
any of the extant works written before
the De Finibus. Cic. may be referring to
some lost work, as the Hortensius, or
to his conversation (see a passage
of Apuleius de Deo Socr. 113, where he
speaks of Latin and Greek much as
Cicero here). The opinion as to the
superior richness of Latin is given below,
3, 5; also N.D. 1, 8; Tusc. 2, 35 (O
verborum inops interdum, quibus tu
abundare te semper putas, Graecia);
3, 10; 4, 10; cf. however below, 3, 51.
The claim made for the Latin language
is not so absurd if the rivalry be restricted to the contemporary Greek.
Cicero's words in speaking of the wealth
of Latin often look like an answer to
the wail of Lucretius about the *patrii
sermonis egestas* (1, 139 and 832; 3, 260)
on which see Munro's remarks in ed. 3,
vol. 11, p. 306 sq. (ed. 4, p. 10). Plin. ep. 4,
18, 1 backs Lucr.; likewise Seneca ep.
58, 1 quanta verborum nobis paupertas,
immo egestas! Cf. also Sen. contr. 10,
4, 23 Latinam linguam facultatis non
minus habere, licentiae minus; Sen.
dial. 11, 2, 6 Graecae linguae gratia,
Latinae potentia.

4. **non inopem:** the insertion of the
non is an absolute necessity. *Non modo*
cannot stand for *non modo non*, excepting where *sed* is followed by *ne...
quidem*. As to the matter see 3, 5 *n*.

5. **vel dicam:** Madvig quotes exx. of
this corrective formula from Fam. 4,
7, 3; Att. 9, 7, 1; Brut. 207 and 246;
Phil. 2, 30; Suet. Cal. 13; also vel dicam
amplius in Varro L. L. 8, p. 106 Bip.
Add Cael. 75; there seem to be no other
parallels in Cicero.

oratoribus bonis aut poetis, postea quidem quam fuit quem imitarentur, ullus orationis vel copiosae vel elegantis ornatus defuit?

IV. Ego vero, cum forensibus operis, laboribus, periculis non deseruisse mihi videor praesidium in quo a populo Romano 5 locatus sum, debeo profecto, quantumcumque possum, in eo quoque elaborare ut sint opera, studio, labore meo doctiores cives mei, nec cum istis tanto opere pugnare, qui Graeca legere malint,

4 cum: ita codd. omnes: *quoniam* edd. fere omnes.   5 videor: *videri* AEP.
6 sum...possum: *sim...possim,* multi, errore vulgatissimo.   8 tanto opere: *tantopere* A et P (ut semper); item *magnopere.*

1. **postea quam,** etc.: i.e. after a few writers had demonstrated the richness of the language. For the words cf. Quint. 10, 2, 3 hoc ipsum quod tanto faciliorem rationem rerum omnium facit quam fuit eis qui nihil quod sequerentur haberent.

2. **orationis:** λέξεως, 'style.'

elegantis: the word indicates compactness, clearness and terseness rather than tasteful literary quality. Cf. my note on Cato M. 13.

ornatus: 'equipment' rather than 'decoration.'

4. **cum forensibus:** the editors practically all change *cum* to *quoniam;* but *cum* is in all the mss. and, as it is not demonstrably erroneous, I think it may be retained. The causal *cum* with the indicative has been elaborately treated by Prof. W. Gardner Hale in his work on 'cum-constructions' (Cornell Studies in Classical Philology, 1887). He, rightly I think, regards the usage as one that was dying out in Cicero's time, and one that would be regarded by his contemporaries as somewhat archaistic. Passages in the De Finibus which have to be considered in this connexion are in 1, 24; 1, 33; 1, 41; 1, 49; 2, 61; 5, 57. See C. F. W. Müller's note to the text of In Verrem 2, 2, 141. Madvig rightly castigates the ignorance of those who (with Bremi) defend *cum...videor* by saying that the indicative is used because the fact is *certain.*

operis: the plur. as here in Sull. 26; Verr. 2, 173; but *forensis opera* of long-continued activity in public business, in Acad. 2, 2; Div. 2, 142. The abl. is one of means or instrument.

periculis: here of actual dangers incurred by Cic., and not with reference to criminal trials in which he was engaged.

5. **praesidium:** φρουρά in Plato Phaedo 62 B means a prison; but cf.

Cato m. 73 vetat Pythagoras iniussu imperatoris, id est dei, de praesidio et statione ('guard-post') vitae discedere. Cf. what Cic. says of himself in Acad. 2, 6; and of Cato in Fin. 3, 7.

6. **locatus sum:** the reading *sim* appears to be quite possible according to Cicero's usage. But *possim* below cannot be right. For the matter that follows cf. Acad. 2, 6.

profecto: not dogmatic but marks merely conviction of speaker. See Landgraf on Rosc. Am. p. 194.

quantumcumque possum: see n. on 3, 58.

7. **elaborare:** Halm (p. 446 of Orelli, ed. 2, vol. 1), I believe wrongly, questioned whether it is sound Latin to say *in eo elaborare* or *id elaborare* followed by *ut* of purpose (the *ut* in 4, 30 below is different). In Verr. 2, 1, 31 (see C. F. W. Müller *ad loc.*) *elab.* has the best mss. support; ib. 3, 130 the Vatican palimpsest gives it as against the other mss.; in Tull. 1 the mss. are divided, and in De Inv. 2, 74. Where *laborare in aliqua re* occurs it seems to mean not so much to expend toil on a thing as to distress oneself over it. This sense clearly comes out in Pro Quinct. 43 and 59; N.D. 3, 62. Hence *elaboret* is to be preferred in Verr. 2, 4, 82. *Elaborare in aliqua re ne...* is in some texts of imp. Pomp. 20 (but mss. there give *lab.* which C. F. W. Müller keeps). Editors are often inconsistent. Thus C. F. W. Müller changes *labor.* to *elab.* in Verr. 2, 3, 124, but leaves it in a similar passage (Fam. 2, 4, 2). Landgraf on Rosc. Am. p. 224 is wrong in calling *condiscipulus* 'vulgar' Latin. It is used here to avoid ambiguity.

8. **tanto opere:** through the omission of the correlative, this becomes merely a stronger *magno opere;* as *tantus* is often the equivalent of *permagnus.*

modo legant illa ipsa, ne simulent, et eis servire qui vel utrisque
litteris uti velint vel, si suas habent, illas non magno opere
desiderent. Qui autem alia malunt scribi a nobis, aequi esse **11**
debent, quod et scripta multa sunt, sic ut plura nemini e nostris,
5 et scribentur fortasse plura, si vita suppetet; et tamen, qui
diligenter haec, quae de philosophia litteris mandamus, legere
assueverit, iudicabit nulla ad legendum his esse potiora. Quid
est enim in vita tanto opere quaerendum quam cum omnia in

---

1 ne: *nec* Orellius.   7 nulla: *ullam* E.

malint: 'poterat expectari indicativus de certo genere hominum ante notatorum,' Madvig. The difference between indicative and subjunctive is merely that between 'those who' and 'any who.'

1. **modo legant, ne simulent:** as Madvig says, when *legunt non simulant* is covered by *modo*, the dividing *non* naturally turns to *ne*. But I know no exact parallel. Acad. 2, 87 videantur sane, ne adfirmentur modo, quoted by Boeckel, is quite different; see my n. there. Cf. Varro r.r. 2, 2, 7 stabula idoneo loco ut sint, ne ventosa. But it can hardly be said that *nec*, read by many older editors, is impossible. If it be true (as it is) that the prohibitive *ne* is sometimes continued by *neque* instead of *neve*, there can be no inherent error in continuing by *nec* the concessive *modo*. The fact that in *ne...neque* the negative occurs in both words, and in *modo...nec* only in one is not essential. Or, to put it differently: if Cic. can cover by an *ut* two verbs linked by *et*, why not two linked by *nec* when *modo* is the covering conjunction?

utrisque litteris: 'literature in both languages.'

2. **habent:** the indicative in the midst of subjunctives, and particularly in a conditional clause, is, as many editors have noticed, very strange. Considering the state of the MSS. there is much to be said in favour of reading *habeant*. See C. F. W. Müller on De Orat. 1, 104.

3. **desiderent:** cf. Acad. 1 § 12.

qui autem, etc.: the works of course consisted mainly of speeches; cf. Orat. § 108 (after a reference to his orations) nemo enim orator tam multa ne in Graeco quidem otio scripsit quam multa sunt nostra. As Madvig remarks, Varro had no doubt surpassed Cicero in the whole compass of his writings.

aequi: cf. § 15.

4. **sic ut:** the *ut* must be consecutive here and thus different from that in N.D. 1, 49 sic tractet ut manu and N.D. 1, 81. *Sic ut* (consecutive) come together in 5, 27 but without ellipse; so Tusc. 3, 27; Fin. 4, 28.

nemini: the dat. is a little curious after *a nobis*, and *a nullo* might have been expected. In the prose of the best period the dative is rare with any part of the passive verb other than the participle. Many passages have been quoted, as illustrating this usage, which are really not pertinent. Thus *cognitus mihi* is to be set beside *mihi amicus, familiaris*; so too *cui non hoc auditum?* Also the dative after gerundive. Such usages as these form a connecting link between the dative of the agent and other datives. The *dativus commodi* has also influenced the passive construction. Thus *pertractata mihi sunt haec* (De Or. 2, 146) is 'I have gotten these things handled,' cf. probatur alicui in § 12. Those instances in Cic. where the dative occurs out of connexion with a participle, generally involve verbs of such a character that the idea of a 'dativus commodi' is possible. The commonest verb so used is *quaerere*. Tillmann in Acta Erlang. II, 71–140 has exhaustively treated this subject and rightly contends that the construction developed naturally in Latin and is no Graecism.

5. **et tamen:** 'and apart from that'; see n. on § 15.

6. **diligenter:** the word implies not industry but close attention to detail.

7. **his:** after *haec* above, *eis* would have been more usual; see n. on § 2.

8. **om. in philosophia:** *om. quae sunt in philosophia* might have been expected; cf. De Or. 3, 79 haec quae sunt in philosophia. Classical Latin had no adjective connected with *philosophus*; see my n. on Acad. 1, 9.

philosophia, tum id quod his libris quaeritur, qui sit finis, quid
extremum, quid ultimum, quo sint omnia bene vivendi recteque
faciendi consilia referenda, quid sequatur natura ut summum ex
rebus expetendis, quid fugiat ut extremum malorum? Qua de
re cum sit inter doctissimos summa dissensio, quis alienum putet 5
eius esse dignitatis, quam mihi quisque tribuat, quid in omni
12 munere vitae optimum et verissimum sit exquirere? An, partus
ancillae sitne in fructu habendus, disseretur inter principes

1 qui Orelli: quis A: *quid* BE.

1. qui sit: it is impossible to say
whether Cic. wrote *qui, quis* or *quid* here.
There are abundant analogies elsewhere
for all three. Our MSS. afford of course no
trustworthy evidence on such a point.
Cf. 4, 5 (A *qui*, cett. *quis*); ib. 14 (where
MSS. evidence is in favour of *quis*, but
edd. read *qui*). Madvig's view that
extremum, ultimum are adjectives is not
necessarily true.

2. extremum...ultimum: representa-
tions of τέλος: cf. §§ 29, 42; 2, 5; 3, 26.

quo...referenda: Cic. thus constantly expresses the Greek ἀναφέρειν
or ἐπαναφέρειν τι εἰς τι, 'to judge of
something by some standard.'

bene vivendi: εὐδαιμονίας. The word
is more often represented by *beate vivere*,
as below, §§ 57, 65 and frequently.
Often both adverbs are combined in
bene beateque vivendum, as above, § 5
and below, § 14.

4: expetendis: thus Cic. renders
αἱρετόν, the word regularly applied by
the later Greek philosophers to all
things which are included in the τέλος.
The opposite φευκτόν is rendered by
fugiendum (below).

5. quis...putet: the question is asked
although Cicero has asserted above that
such persons *do* exist; see n. on § 1.

alienum ... dignitatis: this gen.
occurs in many authors. Imitation of
the Greek construction with ἀλλότριος
has been supposed by some scholars,
but improbably. Cf. Acad. 1, 42 al.
adsensionis; Fin. 5, 78 alienum naturae;
similarly N.D. 2, 77. The abl. with *ab* is
of course common after *alienus*; the abl.
without *ab* is given by the MSS. in Div.
1, 82; 2, 102; 2, 105; Quint. 66; 98;
Verr. 5, 173; Tull. 5; Leg. Agr. 2, 65;
Phil. 11, 16 and 21; and perhaps in
a few other passages, but considering
the state of the MSS. and the analogies
in Cicero, can hardly be regarded as
certain. The dative in Caec. 24 ex illa
parte id dicit quod illi causae sit

alienum is a rare, perhaps an isolated
example of the dative (if the text be
sound) and *illi* may well be an error for
illius. Cf. *ambitioni alienus* in Sen. n.
q. 4, 1, 1.

6. tribuat: So A[1]. Madvig remarks
that *tribuit*, with *quid alienum putem*
above (favoured by Davies and Ernesti),
would lead to this conclusion, 'ut Cicero
certam quandam dignitatem ab omnibus tribui dicat, satis arroganter.' The
assertion, arrogant or not, is involved in
what was said in § 1. Madvig further
lays down that *quisque* is never the
equivalent of *omnes* but 'semper cum
aliqua distributione singulos separatim
significat.' The sense here, he says, is
'eius dignitatis quam mihi prose quisque,
sive magnam sive parvam, tribuit.' Here
the words 'sive magnam sive parvam'
are interposed in defence of Cicero's
modesty; they are not inherent in
Cicero's Latin. It is true that in most
instances the distinction between *quisque* and *omnes* is perceptible; but in
others it is shadowy (as in § 18 *quidque*
and *res quaeque*), and in some phrases
like *cuiusque modi* it vanishes altogether.
[Madvig's assertion that the nexus of
clauses makes *tribuat* a necessity can
hardly be accepted.]

7. munere: 'task,' 'function.'

an, etc.: for the form of the sentence cf. § 5 *n*. There is an imitation of
the whole passage in Lactant. Inst.
1 c. 1: et si quidam prudentes et arbitri
aequitatis institutiones civilis iuris com-
positas ediderunt, quibus civium dissi-
dentium lites contentionesque sopirent,
quanto melius nos et rectius divinas
institutiones litteris persequemur; in
quibus non de stillicidiis aut aquis
arcendis aut de manu conserenda, sed de
spe, de vita, de salute, de immortalitate,
de deo loquemur, ut superstitiones morti-
feras erroresque turpissimos sopiamus?

partus ancillae, etc.: i.e. the question
whether, if the owner of a slave-

civitatis, P. Scaevolam, M'.que Manilium, ab eisque M. Brutus
dissentiet (quod et acutum genus est et ad usus civium non
inutile, nosque ea scripta reliquaque eiusdem generis et legimus
libenter et legemus); haec, quae vitam omnem continent,
5 neglegentur? Nam, ut sint illa vendibiliora, haec uberiora certe
sunt. Quamquam id quidem licebit eis existimare, qui legerint.
Nos autem hanc omnem quaestionem de finibus bonorum et
malorum fere a nobis explicatam esse his litteris arbitramur, in
quibus, quantum potuimus, non modo quid nobis probaretur,

9 modo: om. E.

woman ceded to another the *usus
fructus* attaching to her as a piece of
property, any child she might bear
should be counted as part of the profit
of the *ususfructuarius*, apart from explicit agreement, or should pass to the
owner. Cf. Ulpian Dig. 7, 1, 68 vetus
fuit quaestio an partus ad fructuarium
pertineret: sed Bruti sententia optinuit,
fructuarium in eo locum non habere:
neque enim in fructu hominis homo
esse potest (see the context); also
Ulpian in Dig. 5, 3, 27; Gaius in Dig.
22, 1, 28; Justin. Inst. 2, 1, 37 (copied
from the preceding passage of Gaius),
also Scaevola in Dig. 50, 16, 26. For
the three lawyers here mentioned cf.
Dig. 1, 2, 2, 39 Publius Mucius et Brutus
et Manilius qui fundaverunt ius civile.
Scaevola is the well-known pontifex;
Manilius is the consul of 149 B.C.

8. **in fructu:** similarly used by Cato
Agr. 150, 2.

1. **Brutus:** for this great jurist see
Digest 1, 2, 2, 39.

2. **genus:** sc. *rerum*, as often.

3. **nosque:** for the succession *et...et
...que* see nn. on 5, 64.

reliquaque: so in 2, 106. Cicero seems
not to have felt the cacophony caused
by the repetition of the sound *qu-*;
see my nn. on Acad. 1 §§ 1, 5.

5. **vendibiliora:** 'more fashionable,'
'more popular'; Brut. 174 (orator) and
Lael. 96 (oratio); Brut. 264 populo non
satis erat v. (of a person).

6. **existimare:** =*iudicare*, as often.

8. **fere:** qualifies *explicatam*: Havet
in the Rev. de Phil. vol. XXII, p. 179,
objects to *fere* being separated from *a
nobis* and calls it (absurdly) pleonastic
beside *his litteris*; also to its separation
from *his litteris* by the verb on which
both depend; and he excises *a nobis* as a
gloss due to *nobis*, near at hand.

litteris: Rath, Orelli and others
desired to read *libris*, and even Madvig

hesitated. But Goerenz in this instance
caught the truth. There is the same
difference between *litterae*, as here used,
and *libri*, as there is between 'writings'
and 'books.' Madvig's contemptuous
remark, 'quasi id aliud sit,' is not to
the point. Cf. Att. 13, 32, 3 Torquatus
Romae est. Misi ut tibi daretur;
Catulum et Lucullum antea: his libris
nova prooemia sunt addita, quibus
eorum uterque laudatur. Eas litteras
volo habeas. [Many scholars have believed this passage to be corrupt, chiefly
because they have restricted the
reference in the word *litteras* to the
nova prooemia, which they say would not
be so indicated. But apparently Cicero
chose the word *litterae* just because
Atticus had received copies of the
'Catulus' and 'Lucullus' already, with
different *prooemia*. He therefore could
not very well say *hos libros volo habeas*.
Why the new *prooemia* should not be
described as 'writings' is hard to see.
But apart from that it is quite possible
that the word *litteras* embraces also the
'Torquatus' (i.e. the Epicurean part of
the De Finibus, which Atticus had not
previously seen). Cf. the dispute about
the meaning of *Graecis litteris* in Caes.
B.G. 5, 48, for which see Rice Holmes[2],
p. 730.] Compare also Brut. 13 where
a work by Atticus is first denoted by
litterae and then by *libri*; also De Orat.
1, 192 litteris...voluminibus; Att. 9,
10, 2 libri...litterae...doctrina; and for
litterae = 'writings,' the following passages (among a large number): Brut. 19
and 205; Fam. 5, 19, 2; ib. 15, 4, 12;
Att. 1, 14, 3 (see Tyrrell); Off. 2, 3;
Div. 2, 5; Mur. 28; Arch. 14; Phil. 2, 20.
In Verr. 3, 167 litterarum libri = 'letter-
books,' i.e. correspondence bound in
volumes. Sen. ep. 14 § 11 hae litterae =
philosophical literature.

9. **quantum potuimus:** cf. § 49 quantum efficere possimus.

sed etiam quid a singulis philosophiae disciplinis diceretur, persecuti sumus.

13 V. Vt autem a facillimis ordiamur, prima veniat in medium
Epicuri ratio, quae plerisque notissima est; quam a nobis sic
intelleges expositam ut ab ipsis qui eam disciplinam probant 5
non soleat accuratius explicari. Verum enim invenire volumus,
non tamquam adversarium aliquem convincere. Accurate autem
quondam a L. Torquato, homine omni doctrina erudito, defensa
est Epicuri sententia de voluptate, a meque ei responsum, cum
C. Triarius, in primis gravis et doctus adulescens, ei disputationi 10
14 interesset. Nam cum ad me in Cumanum salutandi causa uterque
venisset, pauca primo inter nos de litteris, quarum summum erat
in utroque studium, deinde Torquatus: Quoniam nacti te, inquit,
sumus aliquando otiosum, certe audiam quid sit quod Epicurum
nostrum non tu quidem oderis, ut fere faciunt qui ab eo dissen- 15
tiunt, sed certe non probes, eum quem ego arbitror unum vidisse

---

1 disciplinis: *disciplinae* A¹.   12 de litteris: *contulimus* addit A².   13 nacti te:
hac tite A¹E; *hac die* A².   15 oderis: *oculis* E.

1. **persecuti sumus:** for the word cf.
my n. on Acad. 1, 12; for the context,
Div. 2, 2 cumque fundamentum esset
philosophiae positum in finibus bonorum
et malorum, perpurgatus est is locus a
nobis v libris, ut quid a quoque et
quid contra quemque philosophum
diceretur intellegi posset.
  3. **facillimis:** Cicero often speaks
scornfully of the want of depth in the
Epicurean writings. See e.g. below
§ 27 illa perdiscere ludus esset; Acad.
1, 6; Tusc. 4, 6.
  4. **quae...quam:** for the repetition of
the relative at the head of successive
clauses, cf. § 22.
  5. **ipsis qui:** n. on 2, 93.
  6. **verum invenire volumus,** etc.: the
boast of the Academic School; see N.D.
1, 5 and 12; Div. 2, 28; Rep. 3, 8;
Off. 2, 7. The words therefore offer no
mere apology for the consideration
accorded to the Epicureans here, as
Usener, Epikurea, p. 264, supposes.
  7. **tamquam:** goes with *adv.* only;
not with the whole phrase *adv. al. conv.*
  8. **omni doctrina:** not merely the
doctrina of Epicurus.
  9. **a meque:** *que* is very rarely
attached to *a.*
  responsum: for the omission of *est* cf.
§§ 3, 18, 59 and n. on Acad. 2, 129.
For the form *interesse in* with ablative
see Landgraf on Pro Rosc. Am. p. 213.

10. **adulescens:** apparently much
younger than Torquatus.
  11. **ad me in Cumanum:** for the prepositions cf. 5, 96 in oppidum ad Pom-
ponium perreximus; pro imp. Cn. P. 46
ad Cn. Pompeium in ultimas prope
terras venerunt; Pis. 77 omnes ad eum...
in Albanum venerant. Many other exx.
may be found; some are given by Clark
on Mil. 51. The tendency in Latin to
change the preposition instead of repeating it is very strong. See n. on 2, 12.
  12. **pauca primo:** sc. *locuti sumus*; cf.
3, 8 deinde prima illa quae in congressu
solemus; and my n. on Acad. 1, 2
  14. **otiosum:** the outset of the discussion in De Rep. 1, 14 is similar (te autem
permagnum est nancisci otiosum, etc.).
  15. **oderis:** Tusc. 1, 77 Epicureorum,
quos equidem non despicio, sed nescio
quo modo doctissimus quisque; ib. 3,
50 et queruntur quidam Epicurei...me
studiose contra Epicurum dicere.
  ut fere, etc.: 'as those who disagree with him generally do,' not 'as
most of those who disagree with him
do'; cf. N.D. 1, 23 ut fere dicitis.
  16. **eum quem:** for the adversative
force, introducing something in sharp
contrast with what precedes cf. § 57;
Sest. 75; Nägelsbach, Stilistik, § 190, 2.
  unum vidisse verum: the constant
boast of the Epicureans. Cf. e.g. Lucian,
Alex c. 61 Ἐπικούρῳ ἀνδρὶ ὡς ἀληθῶς

verum maximisque erroribus animos hominum liberavisse et
omnia tradidisse quae pertinerent ad bene beateque vivendum.
Sed existimo te, sicut nostrum Triarium, minus ab eo delectari,
quod ista Platonis, Aristoteli, Theophrasti orationis ornamenta
5 neglexerit. Nam illud quidem adduci vix possum ut ea quae

ἱερῷ καὶ θεσπεσίῳ τὴν φύσιν καὶ μόνῳ
μετ' ἀληθείας τὰ καλὰ ἐγνωκότι καὶ παρα-
δεδωκότι καὶ ἐλευθερωτῇ τῶν ὁμιλησάντων
αὐτῷ γενομένῳ: ib. 25 and 47; Cleomedes
2, I (p. 164, ed. Ziegler) οὗτος δὲ ὑπὸ
πολλῆς τῆς σοφίας καὶ ἐπιστήμης μόνος
ἀνευρηκέναι τὴν ἀλήθειαν διαβεβαιοῦται:
Lucretius *passim*.

1. **erroribus**: it has been proposed to
read *terroribus* as in N.D. 1, 56 his terroribus ab Epicuro soluti et in libertatem
vindicati. But in § 43 three liberations
are said to be conditions of *voluptas*:
(1) freedom from ~~terrores~~; ~~(2)~~ from
cupiditates; (3) from *opinionum temeritas*. Here *erroribus* refers back to
unum vidisse verum, while *omnia* includes all the three necessary liberations. Cf. § 42 errore maximo liberabuntur.

2. **pertinerent**: the subj. is of course
a necessity here.

3. **sicut...Triarium**: 2, 8 quam ceteros: the attraction in the parenthetic
clause where the verb is omitted is
common but mostly occurs after relatives or relative particles, as 4, 56; cf.
3, 64 quod deceat cariorem nobis esse
patriam quam nosmet ipsos; Cato m. 1
te suspicor isdem rebus quibus me ipsum
interdum gravius commoveri; ib. 26;
Div. 2, 61; N.D. 1, 86; T.D. 5, 63 poetam tragicum, quam bonum, nihil ad
rem (a rare example of attraction in
a dependent clause); Leg. 1, 52; Verr. 3,
215; Fam. 5, 7, 3; pro Ligar. 2; in Pis.
79; many instances are in Livy, some
of which are given by Weissenborn in
n. on 29, 31, 2. With *ut* (as), *sicut, ceu*
and the like the nominative often remains unattracted; see Lachmann on
Lucret. 3, 614; Munro on 3, 456. Other
examples of a somewhat similar attraction are given below in n. on 2, 88; cf.
also 4, 20 *n.* (*potius quam* with infin.). In
Fam. 5, 7, 3 we have examples of
attraction and no attraction in the same
sentence.

ab eo delectari: Davies denied the
Latinity of this rare construction, but
Madvig, quoting parallels from Div. in
Caec. 44, Orat. 195, Brut. 193, Rep. 3,
42, thus defines: 'delector aliquo est

universe: *probo, placet mihi; delector
ab aliquo* est: *delectationem mihi*
(aliquo temporis momento) *parit*"; i.e.
the preposition lays stress on the fact
that some activity or effect proceeds
from the person or thing in question.
But where *ab* goes with a personal noun,
agency is implied, and where (as in
Orat. l.l.) the noun is non-personal,
there is personification, for which see n.
on 4, 17. For *delectari* followed by *in* cf.
n. on § 39.

4. **Aristoteli**: this form of the gen. of
Greek names in -ης is frequently given
by the better mss., where the inferior
add the final *s*. For the facts see Neue
1[2], 332. There is good reason to believe,
with Madvig, that Cic. used only the
form in -*i*. Cp. § 4 Euripidi.

Theophrasti orationis orn.: the two
words *orationis ornamenta*, 'stylistic
adornments,' must be taken together
and the gen. made dependent on the
notion conveyed by the two. For the
two genitives juxtaposed, where one is
dependent on the other, Madvig quotes
Brut. 163 Scaevolae dicendi elegantia;
Tusc. 4, 31; Off. 1, 43; add below 3, 51;
Ligar. 12 studia denique generis ac
familiae vestrae virtutis; Fam. 1, 1, 3
suspicionem Pompei voluntatis; N.D.
2, 156; Tusc. 3, 38 habes formam
Epicuri vitae beatae; ib. 1, 28; 4, 13;
Att. 4, 1, 2. But more commonly the
two genitives are separated either by
the governing word or by some other
word or words, as in Verr. 5, 131 multorum naufragia fortunae; Leg. 2, 42;
Att. 2, 4, 7; etc. Cicero, like Tacitus and
some other writers, often combines a
subjective and an objective genitive in
dependence on the same noun; see
Ellendt on De Or. 1, 219; and the index
to Mayor's ed. of the N.D. sub v. 'genitive.'

5. **illud adduci**: for the pronominal
accus. cf. Att. 7, 3, 8 id quod animum
induxerat (wrongly attacked by some
scholars); Draeger, Hist. Syn. 1[2], 376.
It is rightly compared by Madvig with
the pronominal accusative in such
phrases as *hoc irascor, illud tibi assentior,
quod quidam auctores sunt, id operam do*

15 senserit ille tibi non vera videantur. Vide quantum, inquam, fallare, Torquate. Oratio me istius philosophi non offendit; nam et complectitur verbis quod volt, et dicit plane quod intellegam;

Cf. Phil. 8, 30 illud non adducor, ut credam esse quosdam, where many edd. wrongly punctuate after *credam*. **adduci...ut videantur:** brief for *ut existimem...videri.* The full expression occurs (as Madvig points out) in Att. 11, 7, 3 si me adduxeris ut existimem me bonorum iudicium non funditus perdidisse; add Fam. 2, 10, 1; N.D. 2, 17 non possis adduci ut putes; Lael. 59; Parad. 14; Phil. 1, 33; 8, 30. Other instances from Plin., Liv., Val. Max., Suet., are given by Krebs-Schmalz, Antibarbarus, s. v. *adduco*; Liv. 2, 18, 6; 4, 49, 10; 6, 42, 6. The exact parallels to the present passage quoted by Madvig are a passage below in 4, 55 and Lucr. 5, 1341 vix adducor ut quierint (a spurious line), and I cannot add to these. Madvig gives passages where the *ut*-clause is replaced by accusative and infinitive, as Att. 11, 16, 2 sed ego non adducor quemquam bonum ullam salutem putare mihi tanti fuisse...; Leg. 2, 6; Cluent. 104; Curt. 10,10(2,19); Festus s. v. Oscos, p. 198 M.; add Div. 1, 35. The following similar abbreviations are noted by Madvig: Sull. 40 nec vero possum meo ingenio tantum dare ut tot res...dispexerim (i.e. me dispexisse credam); and *ratio cogit verum esse* for *ut credamus verum esse*, as below, 3, 42, and often; Leg. Agr. 3, 3 numquid est causae quin illa criminatione...vestram diligentiam prudentiamque despexerit (i.e. despexisse iudicetur); De Or. 1, 115 neque haec ita dico ut ars aliquos limare non possit; Pro Marcello 34; Att. 10, 18, 3 conficior ...venisse tempus; Leg. 3, 33 ego in ista sum sententia......nihil ut fuerit in suffragiis voce melius; Fam. 15, 2, 8 hac opinione ut...meus adventus liberarit; and similar ellipses with *definire ut* (5, 90); *efficere ut* [add *describere ut*, Tusc. 4, 20; and the same verb with acc. and infin. De Or. 2, 138; also similar ellipses with *restat ut*, *relinquitur ut* and other like phrases, such as *pugnare* with acc. and inf., for which see below, 3, 41]; *constituere ut*, below 2, 11; 2, 75 (nomen imponis in motu ut sit); *sequi ut* 3, 55; 5, 46. Not essentially different are § 31 cum...permulta dicantur cur nec voluptas in bonis sit numeranda nec in malis dolor; 2, 70 quid affers cur...Thorius vixerit; N.D. 3, 79; Tac. An. 4, 57 plerumque per-

moveor num ad ipsum referri verius sit (i.e. permoveor ut ambigam); ib. 16, 16 should probably be struck out—see Furneaux and Nipp. (Draeger reads oderint)—neque aliam defensionem ab eis quibus ista noscentur, exegerim, quam ne oderim tam segniter pereuntes (sc. odisse dicar). Cic. Div. 2, 41 vide quam temere committant...ut nulli sint di; ib. 2, 127; Acad. 2, 68 nitamur igitur nihil posse percipi; Plaut. Mil. 332 me nemo homo deterruerit quin ea sit in his aedibus. C. F. W. Müller, in his Plautinische Prosodie, p. 577, so interprets Plaut. Epid. 550 si ego te novi, animum inducam ut noveris (i.e. *ut credam te novisse*); cf. Poenul. 877 animum inducam facile ut tibi istuc credam. The poets put brevity to a further use still; thus Lucr. 3, 765 scilicet in tenero tenerascere corpore mentem confugient = ad id confugient ut dicant tenerascere; ib. 2, 1128 fluere...manus dandum est (=m. d. est et concedendum); Ovid, Fast. 5, 74 hinc sua maiores tribuisse vocabula Maio tangor; Hor. sat. 1, 4, 115 sapiens vitatu quidque petitu sit melius, causas reddet tibi; Aetna 392 atque hanc materiam penitus discurrere fontes, infectae rumpuntur aquae radice sub ipsa.

2. **oratio:** see most of the ancient opinions concerning the style of Epicurus collected in Usener's Epicurea, pp. 88 sq. The adverse verdicts rest on two things: (1) the contempt shown by Epicurus for the teaching of the rhetoricians about style; (2) his introduction of novel technical terms. Cicero speaks of his diction as *volgaris* (Acad. 1, 5) which merely implies the absence of technique (cf. Ad Herenn. 4, 69). But although Epicurus repudiated the teaching of the professed rhetoricians, as he did that of the professed dialecticians, yet he had his own views about rhetoric, and wrote of it, just as he had his own views of logic. He inculcated lucidity (σαφήνεια); see Diog. L. 10, 13. Usener (pref. pp. xli, xlii) detects a good deal of art in some of the extant writings of Epicurus.

3. **quod intellegam:** 'language such that I understand it.' But in 2, 21 plane dicit quod intellegit (Epicurus); ib. 16 (Hieronymus) quid dicat intellegit; cf. Tusc. 2, 44. These passages lend some

et tamen ego a philosopho, si afferat eloquentiam, non asperner,
si non habeat, non admodum flagitem. Re mihi non aeque
satisfacit, et quidem locis pluribus. Sed quot homines, tot

3 satisfacit: *satisfecit* codd. omnes.

colour to the supposition that Cicero
wrote here *intellegat* or *intellegit*; the
reading of A¹, *quam intellegam*, may
betray the cause of the corruption, viz.
that *quod* was accidentally changed to
quam, intellegam following suit; *quam*
was then seen to be wrong and corrected.
But *intellegam* is supported by § 26 quid
ei reliquisti nisi te, quoquo modo
loqueretur, intellegere quid diceret. The
question, however, remains whether the
subjunctive is correct; the true reading
may be *intellegit* or *intellegimus*.

1. **et tamen:** 'tamen Cicero dixit,
quod generalem sententiam de ea re
adiungit, de qua quaeri non necesse sit,
cum iam concesserit Epicurum satis
bene loqui' (Madvig). The reasoning is
hard to follow. It is not the special
statement which makes it unnecessary
to argue about the general statement,
but *vice versa. Et tamen* is often thus
idiomatically used when some point is
dismissed as of no consequence; here the
personal question concerning Epicurus
is marked as unimportant because Cicero
in the general way cares little about
rhetoric in a philosopher. Here *et tamen*
puts out of sight a particular instance,
in view of a general principle; but the
relation of the matter which precedes
et tamen to the matter which follows
need not be of that character. The
parallels in the De Fin. will show this,
viz. I §§ 11, 51; 2 §§ 15, 21, 84; 3 §§ 15,
24. In n. on 2, 84 Madvig thus puts the
matter: 'et etiam si illa, quae dixi,
defecerint, tamen cet. Itaque refertur
particula ad tacitum intellectum et con-
cessionem contrarii eius quod antea
positum est.' But there is in these
passages no tacit 'concessio contrarii.'
Tamen, indeed, does not here imply an
irreconcilability. The fact which is
dropped out of sight is not indicated
(even in the way of a momentary concession) as irreconcilable with the fresh
fact which is introduced. *Tamen* was
not originally and is not of necessity a
particle indicating opposition. The
idiom of which we have been treating
has either been misunderstood by editors.
Thus in the famous passage of Cic. ad
Qu. Fr. 2, 9 (11), 3 Lucreti poemata, ut
scribis, ita sunt, multis luminibus ingeni, multae tamen artis, it has been

assumed that the *art* is affirmed *in spite
of* the genius, which appears nonsensical, but *tamen* merely means 'even if
the genius were not there.' In Fam.
1, 7, 10 a similar *tamen* is altered by
many editors and marked as corrupt by
Mendelssohn; the critical note of
C. F. W. Müller on the passage supplies
other examples of the same misappre-
hension. See an admirable note by
Munro on Lucret. 5, 1177; and Lehmann on Cic. ad Att. p. 195; also my
n. on Cato m. 16. [Of course *et tamen*
often occurs where *tamen* does imply
strong opposition; so 2 §§ 24, 64; 3
§§ 22, 33; 5 §§ 10, 26, 69.]

a philosopho: Madv. Em. Cic. p. 50
accounts for the construction by saying
that the 'primaria sententia' is *a philosopho non flagitem*, and that the exception, which might have been conveyed by *etsi non asperner*, is expressed
in a clause parallel to, and imitating the
construction of, the 'primaria sententia.'
He quotes Fam. 3, 8, 7 hos ego sermones,
quod et multi sunt et tuam existima-
tionem, ut ego sentio, non offendunt,
lacessivi numquam, sed non valde repressi. It is obvious here that the chief
idea is *non valde repressi quod*, etc., and
that *non lacessivi quod* is strictly illogical.
Madvig gives other passages of the kind,
but it is not necessary to consider them
here, on account of a fact which he has
overlooked; viz. that *aspernari aliquid
ab aliquo*, 'to put away something from
a person or thing,' is good Latin in
itself. Cf. Clu. 194 cuius ego furorem
atque crudelitatem deos immortalis a
suis aris atque templis aspernatos con-
fido; Rosc. Am. 153 proscriptionem...a
vobis reicitis atque aspernamini; Sen.
ep. 121, 21 naturales ad utilia impetus,
naturales a contrariis aspernationes.

eloquentiam: so applied in 3, 41 to
others than orators, and often.

2. **aeque satisfacit:** the attachment
of *aeque* seems to show that Cicero
treated *satisfacere* as a compound verb;
cf. N.D. 1, 93 turpissime maledicere;
Vatin. 29 contumeliosissime maledicere;
also n. on 2, 80. But *abunde satis* occurs
separately and also *ab. satis facere.
A eque satis*, however, could hardly occur
alone.

3. **quot homines**, etc.: from Ter.

sententiae; falli igitur possumus. Quam ob rem tandem, inquit,
non satisfacit? te enim iudicem aecum puto, modo, quae dicat
16 ille, bene noris. Nisi mihi Phaedrum, inquam, mentitum aut
Zenonem putas, quorum utrumque audivi, cum mihi nihil sane
praeter sedulitatem probarent, omnes mihi Epicuri sententiae 5
satis notae sunt. Atque eos, quos nominavi, cum Attico nostro
frequenter audivi, cum miraretur ille quidem utrumque, Phaedrum autem etiam amaret, cottidieque inter nos ea quae audiebamus conferebamus, neque erat umquam controversia quid ego
intellegerem, sed quid probarem.   10
17 VI. Quid igitur est? inquit; audire enim cupio quid non probes.
Principio, inquam, in physicis, quibus maxime gloriatur, primum

3 nisi: *hic* P, alii.   5 sedulitatem dett.: *sed utilitatem* AE et P¹ (corr.
postea in *sedulitatem*).   7 Phaedrum: *Ph. pulchrum* E (cum in quodam codice
scriba *phelcrum* scriptum invenisset).

Phorm. 454; cf. Hor. sat. 2, 1, 27 quot
capitum vivunt totidem studiorum milia.
For the omission of the verb cf. n. on 2,
105 iucundi acti labores.

2. **aecum**: cf. 2, 119 eiuro inicum.

4. **audivi**: as to Cicero's early attachment to Epicureanism, see the Introd.
to my ed. of the Academica, especially
pp. 1, 3. Philodemus, of whose writings
much has been preserved in the Herculanean rolls, was a pupil of Zeno, and
drew much from him, particularly in
the well-known treatise "περὶ σημείων
καὶ σημειώσεων." Cf. ὁ φίλτατος Ζήνων
in roll no. 1012, col. 21 (Scott's Fragmenta Herculanensia, p. 29).

5. **probarent**: n. on 2, 1 significarent.

6. **atque...audivi**, etc.: as confirma-
tion and expansion of *audivi* above,
which, if left unmodified, might have
been taken to refer to a single occasion
only.

7. **frequenter**: as in 2, 12; 5, 8 and
often. Note that Cicero does not express
the idea of a repeated action by the
perfect *alone*. Sometimes editors have
wrongly altered perfects, because they
imagined the notion of frequency to
be wrongly attached to them by MSS.;
e.g. Fam. 6, 6, 2 non putarunt seems to
be suspected even by C. F. W. Müller;
but the sense is 'never (at any one time)
supposed.' So e.g. De Or. 3, 52; Parad.
9; fragm. ap. C. F. W. Müller, v, 103.

cum...amaret: the facts are somewhat illogically introduced, as they add
nothing to the proof of Cicero's familiarity with Epicureanism.

Phaedrum...amaret: there is the same

contrast between these two in N.D. 1,
93; for Zeno was not lovable; see Tusc.
3, 38.

8. **audiebamus conferebamus**. a rare
example of the juxtaposition of two imperfect tenses.

9. **quid ego intellegerem**: dependent
clauses whether involving subjunctives
or infinitives often depend on substantives, but there is always slight ellipse.
Here controversia, qua disputabamus.
For infinitive clauses dependent on substantives see my n. on Acad. 2, 120.
Excusationem cur in Fam. 4, 4, 1; Lucan
1, 68 opus followed by quid.

11. **quid igitur est?** Davies proposed
to remove the note of interrogation, to
bracket *audire enim cupio*, and to change
quid to *quod*. But in that case *est igitur*,
rather than *igitur est*, would have been
natural; see n. on § 43. While *quid ergo
est?* ('what is the meaning of this?') is
common, the form *quid igitur est?* is
found only here in the philosophical
works and once only in the speeches,
viz. Rosc. Am. 36. In a note on the
latter passage, Landgraf gives a good
deal of information, partly based on
Seyffert, Scholae Latinae, 1 § 48. Cf.
n. on 2, 7 quid ergo?

12. **principio...primum**: the idea of
some old scholars that one of these
words is superfluous was long since
refuted; *principio* refers to the division
of philosophy into φυσική, διαλεκτική,
ἠθική (for which see my n. on Acad.
1, 19). The second of these divisions is
treated in § 22, the third in §§ 23 sq.
Primum introduces the first of several

totus est alienus; Democritia dicit perpauca mutans, sed ita
ut ea quae corrigere volt, mihi quidem depravare videatur. Ille
atomos quas appellat, id est corpora individua propter soliditatem, censet in infinito inani, in quo nihil nec summum nec
5 infimum nec medium nec ultimum nec extremum sit, ita ferri ut

1 Democriti adicit: sic E (sec. Madvig); *Democrite adicit* A[1]; *Democrito adicit* A[2].
4 inani: *innatu* E.   5 ultimum: '*intimum* recte videtur coniecisse Jonas in
dissert. Berol. 1870' Müller; vid. comm.

objections taken to the φυσική of
Epicurus, viz. that he is a plagiarist.
The omission of *deinde* after *primum* has
numerous parallels not only in Cicero,
but in other authors; and there are a
good many instances in this treatise.
Primum twice over in N.D. 2, 142.

quibus maxime gloriatur: see n. on
§ 63 in physicis plurimum posuit.

1. **alienus:** this sense is developed by
contrast from the commoner *suus*,
'original'; cf. 4, 10; 5, 14; Leg. 2, 17
nisi plane esse vellem meus. There is
no reason to think (with Iwan Müller,
progr. Erlang. 1869) that Cic. here imitated a Greek phrase, πάντα ἀλλότριος.
The development of meaning by which
alienus acquires the sense of 'unoriginal'
in Latin is quite as natural as that which
attached the same sense to ἀλλότριος.
Cf. § 26 aliena dixit in physicis. The
reproach of plagiarism hurled against
Epicurus was widespread in ancient
times. Diog. L. 10, 4, quotes as though
from several writers: τὰ δὲ Δημοκρίτου
περὶ τῶν ἀτόμων καὶ τὰ Ἀριστίππου περὶ
τῆς ἡδονῆς ὡς ἴδια λέγειν, and Plut.
Colot. c. 3 asserts that Epicurus called
himself ὁ Δημοκρίτειος in early days.
According to Cic. N.D. 1, 73 he admitted
that he had listened to lectures by
Nausiphanes, a pupil of Democritus;
nevertheless he is said to have overwhelmed both the pupil and the
master with coarse abuse (n. on § 21),
as he did almost every other philosopher
of distinction. Cic. often repeats the
charge about Democritus, as below 2,
102; 4, 13; Acad. 1, 5; N.D. 1 §§ 73, 93,
120. In the fragment περὶ αἰσθήσεως,
preserved in one of the Herculanean
rolls (Scott, Fragmenta Herculanensia,
pp. 275 sq.), there seems to be a polemic
against the plagiarism of Epicurus, and
his 'ungrateful quackery' (ἀχάριστος
ἀλαζονεία) seems to be condemned.

Democritia dicit, etc.: cf. the closely
parallel passage in 4, 13. Boeckel brings
two objections against the reading
of E: (1) that *Democritia dicere* is a

harsh phrase; (2) that Cicero would
have written *perpaucis mutatis* not
mutans (which he thinks has come from
§ 21). As to (1) the phrase *Democritia
dicere* seems to be no harsher than *aliena
dicere* (§ 26 and Phil. 2, 42). Objection
(2) has nothing in it; *mutans* is just as
good as *paucis mutatis* or *cum pauca
mutavisset*; cf. e.g. Att. 10, 7, 3 Curio
mecum vixit, iacere Caesarem putans...
Siciliaeque diffidens, where *cum putaret*
might have been substituted; see
Kühner, Gram. § 136, 4.

2. **ille:** as though *Democritus*, not
Democritia had preceded; see n. on 5, 16.

3. **quas appellat:** =eas quas atomos
appellat; cf. Leg. 2, 5 astu, quod appellatur.

individua: so below 2, 75; the word
first occurs in Acad. 2, 55; but ib. 125
atomus is already used as a Latin word.
Amafinius, the Epicurean writer, had
rendered ἄτομος by *corpusculum* which
Cicero sometimes employs; see Acad.
1, 6 with my n. But Cicero does not
use *insecabilia* (Vitruv., etc.). *Dividuus*
is as old as Terence.

propter soliditatem: so Cicero connects the words *individua* and *solida* in
speaking of the atoms, below § 18; N.D.
2, 93. Galen, de elem. sec. Hippocr.
1, 2, vol. 1, p. 418 K., says that the
followers of Epicurus held the atoms to
be ὑπὸ σκληρότητος ἄθραυστα, while
the school of Leucippus deemed them
ὑπὸ σμικρότητος ἀδιαίρετα. The
soliditas of Cicero is the *solida simplicitas* of Lucret. in the oft-repeated
phrase *solida pollentia simplicitate*.

4. **infinito inani:** n. on 2, 54 callido
improbo. For the boundlessness of the
void see Lucr. 1, 958 ff.; N.D. 1, 54 in
hac immensitate latitudinum longitudinum altitudinum infinita vis innumerabilium volitat atomorum.

in quo...sit: see n. on 4, 16 in quibus
...numeretur.

5. **ultimum:** C. F. W. Müller interprets *extremum* as περιφέρεια 'superficies,'
'surface,' with which he thinks *intimum*,

concursionibus inter se cohaerescant, ex quo efficiantur ea quae
sint quaeque cernantur omnia, eumque motum atomorum nullo
18 a principio, sed ex aeterno tempore intellegi convenire. Epicurus
autem, in quibus sequitur Democritum, non fere labitur. Quamquam utriusque cum multa non probo, tum illud in primis, quod, 5
cum in rerum natura duo quaerenda sint, unum, quae materia

3 ex aeterno: *extremo* E.

'inmost point,' stands in contrast; the
word would also be contrasted with
summum and *infimum*. This is no doubt
a possible meaning of *extremum*, and
Müller quotes for it N.D. 2, 47; Timaeus
§ 17; Varro r. r. 1, 51, 1. The same sense
attaches to *extremitas*; for which see n.
on 2, 102. But Müller, in order to avoid
the tautology involved in *ultimum*...
extremum, introduces another of the
same kind, for it is just as hard to draw
a distinction between *medium* and *intimum*. Numerous attempts to lay down
a difference in sense between *ultimum*
and *extremum* here have been made, but
with no success. If Cicero were here
writing apart from a Greek original,
there would be nothing unnatural in his
using synonymous phrases; indeed,
these two very words occur together
many times as twin renderings of the
word τέλος in its ethical senses (see n.
on 3, 26). But there is reason to think
that Cicero has here badly represented
some words which he found in a Greek
source. This may be seen from Cleomedes, Met. 1, 1, 8: ἄπειρον τοίνυν ἅμα
καὶ ἀσώματον ὂν οὔτε ἄνω τι ἂν ἔχοι οὔτε
κάτω, οὔτε ἔμπροσθεν οὔτε ὄπισθεν, οὔτε
ἐκ δεξιῶν οὔτε ἐξ εὐωνύμων οὔτε μέσον·
αὗται γὰρ αἱ σχέσεις ἑπτὰ οὖσαι περὶ
σώματα θεωροῦνται. This classification of
σχέσεις was evidently hackneyed. All
seven are mentioned in Aristot. 665 *b*, 19
and 667 *b*, 33, and six of them (omitting
μέσον) ib. 284 *b*, 30 and 665 *a*, 23. In
fragm. 195 it is said by Simplicius, on
the authority of Aristotle, that to three
of these σχέσεις, viz. δεξιόν ἄνω ἔμπροσθεν,
the Pythagoreans gave the name ἀγαθόν,
and to the three contrasts the name
κακόν. Cf. also Aristot. Physica 205 *b*,
30 ἢ πῶς τοῦ ἀπείρου ἔσται τὸ μὲν ἄνω,
τὸ δὲ κάτω, ἢ ἔσχατον ἢ μέσον; ἔτι πᾶν
σῶμα αἰσθητὸν ἐν τόπῳ, τόπου δὲ εἴδη καὶ
διαφοραὶ τἄνω καὶ κάτω καὶ ἔμπροσθεν
καὶ ὄπισθεν καὶ δεξιὸν καὶ ἀριστερόν.
From this last passage it would seem
probable that ἔσχατον and some contrasted word sometimes took the place
of ἔμπροσθεν and ὄπισθεν; and so that

Cicero has obscured by his rendering a
real contrast.

ferri: Epic. ap. Diog. L. 10, 43
κινοῦνται συνεχῶς αἱ ἄτομοι. The *clinamen*
(παρέγκλισις) is omitted here, to be
introduced more prominently later.

1. **concursionibus:** by *concursus* or
concursio (for the two forms cf. Nägelsbach, Stilistik, § 56, 1 *b*), Cicero represents ἀντικοπή, σύγκρουσις in the Epicurean texts.

2. **cernantur:** the atoms themselves
being invisible as lying *infra nostros
sensus* (Lucr. 4, 112).

nullo a principio: Epicurus ap. Diog.
L. § 44 ἀρχὴ δὲ τούτων οὐκ ἔστιν.

3. **a...ex:** for the change of the preposition cf. 2, §§ 12, 22. Cicero says both
ab omni aeternitate and *ex o. a.*, both *ab
aeterno tempore* and *ex a. t.*; but *ex* is far
commoner than *ab*.

convenire: infinitive of the impersonal *convenit*. The omission of *fuisse* is
rather awkward.

4. **in quibus:** =in eis, in quibus; so
Fam. 12, 15, 1 per quos celerrime possent;
Sen. d. 12, 6, 8 iterum ibunt per quae
venerant; Fin. 2, 3 inter quos disseritur
conveniat; De Or. 2, 245 quae cadere
possunt in quos nolis; Phil. 1, 10 parum
erat...a quibus debuerat adiutus; N.D.
2, 10 senatus, quos ad soleret, referen-
dum censuit.

fere: very rarely goes before a negative word at all or a positive word which
it qualifies; see Krebs-Schmalz, Antibarbarus, s. v. Madvig in Brut. 150
reads nihil fere aut non multum for nihil
aut non fere multum.

labitur: i.e. does not stumble by
getting confused.

5. **utriusque multa:** n. on 4, 32.
Madvig illustrates the common omission
of *alia* after *multa*.

6. **duo quaerenda sint,** etc.: all this
is set forth in more detail in Acad. 1,
24 sq. where the doctrine, which is
essentially Stoic, is called (after Antiochus of Ascalon) 'Old Academic.' See
my nn. there; and add to the references
Lactant. div. inst. 7, 3 Stoici naturam

sit, ex qua quaeque res efficiatur, alterum, quae vis sit, quae quidque efficiat, de materia disseruerunt, vim et causam efficiendi reliquerunt. Sed hoc commune vitium; illae Epicuri propriae ruinae: censet enim eadem illa individua et solida corpora ferri
5 deorsum suo pondere ad lineam; hunc naturalem esse omnium

1 ex qua: *ex quo* AE. 2 disseruerunt: *deseruerunt* A[1]. 5 hunc: *habent* BE, cum scriba h^c ut h^t interpretatus sit.

in duas partes dividunt, unam quae efficiat, alteram quae se ad faciendum tractabilem praebeat; in illa prima esse vim sentiendi, in hac materiam, nec alterum sine altero posse; 'Ocellus Lucanus,' c. 2, 2 τὸ ἀειπαθὲς μέρος τοῦ κόσμου καὶ τὸ ἀεικίνητον: Stob. Flor. 3, 75. **materia**: for the renderings in Latin of ὕλη see my n. on Acad. 1, 24, and add Aetna 388 silvae (plural); ib. 446 materiam silvamque; in Rutil. Namat. 1, 488 *fomes* is used like *materia*.

2. **vim...reliquerunt**: thus broadly stated, the reproach is not true, for all force in the Epicurean system is traced back to the downward motion of atoms in space. The same charge is brought in Acad. 1, 6; and is over and over again advanced by Aristotle against the Atomists. See Zeller, 1³, p. 788.

et causam efficiendi: *et* is explanatory, *vim* and *causam efficiendi* being identical in meaning. The genitive *efficiendi* is one of definition or equivalence: 'the cause, that is the efficient force' or 'the cause which lies in the efficient force.' Examples of this genitive attached to *causa* are given in my n. on Acad. 1, 6 causas rerum efficientium; add Off. 2, 16 causas eluvionis; De Or. 2, 63 causae...vel casus vel sapientiae vel temeritatis; Div. in Caec. 6 causam tantae necessitudinis. Cf. 3, 45 *n.*

3. **sed hoc commune vitium**: the omission of the substantive verb is common in brief clauses where great emphasis is laid on some one word, often a pronoun, as here; often an adverb or adjective. Cf. § 20 ne illud quidem physici; 2, 6 hoc vero optimum; 2, 93; 3, 27. Many examples are given in my nn. on Acad. 2, 86 and 94 from different authors; and many more might be added.

commune: Lactant. div. inst. 3, 17, 22 Democritus eruditus hereditatem stultitiae reliquit Epicuro.

illae...enim: n. on 3, 26. Madvig notes that the clause with which *enim* or other inferential particle (as *itaque, quare*, etc.) stands is in Cicero often merely introductory to a long demon-

stration, and if taken by itself would seem illogical. Here the 'peculiar downfall' of Epicurus does not lie in his assertion of downward movement attaching to the atoms (which is equally a doctrine of Democritus) but in his subsequent abandonment of that principle, by the invention of the 'swerving aside.' Many passages of the kind have caused unnecessary trouble to editors. Madvig illustrates by reference to Tusc. 2, 62; N.D. 1, 85; Verr. 4, 108; De Or. 2, 217. Hartman in Mnem. XXII ejects an *enim* like this in Clu. 115; Brut. 1, 15, 4.

4. **ruinae**: cf. 2, 18 (Epicurus) ruit in dicendo; 5, 83 iam ruinas videres; Leg. 1, 39 Academia nimias edet ruinas; Lucr. 1, 740 principiis tamen in rerum fecere ruinas.

solida: ναστάς of the atoms in Simplic. on Arist. de caelo 275 *b*, 29 (Usener, p. 202).

5. **deorsum**: the *r* was probably not pronounced, even when written; see Gröber in Archiv 2, 101 sq. The form *deorsus*, though found occasionally in our MSS. (as in A in § 19), was probably not used by Cic. The word is not employed by Cicero as an adverb of rest, in which sense it occurs in old Latin and in Varro r. r. 1, 6, 3.

suo pondere: cf. N.D. 1, 69 suopte pondere; De Fato 23 gravitate naturali ac necessaria; N.D. 1, 69 pondere et gravitate; Lucr. 2, 84 gravitate sua. Madvig quotes from Diog. L. 10, 61 ἡ κάτω (φορὰ) διὰ τῶν ἰδίων βαρῶν. Cf. Usener, p. 19, 1.

ad lineam: for *ad lineas* in late writers see Otto in Archiv 7, 10, 11; κατὰ σταθμήν of the atoms in Plut. Plac. 1, 12, 3 and 1, 23, 4 (Aetius ap. Diels, p. 311 *a*, 10 and p. 319); cf. *rectis lineis*, De Fato 22; *derecto deorsum*, N.D. 1, 69; *rectum per inane*, Lucr. 2, 217 (where see Munro's n.). Guyau, Morale d'Épicure, p. 74, tries, but unsuccessfully, to relieve Epic. from some of the absurdity of assuming perpendicular lines in space. See Plut. de def. orac. p. 425 D.

19 corporum motum. Deinde ibidem homo acutus, cum illud occurreret, si omnia deorsum e regione ferrentur et, ut dixi, ad lineam, numquam fore ut atomus altera alteram posset attingere, † itaque attulit rem commenticiam: declinare dixit atomum

2 deorsum BE, cf. n. ad § 18: *deorsus* A. Vide Neue-Wagener II 744 f.   2 ad lineam: *adlimam* A¹.   3 fore ut: *fore unquam* E.

1. **corporum**: 'heavy bodies,' not atoms, for which Cicero does not employ *corpora* alone, but *c. individua*. Below (§ 19) he has *ponderum*, for which cf. Lucr. 2, 190 pondera, quantum in se est, cum deorsum cuncta ferantur. Madvig's remark that Epic. denied to the atoms a third motion, the only one assigned to them by Democritus, and called πληγή, is erroneous, in two ways. See Zeller, I³, 794, 5. There is no doubt that D. attributed downright rectilinear motion to the atoms as well as πληγή, which implies the collision of atom with atom after they had met; and the conceptions of Ep. and Dem. as to the movement of the atoms after their meeting do not differ essentially.

deinde ibidem: the same combination of particles is found in Acad. 2, 44. In my n. there examples are given of *deinde* combined with *tum, post, postea, statim, mox* and *hinc*; also of the phrase *ibidem ilico* [*deinde post* wrongly attacked by Novák in Vell. P. 2, 23, 3].

2. **occurreret**: 'confronted him'; not essentially different from the use of the word in 2, 108, where see n. Madvig, objecting to an old interpretation, which made the word equivalent to *adversaretur* or *repugnaret*, explains 'in mentem veniret et cogitanti contrarium videretur.' But the distinction is trivial; if the idea of opposition is attached to *occurreret* at all, it matters nothing here whether the opposing circumstance is treated as a reflexion, or a fact. And the notion of opposition is conspicuously present here, differentiating the use of the verb from those we find, e.g., in 3, 53; 4, 24.

e regione: 'in a straight line'; the meaning of *e* in this phrase seems to be 'in accordance with,' as in *e natura*, 5, 26, where see n. The original sense of *regio* is well seen in this phrase, as in *recta regione, regione viarum*, etc. Sometimes *e regione* means 'straight opposite,' as in N.D. 2, 103 e. r. solis, 'straight in the path of the sun' and Acad. 2, 123.

3. **numquam fore**, etc.: so Epic. ap. Diog. L. 10, 42 οὐδαμοῦ ἂν ἔμενε τὰ σώματα, ἀλλ' ἐφέρετο κατὰ τὸ ἄπειρον κενὸν διεσπαρμένα, οὐκ ἔχοντα τὰ ὑπερείδοντα καὶ στέλλοντα κατὰ τὰς ἀνακοπάς, i.e. there would have been nothing underneath the atoms to stay them and place them in a position to knock up against one another. Democritus believed that the heavier atoms would overtake the lighter and so the vortex of atoms (δίνη) would be started; see Zeller, I³, 793–5, and the refutation by Lucr. 2, 225 sq.

altera alteram: De Fato 22 atomus ab atomo pulsa. Cicero's words here lie close to those of Simplicius on Arist. phys. 4, 8 (p. 216 *a*, 17) οὐδέποτε καταλήψεται ἡ ἑτέρα τὴν ἑτέραν οὐδὲ ἀλληλοτυπήσουσιν ἢ περιπλακήσονται. οὐδὲ γὰρ ἡ τῶν σχημάτων διαφορὰ οἷα τέ ἐστιν ἄνισον αὐτῶν ποιεῖν τὴν φοράν· καὶ γὰρ τὰ σχήματα τῷ διαιρεῖν (sc. τὸν ἀέρα) ἢ τῷ μὴ διαιρεῖν ἄνισον τὴν φορὰν ποιεῖ. ἐν δὲ τῷ κενῷ οὐδέν ἐστι τὸ διαιρούμενον. ὥστε οὐδὲ γένεσις ἔσται τινός. Cf. Us. § 279.

4. **itaque**: no real example has been produced of *itaque* used to introduce an apodosis. It has been suggested that it is here used as a resumptive particle; but as Madvig says, the circumstances are not such as to call for a resumptive particle; and moreover, although *ergo* and *igitur* are freely used so, the one passage quoted for such an employment of *itaque*, viz. Liv. 2, 12, 2, is not above suspicion. [The instances quoted by Draeger, II², p. 184, are quite different; they all occur at the beginning of a sentence, not in the middle.] We are driven to choose between emending the text and assuming a lacuna in the archetype of our MSS. The supposition that the words *itaque...commenticiam* are a gloss is improbable; if there is corruption, it lies in *itaque*, and the only word of which this could well be a depravation is *inique*, which does not fit in with the context. It is better to suppose that a few words have dropped out, and a clue to their general sense is afforded by the passage of Simplicius quoted above and Cicero's own words below. The drift of the omitted words may be thus represented: *neque ut complexiones atomorum inter se extarent, quibus mundus crearetur, alio confugiendum sibi videbat, itaque*.

perpaulum, quo nihil posset fieri minus; ita effici complexiones et copulationes et adhaesiones atomorum inter se, ex quo efficeretur mundus omnesque partes mundi quaeque in eo essent. Quae cum res tota ficta sit pueriliter, tum ne efficit *quidem*, quod 5 volt. Nam et ipsa declinatio ad libidinem fingitur (ait enim declinare atomum sine causa, quo nihil turpius physico quam

2 adhaesiones: *adhaesitationes* A.   4 quidem: om. AB.

commenticiam: so Fat. 23 commenticia declinatio; also ib. 48.

1. **perpaulum**: Fat. 22 declinat atomus intervallo minimo—id appellat (Epicurus) ἐλάχιστον: so ib. 46; N.D. 1, 69 ait atomum declinare paullulum; Lucr. 2, 217 sq. corpora...se incerto tempore ferme | incertisque locis spatio depellere paulum, | tantum quod momen mutatum dicere possis; ib. 243 sq. paulum inclinare necesse est | corpora, nec plus quam minimum ne fingere motus | obliquos videamur et id res vera refutet. [In favour of *depellere*, the reading of the MSS. in Lucr. 1, 219, the occurrence of *pellere depellere* with reference to the atoms in Fat. 22 may be adduced.]

posset: the subj. is solely due to the *oratio obliqua*; not perceiving this, and supposing it to be 'potential,' Otto and some others among the older editors make unnecessary trouble. See below, § 30 n.

complexiones: περιπλοκή is the word of Epicurus ap. Diog. L. 10, 43.

2. **quo**: for the neut. sing. here see n. on § 20 and Acad. 1, 32.

3. **partes mundi**: the larger divisions of the *mundus*, such as sea, sky, land (which are defined as *mundi membra* in N.D. 1, 100) seem to be here intended. Cf. 4, 12, and for illustrations of the expression see my n. on Acad. 1, 28.

4. **efficit**: the subject is *Epicurus*, not *res*; see below, *nec tamen id cuius causa haec finxerat assecutus est.*

5. **nam**: the sentence which follows does not prove or confirm the preceding but awkwardly repeats its sense. But *nam* in Cicero often corresponds not so much to our 'for' as to 'indeed,' used as a continuative particle; see n. on *enim* in 1, 18.

declinatio: the word of Lucretius is *clinamen*; cf. Philod. περὶ σημείων καὶ σημειώσεων col. 36, 7 τὰς ἐπ᾽ ἐλάχιστον παρεγκλίσεις τῶν ἀτόμων.

fingitur: the very word which is deprecated by Lucr. 2, 244.

6. **sine causa**: two reasons for the

declinatio were always given by the Epicureans: (1) that without it the atoms would never have come together to create things; (2) that free-will can only be explained by some deviation from rigid law in the atoms out of which all things arise. Cf. De Fat. 23 Epicurus ...veritus est ne, si semper atomus gravitate ferretur naturali ac necessaria, nihil liberum nobis esset, cum ita moveretur animus, ut atomorum motu cogeretur. The *declinatio* is therefore a hypothesis intended to explain the present by the past. But atomism was from the first described by its opponents as being a scheme without cause: so Arist. gen. an. 789 *b*, 2 Δημόκριτος δὲ τὸ οὗ ἕνεκα ἀφεὶς λέγειν πάντα ἀνάγει εἰς ἀνάγκην οἷς χρῆται ἡ φύσις. The physical cause of movement, in the eyes of the atomists, lies solely in the void: Arist. phys. 265 *b*, 23 διὰ δὲ τὸ κενὸν κινεῖσθαι φασίν. And the word *fortuitus* is often applied to the meeting of the atoms by critics of Democritus as well as by those of Epicurus. Generally the critics have in view the absence from both systems of a controlling divine mind. But sometimes the *declinatio* is said to be without cause merely because there is no external physical impulse to give rise to it. This is the case in De Fato 22, declinationem si minus verbis, re cogitur confiteri. Non enim atomus ab atomo pulsa declinat [as in the system of Democritus, which therefore has the advantage over that of Epicurus]. Nam qui potest pelli alia ab alia, si gravitate feruntur ad perpendiculum corpora individua rectis lineis ut Epicuro placet? [Of the atoms descended according to the view of Democritus, the impinging of the heavier atoms on the lighter would account for the abandonment of the rectilinear motion.] Sequitur enim ut si alia ab alia numquam depellatur ne contingat quidem alia aliam. [If there is no knocking aside, there is no touching, because touching would lead to knocking aside. This is assumed, and rightly;

fieri quicquam sine causa dicere), et illum motum naturalem omnium ponderum, ut ipse constituit, e regione inferiorem locum petentium sine causa eripuit atomis nec tamen id, cuius causa
20 haec finxerat, assecutus est. Nam si omnes atomi declinabunt, nullae umquam cohaerescent, sive aliae declinabunt, aliae suo 5 nutu recte ferentur, primum erit hoc quasi provincias atomis dare,

2 e regione: *a r.* E; *regionem* om. *e* P.

a point missed by Madvig, in his n. on *declinare atomum perpaulum.*] Ex quo efficitur etiamsi sit atomus eaque declinet, declinare sine causa. Plut. de anim. procr. in Tim. p. 1015 *c* Ἐπικούρῳ ἀναίτιον ἐπεισάγοντι κίνησιν. Carneades argued (De Fato, 23) that so far as free-will is concerned, Epicurus could have done without the παρέγκλισις.

quo nihil turpius...quam: for *quam* along with the ablat. of comparison cf. Acad. 1, 45 neque hoc quicquam esse turpius quam...; De Or. 1, 169 quid ergo hoc fieri turpius potest quam...; ib. 2, 38 and 302; N.D. 1, 38; Div. 1, 87; Att. 4, 8 *b*, 2; ib. 8, 9, 3; pro Quinct. 8; Prov. cons. 36; Phil. 12, 9. A similar idiom occurs in Greek, ἤ following the genit. of comparison.

physico: Fat. 25 ne omnibus a physicis irrideamur, si dicamus quicquam fieri sine causa; Galen, de plac. 4, 389 (ed. Müller) εἰ οὖν μηδὲν ἀναιτίως γίνεται καὶ τοῦτό ἐστιν ἁπάντων σχεδόν τι τῶν φιλοσόφων ὁμολόγημα κοινόν: Quint. 7, 2, 36 at nihil credibile sit factum esse sine causa.

3. **sine causa...cuius causa**: for the repetition of *causa* cf. Lael. 57.

4. **si omnes...sive aliae**: this is a very rare use for *sive...sive* or *si...sin*, the former mode being employed when the two alternatives are on the same level, the latter when there is a contrast between them. It is hard to trust our мss. in such matters, and easier here to believe that they have dropped the second syllable of the first *sive* than that Cicero departed once from his own constant usage and that of his time. There are two passages in which *si quid* or *si quis* is succeeded by *sive*, viz. Att. 10, 18, 2 si quid de Hispaniis sive quid aliud, perge quaeso scribere; and Rep. 4, 12 si quis occentavisset sive carmen condidisset. But the latter passage is archaistic, and modelled after the language of the statutes; while in the former *si quid* is the equivalent of *quidquid* and *sive* is used as e.g. in Off. 1, 33 Q. Fabium Labeonem seu quem alium. The мss.

of Caesar's *De Bello Gallico* are so bad that little importance can be attached to the reading in 4, 17 si arborum trunci sive naves...essent immissae; cf. too Val. M. 2, 6, 5 (where *si...sive* is retained by the recent editor, Kempf); Phaedr. App. 18, 8. Apart from the passages quoted there are no real exceptions before Seneca excepting in archaic writers (Ennius Plaut. Ter. etc.) and archaizing Latin (statutes, formulae, and the like). Some apparent exx. are to be explained by anacoluthon; for which see my n. on Acad. 1, 7 sive...sin vero and Madvig, Excursus to 1, 23. [The reference in Draeger to Virg. Aen. 1, 218 is an error.] Where *si...sive* occurs in archaic or archaistic Latin, the two particles usually belong to two complete protases which have a common apodosis. The appearance in the present passage of an apodosis to each of the protases is especially unusual; as also is the connexion of the two particles in Att. 10, 18, 2 and Caes. B. G. 4, 17 with a common verb. Cicero occasionally uses *si...si* for *sive...sive* or *si...sin*, as to which see my n. on Acad. 1, 7; but not when the particles lie so close together as in Pl. Rud. 1257 si aurum, si argentumst; Lucr. 4, 783 si mare, si terrast cordi, si denique caelum.

si declinabunt ... cohaerescent: sentences of this form (fut. ind. both in protasis and apodosis) are especially common in Cicero; see Blase in the 'Commentationes in honorem G. Studemund' (Strassburg, 1889).

5. **nullae cohaerescent**: this only holds good if all the atoms swerve at exactly the same angle, and continue to move in parallel lines.

6. **nutu**: 'tendency to move'; cf. Tusc. 1, 40 ut...terrena et umida (corpora)...suopte nutu et suo pondere... ferantur; Rep. 6, 17 in eam (tellurem) feruntur omnia nutu suo pondera; N.D. 2, 98 terra...undique ipsa in sese nutibus suis conglobata (here the tendency of every portion of the earth towards its centre); so De Or. 3, 178 and Lucr.

quae recte, quae oblique ferantur, deinde eadem illa atomorum,
in quo etiam Democritus haeret, turbulenta concursio hunc
mundi ornatum efficere non poterit. Ne illud quidem physici,
credere aliquid esse minimum; quod profecto numquam puta-
5 visset, si a Polyaeno, familiari suo, geometrica discere maluisset

5 geometrica I. F. Gronovius: *geometricam* codd.

Possibly in Virg. Ecl. 4, 50 aspice con-
vexo *nutantem pondere* mundum we have
an echo of Epicurean phraseology.
provincias dare: cf. Fat. 46 num sor-
tiuntur (atomi) inter se quae declinent,
quae non?
1. **quae...ferantur:** for the indirect
question loosely dependent on *provincias dare* (really dependent on some
such idea as *ut decernatur* omitted) cf.
n. on 1, 14 above and 1, 30 itaque negat
opus esse ratione neque disputatione
quamobrem voluptas expetenda, fugiendus dolor sit (i.e. *disputatione qua
demonstretur*, etc.).
2. **in quo:** 'wherein' =*in qua re.* The
neut. pron. is often used in place of a
relative agreeing with the preceding
substantive, whatever be the gender or
number of the substantive. The same
usage attaches to *in eo* (2, 6). Many
passages in which this idiom occurs have
been wrongly changed by editors, and
no doubt many examples of its occurrence have been obscured by the writers
of MSS.; Fin. 1, 56; 2, 6; 3, 21 and 5, 37;
Leg. 1, 45. A good many examples of
the idiom will be found in a n. of mine
on Acad. 1, 32; add to these Div. 1, 72;
De Or. 1, 246 (where *in quo* is an almost
certain correction for *in qua*); 1, 253;
2 §§ 72, 83 (bis), 110, 142; Fam. 1, 9, 7
and 9, 1, 2 (where C. F. W. Müller
rightly keeps *in eo* against Wesenberg
and others); Att. 2, 18, 2 mentionem
facere, quo (kept by edd.); ib. 4, 15, 6;
Fam. 4, 3, 4; Off. 1, 35; De Or. 2, 122; ib.
1, 144 (in quo, some editors for *in qua*);
2, 239; 331; Qu. Fr. 2, 3, 4 (where
Tyrrell vainly defends the reading of
the M.SS. *in ea*); Varro r. r. 1, 13, 7 (*in eo*
needlessly altered, even by Keil); ib.
1, 17, 3. [See Keil's n. on the last passage, and also Spengel, praef. to Varro
de Ling. Lat. ed. 1885, pp. lxvii sq.] In
all the passages to which reference has
been made above one or other of the
expressions, *in eo, in quo*, occurs. But
a similar use of the neut. pron. is found,
though less commonly, in other forms;
see n. on 4, 65.
haeret: the word, as Madvig notes,
does not imply that Dem. admitted the

difficulty. So 2, 18 quam (voluptatem)
si (Epicurus) explicavisset, non tam
haesitaret; cf. too 5, 84 haeret (oratio)
in salebra.
turbulenta concursio: a rendering
of the δίνη of Democritus (or δῖνος, Epic.
in Diog. L. 10, 90), for which see Zeller,
I[3], p. 793 sq. So *concursio fortuita* is
applied to the scheme of Dem. in Tusc.
1, 42, and to that of Epic. in Acad. 1, 6;
N.D. 2, 93.
3. **mundi ornatum:** a rendering of
κόσμον; so often, with or without *mundi.*
Below, 3, 18 *ornatus* renders κόσμος in
another sense. The argument in the
context is hackneyed.
ne illud, etc.: so Div. 2, 14 ne illa
quidem divinantis esse dicebas...ventos
praesentire signis. On *ne...quidem* see
my n. on Acad. 1, 5.
4. **minimum:** so the existence of the
atom is denied (after Antiochus) in
Acad. 1, 27 cum sit nihil omnino in
rerum natura minimum quod dividi
nequeat; cf. too Galen, de plac. p. 663
περὶ δὲ τῆς κατὰ μέγεθος τομῆς τῶν
σωμάτων ἐπιδέδεικται τοῖς γεωμετρικοῖς
ἀνδράσιν ὡς οὐδέποτε στῆναι δυναμένης,
ἀλλὰ ἀεὶ τοῦ τεμνομένου σμικρότερον
ἑαυτοῦ τὸ μέγεθος ἔχοντος: Arist. de
cael. 303 *a*, 20 ἀνάγκη μάχεσθαι ταῖς
μαθηματικαῖς ἐπιστήμαις ἄτομα σώματα
λέγοντας (Democritus and Leucippus).
There is in the Revue de Philologie,
XIII, 86 sq., an unconvincing argument
by Riemann to show that *minimum*
here does not refer to the atom,
but to the 'least possible' swerving
aside of the atom of which mention
was made above. He holds that §§ 18–
20 entirely deal with those points wherein Epicurus differed from Democritus,
and that only in § 21 do we get to what
is common to the two, including the
atom. But in § 20 one weakness at
least is indicated as affecting the two
alike, viz. the *concursio* or δίνη. And it
is not likely that the mathematical
argument, invoked elsewhere to show
that the atom is impossible, should be
here directed against the 'least possible'
swerving.
5. **Polyaeno:** his renunciation of

quam illum etiam ipsum dedocere. Sol Democrito magnus videtur, quippe homini erudito in geometriaque perfecto, huic pedalis fortasse; tantum enim esse censet quantus videtur, vel
21 paulo aut maiorem aut minorem. Ita, quae mutat, ea corrumpit,

2 geometriaque: *geometricaque* P (m. 2).

mathematics at the bidding of Epicurus is mentioned in Acad. 2, 106. He was an interlocutor in the 'Symposium' of Epicurus (see Usener, pp. 115, 116), and his name often occurs in the Herculanean fragments. The title of one of the rolls (Scott, p. 46) is Δημητρίου πρὸς τὰς Πολυαίνου ἀπορίας. In another (Scott, p. 67) reference is made to τὰς ἐπιτομὰς τῶν ἐπιστολῶν τῶν Ἐπικούρου, Μητροδώρου, Πολυαίνου, Ἑρμάρχου καὶ τῶν γνωρίμων. Pol. is ranked with Metrodorus and Hermarchus by Seneca, Ep. 6, 6. There is more about him in Zeller, III, 1, p. 369, n. 4, and particularly in the index to Usener's Epicurea, s.v.

geometrica: Tusc. 1, 57 si geometrica didicisset. Cicero uses musica (fem. subst.) as well as musica (neut. plur.); so with dialectica; physica; see my n. on Acad. 1, 25. For the succession *geometrica...geometria* Madvig compares De Or. 1, 187 in musicis...in geometria.

1. dedocere: as to the attitude of Epicurus and his followers towards mathematics see Usener, Epicurea, §§ 229 *a*, 229 *b*, 230; and cf. N.D. 2, 48 numquam eruditum illum pulverem attigistis; and n. on § 71. Aristippus also attacked mathematics (Arist. Met. III, 2, p. 996 *a*, 32).

2. erudito: 'solet Cicero etiam magnificentius de Democrito loqui, famam quandam sequens, etiam ut Epicurum deprimat' (Madvig). Diog. L. 9, 37 and Plut. 1079 *e* refer to the familiarity of Dem. with mathematics.

3. pedalis: the same word is used in the same connexion in Acad. 2, 82 and Sen. N. Q. 1, 3, 10; Tertull. ad. nat. 2, 4; Arnob. 2, 61 pedis unius. In my comments on Acad. 2, 82 I have given information concerning this opinion of Epicurus, most of which I will not here repeat. Madvig is clearly wrong in supposing that Epic. derived his doctrine about the size of the sun (and the other heavenly bodies—see Diog. L. 10, 91) from his *general* belief in the infallibility of the senses, as well as his ideas concerning the εἴδωλα or *imagines* which all bodies emit, to which the cognisance of all things is due. Only in the case of luminous bodies did Epic.

identify apparent size with real size; and the discrepancy between the two in the case of other objects was explained by the theory that their εἴδωλα become diminished in amplitude as they pass through the air (Lucr. 4, 355 sq.). Although we have no definite record of the fact, we must suppose that for some reason Epic. believed the εἴδωλα proceeding from the sun and other luminous bodies to be exempt from wear and tear. The problem seems to have been handled on these lines in the treatise of which the Herculanean roll no. 1013 has preserved a few miserable remnants; see especially Scott, p. 311. Epicurus discussed the matter in his περὶ φύσεως (Usener, §§ 80, 81), and there is a reference to it in Philod. περὶ σημείων, col. 10. It would appear that the estimate of the sun's apparent size, viz. a foot broad, was a commonplace, as it is given several times by Aristotle, viz. 428 *b*, 3; 458 *b*, 29; 460 *b*, 18; and by Cleomedes many times. The writer last named argues (probably after Posidonius) that the apparent size of the sun is not invariable. It may have been with the purpose of meeting this argument that Epic. allowed the possibility of the sun being in reality a little larger or a little smaller than his apparent size. The Stoic objector in Philod. περὶ σημείων urges that on the view of Epic. the sun becomes one of the μοναχά, i.e. exceptional objects, which throw difficulties in the way of using ἀναλογία. But it was by an application of ἀναλογία that Epic. attempted to defend his position. Absurd as it may seem he, and Lucretius after him (Diog. L. 10, 90, 91 and Lucr. 5, 594 sq.), contended that the apparent size of luminous objects on earth does not diminish with distance. This Epic. treated as an ἐνάργημα, i.e. a self-evident fact which needed no argument (Diog. L. l.l.). [Diels, Dox. 221, treats εὖρος ποδὸς ἀνθρωπείου attributed to Heracl. very oddly; it is a tag of verse from Cleanthes. And in a n. he says the more recent Epicureans saw the puerile opinion of Heraclit. to be unthinkable. He refers to Diog. L. 10, 91.]

quae sequitur, sunt tota Democriti, atomi, inane, imagines, quae
idola nominant, quorum incursione non solum videamus, sed
etiam cogitemus; infinitio ipsa, quam ἀπειρίαν vocant, tota ab
illo est, tum innumerabiles mundi, qui et oriantur et intereant
5 cottidie. Quae etsi mihi nullo modo probantur, tamen Demo-

1 inane: *inanes* P.   2 idola: sic AP; *ydola* codd. multi.   2 quorum: *quarum*
Nonius, et *incursionem.*   3 infinitio: *invitricio* E, miro errore.   3 ἀπειρίαν:
apirian codd. et Nonius.   5 nullo: *in illo* E.

1. **sunt tota D.**: 'are wholly the property of D.' For the slight pleonasm
Madvig compares 5, 22 cum a Peripateticis et Academicis omnia transtu-
lissent, nominibus aliis easdem res
secuti sunt. As to the relation in which
Epic. stood to Dem. cf. 4, 13; N.D. 1, 73
quid est in physicis Epicuri non a
Democrito? Nam etsi quaedam commu-
tavit, ut quod paulo ante de inclinatione
atomorum dixi, tamen pleraque dicit
eadem, atomos inane imagines infini-
tatem locorum innumerabilitatemque
mundorum, eorum ortus interitus, omnia
fere quibus naturae ratio continetur.

atomi, inane, imagines: all these are
said to have formed part of the system
of Leucippus. Democritus appears to
have used the term δείκελα (Zeller, 1³,
p. 818), and it is possible that the term
εἴδωλα, attributed to him in the ancient
sources (as e.g. Fam. 15, 16, 1 and
here), may really have been introduced,
like many other novel terms, by Epicurus. The distinction may have been
set out in the source from which Cicero
drew N.D. 2, 76: et Democritus simulacra et Epicurus imagines inducens.
Mayor, *ad loc.*, thinks the reference is
to a difference between the two philosophers in the *applications* which they
made of the theory of images; if that be
the case, the language is strangely ill
chosen. Timagoras, an Epicurean
teacher, called the images ἀπορροαί (Stob.
ap. Diels, p. 403). Cicero mostly renders
εἴδωλον by *imago*, but here and there
he uses *simulacrum*, which also occurs
occasionally in later prose writers, while
Lucretius employs both words in-
differently. In Fam. 15, 16, 1 (addressed
to Cassius) the rendering *spectrum* is
quoted from the Roman Epicurean
writer Catius. The letter was written
very early in 45 B.C., before the time
at which Cicero began to compose the
De Finibus. Catius no doubt invented
spectrum, lit. 'an instrument of vision,'
from *spec-* of *spec-ies*. The word only
occurs once again in Latin; in a letter

of Cassius ap. Fam. 15, 19, 1, which is
a reply to the one just mentioned.

2. **quorum**: after the introduction of
εἴδωλα, Cicero is not likely to have given
the relative the gender of *imagines*.

3. **cogitemus**: the ancient authorities for this doctrine are nearly all
given by Zeller, III³, 1, p. 421 sq. Cf.
N.D. 1, 107 fac imagines esse, quibus
pulsentur animi; ib. 108 vos autem non
modo oculis imagines, sed etiam animis
inculcatis. The atomists explain all
sensation and all thought as physical
contact.

infinitio ipsa: it seems by Cicero's
use of *ipsa* that Epicurus made more
claim to originality in respect of the
ἀπειρία than in other parts of his physics.
The word ἀπειρία (found in Plut. Colot.
1114 *b* and De def. orac. 420 *b*) applies
both to the unlimitedness of space, and
to the unlimitedness of matter; proof
of both these doctrines is given by
Epicurus, ap. Diog. L. 10, 41, and Lucr.
1, 1008 sq. See Usener, p. 375. The
expression *infinitio* is isolated in Latin.
Whenever Cicero elsewhere has occasion
to render ἀπειρία, he uses *infinitas*
(see Wölfflin in Archiv 4, 411). Nägelsbach, Stil. § 57, 1, has well remarked
that the Latin language obstinately
refused to adopt many verbal nouns,
not merely technical terms, such as
infinitio here and *effectio* (below, 3, 45),
and *praenotio* (for πρόληψις in N.D. 1, 44),
but formations which might have played
a useful part. He gives a long list of
such ἅπαξ εἰρημένα or rarities from
Cicero; and many more might be added,
as (taking only words which begin with
the first letter of the alphabet) *accuratio,*
assensio, ascriptio, aspersio, asportatio,
assessio, asseveratio. Cf. n. on § 25,
evolutio.

ab illo: so est...*a Democrito* in N.D.
1, 73 quoted above; ib. 107; Mur. 61,
ea sunt omnia non a natura sed a
magistro.

4. **mundi**: see Usener, pp. 213–15, 380,
382; and my n. on Acad. 2, 125.

critum, laudatum a ceteris, ab hoc, qui eum unum secutus esset,
nollem vituperatum.

22 VII. Iam in altera philosophiae parte, quae est quaerendi ac
disserendi, quae λογική dicitur, iste vester plane, ut mihi
quidem videtur, inermis ac nudus est. Tollit definitiones, nihil 5
de dividendo ac partiendo docet, non quo modo efficiatur con-
cludaturque ratio tradit, non qua via captiosa solvantur, ambigua distinguantur ostendit; iudicia rerum in sensibus ponit,

2 vituperatum: *vituperare* A¹ (fort. ex *vituperari*).   5 nudus: *mundus* E.

oriantur...cottidie: cf. N.D. 1, 67
mundis innumerabilibus omnibus mini-
mis temporum punctis aliis nascentibus,
aliis cadentibus.

1. **unum**: sc. *in physicis*; so 2, 102
quem ille unum secutus est; Plut. non
posse suav. vivi, p. 1100 *a* τὰ δόγματα
ῥήμασιν αὐτοῖς ὑφαιρούμενος.

2. **nollem vituperatum**: *esse* is thus
constantly omitted by Cicero; so § 35;
2, 8 reprehensum velim.

Epic. criticised Democritus, possibly
in a special work (see Usener, Epic.
p. 97); so, too, Metrod.; see D.L. 10, 24.
It is often said that Epic. abused Dem.
as he abused other philosophers; cf.
Diog. L. 10, 8 (Δημόκριτον Ληρόκριτον);
Sext. A. M. pr. § 3; Plut. contra Epic.
beat. 1100 *a*; N.D. 1, 93. The criticisms
of Dem. which are to be found in existing documents, coming direct from the
Epicurean school, are respectful enough;
and Plut. adv. Colot. 1108 *e* repeats an
assertion of Leonteus, who lived in the
closest friendship with Epicurus and
Metrodorus, that Epic. called himself a
Democritean, and that the atomistic
philosophy continued to be called Democritean; and also an assertion of Metrodorus, that Epic. would never have
become a philosopher but for the lead
given him by Dem. Cf. Usener's index
s. v. Δημόκριτος.

3. **quaerendi ac disserendi**: the
Stoics (who were the dialecticians par
excellence of the post-Aristotelian
period) described this branch of philosophy as λογική, and subdivided it
into ῥητορική and διαλεκτική. Cicero
often represents the latter branch by
disserendum, as here. [Rhetoric is at
this point left out of consideration,
having been dealt with above.] But
disserendum also figures as a rendering
of λογική; so below, 5, 9 una pars est
naturae, disserendi altera, vivendi tertia.
For the scorn with which Epic. treated
the logic of the other schools see n. on § 63.

quae est...quae dicitur: this slightly
inelegant succession of clauses beginning with a relative is not uncommon;
so § 13 and 2 §§ 13, 16.

5. **inermis ac nudus**: Lucr. 5, 1292
omnia cedebant armatis nuda et inerma.
In Acad. 2, 46 *armatos*, of those equipped
with dialectic.

tollit definitiones: this is contradicted
by § 29; 2, 4; and by much else that is
told us about Epic., as in Sext. A.M.
11, 169 (definition of philosophy),
Usener, fr. 228 *b* (of τέχνη), Sext. A.M.
7, 267 (of ἄνθρωπος); Epicurean definitions of physical things are common.
Because he rejected the Stoic techni-
calities concerning definition, Cicero
here says that he rejected definition
altogether. The same holds of the words
that follow; cf. § 63 and 3, 40.

6. **ac partiendo**: but for the fact that
the words *dividendo ac p.* are treated as
a compound phrase, *ac* would have been
changed to *aut* after *nihil*.

efficiatur...ratio: in Cicero *rationem
concludere* is the usual rendering of
συλλογίζεσθαι: so συλλογισμός = *rationis conclusio*, § 30, and 3, 59; and
conclusio alone, 3, 27; 4, 52 and 55. With
efficiatur ratio cf. *e quibus effecta conclusio est* in 3, 27.

7. **captiosa**: σοφίσματα: cf. 2, 17
dialecticas captiones; also 3, 72; 4, 9.
In the character of a New Academic,
Cicero himself denounces dialectic in
Acad. 2, 91–5, and declares many
sophisms to be insoluble.

ambigua: ἀμφίβολα: so 4, 75 am-
biguo ludimur; Acad. 2, 92 (dialectica)
tradit ambiguorum intellegentiam.

8. **iudicia rerum**: *iudicium* is the
word by which Cicero regularly renders
κριτήριον: see 3 § 3, Acad. 1, 30 with
my n. The plural seems to be used here
because Epicurus sometimes laid down
as κριτήρια three things, αἰσθήσεις,
προλήψεις, πάθη (Diog. L. 10, 31).
But the two last are totally dependent

quibus si semel aliquid falsi pro vero probatum sit, sublatum esse
omne iudicium veri et falsi putat....Confirmat autem illud vel **23**
maxime, quod ipsa natura, ut ait ille, sciscat et probet, id est

2 confirmat autem: ante haec verba non nulla excidisse ex rerum nexu patet.

on the first, so that sense becomes sole
test of truth. The difficulty is to avoid
making false inferences from sense,
which gives true evidence always, if we
can get at it. See my n. on Acad. 2, 79
eo enim rem demittit Epicurus, si unus
sensus semel in vita mentitus sit, nulli
umquam esse credendum.

2. **confirmat autem**, etc.: the transition to ethics, intimated merely by an
autem, has seemed to nearly all scholars
who have handled the text, incredibly
abrupt. Probably a page of the archetype has been lost; it may be, through
the occurrence of the word *confirmat* at
the beginning of two successive pages.
In the omitted passage there was, most
likely, further criticism of the κανονικόν
of Epicurus, then some words introduced
the topic of ethics; these corresponded
to the opening words of § 22, and were
followed by an attack on Epic. for
having adopted *voluptas* as *summum
bonum* (and for having borrowed this
very doctrine from Aristippus (§ 26 *n.*)).
Allen alone has attempted to point out
a connexion between the subject-matter
of § 22 and that of § 23 as the text
stands. He supposes that *illud* is
sensuum iudicium. But there is no
Epicurean text which warrants us in
believing that Epic. connected the
ethical test of good and bad with the
intellectual test of true and false. And
(though Allen does not point it out) this
explanation would make *id*, the sup-
pressed antecedent of *quod*, into the
subject of *confirmat* (in spite of *tradit*,
putat, etc. in the context). The only
possible interpretation of the sentence
beginning with *confirmat*, as it stands,
is this: 'he strongly maintains the
principle which nature sets up and
approves, viz. pleasure and pain.'
Madvig objects as follows to the rendering just given of *confirmat*: 'pravis-
sime dicitur Epicurus *confirmare* id
quod natura sciscat, pro eo quod est
probare et tenere.' But the objection is
unfounded; cf. De Fato 48 nec...quis-
quam magis confirmare mihi videtur
non modo fatum verum etiam necessi-
tatem et vim omnium rerum, quam hic;
also ib. §§ 20, 39. Madvig proceeds 'nisi
quod pravius est: *quod natura probet,
id est, voluptatem et dolorem*.' Whether

the objection is to *quod* followed by the
two words *voluptatem et dolorem* or to
probet brought into connexion with
dolorem, is not clear. With regard to
the former of the two points, it is quite
natural that pain and pleasure should
be regarded as forming, combined
together, a single κριτήριον of good and
bad. So it is sometimes said that Epicurus had a κριτήριον τοῦ ἀληθοῦς καὶ
ψευδοῦς, sometimes that he had κριτήρια,
because the κριτήριον consisted of three
parts, αἰσθήσεις προλήψεις πάθη. Cf.
Democritus, qu. in § 30. In this sense
nature may be said to 'set up and
approve of' pleasure and pain, just as
below (§ 30) nature is said to grasp and
determine upon pleasure and pain for
the purpose of testing the desirability
of objects. The words *ad haec...omnia*
seem to support this explanation. But
another elucidation is possible; Cicero
may have written *sciscat et probet*, in-
tending to introduce *voluptatem* only,
and he may have added *et dolorem* as an
after-thought, in spite of the incongruity
of *dolorem* with *sciscat et probet*. Irregularities of the kind are found in all
languages. For illustrations I must refer
to my n. on 3, 52 quae secundum locum
obtinent, προηγμένα, id est producta
nominentur, quae vel ita appellemus
vel promota et remota. But the interpretation given above, though possible,
is open to suspicion. In the first place
it is strange that Epic. should be said
to maintain strongly the ethical test,
instead of the *summum bonum*. If, as
is most probable, the adoption by Epic.
of pleasure as the supreme good was
mentioned in the lost passage, *confirmat*
would naturally mean 'corroborates'
and *illud* would refer back to the
Epicurean view of the *summum
bonum*. This is the opinion I have
adopted, supposing *eo* to have fallen
out between *maxime* and *quod*. It is
conceivable also that *id est* has been
inserted here, as in other places, by the
copyists. In that case *quod* would be a
conjunction.

3. **sciscat**: 'lays down as an ordi-
nance,' a metaphor from legislation.
But *asciscat* may be the right reading;
cf. Tusc. 2, 30 omnia quae natura
aspernetur in malis esse, quae asciscat,

voluptatem et dolorem. Ad haec et quae sequamur et quae fugiamus refert omnia. Quod quamquam Aristippi est a Cyrenaicisque melius liberiusque defenditur, tamen eius modi esse iudico ut nihil homine videatur indignius. Ad maiora enim quaedam nos natura genuit et conformavit, ut mihi quidem 5 videtur. Ac fieri potest ut errem, sed ita prorsus existimo, neque eum Torquatum qui hoc primus cognomen invenit, aut torquem

6 neque eum: *ne enim* E.   7 invenit: *invenerit* AP, alii.

in bonis; Acad. 2, 138 asciscam et comprobem, and below, 3, 70 ascisci aut probari; 3, 17 and 5, 17 (18). The subjunctives are retained though the insertion of *ut ait ille* would have justified the indicative. As Madvig notes, *reprobet* (read here by some) is a late word. Tertullian uses both the verb and the noun *reprobatio* in a theological sense.

1. **ad haec...refert omnia:** *referre* is constantly used like ἀναφέρειν, ἐπαναφέρειν of referring something to a standard, to be judged or tested by it. *Quae sequamur* = αἱρετά: *quae fugiamus* = fugienda, φευκτά: see n. on § 11.

2. **quamquam:** the advocacy of Aristippus is presumed to be more attractive than that of Epicurus. For the differences between Aristippus and Epic. see Usener, p. 293 f.

3. **melius liberiusque:** in 2, 114 the Cyrenaics are said to defend the doctrine more consistently (*constantius*).

4. **homine:** because the Epicureans *pecudis et hominis idem bonum esse censent* (Acad. 1, 6); see below, n. on 2, 18.

ad maiora: so 5, 21 and 2, 113 ad altiora...nati sumus. The latter passage shows that *conformavit* here applies to body as well as mind; so 2, 41.

6. **ita prorsus:** so in 5, 27 and often.

neque eum: the second *neque*, which should have accompanied the mention of the second Torquatus (§ 24), is forgotten and the exposition becomes slightly anacoluthic. Madvig illustrates the usage in an excursus to this passage, pp. 787 ed. 3 'De turbatis et dissolutis orationis connexae...membris.'

7. **invenit:** the untrustworthiness of the MSS. here is shown by the necessity for changing *percusserit*, two or three lines below, to *percussit*. Madvig compares Tusc. 4, 49 ego ne Torquatum quidem illum, qui hoc cognomen invenit, iratum existimo Gallo torquem detraxisse. But Madvig goes too far in asserting that

the indicative is a *necessity* in these two passages.

Descriptive relative clauses of all kinds are from time to time drawn into the vortex of neighbouring subjunctive constructions, and it is hard to see why the *invenerit* should be condemned as a syntactical impossibility, and *finxerit* retained in 5, 49 mihi quidem Homerus huius modi quiddam vidisse videtur in eis quae de Sirenum cantibus finxerit. For the indic. cf. 3 §§ 17, 70; N.D. 1, 117; Div. 1, 93; Tusc. 1, 12. For the words here cf. 2, 73 and Off. 3, 112 hic T. Manlius is est qui ad Anienem Galli, quem ab eo provocatus occiderat, torque detracto cognomen invenit, cuius tertio consulatu Latini ad Veserim fusi et fugati, magnus vir in primis, et qui perindulgens in patrem, idem acerbe severus in filium. Liv. 6, 42, 5 has only a brief mention of the combat with the Gaul; but Gell. 9, 13, 4 sq. has preserved a detailed account by Claudius Quadrigarius, according to whom the fight took place on a bridge over the river Anio, the Gaulish army being on one side of the river and the Roman on the other (about 360 B.C.). Gellius 9, 11 also quotes from the same historian his very similar account of the combat between Valerius and a Gaulish chief, in which the Roman was helped by a *corvus* and so won the name 'Corvinus.' According to Suet. Tib. 3, the name Drusus came from that of a Gaulish chief Drausus, slain by an ancestor of the Drusi. *Torques* is the στρεπτὸς περιαυχένιος of Herodotus, worn by barbarians from east to west, and familiar to us from ancient art and specimens in our museums. It was commonly bestowed as a reward on Roman soldiers and on athletes; see Suet. Aug. 43 in hoc ludicro Nonium Asprenatem lapsu debilitatum aureo torque donavit passusque est ipsum posterosque Torquati ferre cognomen. The Manlii Torquati had probably died out before this occurred.

illum hosti detraxisse ut aliquam ex eo perciperet corpore
voluptatem, aut cum Latinis tertio consulatu conflixisse apud
Veserim propter voluptatem. Quod vero securi percussit filium,

2 apud Veserim: *Vesuvium* C (editio Coloniensis et Romana). 3 percussit:
percusserit codd. omnes.

1. **corpore**: the opposite phrase *p.
animo voluptatem* is common. As to
corpore cf. 2 §§ 98, 106, 108, 115. Note the
emphatic repetition of *voluptatem*, at
the end of the two clauses.

2. **tertio consulatu**: 340 B.C., the first
in 347, the second in 343. He was no
doubt a young man at the time, so that
it was natural that he should not have
obtained the consulship until a good
many years after.

apud Veserim: excepting in Victor de
Vir. Ill. 26 and 28, where V. is called
a stream, the name only occurs in the
phrases *ad Veserim* or *apud Veserim*.
The words of Livy 8, 8, 19, haud procul
radicibus Vesuvii montis qua via ad
V. ferebat, point either to a town or a
river. If a river, it must have been the
Sarnus or some tributary. But there is
great difficulty in supposing that the
decisive battle in the Latin war was
fought anywhere near Vesuvius. Diodorus (16, 90) mentions only a battle
near Suessa. Some confusion of names
between *Vescia*, *Vescinus ager* and
Veseris, may have led to the traditional
account. The name Trifanum, where the
Romans defeated the Latins and Cam-
panians, is unknown but for one passage
of Livy (8, 11, 11). Cf. *ad Mecium* in Liv.
6, 2, 8.

3. **securi percussit filium**: Virg. Aen.
6, 825 saevumque securi aspice Torquatum. The story is told by Livy 8, 7,
as an incident of the Latin war; by
others (with less probability) it is referred to a Gaulish war. The traditional
tale of the son's single combat with the
Latin closely resembles the tale of the
father's combat with the Gaul. [See
Val. M. 2, 7, 6.] To another legend of
the kind, belonging to an earlier date,
Livy, 4, 29, 6, refuses credit.

percussit: it must be admitted that
the subjunctive appears sometimes in
quod-clauses in a manner for which it is
very difficult to account. Madvig seems
to give three reasons against the subjunctive: (1) that the fact embodied in
the clause is historical; (2) that the
clause is separated off from *videtur* ('it
is thought') so that *oratio obliqua* does
not operate; (3) 'ne sic quidem defendi

coniunctivum verborum ordo sinit, ut
ultra veros fines progressa infinitae
orationis vis putetur.' He appends,
however, to (3) the remark 'scrupulum
tamen hoc inicit.' Objection (1) seems
to have no relevancy; the certainty or
even notoriousness of the fact embodied
in the clause would not protect the verb
from passing into the subjunctive; see
n. on § 52. As to (2) it is hard to
set bounds to the levelling effect of
oratio obliqua over the whole range of
a sentence. As to this see n. on quod
arguerint, § 24. With respect to (3),
Madvig sometimes uses the phrases
finita oratio, *infinita oratio* in a very
confusing manner. He seems here to
mean that if *percusserit* be right a clause
containing a definite and certain fact is
treated as though the fact were indefinite and uncertain. Objection (3)
therefore seems to coincide with objection (1). I have changed the reading,
not because I think the subjunctive impossible, but for the reason that in
Cicero there are a very large number of
examples of a *quod*-clause made introductory to a sentence, and that in nearly
all of these the indic. stands in the best
MSS. even when there is in the context
some influence which might well have
changed it. In view of the ease with
which a perfect indic. passes into a
perfect subj. in the MSS., it is on the
whole more likely that in passages like
the present the codices are in fault than
that Cicero changed his usage. But the
matter is far from certain. In Div. 2, 37
the MSS. give: tu vero quid habes quare
putes, si paulo ante cor fuerit in tauro
opimo, subito id in ipsa immolatione
interisse? an quod aspexerit vestitu pur-
pureo excordem Caesarem, ipse corde
privatus est? All recent edd. read
aspexit, and if the subjunctive be right,
there is nothing to explain it, but the
vague idea of oratio obliqua. The same
is the case with some exx. quoted by
Madvig, as Div. 2, 67 (conciderit, potuerit); Phil. 5, 17 habuerit; but the quod-
clause in these passages comes after the
beginning of the sentence; cf. also
Opusc. p. 591.

Madvig notes three passages, Pis. 66

privavisse se etiam videtur multis voluptatibus, cum ipsi naturae
24 patrioque amori praetulerit ius maiestatis atque imperi. Quid?
T. Torquatus, is qui consul cum Cn. Octavio fuit, cum illam
severitatem in eo filio adhibuit quem in adoptionem D. Silano
emancipaverat, ut eum Macedonum legatis accusantibus quod 5

3 cum Cn.: *cum G. N. A.*

and Verr. 2, 15; 5, 175, where he traces
a survival of the old comic use of a *quod*-
clause at the beginning of the sentence
with a verb in subj. but referring to a
supposed or future, not to a past and
actual, fact (*si forte, etiam si*). But these
passages can be easily brought within
the range of those just mentioned. See
his n. also for exx. of *quod* with subj.
in Ovid=*quamquam*, e.g. Her. 4, 157.
[Note the difference between § 23, cum
praetulerit, and § 24, cum adhibuit.]

2. **maiestatis atque imperi:** cf. Part.
Or. 105 maiestas est in imperi atque in
nominis populi Romani dignitate.

3. **consul...fuit:** in 165 B.C.

4. **D. Silano:** the Manlii were an old
patrician family; the Iunii Silani were
plebeians and their first consulship came
in 109 B.C. Nothing is known of this
Silanus, unless he be the D. Silanus who
was one of those commissioned by the
Senate after the destruction of Carthage
to translate into Latin the agricultural
writings of the Carthaginian Mago
(Plin. n. h. 18, 22).

5. **emancipaverat:** this verb is used
both of the process by which a son under
patria potestas was passed over to an
adoptive father's authority, and of the
process by which a father extinguished
his *patria potestas* and left the son *sui
iuris*. The two processes were similar
up to a certain point. The cumbrous
forms used are described by Gaius, 1,
§§ 132-4. The son was praetor in 142 B.C.

accusantibus quod, etc.: we have
another short statement of the case in
Livy, Epit. 54, and one much more
detailed in Val. Max. 5, 8, 3, taken in all
probability from the full text of Livy.
According to this account the envoys
laid complaint before the Senate, when
the father begged 'ne quid ante de ea re
statuerent quam ipse Macedonum fili-
que sui causam inspexisset.' The
request was unanimously granted and,
having undertaken the investigation
(*cognitione suscepta*), he took his seat
alone, without advisers, on the bench.
The hearing lasted three days; on the
third witnesses were heard and this

sentence was given: 'cum Silanum filium
meum pecunias a sociis accepisse probatum mihi sit, et re publica eum et
domo mea indignum iudico protinusque
e conspectu meo abire iubeo.' On the
following night the son hanged himself,
and the father, true to the traditional
character of the Manlii, ignored the
funeral, and ostentatiously gave his
attention to his clients as *patronus* in his
atrium while it was proceeding. The
epitomator of Livy makes the inquiry
held by the father appear somewhat
more formal; he evidently thought the
Senate in the first instance meant to sit
in judgment and to pronounce sentence
(*cum...vellet cognoscere*) and that Torquatus, having asked to be entrusted with
the inquiry (*ut sibi cognitio mandaretur*),
was appointed criminal judge in place of
the Senate (*causa cognita filium condem-
navit abdicavitque*); in fact that he was
entrusted with a *quaestio extraordinaria*.
None of the three accounts give the
least warrant for supposing that the
inquiry was a *iudicium domesticum* connected with the *patria potestas*. This
supposition led to much useless discussion in the editions before Madvig's,
and in some books on Roman law. And
the loose, non-legal use of the technical
words *cognoscere, cognitio* by Val. Max.
and the epitomator of Livy, and of
pronuntiaret, videri by Cicero, has be-
trayed some writers into the assumption
that the Senate took the matter out of
the cognisance of the *quaestio repetundarum*, which was established eight
years before these events took place.
But the complaint in the Senate was
merely the natural and ordinary first
step towards a prosecution before that
court. The informality of the pro-
ceedings before the father is clearly
shown by the fact that he sat without
assessors; this, had he been acting
officially, whether as president of a
quaestio extraordinaria, or by virtue of
patria potestas, would have been an
offensive breach of traditional practice;
and was unlikely to be committed by
one who was himself a distinguished

pecunias praetorem in provincia cepisse arguerent, causam apud
se dicere iuberet reque ex utraque parte audita pronuntiaret
eum non talem videri fuisse in imperio quales eius maiores
fuissent, et in conspectum suum venire vetuit, numquid tibi
5 videtur de voluptatibus suis cogitavisse? Sed ut omittam pericula, labores, dolorem etiam quem optimus quisque pro patria
et pro suis suscipit, ut non modo nullam captet, sed etiam prae-
tereat omnis voluptates, dolores denique quosvis suscipere malit
quam deserere ullam offici partem, ad ea quae hoc non minus
10 declarant, sed videntur leviora, veniamus. Quid tibi, Torquate, **25**

10 veniamus: *videamus* A[1].

lawyer (Val. Max. l.l.). The case of
Tubulus, mentioned in 2, 54, presents
some of the same difficulties as that of
Silanus; see n. there; also on 2, 60.

quod...arguerent: for *quod, ut argue-
bant*. This illogicality of drawing the
verb of statement into the *oratio
obliqua* construction is common; see
above § 4 quod...dicat; Madv. Gram.
§ 357 a, Obs. 2; Roby § 1746. Mayor is,
I think, right in explaining *dixerit* thus
in N.D. 1, 20 illa palmaria quod, qui non
modo natum mundum introduxerit, sed
etiam manu paene factum, is eum dixerit fore sempiternum (=*quod...ut dixit,
sempiternus sit futurus*). So too *responderint* in Div. 2, 66 nam quod
haruspices responderint nihil illo clarius,
nihil nobilius fore, miror deos immortales
histrioni futuro claritatem ostendisse,
nullam ostendisse Africano.

1. **pecunias...cepisse**: technical in
this sense: cf. e.g. lex Acilia §§ 2, 3 pecuniae quod...ablatum captum coactum
conciliatum aversumve siet; Leg. 3, 46
sequitur de captis pecuniis et de am-
bitu. Sometimes (but rarely) *contra leges*
is added.

4. **et...vetuit**: a return is made to the
construction of *adhibuit*, instead of continuing that of *iuberet* and *pronuntiaret*.
As the order given to the son not to
come into his father's presence was part
of the *severitas*, it is strange that *et
vetaret* was not written. Cf. nn. on 2, 61;
4, 43; Verr. 2, 5, 112 non solum ut
laederet...verum scripsit.

5. **ut omittam...veniamus**: so Ligar.
20.

6. **pro...et pro**: so *inter* repeated in
§ 30 and *in* in § 34.

8. **dolores denique**, etc.: Goerenz and
Otto, who defended these words as well
written, are ranked by Madvig with the

'natio superstitiosorum Ciceroniano-
rum.' On the other hand he says of
Davies and others who treated the
passage as spurious, on account of its
careless phrasing: 'non tulerunt in
Cicerone naevum; at quam multos in
hoc opere et in omni hoc genere eius
scriptorum non viderunt!' Davies says
it is 'nefas vel suspicari' that Cicero
could have written thus. But Cicero
often awkwardly repeats or expands or
emphasises something which has already
been said earlier in the sentence. Similarly in 3, 12 instead of writing *qui
omnia sic in utramque partem exaequa-
verunt uti nulla selectione uterentur* he says
*qui omnia sic ex. ut in utramque partem
ita paria redderent ut n. s. uterentur*. Cf.
also 5, 57; and Att. 14, 20, 4 ut suscipiam
cogitationem...quidnam putem.

quosvis: Landgraf's notion (on Pro
Rosc. Am. 132) that this word is characteristic of Cicero's early style seems
baseless.

suscipere malit quam d.: see n. on
2, 87.

10. **quid tibi**, etc.: it is assumed that
devotion to study springs from some
other impulse than that of pleasure.
Cf. 5, 57 tantaque est vis talibus in
studiis ut eos etiam qui sibi alios pro-
posuerunt finis bonorum, quos utilitate
aut voluptate derigunt, tamen in rebus
quaerendis explicandisque naturis
aetates conterere videamus. So Epict.
Diss. 1, 20, 19 taunts Epicurus with
inconsistency: τί δὲ καὶ λύχνον ἅπτεις
καὶ πονεῖς ὑπὲρ ἡμῶν καὶ τηλικαῦτα
βιβλία γράφεις; ib. 2, 20, 15 τί οὖν ἦν
τὸ ἐγεῖρον αὐτὸν ἐκ τῶν ὕπνων καὶ
ἀναγκάζον γράφειν ἃ ἔγραφεν; τί γὰρ
ἄλλο ἢ τὸ πάντων τῶν ἐν ἀνθρώποις
ἰσχυρότατον, ἡ φύσις ἕλκουσα ἐπὶ τὸ
αὐτῆς βούλημα ἄκοντα καὶ στένοντα;

quid huic Triario litterae, quid historiae cognitioque rerum, quid
poetarum evolutio, quid tanta tot versuum memoria voluptatis
affert? Nec mihi illud dixeris: 'haec enim ipsa mihi sunt
voluptati, et erant illa Torquatis.' Numquam hoc ita defendit
Epicurus neque Metrodorus aut quisquam eorum qui aut 5
saperet aliquid aut ista didicisset. Et quod quaeritur saepe cur
tam multi sint Epicurei, sunt aliae quoque causae, sed multitu-

5 Metrodorus aut: ita P. Manutius: *vero tu aut* AE; *vero tu Triari aut* ed. Colon.;
alia etiam magis mira sunt in codd. dett. Pro *vero tu* J. Adam coniecit *Erotion*;
pro *Metrodorus, Patron* Gustafson

1. **historiae**: the plur. because the
reference is to the writings of different
historians, as below 5, 64; Acad. 2, 5;
Att. 2, 5, 1; Fam. 5, 12, 2; Div. 2, 69;
Scaur. 42 (the only passage in Cicero's
speeches where *historia* is used). Thus
in sense the word comes to differ little
from the abstract *historia*; but in some
uses, such as *leges historiae* (Fam. 5,
12, 3; cf. Leg. 1, 5; De Or. 2, 62), Cicero
apparently does not use *historia* in the
sense of 'anecdote,' 'fable,' 'myth,'
which is so common in poets and later
prose writers.

cognitio rerum: 'knowledge of facts'
in the widest sense; so often, as below
4, 19; 5, 87; cf. 3, 37 rebus cognitione
dignis. For another sense of *cognitio
rerum* see n. on 3, 17.

2. **evolutio**: *evolvere librum* must
have been first applied to the book in
the form of a roll; but the phrase is extended to all books; e.g. Att. 9, 10, 4. The
noun appears to be ἅπαξ εἰρημένον here.

tanta tot: cf. 2 § 68 *n.*

3. **nec...dixeris**: *nec=et ne*, rare in
Cicero.

enim: here corresponds to our 'why'
(non-interrogative) at the beginning of
a sentence.

4. **numquam...defendit**: because *ipsa*
above (=αὐτὰ καθ' αὐτά) implies that
the pleasure taken in such things was
for their own sake; so *ipsa per sese* below.
Cf. 2, 107 and Plut. non posse suaviter
vivi, etc., p. 1093 c ἐξωθοῦσι δὲ (οἱ
Ἐπικούρειοι) καὶ τὰς ἀπὸ μαθημάτων
ἡδονάς. See n. on 1, 72 (puerilis).

hoc ita: n. on 2, 17 quod...ita me
malle dixeram.

5. **Metrodorus**: we need here the name
of one of the καθηγεμόνες or leaders of
the school (see Usener, Ind. s. v. and
p. 108, 28) or the μεγάλοι to whom Ep.
wrote (ib. p. 134, 18); the constant
conjunction of Metrod. with Epic. in

the Epicurean texts, as of almost equal
authority with him, forbids us to suppose that Cicero made mention of any
other Epicurean here. The whole context requires that the appeal should be
to the strongest authorities in the
Epicurean school. The corruptions of
proper names in the MSS. notoriously
take a far wider range than errors in
common words. [As to Epicurus or
Metrodorus see Sen. ep. 33, 4.]

aut quisquam: although *neque* precedes; see 3, 71; Draeger § 343, 1, *c, β*.
[Sen. ep. 14, 17 Epicuri est aut Metrodori aut alicuius ex illa officina.]

6. **saperet**: the verb here means 'to
have sense' as in many common phrases,
si sapis, nihil sapere, etc. There is no
allusion to the use of the title *σοφός* in
the Epicurean school (2, 7 *n.*); certainly
none (as Dr Adam supposed) to the
palate (2, 24 *n.*). *Sapere aliquid* is
of course a common phrase in all
periods; but an accusative like *recta*
[given in MSS., cf. Att. 14, 5, 1] is hardly
possible. My correction *recte* for *recta*
in Att. l. c. was adopted by Tyrrell and
Purser.

cur tam multi, etc.: Cicero discusses
in Tusc. 4, 6 the question why there are
so many Epicureans in Italy, and gives
three reasons: (1) that the multitude
were enticed *illecebris blandae voluptatis*;
(2) that the only philosophical writings
accessible in Latin were Epicurean; (3)
the system was *cognitu perfacilis*. Cf.
2, 44 nescio quo modo populus cum
illis facit; and Introd. to my ed. of
Acad. p. 21. On the other hand Epic.
himself said: οὐδέποτε ὠρέχθην τοῖς
πολλοῖς ἀρέσκειν· ἃ μὲν γὰρ ἐκείνοις
ἤρεσκεν, οὐκ ἔμαθον· ἃ δ' ᾔδειν ἐγώ,
μακρὰν ἦν τῆς ἐκείνων αἰσθήσεως (Gnomologion Parisinum, qu. by Usener, p. 157;
rendered by Sen. ep. 29, 10).

7. **aliae**: proleptic, as *ceteri* often is.

dinem haec maxime allicit, quod ita putant dici ab illo, recta et
honesta quae sint, ea facere ipsa per se laetitiam, id est voluptatem. Homines optimi non intellegunt totam rationem everti,
si ita res se habeat. Nam si concederetur, etiamsi ad corpus nihil
5 referatur, ista sua sponte et per se esse iucunda, per se esset et
virtus et cognitio rerum, quod minime ille volt, expetenda. Haec 26
igitur Epicuri non probo, inquam. De cetero vellem equidem aut

2 laetitiam: *licenciam* E.   5 esse iucunda: *esset iocunda* A.

1. **putant**: substantially, the view of
the *multitudo* concerning the teaching of
Epicurus is correct; see nn. on § 42.
Cicero does not make a collective noun
and a plural verb agree together, when
the noun and the verb stand in the same
clause. The doctrine which Cicero here
says the crowd falsely attribute to
Epicurus is indistinguishable from that
which we know him to have actually
taught (see nn. on § 42; 2, 48). The
argument in the source on which Cicero
drew must here have been abbreviated
and obscured. The supposed doctrine is
modified below by the introduction of
the words *etiamsi ad corpus nihil
referatur*.

3. **homines optimi**: a phrase rare in
Cicero compared with *viri optimi*, which
is often applied to the Epicureans, as
in Tusc. 1, 6; 2, 44; 3, 50.

4. **si ita res se habeat**: this order and
s. i. se res h. are, as Madvig shows, both
common.

5. **referatur**: in all Latin the tendency is to accommodate the tense of
the verb in the secondary clause to that
of the verb in the primary clause, even
in cases where, as here, the secondary
clause gives expression to a present or
abiding fact. Cicero carries this accom-
modation of tenses farther than other
writers; cf. below § 27 quae diceret;
§ 66 quae pertinerent; § 68 inhaererent;
2, 22 cum esset, ut ais tu, voluptas nihil
dolere; 2, 119. But the clause *etiamsi...
referatur* is here really correlated with
ista...iucunda, rather than with *si concederetur*. For similar exceptions cf.
N.D. 3, 10 (where there are two verbs,
one accommodated and one not); ib.
2, 1; Tusc. 1, 60; Div. 2, 122; Fam.
13, 6 a, 4. See also below, 4, 31. As to
the form of the conditional see Draeger,
Hist. Synt. § 151.

esset et virtus et cognitio: for the
concord cf. Draeger, § 102. Cicero's argument trifles. He wants to prove that
recta et honesta, apart from pleasure, are
expetenda, but he cannot deduce this

from the assumption that virtue and
pleasure are organically inseparable.

6. **quod minime...volt**: so Acad. 2,
138 quod m. voltis; ib. 2, 18.

haec Epicuri: so below, § 27 quid...
eius; n. on 4, 32.

7. **de cetero**: small clauses of this form
with *de* are frequent in Cicero at the
beginning of the sentence, particularly
in the Letters; see exx. in a n. of
C. F. W. Müller on Fam. 1, 9, 19.
Clauses of the kind are common in the
less formal parts of Latin literature; so
often in Varro r. r. (exx. in Keil's n.
on 2, 3, 2); Ad Herenn. 2, 15 (see
Marx); Martial, 1, 18, 5 (with the quotations in Friedländer's n.).

vellem...instructior: the Epicureans
passed everywhere for ἀπαίδευτοι, like
the Cynics at an earlier time (Arist.
Met. 1043 b, 24). A passage in a letter
of Epicurus addressed to Pythocles was
much quoted and sometimes misquoted:
παιδείαν δὲ πᾶσαν, μακάριε, φεῦγε, τἀκά-
τιον ἀράμενος (Diog. L. 10, 6). 'Culture'
was thus compared with the Sirens, and
the youth was exhorted, like Odysseus,
to drive his bark at high speed past the
rocks: so in a letter to one Apelles:
μακαρίζω σε, ὅτι καθαρὸς πάσης παιδείας
ἐπὶ φιλοσοφίαν ὥρμησας. But Quintilian
goes too far when he renders παιδείαν
πᾶσαν by disciplinas omnis (2, 17, 15;
cf. 12, 2, 24). Doubtless Epic. had his
own idea of education, though he dis-
liked the ordinary rhetorical and literary
education of his day; cf. Athen. 13,
588 a ἐγκυκλίου παιδείας ἀμύητος ὤν.
That, with Plato, and Xenophanes and
many another, he depreciated Homer,
and poetry generally, is clear (Usener,
fragm. 228, 9). Considering the view
held by him about the share which
mythology had in creating the misery of
life, he could hardly do otherwise. His
opinion of mathematics we have had
already, and he felt no respect for
rhetoric or music, at least as ordinarily
taught. Yet it is likely that Epic. held
views of his own as to the form which all

ipse doctrinis fuisset instructior (est enim, quod tibi ita videri
necesse est, non satis politus eis artibus, quas qui tenent, eruditi
appellantur) aut ne deterruisset alios a studiis. Quamquam te
quidem video minime esse deterritum.

VIII. Quae cum dixissem, magis ut illum provocarem quam 5
ut ipse loquerer, tum Triarius leniter arridens: Tu quidem, inquit,
totum Epicurum paene e philosophorum choro sustulisti. Quid
ei reliquisti nisi te, quoquo modo loqueretur, intellegere quid
diceret? Aliena dixit in physicis nec ea ipsa quae tibi pro-
barentur; si qua in eis corrigere voluit, deteriora fecit; disserendi 10
artem nullam habuit; voluptatem cum summum bonum diceret,
primum in eo ipso parum vidit, deinde hoc quoque alienum; nam
ante Aristippus, et ille melius. Addidisti ad extremum etiam
27 indoctum fuisse. Fieri, inquam, Triari, nullo pacto potest ut non

6 leniter: *leviter* AE.   8 quoquo: *quoque* A¹.   10 *deteriora...voluptatem*: om. E.
13 ille: *illo* C. F. W. Müller.   melius: post hoc inserunt codd. multi additamen-
tum insulsum '*etenim quoniam detractis de homine sensibus,*' quae verba sunt in
§ 30. Eiecit primus Manutius.   addidisti: *disti* E.

these arts ought to take. At least his
'wise man' will alone be able to discourse rightly of poetry and music
(Diog. L. 10, 121), while treatises were
written on these subjects by pupils of
the school, as Diogenes of Tarsus,
Philodemus and even Metrodorus,
though with his master he denounced
Homer roundly. It may be noted that
Epicurus regarded Pyrrho as ἀμαθῆ καὶ
ἀπαίδευτον (Diog. L. 10, 8). Cf. § 72
with *n*. [Aristippus also denounced
πολυμάθεια, Diog. L. 2, 71, 79.] So
Democritus (Hirzel, I, 159) and Heraclitus.

1. **quod...ita:** see 2, 17 *n*.

2. **artibus:** so Rep. 1, 28 politi pro-
priis humanitatis artibus. In Pis. 59
Cicero ironically speaks of Piso the
Epicurean as *politus e schola*; and in
writing to Memmius (Fam. 13, 1, 5) he
begs him to believe that Atticus is not
to be ranked with the school: 'est enim
omni liberali doctrina politissimus.'

quas qui: the tendency to place
relatives side by side is common; so
in this book, §§ 49, 52, 60, 64, 67,
72.

eruditi: cf. *ineruditus* in § 72.

5. **provocarem:** so κινεῖν, 'to draw
out,' in Plat. Rep. 329 D βουλόμενος ἔτι
λέγειν αὐτὸν ἐκίνουν.

7. **choro:** perhaps imitated from
Plato's frequent use of χορός applied
to a school of philosophers. So Plato's

κορυφαῖος, a leader in philosophy, is
copied in N.D. 1, 59, where see Mayor's
n. Cf. Dion. Hal. de comp. verb. 24,
p. 188 Ἐπικουρείων χορόν: and an inscr.
in Orelli, 1193 (Dessau 7781, Büch. 961)
Stallius Gaius has sedes Hauranus tue-
tur | ex Epicureio gaudivigente choro.

9. **aliena dixit:** so Plat. Phileb. 29 A
ἀλλότρια ἄνευ κινδύνου λέγειν.

10. **in eis:** sc. *physicis*.

12. **primum...Aristippus:** reference is
here made to words which existed in
the lacuna at § 23.

13. **et ille:** *et is* or *atque is* or *isque*
might have been expected; see Kühner,
Gram. § 118, Anmerk. 16. Although I
cannot quote an example of *et ille*
exactly like the present one, yet in other
connexions *ille* is substituted for *is* in
order to gain emphasis, and I see no
reason for changing it to *illo* here. [Cf.
Tusc. 2, 67 M. Cras ergo ad clepsydram
...A. Ita prorsus, et illud quidem ante
meridiem.] Havet says *illo* is contrary
to laws of rhythm which require trochee
not spondee before final ‿‿≅. Indeed
‿‿≅ is rare at end of sentence. It is
absent from many of Cicero's writings,
but is found in Lael. 17 quamvis subito,
23 cadere patitur, 25 a te potius;
Off. 3, 39 quidnam facerent, 63 quod
non liceat, 75 nulla fraus aberit, nullum
facinus; Parad. 19 si esset misera.

ad extr.: so Div. 2, 25 addunt ad
extremum.

dicas quid non probes eius a quo dissentias. Quid enim me prohiberet Epicureum esse, si probarem quae ille diceret, cum
praesertim illa perdiscere ludus esset? Quam ob rem dissentientium inter se reprehensiones non sunt vituperandae; maledicta,
5 contumeliae, tum iracundae contentiones concertationesque in
disputando pertinaces indignae philosophia mihi videri solent.
Tum Torquatus: Prorsus, inquit, assentior; neque enim disputari 28
sine reprehensione nec cum iracundia aut pertinacia recte dis-

1 eius: om. E.   3 dissentientium: *disserentium* non nulli, etiam P.
5 iracundae: sic Lambinus, alii; quod probat, non tamen scribit C. F. W. Müller.
iracundiae codd. quod fort. retinendum est.   7 tum: *tunc* ed. Colon. (non P).

1. **quid...eius:** cf. τοῦτο αὐτῶν, τόδε
αὐτῶν, common in Plato.
prohiberet...esse: while the infinitive
constr. is common after *prohibere* in
Cicero, in the philosophical works there
is no ex. of *quo minus* with this verb,
and in the speeches it only occurs twice
(Verr. 2, 1, 85 and 2, 2, 14). There is
no instance of *pr. quo minus* in Caesar;
but in Tac. there are three, and one of
pr. quin, while in both authors the infin.
with or without acc. is frequent.
3. **perdiscere ludus esset:** similarly
Virg. Aen. 9, 606 flectere ludus equos et
spicula tendere cornu; Hor. s. 2, 2, 123;
Stat. Ach. 2, 440. Cf. De Or. 2, 72
omnium ceterarum rerum oratio...ludus
est homini non hebeti. Below, 4, 1,
speaking of the Stoic scheme, Cicero
says 'non est facile perdiscere.'
5. **iracundae:** there would be nothing
unnatural in the plural noun *iracundiae*,
cf. Tusc. 3, 7: Rep. 1, 60.
6. **indignae philosophia:** Cicero
often thus speaks in the New Academic
vein; cf. Tusc. 4, 7; Plut. non posse s. v.
(of Epicureans) 19, 1100 d καὶ βιβλία μὴ
λέγωμεν μηδὲ ψηφίσματα βλάσφημα πό-
λεων ὅσα γέγραπται πρὸς αὐτούς· φιλα-
πεχθῆμον γάρ: also the Epicurean γνῶμαι
published by Wotke-Usener, § 74 ἐν
φιλολόγῳ συζητήσει πλεῖον ἤνυσεν ὁ
ἡττηθείς, καθ᾽ ὃ προσέμαθεν.
7. **tum:** it would be hard to prove
the dictum of Madvig in his n. here: 'in
transitu et progressu orationis numquam
ponitur *tunc*, quae particula rem uno
aliquo temporis puncto definit.' Certainly the MSS. of Caesar give *tunc* in
cases like the present. But the MSS.
have a tendency to substitute *tunc* for
tum, improperly; even where e.g. there
is correspondence with *tum*, for which
see C. F. W. Müller's n. on Fam. 3, 5, 3.
It is even doubtful whether Cicero wrote

tunc before consonants. The three exx.
given by the MSS. of Lucr. are corrected
by Lachmann and Munro. In Ovid
(excluding the Metamorphoses) the MSS.
give about 25 exx. of *tunc* before a
consonant; in all, however, but a few,
the following word begins with *c* or *q*,
so that this may well have been the
cause of the change from *tum* to *tunc*.
Ellis gives *tunc* twice before consonants
in Catullus (66, 24; 44, 21). Eight exx.
in Tibullus. Merguet qu. from Caesar
eight exx., four before *c* or *q*. *Tunc* is
extraordinarily rare in Cicero compared
with *tum*. Merguet quotes over 800
passages from the philosophical works
for *tum* as against eight for *tunc*. Two
are marked as doubtful, and suspicion
must rest on some of the remainder. Is
it conceivable that Cicero should (in
his philosophic works) have written
tum...cum, and *cum...tum* very many
times, and have substituted *tunc* in two
instances? In speeches about 21 exx.
(seven before guttural). But some later
authors prefer *tunc*; e.g. Lucan, in
whose text the few exx. of *tum* given
by MSS. have been for the most part
changed by edd.
8. **iracundia:** fragments of a treatise
by Philodemus on anger have been preserved in one of the Herculanean rolls,
and disquisitions on this and other
vices destructive of quietude were no
doubt common in the Epicurean school.
pertinacia: usually vicious per-
sistency; see my n. on Acad. 1, 44;
below, 2 §§ 9, 107.
recte disputari: there is a sort of
chiasmus here, these words coming after
the prepositional phrases with *cum*, and
corresponding to *disputari* above, which
precedes the prepositional phrase with
sine. See illustrations in Nägelsbach,
§ 167, I, 1.

putari potest. Sed ad haec, nisi molestum est, habeo quae velim.
An me, inquam, nisi te audire vellem, censes haec dicturum
fuisse? Vtrum igitur [inquit] percurri omnem Epicuri disciplinam
placet, an de una voluptate quaeri, de qua omne certamen est?
Tuo vero id quidem, inquam, arbitratu. Sic faciam igitur, in- 5
quit: unam rem explicabo, eamque maximam, de physicis alias,
et quidem tibi et declinationem istam atomorum et magnitudinem solis probabo et Democriti errata ab Epicuro reprehensa
et correcta permulta. Nunc dicam de voluptate, nihil scilicet
novi, ea tamen quae te ipsum probaturum esse confidam. Certe, 10
inquam, pertinax non ero tibique, si mihi probabis ea quae dices,

2 an: ita P¹; *at* ceteri.   3 igitur percurri: *qui percurri* E; *igitur inquit percurri*
A²; *inquit* servat C. F. W. M.   5 inquam: om. P (sed litura subest).

1. **nisi molestum est:** Plat. Tim. 17 B
εἰ μή τί σοι χαλεπόν: my n. on Acad. 1, 14.
quae velim: sc. *dicere*; the ellipse as
in 2, 59 sed nimis multa; 4, 1 omittamus
contra omnino velle aliquid; 4, 2 non
soleo temere contra Stoicos; ibid. quare
ad ea primum (sc. respondeatur); 4, 7
ista ipsa quae tu breviter; 5, 85 ne
longius; so too in numerous other passages of Cicero, and ordinary phrases,
like *sed haec hactenus*; and *de physicis
alias* below.
2. **an:** the confusion between *at* and
an in the codd. is constant and begins
early; and *at* does not introduce a
question in Cicero. On the other hand
such interrogations as this are frequently introduced by *an*; see e.g. 2, 74.
3. **utrum igitur:** the change from one
speaker to another is not indicated by
inquit; the omission may be found elsewhere, and the insertion of the word in
A² is an idle correction.
percurri omnem: cf. the inscr. of
Oinoanda, where the reader is implored to
study the system οὐ κατὰ τμήματα, but as
a whole (Bull. de Corr. Hell. xxi, p. 407).
4. **omne certamen:** the present book
being entirely ethical. But it is incorrect to put these words into the mouth
of Torquatus, as they do not agree
with his next speech. Cf. 2, 5 quid sit
voluptas, de quo omnis haec quaestio
est. [In a sense, everything in the Epicurean system hangs on pleasure; even
physics are only to be studied in order
to pave the way to it.] Torquatus does
in §§ 63, 64 touch the subject of physics, but from an ethical point of view.
5. **igitur:** here in the third place in
the sentence, as often; but the word

rarely appears in the fourth place, and
in the fifth only in special circumstances,
as Acad. 2, 129 qua de re est igitur,
owing to the tendency of *igitur* to
follow *est*; cf. too Tusc. 1, 82 ne in
animo quidem igitur, owing to the
accident of a prepositional phrase in-
tervening between *ne* and *quidem*.
(These are the only two passages in
Cicero's philosophical writings where
igitur occupies a place later than the
fourth.)
6. **alias:** contrasted with *nunc* down
below; the same contrast in 5, 77, and
often; cf. 4, 5 qui sit finis bonorum, mox,
hoc loco tantum dico...; 5, 22 sed nunc
quod agimus, de illis cum volemus; my
n. on Lael. § 1.
8. **reprehensa et correcta:** the words
go closely together, 'detected and
amended.' Possibly *et* has fallen out
before *reprehensa*. For the meaning of
reprehensa see n. on 2, 3 apprehendas.
Bremi, because the fact of the adverse
criticism was notorious, and because
there is no particular merit in it, conjectured *deprehensa*; but *deprehendere*,
meaning 'to detect,' is only used in good
Latin of something morally wrong. It
may be noted that the only reforms in
the scheme of Democritus which are
here attributed to Epicurus are in the
region of physics. Possibly one of the
corrections thought of here is that which
lies in the notion that Democritus did
not attribute weight to the atoms
[Diels, Doxogr. 219]. See curious passage,
Aetius Plac. 1, 12, 6; cf. 1, 3, 18. Also the
possibility of a gigantic atom (cf. Lucr.
2, 481–98)—see also Diels, 252, 311.
10. **confidam:** consecutive subj.

libenter assentiar. Probabo, inquit, modo ista sis aequitate 29
quam ostendis. Sed uti oratione perpetua malo quam interrogare
aut interrogari. Vt placet, inquam. Tum dicere exorsus est.

IX. Primum igitur, inquit, sic agam, ut ipsi auctori huius
5 disciplinae placet: constituam quid et quale sit id, de quo
quaerimus, non quo ignorare vos arbitrer, sed ut ratione et via
procedat oratio. Quaerimus igitur quid sit extremum et ultimum
bonorum quod omnium philosophorum sententia tale debet esse
ut ad id omnia referri oporteat, ipsum autem nusquam. Hoc
10 Epicurus in voluptate ponit, quod summum bonum esse volt,
summumque malum dolorem, idque instituit docere sic: Omne 30

3 tum: *tunc* non nulli (non P).   9 ut: om. E.   11 idque...docere: om. BE.

1. **sis**: 'continue all the while to
show.'
2. **quam**: Madvig has an interesting
note on the reading of Victorius (*qua*),
pointing out the limits of this kind of
attraction in Latin. It comes from the
compression of an infinitive construction; thus Hor. (s. 1, 6, 15), iudice quo
nosti populo is for *iudice quem iudicem
esse nosti populo*; and Fam. 5, 14, 1 cum
aliquid agas eorum quorum consuesti,
for *eorum quae consuesti agere*. But the
only ex. of the sort which the MSS. give
us in Cicero is Att. 10, 8, 7 nos tamen
hoc affirmamus eo augurio quo diximus,
and the text is almost certainly wrong
there, *quo* being an error either for *quod*
or for *quo de*.
ostendis: 'promise,' as in Fam. 9, 8, 1
and often.
oratione perpetua: after Plato's time,
the philosophic dialogue, in the hands
of Aristotle, Theophrastus, Heraclides
and others, preferred what the Platonic
Socrates called 'long speech' to 'short
speech' with its rapid interchange of
question and answer. See the Introd.
to my ed. of the Academica, p. 25; Fin.
2, 2; Diog. L. 9, 111 αὐτοδιήγητος
ἑρμηνεία.
quam...interrogari: 'than to question
you (about your difficulties) or let you
question me.' There is no need (as has
been proposed) to read *et interrogari*, so
as to bring about a correspondence with
Plato's phrase δοῦναι καὶ δέχεσθαι λόγον.
5. **quid et quale**: τί καὶ ποῖόν τι:
so below, § 37 and 2, 6. In spite of the
statement of Torquatus here concerning
Epicurus, Cic. in 2, 5 describes this particular definition as having been given
by Torquatus 'inadvertently' (*imprudens*). Epic., as we have seen, regarded

as useless the rules propounded for
definition by the διαλεκτικοί. Yet he
laid great stress on accuracy in the use
of terms, so that they may represent
precisely the things signified. See
§ 63 *n.* and 2, 6 *n.*
6. **ratione et via**: so 2, 18 and 3, 18,
but 2, 3 via quadam et ratione; cf. Top.
2 via atque arte; Pro Quinct. 28 modo
et ratione. Here *via* has a κατ᾽ ἐξοχήν
sense, 'the right way,' like τρόπος in the
expressions κατὰ τρόπον, οὐκ ἀπὸ τρόπου:
so often *locus* for 'the right place' (Sen.
ep. 46, 2).
8. **tale debet esse**, etc.: i.e. it must be
chosen for its own sake and not as a
means for the attainment of something
beyond. See § 42, and cf. Plato, Gorg.
499 E τέλος εἶναι ἁπασῶν τῶν πράξεων τὸ
ἀγαθὸν καὶ ἐκείνου ἕνεκεν δεῖν πάντα τἆλλα
πράττεσθαι, ἀλλ᾽ οὐκ ἐκεῖνο τῶν ἄλλων:
Arist. Eth. N. 1, 2, 1 (1094 a, 18) εἰ δή τι τέλος ἐστὶ τῶν πρακτῶν ὃ δι᾽ αὑτὸ βουλόμεθα,
τἆλλα δὲ διὰ τοῦτο καὶ μὴ πάντα δι᾽ ἕτερον
αἱρούμεθα...δῆλον ὡς τοῦτο ἂν εἴη τἀγαθὸν
καὶ τὸ ἄριστον: Arist. Met. 1. 994 b, 9 τὸ
οὗ ἕνεκα τέλος τοιοῦτον ὃ μὴ ἄλλου ἕνεκα
ἀλλὰ τἆλλα ἐκείνου: Stob. Eth. 2, 6, 3
λέγεται δὲ ὑπὸ τῶν Στωικῶν ὁρικῶς 'τέλος
ἐστὶν οὗ ἕνεκα πάντα πράττεται καθηκόντως, αὐτὸ δὲ πράττεται οὐδενὸς ἕνεκα'·
βραχιόνως 'οὗ χάριν τἆλλα, αὐτὸ δ᾽
οὐδενός.' καὶ πάλιν 'ἐφ᾽ ὃ πάντα τὰ ἐν
τῷ βίῳ πραττόμενα καθηκόντως τὴν
ἀναφορὰν λαμβάνει, αὐτὸ δὲ ἐπ᾽ οὐδέν.'
The last definition agrees closely with
the one we have here and in § 42; cf. 2, 5.
9. **hoc...idque**: see n. on 2, 49.
11. **docere**: 'to prove'; for the context
cf. 3, 27 concluduntur igitur eorum
argumenta sic.
omne animal, etc.: the same foundation had been laid for the hedonistic

animal, simul atque natum sit, voluptatem appetere eaque
gaudere ut summo bono, dolorem aspernari ut summum malum
et, quantum possit, a se repellere, idque facere nondum depravatum, ipsa natura incorrupte atque integre iudicante. Itaque
negat opus esse ratione neque disputatione, quam ob rem voluptas 5

ethics by predecessors of Epicurus: see
Arist. Eth. Nic. 10, 2, 1 (1172 *b*, 9 sq.)
Εὔδοξος μὲν οὖν τὴν ἡδονὴν τἀγαθὸν ᾤετ᾽
εἶναι διὰ τὸ πάνθ᾽ ὁρᾶν ἐφιέμενα αὐτῆς
καὶ ἔλλογα καὶ ἄλογα: and by Aristippus;
cf. Diog. L. 2, 88. The criticism which
Aristotle makes is that the fact adduced
proves ἡδονή to be *an* ἀγαθόν, but not
the ἀγαθόν, the supreme good. Further,
the Hedonists assumed pleasure to be
the same for all sentient beings, but
'δοκεῖ εἶναι ἑκάστῳ ζῴῳ ἡδονὴ οἰκεία,
ὥσπερ καὶ ἔργον' (Arist. Eth. N. 10,
5, 8 or 1176 *a*, 3). Aristotle explains
the universal desire for pleasure by the
universal desire for life, of which pleasure is an accompaniment (ib. 10, 4, 10
or 1175 *a*, 15). Cf. nn. on 2, 31 sq. where
Cicero refutes the fundamental doctrine
of the Epicurean ethics. Aristippus
(Diog. L. 2, 88) argued on the same lines
as Eudoxus.

1. **appetere**: οἰκειοῦσθαι πρὸς αὐτὴν
(sc. τὴν ἡδονήν) is the phrase attributed
to Aristippus by Diog. L. 2, 88. In
Diog. L. 10, 137 the curious word εὐ-
αριστεῖσθαι is quoted from Epicurus,
which should be εὐαρεστεῖσθαι.

2. **dolorem**: Eudoxus and other Hedonists appealed to the universal in-
stinctive repulsion from pain: see Arist.
Eth. Nic. 10, 2, 2 (1172 *b*, 18) οὐχ ἧττον δ᾽
ᾤετ᾽ εἶναι φανερὸν ἐκ τοῦ ἐναντίου· τὴν
γὰρ λύπην καθ᾽ αὑτὸ πᾶσι φευκτὸν εἶναι·
ὁμοίως δὴ τοὐναντίον αἱρετόν.

aspernari: Epic. used προσκρούειν
(Diog. L. 10, 137) as well as φεύγειν
and ἀλλοτριοῦσθαι. For the latter cf.
Democritus as quoted by Diotimus ap.
Sext. A. M. 7, 140 αἱρέσεως δὲ καὶ
φυγῆς (κριτήρια) τὰ πάθη· τὸ μὲν γὰρ ᾧ
προσοικειούμεθα, τοῦτο αἱρετόν ἐστι, τὸ
δὲ ᾧ προσαλλοτριούμεθα, τοῦτο φευκτόν
ἐστι. For αἱρετόν and ἀλλότριον the
words ὁμόφυλον and ἀλλόφυλον seem to
be substituted by Philodemus in his
treatise περὶ θεῶν διαγωγῆς, the fragments of which have been edited by
Scott, Fragmenta Herculanensia, pp.
93–203. In fr. 1, l. 14, it is intimated
that there is no such thing as ἀλλο-
τρίωσις in the case of a god. All his
experiences are pleasurable; he συνεχῶς

ἥδεται (fr. 18, l. 1). He must experience
nothing ἀλλόφυλον, but πάντα οἰκεῖα
(ib. l. 5). Again in fr. 41 οἰκεῖα and
ἀλλόφυλα are contrasted (in the context
are the words ὠκειωμένα ἀδιαλείπτως).
So in fr. 32 the ἀλλόφυλον is set over
against freedom from all ὄχλησις, because
the god enjoys only τὰς καθ᾽ ἡσυχίαν
λεγομένας ἡδονάς (fr. 25). Prof. Scott
gives a somewhat different interpretation
to ἀλλόφυλον, but it seems to me not
so suitable; he refers the word to the
theory of the nutriment by which
the substance of the divine body was
sustained, a matter certainly touched
on in the treatise (see τροφήν in fr. 52
and 77).

3. **nondum depravatum**: Sext. P. H.
3, 194 ὅθεν καὶ οἱ Ἐπικούρειοι δεικνύναι
νομίζουσι, φύσει αἱρετὴν εἶναι τὴν ἡδονήν·
τὰ γὰρ ζῷά φασιν ἅμα τῷ γενέσθαι
ἀδιάστροφα ὄντα ὁρμᾶν μὲν ἐπὶ τὴν
ἡδονήν, ἐκκλίνειν δὲ ἀλγηδόνας. So Sext.
A. M. 11, 96 quotes Epic. as saying that
τὸ ζῷον feels this attraction and repulsion 'φυσικῶς καὶ ἀδιδάκτως,' while it is
not yet enslaved by vain imaginations,
'μηδέπω κατὰ δόξαν δουλεῦον.' In 2, 31
Cicero rallies Epicurus for regarding
animals as 'mirrors of nature,' and
ib. 109 protests against the evidence of
beasts in the matter of the supreme
good. Cf. also 2, 33 bestiarum vero
nullum iudicium puto; quamvis enim
depravatae non sint, pravae tamen
esse possunt; 1, 50 natura non depravata. Aristippus held (Diog. L. 2, 89)
that if men reject pleasure it is κατὰ
διαστροφήν.

4. **incorrupte atque integre**: § 71 incorruptis atque integris testibus;
Acad. 2, 19.

5. **negat**, etc.: so Epic. ap. Diog. L.
10, 137 says that the attraction to
pleasure and the repulsion from pain
are experienced 'φυσικῶς καὶ χωρὶς λόγου·
αὐτοπαθῶς οὖν φεύγομεν τὴν ἀλγηδόνα.'
So Eudoxus urged 'οὐδένα ἐπερωτᾶν
τίνος ἕνεκα ἥδεται, ὡς καθ᾽ αὐτήν....' Cf.
Galen, de plac. H. et P. p. 487, 8 (ed.
Müller) οὐ μακρῶν λόγων οὐδὲ ἀποδείξεων
ἀκριβεστέρων δεόμενα, μόνης δὲ ἀναμνήσεως ὧν ἑκάστοτε πάσχομεν, ὡς καὶ Ποσει-

expetenda, fugiendus dolor sit. Sentiri haec putat, ut calere ignem, nivem esse albam, mel dulce; quorum nihil oporteret exquisitis rationibus confirmare, tantum satis esse admonere. Interesse enim inter argumentum conclusionemque rationis et

2 oporteret: sic codd. omnes.　　　4 argumentum: *augmentatum* A.

δώνιος εἶπεν. Usener (p. 350 n.) says it is clear from the passage of Galen that Cicero wrote in the text *oratione* not *ratione*. I do not see that the words of Galen have any direct bearing on the terms used here; but if they have, they support *ratione*, as far more likely to be chosen by Cicero to represent λόγων.

neque: for the negative after *negat* see Draeger § 325 (=ii, p. 85).

quam ob rem: for the ellipse (*ut demonstretur*) see n. on 1, 14.

1. **sentiri haec putat**: cf. Plut. in Colot. c. 27 (1122 *d*) αἴσθησιν ἔχειν δεῖ καὶ σάρκινον εἶναι καὶ φανεῖται ἡδονὴ τἀγαθὸν (MSS. ἀγαθόν). The desirability of pleasure (so Dem. as reported by Diotimus ap. Sext. A. M. 7, 140) is to the Epicurean attested by πάθος, a test of truth behind which no reasoning can get. The notion of it (πρόληψις) is impressed on the mind by repeated experience, and no argumentation can make it clearer. For the Epicurean πρόληψις and its relation to φθόγγοι see n. on 2, 6. So in 5, 27 Piso treats the impulse to self-preservation as 'infixum in ipsa natura.' It also 'comprehenditur suis cuiusque sensibus' (i.e. is matter of πάθος) and reasoning about it is superfluous. Much in the same spirit Aristotle discourses of the difficulty of demonstrating ἀρχαί in Ethics and says that in some cases we must be content to have a clear statement of fundamental assumptions (δειχθῆναι τὸ ὅτι καλῶς).

haec: for the reading *hoc*, 'this kind of thing,' cf. Acad. 2, 49 soritas hoc vocant, with my n.; Ovid, Tr. 2, 501 and also 2, 285 cum quaedam spatientur in hoc, ut amator eodem | conveniat, quare porticus ulla patet, where *hoc*, 'this kind of place,' is a far better reading than *hac*. The generic use of *id*, *quod* is common in Varro; see Keil on r. r. 2, 3, 6. So often τοῦτο in Greek, as e.g. Dem. Leoch. § 63.

2. **nivem esse albam**: a fact which Anaxagoras paradoxically contested; see Acad. 2 §§ 72, 100, with my nn.

oporteret: Madv. says that if we read *oporteret* we must also read *esset*, but the presence of the relative in the earlier

clause makes all the difference. This passage is strictly parallel with § 19 quo nihil posset fieri minus; ita effici, and many others in Latin authors. Cf. Acad. 1, 41 and the passages to which reference is made in my note there.

3. **confirmare**: after the impersonal expressions *oporteret* and *satis esse*, it would have been more usual to write *confirmari...admoneri*; but there is no need to change the readings, as Latin writers easily pass from the one form to the other in such cases; cf. e.g. Ad Herenn. 2, 11; but ib. § 2 the reading *quales sequi quales vitari oporteret* can hardly be right.

tantum satis esse: a not very common form of phrase. Madvig partly from preceding editors cites De Or. 2, 139 tantum satis est intellegi ne hoc quidem eos consecutos...; Div. 2, 104; Nep. Hann. 10, 5; also Cic. Sull. 39 iam non quaero purgetne Cassius Sullam; illud mihi tantum satis est contra Sullam nihil esse in indicio. In the last passage *illud tantum* is restrictive, 'merely this one fact is enough'; but Madvig strangely supposes *tantum satis* to have coalesced so as almost to form a single phrase, and the sense to be *illud est tantum-satis* ('schon genug'). For *tantum illud*, 'that one thing,' cf. (*si tanti est*) Sall. Iug. 14 § 20.

admonere: cf. the closely similar passage in 3, 3.

4. **argumentum conclusionemque rationis**: Cicero's most ordinary rendering of συλλογισμός is *conclusio rationis*; so συλλογίζεσθαι is *concludere rationem*; but the Latin words correspond more closely to συμπεραίνειν and συμπέρασμα. Also *concludere argumentum* and *argumenti conclusio* are common phrases; cf. also 4, 9 argumentorum ratione concludentium. Here *argumentum* seems to represent some word of wider meaning than συλλογισμός, such as ἀπόδειξις, although argumenti conclusio and ἀπόδειξις are sometimes identified (Ac. 2, 26). For *argumentatio* see 5, 9 *n*. Madvig's contention that *argumenti sententiam concludere* in N.D. 1, 89 is an impossible phrase is confuted by C. F. W. Müller *ad loc*. In all proba-

inter mediocrem animadversionem atque admonitionem; altera
occulta quaedam et quasi involuta aperiri, altera prompta et
aperta iudicari. Etenim quoniam detractis de homine sensibus
reliqui nihil est, necesse est, quid aut ad naturam aut contra sit,
a natura ipsa iudicari. Ea quid percipit aut quid iudicat, quo 5
aut petat aut fugiat aliquid, praeter voluptatem et dolorem?
31 Sunt autem quidam e nostris, qui haec subtilius velint tradere

3 iudicari: *indicari* Orelli. Post hoc inserunt *voluptatem etiam et per se expetendam
esse et dolorem ipsum per se esse expetendum* P et alii non nulli. 5 ea quid: *ei
quid* E; *en quid* P¹ (in marg. 'vel *ea*').

bility Epicurus made little use of the
Aristotelian scheme of deductive reasoning, but we have no reason to suppose
that here Cicero's authority has put into
the mouth of Epic. words that he could
not have used himself.

et inter: the illogical repetition of
inter is found a few times in the philosophical works of Cicero (see Merguet
s. v. *intersum*) but I think not in the
speeches; and seldom elsewhere.

1. **mediocrem animadversionem:** reminds one of βραχεῖα ὑπόμνησις in Sext.
See Diels, p. 247; cf. ἀναμνήσεως in the
passage from Galen given above in n. on
negat.

2. **quasi involuta:** there is a strong
metaphor in *involuta* (cf. *involucrum*, 'a
veil'), hence the apologetic *quasi*; cf.
Acad. 2, 26 cum ea quae quasi involuta
fuerunt, aperta sunt, and my n. there.

3. **iudicari:** this reading is superior
to *indicari* because there is a reference
to the use of κριτήριον (*iudicium*) in the
Greek texts.

detractis...nihil est: so this doctrine
is common to the Epicurean school with
other post-Aristotelian systems. The
mind 'ἤρτηται ἀπὸ τῶν αἰσθήσεων'
(Diog. L. 10, 32). Cf. below, § 64, quicquid
animo cernimus, id omne oritur a sensibus. Acad. 2, 30 (from Antiochus of
Ascalon) mens ipsa quae sensuum fons
est atque etiam ipse sensus est; in my
note there illustrations will be found.
Add Theophr. de sensu 4 (Diels, Doxogr.,
p. 499) τὸ γὰρ αἰσθάνεσθαι καὶ τὸ
φρονεῖν ὡς ταὐτὸ λέγει (of Parmenides).
On p. 392 of Diels' book much the same
statement occurs, in reference to Em-
pedocles (cf. p. 506), Parmenides and
Democritus. The maxim of Hobbes and
Locke, 'nihil est in intellectu quod non
antea fuerit in sensu,' was practically
accepted by Aristotle and by all teachers
after his time. As to the Stoics, see Zeller,
Stoics, p. 79, Eng. Trans. (ed. 1880).

4. **necesse est:** the exposition passes
suddenly into *oratio recta*, as below, 2,
48 and 3, 64, Acad. 2, 99 and often
elsewhere. Madvig without warrant
casts doubt on the opposite change in
Acad. 2, 40; but it is found elsewhere, as
in Acad. 2, 101; both changes occur in
Livy, for whom see Kuhnast², p. 236.

ad naturam = *secundum nat.*, as in
Att. 4, 18, 2 quae vita est maxime ad
naturam ad eam me refero. [Verr. 2, 1,
133, quoted by Madvig, is not in point.]
For *ad* = *secundum* see Draeger § 252,
6 a. Sen. ep. 16 § 7 ad naturam vivere
...ad opiniones.

5. **a natura:** cf. n. on 2, 33.

ea quid...dolorem? So Democritus,
fragm. mor. 8 (Mullach): οὗρος ξυμφο-
ρέων καὶ ἀξυμφορέων τέρψις καὶ ἀτερπίη.
percipit: καταλαμβάνεται: see Acad.
1, 31.

quo: 'whereby'; see n. on § 41. Also
for the combination of pleasure and
pain, which are regarded as constituting
together a single κριτήριον, see n. on § 23
confirmat autem etc.

7. **sunt quidam...qui velint:** how fine
the line is which divides indic. from
subj. in such expressions may be seen
from § 69 sunt quidam...qui verentur.
In what way these Epicureans modified
the teaching of the founder, cannot be
precisely stated. Madvig remarks, with
great probability, 'ut fiebat in illa
schola, eadem mutatis verbis dixisse
videntur'; but the words *ut fiebat in illa
schola* convey a wrong impression. The
insita in animis notio must be what the
Epicureans called πρόληψις, while the
conceptions mentioned above (*nivem esse
albam*, etc.) are also προλήψεις. It
may be that the later school distinguished between προλήψεις, regarding
some of them as simple, elementary,
and easy of attainment, while others
were less easily attained, and perhaps
even called for the conscious exercise

et negent satis esse, quid bonum sit aut quid malum, sensu iudicari, sed animo etiam ac ratione intellegi posse et voluptatem ipsam per se esse expetendam et dolorem ipsum per se esse fugiendum. Itaque aiunt hanc quasi naturalem atque insitam 5 in animis nostris inesse notionem, ut alterum esse appetendum, alterum aspernandum sentiamus. Alii autem, quibus ego assentior, cum a philosophis compluribus permulta dicantur cur nec voluptas in bonis sit numeranda nec in malis dolor,

7 compluribus: *quam pluribus* E.

of reason, working upon experience. But even in the scheme of Epicurus the mind is not the passive recipient of impressions from the senses; it contributes something to sensation (Diog. L. 10, 32 συμβαλλομένου τι καὶ τοῦ λογισμοῦ). Compare Cicero's remarks on the point in 2, 36.

subtilius: ἀκριβέστερον: see my n. on Acad. 1, 6.

tradere: but *iudicari*: for the change of voice cf. 2, 21 and 2, 48.

1. **negent**: apparently, while leaving αἴσθησις as the criterion of things physical, they deemed it insufficient for things moral. They may possibly have Stoicised and held, as the Stoics would say, that the notion of good and evil is not a πρόληψις but an ἔννοια.

2. **sed**: for the positive verb to be supplied from *negent* cf. § 61; 2, 68.

animo: Madvig: 'insolentius dixit *animo* cum mentis rationes intellegantur'; but Cicero nowhere draws so strict a line between *mens* and *animus*.

posse: loosely put where *necesse esse* is required by the argument.

4. **quasi**: here, as often, indicates that Cicero is translating tentatively from the Greek. See 2, 5 and 3, 19 and my n. on Acad. 1, 17.

insitam: on this Madvig remarks 'loquitur Cicero paene ita, tamquam Epicurus eam innatam putaverit; atque aperte id dicit N.D. 1, 44, a Platone et Stoicis colorem ducens. Itaque iure in hoc Cicero reprenditur ab iis, qui philosophiae historiam scripserunt.' The charge of inaccuracy thus formulated by Madvig has been copied from him by many, and much hard language has been used of Cicero concerning it. I venture to think that there is no solid ground for supposing that Cicero intended to attribute anything like what we know as the theory of 'innate ideas' to Epicurus. His critics have erred through identifying the meaning of *insitus* and

innatus with that of *innate* and its representatives in other languages. Cicero merely uses these words as renderings of ἔμφυτος. Why Madvig links the Stoics with Plato in his note I do not understand. They as well as the Epicureans held strongly to the idea that the mind at birth is a *tabula rasa*. Bonhöffer,1,191sq., denies this for Epictetus, but on insufficient grounds. He quotes Plut. Sto. Rep. 17 (1042 *a*) ταῦτα συμφωνεῖν τῷ βίῳ φάσκων καὶ μάλιστα τῶν ἐμφύτων ἅπτεσθαι προλήψεων without saying that it goes back to Chrysippus. Yet they could talk of ἔμφυτοι προλήψεις, meaning thereby that πρ. spring up in the mind after birth by a natural and inevitable process. Cf. Epict. 2, 11, 3 ἔμφυτον ἔννοιαν. The meaning of ἔμφυτος is well exhibited by the corresponding use of ἐμφύεσθαι in Stob. Ecl. c. 40 § 8 περὶ τοῦ νοῦ οἱ μὲν Στωικοὶ λέγουσι μὴ εὐθὺς ἐμφύεσθαι τὸν λόγον. The term ἔμφυτος probably, like many others, was current in Epicurean as well as in Stoic literature. In N.D. 1, 44 insitas vel potius innatas cognitiones, Cicero gives (more suo) a choice of renderings for ἐμφύτους προλήψεις (see Mayor ad l.); but even *a principio innasci* in 2, 34 does not imply (as he thinks) the doctrine of *innate* gifts. Epic.(Diog. L. 10,129) applied σύμφυτον to ἀγαθόν. Much else that bears on the Stoic and the Epicurean πρόληψις I must leave over for later nn.

5. **alterum ... alterum**: referred to *voluptatem* and *dolorem*. See n. on 3, 48 utrumque.

6. **sentiamus**: the word combines the senses of 'thinking' and 'feeling.'

7. **dicantur cur**: for the slight ellipse cf. 2, 117.

8. **voluptas...dolor**: chiasmus.

in bonis: Torquatus does not seem to be alluding to any direct polemics against the Epicurean school, but rather to the contention of the Stoics and

non existimant oportere nimium nos causae confidere, sed et argumentandum et accurate disserendum et rationibus conquisitis de voluptate et dolore disputandum putant.

32 X. Sed ut perspiciatis unde omnis iste natus error sit voluptatem accusantium doloremque laudantium, totam rem aperiam 5 eaque ipsa quae ab illo inventore veritatis et quasi architecto beatae vitae dicta sunt, explicabo. Nemo enim ipsam volup-

2 accurate: *caute* ed. Colon.

Cynics that pleasure is not even *an* ἀγαθόν, much less τὸ ἀγαθόν.

1. **non existimant**: the *non* practically coalesces with the verb here as often; see n. on § 1. For the Stoic point of view cf. Seneca ep. 11 § 1 quicquid infixum et ingenitum est; 14 § 1.

argumentandum: does this mean that these Epicurean heretics advocated the use of the ordinary dialectic which their founder repudiated? The words used (*argumentandum, disserendum, rationibus conquisitis, disputandum*) seem to point to this. Diog. L. 10, 31, after quoting from the κανὼν of Epicurus the doctrine that the κριτήρια τῆς ἀληθείας are the αἰσθήσεις, the προλήψεις and the πάθη, adds: ‘οἱ δὲ Ἐπικούρειοι τὰς φανταστικὰς ἐπιβολὰς τῆς διανοίας.’ Gassendi and Hirzel (1, 186 sq.) understand the words to refer to the vain imaginations of madmen and dreamers; but rather they indicate the faculty whereby the mind is able to transcend the actual impressions of sense and win such conceptions as that of the void, the atoms. This is animi *iniectus* (*iactus*) in Lucr. 2, 740, 1047 (ἐπιβολὴ τῆς διανοίας). The letter of Epic. to Herodotus, c. 50, shows that Epic. himself held this tenet; therefore no stress can be laid on the contrast loosely put by Diog. L. between Epicurus and the Epicureans. So Sext. A. M. 11, 96 attributes to τινὲς τῶν Ἐπικουρείων the theory that ‘φυσικῶς καὶ ἀδιδάκτως τὸ ζῷον φεύγει μὲν τὴν ἀλγηδόνα, διώκει δὲ τὴν ἡδονήν,’ though the theory was indubitably Epicurus’ own; see Hirzel, 11, 671 sq. Madvig notes a point overlooked by Hirzel, that Torquatus proceeds to draw his arguments not from those followers of Epicurus to whom he has just given his assent, but from Epicurus himself. It may, however, be pointed out that Torquatus does not assert that *the whole* of the demonstrations which follow are borrowed from Epicurus.

5. **doloremque laudantium**: while

there were philosophers (like the Cynics) who denounced pleasure *per se*, there were none who lauded pain *per se*; the expression here is rather exaggerated.

6. **inventore veritatis**: the extravagant eulogies heaped on Epicurus by his disciples are well illustrated by the proems to Lucret. 1 and 111. Cf. especially 3, 9 tu pater es rerum inventor (where Davies wrongly conjectured *veri* for *rerum*, which reading is sufficiently protected by 5, 2 pro rerum maiestate). Cf. n. on § 14 unum vidisse verum. Lucretius calls Epicurus a god, as does the Epicurean speaker in N.D. 1, 43. Athen. v. 182 *a* speaks of the interlocutors in the Symposium of Epicurus as ‘κολάκων ἄγυρις ἀλλήλους ἐπαινούντων.’ Cf. N.D. 1, 72 ista enim a vobis quasi dictata redduntur quae Epicurus oscitans halucinatus est, cum quidem gloriaretur, ut videmus in scriptis, se magistrum habuisse nullum. Quod ei non praedicanti facile equidem crederem, sicut mali aedifici domino glorianti se architectum non habuisse.

quasi architecto beatae vitae: similarly in § 42 *sapientia* is spoken of as tamquam artifex conquirendae et comparandae voluptatis. Cicero has only *architectus*; Plaut. has also *architecton* and *architectonus*.

7. **nemo enim**, etc.: cf. Epicurus’ letter to Menoeceus (Diog. L. 10, 129): οὐ πᾶσαν ἡδονὴν αἱρούμεθα, ἀλλ’ ἔστιν ὅτε πολλὰς ὑπερβαίνομεν, ὅταν πλεῖον ἡμῖν τὸ δυσχερὲς ἐκ τούτων ἔπηται· καὶ πολλὰς ἀλγηδόνας ἡδονῶν κρείττους νομίζομεν, ἐπειδὰν μείζων ἡμῖν ἡδονὴ παρακολουθῇ πολὺν χρόνον ὑπομείνασι τὰς ἀλγηδόνας. πᾶσα οὖν ἡδονὴ διὰ τὸ φύσιν ἔχειν οἰκείαν ἀγαθόν, οὐ πᾶσα μέντοι αἱρετή· καθάπερ καὶ ἀλγηδὼν πᾶσα κακόν, οὐ πᾶσα δὲ ἀεὶ φευκτὴ πεφυκυῖα. τῇ μέντοι συμμετρήσει καὶ συμφερόντων καὶ ἀσυμφόρων βλέψει ταῦτα πάντα κρίνειν καθήκει. χρώμεθα γὰρ τῷ μὲν ἀγαθῷ κατά τινας χρόνους ὡς κακῷ, τῷ δὲ κακῷ τἄμπαλιν ὡς ἀγαθῷ. Also No. 8 of the κυρίαι δόξαι (Diog. L.

tatem, quia voluptas sit, aspernatur aut odit aut fugit, sed quia consecuntur magni dolores eos qui ratione voluptatem sequi nesciunt, neque porro quisquam est qui dolorem ipsum, quia dolor sit, amet, consectetur, adipisci velit, sed quia non numquam 5 eius modi tempora incidunt ut labore et dolore magnam aliquam quaerat voluptatem. Vt enim ad minima veniam, quis nostrum

10, 141): οὐδεμία ἡδονὴ καθ᾽ ἑαυτὸ κακόν· ἀλλὰ τὰ τινῶν ἡδονῶν ποιητικὰ πολλαπλασίους ἐπιφέρει τὰς ὀχλήσεις τῶν ἡδονῶν. The same doctrine is represented in Tusc. 5, 95; see also Usener §§ 181, 442, 443, 449; and below, § 47. The same Bentham-like calculus of pleasure and pain is inculcated by Democritus, fr. 1 (Mullach): συνίστασθαι δὲ αὐτὴν (τὴν εὐθυμίην) ἐκ τοῦ διορισμοῦ καὶ τῆς διακρίσεως τῶν ἡδονῶν: cf. fr. 20; also a saying attributed to Solon (Mullach, p. 212) ἡδονὴν φεῦγε ἥτις λύπην τίκτει, and a line of Menander ap. Stob. VI, p. 72 φεῦγ᾽ ἡδονὴν φέρουσαν ὕστερον βλάβην.

1. **quia sit…quia consecuntur**: the change of mood is noticeable. Possibly in Cicero's original text the words quia cons.…nesciunt formed a protasis to an apodosis which has fallen out.

2. **consecuntur magni dolores eos**: for *aliquid sequitur* or *consequitur aliquem* Madvig quotes Verr. 5, 189; Tusc. 2, 28; Sest. 51; Div. 2, 62; Ter. Phorm. 750; Sall. or. Phil. § 9; Quintil. 4, 2, 44 and 8, 3, 82; Sen. Ben. 6, 4, 6; De Ira 2, 2, 1. Add Nep. Att. 19, 3; Caes. Bell. Gall. 8, 31, 3; Quint. 2, 10, 14; 7, 4, 19; 8, 6, 24; 10, 2, 26; 12, 11, 4 (prosequi); Sall. Cat. 3, 2 and 54, 5 and ep. Mithr. 22; or. Phil. 21; Virg. G. 3, 564 immundus sudor sequitur membra; Ovid, Met. 9, 358; ib. 2, 611 (frigus secutum est corpus); 6, 234; Phaedr. 1, 5, 9; Curt. 8, 5, 16; 4, 14, 25; Liv. 28, 21, 5; 33, 13, 10; Virg. Aen. 12, 375; Hor. Od. 3, 27, 59 zona bene te secuta; Tac. H. 4, 32; An. 4, 28; Dial. 10.

ratione: so 3, 58 quod ratione actum est. There is an example of *ratione* in Rep. 6, 18 which is exactly like this where Meissner, ed. 4, strikes it out. We may also compare Off. 3, 55 etiam si illa (villa) nec bona est nec aedificata ratione; Planc. 26 me…ratione cedentem. Cf. 1, 62. It is strange that many scholars should have attacked the reading in Att. 12, 44, 3 quod domi te inclusisti, ratione fecisti (Wesenb. and others *recte*). Expressions like rationem facti probare etc. are common enough and lie near to *ratione fecisti*; Off. 1, 7

a ratione and ratione. In MSS. *recte* and *ratione* are often confused; see C. F. W. Müller's n. to S. Rosc. 113. [A passage in pro Cael. 42 is hardly sound as it stands: 'revocet se aliquando ad curam rei domesticae, rei forensis reique publicae, ut ea quae ratione antea non perspexerat, satietate abiecisse, experiendo contempsisse, videatur.' *Antea* is corrupt; under it perhaps lurks *abicienda*, agreeing with *quae*.]

3. **neque porro quisquam**, etc.: the language is like that of a passage in the collection of Epicurean sayings discovered in the Vatican by Wotke and published by Usener in Wiener Stud. 10, 192 (§ 16): οὐδεὶς βλέπων τὸ κακὸν αἱρεῖται αὐτό, ἀλλὰ δελεασθεὶς ὡς ἀγαθῶν προσόντων μειζόνων ὑπὸ τοῦ κακοῦ ἐθηρεύθη (so Gomperz, Wien. St. 10, 203 corrects the MS. which has ἀγαθὸν προσὸν μεῖζον ἄν). The Greek words raise a suspicion that *non magno* may have fallen out before *magnam*. The Latin sentence is slightly illogical, or rather elliptical, and needs for the completion of the sense words like *idcirco dolorem amplectitur*

porro: see n. on 2, 25.

5. **tempora**: § 33 temporibus quibusdam. The observation of καιρός or εὐκαιρία in the pursuit of pleasure is often inculcated in the hedonistic texts. It is even said that constant opportunity for pleasure would be a bad thing. Cf. Vol. Herc. 132 fr. 89 (Scott p. 139): (the wise man or the god) οὐκ ἀφέτως ἀπολαύει παρὰ πάντα τῆς εὐκαιρίας, καὶ πλήθους καὶ ποιότητος (sc. τῶν ἡδονῶν) ἀστοχάστων· ἥλγει γὰρ ἂν καὶ κατέστρεφεν οὕτως ἀναστρεφόμενος· ἀλλ᾽ ἐπὶ πάντων χρείας (*real* utility) ἐλαύνει κατὰ τὴν διαστάθμησιν (the calculus of pleasures and pains). So Democr. fr. 19 M.: ἡδοναὶ ἄκαιροι τίκτουσι ἀηδίας.

labore et dolore: jingles of the kind are not avoided by Cic. For the sense cf. Max. Tyr. 32 (3), 10 (ap. Usener, p. 313) σμικρῶν πόνων μεγάλας ἡδονὰς ἀντεισάγεις.

6. **ut…veniam**: so 5, 7 ut ad minora veniam.

nostrum: not = *Epicureorum* (as some

exercitationem ullam corporis suscipit laboriosam, nisi ut aliquid ex ea commodi consequatur? quis autem vel eum iure reprehenderit, qui in ea voluptate velit esse quam nihil molestiae consequatur, vel illum qui dolorem eum fugiat quo voluptas **33** nulla pariatur? At vero eos et accusamus et iusto odio dig- 5 nissimos ducimus, qui blanditiis praesentium voluptatum deleniti atque corrupti, quos dolores et quas molestias excepturi sint, occaecati cupiditate non provident, similique sunt in culpa, qui

5 iusto: fort. *isto.*　　6 blanditiis: *per blanditus* E.　　6 deleniti: *deliniti* EP.

have supposed), but=*hominum* generally.

1. **laboriosam:** emphatic at the end of the clause.

3. **quam:** doubtless the right reading; but Madvig's grounds of defence are not quite satisfactory. He may be right in repeating an old rule (which many have repeated after him, cf. Mayor on Phil. 2, 26; Kühner-Stegmann II, § 112 c (a) p. 581) that the omission of *in* before *qua* would be against the usage of good writers, because we cannot supply to the relative clause the same verb that goes with the preceding clause, and in the instances usually quoted this is so, as in 4, 56; N.D. 1, 31; Tusc. 1, 94 and 111; Phil. 2, 26; **Att.** 3, 19, 2; ib. 8, 11 D, 3; Fam. 3, 4, 1; 4, 9, 1 (with the reading de rebus); De Or. 2, 208; ib. 277; Pro Lig. 2; Rosc. Am. 127; Nep. Cim. 3; Liv. 22, 33, 9; 29, 25, 8. Compare also § 49 in eadem causa sunt qua antequam nati (sc. in qua fuerunt antequam nati sunt); Leg. 3, 33 ego in ista sum sententia, qua te semper fuisse scio; Phil. 2, 37 fateor me...tanta in maestitia fuisse, quanta ceteri optimi cives, si idem providissent, fuissent. For examples from other authors cf. Liv. 10, 31, 13 socios...in eadem fortuna videbant, qua ipsi erant; 22, 9, 10 resque publica in eodem quo ante bellum fuisset, statu permansisset; 27, 22, 5 (same vb. changed from imp. to plup.); similarly 34, 28, 9; Varro, r. r. 1, 40, 6. This restriction may be right; it does not perhaps hold so widely in Greek, cf. Thuc. 3, 17, 1; though it is usual, Jelf § 650, 3. But Madvig's other reason against *qua* is hard to understand: 'non potest sic absolute dici *consequi*, ut pro accusativo per praepositionem *in* adiungatur res praecedens (*in hac voluptate nihil molestiae consequitur*); nam aliter longe dicitur: *in hac consequitur* (accidit) *obscuratio* (IV, 29).' But if *qua* be read there is no reason why *consequatur*

should not have the same subject as *velit*, and take *nihil molestiae* as object, just like *aliquid...consequatur* above.

4. **illum qui:** after *eum qui*; cf. Landgr. on Rosc. p. 247.

5. **at vero,** etc.: the sentence is incomplete. Each part describes a motive for mistaken action: (1) the passion for the pleasure of the moment; (2) the desire to avoid pain at the moment. The two sets of people who are subject to these two motives are said to be *simili in culpa*; but the sin of the one set is alleged to consist in mere want of foresight (*non provident*), that of the other in desertion of duty (*officia deserunt*). The want of balance between the two sins is obvious. Probably some words have fallen out after *corrupti*, which described a sin as heinous as that of deserting duty. A close comparison of this section with § 47 suggests that the reference was to *libido*; in fact the words *tradunt se libidinibus constringendos et* (almost taken from § 47) would cure the passage.

accusamus: a word designedly heavier than *reprehenderit* above.

iusto...dignissimos: slightly pleonastic.

6. **blanditiis:** Fam. 15, 16, 3 delenitus illecebris voluptatis.

8. **occaecati:** there are many denunciations in Epicurean literature of the *blindness* of the non-philosophic herd. Cf. ἀβλεψία in Polystratos, περὶ ἀλόγου φρονήσεως (Gomperz ap. Hermes, XI, p. 420; τὸ ταραχῆς ὕπουλον καὶ τυφλόν in Hercul. Papyr. 26, col. 24 (Scott, p. 234); Lucret. 2, 14 o pectora caeca! The *pectus caecum* is opposed to the *purum* or *purgatum pectus* (Lucr. 5, 18, 43) in which passion and terror have been subjugated to reason; Democr. fr. 13 Mullach: διὰ νόου τυφλότητα καὶ ἀγνωμοσύνην: id. 82 αἱ περὶ τι σφοδραὶ ὀρέξιες τυφλοῦσι εἰς τἆλλα τὴν ψυχήν.

officia deserunt mollitia animi, id est laborum et dolorum fuga. Et harum quidem rerum facilis est et expedita distinctio. Nam libero tempore, cum soluta nobis est eligendi optio, cumque nihil impedit quo minus id quod maxime placeat facere possimus, 5 omnis voluptas assumenda est, omnis dolor depellendus. Temporibus autem quibusdam et aut officiis debitis aut rerum necessitatibus saepe eveniet, ut et voluptates repudiandae sint et molestiae non recusandae. Itaque earum rerum hic tenetur a sapiente delectus ut aut reiciendis voluptatibus maiores alias

5 depellendus A: *repellendus* BE; in P littera *d* est in rasura.

1. **mollitia animi:** μαλακία: so often, as Liv. 28, 22, 11; cf. *debilitas animi* in § 49 where the *officia* are mentioned in detail; also Caes. B.G. 7, 20, 5 (speech of Vercingetorix) ne is multitudinis studio ad dimicandum impelleretur, cui rei propter animi mollitiem studere omnes videret, quod diutius laborem ferre non possent.

id est: here, as Madvig points out, corrective rather than explanatory: 'or, to put it differently.' See exx. of this use in my n. on Acad. 1, 5.

2. **distinctio:** 'possibility of distinguishing'; the verbal noun often conveys this idea. With *expedita* cf. *sese expediunt* below.

3. **soluta:** a mere adjective, as often. **eligendi optio:** the same phrase in Att. 4, 18, 3; Brut. 189. Instead of the explanatory genitive, an *ut*-clause occurs in div. Caec. 45 (optionem...ut eligas). The explanatory genitive often lies very close in meaning to the substantive on which it depends; as e.g. Liv. 7, 25, 4 ora littoris Antiatis.

5. **depellendus:** Madvig says '*depellitur* quod locum iam tenet, ut febris corpore...*repellitur* quod appropinquat et instat; *pellitur* omnino quidquid loco movetur; *pellitur* hostis in acie stans, *repellitur* irruens, *depellitur* praesidium colle; *repellitur* quod admitti vult.' But usage is not so rigid; cf. e.g. 5, 17 (18) voluptatis alii primum appetitum putant et primam depulsionem doloris; C. F. W. Müller's n. is far from clear; 2, 41 depulsione mali...adeptione; in Brut. 1. 14, 2 servitutem...depulisti is right; depulisti Ern. Wes. T.P., reppulisti C. F. W. M. Tusc. 3, 25 aegritudinem depellamus; prov. cons. 6 virgines...morte voluntaria necessariam turpitudinem depulisse. According to Madvig's rule the common phrase *mortem depellere* ought not to exist. Part. Or. 42 depellendi aut

ulciscendi doloris. In Sen. dial. 2, 7, 5 repellere (Ambr.) conforms to Madvig's rule, yet Gertz considers dep. probable. For other interchanges of *re* and *de* see his Index.

temporibus quibusdam: this abl. is not purely temporal; *temporibus* as in § 32 means 'critical moments' and the abl. becomes really causal and of the same nature as the ablatives after *et*. There is therefore no real awkwardness in the *et* which many editors have desired to remove, because they thought that it was used to link together ablatives of different classes. Madvig (whose note is obscure) seems to treat *tempora* as species and *officia debita* and *rerum necessitates* as particulars, and to think that the conjunction is due to a sort of logical confusion, whereby a difference is set up between the species and the particulars. For the strongly causal abl. here see n. on 1, 42. *Debitis* must not be taken with *necessitatibus*, an error which led Davies and others to propose needless changes.

7. **repudiandae:** Metrodorus ap. Plutarch, non posse suaviter vivi etc., c. 3, 1088 *d* πολλάκις προσεπτύσαμεν ταῖς τοῦ σώματος ἡδοναῖς; see the context there.

8. **non recusandae:** 'are to be accepted without protest.' On the meaning of *recusare* see 3, 9 *n.*; pro Caec. §§ 81–2.

9. **delectus:** as to the form *dilectus* see C. F. W. Müller.

ut aut, etc.: possibly Cicero wrote *ut aut...aut ut*; see n. on 2, 15. I do not understand Madvig's statement that if the *ut* be repeated, the *delectus* becomes '*duplex non unus*'; the *delectus* is really made *duplex* by the repeated *aut*, and it makes no difference whether a second *ut* is written or not.

reiciendis: Epic. ap. Diog. L. 10, 129 πολλὰς ἡδονὰς ὑπερβαίνομεν ὅταν πλεῖον

34 consequatur aut perferendis doloribus asperiores repellat. Hanc ego cum teneam sententiam, quid est cur verear ne ad eam non possim accommodare Torquatos nostros? quos tu paulo ante cum memoriter, tum etiam erga nos amice et benivole collegisti, nec me tamen laudandis maioribus meis corrupisti nec segniorem ad respondendum reddidisti. Quorum facta quem ad modum, quaeso, interpretaris? Sicine eos censes aut in armatum hostem impetum fecisse aut in liberos atque in sanguinem suum tam

2 ad eam: *eadem* E.   5 me: om. A¹.   5 tamen: *cum* E (ex contracta forma tm̄ non intellecta); vid. Lindsay, *Notae Latinae*, p. 305.   5 corrupisti: *corripuisti* multi (etiam A).

ἡμῖν τὸ δυσχερὲς ἐκ τούτων ἕπηται· καὶ πολλὰς ἀλγηδόνας ἡδονῶν κρείττους νομί- ζομεν, ἐπειδὰν μείζων ἡδονὴ παρακολουθῇ πολὺν χρόνον ὑπομείνασι τὰς ἀλγηδόνας: also ap. Stob. Flor. 17, 34 βρυάζω τῷ κατὰ τὸ σωμάτιον ἡδεῖ, ὕδατι καὶ ἄρτῳ χρώμενος, καὶ προσπτύω ταῖς ἐκ πολυτε- λείας ἡδοναῖς οὐ δι' αὐτὰς ἀλλὰ διὰ τὰ ἐξακολουθοῦντα αὐταῖς δυσχερῆ. Metrod. fr. 16, p. 53 ed. Düning. Aristocles ap. Euseb. Praep. Evang. 14, 21, 3, p. 769 *a* quotes Epicurean γνῶμαι to the same effect in somewhat different lan- guage. See Usener § 442 and Sen. also quoted there. A fragment attributed to Democritus (Mullach, 3) introduces τὸ καλόν strangely: ἡδονὴν οὐ πᾶσαν ἀλλ' ἐπὶ τῷ καλῷ αἱρέεσθαι χρεών; cf. id. 1 where it is said that happiness (εὐθυμίη) depends on the διορισμὸς καὶ διάκρισις τῶν ἡδονῶν; see also fr. 47; Sen. d. 2, 12, 1 voluptatium sine dilectu appetentes.

maiores: the hedonist must see that the *balance* is on the right side: Democr. fr. 2 ἄριστον ἀνθρώπῳ τὸν βίον διάγειν ὡς πλεῖστα εὐθυμηθέντι καὶ ἐλάχιστα ἀνιηθέντι.

2. verear ne...non: so *timere ne non*, Verr. 5, 171; these are the only certain passages, I think, where Cicero sub- stitutes *ne...non* for *ut* after a verb of fearing. But he is sparing even in his use of *ut*; it occurs only once in the philosophical works.

3. cum...tum: see M.

4. memoriter: Madvig shows that this word never bears the meaning 'from memory,' 'by heart,' as the opposite of *de scripto*, but 'semper laudem habet bonae et copiosae memoriae' (like μνημονικῶς). Several scholars have criti- cised Madvig's opinion; and indeed it is easy to find passages where the meaning 'from memory' will just make sense;

but until examples are pointed out where this sense is *necessary*, the matter will not be worth discussion. In ancient times when reference from book to book was difficult beyond our conceptions, a strong and accurate memory was held in higher esteem than now, and the praises of it throughout ancient litera- ture are numerous. [Macrob. Sat. 1, 2, 2 admirantibus memoriae tuae vires; ib. 1, 3, 1; 2, 8, 1 memoria florida.]

nos: 'our school'; wrongly rendered 'me' in some translations.

collegisti: 'quoted'; so below, 2, 62 and often.

6. **quem ad modum...interpretaris:** 'how do you explain?' Cf. De Or. 2, 21 omnia ista ego alio modo interpretor; and Nägelsbach § 113.

7. **quaeso:** all the examples of this verb in Cicero's philosophical writings are parenthetic; elsewhere he has *ut-* and *ne-*clauses dependent on it.

sicine: Madvig points out that *siccine, huiccine, hicce* and the like are barbarous forms; as also are *sicne, hocne*, etc. for *sicine*, etc. The evidence is now collected in Neue, II³, p. 422.

8. **liberos:** on the uses of *liberi* see an elaborate article by Funck in Archiv 7, 73 sq.

atque in: *atque* explanatory. For *in* re- peated see 1, 30 (*inter*), and 2, 40 (*ad*), and cf. Liv. 7, 4, 3 cognomen Imperiosi...ab ostentatione saevitiae ascitum, quam non magis in alienis quam in proximis ac sanguine ipse suo exerceret. This passage of Livy is almost in itself enough to refute the contention of Havet, Rev. de Phil. XXII, 251, that *in liberos* refers to the earlier Torq. who put his son to death and *in sanguinem* to the later who had given away his son in adoption.

sanguinem: 'flesh and blood'; Sest. 130 homo eiusdem sanguinis.

crudelis fuisse, nihil ut de utilitatibus, nihil ut de commodis suis
cogitarent? At id ne ferae quidem faciunt ut ita ruant itaque
turbent, ut earum motus et impetus quo pertineant non intellegamus; tu tam egregios viros censes tantas res gessisse
5 sine causa? Quae fuerit causa mox videro; interea hoc tenebo, 35
si ob aliquam causam ista quae sine dubio praeclara sunt
fecerint, virtutem eis per se ipsam causam non fuisse.—Torquem
detraxit hosti.—Et quidem se texit, ne interiret.—At magnum
periculum adiit.—In oculis quidem exercitus.—Quid ex eo est
10 consecutus?—Laudem et caritatem, quae sunt vitae sine metu
degendae praesidia firmissima.—Filium morte multavit.—Si sine
causa, nollem me ab eo ortum, tam importuno tamque crudeli;
sin ut dolore suo sanciret militaris imperi disciplinam exercitum-

6 si ob aliquam: *si obliquam* A¹.

1. **nihil ut**: in Cicero *ut* generally
follows a negative word; see my n. on
Acad. 2, 48; *ut nihil* in Fam. 6, 1, 4 and
De Or. 2, 2 (where there is *nullam ut* a
little before).

utilitatibus: the temptation to read
voluptatibus has overcome several
editors; but *utilitas* is often held to
imply *voluptas* (though cf. 3, 37); and the
similarity in sense of the two words *ut*.
and *commodis* is quite in Cicero's style.

2. **at**: the form of the sentence
naturally leads to the suspicion that *at*
has here replaced *an* (a very common
interchange in MSS.).

ne ferae quidem: in the Herculanean
roll, no. 26, edited by Scott, there is
an elaborate comparison between the
ταραχή of beasts and men, and a polemic
is carried on against someone who had
argued that the life of animals is happier
than that of mankind because they fear
not gods nor death. In one fragment
(Scott, p. 216) it is asserted that in the
two cases the ταραχαὶ ἐκ τῶν παθῶν καὶ
κακιῶν are similar. The speaker in Liv.
7, 4, 6 contrasts Manlius Imperiosus
with the beasts, unfavourably.

ut...ut: the repetition of *ut* is often
as inelegant as the repetition of *that*
in English, and it is quite as difficult to
avoid. Three clauses with *ut* succeed one
another in Att. 9, 7, 3.

itaque: for *et ita*; not uncommon.

4. **tu...sine causa?** perhaps a retort
on what was said about the Epicurean
physics in § 19. For *sine c.* here cf. n.
on *cum causa* in 2, 56.

5. **videro**: as in 2, 9. In the 3rd pers.
plur. once *videant* (Rep. 6, 25, which is

one reason why Meissner, ed. 4, suspects
the passage), but there is attraction
there to another subj.

8. **et quidem**: frequently used thus in
refutations (as in 2 §§ 9, 13 and Div.
2, 114, about which there is nothing
strange, as M. asserts). Draeger § 311,
13; Seyffert, Schol. Lat. 1 § 66; so
quidem alone just below. Often also the
phrase *et quidem* intensifies a statement
made by the speaker himself; so § 15.
Stamm, Die Partikel-verbindung *et
quidem* bei Cicero (noticed in Archiv
3, 156), points out the avoidance of *et
quidem* by Caesar and Sallust [*et quidem*
in concession, below, 2 § 81].

texit: sc. *armis* (Fam. 3, 10, 10). Sen.
dial. 4, 35 § 5.

10. **vitae...praesidia**: *vitae* may be
either gen. or dat., prob. the former.

11. **praesidia**: cf. 2, 84 praesidium
amicorum. One is reminded of the 7th
κυρία δόξα of Epicurus: ἔνδοξοι καὶ περί-
βλεπτοί τινες ἐβουλήθησαν γενέσθαι τὴν
ἐξ ἀνθρώπων ἀσφάλειαν οὕτω νομίζοντες
περιποιήσεσθαι. But the opinion of Epicurus is given in the 14th, viz. that
ἡ ἐξ ἀνθρώπων ἀσφάλεια is best secured
by ἡσυχία and by withdrawing from
the multitude.

12. **ortum**: the omission of *esse* is frequent, as in §§ 13, 21, 39 and 2, 54.

importuno: the omission of *homine*
or *viro* is unusual; the contracted form
of *homine* (oĩe) may have dropped out
after *imp*.

13. **sanciret**: Manlius to his son ap.
Liv. 8, 7, 19: 'cum aut morte tua
sancienda sint consulum imperia aut
impunitate in perpetuum abroganda.'

que in gravissimo bello animadversionis metu contineret, saluti
36 prospexit civium, qua intellegebat contineri suam. Atque haec
ratio late patet. In quo enim maxime consuevit iactare vestra
se oratio, tua praesertim, qui studiose antiqua persequeris, claris
et fortibus viris commemorandis eorumque factis non emolu- 5
mento aliquo sed ipsius honestatis decore laudandis, id totum
evertitur eo delectu rerum, quem modo dixi, constituto, ut aut
voluptates omittantur maiorum voluptatum adipiscendarum
causa aut dolores suscipiantur maiorum dolorum effugiendorum
gratia.   10
37   XI. Sed de clarorum hominum factis illustribus et gloriosis
satis hoc loco dictum sit. Erit enim iam de omnium virtutum
cursu ad voluptatem proprius disserendi locus. Nunc autem
explicabo voluptas ipsa quae qualisque sit, ut tollatur error

3 vestra: *nostra* E (cf. Lindsay, *N.L.*, pp. 146 sq.).   7 delectu: *deflectu* A
(etiam P); *defluxu* E.   8 adipiscendarum: *adipiscarum* A[1].   9 dolores: *lores* A[1].
12 dictum sit: ita codd.; *dictum est* Madv.; vid. comm.

1. **contineret:** of the cruel punishment Livy 8, 8, 1 says: 'fecit atrocitas
poenae obedientiorem duci militem.'
The occurrence of *contineret, contineri* in
different senses so close together is
awkward.
  saluti: as in Verr. 2, 1, 158; cf. Tac.
Ann. 1, 46.
2. **prospexit ...... intellegebat:** note
change of tense and cf. 2 § 4.
  qua...contineri: occasionally Cicero
writes *in* with the abl. as Cat. 4, 2 forum
in quo aequitas continetur, Verr. 2, 118;
Mur. 31; Clu. 49.
3. **late patet:** less commonly *l.
manare*; similarly N.D. 1, 98 genus hoc
argumenti attende quo serpat.
4. **claris......laudandis:** grammatically these clauses are epexegetic of *quo*;
cf. Nägelsbach, Stil. § 32, 2. But *iactare
se* is sometimes accompanied closely by
the gerundive construction, as in Cat.
4, 10 ne quis huius supplicio levando se
iactare...possit.
5. **factis...emolumento...decore:** n.
on 42 (*utilitate*).
6. **id totum:** so 2, 11.
7. **aut...aut:** on the very close
parallelism of these clauses see Nägelsbach, Stilist. § 168.
9. **causa...gratia:** the same transition (or *vice versa*) in N.D. 2, 158;
Att. 14, 19, 3; Mur. 78; orat. ad
Quir. 1; Cael. 3, where Vollgraff needlessly changes the text. A similar
change in Tusc. 5, 71 quid ex-

tremum sit in bonis, quid in malis
ultimum.
11. **gloriosis:** often thus used in a
good sense.
12. **dictum sit:** Madvig was undoubtedly wrong in departing from the
MSS. The subjunctive often occurs in
little sentences like this where a speaker
intimates that he has said enough on a
particular topic, and then passes on to
another. Some examples will be found
in my n. on Acad. 2, 29; others from
Pliny (the elder), Auson., Augustin.,
Sulp. Sev. are given by C. F. W.
Müller in his critical note on Acad. l.l.;
others from Liv., Val. Max., Pliny,
Colum. in n. on Lael. 50 ed. Seyffert-
Müller, p. 346. Add Plin. n. h. 17, 140
and 19, 189. Of course *satis est dictum*
often occurs in similar circumstances.
A rather strange form is *satis erit dictum*
in Ad Herenn. 1, 11 (where only one of
Marx's MSS. has *est*) and ib. 3, 22 (no
variants). Madvig says that in Att.
6, 9, 1 quare de hoc satis, not *sit* but *est*
is to be understood, but Cicero's usage
admits either.
13. **cursu:** 'non de studio dicitur sed
de via et, ut barbare dicitur, directione,
ut *eo cursu* pro Planc. 17; cfr. de leg.
agr. 11, 44' (Madvig). But *cursus* does
often indicate eager speed, and it may
well connote that here.
  locus: § 42 sq.
14. **quae qualisque:** cf. n. on § 29
quid et quale.

omnis imperitorum intellegaturque ea quae voluptaria, delicata,
mollis habeatur disciplina, quam gravis, quam continens, quam
severa sit. Non enim hanc solam sequimur, quae suavitate
aliqua naturam ipsam movet et cum iucunditate quadam per-
5 cipitur sensibus, sed maximam voluptatem illam habemus, quae
percipitur omni dolore detracto. Nam quoniam, cum privamur
dolore, ipsa liberatione et vacuitate omnis molestiae gaudemus,

1 omnis: *omnium* E. 3 sequimur: *sequuntur* P.

1. **imperitorum**: so Epicurus speaks
in a passage of the letter to Menoeceus
(Diog. L. 10, 131 sq.) of ʼτινὲς ἀγνοοῦντες
καὶ οὐχ ὁμολογοῦντες ἢ κακῶς ἐκδεχόμενοιʼ
who misjudge the Epicurean doctrine of
pleasure; cf. 2, 12 non intellegere nos
quam dicat Epicurus voluptatem; Tusc.
3, 37 (of the same matter) solent isti
negare nos intellegere quid dicat
Epicurus. Later (§ 55) Torquatus uses
imperiti of heretical Epicureans.

intellegatur: the word is probably
not impersonal here, and so the comma
after it should be removed.

2. **quam gravis**, etc.: cf. Sen. de vit.
beat. 13, 1 in ea quidem ipsa sententia
sum, invitis hoc nostris popularibus
dicam, sancta Epicurum et recta prae-
cipere et, si propius accesseris, tristia:
voluptas enim illa ad parvum et exile
revocatur et quam nos virtuti legem
dicimus, eam ille dicit voluptati...
itaque non dicam quod plerique nostrorum, sectam Epicuri flagitiorum magis-
tram esse, sed illud dico: male audit,
infamis est, et immerito. See the context; there is much else in Seneca,
written in the same vein, about Epicureans.

continens: an example of an active
participle which has acquired a neutral
meaning.

3. **solam**: we have here the Epicurean
doctrine of the two kinds of pleasure,
the active and the passive, ἡδονὴ ἐν
κινήσει and ἡδονὴ ἐν στάσει or καταστη-
ματική (so named by Epicurus himself,
quoted by Diog. L. 10, 136) which terms
Cicero represents in 2, 16 by *in motu* and
in stabilitate, 2, 31 by *stans* and *movens
voluptas*; cf. *stabilem* in 2, 75; and n. on
2, 9. The combination of this passive
pleasure with the active is often said
to distinguish the doctrine of Epicurus
from that of Aristippus, who regarded
the active alone. So Diog. L. 10, 136
διαφέρεται δὲ Ἐπίκουρος πρὸς τοὺς Κυρη-
ναικοὺς περὶ τῆς ἡδονῆς· οἱ μὲν γὰρ τὴν
καταστηματικὴν οὐκ ἐγκρίνουσι, μόνην
δὲ τὴν ἐν κινήσει· ὁ δὲ ἀμφοτέραν : Clem.

Al. Strom. 11, 21, pp. 178, 43; quoting
perhaps from Antiochus of Ascalon:
ὁ δὲ Ἐπίκουρος καὶ τὴν τῆς ἀλγηδόνος
ὑπεξαίρεσιν ἡδονὴν εἶναι λέγει: cf. 179,
36; Us. §§ 450, 451. As to the necessity
of passing by much of the 'movens voluptas' in order to secure the 'stans'
see § 47 with nn.

4. **naturam**: the physical frame.
Nägelsbach is right (§ 91, 1) in repre-
senting *ipsam* by 'unmittelbar'; the
word indicates that the effect exercised
is *direct*. Madvig seems to miss the
meaning, drawing the conclusion from
ipsam that the *stans voluptas* is not
regarded as affecting the physical frame,
and hence landing Cicero in a sort of
contradiction: 'atqui non dolendi
voluptas sentiri tamen debet.' True,
but what is meant is that the active
pleasure affects the senses more immediately and directly than the passive.

iucunditate: commonly used of the
subjective feeling of the percipient,
suavitas of the quality in the pleasure
itself; cf. 2 §§ 6, 13, 14.

5. **sed...habemus**: in order to bring
this into closer correspondence with
non...solam sequimur, Gruter desired to
read *avemus*; but Cicero only has *avere*
here and there in the Speeches and the
Letters; cf. n. on 2, 46.

maximam: see n. on § 38 terminari.
After this statement that the passive
pleasure is the highest, we have a
parenthesis (ending just before the last
sentence in the section) to justify the
application of the name pleasure to the
absence of pain. The words in this
parenthesis seem to imply, though they
do not definitely assert, the doctrine
that *all* pleasure springs from the removal of pain. Thus the distinction
between active and passive pleasure is
swept away. The argument in the
parenthesis is a *sorites*; for this see my
n. on Acad. 2, 49.

7. **liberatione**: the context often
throws on verbal nouns from active
verbs a kind of passive meaning; and in

omne autem id quo gaudemus voluptas est, ut omne quo
offendimur dolor, doloris omnis privatio recte nominata est
voluptas. Vt enim, cum cibo et potione fames sitisque depulsa est,
ipsa detractio molestiae consecutionem affert voluptatis, sic in
38 omni re doloris amotio successionem efficit voluptatis. Itaque 5
non placuit Epicuro medium esse quiddam inter dolorem et

1 omne...gaudemus: om. ed. Colon.

a similar manner the gerund often takes
a passive tinge (Nägelsbach § 59 *a*, 1).

omnis: this may be an error for
omni; in that case *vacuitate omni* would
correspond to *omnis privatio* below.

molestiae: possibly a rendering of the
common Epicurean term ταραχῆς: or
perhaps *vacuitate molestiae* represents
ἀπαθείᾳ, a word often rendered by *non
dolendi* (2 § 38), or perhaps ἀπονίᾳ, or
ἀνοχλησίᾳ (Diog. L. 2, 87–9).

gaudemus: the distinguishers of
synonyms in ancient and modern times
have sometimes asserted that *gaudere* is
not used in close connexion with pleasure
of the senses. The restriction is disregarded by Cic. Tusc. 5, 96 corpus
gaudere tam diu, dum praesentem sentiret voluptatem.

  1. **omne...gaudemus:** πᾶν τὸ χαρτόν.

  2. **doloris...privatio...voluptas:** on
the surface (but only on the surface) the
tendency of Epicurus would seem to be
to treat pain as something positive,
pleasure as something negative. A
writer (E. J. Dillon) in the 'Contemporary Review' for Feb. 1894 traces
this tendency in the author of Ecclesi-
astes and illustrates it from Schopenhauer ed. Grisebach, II, 676, 677: 'We
feel pain but not painlessness; we feel
care but not exemption from it; fear
but not safety....Only pain and priva-
tion are perceived as positive and
announce themselves; well-being on the
contrary is merely negative. Hence it is
that we are never conscious of the three
greatest boons of life, health, youth and
freedom, as such, so long as we possess
them, but only when we have lost them:
for they too are negations....The hours
fly the quicker the pleasanter they are;
they drag themselves on the slowlier,
the more painfully they are passed,
because pain not enjoyment is the something positive whose presence makes
itself felt.' So the haters of pleasures
mentioned in Plat. Phileb. 44 c contend
that they have no real existence, being
merely λυπῶν ἀποφυγαί. Plut. non posse

etc. 7 (1091 *a*) makes Epic. identify
κακῶν ἀποφυγή with τὸ χαρτόν and
τἀγαθόν. Aristippus denied the middle
state; and the followers of Anniceris
called the pleasure of Epicurus 'νεκροῦ
κατάστασιν' (Clem. Al. Strom. II, 21,
p.179, 36). But Epic. holds rather with the
writer of Eth. N. 7,14,8(1154 *b* 26) οὐ μόνον
κινήσεώς ἐστιν ἐνέργεια ἀλλὰ καὶ ἀκινη-
σίας, καὶ ἡδονὴ μᾶλλον ἐν ἠρεμίᾳ ἐστὶν ἢ
ἐν κινήσει: while in c. 11 § 4 the doctrine
that ἡδονή is ἀγαθόν is met by the statement that ὁ φρόνιμος τὸ ἄλυπον διώκει οὐ
τὸ ἡδύ. [Plut. n. p. s. v. c. 30 (1106 *f*)
argues that if κακῶν ἀποφυγή is ἀγαθόν,
then στέρησις ἀγαθῶν is κακόν: therefore
Epic. must allow death to be κακόν.]

  3. **cibo et potione:** *potus* occurs in
Cicero only in a very doubtful passage,
Div. 1, 60 immoderato potu atque pastu,
where probably the writers of the MSS.
have assimilated *potione* (written con-
tractedly) to the word *pastu*. *Potus* is
common in the imperial period of
literature, but I have found no example
of certainly earlier date than those
which occur in the elder Pliny.

  4. **detractio,** etc.: Nägelsb. § 61
quotes this passage as illustrating what
he calls the 'rhetorical' use of verbal
nouns, by which artificial evenness and
uniformity are secured. He thinks that
many of these nouns probably owe their
existence to this striving after 'concinnitas.'

  5. **successionem:** this, like many
other verbal nouns, is rare in Cicero.
Nizoli quotes two exx., one from 'Hortensius' is given by Aug. vit. beat. and
it does not seem to occur in the ordinary
collections of fragments, the other is described as Brut. 17, and is in a letter of
Brutus to Atticus (1, 17, 2).

  6. **non placuit:** in many such
phrases the negative coalesces with
the verb and gives a meaning stronger
than the mere negation of the original
verb; here *non placuit*='he rejected the
idea.' In Phileb. 44, 45, Plato mentions
people (Grote thinks Pythagoreans,

voluptatem; illud enim ipsum quod quibusdam medium videtur,
cum omni dolore careret, non modo voluptatem esse, verum etiam
summam voluptatem. Quisquis enim sentit, quem ad modum sit
affectus, eum necesse est aut in voluptate esse aut in dolore.
5 Omnis autem privatione doloris putat Epicurus terminari sum-

1 videtur: recte tuetur hanc codicum omnium lectionem C. F. W. Müller; *videretur* edd. non nulli post Manutium (etiam Madvigius. Vid. comm.). 4 affectus:
effectus E; (ita *effecta* in § 39).

Zeller Antisthenes), μάλα δεινοὺς λεγο-
μένους περὶ τὴν φύσιν, who held a
view like that of Epicurus, and condemns them, cf. Phil. 51 A. So elsewhere, as Rep. 584 C λυπῶν τινὲς
ἀπαλλαγαί. Plut. adv. Col. 27 (1123 a)
contends much like Plato, τὸ δὲ πόνου
καὶ ἡδονῆς μηδὲν εἶναι μέσον οὐκ ἀποφαί-
νεσθε παρὰ τὴν πάντων αἴσθησιν ἤδεσθαι
τὸ μὴ ἀλγεῖν καὶ πονεῖν τὸ μὴ ἤδεσθαι
λέγοντες.
medium: somewhat similarly, the
writer of Eth. Nicom. 7, 14, 5 contends
that the mere absence of pleasure and
actual pain (τὸ μηδέτερον) may be
actually λυπηρόν. The school of Aristippus contended that ἀπονία is only οἱονεὶ
καθεύδοντος κατάστασις (Diog. L. 2, 89),
like νεκροῦ κατάστασις in Clem. Al. qu.
above.
1. videtur: Matthiae (followed by
several scholars) proposed to treat the
words *quod...videtur* as a parenthesis,
giving the opinion of Torquatus; but
Madvig rightly asserts that the words
belong, grammatically and by sense, to
the quotation from Epicurus. From this
he draws the conclusion that the change
to *videretur* is a necessity. C. F. W.
Müller says alteration is no more
necessary here than in § 20 tantum enim
esse censet quantus videtur, and in
other passages which he quotes. That
the *tense* of careret does not decide the
matter may be seen from such passages
as § 25, *referatur*, where see n.
2. cum...careret: the subject is *illud
ipsum*. A comparison with 2, 10 quod
ais cum dolore careamus, suggests that
carerent may be the right reading here.
Phileb. 43 D ὡς ἥδιστον πάντων ἐστιν
ἀλύπως διατελεῖν τὸν βίον ἅπαντα: Plut.
non p. s. v. 1088 c (Us. § 417).
3. summam voluptatem: the most
famous passage of Epicurus bearing on
this doctrine was the third of the κυρίαι
δόξαι, which Cicero had in mind here:
ὅρος τοῦ μεγέθους τῶν ἡδονῶν ἡ παντὸς
τοῦ ἀλγοῦντος ὑπεξαίρεσις. ὅπου δ' ἂν τὸ
ἡδόμενον ἐνῇ, καθ' ὃν ἂν χρόνον ᾖ, οὐκ

ἔστι τὸ ἀλγοῦν ἢ τὸ λυπούμενον ἢ τὸ
συναμφότερον (cf. the 18th δόξα). The
references in ancient literature to the
maxim are numerous: so Gell. 2, 9, 2,
where a trivial criticism of the definition
by Plutarch is repelled; ib. 2, 6, 12 (repeated by Macrob. 6, 7, 15); Plut. Qu.
Conviv. 635 a; Sext. Emp. A. M. 1,
273, 283. [A curious Herculanean fragment is quoted by Usener, p. 72, in
which the text of the maxim is discussed; some of the MSS., it is said, give
παντός, some omit it, while the good MSS.
present ἐξαίρεσις not ὑπεξαίρεσις.] See
Tusc. 3, 47; below 2 §§ 28, 41; Plutarch,
non posse, etc. 7 (1091 b); Lact. inst.
3, 8, 10 (Usener § 419); an unknown
Epicurean author qu. by Us. § 434.
quisquis, etc.: Olympiod. in Plat.
Phil. p. 275 ὁ Ἐπίκουρος οὐκ οἴεται
μίγνυσθαι λύπην ἡδονῇ μηδὲ γὰρ ἀγαθῷ
τὸ κακόν (a direct denial of the μῖξις
λυπῆς καὶ ἡδονῆς in Phil. 48). Epicurus
ap. Stob. flor. 17, 35 τότε χρείαν ἔχομεν
τῆς ἡδονῆς ὅταν ἐκ τοῦ μὴ παρεῖναι αὐτὴν
ἀλγῶμεν· ὅταν δὲ τοῦτο μὴ πάσχωμεν ἐν
αἰσθήσει καθεστῶτες, τότε οὐδεμία χρεία
τῆς ἡδονῆς. The words ἐν αἰσθήσει καθεστῶτες are so like the clause quisquis...
sentit, that Cicero must be drawing on
the same passage of Epicurus. Inscr. of
Oinoanda, p. 409, ἡμεῖς δὲ ζητῶμεν ἤδη
πῶς ὁ βίος ἡμεῖν ἡδὺς γένηται καὶ ἐν τοῖς
καταστήμασι καὶ ἐν ταῖς πράξεσιν· περὶ
δὲ τῶν καταστημάτων πρῶτον εἴπωμεν
ἐκεῖνο τηροῦντες τὸ δὴ ὅτι τῶν ὀχλούντων
τὴν ψυχὴν παθῶν ὑπεξαιρεθέντων τὰ
ἡδοντα αὐτὴν ἀντιπαρέχεται.
5. omnis...doloris:=παντὸς τοῦ ἀλγοῦντος: here omnis not omni is necessary.
terminari: a representation of ὅρος
ἐστίν in the third δόξα. Sometimes πέρας
is substituted in the quotations for the
actual word used by Epicurus; so Porphyr. de abstin. 1, 51 (Us. § 463); Plut.
Qu. conviv. 635 a ὅρον καὶ πέρας. Cf.
Sidon. Ep. 1, 6, 5 (Epicurus) summum
bonum sola corporis voluptate determi-
nat (πέρας in δόξα 18; cf. Us. § 434).

mam voluptatem, ut postea variari voluptas distinguique possit,
39 augeri amplificarique non possit. At etiam Athenis, ut a patre
audiebam facete et urbane Stoicos irridente, statua est in Cera-
mico Chrysippi sedentis porrecta manu, quae manus significet
illum in hac esse rogatiuncula delectatum: 'Numquidnam manus 5

2 a patre: *e patre* E.   3 irridente: *arridente* AEP.

1. **variari**: the highest pleasure lies in
the κατασταστηματικὴ ἡδονή: if the ἡδονὴ ἐν
κινήσει be added to this, it does not increase the intensity of the pleasure, but
merely gives it variety. So the 18th
δόξα: οὐκ ἐπαύξεται ἐν τῇ σαρκὶ ἡ ἡδονή,
ἐπειδὰν ἅπαξ τὸ κατ' ἔνδειαν ἀλγοῦν
ἐξαιρεθῇ, ἀλλὰ μόνον ποικίλλεται: Plut.
n. p. s. c. 3 (1088 *c*) speaks of ποικιλμούς
τινας. Cf. below 2, 10, where the notion
of ποικιλμός is criticised; see also the
criticism in 2, 75 and an important
passage in Sen. ep. 66, 45 f. Cicero here
(more suo) represents the verb ποικίλλεσθαι by two Latin verbs, *variari* and
distingui; ἡδονή when once grasped is
like ἀρετή when won by the Stoic σοφός,
'rigidari quidem, amplius intendi non
potest.' Sen. ep. 71, 20.
The function of the active pleasure is
therefore to do away with monotony;
but as we shall see, much of it cannot be
admitted without the danger to the
existence of ἀπονία itself.

2. **at etiam**: these are hardly the
words by which we should have expected
a criticism like this to be introduced.

a patre: Madvig: 'saepius Cicero
audire ex aut *de aliquo* dixit, rarius
audire ab al.' This is not quite borne
out by the quotations in Merguet's
lexicons, which yield (approximately)
58 instances of *ex*, 18 of *ab*, and only
6 of *de*. In the case of *quaerere*, *ab* is
nearly as common as *ex*, the numbers
being about 47, 58 and 9. Of the
passage in Fam. 10, 28, 3 illa cognosces
ex aliis, a me pauca, Madvig says: 'mire
haec (*ex* and *a*) coniunguntur.' But most
writers do thus occasionally avoid repeating a preposition; cf. Verr. 3, 130
non hoc nunc primum audit privatus
de inimico, reus ab accusatore; N.D.
1, 60 Simonide, de quo cum quae-
sivisset hoc idem tyrannus Hiero, de-
liberandi sibi unum diem postulavit;
cum idem ex eo postridie quaereret...;
Cato m. 43 audisset a Cinea...ex eo
audientes. So, too, in Verr. 2, 1, 32
nihil a me de pueritiae flagitiis audiet,
nihil ex illa impura adulescentia sua;
the change from *de* to *ex* is merely for

change's sake; cf. Varro de r. r. 1, 22, 2
potius ad utilitatem quam ob speciem
(unreasonably suspected by Keil);
Clark on Mil. 51. [With *quaerere* Caes.
has *ab* thrice, *ex* six times, *de* not at all;
Tac. has no exx. of *ab* or *de*, and only
two of *ex*, both in the legal phrase *in
aliquem ex servis quaerere*. Fügner's
Lexicon gives 12 or 13 exx. of *quaerere
ab aliquo* in Livy and about the same
number of *audire ab aliquo*.]
patre: L. Manlius Torquatus cons.
65 B.C.

3. **facete et urbane**: n. on 2, 103.
statua: Diog. L. 7, 182 ἦν δὲ Χρύσιππος καὶ τὸ σωμάτιον εὐτελής· ὡς δῆλον
ἐκ τοῦ ἀνδριάντος τοῦ ἐν Κεραμεικῷ· ὃς
σχεδόν τι ὑποκέκρυπται τῷ πλησίον ἱππεῖ·
ὅθεν αὐτὸν ὁ Καρνεάδης Κρύψιππον ἔλεγεν. Pausan. 1, 17, 2, speaks of a statue of
Chrysippus as being ἐν τῷ γυμνασίῳ τῆς
ἀγορᾶς ἀπέχοντι οὐ πολύ. The Ceramicus
contained the ἀγορά and the name was
sometimes used to indicate the market.
The γυμνάσιον is that of Ptolemy, which
seems from certain inscriptions to have
contained a library and to have been
used for philosophical lectures. The
identity of the statue mentioned by
Pausanias with that to which allusion is
made by Cicero is doubtful; see Iwan
Müller's Handb. III, p. 319, n. 3;
Wyttenbach says the statue is mentioned by Plut. Sto. Rep. 1033 E.

4. **quae manus**: for the repetition see
Div. in Caec. § 41 illius temporis quo die.
Thomas says Eberhard gives 4 exx.
from Epp. He adds Hor. od. 4, 11, 15.

5. **in hac...delectatum**: Cicero uses
delectari in only twice elsewhere: Leg.
2, 17 in hoc admodum delector, and
Fam. 6, 4, 4 in hac inani prudentiae
laude delector; for two other passages,
viz. Att. 16, 5, 2 incredibile est quam
me in omni genere delectarit and Rep.
1, 1 Catoni licuit se in otio delectare, are
clearly not parallel; cf. Att. 2, 4, 2
cum Musis nos delectabimus; Hyg. astr.
2, 27 cum Musis solitus est delectari.
[In Leg. 1, 5 the *in* has no authority.]
A rare construction is found in De Off.
1, 135 neque enim omnes isdem de

tua sic affecta, quem ad modum affecta nunc est, desiderat?'
—'Nihil sane.'—'At, si voluptas esset bonum, desideraret.'—
'Ita credo.'—'Non est igitur voluptas bonum.' Hoc ne statuam
quidem dicturam pater aiebat, si loqui posset. Conclusum est
5 enim contra Cyrenaicos satis acute, nihil ad Epicurum. Nam si
ea sola voluptas esset quae quasi titillaret sensus, ut ita dicam,

2 at si...credo: om. ed. Colon.

rebus...delectamur. The *de* there may be
caused by dittography from *dem (dē)*; or
perhaps may possibly be due to the
occurrence of *sermones...de negotiis* in
the preceding sentence. But *gaudere
de* occurs in Cic. Tac. Treb. Poll.
Valer. ap. Georg. Mühlmann, Lex. s. v.
Gaudere in occurs in Lucr. 3, 72 crudeles
gaudent in tristi funere fratris; Catull.
22, 17 tam gaudet in se tamque se
ipse miratur; Prop. 4, 18, 28; 5, 8,
63. Similarly *gloriari in* below (4, 51);
N.D. 3, 87; Tusc. 1, 48; Rep. 1, 11;
Off. 2, 59; Ligar. 25 (cf. 20). *Laetari in*,
Phil. 11, 9.
Fin. 2, 106 is an example of *in* of a
different kind.

rogatiuncula: '*rogatiunculam Cicero
dixit totum syllogismum, ut alibi interro-
gationem, interrogare*' (Madvig). So
were used very frequently ἐρώτημα,
ἐρωτᾶν from Aristotle's time onward,
whether the argument was in question-
form or not; see the material collected
in my n. on Acad. 1, 5. *Rogatiuncula*
seems to occur here only in this sense;
but in De Dom. 51 it is the diminutive
of *rogatio*, 'a proposal for legislation.'
On the other hand, *rogatio* is not employed to denote the syllogism, although
interrogatio occurs a good many times
with this meaning. [*Interrogatiuncula*
below, 4, 7; Parad. prooem. 2, and in
Sen. and Macrob.]
numquidnam: twice in the philosophical writings; and Planc. 65; *num-
quisnam* two or three times in the
speeches.
1. sic...quem ad modum: Draeger,
Hist. Synt. II², p. 632.
3. credo: not ironical here. Prof.
Ellis in Journ. of Phil. XIX, p. 150
defends with plausibility the reading of
the Avranches MS. in Orat. 155 ita
credo, hoc illi nesciebant, where edd.
give *id credo*, omitting *hoc.*
ne statuam quidem: 'Ruhnkenius (ad
Rutil. p. 129) cum in cod. Leidensi
quidem abesse vidisset, probavit omis-
sionem habuitque adsentientem Goeren-
zium, qui nescio quid de sono balbutit.'

2 desideraret...bonum: om. E.

M. then demonstrates the idea that *ne*
could stand for *ne...quidem* to be a
delusion, based on errors in MSS. There
is an elaborate examination of the history
of *ne...quidem* in Latin by Grossmann
(Allenstein progr. 1884) known to me
only from a review by Jordan in Archiv
1, p. 600. Grossmann proves that Cicero
greatly developed its uses after Terence.
5. nihil ad: for this phrase (used only
with ellipse of verb) see my n. on Acad.
1,15. The comma after *acute* (Madv. etc.)
is insufficient, as the words *nihil ad
Epicurum* stand by themselves and have
no connexion with *conclusum est.*
6. ea: slight attraction; cf. 2 §75.
quasi titillaret: *quasi* is here as often
the mark of a tentative translation from
the Greek; *titillare, titillatio* occur in
Cicero only in connexion with ἡδονή and
are always preceded by *quasi*. Cf. N.D. 1,
113 quasi titillatio, Epicuri enim hoc verbum est; Cleomedes 2, 1, p. 166 Ziegler
γαργαλισμοὺς σώματος (given as a characteristic phrase of Epicurus); Athenaeus,
12, 546 e οὐ μόνος δὲ Ἀρίστιππος καὶ οἱ
ἀπ' αὐτοῦ τὴν κατὰ κίνησιν ἡδονὴν ἠσπά-
ζοντο, ἀλλὰ καὶ Ἐπίκουρος καὶ ἀπὸ
τούτου. καὶ ἵνα μὴ τοὺς καταιγισμοὺς
λέγω καὶ τὰ ἐπεντρώματα, ἅπερ πολλάκις
προφέρεται ὁ Ἐπίκουρος, καὶ τοὺς γαργαλισμοὺς καὶ τὰ νύγματα...; also Plutarch
1090 b quoted by Usener, fragm. 411–13.
The verb γαργαλίζειν often occurs in
Philodemus περὶ ποιημάτων in reference
to the 'ear-tickling' qualities of poetry;
see Gomperz, Philodem u. d. aesthe-
tischen Schriften des Epicurus, p. 16;
and cf. Varro, Ep. ad Fufium ap. Non.
117 Quintiporis Clodius Antipho fies; ac
poemata eius gargaridians ('savourant')
dices 'o fortuna, o fors.' The word
γαργαλισμός occurs with a kind of ref.
to pleasure in Plato, Phileb. 46 D, where
the ἡδοναὶ τῆς ψώρας and τῶν γαργαλισ-
μῶν are mentioned together, but the word
is used in a different manner from that
of Epicurus; it denotes there not any
pleasurable excitation of the senses, but
the counter-irritation applied to a sore
or uneasy spot in the flesh, which some-

et ad eos cum suavitate afflueret et illaberetur, nec manus esse
contenta posset nec ulla pars vacuitate doloris sine iucundo motu
voluptatis. Sin autem summa voluptas est, ut Epicuro placet,
nihil dolere, primum tibi recte, Chrysippe, concessum est, nihil
desiderare manum, cum ita esset affecta, secundum non recte, 5
si voluptas esset bonum, fuisse desideraturam. Idcirco enim non
desideraret quia quod dolore caret id in voluptate est.

40   XII. Extremum autem esse bonorum voluptatem ex hoc
facillime perspici potest: Constituamus aliquem magnis multis
perpetuis fruentem et animo et corpore voluptatibus nullo dolore 10
nec impediente nec impendente, quem tandem hoc statu praesta-
biliorem aut magis expetendum possimus dicere? Inesse enim

2 nec ulla: *ut ulla* E.   2 pars E: *par* A: om. *nec* et *pars* dett.
5 non recte, si: *si non recte* E.

times may produce a satisfaction: cf. Cic.
Leg. 1, 47 dulcedine hac et scabie (contemptuous substitution of ψώρα for
γαργαλισμός—scabis in Sen. ep. 75, 7
(sc. *auris*)). The verb *titillare* occurs
in Lucret. 2, 429 (but in a different connexion), and Hor. sat. 2, 3, 179 ne vos
titillet gloria; the noun *titillatio* in Sen.
ep. 92, 6. Cognate words found in late
writings are *titillus, titillosus, titillatus,*
titillamentum; see the large collection of
exx. by A. Funck in Archiv 4, 240 sq.
Add C.G.L. III, 132, 55 (γαγγαλίζειν expl.
by *titillicare*). Many attempts have been
made to explain the etymology of this
group of words. Some have regarded
titillare as reduplicated from the same
root as that of τίλλειν. But for the
barrier of quantity, one would be inclined to suspect a connexion with *titio*,
a firebrand, *titulus*, something branded.
A. Funck (l.l.) hints at a relationship
with *titus*=*penis* (Bücheler in Archiv
2, 118); but the difference of quantity is
an insuperable barrier.
   1. **afflueret**: the word is here used
(and in N.D. 1, 49; Qu. Fr. 3, 3, 1) in
a sense more nearly literal than is common in Cicero, who usually attaches to
it an idea of richness and abundance;
so 2, 93 afflueret voluptatibus; Tusc. 5,
16 voluptates affluentius hauriat; Div.
1, 61 eaque parte animi quae voluptate
alitur nec inopia enecta nec satietate
affluenti—quorum utrumque prae-
stringere aciem mentis solet, sive deest
naturae quippiam sive abundat atque
affluit. [In the last passage the readings
of many editions, *afluenti* and *afluit*, are
insupportable.]

   4. **primum...secundum**: the premisses are denoted by *superius, in-
ferius* in Acad. 2, 96.
   5. **cum**: here *temporal*; cf. above
quem ad modum affecta nunc est.
   6. **idcirco**: this word, common in the
dramatic writers, is of very frequent
occurrence in Cicero, but is sparely used
by most other authors (twice by Caes.,
once by Sall., once by Tac.).
   7. **desideraret**: it is possible that
Cicero wrote *desideratura erat.*
   8. **non recte**: referring on, not back; see 2, 16.
   9. **constituamus**, etc.: this is the un-
realised picture of the happiness of the
sapiens (see 2, 88 *n.*) or that of the gods.
In Philod. περὶ θεῶν διαγωγῆς (Herc.
fragm. 152, 18; Scott, p. 112) συνεχῶς
ἥδεσθαι seems to be applied to the life of
the gods, and in the same treatise
(Scott, p. 134) it appears to be inculcated that the mortal nature does per-
mit of long-continued positive enjoyment. Ibid. (Scott, p. 135) τελειοτάτη
ἀκαταπληξία πρὸς τὰ δεινὰ is attributed
to the divine nature. [See the remarks
made on this section in 2, 63.]
   10. **animo**: the *voluptas animi* first
appears here in the exposition of Torquatus; see n. on 55.
   11. **impediente...impendente**: an intentional jingle; so *necesse, inesse* below.
See § 32. Cicero had in mind here, or
was perhaps translating from a Greek
original, the word ἀνεμπόδιστος: cf. § 33
nihil impedit etc.
   12. **possimus**: the mood is influenced
by that of *constituamus*. The context
bears some resemblance to a passage
in the letter of Epicurus to Menoeceus

necesse est in eo qui ita sit affectus et firmitatem animi nec
mortem nec dolorem timentis, quod mors sensu careat, dolor in

(Diog. L. 10, 133): ἐπεὶ τίνα νομίζεις
εἶναι κρείττονα τοῦ καὶ περὶ θεῶν ὅσια
δοξάζοντος καὶ περὶ θανάτου διὰ παντὸς
ἀφόβως ἔχοντος καὶ τὸ τῆς φύσεως ἐπιλε-
λογισμένου τέλος, καὶ τὸ τῶν ἀγαθῶν
πέρας ὡς ἔστιν εὐσυμπλήρωτόν τε καὶ
εὐπόριστον διαλαμβάνοντος, τὸ δὲ τῶν
κακῶν ὡς ἢ χρόνους ἢ πόνους ἔχει βραχεῖς.
Madvig remarks that in Epicurus this
passage follows on one asserting the
close connexion between virtue and
pleasure, and he seems to blame Cicero
for introducing a similar passage before
that connexion has been discussed. But
the passage in Epicurus has no intimate
reference to the passage that precedes it,
and no harm is done by severing it from
the context. And Cicero's authority
here can hardly be the letter to Menoeceus itself. Doubtless the same ideas
were propounded by Epicureans in other
writings where the context was different.
Madvig again criticises Cicero because
'non ex voluptatis perceptione sequitur
ut is, qui eam percipiat, sit sapiens
Epicureus.' But the picture drawn is
nothing else but a picture of the Epicurean ideal wise man; for he alone (with
the exception of the gods) can experience
continuous pleasure. Cf. § 57.
inesse enim, etc.: the passage is
slightly illogical, as was seen by Guyet
and some other editors, who wrongly
inferred that it was corrupt. Torquatus
has pictured his ideal man as un-
assailed by pain. He now says that he
must meet pain with fortitude. It is
implied, though not stated, that the
ideal man's intellectual firmness will
win such a victory over pain as to leave
his state of pleasurable happiness practically unaffected. See § 62 n.
1. et firmitatem: slight anacoluthon.
'Volebat Cicero adiungere et tranquillitatem, cum divinum numen non horreat,
et memoriam praeteritarum voluptatum;
pro his subiecit: Ad ea cum accedit,
etc.' (Madvig).
firmitatem: εὐστάθειαν, a common
Epicurean term; see 2, 9 n.
2. mors: Torquatus only touches on
the subject of death here and again
briefly in §§ 49 (where see nn.) and 62;
but in 2, 100 Cicero criticises the Epicurean view of death at some length.
See the notes there. Madvig here remarks: 'ut alii, Epicurus statum post
mortem consolabatur; ipsum vitae

desiderium et timorem dissolutionis non
attingebat.' In the tract 'non posse
suaviter vivi, etc.' Plutarch brings the
same charge (cc. 27, 29, pp. 1105, 6). But
there is much in the fragments of Epicurus to show the injustice of the allega-
tion. The words of Epic. (ap. Porphyr.
ad Marcellam, 31, p. 209, 21, Us. § 457)
supply the answer: 'ἔρωτι φιλοσοφίας
ἀληθινῆς πᾶσα ταραχώδης καὶ ἐπίπονος
ἐπιθυμία ἐκλύεται.' But, further, the
whole scheme of Epicurus had for one of
its chief aims the uprooting of the 'timor
dissolutionis' and the 'vitae desiderium.'
These are inextricably bound up with the
dread of pain, gods, and the hereafter,
and would in large measure disappear
when true views on these subjects had
been grasped; the purification of the
intellect and the passions by philosophy
would accomplish the rest. Cf. Diog. L. 10,
124 γνῶσις...τὸν τῆς ἀθανασίας ἀφελομένη
πόθον. Thus, 'the sense of death is most
in apprehension' (Measure for Measure,
3, 1, 78). For the unfortunate man there
can be, rationally, no πόθος τοῦ ζῆν, for
death is to him a λίμην τῶν κακῶν: while
the happy philosopher will not prove
himself to have been unworthy of his
happiness by grumbling like a thankless
guest when he has to leave the bountiful
banquet of life (see Lucr. 3, 931–77).
Epicurus, indeed, dealt with the desiderium vitae much as did the Stoics and
Peripatetics; cf. Usener, notes to p. 310.
The following passage has quite a Stoic
form: 'ὥσπερ δὲ σιτίον οὐ τὸ πλεῖον πάντως
ἀλλὰ τὸ ἥδιον αἱρεῖται (ὁ σοφός), οὕτω καὶ
χρόνον οὐ τὸν μήκιστον, ἀλλὰ τὸν ἥδιστον
καρπίζεται' (Diog. L. 10, 126). Cf. 3, 60, 61.
dolor...consoletur: Diog. L. 10, 133
τὸ τῶν κακῶν (πέρας) ἢ χρόνους ἢ πόνους
ἔχει βραχέας: ib. 140 (κυρία δόξα iv) οὐ
χρονίζει τὸ ἀλγοῦν συνεχῶς ἐν τῇ σαρκί,
ἀλλὰ τὸ μὲν ἄκρον τὸν ἐλάχιστον χρόνον
πάρεστι, τὸ δὲ μᾶλον ὑπερτεῖνον τὸ ἡδόμενον κατὰ σάρκα οὐ πολλὰς ἡμέρας
συμβαίνει. αἱ δὲ πολυχρόνιοι τῶν ἀρρω-
στιῶν πλεονάζον ἔχουσι τὸ ἡδόμενον ἐν
τῇ σαρκὶ ἤ περ τὸ ἀλγοῦν: Wotke-Usener,
Vatican γνῶμαι § 4 πᾶσα ἀλγηδὼν εὐ-
καταφρόνητος· ἡ γὰρ σύντονον ἔχουσα τὸ
πονοῦν σύντομον ἔχει τὸν χρόνον, ἡ δὲ
χρονίζουσα περὶ τὴν σάρκα ἀβληχρὸν ἔχει
τὸν πόνον: cf. § 49, below. Inscr. of
Oinoanda (Heberdey and Kalinka, ap.
Bull. de Corr. H. xxi, 375) τῶν ἀλγηδόνων
αἱ ἄκραι χρονίζειν οὐ δύνανται· ἢ γὰρ ταχὺ

longinquitate levis, in gravitate brevis soleat esse, ut eius magni-
41 tudinem celeritas, diuturnitatem allevatio consoletur.   Ad ea cum
accedit ut neque divinum numen horreat nec praeteritas
voluptates effluere patiatur earumque assidua recordatione
laetetur, quid est quod huc possit, quod melius sit, accedere? 5

1 levis: *lenis* AP.   2 allevatio: *elevatio* E.   3 numen: *nomen* E.   5 quod
melius: *quo m.* C. F. W. Müller; vid. comm.   5 accedere: *accidere* E.

τὸ ζῆν ἀναιροῦσαι συναναιροῦνται καὶ
αὐταί, ἢ ὑφαίρεσιν λαμβάνουσι τῆς ἀκρό-
τητος.
    1. **in longinquitate**: 'when it is last-
ing'; Draeger § 298, 7.
    levis...brevis: for the jingle see 2,
22 and n. there. Seneca often adopts this
consolation of Epicurus: so ep. 24, 2
(without mentioning Epic.) timorem
tuum taxa et intelleges profecto aut non
magnum aut non longum esse quod
metuis; so § 14 (of *dolor*) levis est si ferre
possum, brevis est si ferre non possum;
similarly in 30, 14 Aufidius Bassus
solaces himself with the words of
Epicurus; cf. too 78, 7 nemo potest
valde dolere et diu: sic nos amantissima
nostri natura disposuit ut dolorem aut
tolerabilem aut brevem faceret; 94, 7
optimam doloris esse naturam, quod
non potest nec qui extenditur, magnus
esse nec qui est magnus, extendi. In
Tusc. 5, 88 Cicero says of Epic.: 'de
dolore certa habet quae sequatur cuius
magnitudinem brevitate consolatur,
longinquitatem levitate,' and then
asserts that for facing death and pain
the grandiloquent Stoics are no better
equipped than Epicurus. See also notes
on § 49 and 2, 22.
    soleat esse: as to the emphatic
position of *esse* at the end of the clause,
see my note on Acad. 2, 22.
    2. **celeritas**: short duration, as Lael.
12 moriendi sensum celeritas abstulit,
Rep. 3, 34.
    allevatio: a rare word; Fam. 9, 1, 1;
Quint. 11, 3, 83 all. umerorum; the only
other references in the lexica are from
late writers.   But *allevamentum* in
Sull. 66 is equally rare. Perhaps (like
many other rarities) these expressions
were colloquial; the verb *allevare* is also
rare in Cicero; once in the philosophical
writings (in a quotation) and once in
the speeches, and rarely elsewhere as
Att. 7, 1, 1 (of relief from bodily pain);
ib. 12, 39, 2; Brut. 12.
    3. **accedit...accedere**: the repetition
of the verb is awkward, but there are
many parallels in Cicero; Madvig

quotes some in his note here; see also
my note on Acad. 2, 31.
    divinum numen: the only passage
where this is mentioned in book 1 (cf. 2,
21). Cicero's whole exposition here is free
from the Epicurea cantilena (Sen. ep.
24, 18) which Lucr. has so largely.
    4. **effluere**: the σοφός 'praeterita grate
meminit,' § 62; 2, 104 (the σοφός takes
care not to remember past pains); ib.
106; Tusc. 5, 96 nec (animum sapientis)
praeteritam (voluptatem) praeterfluere
sinere: ita perpetuas et contextas voluptates in sapiente fere semper, cum expectatio speratarum voluptatum cum
perceptarum memoria iungeretur; Plut.
non posse suaviter vivi etc. c. 18, p.
1099 *d* τὸ μεμνῆσθαι τῶν προτέρων ἀγαθῶν
μέγιστόν ἐστι πρὸς τὸ ἡδέως ζῆν (in c. 4,
p. 1089 *c* some coarse jests of Carneades
on this doctrine are quoted); see also
Jerome and Augustine quoted in Usener
§ 437. Madvig complains that Epic. does
not show how memory of past pleasure,
mental or bodily, can influence a
present pain of body or mind; but Epic.
was no more to seek than most ancient
and many modern philosophers in his
views of the relation of mind to body.
Effluere for *effluere ex memoria* or *animo*,
Verr. 4, 57; Sil. 2, 627; ib. 3, 188; so
excidere (often) and *dilabi* (Tusc. 4, 10;
Sall. Iug. 27, 2).
    5. **huc...accedere**: as Madvig says,
accidere is out of place here, and if *accedere* be read, *huc* is necessary.
    quod melius sit: in support of his
reading (*quo*) C. F. W. Müller writes:
'non quale sit id quod accedat quaeritur;
sed negatur quidquam posse accedere,
quo voluptas augeatur.' This is logically
correct; but many slight irregularities
of the kind are to be found in Cicero.
The question which of two things is
more likely, viz. that Cicero was guilty
of the illogicality, or that the writers
of the MSS. made the easy passage from
quo to *quod* (influenced by the neighbouring *quod*), is a very nice one. If *quo*
be read it will be like § 30 quid percipit...
quo...; § 57 quam nihil praetermittatur,

Statue contra aliquem confectum tantis animi corporisque
doloribus quanti in hominem maximi cadere possunt, nulla spe
proposita fore levius aliquando, nulla praeterea neque praesenti
nec exspectata voluptate, quid eo miserius dici aut fingi potest?
5 Quod si vita doloribus referta maxime fugienda est, summum
profecto malum est vivere cum dolore; cui sententiae consentaneum est ultimum esse bonorum cum voluptate vivere. Nec

2 maximi: *maxime* EP.   3 levius: *cuius* ed. Colon.   3 aliquando: *aliquanto*
AEP (ut coniecit Manutius).

quod vitam adiuvet, quo ('whereby,'
not 'to the intent that') facilius id...
consequamur; so § 72. [I have made a
similar change from *quod* to *quo* in my
text of Mil. 2, where my reading has
been strangely misunderstood by Prof.
Clark *ad loc.*; see the appendix to the
revised edition.]

1. **statue:** so *constitue* above; so
Acad. 2, 117 finge aliquem nunc fieri
sapientem; Verr. 3, 23 fingite vos aliquem qui; cf. Plato, Rep. 488 A νόησον
γὰρ τοιουτονί. So τιθέναι (pone Sen. ep.
66, 22).

2. **quanti...maximi:** cp. Brutus in
Ep. ad Brut. 1, 16, 1.

cadere in: so below, 3, 29 and 5, 93.

3. **levius:** sc. τὸ πρᾶγμα: there is no
need to read *leviores*, as has been proposed.

praeterea: merely continuative, as in
§ 42 *init.*; not like *pr.* at the end of this
section.

4. **exspectata:** the construction is not
abl. absolute, in which case *praesente*
must have been written; *exspectata* is
here a mere adjective; see note on
dolore futuro in 2, 63. *Adiuncta* is
substituted there for *praesenti* here.

dici aut fingi: so Flacc. 56; Mil. 5. For
fingere, 'to imagine,' see 5, 53; generally with *animo* or *cogitatione.*

6. **profecto:** on this word see Lindsay,
Lat. Lang. p. 590.

cui...vivere: Th. Bentley, Walker,
Davies and other scholars treated these
words as a gloss, because, without them,
the whole passage from *statue contra
aliquem* above to the end of this section
would refer to the *summum malum.*
Others (among them Madvig) while
believing the passage to come from
Cicero's hand, think that he would have
done better to omit it. But (to defer for
a moment the consideration of the sentence which follows) the whole exposition
of Torquatus is much more directed to
prove that *voluptas* is *summum bonum*

than that *dolor* is *summum malum,* and,
like Eudoxus, Epicurus thought the
main doctrine 'οὐχ ἧττον εἶναι φανερὸν
ἐκ τοῦ ἐναντίου' (Eth. N. 10, 2, 2); cf. § 30.
Speusippus denied the validity of the
argument; see Eth. 10, 2 and 7, 13, 1.
The argument ἐκ τοῦ ἐναντίου is of
course very common; so from *falsa* to
vera in Acad. 2, 43 f. and from *mortalis*
to *immortalis* in N.D. 1, 109. Madvig
says of the next sentence 'pergit de
summo malo.' But it is far from certain
that *quidquam* refers to the *summum
malum.*

7. **cum voluptate vivere:** so § 54; 2,
20 esse cum vol.; 1, 62 esse in v.; § 43
in tranquillitate vivi.

nec enim, etc.: the difficulties of this
sentence are considerable. The omission
of *aliud* with *quicquam* is very harsh;
Madvig refers to § 18 and the exx. of
alius omitted which he quotes in his
note there; but not one of them is so
awkward as this. It is most unlikely
that Cicero wrote the words *nec...
extremo* with a reference to the *summum
malum.* It is natural to connect the
words with those that precede; again
consistat implies effort and desire, and
extremo, if referred to evil, would have
been made clear by some addition. Cf.
below, 5, 44 confitendum est, cum id
adepti simus, quod appetitum sit, in eo
quasi in ultimo consistere naturam,
atque id esse summum bonum. So
consistere is 'to arrive at the goal of good'
in 5, 40 and 86; Acad. 2, 139; Tusc.
5, 40 eorum, in quibus vita beata con-
sistit. Cf. the word σταθῇ in Epic. ap.
Plut. non posse suaviter vivi, c. **7**,
p. 1091 *b*: τὸ γὰρ ποιοῦν ἀνυπέρβλητον
γῆθος τὸ πάραυτα πεφυγμένον μέγα
κακόν· καὶ αὕτη φύσις ἀγαθοῦ, ἄν τις
ὀρθῶς ἐπιβάλῃ, ἔπειτα σταθῇ, καὶ μὴ κενῶς
περιπατῇ περὶ ἀγαθοῦ θρυλῶν. The
sudden transition to pain again in
the words *omnesque et metus* etc. is in-
convenient, but after all that has been

enim habet nostra mens quicquam ubi consistat tamquam in
extremo, omnesque et metus et aegritudines ad dolorem referuntur, nec praeterea est res ulla quae sua natura aut sollicitare
42 possit aut angere. Praeterea et appetendi et refugiendi et omnino
rerum gerendarum initia proficiscuntur aut a voluptate aut a 5
dolore. Quod cum ita sit, perspicuom est omnis rectas res atque
laudabilis eo referri ut cum voluptate vivatur. Quoniam autem
id est vel summum vel ultimum vel extremum bonorum (quod
Graeci τέλος nominant), quod ipsum nullam ad aliam rem, ad id
autem res referuntur omnes, fatendum est summum esse bonum 10
iucunde vivere.

4 angere: *tangere* AEP ed. Rom.; *frangere* dett. non nulli: corr. Victorius.
7 referri: *ferri* dett.   10 referuntur: *feruntur* A et P (sed *res* est in rasura).

said about the identity of the highest
pleasure with the absence of pain, is
not misleading. This same identity is
again assumed in § 42. If the whole
passage to the end of § 42 be read con-
tinuously it will be seen that the consideration of pain looks altogether to the
conclusion that pleasure is the *summum
bonum*. Usener, p. 267, places a full
stop at *extremo* and says, 'hiat oratio,
Ciceronis culpa an librariorum mihi non
liquet.' (Why should the Epicurean
friend who, as Usener imagines, supplied
Cicero with an epitome, be here left
out?) Usener then refers to certain
passages, but they do not help us to
understand exactly what he thinks
ought to have been added to the exposition here.

2. **omnesque:** for *que* after negative
see Draeger, Hist. Synt., § 326, 4.

3. **sua natura:** the words are important. The other things besides pain
which do as a matter of fact torment
men are due to κενοδοξία.

sollicitare aut angere: Cato m. 66
angere et sollicitam habere; Qu. Fr.
3, 3, 1; Att. 1, 18, 1. In Cicero the verb
angere is not common excepting in the
passive (below, 2, 14; 4, 69). Here
angere refers back to *aegritudines,
sollicitare* to *metus*.

4. **appetendi:** ὁρμῆς or τοῦ ὁρμᾶσθαι:
refugiendi, ἀφορμῆς: see my n. on Acad.
2, 30.

5. **rerum gerendarum initia:** πρά-
ξεως ἀρχή (Eth. Nic. 1139 a, 31) or
πρακτικαὶ ἀρχαί (ib. 1144 a, 35, where
the context should be compared).

initia proficiscuntur: slight pleonasm as in the common phrase *initium
ortum est* and the like; similarly Lael. 30

sed quamquam utilitates multae et
magnae consecutae sunt, non sunt
tamen ab earum spe causae diligendi
profectae; Rep. 2, 4 huius urbis
condendae principium profectum a
Romulo.

6. **perspicuom:** in Cicero the common
rendering of ἐναργές: see my n. on
Acad. 2, 17.

rectas res atque laudabilis: πράγ-
ματα ὀρθὰ καὶ ἐπαινετά. In note on § 29
Madvig charges Cicero with incorrect-
ness here and in 2, 5 omnia quae recte
fierent, thinking (apparently) that the
words employed are proper only in
describing the Stoic view. The reference should rather be to the Stoic
term κατόρθωμα than to καθῆκον (see
note on 3, 24). But the Epicureans
claimed as much right as the Stoics to
divide actions into the virtuous and the
vicious, the praiseworthy and the un-
praiseworthy; nor did they differ much
from the Stoics in regard to the particular actions which deserve these
titles, but only in regard to the reason
for pursuing the right action and shun-
ning the wrong. Why the words *rectas,
recte* should be unsuitable for describing
right action from the Epicurean point
of view, is hard to see.

7. **referri:** note on § 11 above.

ut...vivatur: to make the argument
fit in precisely with the words above
(*aut a voluptate aut a dolore*) there should
have been added here *aut ne cum dolore*.

8. **id est vel summum,** etc.: note on
§ 29.

9. **quod ipsum...ad id:** 'relativa sententia cum adversativa sic continuatur,
ut opus sit pronomine expresso, naturali
quodam orationis flexu transit in demon-

XIII. Id qui in una virtute ponunt et splendore nominis capti, quid natura postulet non intellegunt, errore maximo, si Epicurum audire voluerint, liberabuntur. Istae enim vestrae eximiae pulchraeque virtutes nisi voluptates efficerent, quis eas

4 voluptates: *voluptatem* AP, al.

strativam; cf. 2, 5. Latini non solum hoc modo saepe locuti sunt, sed, ut opinor, altero (*ad quod autem*) numquam' (Madvig).

1. una virtute: = *virtute per se ipsam*. The Epicureans contended that virtue cannot exist apart from pleasure, and that the Stoics erred in severing the two; and in emphasising the severance by their vaunts concerning τὸ καλόν or *honestum*. Cf. § 61.

splendore nominis: cf. § 61 quod appellant honestum, non tam solido quam splendido nomine; Off. 3, 101 utilitatis nomen non tam splendidum quam necessarium; Hortens. fragm. 75 (Müller) hi nostri amici verecundantur capti splendore virtutis. Words strikingly similar occur in a passage of the Greek elegiac poet Hermesianax (*v.* 79 sq.; Bergk's Anthologia Lyrica, p. 137): οὐδὲ μὲν οὐδ' ὁπόσοι σκληρὸν βίον ἐκτίσσαντο | ἀνθρώπων, σκολιὴν μαιόμενοι σοφίην, | οὓς λεπτὴ περὶ πικρὰ λόγοις ἐσφίγξατο μῆτις, | καὶ δεινὴ μύθων κῦδος ἔχουσ' ἀρετή. Hermesianax entitled his poems 'Leontion,' and the name has been identified with that of the well-known female disciple of Epicurus. But, although the lines just quoted would well fit an Epicurean speaking of Stoics, dates forbid the identification. Cf. note on 2, 48 voce inani sonare.

2. capti: here almost = *occaecati*; cf. 4, 37.

quid natura postulet: 5, 36 and 44.

3. istae...virtutes: cf. 3, 11 istam gloriosam memorabilemque virtutem.

vestrae: Torquatus seems here to indicate all schools other than the Epicurean. Cf. § 54 virtutum laus in qua maxime ceterorum philosophorum exultat oratio. We seem here to have a trace of the 'Old Academic' views of Antiochus of Ascalon, for which see my nn. on Acad. 1, §§ 7, 17, 18.

4. nisi voluptates efficerent, etc.: this is opposed to the doctrine of the Stoics and others, τὴν ἀρετὴν δι' αὐτὴν αἱρετὴν εἶναι: see note on 3, 32. In the Epistle to Menoeceus (Diog. L. 10, 132) Epicurus teaches: τούτων δὲ πάντων ἀρχὴ καὶ τὸ μέγιστον ἀγαθὸν φρόνησις... ἐξ ἧς αἱ λοιπαὶ πᾶσαι πεφύκασιν ἀρεταί,

διδάσκουσα ὡς οὐκ ἔστιν ἡδέως ζῆν ἄνευ τοῦ φρονίμως καὶ καλῶς καὶ δικαίως <οὐδὲ φρονίμως καὶ καλῶς καὶ δικαίως> ἄνευ τοῦ ἡδέως. συμπεφύκασι γὰρ αἱ ἀρεταὶ τῷ ζῆν ἡδέως, καὶ τὸ ζῆν ἡδέως τούτων ἐστὶν ἀχώριστον. (Cf. below, § 57.) Virtue is inseparable from pleasure, all other things are separable (Diog. L. 10,138): ὁ δ''Επίκουρος καὶ ἀχώριστόν φησι τῆς ἡδονῆς τὴν ἀρετὴν μόνην, τὰ δ' ἄλλα χωρίζεσθαι, οἷον βρωτά. In κυρ. δόξα 5 it is insisted that all three elements, φρονίμως ζῆν, καλῶς ζῆν, δικαίως ζῆν are necessary for happiness (cf. §§ 50, 62 below; and Tusc. 5, 26). The words of Epic. are repeated in many passages of ancient literature, as Cic. Tusc. 3, 49; Sen. dial. 7, 6, 3 and 10, 1 and 12, 3; id. Ep. 85, 18; Clem. Alex. Strom. 2, 21, p. 178, 51, Sylb. The virtues are not directly, but indirectly desirable, for the pleasure they bring. Athen. 12, 546 *f* (quoting from Epic. περὶ τέλους) τιμητέον τὸ καλὸν καὶ τὰς ἀρετὰς καὶ τὰ τοιουτότροπα, ἐὰν ἡδονὴν παρασκευάζῃ· ἐὰν δὲ μὴ παρασκευάζῃ, ἐατέον: Plut. Col. c. 2, p. 1108 *c* οἱ περὶ γαστέρα τἀγαθὸν εἶναι βοῶντες, οὐκ ἂν δὲ τὰς ἀρετὰς ὁμοῦ πάσας τετρημένον χαλκοῦ πριάμενοι δίχα τῆς ἡδονῆς πάσας παντα-χόθεν ἂν ἐξελαθείσας [I have inserted ἂν and read, with Usener, p. 315, πάσας... ἐξελαθείσας for -ης]; Quint. 12, 11, 29 eorum qui a se non virtutes, sed voluptatem quae fit ex virtutibus peti dicunt; also the jocular treatment of the theme by Cassius, Fam. 15, 19. Diog. L. 10, 138 διὰ δὲ τὴν ἡδονὴν καὶ τὰς ἀρετὰς αἱρεῖσθαι, οὐ δι' αὐτάς, ὥσπερ τὴν ἰα-τρικὴν διὰ τὴν ὑγίειαν, καθά φησι καὶ Διογένης (of Tarsus); Max. Tyr. diss. 3, 5, p. 34 Reisk. The Stoic conception of a virtue dissoluble from pleasure was treated by Epic. with contempt: Athen. 12, 547 *a* (from Epic. περὶ τέλους) προσπτύω τῷ καλῷ καὶ τοῖς κενῶς αὐτὸ θαυμάζουσιν, ὅταν μηδεμίαν ἡδονὴν ποιῇ: so Plut. Col. c. 30, p. 1124 *e*; and de occulte vivendo, c. 4, p. 1129 *b*. Sen. ep. 85, 18, 19 argues that as virtue invariably produces pleasure, virtue is *per se* enough to produce happiness. The view of Aristippus and other Hedonists was of course the same; Diog. L. 2, 91; Off. 3, 116. In his system the wise

aut laudabilis aut expetendas arbitraretur? Vt enim medicorum
scientiam non ipsius artis, sed bonae valetudinis causa probamus,
et gubernatoris ars, quia bene navigandi rationem habet, utilitate,
non arte laudatur, sic sapientia, quae ars vivendi putanda est,

1 arbitraretur: *arbitretur* A¹.   2 scientiam: *sententiam* ed. Col. (vulgato errore).

man avoids immoral action, because of
the pains and penalties which it entails
(Diog. L. 2, 93). Against the Stoic τὸ καλόν Epic. wages an ἄσπονδον καὶ ἀκήρυκ-
τον πόλεμον (Plut. non posse suaviter
vivi etc. c. 13, p. 1095 *f*). Naturally his
enemies treat everything that he ad-
vances against the Stoic conception of
virtue as being directed against virtue,
sans phrase. Thus e.g. Plut. non posse
etc. 12 (1095 *b*) accuses the Epicureans
of saying that virtue is a πραγματεία
ἀτερπὴς καὶ ξηρά, which is the very
opposite of what they did teach. Aristotle
often speaks of the connexion between
ἀρετή and ἡδονή: thus Eth. N. 2, 3, 2 εἰ
ἀρεταί εἰσι περὶ πράξεις καὶ πάθη, καὶ
πάσῃ πράξει ἕπεται ἡδονὴ καὶ λύπη, καὶ
διὰ τοῦτ' ἂν εἴη ἡ ἀρετὴ περὶ ἡδονὰς καὶ
λύπας: ib. 10, 3, 12 οὐδεὶς ἂν ἕλοιτο...
χαίρειν ποιῶν τι τῶν αἰσχίστων μηδέποτε
μέλλων λυπηθῆναι. περὶ πολλά τε σπουδὴν
ποιησαίμεθα ἂν καὶ εἰ μηδεμίαν ἐπίφεροι
ἡδονήν, οἷον ὁρᾶν, μνημονεύειν, εἰδέναι,
τὰς ἀρετὰς ἔχειν. εἰ δ' ἐξ ἀνάγκης
ἕπονται τούτοις ἡδοναί, οὐδὲν διαφέρει.
ἑλοίμεθα γὰρ ἂν ταῦτα καὶ εἰ μὴ γίνοιτ'
ἀπ' αὐτῶν ἡδονή. Cf. also 7, 13, 7 where
it is argued that pleasure must be an
ἀγαθόν because it is the concomitant of
(morally) good acts.

1. laudabilis: ἐπαινετάς: note on 3, 27.
medicorum: the comparison between
medicine and philosophy frequently
occurs in ancient texts, Epicurean and
other. In Plato it is argued that the end
pursued by these looks to something
beyond themselves, see 3, 24 *n*. There
is no reason to suppose (with Usener)
that our passages are drawn from Plato,
Rep. 341 C—342 E in which there is a
discussion of ἰατρική and κυβερνητική:
the two passages are not strikingly
similar. Cf. esp. Diog. L. 10, 138; Tusc.
3, 6; Epic. ap. Porphyr. ad Marcellam,
p. 209, 23 Nauck: κενὸς ἐκείνου φιλο-
σόφου λόγος ὑφ' οὗ μηδὲν πάθος ἀνθρώπου
θεραπεύεται: ὥσπερ γὰρ ἰατρικῆς οὐδὲν
ὄφελος μὴ τὰς νόσους τῶν σωμάτων ἐκβαλ-
λούσης, οὕτως οὐδὲ φιλοσοφίας εἰ μὴ τὸ
τῆς ψυχῆς ἐκβάλλει πάθος. So Democritus
fragm. 80 ἰατρικὴ μὲν γὰρ σώματος νοῦσον
ἀκέεται, σοφίη δὲ ψυχὴν παθέων ἀπαιρέεται

(? καθαίρεται). The Stoics from their
point of view denied the resemblance
assumed here between *sapientia* and
medicine and navigation; see note on
3, 24.
3. habet: 'brings with it'; 2, 9;
Nägelsbach § 110.
utilitate: a strong abl. of cause,
like § 36 factis non emolumento aliquo
sed ipsiu s honestatis decore laudandis;
2, 83 si fructibus et emolumentis et
utilitatibus amicitias colemus; Div. 1, 13
quorum...utilitate et ars et inventor
probatus; Ov. Pont. 2, 3, 8 volgus
amicitias utilitate probat (Roby § 1228).
Here as often elsewhere, *utilitas* (τὸ
συμφέρον) and *voluptas* are treated as
identical; so by Epicurus ap. Diog. L.
10, 120; cf. Usener, fr. 510 (p. 358).
4. ars vivendi: τέχνη τοῦ βίου or περὶ
τὸν βίον: a commonplace definition of
philosophy in post-Aristotelian writers;
see my note on Acad. 2, 23. Shakespeare
seems to have this definition in view in
Love's Labour's Lost, 1, 1, 13: 'our court
shall be a little Academe | still and con-
templative in living art' (see the context). But here and in § 46 *sapientia* is
a rendering, not of φιλοσοφία, but of
φρόνησις, which Epicurus made supreme
among virtues; Diog. L. 10, 132 τούτων
δὲ πάντων ἀρχὴ καὶ τὸ μέγιστον ἀγαθὸν
φρόνησις. διὸ καὶ φιλοσοφίας τιμιώτερον
(? read τιμιώτατον) φρόνησις: Polystratos
περὶ ἀλόγου καταφρονήσεως (Gomperz in
Hermes, xi, p. 405)...τὸν ἐκ τῆς ψυχῆς
φόβον λῦσαι καὶ τὴν ὑποψίαν, τοῦτο δ'
εἶναι φρονήσεως ἔργον νομίζων...τὸ τὴν
μάταιον ταραχὴν ἀφαιρεῖν. Epic. himself
seems sometimes to have treated φρόνησις and φιλοσοφία as convertible terms;
compare Plut. de Sto. Rep. c. 26, p.
1046 e εἰ μὲν οὖν τὴν φρόνησιν ἡγεῖτο
(Χρύσιππος) ποιητικὸν εἶναι τῆς εὐδαιμονίας τι ἀγαθόν, ὥσπερ ὁ Ἐπίκουρος,
with Sext. A.M. 11, 169 ἐπαγγέλλονται
γὰρ τέχνην τινα περὶ τὸν βίον παραδώσειν,
καὶ διὰ τοῦτο Ἐπίκουρος μὲν ἔλεγε τὴν
φιλοσοφίαν ἐνέργειαν εἶναι λόγοις καὶ
διαλογισμοῖς τὸν εὐδαίμονα βίον περι-
ποιοῦσαν. So in § 44 *sapiens* is φρόνιμος,
a word applied in all late systems more
or less the ideal philosopher. [Cf. the

non expeteretur, si nihil efficeret; nunc expetitur, quod est tamquam artifex conquirendae et comparandae voluptatis. (Quam **43**
autem ego dicam voluptatem iam videtis, ne invidia verbi
labefactetur oratio mea.) Nam cum ignoratione rerum bonarum
5 et malarum maxime hominum vita vexetur, ob eumque errorem
et voluptatibus maximis saepe priventur et durissimis animi
doloribus torqueantur, sapientia est adhibenda quae et terroribus
cupiditatibusque detractis et omnium falsarum opinionum te-
meritate derepta certissimam se nobis ducem praebeat ad volup-

---

6 durissimis cod. Leidensis: *purissimis* AEP al.; *pravissimis* ed. Colon.;
gravissimis Orelli.   7 terroribus: *erroribus* E.

---

identification of σοφία with σωφροσύνη
in Xen. Mem. 3, 9, 4.] Perhaps in his
treatment of φρόνησις Epicurus followed
the lead of Democritus, who in his
Τριτογένεια assigned to it a wide sphere:
'τρία γίνεται ἐξ αὐτῆς ἃ πάντα τὰ ἀνθρώ-
πινα συνέχει, εὖ λογίζεσθαι, λέγειν καλῶς,
ὀρθῶς πράττειν.' In an examination of
the Epicurean view of the four cardinal
virtues in Off. 3, 117 sq. φρόνησις is
rendered by *prudentia* (cf. Ad Her. 3, 6).
Cf. Off. 1, 153 where *sapientia* is indicated as a possible equivalent for both
σοφία and φρόνησις: so Tusc. 5, 13
constantia, gravitas, fortitudo, sapientia
reliquaeque virtutes; below, 2, 51.

1. **nihil:** i.e. nothing over and above
its own presence.

tamquam artifex: a tentative rendering of ἀρχιτέκτων (§ 32) or δημιουργός.
Cf. 2, 116.

3. **ne:** the slight ellipse is of a very
common sort; cf. 2 §§ 20, 77; 4, 36.

invidia verbi: 2, 12 invidiosum nomen; Sull. 25 verbi invidiam; Planc. 75;
Cat. 3, 3; Rep. 2, 52 odium regalis
nominis.

4. **ignoratione:** Cicero avoided *igno-
rantia,* which the inferior MSS. sometimes introduce, as in 3 § 72 and Acad.
1, 42, where see my note. It is to be
noted that this ignorance is not to be
ousted without the aid of φυσιολογία; see
1, 63 *n.*

6. **durissimis:** 'fateor, *durum* dolorem apud Ciceronem alibi non dici, et
in hoc substantivo scriptores prosae
orationis iis potius adiectivis uti, quae
ab onere aut a tactu aut gustu imaginem
traducant, cum hoc magis ad rigorem
quemdam spectet, ut aliter *dura con-
dicio* dicatur et servitus. Sed admodum
propinqua haec sunt: et transierunt
illum finem poëtae, quin ipse antiquus
usus cotidianus, ut in *duro vino* apud

Catonem' (Madvig). The readings
purissimis and *pravissimis* are impossible; if emendation were needed we
should have to resort to *asperrimis* (§ 33)
or *amarissimis* (§ 44) or *miserrimis* (2, 88);
cf. *duros dolores* in poet. ap. Div. 1, 106.

7. **est adhibenda:** Madvig condemns
the assertion of Beier and others that
Cicero constantly omits *esse* with the
gerundive. 'Non omittit, nisi in brevi
sententia, initio periodi, cum rhetorica
quadam gravitate.' This canon is probably too strict. [A large number of exx.
occur in Varro, de re rust.] Madvig
doubtless had in mind passages like
2, 41 nec vero audiendus Hieronymus
etc., where see note. But sometimes the
verb is left to be supplied from a neighbouring clause, as in Cato m. 35; Off. 1,
150; sometimes it is omitted in two
parallel clauses, as Off. 3, 113 ut laudandus Regulus...sic decem illi...vitupe-
randi; also in the middle of the 'periodus'
when emphasis is intended, as Cato m. 29.

terroribus cupiditatibusque : but
for the fact that *cupiditatibus* begins
with a guttural, Cicero would probably
have written *ac cup.* here; see my note
on Acad. 2, 34. The reading *erroribus*
is certainly wrong. *Terror* and *passion*
are constantly linked together by the
Epicureans as the two great torments
of life; cf. 2 §§ 18–22; Epic. ap. Porphyr.
ad Marc. 29, p. 208, Nauck (Us. § 485): ἦ
γὰρ διὰ φόβον τις κακοδαιμονεῖ ἢ διὰ κενὴν
ἐπιθυμίαν· ἃ τις χαλινῶν δύναται τὸν
μακάριον ἑαυτῷ περιποιῆσαι λογισμόν.

8. **opinionum:** οἰήσεων: a word used
in all later systems to denote an ill-
grounded and unphilosophic persuasion.
Epic. called οἴησις a ἱερὰ νόσος (Flori-
legium Monacense, 195). Cf. my note on
Acad. 1, 42 and Timon ἄνθρωποι κενεῆς
οἰήσιος ἔμπλεοι ἀσκοί.

9. **derepta:** Madvig qu. Sull. 2 quan-

tatem. Sapientia enim est una quae maestitiam pellat ex animis,
quae nos exhorrescere metu non sinat; qua praeceptrice in
tranquillitate vivi potest omnium cupiditatum ardore restincto.
Cupiditates enim sunt insatiabiles, quae non modo singulos
homines, sed universas familias evertunt, totam etiam labe- 5
44 factant saepe rem publicam. Ex cupiditatibus odia discidia dis-
cordiae seditiones bella nascuntur, nec eae se foris solum iactant
nec tantum in alios caeco impetu incurrunt, sed intus etiam in
animis inclusae inter se dissident atque discordant, ex quo vitam
amarissimam necesse est effici, ut sapiens solum amputata cir- 10

6 discidia: *dissidia* Orelli (non bene).

tum de mea auctoritate deripuisset;
Prov. Cons. 13; Val. Max. 3, 2 E, 4
dereptam hostibus victoriam; Tac. An.
2, 45 tela Romanis derepta; but doubts
Val. Max. 2, 9, 8 dereptis publicis equis
for ademptis. Many similar things occur
in the poets. Add Off. 3, 42; Quinct. 64.

I. sapientia...est una: cf. Lael. 86 una
est enim amicitia de cuius utilitate, etc.
Cf. Inscr. of Oinoanda, Heberdey and
Kalinka, in Bull. de Corr. Hell. xxi, 403:
τὸ δὲ ἡμῶν κατασκευαστικὸν τῆς μετ'
εὐθυμίας χαρᾶς οὐ τὰ θέατρα καὶ μουσεῖα
καὶ βαλανεῖα καὶ ἀλείμματα, ἀλλά...τὸ
ἐπιζητούμενον ὑπὸ τῆς φύσεως τέλος· τί
δ' ἔστι τοῦτο, ὅτι τε μήτε πλοῦτος αὐτὸ
δύναται παρασχεῖν μήτε δόξα πολειτικὴ
μήτε βασιλεία μήθ' ἀβροδίαιτος βίος καὶ
τραπεζῶν πολυτέλεια μήτ' ἀφροδεισίων
ἐγλελεγμένων ἡδοναὶ μήτ' ἄλλο μηδὲν
φιλοσοφία δὲ περιποιεῖ μόνη. With *quae*
pellat here cf. § 47 temperantia est enim
quae...monet.

enim est: Madvig asserts that with
the collocation *est enim* the stress falls
on the word that precedes, while with
the other collocation (*enim est*) the stress
falls on the words that follow. At the
same time he allows that in matters of
this kind it is hard to find a rule, and
dangerous to follow uniformity in
editing texts. Madvig's statement that
collocations like *sapientia est enim*, etc.
are commoner in Cicero than *sapientia*
enim est seems correct. But when *enim*
takes the third place in the sentence
and is preceded by some part of *sum*,
the part is almost always *est* or *sunt* or
sit or *sint*, rarely fut. or a past tense.

2. qua praeceptrice...potest: 'paulo
durius hoc propter adiectum *praeceptrice* seorsum extulit: expectabatur
possit' (Madvig). In separate relative
clauses, there is considerable caprice in
the choice between indic. and subj.; cf.

10 necesse est: *esse* (om. *necesse*) E.

e.g. § 47 temperantia est enim quae
monet, with § 54 voluptas est sola quae
nos vocet....

praeceptrice: quoted only besides
from Vitruvius 10, 1, 4 natura p.

3. **tranquillitate:** γαλήνη, γαληνίζειν
(so ἡσυχία, etc.) occur in Epicurean texts.
Epicurus placed human life *in tranquillo*
(Lucret. 5, 12). Lucil. fragm. 430 Baehr.,
'quodque te in tranquillum ex saevis
transfert tempestatibus,' may be an
Epicurean echo. Cf. λύεται πᾶς ὁ χειμών:
and Epic. ap. Porphyr. ad Marcellam,
31, p. 209, 21 (Usener, p. 296): ἔρωτι
φιλοσοφίας ἀληθινῆς πᾶσα ταραχώδης
καὶ ἐπίπονος ἐπιθυμία ἐκλύεται. Usener
says of the first three words that they
are hardly Epicurean; but φιλοσοφία
ἀληθινή is certainly an Epicurean expression, occurring in Polystratos
(Gomperz in Hermes, xi, 409) and
represented often in Lucret. by *vera*
ratio as below, § 52. Lucretius says
much that is similar of *vera ratio*.

ardore restincto: the passionate are
compared to πυρέττοντες in an Epicurean fragment (Usener, §471).

6. **discidia:** in an excursus to this
passage Madvig shows that *dissidium*,
often given by mss., is a 'vox nihili.'

7. **nec eae se,** etc.: cf. § 58 animus a
se ipse dissidens secumque discordans.
The verb *discordare* was archaic, and
was revived (in these two passages only)
by Cicero, who was followed in its use by
Horace and later writers. A great deal
of the language about internal discord
of mind is common to Stoics and Epic.;
cf. e.g. Sen. dial. 7, 8, 5, 6, which might
be adopted by Epic.; also Sen. de ben.
1, 10, 3.

8. **incurrunt:** figure from beasts; Sen.
dial. 3, 3, 4.

10. **sapiens solum:** Davies and others
write *solus* quite unnecessarily: cf. Otto's

cumcisaque inanitate omni et errore naturae finibus contentus
sine aegritudine possit et sine metu vivere. Quae est enim aut **45**
utilior aut ad bene vivendum aptior partitio quam illa, qua est
usus Epicurus? qui unum genus posuit earum cupiditatum quae
5 essent et naturales et necessariae, alterum, quae naturales essent
nec tamen necessariae, tertium, quae nec naturales nec necessariae. Quarum ea ratio est ut necessariae nec opera multa nec
impensa expleantur; ne naturales quidem multa desiderant,
propterea quod ipsa natura divitias, quibus contenta sit, et

3 qua est usus: *que e usu* A[1].

note: 'monendum *solum* ad rationem
non ad personam referri. Sensus est;
nulla ratione nisi sapientia sine aegritudine vivi posse: *sapiens solus* significaret
nemo nisi sapiens.' Below, 4, 36
Stoicos solum; 2, 17 rhetorum s.

amputata circumcisaque: these verbs
are often combined, as in 5, 39; Acad.
2, 138; in my note on the latter passage
will be found illustrations, to which add
Tac. dial. 32 (eloquentia) circumcisa et
amputata; Plin. ep. 1, 20, 19 amputata
oratio et abscisa. In Mar. Vict. p. 24,
l. 20 (ed. Stangl) circumcisa et ablata
notarum rerum cognitione, we should
probably read c. et amputata (āp'tata).
Aug. ep. 118, 4 puns on the original
meaning of *putare*; non esse...sed putari.
at ego te admoneo eum, qui talium puta-
torum linguis tanquam falcibus concidi
timet, lignum aridum esse.

1. inanitate: note on § 45 inanium.
errore...metu: cf. *errore...terrore* in
§ 46.
naturae finibus: so of the repression
of the passions, Ad Her. 3, 5 si unam
quamque rem certae naturae termino
definiemus.

3. partitio: the 29th κυρία δόξα is: τῶν
ἐπιθυμιῶν αἱ μέν εἰσι φυσικαὶ < καὶ ἀναγ-
καῖαι· αἱ δὲ φυσικαὶ > καὶ οὐκ ἀναγκαῖαι·
αἱ δὲ οὔτε φυσικαὶ οὔτε ἀναγκαῖαι ἀλλὰ
παρὰ κενὴν δόξαν γινόμεναι. The words
in brackets are absent from Diog. L.
and were supplied by H. Stephanus
from Cicero, particularly 2, 26; cf.
Tusc. 5, 93 sq.; see Nemesius and
Olympiod. referred to in Us. p. 397.
The Latin here agrees better with a
slightly different version of the δόξα
given in the Vatican Gnomologion...
'αἱ δὲ φυσικαὶ μὲν οὐκ ἀναγκαῖαι δέ' (see
Usener in Wiener Stud. 10, 179); so also
in a scholion on Arist. Eth. Nic. (Us.
§ 456); and Plut. Gryllus, p. 989 b (ibid.).
The division of ἐπιθυμίαι into ἀναγκαῖαι

and οὐκ ἀναγκαῖαι repeatedly occurs in
Plat. Rep. VIII, IX. Varro in a difficult
fragment of the Menippean Satires (316
Bücheler) alludes to this 'partitio':
asse vinum, asse pulmentarium: secundas quo natura aurigatur non
necessitudo.' The passage is twice
quoted by Nonius, pp. 70, 353 M. L.
Müller reads *quoi* for *quo* with Mercer.,
understanding *mensas* with *secundas*,
and remarking 'hominis divitis eiusdemque sobrii mores describi apparet.' Riese
remarks on *necessitudo* 'sc. restringit,
non luxuries effrenat.' But *secundas* is
obviously corrupt, and the first syllable
conceals *asse*, the other two *ludus* in the
sense of *venus*. Martial had the passage
of Varro in mind when he wrote (1, 103,
ll. 9, 10): 'et Veientani bibitur faex
crassa rubelli: asse cicer tepidum constat et asse venus.' For *ludus* see note
on 2, 23, and for *asse* in this connexion
Lucil. 5, 30 (ed. L. Müller). In Martial
cicer tepidum may well represent *pulmentarium*; see Marq.-Momms. 7,
p. 298 *n.*; for the word cf. Hor. s.
2, 2, 20; Lucil. 20, 3. The Menippean
satires, like those of Lucilius and
Horace, are full of allusions to Epicureanism.

7. quarum: it is possible that
quorum=generum should be read.

8. ne naturales quidem: *naturales* is
briefly put for *n. nec tamen necessariae*,
just as above *necessariae* stands for *et
naturales et n.*; there is no need to
suppose (with Usener) that words have
been lost from the text. Lower down,
inanium replaces *nec naturalium nec
necessariarum.* For the abandonment
of the *ut*-construction here cf. 2, 16 and
4, 4 and Madvig's first Excursus, p. 798
(ed. 3); above, note on 1, 23.

9. ipsa natura, etc.: Epic. κυρ. δ. 15
ὁ τῆς φύσεως πλοῦτος καὶ ὥρισται καὶ
εὐπόριστός ἐστιν· ὁ δὲ τῶν κενῶν δοξῶν

parabilis et terminatas habet; inanium autem cupiditatum nec
46 modus ullus nec finis inveniri potest. XIV. Quod si vitam omnem
perturbari videmus errore et inscientia, sapientiamque esse
solam quae nos a libidinum impetu et a formidinum terrore
vindicet et ipsius fortunae modice ferre doceat iniurias et omnis 5
monstret vias, quae ad quietem et tranquillitatem ferant, quid
est cur dubitemus dicere et sapientiam propter voluptates expetendam et insipientiam propter molestias esse fugiendam?
47 Eademque ratione ne temperantiam quidem propter se expetendam esse dicemus, sed quia pacem animis afferat et eos 10
quasi concordia quadam placet ac leniat. Temperantia est enim,
quae in rebus aut expetendis aut fugiendis ut rationem sequamur
monet. Nec enim satis est iudicare quid faciendum non facien-

3 inscientia: *inscitia* ed. Colon.   6 monstret: *doceat* P et ed. Rom.; om. non
nulli.

εἰς ἄπειρον ἐκπίπτει; and ap. Diog. L.
10, 130 τὸ μὲν φυσικὸν πᾶν εὐπόριστόν
ἐστι, τὸ δὲ κενὸν δυσπόριστον: also κυρ.
δ. 21 ὁ τὰ πέρατα τοῦ βίου κατειδὼς οἶδεν
ὡς εὐποριστόν ἐστι τὸ τὸ ἀλγοῦν καὶ
ἔνδειαν ἐξαιροῦν καὶ τὸ τὸν ὅλον βίον
παντελῆ καθιστάν, below, 2, 90 and 91;
very many writers report and harp upon
this saying of Epicurus. See references
in Usener, p. 396; and in a note by Mayor
on Juv. 14, 319. Democritus inculcated
the same lesson; fragm. 22 M. τῶν τὸ
σκῆνος ('earthly tabernacle') χρῇζει,
πᾶσι πάρεστι εὐμαρέως ἄτερ μόχθου καὶ
ταλαιπωρίης, ὁκόσα δὲ μόχθου καὶ ταλαιπωρίης χρῇζει καὶ βίον ἀλγύνει, τούτων
οὐκ ἱμείρεται τὸ σκῆνος, ἀλλ' ἡ τῆς γνώμης
κακοφυίη: id. fr. 24 σμικρὴ ὄρεξις πενίην
ἰσοσθενέα πλούτῳ ποιέει: cf. too Theognis
719 sq. ed. Bergk. Petronius (fragm.
xxxv Büch.) has a poem on the theme
ending 'quod satiare potest dives natura
ministrat; quod docet infrenis gloria,
fine caret.' So Lucil. fragm. 150 Baehr.
1. **parabilis**: the ordinary rendering
of εὐπόριστος as in 2, 90, 91; Sen. ep.
4, 10.
inanium: cf. vana Sen. ep. 16, 9.
cupiditatum modus: on the gen. see
n. on § 3, and for the words *modus, finis*
note on § 62.
3. **errore et inscientia**: Polystratos
περὶ ἀλογ. καταφρ. (Gomperz in Hermes
xi, 409): πάσης ἀγνοίας καὶ ἀπάτης καὶ
ψευδοδοξίας ἀπολυθείσης, ὅπερ ἦν τέλος
τοῦ ἀρίστου βίου. On the reading *inscitia*
Madvig remarks 'facultati aliquid recte
et ordine, hoc est scite agendi contraria
est (ut *inscitia loquendi negotii gerendi*)

non cognitioni et intellegentiae.' But
his rule is too tightly drawn; cf. 2, 34
summae videtur inscitiae, of a philosophic doctrine. In De Inv. 1, 2 *error*
and *inscientia* are joined.
4. **libidinum**: hitherto *cupiditatum*
for ἐπιθυμῶν.
5. **ipsius fortunae**: *even* of fortune.
Cf. 1, 63 *n*.
8. **molestias**: §§ 51, 59.
10. **animis**: 'the mind'; in this general
or abstract sense the plural is far commoner than the singular; see my note
on Acad. 1, 20 ingeniis ('genius'); to
the exx. given there add De Or. 1, 115;
Fam. 4, 8, 2.
11. **quasi concordia quadam**: the
words *quasi...quadam* indicate a rendering of some particular Greek word,
ὁμονοίᾳ or ἁρμονίᾳ. See my n. on Acad.
1, 17.
placet ac leniat: the two verbs are
joined thus in Phil. 7, 25.
12. **aut exp. aut fug.**: *et...et* might
have been expected.
13. **monet**: the succeeding words show
that perpetual or repeated admonition
is meant. Only the perfect σοφός is
unwavering in practice; cf. Plut. Colot.
19, p. 1117 *f* ἐν γάρ ἐστι τῶν Ἐπικούρου
δογμάτων τὸ μηδέν' ἀμεταπείστως πεπεῖ-
σθαι μηδένα πλὴν τὸν σοφόν.
satis est: in the philosophical writings
there are six exx. of *sat*, all before *est*,
erat, *esse*; in the speeches two, one in a
quotation, the other in the phrase
sat bonus (S. Rosc. 89; cf. Att. 14, 10, 1).
See Neue-Wag. ii³, 595 f. On *sat bonus*
see Landgr. p. 299 on S. Rosc. l.c.

dumve sit, sed stare etiam oportet in eo quod sit iudicatum.
Plerique autem, quod tenere atque servare id quod ipsi statuerunt
non possunt, victi et debilitati obiecta specie voluptatis tradunt
se libidinibus constringendos nec quid eventurum sit provident
5 ob eamque causam propter voluptatem et parvam et non
necessariam, et quae vel aliter pararetur, et qua etiam carere
possent sine dolore, tum in morbos gravis, tum in damna, tum
in dedecora incurrunt, saepe etiam legum iudiciorumque poenis
obligantur. Qui autem ita frui volunt voluptatibus ut nulli **48**
10 propter eas consequantur dolores, et qui suum iudicium retinent,
ne voluptate victi faciant id quod sentiant non esse faciendum,
ei voluptatem maximam adipiscuntur praetermittenda voluptate.
Idem etiam dolorem saepe perpetiuntur ne, si id non faciant,
incidant in maiorem. Ex quo intellegitur nec intemperantiam
15 propter se esse fugiendam temperantiamque expetendam, non
quia voluptates fugiat, sed quia maiores consequatur.

XV. Eadem fortitudinis ratio reperietur. Nam neque laborum **49**
perfunctio neque perpessio dolorum per se ipsa allicit nec
patientia nec assiduitas nec vigiliae nec ipsa quae laudatur in-

---

4 eventurum: *proventurum* dett. (etiam P). 9 nulli: *nullos* E. 10 dolores:
om. E. 19 assiduitas: *assiduitates* AP; cf. *dictatas* (§ 7). 19 nec ipsa BE: *ea ipsa*
(om. *nec*) A; *nec ea ipsa* codd. dett. vulgo.

iudicare...stare: cf. § 55 stabili; and
2, 9.

non faciendumve: so De Inv. 1, 36
and 2, 31 aliquid faciendi non facien-
dive; below, 2, 38 non dolendive.

1. sit iudicatum: see C. F. W. Müller.

3. victi et debilitati: 5, 42 victi de-
bilitantur; and below § 49 debilitatem.

obiecta specie: Hor. ep. 1, 6, 11 im-
provisa species. For the context cf. § 33.

4. constringendos: cf. 2, 62: the
Vatican Gnomologion (see Wiener Stud.
10, 195) shows that Metrodorus used the
expression ἐκδότους ἑαυτοὺς παρέχειν in a
context like this. Possibly Cicero either
found ἐκδέτους in a similar passage or
mistook ἐκδότους for it. Seneca repeatedly
defended Epicurus on this head: cf.
dial. 7, 12, 4 (Epicuri) voluptas sobria
et sicca.

quid eventurum sit: Gnom. Vatic.
§ 71 πρὸς πάσας τὰς ἐπιθυμίας προσακτέον
τὸ ἐρώτημα τοῦτο· τί μοι γενήσεται ἂν
τελεσθῇ τὸ κατὰ τὴν ἐπιθυμίαν ἐπιζητούμενον, καὶ τί ἐὰν μὴ τελεσθῇ;

8. saepe etiam: the triple *tum*
followed by *saepe etiam* is well illustrated by Wölfflin, Archiv 2, p. 252, 3.

10. suum iudicium retinent: as above,
tenere atque servare id quod ipsi
statuerunt.

12. praetermittenda v.: n. on § 33.

14. nec...que: so § 3 and often.

18. perfunctio: a rare word, which,
but for De Or. 3, 7, is only found here
and in late Latin.

19. patientia: 'endurance'; cf. Sen.
ep. 67, 10 fortitudo, cuius patientia et
perpessio et tolerantia rami sunt.

ipsa...industria: for *ipsa* see 1, 13 *n.*
Madvig: '*ipsa, quae laudatur* ideo dicitur quod haec tamquam propria quaedam virtus laudari in hominibus solet,
non vigiliae quae in hominibus non sunt,
nec assiduitas quae in certis actionibus
spectator non in toto ingenio.' But
patientia (which Madvig neglects) is
certainly 'propria quaedam virtus.'
Rather Cicero means that *industria*,
'energy,' is more specially a subject of
eulogy than the rest. Yet it is surprising that the words *ipsa quae
laudatur* should be attached to *industria*
rather than to *fortitudo*; perhaps they
have been displaced in our MSS. and
should come after *quidem*.

dustria, ne fortitudo quidem, sed ista sequimur ut sine cura
metuque vivamus animumque et corpus, quantum efficere
possimus, molestia liberemus. Vt enim mortis metu omnis
quietae vitae status perturbatur, et ut succumbere doloribus
eosque humili animo imbecilloque ferre miserum est, ob eamque 5
debilitatem animi multi parentes, multi amicos, non nulli
patriam, plerique autem se ipsos penitus perdiderunt, sic robustus
animus et excelsus omni est liber cura et angore, cum et mortem
contemnit, qua qui affecti sunt in eadem causa sunt qua ante
quam nati, et ad dolores ita paratus est ut meminerit maximos 10

4 et ut: *et* om. A.　　　9 qua qui: *qua quia* A¹E.

1. **fortitudo**: here contrasted with
patientia, etc., as specially connected
with *danger*. According to Epicurus,
ἀνδρεία does not exist φύσει, λογισμῷ δὲ
τοῦ συμφέροντος (Diog. L. 10, 120). In
connexion with courage, as in other connexions, pain must be endured to avoid
greater pain; Orig. contra Celsum, v, 47,
p. 270 Hoesch. οὕτω δὲ καὶ ἄλλη μὲν ἡ
Ἐπικούρου ἀνδρεία ὑπομένοντος πόνους
διὰ φυγὴν πόνων πλειόνων, ἄλλη δὲ ἡ τοῦ
ἀπὸ τῆς στοᾶς δι' αὐτὴν αἱρουμένου πᾶσαν
ἀρετήν. Cf. Ad Herenn. 3, 3; 4, 35. In
the Hercul. Fragm. there are remains of
a treatise περὶ φοβερῶν (No. 57).

4. **perturbatur**: cf. Gnom. Vat. § 57
ὁ βίος αὐτοῦ πᾶς δι' ἀπιστίαν συγχυθή-
σεται καὶ ἀνακεχαιτισμένος ἔσται.

6. **parentes...patriam**: Lucr. 3, 83 sq.
hunc vexare pudorem, hunc vincula
amicitia | rumpere et in summa pietatem
evertere suadet; | nam iam saepe homines
patriam carosque parentes | prodiderunt
vitare Acherusia templa petentes; and
Sen. ep. 70, 8 stultitia est timore
mortis mori. Possibly *perdiderunt* in
Cicero is an error for *prodiderunt*.

7. **rob. animus**: so Off. 1, 67; 1.
fortitudo, Tusc. 4, 51.

8. **cum...contemnit**: n. on § 10.
mortem: n. on § 40.

9. **in eadem causa**: this use of *causa*,
meaning 'circumstances,' is not uncommon. The words *in ead. c.* occur in
Caec. 38 and Off. 1, 112 (but in the latter
passage only in inferior mss.); Caes.
B.G. 4, 4, 1; Sen. d. 4, 19, 5.

qua ante quam nati: for the omission
of *in* see n. on § 32; for the doctrine in
the context cf. Eur. Tro. 636 κείνῃ δ'
ὁμοίως ὥσπερ οὐκ ἰδοῦσα φῶς | τέθνηκε
κοὐδὲν οἶδε τῶν αὐτῆς κακῶν: Lucret.
3, 866 sq. and passages from Sen.
ep. 22, 15 nemo, inquit (sc. Epi-

curus), aliter quam qui modo (*quo modo*
mss., corr. Wolters) natus est, exit e
vita; but Sen. sometimes treats death
as the beginning of a new life for which
our mortal life is a preparation; see
Sen. ep. 102, 23, and cf. the well-known
passage in Cicero's letters; Sen. ep.
54 §§ 4, 5. Axiochus, p. 365 D εἰς παντελῆ
μεταβαλὼν ἀναισθησίαν καὶ τὴν αὐτὴν τῇ
πρὸ τῆς γενέσεως: pseud.-Plut. cons. ad
Apollonium, p. 109 f ἡ γὰρ αὐτὴ κατά-
στασίς ἐστι τῇ πρὸ τῆς γενέσεως ἡ μετὰ
τὴν τελευτήν. Schopenhauer, Die Welt als
Wille, 11, c. 41 and 1, l. iv argues exactly
as Epicurus that the nothingness which
death brings concerns us no more than
the nothingness which preceded our life.
On which Guyau remarks 'on se console
aisément de n'avoir pas toujours
possédé un bien, on se console plus
difficilement d'être condamné à le
perdre.' Democritus handled the topic
of death much in the fashion of Epicurus: see fragm. 53–5, 119 (Mullach);
the Epicurean view is picturesquely
given in ep. 54. Stoics differed. See
interesting passages in Sen. ep. 57, 7;
77, 11, 12.

10. **ita paratus est**, etc.: Sen. ep. 30,
14 gives account of a friend who applied
practically these precepts.

maximos morte finiri: The native
Italian was averse to suicide: this is
strongly shown by the fact that the
collegia tenuiorum regard all suicides as
infames: see Waltzing les corp. pro-
fessionnelles, 1, p. 267 sq., where it is
pointed out that Roman lawyers re-
cognized suicide as justifiable in some
cases. The Stoic view of the worthlessness of life induced suicide: Sen. d.
1, 6, 6 contemnite dolorem: aut solvetur
aut solvet. Epicurus ap. Plut. de aud.
poet. p. 36 b οἱ μεγάλοι πόνοι συντόμως

morte finiri, parvos multa habere intervalla requietis, mediocrium nos esse dominos, ut, si tolerabiles sint, feramus, si minus,
animo aequo e vita, cum ea non placeat, tamquam e theatro
exeamus. Quibus rebus intellegitur nec timiditatem ignaviamque
5 vituperari nec fortitudinem patientiamque laudari suo nomine,
sed illas reici quia dolorem pariant, has optari quia voluptatem.
XVI. Iustitia restat, ut de omni virtute sit dictum; sed 50
similia fere dici possunt. Vt enim sapientiam temperantiam
fortitudinem copulatas esse docui cum voluptate, ut ab ea nullo

1 mediocrium: *medicorum* E.   2 si minus: ita codd. (etiam P); *sin minus* Orelli.

ἐξάγουσιν, οἱ δὲ χρόνιοι μέγεθος οὐκ
ἔχουσιν, and id. non posse suaviter vivi,
p. 1103 e ὁ γὰρ πόνος ὁ ὑπερβάλλων
συνάψει θανάτῳ: see also passages quoted
in n. on § 40 (mors). Plutarch in the
former passage quotes a line of Aes-
chylus: 'θάρσει· πόνου γὰρ ἄκρον οὐκ
ἔχει χρόνον.' Also Marc. Aurel. 7, 33
περὶ πόνου· τὸ μὲν ἀφόρητον ἐξάγει· τὸ
δὲ χρονίζον, φορητόν; id. 7, 64.
1. **intervalla:** so Sen. ep. 78, 7
magnos cruciatus habet morbus; sed hos
tolerabiles intervalla faciunt, nam
summi doloris intentio invenit finem;
below, 2, 94 *n.*
2. **ut, si tol....exeamus:** cf. Tusc.
5, 117 sin forte longinquitate producti
(dolores) vehementius tamen torquent
quam ut causa sit cur ferantur, quid
est tandem, di boni, cur laboremus?
Portus quidem praesto est, aeternum
nihil sentiendi receptaculum; ib. 118
mihi quidem in vita servanda videtur
illa lex, quae in Graecorum conviviis
obtinetur: 'Aut bibat,' inquit, 'aut
abeat.'...Sic iniurias fortunae, quas
ferre nequeas, defugiendo relinquas.
Haec eadem, quae Epicurus, totidem
verbis dicit Hieronymus. Also Epic.
ap. Sen. ep. 12, 10 malum est in
necessitate vivere, sed in necessitate
vivere nulla necessitas est; Wotke-
Usener, § 9 κακὸν ἀνάγκη ἀλλὰ οὐδεμία
ἀνάγκη ζῆν μετ' ἀνάγκης. For the Stoic
doctrine of suicide see 3, 61 *n.* The
Epicureans were more cautious in their
treatment of the subject than the Stoics:
cf. Epic. ap. Sen. ep. 24, 22 ridiculum
est currere ad mortem taedio vitae, cum
genere vitae, ut currendum ad mortem
esset, effeceris. In the case of many,
the very fear of death leads to irrational
suicides, Lucr. 3, 79–82; Sen. ep. 70,
8 stultitia est timore mortis mori
(cf. Lucr.); ib. 24, 23; ps.-Plut. ad
Apollon. p. 110 *a*. See also Usener,

p. 310, n. 1. Sen. dial. 7, 19, 1 refers to a
case of an Epicurean philosopher who
committed suicide and was condemned
by his fellow-disciples for having acted
contrary to the spirit of his master.
[See also § 62 migrare de vita.] Cf. the
story in Sen. 77, 5 ff. which is from a
Stoic source.
3. **animo aequo:** (in re simili) Lucr.
3, 939 and 962.
theatro: the comparison of life with
the theatre has been common at all
times. Sometimes the human being is
treated as spectator, sometimes as
actor. Philodemus, Us. p. 269 *n.*; below
3, 67. Cf. a fragment of Democritus (249
M.) adapted by Caesar in his 'veni,
vidi, vici': ὁ κόσμος σκηνή· ὁ βίος
πάροδος· ἦλθες, εἶδες, ἀπῆλθες: Cicero,
Cato m. §§ 5, 64, 70, 85; Sen. ep. 80
§§ 7–10 (*vitae mimus*). The celebrated
question addressed by Augustus on his
deathbed, to the bystanders, 'ecquid eis
videretur mimum vitae commode trans-
egisse?' has often been misunderstood.
The emperor was not jesting at life as
Dio Cass. 56, 30 supposed. The *mimus*
came commonly at the end of a series
of performances; the question therefore
meant 'have I acquitted myself credit-
ably in the closing scene?' The comparison of life with a banquet is equally
common; so in Tusc. 5, 117 quoted
above, in Lucr. 3, 935–43, and in other
passages to which reference is made by
Usener, p. 310, n. on l. 19; and by
Munro on Lucr. l.l.; cf. Sen. ep. 26, 5.
7. **iustitia:** Diog. L. 10, 28 mentions
a work of Epic. 'περὶ δικαιοσύνης καὶ
τῶν ἄλλων ἀρετῶν' and another 'περὶ
δικαιοπραγίας.' As to the former see
Usener, p. 92. There was doubtless much
Epicurean literature relating to the
ἀρεταί, as well as the κακίαι (n. on
§ 61).
restat, ut, etc.: there is ellipse of

modo nec divelli nec distrahi possint, sic de iustitia iudicandum est, quae non modo numquam nocet cuiquam, sed contra semper *impertit* aliquid cum sua vi atque natura, quod tranquillet animos, tum spe nihil earum rerum defuturum quas natura non depravata desideret. *Et* quem ad modum temeritas et libido et 5 ignavia semper animum excruciant et semper sollicitant turbulentaeque sunt, sic *improbitas si* cuius in mente consedit, hoc ipso, quod adest, turbulenta est; si vero molita quippiam est, quamvis occulte fecerit, numquam tamen id confidet fore semper occultum.   Plerumque improborum facta primo suspicio in- 10

3 aliquid: *alit...quid* P; cum lacuna inter *alit* et *quid*; quam lacunam indicant codd. meliores; *allicit* Rath et Orelli; *impertit aliquid* C. F. W. Müller; *affert aliquid* Th. Bentley: item Iwan Müller (Erlangen progr. 1869) et Baiter; cf. § 43. 4 non: om. P.   5 et: om. omnes; addidit Lambinus.   7 improbitas si: om. omnes, add. Madv. (cf. § 53); *impietas si* Manutius et Gruter.   8 est; si: *et si* AE. corr. Gruter.

words such as *quae tractanda est*; cf. Div. 2, 49 and 84.

1. **nec divelli nec distrahi**: 'repetita particula oratorie unam notionem dissolvit in duas' (Madvig).

3. **tranquillet**: cf. Epicurus ap. Cl. Alex. Strom. VI, 2, p. 266, 39 δικαιοσύνης καρπὸς μέγιστος ἀταραξία; κυρ. δόξ. 17 ὁ δίκαιος ἀταρακτότατος ὁ δὲ ἄδικος πλείστης ταραχῆς γέμων. Cf. Dem. fr. 111 δίκης κῦδος γνώμης θάρσος καὶ ἀθαμβίη, ἀδικίης δὲ δεῖμα συμφορῆς τέρμα. But some of Democritus' sentences about justice have a different ring; see esp. fragm. 117. Usener (§ 518) quotes Augustin. serm. 348 Epicurei...iustitiam venalem habent carnalis pretio voluptatis. Cf. also Hor. s. 1, 3, 98 utilitas iusti prope mater et aequi; and Cic. Off. 3, 117.

4. **spe**, etc.: the argument is not easy to follow. How does justice inspire a hope that the necessaries of life will never be wanting to its possessor? If Cicero has not here by compression misrepresented some Epicurean text, the sense must be that the right-minded man knows how little is needed.

nihil earum rerum: not *nullam*; cf. Du M. on Flacc. 32.

natura non d.: n. on § 30.

7. **improbitas si**: the correction of Madvig is rendered certain by the parallel passage in § 53. The loss of the words *improbitas si* was doubtless caused by the similarity of *sic* and *si* before *cuius*.

8. **molita...fecerit**: conception and execution are contrasted.

9. **quamvis**, etc.: in the κυρ. δόξαι 31–9, Epicurus states his view of justice.

It rests on expediency (τὸ συμφέρον), leading to a covenant among men not to injure one another. It is nothing by itself (οὐκ ἦν τι καθ' ἑαυτὸ δικαιοσύνη) but rests on a social compact. Injustice also is nothing by itself, ἀλλ' εἰ μὴ λήσει τοὺς ὑπὲρ τῶν τοιούτων ἐφεστηκότας κολαστάς. No man who contravenes the compact can feel secure: οὐκ ἔστι τὸν λάθρα τι κινοῦντα ὧν συνέθεντο πρὸς ἀλλήλους εἰς τὸ μὴ βλάπτειν μηδὲ βλάπτεσθαι πιστεύειν ὅτι λήσει, κἂν μυριάκις ἐπὶ τοῦ παρόντος λανθάνῃ. μέχρι γὰρ καταστροφῆς ἄδηλον εἰ καὶ λήσει. Justice is not necessarily the same all the world over; in other words, although in a certain sense there is a φύσεως δίκαιον (31), the φύσει δίκαιον of Plato and Aristotle does not exist. These views of course are by no means peculiar to Epicurus; they were shared by Aristippus, many of the sophists, Carneades and others. See the references in the notes of Usener to these κυρ. δόξαι. The doctrine of Epicurus is reported by many writers; Lucret. 5, 1152–7 agrees to some extent verbally with Cicero, especially in the line 'perpetuo tamen id fore clam diffidere debet.' See also Usener, §§ 530–4; especially Plut. non posse, etc. c. 6 ; add Gnomol. Vat. 7 ἀδικοῦντα λαθεῖν μὲν δύσκολον, πίστιν δὲ λαβεῖν ὑπὲρ τοῦ λαθεῖν ἀδύνατον; ib. § 70 μηδέν σοι ἐν βίῳ πραχθείη δ φόβον παρέξει σοι εἰ γνωθήσεται τῷ πλησίον. Petron. § 125.

10. **primo...dein**: this form of expression indicates usually succession of two events in *time*, as here; while

sequitur, dein sermo atque fama, tum accusator, tum index; multi etiam, ut te consule, ipsi se indicaverunt. Quod si qui satis **51** sibi contra hominum conscientiam saepti esse et muniti videntur, deorum tamen horrent easque ipsas sollicitudines quibus eorum
5 animi noctesque diesque exeduntur, a dis immortalibus supplici causa importari putant. Quae autem tanta ex improbis factis ad minuendas vitae molestias accessio potest fieri, quanta ad augendas, cum conscientia factorum, tum poena legum odioque civium? Et tamen in quibusdam neque pecuniae modus est
10 neque honoris neque imperi nec libidinum nec epularum nec reliquarum cupiditatum, quas nulla praeda umquam improbe parta minuit potius*que* inflammat, ut coercendi magis quam

1 dein: *deinde* P.   1 index: ita A; *iudex* B Madv.   2 si qui satis: *sequi* (om. *satis*) E.   5 a dis: *ad his* A[1]; *a diis* A[2]P.   8 odioque: *odique* A[1]. 11 improbe: om. E.   12 potiusque Madvigius: om. *que* AE; *potius atque* P et ed. Rom. et Orelli; *sed auget potius atque* dett. unde *sed potius* Baiter.

primum...deinde conveys succession as a matter of *arrangement*.
   1. **tum accusator, tum index**: Madvig prefers *iudex*, because the *indicium* precedes the *accusatio*; Müller *index* because 'ascendi videtur quasi gradibus a levi suspicione usque ad certum testimonium indicis, qui ipse pro teste est.' Cf. Liv. 7, 39, 5 iam quaestiones, iam indicia.
   2. **quod si...tamen**: so 2, 79; 4, 27 and often elsewhere.
   3. **saepti et muniti**: these words often thus go together, as in Tusc. 5, 41; Verr. 2, 5, 39; Sest. 95. I would read *muniti* for *magni* in Att. 14, 5, 2 orbis terrae custodes non modo saepti verum etiam magni esse debebant.
   5. **noctesque diesque**: this form is common in Cicero, also *noctes et dies* and *et noctes et dies, dies noctesque, noctes atque dies* (rarely), *diem noctem* or *diem ac noctem* (in a very few passages). The notion that Cicero, in a serious passage like this, quoted a little tag such as *noctesque diesque* from a line of Ennius to which he refers in Cato m. 1, seems to me most improbable; particularly as Cicero himself, in translating a line of Aratus, uses the phrase (N.D. 2, 104).
   exeduntur: cf. Σέξτου γνῶμαι 4 ap. Mullach, II, p. 116 ὥσπερ δὲ σκώληξ ἀναλίσκει τὸ ξύλον ὅπου εἰσέρχεται, οὕτω καὶ ἡ ἁμαρτία μένουσα ἐν τῷ ποιήσαντι αὐτήν.
   6. **importari**: this verb when employed in a secondary sense is nearly always connected with things evil.
   ad minuendas...accessio: 'paulo minus proprie dixit, ut concinne diceret:

quanta ad augendas' (Madvig). Havet, Rev. XXIII, 118, takes other objections; some very flimsy: (1) la phrase semble terminée à potest fieri...le quanta qui arrive inopinément déroute le lecteur; (2) he strongly objects to the additional explanatory clause 'cum' and ends by supposing a gap after *molestias* and transferring *accessio potest fieri* to the end.
   8. **poena legum**: parallel to *legis beneficium, praemium*; see my n. on Acad. 2, 1.
   9. **pecuniae ... cupiditatum**: 'non prorsus accurate coniunxit cupiditates et ea quae cupiuntur' (Madvig). Just as here *pecunia* is put for *pecuniae cupiditas*, so below, 72 se in musicis, geometria, numeris, astris contereret, *astris* stands for *astrorum scientia*. And *gloria* stands often for *gloriae studium* (as Arch. 26). The subject of φιλαργυρία was largely treated by Philodemus περὶ κακιῶν (Scott, p. 72), and appears in other fragments (ib. p. 50). Epicurus himself wrote περὶ πλούτου, and there are remnants of a work by Philodemus with the same title (Us. p. 108).
   10. **neque honoris**, etc.: it is curious to find triple *neque* followed by triple *nec*. Here only does Torquatus touch on the evils of political and military ambition which Epicureans generally denounce with vigour. Cf. what Timon says of Pyrrho.
   12. **potiusque**: this form and *et p.* and *ac p.* are all used by Cicero after negatives; but not *atque p.*; though *atque* sometimes is in the same clause, followed by a vowel.
   coercendi, etc.: 2, 30 quae oratio

52 dedocendi esse videantur. Invitat igitur vera ratio bene sanos ad iustitiam, aequitatem, fidem. Neque homini infanti aut impotenti iniuste facta conducunt, qui nec facile efficere possit quod conetur, nec obtinere, si effecerit, et opes vel fortunae vel ingeni liberalitati magis conveniunt, qua qui utuntur, benivolen- 5

1 dedocendi: *docendi* E.   2 neque homini...conveniunt: Usenero haec videntur a scribis in alienum locum translata esse.   4 fortunae: *fortuna* E,   5 ingeni edd.: *ingenia* AEP.

non a philosopho aliquo, sed a censore opprimenda est; Off. 3, 73 qui non verbis sunt et disputatione philosophorum, sed vinclis et carcere dedocendi.

1. **bene**: § 71.

2. **aequitatem, fidem**: here first mentioned. Compare as regards this section De Or. 2, 342 ut opes et copiae non superbiae videantur ac libidini, sed bonitati et moderationi facultatem et materiam dedisse.

neque homini...conveniunt: I cannot agree with Usener in thinking these words out of place. They supply additional reasons for practising justice. Eloquence and wealth are needed to protect a man from the consequences of injustice; but if a man has these, he can make a better use of them. On eloquence as an aid to injustice cf. Plato, Gorg. p. 454 sq.; on wealth as a protection against the consequences of wrong see 2, 84.

infanti: = *non eloquenti*: a common enough sense, though scholars have often failed to understand it, here and elsewhere. Cf. esp. Brut. 77 Scipionem accepimus non infantem fuisse; ib. 101 historia ipsius...quae neque nimis est infans neque perfecte diserta; Att. 9, 14, 2 homo non infans, sed qui de suo illa non dicat. In the last passage I accept the fine correction of Tyrrell and Purser (*qui de suo illa* for *quis ulli*); but they, like other editors, interpret *non infans* as 'no fool,' a sense which belongs to a much later time than that of Cicero; for Att. 10, 18, 1 Hortensina omnia fuere infantia, is obviously corrupt. *Fuerunt* must be substituted for *fuere*, which Cicero did not write; the first letters of *infantia* have come from that word. Then read *fatua*. Even in Inv. 1, 4 infantes et insipientes homines, and in Varro, '*ὄνος λύρας*' (ap. Non. 55 M.) infantiorem quam meus est mulio, *infans* does not mean 'silly.' [In the latter passage the context and the other fragments of the same satire show this.]

Exx. of *infans* = *non eloquens* are rare after Cicero's time; so Quint. 11, 1, 21; Arnob. 3, 6 has one instance, imitated from Cicero. The noun *infantia* in Cicero always means 'incapacity to speak,' as several times in Quint. and Ad Her. 2, 16, not 'infancy'; much less 'childishness,' which usage is late, as in Juv. 10, 199 madidique infantia nasi. [Suet. Gram. 4 is wrongly quoted for this meaning in Dictt.]

impotenti: Cicero doubtless had in his original ἀσθενής, which often means 'poor.' This sense of *impotens* is rare; the only other instance in Cicero is Mur. 59; Terence employs *impotentia*, meaning 'poverty.' Even the meaning 'powerless' is not common; so Sall. or. Macri 3 (p. 127 Maur.) solus impotens inani specie magistratus. As to the context cf. Stob. flor. 45, 25 Ζάλευκος ὁ τῶν Λοκρῶν νομοθέτης τοὺς νόμους ἔφησε τοῖς ἀραχνίοις ὁμοίους εἶναι, ὥσπερ εἰς ἐκεῖνα ἐὰν ἐμπέσῃ μυῖα ἢ κώνωψ, κατέχεται, ἐὰν δὲ σφὴξ ἢ μέλιττα, διαρρήξασα ἀφίπταται. οὕτω καὶ εἰς τοὺς νόμους ἐὰν μὲν ἐμπέσῃ πένης συνέχεται, ἐὰν δὲ πλούσιος ἢ δυνατὸς λέγειν διαρρήξας ἀποτρέχει.

3. **qui...possit**: causal subj., to which *conetur* is assimilated.

4. **fortunae**: for the explanatory gen. cf. Tac. an. 1, 8, 7 heredum opibus (cf. our vulgar phrase, 'a wealth' of anything).

5. **liberalitati**: (cf. 2, 84) includes a generous use of talent as well as property. *Liberalitas* implies justice, being an expansion of it; the two notions are often joined by Cicero as e.g. in Off. 1, 43 nihil est...liberale quod non idem iustum. Hence the reference of *qua* in the next sentence to *liberalitate* is quite natural. [Usener thought it should refer to *iustitia* and so conjectured dislocation.]

qua qui: see my n. on Acad. 1, 6.

benivolentiam: Philod. Vol. Rhet. ed. Sudhaus, p. 60, l. 21 ἔχειν δὲ ὥσπερ τι ἐφόδιον ἐπὶ τὸν βίον ἔφασαν διὰ παντὸς

tiam sibi conciliant et, quod aptissimum est ad quiete vivendum, caritatem, praesertim cum omnino nulla sit causa peccandi. Quae **53** enim cupiditates a natura proficiscuntur, facile explentur sine ulla iniuria, quae autem inanes sunt, iis parendum non est. Nihil 5 enim desiderabile concupiscunt, plusque in ipsa iniuria detrimenti est quam in iis rebus emolumenti, quae pariuntur iniuria. Itaque ne iustitiam quidem recte quis dixerit per se ipsam optabilem, sed quia iucunditatis vel plurimum afferat. Nam diligi et carum esse iucundum est propterea, quia tutiorem vitam et voluptatum o pleniorem efficit. Itaque non ob ea solum incommoda, quae eveniunt improbis, fugiendam improbitatem putamus, sed multo etiam magis, quod, cuius in animo versatur, numquam sinit eum respirare, numquam acquiescere. Quod si ne ipsarum quidem **54** virtutum laus, in qua maxime ceterorum philosophorum ex- 5 sultat oratio, reperire exitum potest, nisi dirigatur ad volup-

---

4 non est: *non* om. A¹.   5 in ipsa iniuria: *iniuria ipsa* A.   9 voluptatum
C. F. W. Müller (vid. comm.): *voluptatem*, ita codd.   11 eveniunt: *et veniunt* AP.

αὐτὴν (sc. τὴν ῥητορικὴν) καὶ κατασκευα-
στικὴν φίλων: Plat. Rep. 351 D ἡ δὲ
δικαιοσύνη ὁμόνοιαν καὶ φιλίαν παρέχει.
On the other hand rhetoric was described by Philod. as a bulwark for the
protection of wealth (p. 235).

2. **praesertim...peccandi**: this clause
is very abruptly introduced, and the exposition from this point to the end of § 54
is in some respects disorderly; whether
the fault lies with Cicero or his source
or the copyists is hard to tell. The
words *praesertim cum...pariuntur iniuria*
hang together; but the following sentence is out of harmony with them; and
again *nam diligi...efficit* has little connexion with what immediately precedes.
The following arrangement would make
the whole context fairly consistent.
Place a full stop at *caritatem*; then let
the sentence *nam diligi...efficit* follow,
with a semicolon at *efficit*. Next should
come *praesertim cum...pariuntur iniuria*.
No proper place can be found for the
sentence *itaque...acquiescere* unless it be
made to succeed *turbulenta est* in § 50.

quae enim, etc.: nn. on § 45; and cf.
Epic. ap. Stob. flor. 17, 35 οὐ γὰρ ἡ τῆς
φύσεως ἡδονὴ τὴν ἀδικίαν ποιεῖ ἔξωθεν,
ἀλλ' ἡ περὶ τὰς κενὰς δόξας ὄρεξις. Here
probably we should read ἀπὸ τῶν ἔξωθεν,
connecting the words with ἡδονή: cf.
κυρ. δ. 39 τὸ μὴ θαρροῦν ἀπὸ τ. ἔξ.

5. **ipsa iniuria**: 'the mere fact of
wrong-doing'; cf. *hoc ipso quod adest* in
§ 50.

8. **quia...afferat**: n. on § 32. Cicero
has *propterea quia* a few times in his
philosophical works but not in his
speeches; cf. Fam. 4, 5, 1 (Sulpicius).

9. **iucundum est**: spite of two subjects, marked off by *et...et*; cf. § 66.
Torquatus here touches on the theme of
friendship, fully debated in §§ 65–70. As
justice is ἀνταπόδοσις, equivalent mutual
service, the two matters lie close
together.

voluptatum: cf. Diog. L. 10, 142 πανταχόθεν εἰσπληρουμένοις τῶν ἡδονῶν : 2,
64 vita conferta voluptatum omnium
varietate; Sest. 23 vita plena et conferta
voluptatibus; above § 41 vita doloribus
referta. With the reading *voluptatem*
cf. Sen. ep. 74 § 15 bona pleniora.

10. **incommoda**: here confined to
trouble from without, though the word
would naturally cover the internal
trouble also. For the unrest of the
φαῦλος see Lael. 92 *n.*

14. **exsultat**: for the metaphor see my
n. on Acad. 2, 112. In Cat. 2, 3 in
hoc ipso in quo exsultat et triumphat
oratio mea; above § 36 iactare vestra se
oratio.

15. **reperire exitum**: see parallels
in my n. on Acad. 2, 27; add N.D.
1, 107; Merguet, Lex. to Cicero's
Speeches s. v. *exitus* (invenio, reperio);
Varro, r. r. 2, 1, 25 exeant = *exitum
habeant*.

dirigatur: cf. 2, 115 ad voluptatem
artes direxisse.

tatem, voluptas autem est sola, quae nos vocet ad se et alliciat suapte natura, non potest esse dubium, quin id sit summum atque extremum bonorum omnium, beateque vivere nihil aliud sit nisi cum voluptate vivere.

55   XVII. Huic certae stabilique sententiae quae sint coniuncta 5 explicabo brevi. Nullus in ipsis error est finibus bonorum et

6 nullus...ignorant: vereor ne haec verba vel insiticia sint vel a scribis alieno loco posita. Cf. Usener, *Epicurea*, p. 271.

1. **sola quae**, etc.: as set forth in § 30 sq.

2. **id sit**: attraction.

5. **stabili**: § 63 stabilem scientiam rerum; 2, 71, 113.

coniuncta: the expression implies that the preceding exposition has given all that is essential to the ethical scheme of Epicurus, and that only details are left which are not of the first importance. We may compare the introduction of the topic of friendship in § 65 restat locus, etc.

6. **explicabo**: so *nunc autem explicabo* in § 37; also §§ 28, 32, 72; 3, 14; 3, 50 deinceps explicatur differentia rerum.

brevi: this may possibly point to compression of an original Epicurean source. The whole xviith chapter presents serious difficulties. The introduction of the sentence *nullus...ignorant* is exceedingly abrupt. It announces a polemic against certain persons who hold wrong notions as to the sources from which pleasure and pain arise. These are immediately declared to be *adherents of the Epicurean school itself* (*si qui e nostris aliter existimant*) and this is confirmed by a reference which Torquatus makes to a criticism by Cicero in § 25. The error of these heretics consists in not admitting that mental pleasures and pains have their ultimate source in the pleasures and pains of the body; in fact they hold that the two sets of pleasures and pains exist independently. (It does indeed happen that these heretics coincide with Aristippus, Diog. L. 2, 89.) Then the exposition seems to turn to the Cyrenaics with the words *quamquam autem* (§ 55); and their doctrine that bodily pleasure is greater than mental is controverted. Next, it is argued (against unknown objectors) that though the removal of pain *ipso facto* produces pleasure, yet the removal of pleasure does not *ipso facto* bring with it pain. Then from the beginning of § 57 to the end of the chapter the pleasures and pains of anti-cipation and memory are treated. The chapter therefore falls into these sections: (*a*) criticism of certain Epicurean heretics; (*b*) criticism of Cyrenaics; (*c*) criticism of some unknown objectors; (*d*) statement of a point in Epicurean ethics not hitherto handled, but appropriately introduced here, as naturally connected with the previous sections. There is no warrant whatever for supposing (as Usener and Hirzel do) that in the original from which Cicero drew, all these four sections formed part of a polemic against the Cyrenaics. In order to include the first section in this supposed polemic, Hirzel (II, 678) is forced to interpret *nostris* as including the Cyrenaics! And he supposes that he strengthens his position by assuming that there were many who wavered about between the school of Epicurus and that of Aristippus. [Usener ignores the difficulty of *nostris* altogether.] It is, moreover, by no means certain that Aristippus denied the ultimate connexion of all mental pleasures and pains with bodily; see Zeller, II, p. 308, 9, ed. 3. Again, it is quite impossible to suppose that the sentence *nullus... ignorant* can apply to Aristippus. See however below. There is further not the least reason for identifying with the Cyrenaics the objectors against whom defence is made in section (*c*). Epicurus held that there was no middle state between pleasure and pain, while Aristippus asserted its existence, but the controversy in the section is not between these two views; it only concerns a minor question of consistency. As to section (*d*) it is true that the Cyrenaics attributed no importance to the pleasures and pains of anticipation and memory. But this is a matter for which a place must have been found in any exposition of Epicurean ethics. Looking to the whole matter, I regard as improbable the assumption of Usener that Cicero's supposed Epicurean friend appended to his epitome of Epicurean ethics a sum-

malorum, id est in voluptate aut in dolore, sed in eis rebus peccant, cum, e quibus haec efficiantur, ignorant. Animi autem voluptates et dolores nasci fatemur e corporis voluptatibus et

2 e quibus: *ei quibus* E.

mary of the whole Epicurean polemic against Aristippus. There would be just as much reason in referring §§ 38, 39 to a polemic against Aristippus. If there had been such an appendix, one would have expected to find it, not here, but at the end of the whole exposition, just as in Diog. it comes at the end of his presentment of the Epicurean scheme. I need hardly say that I regard as unjustified the abuse aimed at Cicero by Usener merely on the strength of a baseless assumption. He practically denies to Cicero the most elementary knowledge of the views of Aristippus, which other passages abundantly prove him to have possessed.

As to the objections (Madvig and Usener) that topics are in this chapter handled which had been brought forward before, it is only what must be expected in ancient philosophy. The argument (Hirzel) from Epicurus' writings is unsound; e.g. justice is mentioned in the 17th κ. δ. and again XXXI–XXXVII.

The contention of Hirzel, Unt. II, 664, that only in the title of the book and in Acad. 2, 132, is *finis* applied to evil, is wrong.

nullus...ignorant: Usener, as proof that the sentence refers to Cyrenaics, quotes Diog. L. 2, 89 δύνασθαι δέ φασι καὶ τὴν ἡδονήν τινας μὴ αἰρεῖσθαι κατὰ διαστροφήν, which is obviously irrelevant. If, as has been supposed, this is a criticism of the Cyrenaics, it is strangely put. The difference between the ἡδονή ἐν στάσει and the ἡδονή ἐν κινήσει goes to the root of the Epicurean system and cannot have been treated as a mere difference of detail. Above, for instance, § 37, the Cyrenaic doctrine of pleasure is called an *error imperitorum*. It is further to be noticed that *in eis rebus* can hardly refer to *voluptas* and *dolor*; if so, *haec* becomes intolerably superfluous; and also there is a contradiction, for the very people who make no error about the ethical standard are said to sin in respect of it. We have thus indications that the whole sentence has been torn from its original context, so that *in eis rebus* has lost its proper reference. Not improbably, the sentence originally came

between §§ 47 and 48 (after *obligantur*). Thus *in eis rebus* means 'in connexion with such circumstances' and *peccant* is much more suitably used; cf. § 52 cum omnino nulla sit causa peccandi, but *peccare in re* of theory; 2, 32; 4, 58. Havet solves the difficulty of *haec* by supposing it to have arisen from *ecficiantur*. He condemns *iis* because it is anacoluthic (Rev. de Phil., XXIII). [The space between Müller's p. 110, l. 19 and 113, l. 2 is just about 93–94 ll., i.e. four times the 23–4 line to a page of archetype of which there are other indications. The sentence in question may have dropped out and been written in 4 pp. too late.]

finibus...dolore: see Acad. 2, 114.

2. animi voluptates: Epicurus used ἥδεσθαι, ἡδονή of the body, χαίρειν, χαρά of the mind; see Plut. n. p. suav. vivi, c. 5, p. 1089 e and Diog. L. 10, 22 τὸ κατὰ ψυχὴν χαῖρον, rendered by *laetitia* in 2, 97; cf. Tusc. 3, 41 mentis laetitia... laetantem mentem; and below 3, 1 dulcedinem corporis ex eave natam laetitiam (sc. animi). Sen. uses the phrase, ep. 78, 22; 84, 11.

3. nasci fatemur, etc.: the utterances of Epicurus and his followers concerning the relation of bodily to mental pleasure are contradictory; and their ancient critics, especially Plutarch in his tract 'non posse suaviter vivi secundum Epicurum,' pushed home vigorously the contradictions. On the one hand we are told that if sensual pleasure be removed, there is no pleasure left (n. on 2, 7); that happiness consists in the stability of bodily welfare, and the confidence that this welfare will continue (n. on 2, 92), and even that the belly is the gauge by which all pleasure must be measured (see next note); on the other hand (as here) that mental pleasure far outweighs bodily; that to be happy we must purge ourselves of bodily contamination. Plato Phaedr. 250 c καθαροὶ καὶ ἀσήμαντοι τούτου ὃ νῦν σῶμα περιφέροντες ὀνομάζομεν, and Metrodorus ap. Plut. Colot. 17, p. 1117 b ἀπαλλαγέντες ἐκ τοῦ χαμαὶ βίου εἰς τὰ Ἐπικούρου ὡς ἀληθῶς θεόφαντα ὄργια. Nearly all the information which we possess concerning the Epicurean school comes from professed opponents who doubtless passed by

doloribus; itaque concedo, quod modo dicebas, cadere causa, si qui e nostris aliter existimant, quos quidem video esse multos, sed imperitos; quamquam autem et laetitiam nobis voluptas animi et molestiam dolor afferat, eorum tamen utrumque et ortum esse e corpore et ad corpus referri, nec ob eam causam non 5 multo maiores esse et voluptates et dolores animi quam corporis. Nam corpore nihil nisi praesens et quod adest sentire possumus, animo autem et praeterita et futura. Vt enim aeque doleamus animo, cum corpore dolemus, fieri tamen permagna accessio

1 cadere causa: *cedere causae* codd. omnes; correxit Victorius.　4 afferat: *afferet* A¹E; *afferret* P et ed. Rom. (sed in P litterae *ret* ex correctione). 8 doleamus: post hoc habent codd. *animo,* quod eiecit Madv.: sed retinendum puto; vid. comm.　9 dolemus: *non dolemus* E.

much that would have served to heal over these inconsistencies. They partly disappear when we remember that to Epicurus perfect happiness means perfect peace, and that peace is only attainable by the restriction of the passions to the narrowest sphere. The ideal sage pays no more heed to the body than is merely necessary for the continuance of life. The resultant peace is a possession of the mind, as is indeed, in a certain sense, the grossest bodily pleasure. Epicurus must have seen how impossible it is to disregard the mental factor, just as he saw it in connexion with sense-perception.

nasci: cf. Acad. 2, 140 (of Epicurus) fontem omnium bonorum in corpore esse; Epic. ap. Athen. 12, p. 546 ἀρχὴ καὶ ῥίζα παντὸς ἀγαθοῦ ἡ τῆς γαστρὸς ἡδονή· καὶ τὰ σοφὰ καὶ τὰ περιττὰ ἐπὶ ταύτην ἔχει τὴν ἀναφοράν. The precise meaning of this utterance is far from certain. It does not deny that τὰ σοφὰ καὶ περιττά are ἀγαθά, but asserts that they are *somehow* dependent on the γαστήρ. It may be that γαστήρ like σάρξ was a symbol of the whole body. Naturally the opponents of Epicureanism took the text to mean that the pleasure of the belly was the sole and only pleasure; so Düning, Metrod. fragm. 47–51. Cic. in N.D. 1, 113 treats *ventre beatam vitam metiri* as the equivalent of *omnia ad voluptatem referre.* Cf. also below 2, 98, 106–107.

1. **dicebas:** in § 25, where, however, the opinion is rather implied than clearly shown.

3. **quamquam...referri:** merely a repetition of *animi...doloribus* above.

4. **eorum...utrumque:** for the neuter,

though both nouns are fem., cf. § 65 eorum utrumvis; Acad. 2, 60 *utrumque* after *ratione, auctoritate*; ib. 2, 138 and n. on 3, 48.

5. **corpore,** etc.: so Tusc. 5, 96 (of Epicurus) corpus gaudere tam diu, dum praesentem sentiret voluptatem, animum et praesentem percipere pariter cum corpore, et prospicere venientem nec praeteritam praeterfluere sinere. Ita perpetuas et contextas voluptates in sapiente fore semper, cum expectatio speratarum voluptatum cum perceptarum memoria iungeretur.

nec...corporis: the opposite view was held by the Cyrenaics, Diog. L. 10, 137; ib. 2, 90. Usener says that Cicero coupled this doctrine with the preceding 'inepte,' but he gives no reasons for his opinion. The two statements seem to me to cohere very naturally: (1) that all mental pleasures and pains are referable to the body; (2) that *nevertheless,* mental pleasures and pains are intenser than bodily. Cf. Philod. V. H.² 7, 177 μυρίῳ μείζονα τὰ ψυχικὰ τῶν ἄλλων ὑπάρχειν. Democritus in the same way sets mental enjoyment above corporeal (fragm. 3–7, 17).

7. **praesens et quod adest:** the same pleonasm in Off. 1, 11; Tusc. 4, 14; Ter. Ad. 393 ades praesens; Plaut. Amph. 977.

8. **et praeterita:** possibly *etiam* should be read.

ut enim, etc.: Madvig (bracketing *animo*) calls it *vocem suppositiciam.* I venture to think this note mistaken; by introducing the words *non maiorem, non minus,* Madvig has confused the issue. In Tusc. 5, 96 it is said 'animum et praesentem (voluptatem) percipere pariter cum corpore.' Exactly similarly it may

potest, si aliquod aeternum et infinitum impendere malum nobis opinemur. Quod idem licet transferre in voluptatem, ut ea maior sit, si nihil tale metuamus. Iam illud quidem perspicuom est, **56** animi maximam aut voluptatem aut molestiam plus aut ad 5 beatam aut ad miseram vitam afferre momenti quam eorum utrumvis, si aeque diu sit in corpore. Non placet autem detracta voluptate aegritudinem statim consequi, nisi in voluptatis locum dolor forte successerit; at contra gaudere nosmet omittendis doloribus, etiamsi voluptas ea, quae sensum moveat, nulla o successerit; eoque intellegi potest quanta voluptas sit non dolere.

4 ad: om. E (bis).   6 utrumvis: *utriusque utrumvis* ed. Rom.

be said, 'aeque dolemus animo, cum (*whenever*) corpore dolemus.' Put this as a concession with *ut* and we have the words in the text. Madvig's interpretation of *cum* is surely perverse.

1. **si...opinemur**: the most extreme specimen is given of the addition to pain which the mind can make and it is one which does not closely correspond to the circumstances just mentioned. From the context *ut*, 'for instance,' might have been expected to introduce the illustration. Cf. the Herculanean Roll, no. 26, in Scott, p. 214, where men and animals are compared, and it is said that the ταραχή of men is greater, 'αἰώνια δεινὰ προσδοκώντων.' In the same treatise (p. 226) it is argued that the fear of death is in reality part and parcel of the dread of the gods. (In the next section it is forgotten that οἴησις may lead to reasonless exaltation as well as to reasonless depression.)

aliquod: for this after *si* see Reisig-Haase (ed. Landgraf) n. 355. The difference between *si quod* and *si aliquod* is just that between 'if any' and 'if some.'

2. **quod idem**: cf. 3, 24, 44.

3. **iam illud...in corpore**: this is in the main a re-statement of the doctrine put forward just above. The two presentments of it differ in these respects: (1) above, the case of pain or pleasure *simultaneously* affecting mind and body is considered; here the case of mind and body being affected by a pain or a pleasure *for equal periods of time* not *at the same time*; (2) the words *si aliquod ...metuamus* are now summed up in the one word *maximam*; (3) the bearing of the case contemplated upon the whole happiness or misery of life is now considered. The distinctions between the two presentments are not fundamental,

but they are sufficient to prevent the re-statement from being looked upon as mere repetition. In the second passage, it may be noted (as sometimes in the *Philebus*) the language implies the possibility of the body being affected entirely apart from the mind, and *vice versa*.

perspicuom: this is not an appeal to popular or general opinion, as Hirzel says; rather Torquatus conveys that the fact has been made clear by his exposition. This is the regular use of the clause *iam illud perspicuom est*, for which see my n. on Acad. 2, 132. The words *eoque...non dolere* are certainly rather loose, especially *quanta*, but the Epicurean use of language is not looser on the whole than that of other ancient philosophical writers, even the greatest. But no exposition of a system can absolutely avoid the repetition of topics, and the incoherence of this sentence with what precedes, on which Madvig insists, is very slight. When speaking of the effect which pleasures and pains of body and mind have on happiness, it was not unnatural to caution against supposing that the moment bodily pleasure vanishes, unhappiness ensues.

6. **non placet**, etc.: we have certainly (as Madvig objects) had this doctrine before (§ 38).

7. **voluptate**: here evidently = *v. quae sensum moveat*, not the ἡδονὴ ἐν στάσει. The repetition *voluptate...voluptatis* should be noticed. Cf. 2, 33.

aegritudinem: πόνον.

8. **successerit**: perf. subj. as in § 22 putat sublatum esse si probatum sit.

omittendis: this word can scarcely be right; *omittere* implies the rejection of something desirable, as in § 36 ut voluptates omittantur.

57 Sed ut eis bonis erigimur, quae exspectamus, sic laetamur eis quae recordamur. Stulti autem malorum memoria torquentur, sapientes bona praeterita grata recordatione renovata delectant. Est autem situm in nobis ut et adversa quasi perpetua oblivione obruamus et secunda iucunde ac suaviter meminerimus. Sed 5 cum ea quae praeterierunt, acri animo et attento intuemur, tum fit ut aegritudo sequatur, si illa mala sint, laetitia, si bona. XVIII. O praeclaram beate vivendi et apertam et simplicem et directam vitam! Cum enim certe nihil homini possit melius esse quam vacare omni dolore et molestia perfruique 1 maximis et animi et corporis voluptatibus, videtisne, quam

5 secunda: secula E.

nulla: cf. my n. on Cat. m. 74.

eoque: qy. *ex eoque* (3, 16 ex quo intellegi debet) and 1 § 48.

1. **erigimur:** as in Acad. 2, 127 and Cato m. 82 = ἐπαιρόμεθα: i.e. we who are wise; cf. *stulti autem.*

2. **stulti:** the stock phrase for the unenlightened.

3. **grata:** 'thankful'; the Epicurean writings contained many denunciations of unphilosophic men as thankless for the good things which nature spreads forth for us. Cf. Sen. ben. 3, 4, 1 Epicuro...qui assidue queritur quod adversus praeterita simus ingrati; id. ep. 15, 10 (from Epicurus) stulta vita ingrata est et trepida; Lucr. 3, 935 nam grato si (so I read for *gratis*, which is unintelligible) anteacta fuit tibi vita priorque | et non omnia pertusum congesta quasi in vas | commoda perfluxere atque ingrata interiere: | cur non ut plenus vitae conviva recedis | aequo animoque capis securam, stulte, quietem? | Sin ea quae fructus cumque es periere profusa | vitaque in offensast, cur amplius addere quaeris | rursum quod pereat male et ingratum occidat omne? Ib. 1003; ib. 5, 43 at nisi purgatumst pectus, quae proelia nobis | atque pericula tumst ingratis insinuandum! Here *ingratis* is an adjective in agreement with *nobis*, not an adverb. The same is the case with 6, 15 atque animi ingratis vitam vexare sine ulla pausa. The Herculanean roll no. 1414 has preserved fragments of the work of Philodemus περὶ χάριτος; and the word χάρις is of frequent occurrence in other fragments, as roll 157 (ed. by Scott), fragm. 69, 70 p. 130; add the Vatican γνῶμαι § 69 τὸ τῆς ψυχῆς ἀχάριστον λίχνον ἐποίησε τὸ ζῷον εἰς ἄπειρον τῶν ἐν

διαίτῃ ποικιλμάτων: § 75 εἰς τὰ παρῳχηκότα ἀγαθὰ ἀχάριστος φωνὴ ἡ λέγουσα 'τέλος ὅρα μακροῦ βίου': Plut. non posse, etc. c. 7, p. 1091 *b* τὴν τοῦ ἀγαθοῦ φύσιν ἐξ αὐτῆς τῆς φυγῆς τοῦ κακοῦ καὶ τῆς μνήμης καὶ ἐπιλογίσεως καὶ χάριτος...γεννᾶσθαι. One of the works of Epic. in Diog. L. is περὶ δώρων καὶ χάριτος.

4. **est situm in nobis:** 'it depends upon our wills'; so 2, 89 and 5, 12 and often elsewhere; also est, non est in nostra potestate, as in Tusc. 3, 35, where this doctrine of Epicurus is attacked.

et...et...ac: cf. et, et, que in 2, 100.

oblivione ob.: so 2, 105; *quasi*, 'almost,' as often with numbers. Cf. Reisig-Haase (ed. Landgraf) n. 415 *i.*

5. **iucunde ac suaviter:** the only distinction between these two adverbs is, as Madvig says, that the former has the wider scope.

meminerimus: Aristippus insisted 'οὐδὲ κατὰ μνήμην τῶν ἀγαθῶν, ἢ προσδοκίαν, ἡδονὴν ἀποτελεῖσθαι...ἐκλύεσθαι γὰρ τῷ χρόνῳ τὸ τῆς ψυχῆς κίνημα' (Diog. L. 2, 89, 90). Plutarch argues (non posse, etc., cc. 4 sq.) that the memory of pleasure is no more than a sort of aroma (ὀσμή), the chief effect of which will be to stimulate to the repetition of the active pleasure. [Cf. Orosius, Hist. IV, praef.]

7. **aegritudo:** the mode in which Epicurus treated this topic is dwelt on in Tusc. 3, 28–35 (where notice the reference to the Cyrenaics).

11. **videtisne:** here *ne* = *nonne*, as often; see Acad. 2 §§ 11, 75, 116.

quam nihil p.: so Att. 9, 2 *a*, 1 quam nihil praetermittis. *Quam n.* is fairly common, *tam nihil* rare and not Ciceronian (Persius, 1, 122).

nihil praetermittatur, quod vitam adiuvet, quo facilius id, quod propositum est, summum bonum consequamur? Clamat Epicurus, is quem vos nimis voluptatibus esse deditum dicitis, non posse iucunde vivi, nisi sapienter, honeste iusteque vivatur, 5 nec sapienter, honeste, iuste, nisi iucunde. Neque enim civitas **58** in seditione beata esse potest nec in discordia dominorum domus; quo minus animus a se ipse dissidens secumque discordans gustare partem ullam liquidae voluptatis et liberae potest. Atqui pugnantibus et contrariis studiis consiliisque semper utens nihil 10 quieti videre, nihil tranquilli potest. Quod si corporis gravioribus **59** morbis vitae iucunditas impeditur, quanto magis animi morbis impediri necesse est! Animi autem morbi sunt cupiditates

---

2 consequamur: *prosequamur* E.   3 vos: om. P et ed. Rom.   7 discordans: *dicordans* A.   8 atqui: *atque* Orelli.   10 tranquilli: fortasse excidit *cernere*.   11 vitae iucunditas...animi morbis: om. E.   12 necesse est: *necesse potest* A (sed *necesse* prima manus indicat delendum esse).

1. **praetermittatur**: the tense seems to indicate that the exposition is not yet at an end.

   quo: not conjunction, but abl. neut.; see n. on § 41.

2. **clamat**: so 2, 51; 5, 93 and often; cf. *vociferari* in Lucret.

4. **non posse**, etc.: see n. on § 42; and cf. Baton comicus (Us. § 427).

   iusteque: for *que* see N.D. 2, 99. Possibly here it should be struck out, as it is not found immediately after. In 2, 51 honeste et sapienter et iuste.

6. **seditione**, etc.: cf. § 44.

   dominorum: the passions; Lucr. 5, 87; 6, 63 acres dominos; Sen. ep. 37, 4.

   dominorum domus: Ihering, Geist d. Röm. Rechts, II, p. 215, shows that the Romans connected in their minds the words *domus, dominus, dominium*; cf. Enn. ap. Off. 1, 139 o domus antiqua, heu quam dispari | dominare domino!

7. **quo minus**:=*et eo minus*; Madv. qu. Fat. 33 ne praeterita quidem ea, quorum nulla signa...exstarent, Apollini nota esse censebat; quo minus futura. So, too, Lucret. 4, 206 quone vides citius debere...ire is equivalent to *eone citius*, etc. rather than *videsne quanto*, etc. (as Munro explains).

   animus...dissidens: there is much talk of this internal στάσις in the Republic of Plato; but no passage is imitated here, as Usener supposes, who points to 352 a. For the comparison was trite, e.g. Rep. 1, 60; Lael. 23; above, § 44.

   a se ipse: cf. 3, 1; Acad. 2, 36.

   dissidens...discordans: so § 44; these

are, I think, the only two instances of *discordare* in Cicero.

8. **gustare**: so often; cf. Fam. 12, 23, 3 nullam partem sanae et salvae rei publicae gustare potuisti.

   liquidae: ἀκεραίου, as often in Epicurean texts; cf. Lucr. 3, 40 neque ullam | esse voluptatem liquidam puramque relinquit. *Liberae* is ἀνεμποδίστου.

   atqui: Madvig combats the proposal to read *atque*, saying that we have the common use of the word as attached to the minor premiss of a syllogism, which he thus sets forth: 'animus a se dissidens beatus esse non potest; atqui animus pugnantibus studiis utens, quod facit, si non honeste sapienterque vivit, non est tranquillus et a se dissidet; ergo animus non honestus non est beatus.' In a great many places *atque* at the beginning of a sentence, introducing a new point like *et*, has been needlessly altered to *atqui* by editors; so in Att. 13, 31, 3; Fam. 5, 12, 7; 10, 14, 1; Qu. Fr. 2, 4, 7 [cf. 2, 34; Flacc. 41 Du M.]. C. F. W. Müller refers to Lehmann in Jahresb. d. phil. Vereins, 1888, p. 259.

10. **quod si...quanto**: the same form in 3, 5 and elsewhere.

11. **animi morbis**: see 3, 35 *n.*; medical metaphors applied to the soul are of course widespread. So Diog. L. 10, 122 ὑγίεια τῆς ψυχῆς: Vat. γνῶμαι § 64 δεῖ...ἡμᾶς γενέσθαι περὶ τὴν ἡμῶν ἰατρείαν: Hor. s. 2, 3, 77 sq. quisquis | ambitione mala aut argenti pallet amore, | quisquis luxuria tristive superstitione | aut alio mentis morbo calet.

immensae et inanes divitiarum, gloriae, dominationis, libidino-
sarum etiam voluptatum. Accedunt aegritudines, molestiae,
maerores, qui exedunt animos conficiuntque curis hominum non
intellegentium nihil dolendum esse animo, quod sit a dolore
corporis praesenti futurove seiunctum. Nec vero quisquam stultus 5
non horum morborum aliquo laborat; nemo igitur *stultus* non
60 miser. Accedit etiam mors, quae quasi saxum Tantalo semper
impendet, tum superstitio, qua qui est imbutus, quietus esse
numquam potest. Praeterea bona praeterita non meminerunt,
praesentibus non fruuntur, futura modo exspectant, quae quia 10
certa esse non possunt, conficiuntur et angore et metu maxime-
que cruciantur, cum sero sentiunt frustra se aut pecuniae
studuisse aut imperiis aut opibus aut gloriae. Nullas enim con-

1 inanes cod. Vat.; *immanes* EP; *inmanes* A.   1 dominationis: ita P²; *-es* AEP¹.
3 exedunt: *excedunt* E.   3 animos: *nos* P et ed. Rom.   4 a dolore: *adere* A¹;
adore A² (ex *do^{re}* pro *dolore*; vid. Cappelli, *Dizionario di abbreviature* (Milan, 1899),
p. 94.   6 stultus: *est* codd.; corr. Baiter.   7 etiam: om. Nonius (p. 324 Merc.).
8 impendet: *impendit* E.   8 qua qui: *quia qui* Nonius (om. *superstitio*).
12 pecuniae: *pecuniis* E.

1. **inanes**: so, of *cupiditates* in §§ 45,
53; 2, 26, and Tusc. 5, 93. Madvig calls
immensae et immanes 'nimium ac paene
ridiculum,' saying that *ingens et immanis* (Verr.) is an expression of another
type. But the reading *immanes* derives
some support from the peculiar use of
the word θηριώδης in Epicurean texts,
for which see n. on § 61 *monstrosi*.

divitiarum: Vat. γνῶμαι § 43 φιλαρ-
γυρεῖν ἄδικα μὲν ἀσεβές, δίκαια δὲ αἰσχρόν.
ἁπρεπὲς γὰρ ῥυπαρῶς φείδεσθαι καὶ μετὰ
τοῦ δικαίου.

3. **exedunt**: § 51; Tusc. 3, 27. Holstein's suspicion that *conficiuntque curis*
has sprung from a gloss on *exedunt* is
not unnatural, but it is not cogent.

5. **praesenti futurove**: see nn. on § 55
and cf. Epictet. d. 3, 7, 9 ἐπὶ τοῖς σωματι-
κοῖς ἥδεσθαι τὴν κατὰ ψυχὴν ἡδονήν.

seiunctum: so 2, 20; 3, 71; 4, 43.

6. **nemo igitur...non miser**: a Stoic
doctrine also; see 3, 61 and Zeller, Stoics,
p. 270; and for the omission of *est* cf.
§ 13.

7. **accedit**: after *accedunt* above.

saxum Tantalo: this form of the
punishment of Tantalus appears in
Pind. Ol. 1, 90 and Isthm. 8, 20; Eur.
Or. 5; and often elsewhere in the poets;
see Tusc. 4, 35; and cf. Lucret. 3, 980 nec
miser impendens magnum timet aere
saxum | Tantalus, ut fama est, cassa
formidine torpens; | sed magis in vita

divom metus urget inanis | mortalis,
casumque timent quem cuique ferat fors.

8. **imbutus**: this word has a weak
and a strong meaning, 'tinged' and
'soaked'; for the former cf. Hortens.
fragm. 23, which is very like Sen. ep.
71 § 31, but he contrasts *colorare* with
inficere; Tusc. 1, 14 an tu dialecticis ne
imbutus quidem es? and for the latter
Fin. 2, 16 extorquere ex animis cognitiones verborum, quibus imbuti
sumus. The phrases *imbui superstitione, religione* are common. Cf. Hor.
ep. 1, 6, 5 (an Epicurean passage)
formidine nulla imbuti; Sen. ep. 36, 3
perfundi, tingui; d. 12, 17, 4, where
eruditi is much stronger than *imbui*.

10. **praesentibus**: Vat. γνῶμαι § 35 οὐ
δεῖ λυμαίνεσθαι τὰ παρόντα τῶν ἀπόντων
ἐπιθυμίᾳ, ἀλλ' ἐπιλογίζεσθαι ὅτι καὶ
ταῦτα τῶν εὐκταίων ἦν.

modo: 'merely'=οὐδὲν ἄλλο ἤ: cf.
Epic. ap. Sen. ep. 15, 10 stulta vita...
tota in futurum fertur; cf. § 62 pendet
ex futuris.

11. **non possunt**: from the point of
view of the *stultus*; the *sapiens* has
πιστὸν ἔλπισμα (Plut., non posse, etc.
4, 1089 d).

12. **sero sentiunt**: cf. the proverb *sero
sapiunt Phryges*. Otto, Sprichwörter,
p. 278.

13. **studuisse**: Nägelsbach, § 177, p. 572,
ed. 7.

secuntur voluptates, quarum potiendi spe inflammati multos labores magnosque susceperant. Ecce autem alii minuti et 61 angusti aut omnia semper desperantes aut malevoli, invidi, difficiles, lucifugi, maledici, monstrosi, alii autem etiam amatoriis

2 alii: *mali* Nonius, p. 345. 2 minuti: *inimici* E. 3 invidi: *aut invidi* ed. Rom.
4 monstrosi: *monstruosi* Nonius: *morosi* Lamb., quod commendat Madvig.

1. **quarum potiendi spe**: the analogy of passages like 5, 19 (below) eorum... adipiscendi causa and Phil. 5, 6 facultas agrorum condonandi makes it probable that *quarum* is not the ordinary genitive which follows, directly governed by *potiendi*. Much has been written about the origin of the construction in which a genitive of the gerund appears, as here, with another gen. plural in connexion. Madvig denounces those who hold that in *spe potiendi, facultas condonandi*, etc. the two words coalesce to form a single notion, on which thereafter the plural gen. depends; and indeed the explanation, when tested by application to many of the examples, comes to seem forced and unnatural. Yet there are some to which it applies well enough, as to Acad. 2, 128 omnium rerum una est definitio comprehendendi; and analogies may be found in such uses as in Att. 2, 5, 1 ab hac hominum satietate nostri. Madvig's own view is that the construction lies midway between the true gerund construction and the true gerundive construction and that *facultas agrorum condonandi* was a compromise, to avoid 'molestiam terminationis longioris et insuavioris repetendae.' Another theory is that of Reisig, in accordance with which we have two parallel genitives both dependent on the same noun. He brings into comparison passages like Dem. Olynth. 2, p. 19 τού- των οὐχὶ νῦν ὁρῶ τὸν καιρὸν τοῦ λέγειν, put for τοῦ λέγειν ταῦτα. A fourth elucidation is possible, viz. to make the construction a case of double genitive so that the gen. of the noun depends directly on the gen. of the gerund. Madvig insists on the necessity of treating phrases like Caes. B.G. 4, 13 venerunt...sui purgandi causa (which contain a possessive pronoun) separately; in them he says *sui*, *mei*, etc. is neut. sing.; this he deduces from the fact that phrases such as *sui purgandorum causa* are unknown. Thus *sui purgandi causa=suae rei purgandae c.* It is, however, highly improbable that *sui* here was realised by the Latins as anything but a gen. plur.

2. **ecce autem**: this form of transition is common in Cicero; also in Livy and many other writers; *ecce enim* occurs once in a speech of Cicero; *sed ecce* two or three times; *ecce iam* is rare and late. See Köhler in Archiv 5, p. 16 sq.

minuti: the writer of the anonymous treatise, Vol. Herc. 1055 (given by Scott, p. 251) contrasts the διαθέσεις ὀργίλας καὶ μεικραιτίους with the διαθέσεις παντὸς τοῦ ταπεινοῦ περιφρονούσας. *Minutus* and *angustus* are joined in De Or. 3, 121; and Cicero several times applies *minutus* to persons, as Cato m. 85 m. philosophi (of the Epicureans). For the use of the word cf. my n. on Acad. 2, 75, and add Petron. 44 populus m.; Pl. Cas. 311 (ed. Ussing) minutos deos. As to the context Madvig writes 'recte Matthiaeus duo genera minuti animi notari docet, alterum positum in timiditate quadam et desperatione, alterum in invidia et morum difficultate.'

3. **omnia desp.**: ἀπονενοημένοι: cf. Usen. § 488 ἡ ταπεινὴ ψυχὴ τοῖς μὲν εὐημερήμασιν ἐχαυνώθη, ταῖς δὲ συμφοραῖς καθηρέθη.

invidi: Vat. γνῶμαι § 53 οὐδενὶ φθονη- τέον· ἀγαθοὶ γὰρ οὐκ ἄξιοι φθόνου, πονηροὶ δὲ ὅσῳ ἂν μᾶλλον εὐτυχῶσι, τοσούτῳ μᾶλλον αὐτοῖς λυμαίνονται. In Vol. Herc. No. 26 (Scott, p. 211) ἐπιχαιρεκακία is mentioned; there was evidently a large Epicurean literature devoted to the treatment of the vices. Thus roll no. 1008 has the title Φιλο- δήμου περὶ κακιῶν and 1470 (Scott, p. 40) Φιλοδήμου τῶν κατ' ἐπιτομὴν ἐξειργασ- μένων περὶ ἠθῶν καὶ βίων ἐκ τοῦ Ζήνωνος σχολῶν ὅ ἐστι περὶ παρρησίας.

4. **lucifugi**: the word occurs here only in Cicero, and is rare elsewhere. In Lucil. 340 (ed. Baehrens) it is joined with *nebulo*; Virg. G. 4, 243 applies it to *blatta*; cf. Min. Fel. 8, 4 vita latebrosa et lucifuga; Rutil. Namat. 1, 440 speaks of the island of Capraria as full of *lucifugi* (monks). [The expression *Lucretiano adiectivo* in Madvig's n. is an error for *Luciliano*.] There is also *luci- fuga*, applied to persons by Sen. ep. 122, 15, and by Ammianus, Appuleius and others; and I would read *lucifugas* for

levitatibus dediti, alii petulantes, alii audaces, protervi, idem

1 alii petulantes: *alii appetendo omnia petulantes* ed. Colon.   1 protervi...
ignavi: fortasse legendum est *protervi idem intemperantesque et ignavi.*

lucrifugas in Plaut. Pseud. 1131 Venus mihi haec bona dat, quom hos huc adigit | lucrifugas, damni cupidos, where *lucrifugas* is a weak doubling of *damni cupidos.* The words *lucifugus lucifuga* are slang formations like Hesiod's ἡμερόκοιτος for a housebreaker, which Plautus represents by *dormitator*; cf. too Corp. Gloss. Lat. 2, p. 60 emansores ἀπόκοιτοι λῆσται. There are a good many words of the same stamp. So *tenebrio* (Afranius, Varro ap. Non. 18, 27); with which compare *tenebrae*=‘a low haunt,’ in Catull. 55, 2 demonstres ubi sint tuae tenebrae, and Varro, Men. sat. fr. 435 (ed. Büch.). Then *nebulo*, for which we have an explanation by Aelius Stilo: ‘dictus est qui non pluris est quam nebula, aut qui non facile perspici potest’; rather, ‘the man under a cloud.’ So, too, *lustro Naevius nubilo* in Hildebr. gl. Paris. p. 220 (I see no reason for questioning the word as W. Meyer does in Archiv 5, p. 226); *vapio* in C.I.L. 9, 6089, 6, related to *vappa*, ‘the man of smoke,’ whom Hor. s. 1, 1, 104 joins with *nebulo*; further, Paul. ex F. p. 75 (s.v. Elucum) halonem, id est hesterno vino languentem; and the names *vesperones, vespillones* are of the same type. Querolus ed. Peiper, p. 21, l. 18 ubinam illa est cohors fuliginosa vulcanosa atra (thieves).

monstrosi: I have no doubt that Cicero is here rendering the word θηριώδεις; cf. Epicur. ap. Marc. 29, p. 209, 5 (Us. § 480) ἐξ ἐργασίας θηριώδους (so Nauck) οὐσίας μὲν πλῆθος σωρεύεται, βίος δὲ ταλαίπωρος συνίσταται: Arist. Pol. 5 (8), 1338 b, 12 (of Spartans) θηριώδεις ἀπεργάζονται τοῖς πόνοις: Eth. N. 7, 1145 a, 30. There is no adjective better suited to render θηριώδης, since there is none connected with *bestia, fera, animal*, while *monstrum* (like *portentum*) is often applied to persons. The frequent occurrence in our MSS. of *monstruosus* has led some scholars to regard that as the true form (so Seyffert-Müller's ed. of Laelius, p. 432, and Usener, p. 273 n., but Seyffert was wrong in saying that Nonius here had *monstrosus*). It seems to me more probable that *monstruosus* has sprung from the late form *monstruum*, which occurs in glosses, as in Corp. Gloss. Lat. 5, p. 466; see also

Weyman in Archiv 9, 138. Weyman writes, ib. 5, 192 sq., about the whole class of adjectives in *-osus. Monstrosus* does not occur in classical verse, but Virgil has *montosus* once, and Statius once. *Montuosus* probably followed the analogy of *monstruosus*; if these forms were really classical, we should have to suppose that they were produced by analogy with *portuosus* and the like. As to *morosi*, it is joined with *difficiles* in Orat. 104 and Cato m. 65. [Hirzel's supposition that Cicero was rendering τερατολόγος is improbable.]

autem etiam: the particles come together often, as above, § 16; below, 2, 113; 5 §§ 35, 55, 63.

amatoriis l.: in the course of a description of the σοφός Diog. L. 10, 118 says: σοφὸς οὐκ ἐρασθήσεται: also that ἔρως is not θεόπεμπτος: then συνουσία δέ, φασίν, ὤνησε μὲν οὐδέποτε· ἀγαπητὸν δὲ εἰ μὴ καὶ ἔβλαψεν (from Diogenes). So Hermias in Plat. Phaedr. p. 76 οἱ μὲν γὰρ ὑπέλαβον ἁπλῶς φαῦλον τὸ ἐρᾶν, ὡς Ἐπίκουρος. More to the same effect in Usener § 483. One of the works of Epicurus in the list of Diog. L. is entitled περὶ ἔρωτος. For the Stoic view of ἔρως see n. on 3, 68.

1. **petulantes...audaces, protervi:** Madvig regards all these words as explanatory of *amat. lev. dediti*, and is probably right. *Petulantes* (a far stronger word than the English one derived from it) befits ἔρως: cf. Lucr. 5, 47 quidve superbia spurcitia ac petulantia? Lucil. 6, 4 (L. Müller) nequitia occupat hos, petulantia prodigitasque (*nequitia* is of course a *vox amatoria*); Cicero, Phil. 3, 35 libidinosis petulantibus impuris impudicis; Cael. 50; Font. 40; Phil. 3, 28; Anth. Lat. 1, 362 (Riese) petulans pariterque insanus amator; ib. 358; Ov. Her. 16, 245; Ausonius, Cento defending himself against a charge of indecency, quotes Martial, Pliny, Sulpicia, Appuleius, Plato and Cicero, of whom he says ‘in praeceptis Ciceronis exstare severitatem, in epistulis ad Caerelliam subesse petulantiam.’ In Cat. 2, 25 *pudor* and *petulantia* are contrasted, and the Schol. Gron. explains *petulans* est ex animo, ex moribus; *impudicus* ex corpore. Also Corp. Gl. where see also *petulantia.*

idem...ignavi: Davies objects to the

intemperantes et ignavi, numquam in sententia permanentes,
quas ob causas in eorum vita nulla est intercapedo molestiae.
Igitur neque stultorum quisquam beatus neque sapientium non
beatus. Multoque hoc melius nos veriusque quam Stoici. Illi
5 enim negant esse bonum quicquam nisi nescio quam illam
umbram, quod appellant honestum non tam solido quam
splendido nomine; virtutem autem nixam hoc honesto nullam
requirere voluptatem atque ad beate vivendum se ipsa esse
contentam.
10 XIX. Sed possunt haec quadam ratione dici non modo non **62**
repugnantibus, verum etiam approbantibus nobis. Sic enim ab
Epicuro sapiens semper beatus inducitur: finitas habet cupidi-

12 beatus: om. P et ed. Rom.

same men being called *audaces* and
ignavi; but the latter word is by no
means restricted to the cowardly; it
implies here general worthlessness.
1. **numquam...permanentes**: the fool
has ἀκρισία καὶ ταραχή (κυρ. δόξα 22);
he cannot attain to εὐστάθεια τῆς γνώμης
(cf. εὐσταθεῖν κατὰ διάνοιαν, Schol. on
Il. 5, 2) or certa stabilisque sententia
(§ 55). Cf. § 40.
2. **intercapedo**: a word rare in Cicero;
Fam. 16, 21, 1. *Capudo*, which occurs in
Rep. 6, 2 and Parad. 11 has nothing to
do with this. Cf. however Corp. Gloss.
vi s.v. *capedo* where it is given as inter
parietem spatium, etc.
3. **igitur**: Quint. 1, 5, 39 an sit
'igitur' initio sermonis positum, dubi-
tari potest, quia maximos auctores in
diversa fuisse opinione video, cum apud
alios sit etiam frequens, apud alios
numquam reperiatur. Cicero often
places the word at the beginning
of a sentence or clause. The variations in the use of *igitur* are well
illustrated by Wölfflin in Archiv 3,
560. Probably Caesar avoided the word
altogether.
sapientium, etc.: see nn. on 5, 80. As
Epicurus held the doctrine 'once a
σοφός, always a σοφός' (Diog. L. 10, 117)
it follows that from the first moment of
attaining to wisdom to the end of life,
nothing can destroy happiness. Yet the
gods alone (Diog. L. 10, 121) have happiness absolute and incapable of increase.
4. **Stoici**: cf. Sen. ep. 85, 18 Epicurus quoque iudicat, cum virtutem
habeat, beatum esse, sed ipsam virtutem non satis esse ad beatam vitam,

quia beatam efficiat voluptas quae ex
virtute esset, non ipsa virtus.
6. **umbram**, etc.: for the Stoic τὸ
καλόν *honestum* see 3, 14. Torquatus
here speaks as though ἀρετή and τὸ καλόν
were distinguished by the Stoics; but
that is not so. Madvig's distinction that
the one phrase indicates virtue sub-
jectively, the other virtue objectively
considered, is not verifiable.
7. **nomine**: n. on § 42, and on 2,
48.
10. **quadam ratione**: n. on § 32 ratione.
12. **sapiens semper beatus**: a short
title for the doctrine, resembling the
short titles of 'controversiae' in
rhetorical writers; e.g. 'pater raptam
continens' (Seneca); 'tyrannicida volens
dedi' (ps.-Quint.).
inducitur: Acad. 2, 99 is quoque qui
a vobis sapiens inducitur; there is a
reference to *inducere*, 'to bring on the
stage.' The ideal picture that follows
keeps close to the lines of Epicurus in
ep. ad Menoeceum § 133.
finitas...cupiditates: to be wise we
must learn 'τὸ πέρας τῶν ἐπιθυμιῶν'
(κυρ. δ. 10); or 'τοὺς ὅρους τῶν ἀλγηδόνων
καὶ τῶν ἐπιθυμιῶν' (ib. 11); or τὰ πέρατα
τοῦ βίου (ib. 21); cf. Lucr. 6, 25 (of
Epic.) finem statuit cuppedinis atque
timoris; Hor. ep. 1, 2, 56 certum voto
pete finem (the whole context of the
passage is from Epicurean sources);
above § 45 inanium cupiditatum nec
modus nec finis. Porphyr. de abst. 1, 53
ἀοριστεῖν γὰρ οὐδαμοῦ δεῖ ἀλλ' ἔχεσθαι
ὅρου καὶ μέτρου. The wise man has
αὐτάρκεια: cf. Diog. L. 10, 130: 'πλου-
σιώτατον αὐτάρκεια πάντων' was a saying
of Epic.; see Usener § 476.

tates, neglegit mortem, de dis immortalibus sine ullo metu vera
sentit, non dubitat, si ita melius sit, migrare de vita. His rebus
instructus semper est in voluptate. Neque enim tempus est
ullum, quo non plus voluptatum habeat quam dolorum. Nam
et praeterita grate meminit et praesentibus ita potitur, ut 5
animadvertat, quanta sint ea quamque iucunda, neque pendet
ex futuris, sed exspectat illa, fruitur praesentibus ab eisque vitiis,
quae paulo ante collegi, abest plurimum et, cum stultorum vitam
cum sua comparat, magna afficitur voluptate; dolores autem si
qui incurrunt, numquam vim tantam habent ut non plus habeat 10
63 sapiens, quod gaudeat, quam quod angatur. Optime vero
Epicurus, quod exiguam dixit fortunam intervenire sapienti,

1 neglegit: *nec legit* A¹E.   6 quanta: fort. *quanti.*   6 sint ea: *sint in ea* A²E;
sit in ea A¹B.

1. **neglegit mortem:** §§ 40, 49. There
is an interesting passage of Polystratos
περὶ ἀλόγου φρονήσεως (Gomperz in
Hermes, 11, p. 406), where a Stoic (or
Cynic) says, in reference to the quietism
of Epicurus, that his school also has
that in view. The answer made by the
Epicurean is that the Stoic or Cynic
gives men no practical aid towards
attaining the end.
   de dis: Torquatus touches very
lightly on the dread of the gods, which
fills so large a space in the poem of
Lucretius. In § 41 neque divinum numen
horreat; so § 51; § 60 superstitio.
   2. **si ita melius sit:** probably *sit* has
sapiens for its subject; cf. the common
phrases *fui libenter*.
   migrare de vita: see § 49; and cf.
Vat. γνῶμαι § 38 οἰκτρὸς παντάπασιν ᾧ
πολλαὶ αἰτίαι εὔλογοι εἰς ἐξαγωγὴν βίου
(directed against the Stoic εὔλογος
ἐξαγωγή, for which see n. on 3, 60, 61).
Migrare de occurs here only in Cicero;
possibly, in classical Latin, here only
and Juv. 15, 152; *m. a* is also rare
(Hor. ep. 2, 1, 187; Juv. 11, 51). Some
authors, as Caesar, Tacitus, seem to
avoid the word.
   3. **neque tempus,** etc.: in 2, 95 Cicero
asks why suicide should be permitted to
the σοφός if the maxim 'semper plus
voluptatis' holds good; cf. too, 5,
93.
   5. **grate:** n. on § 57. Cf. Hor. ep.
2, 2, 210 natales grate numeras? The
σοφὸς differs from the ordinary man
largely in the vividness which past
pleasures retain in his recollection; so
says Plut. n. p. s. v. 4, 1089 *b*; this

doctrine gave Carneades an opening for
bitter jests (ib. 1089 *c*).
   potitur: so 2, 14 potiatur...voluptati-
bus. The thankful heart which cherishes
the memory of past pleasures, also
heightens the enjoyment of those which
are present. The unthankful man is
blind to the true importance of the
present.
   6. **pendet:** Porphyr. de abst. 1, 54
οὐκ ἐπ' ἐλπίδι κρεμήσεται μεγίστης ἡδονῆς
πίστιν οὐκ ἐχούσῃ; Hor. ep. 1, 18, 110
dubiae spe pendulus horae; Sen. ep. 15,
10, 10 stulta vita...tota in futurum fertur;
ep. 22, 13 (Us. § 495); 98, 6 calami-
tosus est animus futuri anxius. Cf. n.
on *modo* in § 60. Sen. ben. 7, 2, 4.
   8. **cum stultorum...voluptate:** this is
the gratification so vividly described by
Lucr. 2, init. In that passage *bene
munita tenere edita doctrina sapientum
templa serena* is imitated from Emped.
52 (Mullach) θάρσει καὶ τότε δὴ σοφίης
ἐπ' ἄκροισι θόαζε, rather than from
Aristophanes, as Munro supposes.
   11. **quod gaudeat:** see n. on § 41
(*quod* or *quo*); and for *quod angatur* n.
on 1 § 14.
   optime vero...quod: for the elliptic
form cf. n. on 2, 41.
   12. **exiguam,** etc.: Epic. κυρ. δόξα 16
βραχεῖα σοφῷ τύχη παρεμπίπτει, τὰ δὲ
μέγιστα καὶ κυριώτατα ὁ λογισμὸς διῴκηκε
καὶ κατὰ τὸν συνεχῆ χρόνον τοῦ βίου
διοικεῖ καὶ διοικήσει: below, 2, 89 fortuna
quam Epicurus ait exiguam intervenire
sapienti; Tusc. 5, 26 quid melius quam
fortunam exiguam intervenire sapienti?
It is hardly likely that in these three
passages of Cicero the MSS. have altered

maximasque ab eo et gravissimas res consilio ipsius et ratione
administrari, neque maiorem voluptatem ex infinito tempore
aetatis percipi posse, quam ex hoc percipiatur, quod videamus
esse finitum. In dialectica autem vestra nullam existimavit esse
5 nec ad melius vivendum nec ad commodius disserendum viam.

3 aetatis: om. E.   3 ex hoc: *extra hoc* ed. Rom.   5 viam AEP; *vim* Or. Madv.;
om. alii.

exiguum into *exiguam* (as Usener appears to suppose); and Cicero would not
have employed the adjective in this adverbial sense had he not found βραχεῖα
in the text of Epic. κυρ. δόξ. 16; and
this reading is confirmed by Stobaeus,
ecl. eth. 8, 28, p. 159, 17 Wachsm.
Sen. dial. 2, 15, 4 substitutes an adverb:
'raro, inquit, fortuna sapienti inter-
venit.' Cicero, Tusc. 3, 49 goes somewhat beyond Epicurus: 'negat (Ep.)
ullam in sapientem esse vim fortunae';
cf. however, Epicurus ap. Porphyr. ad
Marc. p. 209, Nauck σοφία δὲ οὐδαμῶς
τύχῃ κοινωνεῖ, Vitruvius 6, pref. 3 Ep....
ait pauca sapientibus fortunam tribuere,
quae autem maxima et necessaria sunt,
animi mentisque cogitationibus gubernari. Metrodorus expresses himself
riotously in a passage most fully quoted
in Vat. γνῶμαι § 47 προκατειλημμαί σε
ὦ τύχη καὶ πᾶσαν σὴν παρείσδυσιν
ἐνέφραξα, καὶ οὔτε σοι οὔτε ἄλλῃ οὐδεμιᾷ
περιστάσει δώσομεν ἑαυτούς· ἐκδότους·
ἀλλ' ὅταν ἡμᾶς τὸ χρεὼν ἐξάγῃ, μέγα
προσπτύσαντες τῷ ζῆν καὶ τοῖς αὐτῷ
κενῶς περιπλεκομένοις ἄπιμεν ἐκ τοῦ ζῆν
μετὰ καλοῦ παίωνος ἐπιφωνοῦντες ὡς εὖ
ἡμῖν βεβίωται (see Tusc. 5, 27). The
utterances of Democritus on the subject
of fortune are similar; cf. fragm. 14
(Mull.) ἄνθρωποι τύχης εἴδωλον ἐπλάσαντο
πρόφασιν ἰδίης ἀβουλίης· βαιὰ γὰρ φρόνησι
τύχη μάχεται, τὰ δὲ πλεῖστα ἐν βίῳ ψυχὴ
εὐξύνετος ὀξυδερκέειν κατιθύνει: also
fragm. 15 τύχη μεγαλόδωρος ἀλλ' ἀβέ-
βαιος, φύσις δὲ αὐτάρκης· διόπερ νικᾷ τῷ
ἥσσονι καὶ βεβαίῳ τὸ μέζον τῆς ἐλπίδος.
In truth every ancient ethical system
regarded its σοφός as impervious to the
attacks of fortune; see e.g. for Diogenes
the Cynic, Diog. L. 6 §§ 63, 105 and
Stob. Ecl. 2, 348. The inscr. of Oinoanda
(Heberdey and Kalinka ap. Bulletin de
Corr. Hell. xxi, p. 374): τὸ κεφάλαιον τῆς
εὐδαιμονίας ἡ διάθεσις ἧς ἡμεῖς κύριοι is like
much in Seneca. Havet, Rev. de Phil.
xxiii, 323, says a link is needed between
administrari and *neque maiorem*, and
he thinks the need of it shows some
dubious words in the κυρία δόξα (Us.
p. 74) to have been represented here.

2. **neque maiorem**, etc.: Epic. ap.
Diog. L. 10, 145 ὁ ἄπειρος χρόνος ἴσην
ἔχει τὴν ἡδονὴν καὶ ὁ πεπερασμένος, ἐὰν
τις αὐτῆς τὰ πέρατα μετρήσῃ τῷ λογισμῷ :
ib. 126 ὥσπερ δὲ σιτίον οὐ τὸ πλεῖον
πάντως ἀλλὰ τὸ ἥδιον αἱρεῖται, οὕτω καὶ
χρόνον οὐ τὸν μήκιστον ἀλλὰ τὸν ἥδιστον
καρπίζεται. The theme is expounded in
Ps.-Plut. cons. ad Apoll. 17, 111 a, where
cf. esp. 'οὐδὲ γὰρ ὁ πλεῖστα κιθαρῳδήσας,
ἢ ῥητορεύσας, ἢ κυβερνήσας, ἀλλ' ὁ καλῶς,
ἐπαινεῖται.' These words resemble a
passage of Feuerbach, quoted by Guyau,
p. 113, in which he compares life to a
sonata, whose perfection is not dependent on duration of time. But the
belief that 'in small measures lives may
perfect be' is expressed a thousand
times in literature. For similar deliverances of the Stoics see 3, 47 *n*.

3. **percipiatur**: although *dixit* not
dicit stands above; cf. 2, 86.

4. **in dialectica**, etc.: Polystratos
περὶ ἀλ. φρον. (Gomperz in Hermes xi,
p. 410) calls dialectic παντοδαπὴν λαλίαν
οὐθὲν οὔτ' αὐτοῖς οὔτε τοῖς ἀκούουσιν εἰς
ἐπανόρθωσιν καὶ τὸ βελτίον ζῆν συντεί-
νουσαν: Diog. L. 10, 31 τὴν διαλεκτικὴν
ὡς παρέλκουσαν ἀποδοκιμάζουσιν (sc. οἱ
Ἐπικούρειοι): ib. 10, 8 τοὺς διαλεκτικοὺς
πολυφθόρους. Epicurus treated with
scorn the Megaric and Stoic logic in
fashion in his day, with its apparatus of
ὁρισμοί, διαιρέσεις, syllogistic ἀπόδειξις
and the rest; see above, § 22; below,
2 §§ 5, 27, 30; 3, 40; Acad. 1, 5. But the
Herculanean fragments afford indications that Epicurus laboured to construct
a logic of his own on inductive lines.
This is especially shown in the treatise
of Philodemus entitled 'περὶ σημείων
καὶ σημειώσεων': see the comments of
Gomperz in Herkulanische Studien 1
(1865) and Bahnsch (Lyck, 1879). Diog.
L. 10, 27 mentions a work of Epicurus
directed against the Megarians. For the
κανών or κανονικόν see below.

5. **viam**: I have retained the reading
of the mss. because: (1) *vim* at the end
of the sentence gives an intolerable
rhythm; (2) because I believe, with
Boeckel that *viam* represents ἐφόδους in

In physicis plurimum posuit. Ea scientia et verborum vis et natura orationis et consequentium repugnantiumve ratio potest perspici; omnium autem rerum natura cognita levamur super-

Diog. L. 10, 30 τὸ μὲν οὖν κανονικὸν ἐφ-όδους ἐπὶ τὴν πραγματείαν ἔχει. Madvig's remark 'in arte esse viam ad melius vivendum,' is inconclusive, if, as I think, there is nothing unnatural in the expression. 'Via ad melius vivendum' for v. quae fert ad m. v. (§ 46; cf. Off. 1, 100) is good enough; cf. si tanti est Leg. agr. 2, 17; and there is nothing strange in saying that a method is contained within an art; cf. Acad. 2, 96 si ars si ratio si via si vis denique conclusionis valet, eadem est in utroque.

1. in physicis plurimum posuit: § 17 physicis quibus maxime gloriatur.

ea scientia, etc.: Madvig blames Cic. for saying that the rules for practical logic which Epicurus laid down were part of his physical doctrine. But Epic. undoubtedly did profess to reduce the divisions of philosophy from three to two by expunging dialectic: Sen. ep. 89, 11 expressly states this and Sext. Emp. A. M. 7, 14 says that Epicurus was by some reckoned as having made philosophy διμερῆ, like Archelaus; while others held that he only rejected the Stoic dialectic, so that his divisions of philosophy were δυνάμει (practically) τρία. Clearly the κανονικόν was no independent branch of philosophy, like the Stoic διαλεκτική. And Epicurus did frequently deal with rules of reasoning in his physical treatises, as in the 28th book of the περὶ φυσικῶν (see Scott, p. 62); cf. too the sharp transition in Diog. L. 10, 31 from the rejection of διαλεκτική to the consideration of physics. The fact that Diog. L. 10, 30 asserts the Epicureans to have 'ranged side by side' Canonic and Physics (τὸ κανονικὸν ὁμοῦ τῷ φυσικῷ συν-έταττον) and that Seneca ep. 89, 11 speaks of Canonic as 'an appendage' to Physics (accessio) cannot justify the blame which Madvig throws upon Cicero. See the passage from the letter of Epic. to Herodotus given below, n. on 2, 6.

verborum vis: Diog. L. 10, 31 τὴν δια-λεκτικὴν ὡς παρέλκουσαν ἀποδοκιμάζουσιν· ἀρκεῖν γὰρ τοὺς φυσικοὺς χωρεῖν κατὰ τοὺς τῶν πραγμάτων φθόγγους: below, 2, 6 Epicurum...qui crebro dicat diligenter oportere exprimi quae vis subiecta sit vocibus, where see n.

2. natura orationis: Orelli referred these words to the theory taught by Epicurus of the origin of language, which he believed to have arisen φύσει not θέσει (Diog. L. 10, 75; Lucr. 5, 1028 sq.; Origenes and Proclus ap. Usener §§ 334, 5). Madvig contends that the reference is merely to rules of reasoning, but the word natura is against this view. He also declares that Epicurus never dealt at all with natura orationis (in the sense which he gives the phrase) nor with conse-quentium repugnantiumve ratio; but that Cicero has ignorantly introduced into the κανονικόν of Epicurus certain elements derived from the Stoic dialectic. This supposition seems to me to be most improbable. Our information concerning the contents of the 'Canonic' is most defective; but it is hardly conceivable that it should not have contained some tests of consistency and inconsistency in reasoning to replace those Stoic tests which Epicurus threw away. As to this see further, 3, 10 n. (see Diog. L. 10, 31 f. on ἀναλογία, etc.). The fact that the phrase consequentium repugnantiumve and similar phrases occur in connexion with the Stoic scheme (as Tusc. 5, 68; Div. 2, 150; Leg. 1, 45; Orat. 16, 115; Brut. 152; De Orat. 2, 166; Top. 53) has no bearing on the matter. The terminology of all schools was in ancient times, as in modern, in many respects alike, and Epicurus was not debarred from employing a particular expression (giving it his own sense) merely because it occurred in the Stoic literature. See above, n. on passage earlier (§ 42), where Madvig made a similar change in an ethical matter.

3. levamur superstitione, etc.: as Madvig remarks, Epicurus valued knowledge of nature not for its own sake, but for its bearing on ethics and happiness. This treatment of nature is conspicuous even in the poem of Lucretius. Cf. κυρ. δόξα 11 εἰ μηθὲν ἡμᾶς αἱ τῶν μετεώρων ὑποψίαι ἠνώχλουν καὶ αἱ περὶ θανάτου, μή ποτε πρὸς ἡμᾶς ᾖ τι, ἔτι τε τὸ μὴ κατανοεῖν τοὺς ὅρους τῶν ἀλγηδόνων καὶ τῶν ἐπιθυμιῶν, οὐκ ἂν προσεδεόμεθα φυσιολογίας: Vat. γνῶμαι § 45 οὐ κόμπου οὐδὲ φωνῆς ἐργαστικοὺς...φυσιολογία παρασκευάζει ἀλλ' ἀφόβους καὶ αὐταρκεῖς καὶ ἐπὶ τοῖς ἰδίοις ἀγαθοῖς οὐκ ἐπὶ τοῖς

stitione, liberamur mortis metu, non conturbamur ignoratione
rerum, e qua ipsa horribiles exsistunt saepe formidines; denique
etiam morati melius erimus, cum didicerimus quid natura
desideret. Tum vero, si stabilem scientiam rerum tenebimus,
5 servata illa, quae quasi delapsa de caelo est ad cognitionem
omnium, regula, ad quam omnia iudicia rerum dirigentur, numquam ullius oratione victi sententia desistemus. Nisi autem 64
rerum natura perspecta erit, nullo modo poterimus sensuum
iudicia defendere. Quicquid porro animo cernimus, id omne
10 oritur a sensibus; qui si omnes veri erunt, ut Epicuri ratio docet,
tum denique poterit aliquid cognosci et percipi. Quos qui tollunt

4 scientiam: *sententiam* E. 7 ullius oratione: *illius ratione* E. 11 et percipi:
et recipi A¹P et ed. Rom.

τῶν πραγμάτων (external advantages)
μέγα φρονοῦντας. The Stoics (who are
aimed at in the first words of the last
passage) held much the same view as
the Epicureans concerning the value of
physical inquiries; see 3, 73 *n.*

1. ignoratione rerum: the word
rerum here corresponds to ἡ τοῦ σύμ-
παντος φύσις which (in κυρ. δόξα 12)
Epic. says men must know if they are
to get quit of terror; so *cognitio rerum*,
as in 5, 11. Cf. § 43 (esp. *ignoratione
rerum bonarum ac malarum*); Epic. ap.
Diog. L. 10, 76–82; ib. 37; ib. 85; ib.
87; below, 4, 11; Lucr. 1, 102–35 (and
elsewhere).

2. e qua ipsa: 'the very thing from
which.'

5. illa...regula: the '*περὶ κριτηρίου ἢ
κανών*' of Epicurus (Diog. L. 10, 27), in
which the precepts of τὸ κανονικόν were
embodied; cf. N.D. 1, 43 illo caelesti
Epicuri de regula et iudicio volumine;
Sen. ep. 89, 11 de iudicio et regula;
Plut. Colot. 1118 *a τοὺς διοπετεῖς ἀνέγνω-
κας κανόνας*. Probably Democritus wrote
a book entitled κανόνες: see Hirzel 1,
125 sq. and 135,'where the view of Zeller,
that Epic. borrowed his Canonic from
Aristippus, is rightly rejected. Aristo
ap. Diog. L. 10, 14, said that the κανών
was written ' from the tripod' ('divining-
stool') of Nausiphanes. Athen. p. 102 *b*
quotes a passage of the comic dramatist
Damoxenus, where a cook speaks:
μάγειρον ὅταν ἴδῃς ἀγράμματον | μὴ
Δημόκριτόν τε πάντα διανεγνωκότα | καὶ
τὸν Ἐπικούρου κανόνα, μινθώσας ἄφες.

delapsa de caelo: many illustrations of this phrase are given by Otto
in Archiv 3, 211. One is especially
reminded of 'de caelo descendit γνῶθι

σεαυτόν.' Cf. n. on 2, 20 quasi oracula.

6. omnium: sc. *hominum* not *rerum*
(as Holstein); cf. Lucr. 1, 75 refert *nobis*
quid possit oriri.

7. oratione: so in Acad. 2, 8 Cicero
says many adopt opinions hastily, *una
alicuius oratione capti*. Cf. a denuncia-
tion of the Sophists who delude
wretched men in the Inscr. of Oinoanda,
p. 409.

8. sensuum iudicia: cf. Acad. 2, 19.
Madvig says 'pugnandum enim erat
contra geometras, astronomos, ceteros';
but surely the reference is to the battle
waged by the Epicureans against the
Sceptics, to which there is much allusion
in Acad. 2 and elsewhere.

9. animo...sensibus: n. on § 30 detractis sensibus. Here *sensibus* indicates 'sensations,' not the five senses.
For *oritur* cf. Lucr. 4, 483.

10. omnes veri erunt: see Acad. 2, 79
sq. with my nn.

11. tum: 'only then will sure knowledge be possible.' For the union of the
two verbs *cognosci* and *percipi* to represent ἐπίστασθαι see my n. on Acad. 2,
23. So below, *cognitione* and *scientia*
together =ἐπιστήμην.

quos qui tollunt: 'pinguius aliquanto
Torquatus *tolli sensus* ab Academicis
dicit, neque enim sensus tollebant, sed
eorum iudicium' (Madvig). But in the
controversies between the Dogmatists
and the Sceptics, the latter are often
said to sweep away the αἰσθήσεις by
rendering them deceptive. In Sext.
Emp. the phrase ἀναιρεῖν τὰς αἰσθήσεις repeatedly occurs; cf. also my n. on Acad.
2, 61 omnibus orbat sensibus; also ib.
103 sensus eripi. Just in the same way
the Sceptics were said 'to bereave us of

et nihil posse percipi dicunt, ei remotis sensibus ne id ipsum
quidem expedire possunt quod disserunt. Praeterea sublata
cognitione et scientia tollitur omnis ratio et vitae degendae et
rerum gerendarum. Sic e physicis et fortitudo sumitur contra
mortis timorem et constantia contra metum religionis et sedatio 5
animi omnium rerum occultarum ignoratione sublata et moderatio natura cupiditatum generibusque earum explicatis, et, ut
modo docui, cognitionis regula et iudicio ab eodem illo constituto veri a falso distinctio traditur.

65   XX. Restat locus huic disputationi vel maxime necessarius 10
de amicitia, quam, si voluptas summum sit bonum, affirmatis
nullam omnino fore. De qua Epicurus quidem ita dicit, omnium
rerum, quas ad beate vivendum sapientia comparaverit, nihil
esse maius amicitia, nihil uberius, nihil iucundius. Nec vero hoc
oratione solum, sed multo magis vita et factis et moribus com- 15
probavit. Quod quam magnum sit, fictae veterum fabulae
declarant, in quibus tam multis tamque variis ab ultima anti-
quitate repetitis tria vix amicorum paria reperiuntur, ut ad

1 ei remotis: *ire motis* A¹; *hi remotis* A²P.   6 occultarum: om. E.   8 eodem
illo: *ea dein illa* A¹; *eadem illa* A² et cett. omnes; correxit Madvig.   10 disputationi vel: *disputationibus* A¹.   14 iucundius: *iucundus* A.   14 hoc: *hos* A¹E.
15 comprobavit: *comprobatur* E.

the light of day' (*lucem eripere*, Acad.
2, 30).
    1. **ne id ipsum quidem**, etc.: the
Epicureans, like the Stoics and other
Dogmatists, argued that the Sceptic cuts
the ground from under his own reason-
ings; see especially Lucr. 4, 469 sq.;
Epic. κυρ. δόξαι 23 and 24. Also that
Scepticism renders life impossible: there
is much to this effect in Cicero's
Academica and other ancient writings
touching on the controversy between
Sceptics and Dogmatists. The Cyrenaics,
among others, discredited the senses,
the result of which is '*μὴ δύνασθαι ζῆν
μηδὲ χρῆσθαι τοῖς πράγμασιν*' (Colotes
ap. Plut. c. 24, 1120 d).
    4. **sic...traditur**: we have here a re-
capitulation of the contents of φυσιολογία, the κανονικὸν coming last in the
enumeration of items, whereas above it
comes first. Madvig remarks on this
summary: 'paulo post, ubi *ἀνακεφα-
λαίωσις* fit (*Sic e physicis*, etc.) nihil de
hac physicorum laude (i.e. the merit
of imparting κανονικὸν) dicit sed a
fortitudine incipit.' The words *nihil...
dicit* contain a strange oversight.
    5. **sedatio animi**: =ἀταραξία.

    6. **rerum occultarum**: a constantly
recurring phrase for physical pheno-
mena; so below, 4, 18 and 5 §§ 9, 10;
also 3, 37 illa quae occulta nobis sunt
(see note there); 5, 51 eorum quae
naturae obscuritate occultantur.
    7. **cupiditatum**, etc.: cf. n. on § 45,
partitio. According to κυρ. δ. 11 it is
φυσιολογία which teaches the ὅρους τῶν
ἐπιθυμιῶν.
    9. **veri a falso**: n. on Acad. 2, 27.
    12. **nullam fore**: so in 2 §§ 80,85, where
see nn.
    Epicurus: κυρ. δ. 27 ὧν ἡ σοφία παρα-
σκευάζεται εἰς τὴν τοῦ ὅλου βίου μακαριό-
τητα, πολὺ μέγιστόν ἐστιν ἡ τῆς φιλίας
κτῆσις: cf. Sen. ben. 3, 12, 2 invenies
qui nihil putet esse iucundius, nihil
maius quam habere in quo calamitas ac-
quiescat; Vat. γνῶμαι § 78 ὁ γενναῖος
περὶ σοφίαν καὶ φιλίαν μάλιστα γίγνεται·
ὧν τὸ μέν ἐστι θνητὸν ἀγαθόν, τὸ δὲ
ἀθάνατον; cf. Sen. ep. 19, 10.
    15. **comprobavit**: 'proved' Div. 1, 11.
    16. **quod**:=*amicitia*. Cf. nn.on 30;2,17.
    fictae...fabulae: a common phrase,
as below, 5, 51 and 64.
    18. **repetitis**: 'when conned over.'
    tria paria: Theseus and Pirithous,

Orestem pervenias profectus a Theseo. At vero Epicurus una
in domo, et ea quidem angusta, quam magnos quantaque amoris
conspiratione consentientes tenuit amicorum greges! Quod fit
etiam nunc ab Epicureis. Sed ad rem redeamus; de hominibus
5 dici non necesse est. Tribus igitur modis video esse a nostris 66
de amicitia disputatum. Alii cum eas voluptates, quae ad amicos
pertinerent, negarent esse per se ipsas tam expetendas, quam
nostras expeteremus, quo loco videtur quibusdam stabilitas

7 ipsas: *ipsos* A¹.

Achilles and Patroclus, Orestes and
Pylades; so classed by Lucian Toxar. 10.
Cf. Lael. 15 ex omnibus saeculis vix tria
aut quattuor nominantur paria amicorum; where there is a reference to
Damon and Phintias, mentioned below,
2, 79 and Off. 3, 45. Plut. de am. mult.
93 *e* adds a fifth pair, Epaminondas and
Pelopidas; and Scipio and Laelius
sometimes appear in the same company
(Lael. l.l.; Val. M. 8, 8, 1); so Charito
and Melanippus ap. Ael. var. hist. 2, 4.
Amicorum is here, as often, for *verorum
am.* '*ideal* friends'; see my n. on Lael. 22.
On the rarity of the ideal friend cf.
Sen. ben. 6, 33, 3 amicum, rem non
domibus tantum, sed saeculis raram;
Mart. 1, 93, 5 iunctus uterque sacro
laudatae foedere vitae | famaque quod
raro novit, amicus erat. (The passage
in Mart. has often been misunderstood.)
Hieron. ep. 3 § 6 (Migne) amicum qui
diu quaeritur, vix invenitur, difficile
servatur.

1. **una in domo**...**greges**: for a loose
use of *domus* cf. Sen. ben. 5, 16, 4; for the
extravagance cf. Diog. L. 10, 9 οἵ τε φίλοι
τοσοῦτοι τὸ πλῆθος, ὡς μήδ' ἂν πόλεσιν
ὅλαις μετρεῖσθαι δύνασθαι: ib. 10 τοὺς
φίλους οἳ καὶ πανταχόθεν πρὸς αὐτὸν
ἀφικνοῦντο καὶ συνεβίουν αὐτῷ ἐν τῷ
κήπῳ: Epictet. fragm. 47 ἀντὶ βοῶν
ἀγέλης πειρῶ φίλων ἀγέλας ἐναγελά-
ζεσθαί σου τῇ οἰκίᾳ: Phaedr. 3, 9 volgare
amici nomen sed rara est fides. | cum
parvas aedes sibi fundasset Socrates... |
ex populo sic nescio quis, ut fieri solet, |
'quaeso tam angustam talis vir ponis
domum?' | 'utinam,' inquit, 'veris hanc
amicis impleam!' See Sen. fragm. of De
Amic. in Haase, § 97 (p. 436) also *domibus*
in Sen. ben. 6, 33, 3. Cic. Orat. 146
doctissimis hominibus referta domus. A
touch of bathos is added by the words
et ea quidem angusta. To obviate this, it
has been proposed (but without probability) to understand *domo* as 'sect'; for
which sense see Hor. od. 1, 29, 14; Sen.

n. q. 7, 32, 3; ben. 5, 15, 3 philosophorum domo; ep. 29, 11 omnes ab
omni domo...Peripatetici Academici
Stoici Cynici. Plut. de frat. am. 16, 487*d*,
33 admires the affection of Epicurus
and his brothers; the close relations of
the μεγάλοι were famous. Two-headed
busts of Epicurus and Metrodorus were
common.

3. **fit nunc**: there is much testimony
to this; below, 2, 81; Acad. 2, 115;
Numen. ap. Eus. pr. eu. 14, 5, 1–3. There
was no doubt a great deal of literature
in the school on the subject of friendship.
Thus Colotes wrote πρὸς Πλάτωνος Λύσιν
(Scott, p. 23), and in the Herculanean roll
no. 1027 (ib. p. 34) we have fragments of a
work by Carneiscus, entitled 'Philistas,'
where an attack is made on the views of
friendship maintained by Praxiphanes,
the Peripatetic whose lectures Epicurus
was alleged to have attended. Hirzel
1, 165 assumes that Epic. got his ideas
about friendship from Theophrastus
through this Praxiphanes. There is no
probability in this theory In roll
no. 157 (Scott, p. 143 sq.) is an interesting discussion of the question whether
the gods need friendship. Cf. Epicurus'
polemic against Stilbon, Sen. ep. 9, 1.

6. **alii**: instead of a second *alii* we have
in § 69 sunt autem quidam, followed in
§ 70 by sunt autem qui dicant. The view
first given is that of Epicurus: see
2, 82, 84; Diog. L. 10, 120 καὶ τὴν φιλίαν
διὰ τὰς χρείας δεῖν μέντοι προκατάρχεσθαι, καὶ γὰρ τὴν γῆν σπείρομεν·
συνίστασθαι δὲ αὐτὴν κατὰ κοινωνίαν
μεγίσταις ἡδοναῖς ἐκπεπληρωμένην (so
Usener § 540): ib. 2, 91 (of Aristippus)
τὸ φίλον τῆς χρείας ἕνεκα; Sen. ep. 9, 8;
Philod. de vit. 9.

7. **tam exp.**: sc. *nobis*. The syntax
is a little irregular; to make it strictly
correct *tam expeti* would be needed.

8. **quo loco**: Madvig denies (I do not
know why) that the relative refers to
what precedes.

amicitiae vacillare, tuentur tamen eum locum seque facile, ut
mihi videtur, expediunt. Vt enim virtutes, de quibus ante
dictum est, sic amicitiam negant posse a voluptate discedere.
Nam cum solitudo et vita sine amicis insidiarum et metus plena
sit, ratio ipsa monet amicitias comparare, quibus partis con- 5
firmatur animus et a spe pariendarum voluptatum seiungi non
67 potest. Atque ut odia invidiae despicationes adversantur
voluptatibus, sic amicitiae non modo fautrices fidelissimae, sed
etiam effectrices sunt voluptatum tam amicis quam sibi; quibus
non solum praesentibus fruuntur, sed etiam spe eriguntur con- 10
sequentis ac posteri temporis. Quod quia nullo modo sine amicitia
firmam et perpetuam iucunditatem vitae tenere possumus neque
vero ipsam amicitiam tueri, nisi aeque amicos et nosmet ipsos
diligamus, idcirco et hoc ipsum efficitur in amicitia et amicitia

5 monet: *manet* E.   7 ut odia: *odia* A²; *odiā* BE; *udia* A¹.   7 invidiae A²:
invidia A¹EP.   8 fautrices: *fotrices* Scaliger, Guyet, Davies.   9 effectrices:
efficatrices E.   13 nisi: *ipsi* AP.

1. **vacillare**: cf. *claudicare* in § 69 and
Off. 3, 118 iustitia vacillat vel iacet
potius (of the Epicureans); N.D. 1, 107
tota res vacillat et claudicat.
    se...expediunt: a military phrase;
Liv. 7, 34, 6.
    3. **discedere**: 2, 79 si utilitas ab
amicitia defecerit; but 82 amicitiam
a voluptate non posse divelli.
    4. **cum solitudo**, etc.: n. on 2, 84
praesidium amicorum.
    5. **amicitias comparare**: so Lael. 60.
    confirmatur animus: 2, 82 cum sine
ea (amicitia) tuto et sine metu vivi non
posset.
    7. **despicationes**: ἅπαξ εἰρημένον. The
context resembles closely words of
Epicurus, reported by Diog. L. 10, 117
βλαβὰς ἐξ ἀνθρώπων ἢ διὰ μῖσος, ἢ διὰ
φθόνον ἢ διὰ καταφρόνησιν γίνεσθαι.
With *despicationes* cf. 2, 84 contemni
non poteris, and Lucr. 3, 65 turpis enim
ferme contemptus et acris egestas |
semota ab dulci vita stabilique videntur
| et quasi iam leti portas cunctarier ante.
Hieron. ep. 14, 7 (Migne) ubi honor non
est, ibi contemptus est; ubi contemptus,
ibi frequens iniuria; ubi autem iniuria,
ibi et indignatio; ubi indignatio, ibi
quies nulla.
    9. **voluptatum**: to be taken both
with *fautrices* and *effectrices*. The word
effectrix occurs only here and Tim. 10.
For the genitive cf. n. on 2, 21 (*fautor*
not in Cicero's philosophical works).
    sibi: 'non sane amicitiis; sed re-
flexivum refertur ad latentem personae

agentis notionem, ut sit: *einem selbst'*
(Madvig). The same indefinite sense,
'oneself,' recurs below, 2, 78; and many
examples are scattered widely in Latin
literature. The same indefinite reference
attaches to *ipse* and *suus*; in the case of
the latter the usage must be distinguished
from another whereby the pronoun
stands for *eius*, in reference to a subject
indicated in the context, and marks the
difference between 'his' and 'his own.' So
se referred to the logical, not grammatical
subject of the clause; 2, 2, and often.
    10. **spe**: cf. Arist. Eth. N. 9, 4, 5
(1166 a, 24) (of friendship) τῶν πεπραγ-
μένων ἐπιτερπεῖς αἱ μνῆμαι, καὶ τῶν
μελλόντων ἐλπίδες ἀγαθαί: Vat. γνῶμαι
§ 34 οὐχ οὕτως χρείαν ἔχομεν τῆς χρείας
παρὰ τῶν φίλων ὡς τῆς πίστεως τῆς περὶ
τῆς χρείας: ib. § 39 οὔθ' ὁ τὴν χρείαν
ἐπιζητῶν διὰ παντὸς φίλος, οὔθ' ὁ
μηδέποτε συνάπτων· ὁ μὲν γὰρ καπηλεύει
τῇ χάριτι τὴν ἀμοιβήν, ὁ δὲ ἀποκόπτει
τὴν περὶ τοῦ μέλλοντος εὐελπιστίαν.
    consequentis...temporis: cf. Tusc.
1, 97.
    11. **quod quia**: n. on 4, 10 quod etsi;
quod si in § 59. For *quod* continuing a
statement see Roby § 2214.
    12. **iucunditatem vitae**: although,
Epicureanly speaking, 'dia voluptas' is
'dux vitae,' yet the phrase 'voluptas
vitae' does not, I think, occur.
    tenere...tueri: these two verbs run
much together; as below, 2, 11; Off. 2, 23
ad opes tuendas ac tenendas; De Or. 3,
108 tenere tuerique.

cum voluptate conectitur. Nam et laetamur amicorum laetitia
aeque atque nostra et pariter dolemus angoribus. Quocirca eodem **68**
modo sapiens erit affectus erga amicum quo in se ipsum, quosque
labores propter suam voluptatem susciperet, eosdem suscipiet
5 propter amici voluptatem. Quaeque de virtutibus dicta sunt,
quem ad modum eae semper voluptatibus inhaererent, eadem
de amicitia dicenda sunt. Praeclare enim Epicurus his paene
verbis: 'Eadem,' inquit, 'sententia confirmavit animum, ne
quod aut sempiternum aut diuturnum timeret malum, quae
10 perspexit in hoc ipso vitae spatio amicitiae praesidium esse
firmissimum.' Sunt autem quidam Epicurei timidiores paulo **69**

2 aeque atque: *aeque ut* P (quod non est Tullianum).   8 sententia BE: *scientia*
AP alii.

aeque…et: as Madvig remarks, two
classes of passages in which *et* follows
aeque must be distinguished: (1) those
in which *et* closely connects two subjects, and *aeque* stands in front of the
combination, as Tusc. 2, 62 eosdem
labores non esse aeque graves imperatori et militi; below, 4, 66; 3, 70 (*ac*);
3, 61; (2) those in which the *aeque…et*
stands between the two things compared, so that the idea of comparison
is made conspicuous; so below 4, 62
catuli qui iam dispecturi sunt, caeci
aeque et ei qui modo nati. *Aeque atque,*
found below, is unusual because *atque*
is there not followed by a vowel; *aeque
ac* is fairly common; *aeque quam* is
avoided by Cicero and Caesar; *aeque ut*
is rare, and indeed doubtful; for the
text of Plaut. Asin. 838 is not quite
certain, and Hor. od. 1, 16, 7 is sus-
ceptible of another explanation, but it
seems to occur in Plin. ep. 1, 20, 1.
Pariter is not used by Cicero with *ac*,
atque, *et*, but either alone or with *cum*,
whereas *aeque cum* belongs to archaic
Latin. See also n. on 2, 21 similiter
et si. Non tantum ac in Sen. N.Q. 2,
22, 3.

1. **nam et laetamur**, etc.: Epic. thus
arrives at the same point with the non-
hedonists, as Arist. Eth. Nic. 9, 4, 5, 1166 *a*
πρὸς δὲ τὸν φίλον ἔχειν ὥσπερ πρὸς
ἑαυτόν: Diog. L. 5, 21 (of Aristotle)
ἐρωτηθεὶς πῶς ἂν φίλοις προσφερόμεθα,
ἔφη ὡς ἂν εὐξαίμεθα αὐτοὺς ἡμῖν προσ-
φέρεσθαι: Sen. ep. 95, 63 ut amicum
habeat eodem loco quo se. For the
Stoic view see n. on 3, 70. For the
friend as 'alter ego' see my n. on
Lael. 80; and for *laetamur … laetitia,*
2, 13.

2. **angoribus:** Vat. γνῶμαι § 56 ἀλγεῖ

μὲν ὁ σοφὸς οὐ μᾶλλον στρεβλούμενος
⟨αὐτὸς ἢ ὁρῶν στρεβλούμενον⟩ τὸν φίλον.
quocirca: on this word see Landgraf
in Archiv 9, 566 sq.
eodem modo, etc.: Lael. 56 ut eodem
modo erga amicum affecti simus quo
erga nosmetipsos.
3. **erga…in:** cf. 1, 17 *n.* for change of
preposition.
quosque labores, etc.: the σοφὸς will
even die for his friend, Diog. L. 10, 121:
Plut. Colot. 1111 *b* καὶ τῆς ἡδονῆς ἕνεκα
τὴν φιλίαν αἱρούμενος (λέγει Ἐπίκουρος)
ὑπὲρ τῶν φίλων τὰς μεγίστας ἀλγηδόνας
ἀναδέχεσθαι. Guyau, p. 135, compares
Bentham's opinions on friendship and
shows that he, like Epicurus, though
basing it on egoistic principles, ends in
making the friend an *alter ego*. In one
of his letters Epicurus attacked Stilpo
for saying that the σοφός, being αὐτάρκης,
would not need friends. He does need
them, 'ut habeat qui sibi aegro adsideat, succurrat in vincula coniecto vel
inopi' (Sen. ep. 9 § 8). The same difficulty
affected other schools (see Chrysippus
quoted by Sen. l.l. § 14 and cf. Plato's
Lysis, 215 B).
6. **inhaererent:** n. on 1, 25 (referatur).
eadem dicenda: Acad. 2, 132; Scott,
Fragm. Herc. p. 224 τὰ πλείω τῶν
εἰρημένων ἀντιστρέφουσι.
7. **praeclare Epicurus:** this is κυρ. δ.
28 ἡ αὐτὴ γνώμη θαρρεῖν τε ἐποίησεν ὑπὲρ
τοῦ μηθὲν αἰώνιον εἶναι δεινὸν μηδὲ
πολυχρόνιον, καὶ τὴν ἐν αὐτοῖς τοῖς
ὡρισμένοις ἀσφάλειαν φιλίαις μάλιστα
κατεῖδε συντελουμένην.
11. **sunt autem quidam:** cf. § 31. It is
quite impossible to determine who, out
of the great number of Epicurean
writers, are here quoted. Hirzel guesses
(1, 170) Siro and Philodemus.

contra vestra convicia, sed tamen satis acuti, qui verentur ne, si amicitiam propter nostram voluptatem expetendam putemus, tota amicitia quasi claudicare videatur. Itaque primos congressus copulationesque et consuetudinum instituendarum voluntates fieri propter voluptatem; cum autem usus progrediens 5 familiaritatem effecerit, tum amorem efflorescere tantum ut, etiam si nulla sit utilitas ex amicitia, tamen ipsi amici propter se ipsos amentur. Etenim si loca, si fana, si urbes, si gymnasia, si campum, si canes, si equos, si ludicra exercendi aut venandi

1 convicia: *convitia* AP.   4 voluntates: om. E.   5 voluptatem: *voluptatum* P.
8 fana: *fama* A.   9 ludicra A¹: *ludicras* A².

1. convicia: the statement of Zumpt (on Mur. 21) that this plural only occurs once in Cicero is incorrect; there are four passages besides this, viz. Att. 2, 18, 1; N.D. 2, 20; dom. 16; Cluent. 39; possibly also Balb. 41 (see my n.). The word originally meant, in the singular, the sound of many voices heard together, and this is still the commonest use of it in Cicero, but the singular is sometimes used of repeated clamour by a single person. Only in N.D. 2, 20 is the *plural* referred to one person.

3. claudicare: n. on § 67 vacillare. If the MSS. may be trusted, Cicero used *claudere* in the same metaphorical sense in Brut. 214 (but 227 claudicabat); Orator 170 (but 173 claudicans); Tusc. 5, 22. The dict. qu. also Caecil. com. 32 and a fragment of Sallust.

itaque: sc. *dicunt*, to be supplied from *verentur*; cf. for zeugma 2, 88.

primos congressus: Diog. L. 10, 120 δεῖν μέντοι προκατάρχεσθαι (καὶ γὰρ τὴν γῆν σπείρομεν) συνίστασθαι δὲ αὐτὴν (sc. τὴν φιλίαν) κατὰ κοινωνίαν ἐν ταῖς ἡδοναῖς. On the other hand Lael. 30 quamquam utilitates multae et magnae consecutae sunt, non sunt tamen ab earum spe causae diligendi profectae; see the context, where the Epicurean view is condemned.

6. amorem: here substituted for *amicitiam*.

efflorescere: a *vox Ciceroniana*; Lael. 100 utilitas efflorescit ex amicitia.

7. ipsi propter se ipsos: for *ipsi... ipsos* see Peterson on Tac. dial. 24. For the context cf. Vat. γνῶμαι § 23 πᾶσα φιλία δι᾽ ἑαυτὴν αἱρετή· ἀρχὴν δὲ εἴληφεν ἀπὸ τῆς ὠφελείας.

8. si: for the repetition of the word cf. 2, 73; 5, 69 and *ut* repeated in 5, 67.

gymnasia: probably regarded here as

a pleasant locality, not as in the Greek fashion as a wrestling-place.

9. ludicra...venandi: Madvig interprets 'ludicrae armorum et corporum exercitationes (*ludicram exercitationem* Cicero dicit 1 N.D. 102, 1 De Orat. 147) et venationes, quae ipsa erat ludicra et assimulata exercitatio belli (N.D. 11, 161).' He explains *exercendi* as =*se ex.*; so that the words *ludicra...venandi* practically repeat what was indicated before by *si gymnasia, si campum, si canes, si equos*. This interpretation is not free from difficulties. It is doubtful whether the passages quoted lend any support to it. The word *ludicra* in good Latin seems always to have some reference, direct or indirect, to public exhibitions, and it is doubtful whether *ludicra exercendi, venandi* could be applied to the exercises in the *campus* or the hunting-field. In De Or. 1, 147 *ludicra exercitatio* means 'sham fight'; in N.D. 1, 102, if the whole context be taken into account, it will be seen probably to refer to a public spectacle; and this interpretation is strongly borne out by Fin. 5, 48 q. v. Even *ludicri sermones* in Acad. 2, 6 refers to trivial gossip such as is presented in comedy, and *ars ludicra armorum* in De Or. 2, 84 refers to something different from the mere private practice with weapons for amusement's sake. As to N.D. 2, 161 beluas nanciscimur venando ut et vescamur eis et exerceamur in venando ad similitudinem bellicae disciplinae (very like Scott's 'mimicry of noble war'), the passage evidently has no bearing on the use of *ludicra* here. Madvig says Cicero could not use the word *ludi* or *lusus* here, because these sports were not *ludi*, and *lusus* did not befit 'exercitationes non inutiles'; he was therefore driven to *ludicra*. But

consuetudine adamare solemus, quanto id in hominum consuetudine facilius fieri potuerit et iustius? Sunt autem qui dicant **70**

1 consuetudine: *consuetudines* AP alii.

ludus and *lusus* are both commonly
applied to bodily exercises; as *exerci-
tatione ludoque campestri*, Cael. 11;
though *lusus* is not a Ciceronian word.
If we turn to the closely parallel
passage, 2, 107, where *locus amoenus,
ludi, venatio* come together, a suspicion
arises that the allusion here is to gladia-
torial (or gymnastic) exhibitions, and
the contests with wild beasts in the
circus. Possibly as above Cicero adds
campus to the *gymnasia* which he found
in his Greek source, so here he has added
the distinctly Roman wild-beast show
to the Greek athletic competitions to
which the Greek source made reference.
The phrase *ludicra exercendi* is better
fitted to express this, than to bear the
meaning which Madvig assigns to it. It
has been objected by commentators on
Hor. ep. 1, 6, 7 that the plural *ludicra*
is unusual, though Livy and others
have *ludicrum* for an exhibition; but
the objection is not important. There
is no reason in the nature of the word
why it should not have a plural; and
many plurals occur rarely, because they
are rarely needed; here the sense is 'the
different forms of gymnastic exhibition.'
Nor is the fact that elsewhere *ludicra*
is only adjectival in Cicero of any great
significance; though in consequence of
this fact Bake read *ludicrā ex. aut ven.
cons.* Madvig answered, 'nude *consuetudine* dici debet, nec *ludicra exerc. aut
venandi consuetudine* fana, urbes ada-
mantur.' The latter reason is fatal to
Guyau's punctuation, whereby the
words *exerc. aut v. cons.* are placed
between commas. Against the reading
ludicras consuetudines it is enough to
say that the causal ablative *consuetudine*
is entirely necessary to the sense. Nor,
in determining the reading, must any
weight be given to the fact that *hominum*
depends on *consuetudine* below; there is
no need to suppose original parallelism
of construction between *venandi consuetudine* and *hominum c.*

exercendi: here a pure verbal noun
=*exercitationis*; so the gerund often
is in Cicero; see 3, 34 *n*. The fact that
Cicero uses *exercentes* for *se exercentes*
(if it be a fact) in De Or. 2, 287 would
have no bearing on the use of the gerund
here.

1. **adamare**: the only passage in ex-

tant writings of the best period where
any part of this verb is used excepting
the perfect and pluperfect tenses. The
present occurs in Columella, Pliny the
elder, Quintilian, the imperf. sub. in
Petronius. As *addiscere* is 'to go on
learning more and more,' so *adamare*
is 'to go on loving more and more,' the
force of *ad* being like that of πρὸ in
προδιδάσκειν, προμανθάνειν. Hence *adamare* is sometimes contrasted with
amare as a stronger word; so in Sen.
ep. 71, 5 and pseud. Quint. 18, 10.

2. **potuerit**: Madvig, dismissing (and
properly) the notion that *potuerit* is
'potential' subj., refers to his own
masterly essay on the future perfect
tense in Vol. II of his Opuscula; remarking that *potuerit* here cannot be
referred to any of the heads under which
he there classified the examples. In the
essay itself (p. 94) his first class is thus
described 'illi (the writers of the best
period) quum de futura actione sic
loquuntur ut perfectae effectus et
fructus maxime animo obversetur, rarius,
sed utuntur tamen futuro exacto';
and as examples of this class Fin. 3, 14
(profecerit) and 4, 41 (effecerit) are
quoted. The second class is said to
present 'et celeritatis et certae affirma-
tionis significationem'; but some of the
examples given exhibit the *affirmatio*
without the *celeritas*. It is under this
head that Madvig says he would rank
potuerit here, were the word sound. The
only reason which he expressly gives
for regarding the word as unsound is
curious. He quotes two passages of
Cicero 'in quibus affirmatio eminet,
simul autem actionis cum altera connexio,' viz. Tusc. 2, 16 quam quis
ignominiam non pertulerit...si decre-
verit? Leg. 3, 43 quis non studiose rei
publicae subvenerit, hac tam praeclara
lege laudatus? He then says that there is
'nulla talis connexio' in Fin. 1, 69. But
as he has classed without hesitation
under this head other examples which
certainly present 'nulla talis connexio,'
it is hard to understand the force of the
objection. Further, there seems to be
no obvious reason why *potuerit* should
not be ranked with Madvig's first group
of instances. In the case of *posse* more
than in that of any other verb, good
writers love to look to 'perfectae actionis

foedus esse quoddam sapientium ut ne minus amicos quam se
ipsos diligant. Quod et posse fieri intellegimus et saepe *evenire*
videmus, et perspicuom est nihil ad iucunde vivendum reperiri
posse quod coniunctione tali sit aptius. Quibus ex omnibus
iudicari potest non modo non impediri rationem amicitiae, si 5
summum bonum in voluptate ponatur, sed sine hoc institutionem omnino amicitiae non posse reperiri.

71 XXI. Quapropter si ea, quae dixi, sole ipso illustriora et
clariora sunt, si omnia hausta e fonte naturae, si tota oratio
nostra omnem sibi fidem sensibus confirmat, id est incorruptis 10
atque integris testibus, si infantes pueri, mutae etiam bestiae
paene locuntur magistra ac duce natura nihil esse prosperum nisi
voluptatem, nihil asperum nisi dolorem, de quibus neque depravate iudicant neque corrupte, nonne ei maximam gratiam
habere debemus, qui hac exaudita quasi voce naturae sic eam 15

1 quoddam: om. E.   1 amicos: *quidem amicos* A; *quam amicos* E; *amicos*
quidem quam ceteri; correxerunt Manutius et Lambinus.   1 se: *sii* A¹.   2 saepe
evenire: *saepe enim* codd.; supplevit Halm.   9 omnia: sequitur *dixi* in codd.,
quod aliis suspectum eiecit Madvig.   9 oratio: *cracio* A¹.   10 confirmat: om. E.

effectus et fructus.' There is often a
rather sudden change from *potero* to
potuero; so e.g. in Leg. 2, 18. (Madvig's
classification is not altogether satisfactory; under 1 he ranks Caes. B.G.
4, 25 ego certe meum rei publicae atque
imperatori officium praestitero; but
under ii, Verg. Aen. 9, 281 me nulla dies
tam fortibus ausis | dissimilem arguerit.
The former passage is supposed to exhibit 'actionis effectus,' the other
'affirmatio'; it would be truer to say
that both passages exhibit both ideas.
C. F. W. Müller, who decisively rejects *potuerit*, unfortunately assigns no
reasons.)

1. **foedus:** the word is often used of
friendship by the poets; see n. on 2, 83.
For the context cf. Diog. L. 10, 121
where Epicurus asserts that the σοφός
will be ready to die for his friend.

esse: the opposition between *fieri* and
esse is not uncommon; so e.g. in Fat. 17;
Acad. 2, 121; below 2, 83 id et fieri
posse et saepe esse factum (referring to
this passage).

4. **coniunctione tali:** i.e. the *foedus*.

5. **non...amicitiae:** 'that the theory
of friendship is not embarrassed.'

6. **institutionem:** the word, like many
nouns in *-tio*, conveys the idea of possibility; see my nn. on Acad. 2 §§ 45, 51.

8. **quapropter:** on the usage of this
word see Landgraf in Archiv 9, 566.

sole illustriora: so *luce clarius*, Tusc.
1, 90; many parallels are given by
Wölfflin in Archiv 6, 455.

9. **naturae:** there is probably no such
direct reference to the φυσιολογία of
Epicurus as Hirzel, 1, 156, makes out.

10. **id est:** n. on 1, 72: 2, 6.

11. **testibus:** n. on 1, 30.

mutae bestiae: Lucr. 5, 1059 pecudes m.; Hor. s. 1, 3, 100, speaking of
men before the convention of language,
calls them *mutum et turpe pecus.*

12. **magistra:** Off. 1, 129 natura ipsa
magistra ac duce.

prosperum: the sense is hardly
'iucundum et gratum' (Madvig) but
fortunatum = εὐδαιμονίας μετέχον. So 2,
19 and elsewhere *prosperitas* represents
εὐδαιμονία. In 4, 52 and 5, 78 and a
good many other places in Cicero,
aspera are associated with things
contra naturam or *aliena naturae*. Tac.
h. 2, 4 contrasts *prosperum* with *as-*
perum (applied to the sea); cf. too Sen.
ep. 66, 21. Cf. Liv. 7, 4, 6 si quid ex
progenie parum prosperum esset (of
physical defects).

13. **neque depravate:** cf. 1, 30 animal
...nondum depravatum, with n.

15. **exaudita:** the verb is always used

firme graviterque comprehenderit, ut omnes bene sanos in viam placatae, tranquillae, quietae, beatae vitae deduceret? Qui quod tibi parum videtur eruditus, ea causa est, quod nullam eruditionem esse duxit nisi quae beatae vitae disciplinam iuvaret.

5 An ille tempus aut in poetis evolvendis, ut ego et Triarius te **72** hortatore facimus, consumeret, in quibus nulla solida utilitas omnisque puerilis est delectatio, aut se, ut Plato, in musicis, geometria, numeris, astris contereret, quae et a falsis initiis profecta vera esse non possunt et, si essent vera, nihil afferrent 10 quo iucundius, id est quo melius viveremus, eas ergo artes perse-

2 vitae: om. E.   5 an ille A¹: *an si ille* A².   6 facimus: *facinus* A¹
7 est: om. P.

of catching sounds with some effort or difficulty; see my n. on Sull. 33.
voce naturae: so 3, 62; Tusc. 1, 35 and often elsewhere.
1. **bene sanos:** § 52 *n.*
viam...vitae: so 5, 15; Off. 1, 118 and often; and *in viam deducere* (of wanderers), Leg. 1, 41.
2. **beatae:** this sums up the three preceding adjectives, all of closely allied meaning, and the whole emphasises the fact that happiness consists in the victory over unrest; Sen. dial. 10, 14, 2 cum Epicuro quiescere. *Tranquillus* and *quietus, tranquillitas* and *quies* are often linked together, as in §§ 46, 58; Tim. 9; Clu. 153; Sull. 26; De Orat. 1, 2; Liv. 27, 12, 13; Vell. Pat. 2, 6 and 103.
3. **nullam...iuvaret:** cf. Sext. A.M. 1, 1 (of Epicureans) ὡς τῶν μαθημάτων μηδὲν συνεργούντων πρὸς σοφίας τελείωσιν ἢ ὥς τινες εἰκάζουσι, τοῦτο προκάλυμμα τῆς ἑαυτῶν ἀπαιδευσίας εἶναι νομίζοντες (ἐν πολλοῖς γὰρ ἀμαθὴς Ἐπίκουρος ἐλέγχεται). Sextus adds another reason, hatred for the followers of Plato and Aristotle, who were πολυμαθεῖς. Cf. nn. on § 26 and 2, 12.
5. **evolvendis:** 25 *n.*
7. **puerilis...delectatio:** Plut. non posse suaviter vivi, p. 1093 *b* ἐξωθοῦσι δὲ (οἱ Ἐπικούρειοι) τὰς ἀπὸ τῶν μαθημάτων (ἡδονάς); so in § 25 literature, history and poetry are not allowed by Epicurus to be fitted to convey pleasure *directly*, although it is not denied that ultimate profit may be obtained from them. Here it is indicated that poetry may reasonably give a child pleasure, but not a man. Plutarch complains, in his attack on Epicurus' view of happiness, p. 1095 *c*, that even kings are not permitted to refresh themselves with μουσικὰ προβλήματα or κριτικῶν φιλόλογα

ζητήματα at their banquets. Cf. N.D. 1, 72 Epicurus...nil olet ex puerilibus disciplinis, where see Mayor's n.; Heraclit. alleg. Hom. c. 4, ap. Usener § 229 ('Επίκουρος) ἅπασαν ὁμοῦ ποιητικὴν ὥσπερ ὀλέθριον μύθων δέλεαρ ἀφοσιούμενος.
se...contereret: *se* is not put for *otium suum* (Nägelsbach); cf. De Or. 1, 249 cum in causis et in negotiis et in foro conteramur; Caec. 14 contriti ad Regiam; Sen. ep. 88, 39 aetatem in syllabis conteram?
musicis...astris: these subjects are just those which, in the Republic, Plato lays down for the education of the φύλακες in his ideal state. According to Sext. A.M. 6, 27, the Epicurean calls μουσικὴ 'ἀσύμφορον and ἀργὸν φίλοινον χρημάτων ἀτημελῆ.' As to mathematics see § 20 *n.*, and cf. also Philod. Rhet. ed. Sudhaus, p. 244 καταγελάστως μὲν τὴν γεωμετρίαν ἡδονῆς καὶ κόσμου παρασκευαστικὴν εἶναι λέγουσιν· οὐ μὴν ἡμεῖς γε πάντα τὸν βίον εἰς ταύτην κατατίθεσθαι λέγομεν.
8. **numeris, astris:** put for scientia numerorum, astrorum.
initiis: i.e. definitions, axioms and postulates; cf. Proclus in Euclidem, p. 199, 9 Friedl. τῶν δὲ τὰς γεωμετρικὰς μόνας ἀρχὰς ἀνατρέπειν προθεμένων, ὥσπερ τῶν Ἐπικουρείων. The Sceptics attacked these ἀρχαί: see Acad. 2, 116, and cf. Lucian, Hermot. 74 γεωμετρία... ἀξιοῖ εἰς ἀπόδειξιν ἀληθῆ λέγειν ἀπὸ ψευδοῦς τῆς ἀρχῆς ὁρμωμένη (with the context).
9. **nihil...quo:** n. on § 41.
10. **id est:** as in 2 §§ 1, 6, 21, 90, 101.
eas...persequeretur : owing to the length of the sentence, this clause sums up the preceding, so as to show clearly the bimembral form. For *ergo* see n. on 2, 23.

queretur, vivendi artem tantam tamque operosam et perinde fructuosam relinqueret? Non ergo Epicurus ineruditus, sed ei indocti qui, quae pueros non didicisse turpe est, ea putant usque ad senectutem esse discenda. Quae cum dixisset, Explicavi, inquit, sententiam meam, et eo quidem consilio, tuom iudicium 5 ut cognoscerem, quae mea facultas, ut id meo arbitratu facerem, ante hoc tempus numquam est data.

1 tantam: om. E.   5 consilio tuom: *consilium* A[1].   6 mea: ita AEP:
mihi dett.

1. **vivendi artem:** § 42 *n.*
perinde: 'correspondingly'; i.e. the
fruit is commensurate with the toil.
Perinde appears not to occur in writings
before Cicero's time, and is generally
followed by some comparative particle,
as *ut, quam, atque.* Havet, Rev. de Phil.
xxiii, 331, argues for writing *et* before
operosam.

2. **non...ineruditus:** *est* omitted as
often with an emphatic word; cf. 1, 3.

3. **non didicisse:** so Sen. ep. 88, 2 non
discere debemus ista (liberalia studia)
sed didicisse.

usque ad senectutem: Philodemus
(Usener § 49) τῶν ἀκουστῶν ἄγαμαι τοῦ
σχολάζειν τοῖς λόγοις ἕως ἀνδρός. Many
of the Epicurean works of which fragments exist in the Herculanean rolls
dealt with portions of the ἐγκύκλιος

παιδεία: so the well-known treatises of
Philodemus about rhetoric, poetry, and
music; see Scott's list, no. 831, 862,
1003, 1039, and his comments, pp. 75,
80, 82. In some Epicurean texts we find
the γνήσιοι Ἐπικούρειοι contrasted with
certain heretics called σοφισταί: these
presumably occupied themselves much
in the 'pueriles disciplinae'; one,
Diogenes, even travelled as lecturer and
improvisatore.

4. **explicavi:** cf. 3, 14; Div. 1, 6.

6. **quae mea facultas:** Havet *quoniam* for *quae mea* in Rev. de Phil.
xxiii, 332.

meo arbitratu: 'unrestrictedly.' The
exposition of Epicurean ethics ends
without mention of important topics,
such as the family and the State.

M. TVLLI CICERONIS
DE FINIBVS BONORVM ET MALORVM
AD BRVTVM
LIBER SECVNDVS

I. Hic cum uterque me intueretur seseque ad audiendum 1
significarent paratos, Primum, inquam, deprecor ne me tamquam philosophum putetis scholam vobis aliquam explicaturum,
quod ne in ipsis quidem philosophis magno opere umquam pro-
5 bavi. Quando enim Socrates, qui parens philosophiae iure dici
potest, quicquam tale fecit? Eorum erat iste mos, qui tum
sophistae nominabantur, quorum e numero primus est ausus

---

3 scholam: *scolam* AB. 3 vobis: om. B. 4 magno opere: *magno pere* A;
om. BE. 4 umquam: *numquam* BE. 7 e: *est* E.

---

1. **cum…intueretur**: Acad. 2, 63 *n.*
intueretur…significarent: for the
change of number cf. 1 § 16 quorum
utrumque audivi cum probarent; Asin.
Pollio ap. Fam. 10, 33, 3 ita porro
festinavit uterque confligere, tamquam
nihil peius timerent quam…; Flacc. 104,
where *quotus quisque* is followed by
three clauses with singular verbs, then
one with a plural verb. In no other
passage of certain reading in Cicero is
uterque construed with a plural verb.
The construction is common in old
Latin and in poetry generally, and sure
exx. of it are found here and there in
the later prose, as Tac. h. 2, 97; 3, 35;
4, 34. Caes. B.C. 2, 6, 5 has *utraque* in
apposition to *naves*, with which the
number of the verb accords, but there
is no ex. in Caes. of the construction
without such complication, for the
reading in B.C. 3, 30, 3 is doubtful; so
with the one instance quoted from
Sallust, i.e. Cat. 49, 2. Livy is said to
have avoided the usage.

2. **tamquam philosophum**: cf. 5, 8
numquam putarem me in Academia
tamquam philosophum disputaturum.

3. **scholam**:=*quaestionem* below;
Schola is sometimes local as De Orat.
1, 102; Off. 2, 87; but often used in
the wider sense of 'discourse' or 'essay'
of any kind (cf. σχόλιον Att. 16, 7, 3),
Tusc. 1, 7, 8, 113; De Or. 2, 13; sometimes the word means 'a commonplace'

as in Fam. 9, 22, 5 habes scholam
Stoicam: ὁ σοφὸς εὐθυρρημονήσει. These
meanings are said not to attach to
σχολή in extant Greek writings earlier
than Plutarch; the reference in L.S.
s. v. to Plato Leg. 820 c is not important.

5. **parens philosophiae**: N.D. 2, 167
Socrates princeps philosophiae; ps.
Quint. decl. 268 Socratis, quo velut
fonte omnis philosophia manasse credi-
tur; see also my n. on Acad. 1, 18.

6. **qui tum**: Cicero speaks similarly
in Acad. 2, 72, the word σοφιστής having
received a somewhat different application in his time.

7. **quorum e numero**: probably only
here (in Cicero) and Acad. 2, 15 for *quo
e numero*; so *ex eo numero* not *eorum*,
excepting in De Or. 2, 56, where however *eorum* follows *numero* and is
succeeded by *qui*. But even where *qui*
follows, *ex eo numero* occurs, as Arch.
31; so below, 3, 70 ex eo genere quae
prosunt. It is probable that De Or.
2, 56 is corrupt. So usually *in eo
numero*, but N.D. 1, 43 venerari Epicurum et in eorum ipsorum numero, de
quibus haec quaestio est, habere debeat,
where, however, *deorum* should probably be read, as in §§ 36, 38; cf. too
in illorum numero once in Vat. 41;
but *in quorum numero* I do not remember to have seen in Cicero. Cf. n.
on *ex eo genere* in 3, 70.

Leontinus Gorgias in conventu poscere quaestionem, id est
iubere dicere qua de re quis vellet audire. Audax negotium,
dicerem impudens, nisi hoc institutum postea translatum ad
2 philosophos nostros esset. Sed et illum quem nominavi, et
ceteros sophistas, ut e Platone intellegi potest, lusos videmus a 5
Socrate. Is enim percontando atque interrogando elicere solebat
eorum opiniones, quibuscum disserebat, ut ad ea, quae ei
respondissent, si quid videretur, diceret. Qui mos cum a pos-

1 Leontinus: *leoncius* BE.   1 Gorgias in conventu: *gorgius hi conventu* A¹.
1 poscere: *posceret* A¹.   4 philosophos nostros: sic A; *nostros philosophos* BE.
4 esset: *esse* A¹.   5 a: om. B (non E).   6 percontando: *percunctando* A¹BE.
7 ei: *hii* A; *hi* B.

1. **Leontinus Gorgias**: 'idem narra-
tur de Orat. 1, 103, 111, 129. Res nota e
Platonis Gorgia 447 c' (Madvig). In the
Hippias of Plato, H. boasts of the
number of subjects with which he is
familiar. Cicero very frequently sets
the epithet of origin in front of the
personal name, as here. [*Leontinus
Gorgias* in De Or. 1, 103: Cato m. 13
and even where the reverse order is
followed in mentioning other people, as
Brut. 30, Orator 39; only in Inv. 1, 7
Gorgias L.]
in conventu poscere: De Or. 3, 129 in
c. p. qua de re quisque vellet audire;
Lael. 17 Graecorum consuetudo, ut eis
ponatur de quo disputent quamvis
subito; Tusc. 3, 7 poposci eorum aliquem,
qui aderant causam disserendi; ib. 1, 7
ponere iubebam de quo quis audire
vellet. For *quaestionem* cf. Fam. 9, 26, 1
ζήτημα Dioni philosopho posuisti;
Quint. 7, 4, 40 quaestiones positionibus
mutantur, where *pos.* is a rendering of
θέσεσιν, as in 2, 10, 15.
id est, etc.: see n. on 1, 71.
2. audax negotium: the use of phrases
like this, in apposition to the preceding
sentence, is common in Cicero; as Lael.
§§ 67, 71, 79. See Draeger § 309; and cf.
n. on § 75, below. *Impudens* is doubtless
accus. not nom., as Cicero would not
repeat the nom. unchanged (spite of
Madv. in Opusc. 2, 307 on Deiot. 2).
The only exx. in Merg. all change
nom. to acc.; so Flacc. 13; Lig. 26; Phil.
2, 48 (a little complicated); ib. 67; in
none of these are variants given.
Deiot. 2 is of uncertain reading; Phil.
14, 22 decreta est...decretam ('decreta
maluit Faernus ut est in 2 Oxonn.' Halm).
Att. 16, 15, 5 rem...Terentiae where
Tyrrell and Purser repeat (after Boot)
Madvig's erroneous dictum and want to

read *res.* Fam. 5, 15, 1 amor tuus...non
ille quidem mihi ignotus sed tamen gratus
et optatus; dicerem 'iucundus' nisi id
verbum in omne tempus perdidissem.
Verbum shows that *iucundus* is treated
as *caseless*; cf. Mayor on Plin. ep. 3, 2, 2.
Add Att. 6, 2, 4; Leg. agr. 2, 95;
Orat. §§ 106, 219. On the other hand
gen. dat. abl. seem always to be repeated unchanged in Cicero. In Sest.
53 Cod. Salisb. has *diem*, but Harl.
with which it generally agrees *die*
(and so Par.). Schmalz Antib. s.v. dico
treats unaltered nom. as post-class. (so
Haacke, Stil. § 83) and refers to his
Synt. § 51.
3. **institutum**: prob. participle, not
noun, 'when once established'; so § 4
hoc positum.
4. **nostros**: 'Academicos praecipue
Cicero significat' (Madvig), no doubt
rightly.
5. **lusos**: the meaning required here
is rather 'foiled' than 'mocked'; and
this would be given by *elusos*; cf. Caec. 24 pueris nobilibus quos adhuc
elusit; Acad. 2, 123 ipsi illum vicissim
eluditis; Leg. 2, 52 hac scientia illam
eluditis. A similar change from *lusit* to
elusit is necessary in De Orat. 2, 222,
where see Wilkins' n. (*Ludificari* only in
Sext. Rosc. 55; Rep. 3, 9; *ludificare* in
Quinct. 54.)
videmus: often employed of what
is got by reading; below, 4, 15 and my
n. on Acad. 2, 129.
6. **percontando atque interrogando**:
τῷ ἐλέγχειν: for the tendency of Cicero in
rendering from the Greek to translate
the same phrase twice, see n. on
1, 38.
elicere: used, *in re simili*, De Or. 1,
158; ib. 3, 79; Acad. 2, 7.
8. **si quid videretur**: Acad. 2, 7.

terioribus non esset retentus, Arcesilas eum revocavit instituitque
ut hi qui se audire vellent, non de se quaererent, sed ipsi dicerent
quid sentirent; quod cum dixissent, ille contra. Sed eum qui
audiebant, quoad poterant, defendebant sententiam suam. Apud
5 ceteros autem philosophos, qui quaesivit aliquid, tacet; quod
quidem iam fit etiam in Academia. Vbi enim is qui audire volt,
ita dixit: 'Voluptas mihi videtur esse summum bonum,' perpetua
oratione contra disputatur, ut facile intellegi possit eos qui
aliquid sibi videri dicant, non ipsos in ea sententia esse, sed
10 audire velle contraria. Nos commodius agimus. Non enim solum **3**
Torquatus dixit quid sentiret, sed etiam cur. Ego autem
arbitror, quamquam admodum delectatus sum eius oratione
perpetua, tamen commodius, cum in rebus singulis insistas et
intellegas quid quisque concedat, quid abnuat, ex rebus concessis
5 concludi quod velis, et ad exitum perveniri. Cum enim fertur

1 que: om. BE.   2 hi: sic A; *hy* B.   2 audire: *audite* A[1]; *audiri* B.
5 quod quidem: *quid quidem* E; *quicquid* B.   6 etiam: om. B.   8 eos: *ut eos*
BE.   9 aliquid sibi: *sibi aliquid* BE.   11 etiam: *esse* B.   14 abnuat: *obnuat* B.
14 ex rebus concessis: *ex quibus concessit* A[1].

1. **Arcesilas**: cf. 5, 10 and De Or.
3, 67 quem (Arcesilan) ferunt...primum
instituisse—quamquam id fuit Socrati-
cum maxime,—non quid ipse sentiret
ostendere, sed contra id, quod quisque
se sentire dixisset, disputare; Att. 2, 3, 3
Σωκρατικῶς εἰς ἑκάτερα: Diog. L. 4, 28;
August. contra Acad. 3, 39; Lactant.
7, 7 Academici quibus ad omnia respondere propositum est; other passages are
quoted in my n. on Acad. 2, 7.
  3. **ille contra**: for the ellipse cf. 1,
3 *n.*
  eum: for position of pronoun cf.
Acad. 1, 1.
  6. **iam...etiam**: not uncommon in
Cicero and elsewhere; Merguet's Lexika
give seven exx. from the speeches and
philosophical works.
  7. **perp. or.**: 1, 29 *n.*
  9. **in ea sententia esse**: this form is
widely scattered in Latin; so *versari,
perseverare in opinione, sententia. Esse
ea* or *eadem sententia*, without *in*, seems
to be un-Latin.
  10. **commodius**: although the plan of
conducting debate by *perpetua oratio*
pitted against short speeches is better
than the current plan, yet quick
question and answer would be better
still (*commodius* below).
  13. **insistas**: Orat. 207 oratio insistat
in singulis; but the MSS. have in Verr.

2, 3, 172 si singulis insistere velim; and
in Acad. 2, 94 illustribus rebus insistis;
and in De Or. 3, 33 quibus vestigiis
institi and in Cael. 41. It is probable
that Cicero used after *insistere* only *in*
and abl.; see my n. on Wilkins' edition
of De Or. l.l. The dative construction
which Wilkins assumes in the passage
of De Or. is improbable; if the MSS.
reading is right *vestigiis* is abl.; cf. ib. 3,
6 vestigium in quo institisset. In Tusc.
4, 41 quo loco volt insistere, *quo loco* is
a mere adverbial phrase, a substitute
for *qua* or *ubi*. Similarly if the MSS. have
preserved the right reading in Verr. l.l.
and Acad. l.l. and Cael. l.l. we must
suppose the construction to be abl. not
dat. as some of the dictionaries assert;
but it is more likely that *in* has fallen
out in these passages, and also in the
isolated passage of Caes. B.G. 2, 27, 3.
It is still harder to believe that Cic. once
(De Or. 3, 176) and Caes. once (B.G.
3, 14, 3) employed the accusative after
insistere. Cicero has not the constr. with
in and accusative which appears in
Caes. B.G. 6, 5, 1.
  14. **ex rebus concessis**: Div. 2, 104
videsne ut ad rem dubiam concessis
rebus pervenerit? [C. F. W. Müller
inserts *a* before *concessis*.]
  15. **ad exitum perveniri**: of debate in
Orat. 116.

quasi torrens oratio, quamvis multa cuiusque modi rapiat, nihil
tamen teneas, nihil apprehendas, nusquam orationem rapidam
coërceas.

Omnis autem in quaerendo, quae via quadam et ratione
habetur, oratio praescribere primum debet ut quibusdam in 5
formulis EA RES AGETUR, ut, inter quos disseritur, conveniat
4 quid sit id de quo disseratur. II. Hoc positum in Phaedro a
Platone probavit Epicurus sensitque in omni disputatione id fieri
oportere. Sed quod proximum fuit non vidit. Negat enim definiri
rem placere, sine quo fieri interdum non potest ut inter eos qui 10
ambigunt conveniat quid sit id de quo agatur, velut in hoc ipso

1 multa: *multi* B.   2 apprehendas: *reprehendas* B.   3 coërceas: *coherceas*
A²B.   4 in quaerendo: *inquirendo* B.   4 quae via...ut quibusdam: om. A¹.
4 ratione: *oracione* B.   5 ut: *ne* (*ut* superscripto) A.   5 in: om. B.   9 proximum: *primum* B.   10 placere...conveniat: om. A¹.   11 agatur...de quo:
om. B.   11 velut: *velit* A¹.

1. **torrens**: often of speech in later
writers; the word occurs here only in
Cicero and apparently not at all in
earlier literature in this connexion.
cuiusque modi: so § 22; Off. 1, 139;
Verr. 4, 7 (a correction of *cuiuscemodi*
in Cod. Reg.).
2. **apprehendas**: this reading is quite
supportable; cf. Clu. 52 ut quidquid ego
apprehenderam accusator extorquebat
e manibus; and *arripiet* in N.D. 2, 162
quod uterque vestrum arripiet fortasse
ad reprehendendum. If *reprehendas* be
the right reading, the word must be used
as it is of witnesses who are brought to
book by their slips; so Att. 2, 24, 3
maxime in eo Vettius est reprehensus;
Flacc. 22 bene testem interrogavit;
callide accessit; reprehendit ('quasi
evolantem et fugientem,' says Madvig,
but that hardly conveys the idea;
rather 'ne institutum iter pergeret');
there are other instances of the same
use in Cicero's speeches. Madvig quotes
some illustrations which are not closely
similar, such as Acad. 2, 139 revocat
virtus vel potius reprehendit manu.
Madvig's argument against *apprehendas*
is not cogent: 'aptus est orationis ascen-
sus: *nihil teneas, nihil* (si non statim
tenueris, postea) *reprehendas*. Contra
apprehendere prius est quam *tenere*.'
4. **in quaerendo**, etc.: the phrase
oratio in quaerendo is condemned by
Davies; but the connexion is rather
or. quae habetur in qu.
5. **praescribere**: Gaius Inst. 4, 130
−7, describes certain *praescriptiones*,

prefaces to the ordinary *formulae*, intended to define more precisely the
scope of the actions raised. These *praescriptiones* began with *ea res agetur*; but
as Madvig remarks, *agetur* may sometimes have occurred also, or Cicero may
have changed the phrase. In Orat. 36
he has *praescriptum aut formulam*
(applied metaphorically).
ut: sc. *solet praescribi*; perhaps, however, *est* has fallen out after *formulis*.
6. **inter quos**: n. on 1, 18.
7. **in Phaedro**: i.e. in 237 b περὶ παντός, ὦ παῖ, μία ἀρχὴ τοῖς μέλλουσι καλῶς
βουλεύεσθαι· εἰδέναι δεῖ περὶ οὗ ἂν ᾖ ἡ
βουλή, ἢ παντὸς ἁμαρτάνειν ἀνάγκη.
There is much in the other dialogues
(especially the 'Theaetetus') touching
the necessity of a ὁμολογία between
disputants as to the meaning of the
terms used and the points at issue.
9. **vidit...negat**: the change of tense
as in 1, 29; 2, 86 and often. Cf. my n.
on Acad. 2, 104 quae cum exposuisset,
adiungit.
negat: for this see n. on 1, 22.
Madvig blames Cicero 'qui non sentiat
ipsam notionem boni in his libris nusquam ab origine sua explicari et certis
finibus comprehendi.' However, no
formal definition of ἀγαθόν was attempted by Plato or Aristotle, and (as
Madvig notes) the attempt when made
by the Stoics was not very successful.
See n. on 3, 33.
11. **ambigunt**: the verb occurs in the
philosophical writings only here and in
N.D. 1, 69.

de quo nunc disputamus. Quaerimus enim finem bonorum.
Possumusne hoc scire quale sit, nisi contulerimus inter nos, cum
finem bonorum dixerimus, quid finis, quid etiam sit ipsum
bonum? Atqui haec patefactio quasi rerum opertarum, cum quid 5
quidque sit aperitur, definitio est; qua tu etiam imprudens
utebare non numquam. Nam hunc ipsum sive finem sive extremum sive ultimum definiebas id esse quo omnia, quae recte
fierent, referrentur, neque id ipsum usquam referretur. Praeclare
hoc quidem. Bonum ipsum etiam quid esset, fortasse, si opus
fuisset, definisses, aut quod esset natura appetendum, aut quod
prodesset, aut quod iuvaret, aut quod liberet modo. Nunc idem,
nisi molestum est, quoniam tibi non omnino displicet definire et
id facis cum vis, velim definias quid sit voluptas, de quo omnis

---

2 hoc scire: sic A; *hac scire* BE.　　2 quale sit: sic A²; *qualisunt* A¹; *qualis sit* B.
2 cum: *meum* B.　　　　3 etiam: *esse* B, ut in § 3.　　　4 patefactio: *patefacio* A¹.
5 sit: om. B.　　　5 definitio: *diffinitio* AB, vulgato errore.　　　6 extremum sive:
om. A¹.　　8 referrentur: *referentur* B.　　9 quidem: *quam* B.　　11 liberet modo.
Nunc: *liberet. Modo nunc* A.　　12 definire: *finire* AB.

in hoc ipso: *hoc ipsum* would have
been more natural; so below, § 18, nec
ea quae docere volt, ulla arte distinguit,
ut haec ipsa, quae modo loquebamur.
　2. contulerimus: indic. though *dixerimus* is subj.
　4. patefactio: Acad. 2, 44 patefac-
turum (of ἀπόδειξις). The noun is ἅπαξ
εἰρημένον in classical literature.
　quasi: here, as often, indicates a
rendering from the Greek; see my n.
on Acad. 1, 17.
　cum, etc.: explanatory clauses with
cum are pretty common; *cum bonum
dixerimus* above is similar; so Tusc. 5,
29; N.D. 1, 121.
　5. imprudens...non numquam: Cicero
is somewhat forgetful; Torquatus gave
his definition of the *summum bonum*
(§§ 29, 42) not as *imprudens*, but in
obedience to the precepts of Epicurus.
For *finem...extremum...ultimum* see n.
on 1, 17; for *recte fierent* 1, 29 *n.*; for
neque id ipsum 1, 42 *n.*; and for *referretur* 1, 11, 42.
　7. id esse: the acc. and inf. constr.
after *definire* occurs elsewhere, as Tusc.
5, 27; Rep. 1, 1. For other forms see
n. on § 13 and on 3, 33 (cf. n. on idem
esse dico in 2, 13).
　8. referretur: in 1, 29 the second verb
is missed out, and perhaps is due to
the copyists here.
　praeclare: as to ellipse of verb cf.
1, 68 and n. on 1, 3.

　9. si opus fuisset: here, as often,
opus conveys the idea of advantage,
rather than of need: 'if you had seen
your advantage in it.' Cf. Fam. 1, 9, 25
legem curiatam consuli ferre opus esse,
necesse non esse.
　10. quod prodesset: = τὸ ὠφέλιμον:
see n. on 3, 33.
　11. quod liberet: Tusc. 4, 44 nihil
quemquam nisi quod lubeat, praeclare
facere posse.
　12. nisi molestum est: see n. on 1, 28.
　definire: in reference to logical definition, *finire* (which ABE have here)
and *finitio* are post-Ciceronian; common
in Quint. Sen.
　13. definias: yet later, in speaking of
honestum (§ 45) Cicero says that the
meaning of the word is rather to be
understood from the general opinion of
mankind than from definition. Cf. ἄν-
θρωπός ἐστιν ὃ πάντες ἴδμεν (Democritus,
ap. Mullach, 1, p. 359 § 9). In the same
way Cicero, Off. 1, 7 abuses Panaetius
for not defining *officium* (καθῆκον)
yet gives no precise definition himself. Edd. there have often unnecessarily
assumed a lacuna. So Rep. 1, 38 Scipio
lays down the need for a definition of *res
publica*, but practically admits that an
exact definition is impossible. It is
strange that the careful definition of
ἡδονή given by Aristotle in Eth. Nic. 10
should (so it appears) have dropped out
of mind very soon; but most of Aris-

6 haec quaestio est. Quis, quaeso, inquit, est, qui quid sit voluptas nesciat, aut qui, quo magis id intellegat, definitionem aliquam desideret? Me ipsum esse dicerem, inquam, nisi mihi viderer habere bene cognitam voluptatem et satis firme conceptam animo atque comprehensam. Nunc autem dico ipsum Epicurum nescire et in eo nutare, eumque, qui crebro dicat diligenter oportere exprimi quae vis subiecta sit vocibus, non intellegere interdum quid sonet haec vox voluptatis, id est quae res huic voci subiciatur.

1 Quis, quaeso: *quis quasi* A¹B; *quis quam* A²; corr. Goerenz.   1 inquit: *inquis* A¹.   1 voluptas: *voluptatis* A.   4 habere: om. B.   4 bene cognitam: *cognitam bene* B.   4 conceptam: *acceptam* B.   5 atque: om. B. 6 et: *ut* B.   6 nutare: *mutare* E.

totle's teaching shared the same fate. [Cf. Sidgwick, Methods of Ethics, p. 29, ed. 2. 'What definition can we give of "ought," "right," and other terms expressing the same fundamental notion? To this it might be answered that the notion is too elementary to admit of being made clearer by any formal definition.']

voluptas, etc.: 1, 28 voluptate de qua omne certamen est.

1. quis…quid: for the repetition of *qu-* here see exx. in my n. on Acad. 1, 6, to which add Brut. 210; Liv. 30, 29, 10; Lucr. 6, 389; Ov. Trist. 1, 1, 18 si quis qui quid agam forte requiret erit; De Or. 2, 235.

2. quo magis: 1, 41 *n.*

4. habere cognitam: not exactly an equivalent for *cognosse*, since each of the two words retains its force; lit. 'to hold after having thoroughly learned.' Later this construction developed into a mere tense-form, as *habere* tended more and more to become a purely auxiliary verb. Cf. 4, 3; 5, 26 and 76, and Thielmann's excellent articles in Archiv 2, 372 sq. and 509 sq.

firme…comprehensam: 1, 71 firme… comprehenderit.

6. in eo: though the pronoun refers to *voluptatem*; see n. on 1, 20 (*in quo*).

nutare: so N.D. 1, 120 Democritus nutare videtur in natura deorum. Cicero has *natare* with the same sense, N.D. 3, 62 (cf. Fam. 7, 10, 2); also Hor. s. 2, 7, 7, and Georges s. v. quotes Varro, Tibull. Sen.

7. quae vis…vocibus: so Tusc. 1, 87 triste est nomen ipsum carendi, quia subicitur haec vis….

8. sonet: the word occurs again with this somewhat strange sense in Off.

3, 83 honestate igitur dirigenda utilitas est et quidem sic ut haec duo verbo inter se discrepare, re unum sonare; cf. August. ep. 118 (in Corp. Scr. eccl. 34, p. 666 hoc enim sonat videri tibi, etc.).

id est, etc.: this clause, like many others prefaced by *id est* in Cicero, has been condemned by scholars who have not sufficiently observed that Cicero never uses such a clause to introduce a *mere* re-statement of what precedes. I have discussed the different applications of these clauses in a n. on Acad. 1, 8. Here, as Madvig points out, Cicero is rendering the phrase τὸ ὑποτεταγμένον τῷ φθόγγῳ used by Epicurus in the letter to Herodotus quoted by Diog. L. 10, 37: πρῶτον μὲν οὖν τὰ ὑποτεταγμένα τοῖς φθόγγοις, ὦ 'Ηρόδοτε, δεῖ εἰληφέναι, ὅπως ἂν τὰ δοξαζόμενα ἢ ἀπορούμενα ἔχωμεν εἰς ταῦτα ἀναγαγόντες ἐπικρίνειν, καὶ μὴ ἄκριτα πάντα ἡμῖν ἴῃ εἰς ἄπειρον δεικνύουσιν ἢ κενοὺς φθόγγους ἔχωμεν. ἀνάγκη γὰρ τὸ πρῶτον ἐννόημα καθ' ἕκαστον φθόγγον βλέπεσθαι καὶ μηθὲν ἀποδείξεως προσδεῖσθαι, εἴπερ ἕξομεν τὸ ζητούμενον ἢ ἀπορούμενον καὶ δοξαζόμενον ἐφ' ὃ ἀνάξομεν. Here τὰ ὑποτεταγμένα τοῖς φθόγγοις are the προλήψεις or conceptions impressed on the mind by repeated experience (πρόληψιν = μνήμην τοῦ πολλάκις ἔξωθεν φανέντος, Diog. L. 10, 33). These προλήψεις are the ultimate bases of all reasoning; they are ἀρχαί: hence 'μὴ δύνασθαι μηδένα μήτε ζητῆσαι μήτε ἀπορῆσαι μηδὲ μὴν δοξάσαι, ἀλλ' οὐδὲ ἐλέγξαι χωρὶς προλήψεως' (Clem. Al. Strom. II, 4, p. 157, 44 Sylb.); so, too, Sext. A.M. 1, 57 and 11, 21; Cic. N.D. 1, 43. Each πρόληψις is ἐναργές, i.e. carries with it its own evidence of

III. Tum ille ridens: Hoc vero, inquit, optimum, ut is, qui

1 inquit: *inquid* A¹, ut in §§ 7, 8, 9.

truth. Diog. L. 10, 33 παντὶ οὖν ὀνόματι τὸ πρώτως ὑποτεταγμένον ἐναργές ἐστιν... ἐναργεῖς οὖν εἰσιν οἱ προλήψεις: Clem. Al. l.l. πρόληψιν δὲ (Ἐπίκουρος) ἀποδίδωσιν ἐπιβολὴν ἐπί τι ἐναργὲς καὶ ἐπὶ τὴν ἐναργῆ τοῦ πράγματος ἐπίνοιαν. We have προλήψεις not only of visible and tangible things like ἄνθρωπος, βοῦς, but of 'god' (N.D. 1, 44), 'pleasure' and qualities such as 'sweetness,' 'whiteness,' etc. (above 1, 30). It is necessary that disputants should agree on the designations of these προλήψεις, but further than that definition could not go (see Usener, fragm. 258). According to Epicurus, it is of no use to attempt to get behind the πρόληψις, and we must assume that it correctly represents its source (τὸ πρᾶγμα).

1. tum ille ridens: so 1, 26; 5, 8; 5, 86, etc. On the reading *tunc* see n. on 1, 28.

hoc vero optimum: see n. on 1, 3 as to the omission of *est.* For *optimum* cf. Suet. Iul. 80 bonum factum: ne quis, etc. In such ironical statements *vero* often appears, as e.g. in Fam. 1, 9, 16 hoc vero probandum, where the reading has been wrongly suspected. Draeger, 2, p. 276 qu. optimum est ut from Gell. praef. 19.

ut, etc.: scholars have differed a good deal in their views concerning the substantive clauses with *ut.* Madvig in his note here criticises Wunder, who had asserted that the *ut* has in them the force of *quo modo:* 'nam illam esse primam huius particulae significationem certum est; illud ambigitur, retineaturne sic interrogativa sententia in hac de qua agitur coniunctione, ut appareat per se et sentiatur, et num haec sit causa hanc particulam potius quam infinitam sententiam ponendi.' He rightly decides that the sense assigned to *ut* requires great forcing in the interpretation of many passages; clauses like *non est veri simile quam* give no support to the theory because here the *quam* clause conveys the notion of degree while the *ut*-clauses in question express merely a fact. Madvig seems to think that clauses expressive of *manner* (*ut = quo modo*) easily glide into expressing *result*, and that the *ut* is the sign of this change. But *ut* now has 'non certa prima significatio sed generalis quaedam vis in sententiis vinciendis.' If I have understood Madvig rightly, he appears

to hold that the notion of result runs through all these clauses more or less conspicuously. On this ground, he says, Cicero did not say *probo, ut ita sit* but sometimes *qui probari potest ut...* and never *veri simile est ut,* but four times *non veri simile est ut....* He then quotes *integrum est ut* (apparently believing the negative *in-* to have something to do with this case); but *integrum est* is only quoted *twice*, both times from Cicero, and both times with negative. Madvig then proceeds to illustrate the difference between the *ut*-construction and the infinitive construction by quoting Flacc. 65 quid in Graeco sermone tam tritum atque celebratum est quam, si quis despicatui ducitur, ut Mysorum ultimus dicatur? This means *quid tam vulgo fit?* whereas the infinitive would mean *quid tam notum et saepe dictum est?* [But as in the previous case the thing that happens is a *saying*, this distinction comes to very little.] Of the present passage it is said: 'si sic dixisset Torquatus: *eum...nescire*, tantum, merum id esse, simpliciter iudicasset (*dass er nicht weiss*), nunc simul dubitare se ostendit, fierine possit (*dass er nicht wissen sollte*).' The questions of syntax raised would need much space for their treatment. I can only mention here summarily the following points: (1) the idea, which Madvig apparently favours, that the *ut*-clauses sprang in all cases out of parallel infinitive clauses, is hardly tenable. In many instances the infinitive form is the later in literature. Possibly infinitive clauses passed into *ut* clauses in a few simple instances and so a grammatical type arose which spread over far more ground than the infinitive clauses had ever covered. In many instances a parallel infinitive construction is inconceivable, as e.g. in Fin. 3, 48 appropinquat ut videat; (2) it is quite impossible to determine with exactness the notions which the users of the construction may have attached to the *ut* in every instance. Quite possibly, the whole clause was realised together as giving completeness to the verb or phrase which it followed, and there was no conscious differentiation of *ut* in any of the class. But if differences were realised as existent, then it is not probable that *all* the clauses were held to convey the idea of result. Most of them can be easily imagined to do so; but some

finem rerum expetendarum voluptatem esse dicat, id extremum,
id ultimum bonorum, id ipsum quid et quale sit, nesciat! Atqui,
inquam, aut Epicurus quid sit voluptas, aut omnes mortales qui
ubique sunt, nesciunt. Quonam, inquit, modo? Quia voluptatem
hanc esse sentiunt omnes, quam sensus accipiens movetur et
7 iucunditate quadam perfunditur. Quid ergo? istam voluptatem,
inquit, Epicurus ignorat? Non semper, inquam; nam interdum

2 quid et: *quid ē* A; *quidem* B; cf. 1 § 29.   4 quonam: *quoniam* ABE.

would more naturally be otherwise conceived, as *eo consilio ut* (1, 72), which
may well be the *ut* of purpose. In the
construction *concedere ut*, scholars have
often seen a reflexion of the concessive
ut (so Draeger, II², p. 252); (3) the language is very capricious in the choice
between the two forms, where the
choice exists: e.g. iubeo + inf., impero +
ut. A great deal depends on the idio-
syncrasy of the writer; Cicero, for example, favours the *ut*- clause; (4) a
distinction in meaning between the two
forms is very far from being always
traceable. Passages may easily be
found, for example, where *sequitur ut*
and *sequitur* followed by infinitive
obviously convey precisely the same
sense (so e.g. in Fat. 28); and in Fin.
5, 78 *concedere ut* and *c.* with inf. follow
each other in two successive sentences.
But (5) the existence of the two forms
did provide a ready means of distinguishing between two senses of the same
verb. Thus *dicere* sometimes has the
sense 'to order'; very naturally after
this sense followed the subjunctive
with *ut*. Yet here and there this construction succeeds *dicere* in its ordinary
sense; as in Varro r.r. 1, 2, 26 verum
dicit ut hoc scripserit. So when *concedere* means 'to give permission' *ut* is
employed. (6) The *ut*-constructions
were probably at first dependent on
verbs of *action* or *desire*, not of being;
then were introduced expressions like
est consilium ut, parallel to *volumus ut*;
then even *est ut*; then *ut*-clauses purely
explanatory, as after *hoc illud*, etc.
(7) The greater the separation in the
sentence between the governing verb
or phrase and the dependent clause, the
greater is the probability of the *ut*-
clause rather than the infinitive clause
where the choice between the two is
open. (8) Some of the more noticeable
ut-clauses in Fin. 1, 7 inciderit ut; 1, 8
usu venit ut (? only Cicero); 1, 14

adducor ut (see n.); 2, 24 sequitur ut
(commoner than inf.); 3, 63 nascitur ut;
3, 68 consentaneum est ut; 4, 80 exigere
ut; 5, 1 constituere ut; 5, 42 coniti ut
(isolated).
  In Caes. where there is *noun + est + ut*
the noun seems almost always to have
a demonstrative with it.
  1. **finem ... extremum ... ultimum**:
three renderings of τέλος: cf. n. on 1,
29 and 42.
  2. **quid et quale**: 1, 29 *n.*
  3. **omnes mortales**: Cicero has this
phrase and *multi mortales, nemo mortalis*, frequently, but not *mortalis or
mortales* alone, like Sallust, Tacitus, and
later writers.
  omnes...qui ubique sunt: § 13; 4,
74.
  5. **sentiunt**: this verb means not
merely to entertain an opinion ('feel' or
'think') but to express it; as often in
connexion with debate in the senate,
and so (probably) here, and below, 3, 34
and 5, 23. Thus *sentio* and *censeo* come
to have precisely the same meaning;
cf. N.D. 1, 27 (*sensit* and *censuit* in two
consecutive sentences); also Acad. 1, 22
compared with 2, 131. As to Madvig's
contention about *esse* see two other exx
in Merguet, and the omission with *puto*
etc. is common, e.g. Leg. 1, 49.
  quam...accipiens: *accipere voluptatem*
for *percipere* is unusual; though *a
dolorem* is common enough.
  6. **perfunditur**: so 2, 114 dulcedine
perfusi, 5, 70 laetitia perfundi; N.D.
1, 112; Tusc. 4, 20; iudicio perfund
Rosc. Am. 80 (strange and much
debated; see Landgr.).
  quid ergo? this form, like *quid igitur*
is always followed by another question
this is not the case with the much les
common forms *quid igitur est?* and *quic
ergo est?* (n. on 1, 17). While *quid erg*
merely points to a coming question
quid ergo est? means, 'what, now, are the
facts?'

nimis etiam novit, quippe qui testificetur ne intellegere quidem
se posse, ubi sit aut quod sit ullum bonum praeter illud quod
cibo et potione et aurium delectatione et obscena voluptate

1 quidem se: om. B.   3 et aurium: *et auri* B; *aut auri* E.

1. **nimis etiam:** Acad.
2, 14 isti vi-
dentur nimis etiam adfirmare quaedam.
novit: Tusc. 3, 42 quivis ut intellegat
quam voluptatem norit Epicurus.
ne intellegere quidem, etc.: this
passage from the work of Epicurus περὶ
τέλους was much quoted. Thus Athen.
12, p. 546 e οὐ γὰρ ἔγωγε ἔχω τι νοήσω
τἀγαθόν, ἀφαιρῶν μὲν τὰς διὰ χυλῶν
ἡδονάς, ἀφαιρῶν δὲ τὰς δι' ἀφροδισίων,
ἀφαιρῶν δὲ τὰς δι' ἀκροαμάτων, ἀφαιρῶν
δὲ καὶ τὰς διὰ μορφῆς κατ' ὄψιν ἡδείας
κινήσεις. Athenaeus quotes the words
also with slight differences in two
other passages, 7, 280 a and 7, 278 f.
The context is more fully given by
Cicero in Tusc. 3, 41–2 than by any
other authority. He translates the
words of Epicurus beyond the point at
which Athenaeus stops, thus: sive quae
aliae voluptates in toto homine gignuntur quolibet sensu; nec vere ita dici
potest, mentis laetitiam solam esse in
bonis. Laetantem enim mentem ita
novi: spe eorum omnium, quae supra
dixi, fore ut natura eis potiens dolore
careat. Then, having omitted something, Cicero goes on 'paulo infra' as he
says: saepe quaesivi ex eis qui appellabantur sapientes quid haberent quod in
bonis relinquerent, si illa detraxissent,
nisi si vellent voces inanis fundere;
nihil ab eis potui cognoscere. Qui si
virtutes ebullire vellent et sapientias,
nihil aliud dicent nisi eam viam qua
efficiantur eae voluptates quas supra
dixi. Cicero then declares that what
follows is in the same vein and that this
whole work of Epicurus is 'crammed
with the like expressions and opinions';
further (§ 44), that the work is 'confertus
voluptatibus.' [In Fin. 2, 20 it is said
that Epic. put forward the same view
'plurimis locis.'] Later (§ 46) there is a
criticism from an imaginary Epicurean:
'tu Epicurum existimas ista voluisse aut
libidinosas eius fuisse sententias?' To
which Cicero answers, 'No; I am aware
that many of his utterances are moral
and many noble. The question is about
his talent, and not about his character;
although he rejects the pleasures which
he lately eulogised, I shall bear in mind
what his view of the supreme good is.
He not only gave it the name of pleasure,
but made clear what he meant thereby.'

It is certain, therefore, that Epicureans did not accept as correct the
description given by Cicero of the exposition by Epicurus of the *summum
bonum.* The gulf between his enumeration of the contents of the idea 'pleasure'
and his numerous eulogies of a simple
and moral life had been bridged somehow; it is hard to say precisely how. It
may be noticed that in the passage of
the 'Tusculan Disputations,' to the list
of particular pleasures is added a vague
class 'sive quae aliae voluptates in toto
homine gignuntur quolibet sensu.' These
pleasures are of a general character and
not specially connected with any particular part of the human frame; the
words *quolibet sensu* meaning, not 'any
one of the five senses,' but 'any kind of
perception.' Among this class is included *mentis laetitia,* which is a good,
but not the only good. When Epicurus
is quoted as saying that mental pleasure
consists in the hope of sensual pleasures,
the hope that our nature by the ac-
quisition of these may be freed from
pain, it must be remembered that,
according to him, the amount of sensual
pleasure sufficient to liberate from pain
is very small, and that when this
liberation is once attained, no increase
of pleasure is possible. This point is
brought forward in the Epicurean interest in connexion with the passage of
the περὶ τέλους, both in Fin. 2, 10 and in
Tusc. 3, 47. This point, then, formed a
principal part of the Epicurean defence
against such criticism as we have here.
Cf. nn. on 1, 55; 2, 92.

2. **ubi sit aut quod sit:** cf. 2, 48
quam aut qualem.

3. **cibo et potione:** 1, 37 *n.*; corresponds to *palato* in § 29.

obscena voluptate: this kind of
pleasure was especially denounced by
the Epicureans: Diog. L. 10, 118 ἐρασ-
θήσεσθαι τὸν σοφὸν οὐ δοκεῖ αὐτοῖς...
οὐδὲ θεόπεμπτον εἶναι τὸν ἔρωτα (see the
context). They objected to the ἔρως
φιλόσοφος of Plato, accepted in a
modified form by the Stoics; see Tusc.
4, 70; and Diog. L.7, 129, 130. There is a
curious quotation from Chrysippus in
Stob. flor. 63, 31 εἰπόντος τινός, 'οὐκ
ἐρασθήσεται ὁ σοφός· μαρτυρεῖ γοῦν
Μενέδημος 'Επίκουρος 'Αλεξῖνος· 'τῇ

capiatur. An haec ab eo non dicuntur? Quasi vero me pudeat, inquit, istorum, aut non possim quem ad modum ea dicantur ostendere! Ego vero non dubito, inquam, quin facile possis, nec est quod te pudeat sapienti assentiri, qui se unus, quod sciam, sapientem profiteri sit ausus. Nam Metrodorum non puto ipsum ſ professum, sed, cum appellaretur ab Epicuro, repudiare tantum beneficium noluisse; septem autem illi non suo, sed populorum 8 suffragio omnium nominati sunt. Verum hoc loco sumo verbis his eandem certe vim voluptatis Epicurum nosse quam ceteros. Omnes enim iucundum motum quo sensus hilaretur, Graece ɪ ἡδονήν, Latine voluptatem vocant. Quid est igitur, inquit, quod requiras? Dicam, inquam, et quidem discendi causa magis, quam quo te aut Epicurum reprehensum velim. Ego quoque, inquit, didicerim libentius, si quid attuleris, quam te reprehenderim. Tenesne igitur, inquam, Hieronymus Rhodius quid dicat ɪ

2 possim: *possunt* A¹.   2 ea: *ista* B.   4 sapienti: om. A¹.   7 beneficium: *bene officium* B.   7 noluisse: *voluisse* A¹.   8 verum...vocant: habet Nonius p. 121; *verum...voluptatis* idem, p. 396.   8 verbis: *de verbis* Nonius, p. 396.   9 nosse: ita AB; *non nosse* Nonius; *notasse* Davies et Orelli.   10 hilaretur: ita Nonius; *hiaretur* AB al.; *titillaretur* Bake.   11 ἡδονήν: *hedonem* AB; *hedoneum* codd. Nonii.   12 quidem: om. B.   13 reprehensum: *repensum* A¹.   15 inquam: *inquit* B.   15 Hieronymus: *hieronimus* AB.   15 quid: ita B; *quod* A.

αὐτῇ,' ἔφη, 'χρήσομαι ἀποδείξει· ἢ γὰρ Ἀλεξῖνος ὁ ἀνάγωγος καὶ Ἐπίκουρος ὁ ἀναίσθητος καὶ Μενέδημος ⟨ὁ λῆρος⟩ οὔ φασιν, ἐρασθήσεται ἄρα.'

1. quasi vero: Otto quotes Lucr. 6, 971 as the only ex. within his knowledge where *quasi vero* has any use other than in indignant denial.

2. istorum...ea: n. on 1, 11.

4. unus...sit ausus: Plutarch, non posse suaviter vivi, c. 18, p. 1100 *a*, puts it more forcibly; he says Epicurus proclaimed himself the only σοφός who had ever lived (some bitter jesting in the context). Cf. Cato m. 43; Epict. Enchir. 46 μηδαμοῦ σεαυτὸν εἴπῃς φιλόσοφον. The title σοφός is often given to Epic. ironically, as by Sext. A.M. 1, 57 and 11, 21. With this passage we may compare what Demosthenes says of Aeschines, De Cor. § 128 ποῦ δὲ παιδείας σοι θέμις μνησθῆναι, ἧς τῶν μὲν ὡς ἀληθῶς τετυχηκότων οὐδ' ἂν εἰς εἴποι περὶ αὑτοῦ τοιοῦτον οὐδέν, ἀλλὰ κἂν ἑτέρου λέγοντος ἐρυθριάσειε. There is an odd argument in Philod. περὶ θεῶν διαγωγῆς to the effect that the gods must speak Greek, because 'μόνον οἴδαμεν γεγονότας θεοὺς Ἑλληνίδι γλώττῃ χρωμένους.' (Us. § 356*.)

5. Metrodorum: ὁ σοφὸς M., Plut. n. posse s. vivi, c. 3; Epicuri collega sapientiae, Cic. N.D. 1, 113. Plutarch (cc. 18, 19) ridicules Colotes for having worshipped Epic. as a god, yet without winning the title of σοφός.

6. professum: for the omission of *esse* cf. 1 §§ 13, 38, 39; 2 § 54.

7. septem: they are commonly spoken of simply as 'the seven' just as the Twelve Tables are merely 'the twelve.' See my n. on Acad. 2, 118.

8. verbis his: briefly put, as Madvig says, for *cum his verbis utitur*.

9. nosse: much as in § 7, for *agnoscere*; so *noscere causam*, 'to admit a plea,' in Leg. 1, 11; Fam. 4, 4, 1; Att. 11, 7, 5; also *ignorare causam* in Phil. 8, 7, with which *ignorat* in § 7 may be compared. In Prop. 2, 2, 4 *ignoro* (MSS.) may perhaps be defended by this usage.

quam ceteros: n. on 1, 14.

10. hilaretur: in Cicero elsewhere only in N.D. 2, 102 and Brut. 44.

15. Hieronymus: a contemporary of Lyco (successor of Strato in the headship of the Peripatetic school), Arcesilas and Timon the Sceptic; Cic. Or. 190 calls him 'Peripateticus nobilis,' but in Fin. 5, 14 questions his title to be called

esse summum bonum, quo putet omnia referri oportere? Teneo,
inquit, finem illi videri nihil dolere. Quid? idem iste, inquam,
de voluptate quid sentit? Negat esse eam, inquit, propter se **9**
expetendam. Aliud igitur esse censet gaudere, aliud non dolere.
5 Et quidem, inquit, vehementer errat; nam, ut paulo ante docui,
augendae voluptatis finis est doloris omnis amotio. Non dolere,
inquam, istud quam vim habeat, postea videro; aliam vero vim
voluptatis esse, aliam nihil dolendi, nisi valde pertinax fueris,
concedas necesse est. Atqui reperies, inquit, in hoc quidem per-
10 tinacem; dici enim nihil potest verius. Estne, quaeso, inquam,
sitienti in bibendo voluptas? Quis istud possit, inquit, negare?
—Eademne, quae restincta siti?—Immo alio genere; restincta
enim sitis stabilitatem voluptatis habet, illa autem voluptas
ipsius restinctionis in motu est. Cur igitur, inquam, res tam
15 dissimiles eodem nomine appellas? Quid paulo ante, inquit, **10**

1 summum bonum: *bonum summum* B.   3 quid: om. B.   5 et quidem:
equidem B.   7 aliam...necesse est: om. B.   11 istud: ita A; *ista* B.   11 possit,
inquit: ita A; *inquit, possit* B al.; *inquit* om. E.   12 eademne: ita A²; *eaedemne*
A¹; *eedem ne* B.   12 siti: *enim sitis* B¹; *enim siti* B².   13 Post *habet* A add
inquit: om. BE.   15 dissimiles: *difficiles* A¹.   15 quid: *quia* B.

a Peripatetic. He seems to have been
a voluminous writer, but only the titles
of some of his works have been preserved,
and the only tenet definitely attributed
to him is this doctrine of ἀοχλησία =
indolentia (§ 19) = *vacuitas doloris* (5, 14;
cf. 5, 73) = *vacare omni molestia* (Acad.
2, 131, 138). Hoyer, de Ant. Asc. init.,
calls the rendering *vacuitas doloris* 'in-
epta'; apparently thinking of *dolor* as
only bodily pain.

3. **propter se**: yet it might have (like
virtue in the Stoic system) an indirect
value as conducing to peace. But,
judging from the tone of the references
elsewhere to the doctrine of Hieronymus, it seems possible that Cicero or
his authority has erred in introducing
these words.

5. **et quidem**: n. on 1, 35.
paulo ante: 1, 37 f., where see nn.

6. **amotio**: used in 1, 37; elsewhere only
in late literature. Similarly *commotio,
permotio, remotio*, are nearly confined to
Cicero and late writers; the nouns for
demoveo, dimoveo, submoveo are wanting.

non dolere istud: n. on 1, 1 totum
hoc philosophari.

7. **videro**: cf. 1, 35.

8. **valde**: see F. Abbott in Archiv
9, 462.

pertinax: the word always conveys

blame = 'obstinate'; cf. my n. on Acad.
1, 44.

11. **istud**: Madvig says of the reading
ista, 'non secutus sum quod hic necessario ad unam illam rem de qua quae-
situm erat, refertur pronomen.' But
actual usage does not follow so strict a
rule. Both in Greek and in Latin neuter
pronouns in the plural are often used in
reference to *una res*. Cf. for ex. *ista*
followed by *istud* in Tusc. 1, 12.

12. **eademne**: for *inquam* omitted see
n. on 2, 17

alio genere: Madvig is right in saying
that *voluptas est ei* is to be understood;
while *alio genere* approaches the sense
of *alio modo*. In the later Latin *genere*
becomes almost indistinguishable from
modo, as e.g. Amm. Marc. 31, 5, 10 qui
(numerus) comprehendi nullo genere
potuit.

13. **stabilitatem...in motu**: n. on 1, 37
solam; for the phrase κατασταματικὴ
ἡδονή in Epicurus; he also spoke of
εὐσταθὲς σαρκὸς κατάστημα and εὐστάθεια
(Usener, fragment 68).

habet: 1, 42 *n*. The position of *inquit*,
placed after this by some MSS., is intolerable.

14. **restinctionis**: apparently ἅπαξ
εἰρημένον.

15. **paulo ante**: 1, 38.

dixerim, nonne meministi, cum omnis dolor detractus esset,
variari, non augeri voluptatem? Memini vero, inquam. Sed
tu istuc dixisti bene Latine, parum plane. Varietas enim Latinum
verbum est, idque proprie quidem in disparibus coloribus dicitur,
sed transfertur in multa disparia: varium poema, varia oratio,
varii mores, varia fortuna, voluptas etiam varia dici solet, cum
percipitur e multis dissimilibus rebus dissimilis efficientibus
voluptates. Eam si varietatem diceres, intellegerem, ut etiam
non dicente te intellego; ista varietas quae sit non satis perspicio,
quod ais, cum dolore careamus, tum in summa voluptate nos

3. dixisti: codd. dett.; *dixti* codd. meliores: de forma confert Baiterus Caec. 82,
Att. 5, 9, 2 (ubi Med. exhibet *rescripsti*). Vide Comm.   3 plane: *plene* A¹.
4 coloribus: *caloribus* B.   5 poema: *pena* A¹.   7 dissimilis: ita A; *dissimiles*
B al.   7 efficientibus: *efficientes* B.

1. **nonne**: for the late position of this
word in the sentence see my n. on Acad.
2, 86. Madvig favours the conjecture of
Bremi, *non* for *nonne*, thinking the
meaning to be *oblitusne es?* But surely
nonne here, as usual, looks forward to
an affirmative answer: 'surely you
remember.'

2. **variari**: see n. on 1, 38.

memini vero: cf. Tusc. 1, 81 oblitine
sumus?...ego vero memineram.

3. **dixisti**: Madvig says of *dixti*
'nolui delere, quod fieri potest ut ipse
Cicero scripserit; etsi si is ea syncopa
in loquendo et scribendo usus est, aut
constanter id fecit aut saltem saepius
quam tribus quattuorve locis (hic et III,
N.D. 23, et ad Att. v, 9, 2; XIII, 32, 3).'
It appears to me immeasurably more
probable that the copyists should have
introduced these forms here and there
than that Cicero should have used the
abnormal form in a very few instances
out of a vast number. C. F. W. Müller
expresses himself in the same terms with
regard to the form *decesse* for *decessisse*,
retained in Fam. 7, 1, 2 by Mendelssohn, who has a fondness for archaic and
poetic forms. Thus in Fam. 8, 16, 1 he
writes *perscripsti neque*, where Med. has
perscripsit without *neque*; and a better
copy of the same letter, preserved in
Att. 10, 9 *a*, presents *perscripsisti neque*.
In the same letter he prefers to alter
praedixi of Med. into *praedixe*, rather
than to accept *praedixisse* from the
better source; but rejects *successe* (MSS.
successa) in Fam. 16, 21, 2 (Schwabe).
Bücheler's conjecture *perscripsti* for
perscripsit in Qu. F. 3, 5, 3, fails on the
score of sense. So far as Cicero's text

is concerned, the worse the sources are,
the more of these forms are found, as a
rule. So, for example, *dixti* is found in
inferior *codices* of Div. 2, 66, and the
Schol. Bob. in quoting Sest. 28 gives
dixet for *dixisset*. In Balb. 16 one of
the better MSS., P, has *extinxet*, but
Gembl. *extinxisset*. The Med. of Att.
5, 9, 2 has *rescripsti* (Lehmann *rece-
pisti*, with probability). Curiously
Quint. 9, 3, 22 quotes Caec. 82 for *dixti*,
though our MSS. of the original have
dixisti. In many MSS. the tendency to
drop syllables in the middle of words
and the opposite tendency to insert
syllables are both very pronounced; for
the former see exx. in C. F. W. Müller's
n. on Fam. 1, 7, 9 [Neue, II², 535 sq.].

5. **transfertur**: here in the technical
sense, like μεταφέρειν, μεταφορά: for this
and *proprie* cf. Orat. 94, 134; De Or. 3,
149.

7. **efficientibus**: n. on 1, 42: 1, 46.

9. **non dicente**: *me indicente*, which
I. F. Gronovius desired to read here, is
a rare expression, probably occurring
(in Classical Latin) only in Ter. Ad. 507
and Liv. 22, 39, 2. Cicero has *insperans,
insciens, insipiens, intemperans*. *In-
cogitans* is confined to Ter. Phorm. 155.
Few of this class of compounds are
really common in the classical period,
inconstans, insipiens, infans, inficiens
(Varro)—in-frequens; ?ingens; inno-
cens; inoboediens (Eccl.); inobsequens
(Sen.); inobservans (Pall.).; inolens
(Lucr. 2, 850); inopinans (Caes.); insons;
intolerans (Liv.).

10. **quod ais**: 'dixit paulo brevius, hac
sententia: *quae in eo posita sit quod, ut
ais,—in summa voluptate simus*, etc.'

esse, cum autem vescamur eis rebus, quae dulcem motum
afferant sensibus, tum esse in motu voluptatem, quae faciat
varietatem voluptatum, sed non augeri illam non dolendi voluptatem, quam cur voluptatem appelles nescio.

5   IV. An potest, inquit ille, quicquam esse suavius quam nihil 11
dolere? Immo sit sane nihil melius, inquam (nondum enim id
quaero), num propterea idem voluptas est quod, ut ita dicam,
indolentia? Plane idem, inquit, et maxima quidem, qua fieri
nulla maior potest. Quid dubitas igitur, inquam, summo bono

1 cum autem: *tunc autem* B.   2 afferant: *afferunt* B.   2 quae: *que* A; 'in
BE est incertum compendium' Baiter; *qui* Davisius.   5 inquit ille: sic A;
ille inquit B.   7 propterea: *praeterea* B.   8 idem: ita A; *quidem* B; om. E.
9 inquam: *inquit* B.

(Madvig). The explanation appears to
be needlessly complex. The use of *quod*
here is not essentially different from its
employment below, 2, 36 (and in many
similar passages): 'nam quod ait sensibus ipsis iudicari voluptatem bonum
esse...plus tribuit sensibus quam nobis
leges permittunt.' In the present
passage the order of the clauses is in-
verted merely because the statement of
the case, introduced by *quod*, is so
lengthy.

1. **vescamur:** used in the same wide
sense (=*frui*) below, 5, 57 paratissimis
vesci voluptatibus. The usage is archaic;
Ribbeck's dramatic fragments give six
or seven instances; and Lucr. 5, 72 has
vesci loquella. But *vesci vitalibus auris*
(Lucr. Virg.) is different, the idea there
being that the air nourishes life; cf.
Soph. Ajax 559 τέως δὲ κούφοις πνεύμασιν
βόσκου νέαν ψυχὴν ἀτάλλων.

dulcem motum: cf. *iucundus motus*,
1, 39; 2, 8; 2, 75; Tusc. 3, 41 suavis
motiones.

2. **quae faciat:** cf. 2, 75 nomen imponis (voluptati) in motu ut sit et
faciat aliquam varietatem. Madvig
argues that the cause of the *varietas* lies
in the *motus* not in the *voluptas* and that
the parallel with 2, 75 does not hold
because 'nec in unam notionem
coniungi potest *in motu voluptatem* ut
in motu divellatur a verbo *esse*, in-
telligaturque ἡ ἐν κινήσει, et additur
voluptatum.' These reasons have no
cogency; *esse in motu* here and *in motu
ut sit* in 2, 75 are strictly comparable;
while there is nothing surprising in the
fact that *voluptas* is said *facere varietatem voluptatum* (cf. n. on 1, 38). The
varietas that is produced is *varietas
voluptatum* and nothing else, so that the

insertion or omission of the word *voluptatum* is immaterial.

5. **inquit:** in Cicero (and indeed in
Latin generally) where the subject of
inquit inquiet precedes the verb, it is
regularly separated from the verb by
one or more words. There are five
passages in the De Or. which conflict
with the rule; viz. 1, 149; 2, 31; 3, 47,
90, 190; but, as Madvig remarks, the
codices are not of much authority. In
Div. 1, 8 *ille inquit* is given by the better
codd.; also in Varro r.r. 3, 17, 8. Liv.
8, 7, 5 has *Manlius inquit*; Varro r.r.
1, 22, 3 Stolo inquit, but as immediately
afterwards (1, 23, 7) we have *Stolo*
without *inquit*, the verb may be inter-
polated. Madvig's reason for omitting
ille, viz. that in the whole of this
conversation, from § 6 to § 17, the pronoun is only added twice, once at the
beginning in § 6 and once at the end,
in § 17, is insufficient. The pronoun is
often inserted where it is not strictly
needed, for lucidity, as e.g. in Caes.
B.G. 7, 38, 6: Aedui...obsecrant ut sibi
consulat. 'Quasi vero,' inquit ille,
'consili sit res.'

6. **nondum id quaero:** so in post-
poning a point, Caec. 34 nondum de iure
nostrae possessionis loquor.

8. **indolentia:** the words *ut ita dicam*
indicate the word to be an unfamiliar
rendering of ἀοχλησία or ἀπάθεια or
ἀπονία, so Tusc. 3, 12 nescio quam in-
dolentiam; but without apology in
Off. 3, 12; Tusc. 5, 85. Seneca follows
Cicero in his use of the term. It is incredible that Cicero should have anywhere written *indoloria* as is asserted by
Sid. Apoll. in the epistle prefixed to
carm. 14. See Wölfflin, 'Substantiva
mit in privativum,' in Archiv, 4, 410.

a te ita constituto, ut id totum in non dolendo sit, id tenere unum,
12 id tueri, id defendere? Quid enim necesse est, tamquam mere-
tricem in matronarum coetum, sic voluptatem in virtutum con-
cilium adducere? Invidiosum nomen est, infame, suspectum.
Itaque hoc frequenter dici solet a vobis, non intellegere nos quam 5
dicat Epicurus voluptatem. Quod quidem mihi si quando
dictum est (est autem dictum non parum saepe), etsi satis clemens
sum in disputando, tamen interdum soleo subirasci. Egone non
intellego quid sit ἡδονή Graece, Latine voluptas? utram tandem
linguam nescio? deinde qui fit ut ego nesciam, sciant omnes, 1(
quicumque Epicurei esse voluerunt? Quod vestri quidem vel
optime disputant, nihil opus esse eum, philosophus qui futurus
sit, scire litteras. Itaque ut maiores nostri ab aratro adduxerunt
Cincinnatum illum, ut dictator esset, sic vos de pagis omnibus
colligitis bonos illos quidem viros, sed certe non pereruditos. 1!
13 Ergo illi intellegunt quid Epicurus dicat, ego non intellego? Vt

1 ita: om. B.   5 quam: *quid* B.   8 soleo: *solet* A¹.   9 ἡδονή: *haedonae*
A; *hedone* B.   10 linguam: *linquam* A¹.   10 qui fit: *qui sit* B.   10 nesciam:
om. B.   11 voluerunt: sic A; *voluerint* B.   11 vestri: *nostri* B.   12 opus esse:
esse opus B.   12 eum philosophus qui futurus sit: ita A; *eum qui futurus sit
philosophus* B.   14 pagis: *plagis* AB al.; corr. Cod. 1 Eliensis Turnebus.
15 pereruditos: *eruditos* A¹.   16 intellegunt: *intelligant* B.   16 quid: *quod* B.

7. **clemens:** this word and its cognates (especially in the older Latin) are
often applied to placidity of temper; so
Lucr. 3, 311 proclivius hic iras decurrat
ad acris, | ille metu citius paulo temp-
tetur, at ille | tertius accipiat quaedam
clementius aequo.

8. **subirasci:** like many words com-
pounded with *sub* this is almost confined
to Cicero's writings.

11. **voluerunt:** the subjunctive is not
a necessity here, as Madvig seems to
think; see note on 1, 43; 2, 15.

quod vestri: 'pronomen *quod* cum
Cicero rettulisset ad id, quod involutum
erat in illis: *sciant, quicumque...voluerint*
(ut voluntas sufficiat, nihil opus sit discere) addidit epexegesin, explicatius idem
subiungens, *nihil opus esse,* etc. notissima
figura (ad Fam. xiii, 40: *si ulla mea
apud te commendatio valuit, quod scio
multas plurimum valuisse*)' (Madvig).

13. **scire litteras:** here *litteras* =
μαθήματα: cf. Sext. A. M. 1, 1 ὡς τῶν
μαθημάτων μηδὲν συνεργούντων πρὸς
σοφίας τελείωσιν (of the Epicureans);
there seems to be an allusion to this
doctrine in Philod. rhet. ed. Sudhaus,
i. p. 141, l. 22 ἀγράμματοι, φησὶν Ἐπίκουρος, ἄνθρωποι, καὶ ἀγροίκους φησὶν

Ἑρμαρχος. Although μαθήματα were
needless, γράμματα were necessary;
Sext. A. M. 1, 49 ἐν οἷς θετέον καὶ τὸν
Ἐπίκουρον, εἰ καὶ δοκεῖ τοῖς ἀπὸ τῶν
μαθημάτων διεχθραίνειν· ἐν γοῦν τῷ
Περὶ δώρων καὶ χάριτος ἱκανῶς πειρᾶται
διδάσκειν ὅτι ἀναγκαῖόν ἐστι τοῖς σοφοῖς
μανθάνειν γράμματα. Also Lactant.
3, 25, 6–7 (after condemning Cicero's
words in Tusc. 2, 4 est philosophia
paucis contenta iudicibus, multitudinem consulto ipsa fugiens) says: maximum argumentum est philosophiam
neque ad sapientiam tendere, neque
ipsam sapientiam esse, quod mysterium
eius barba tantum celebratur et pallio.
Senserunt hoc adeo Stoici, qui et servis
et mulieribus philosophandum esse dixerunt, Epicurus quoque, qui rudes omnium litterarum ad philosophiam invitat.
Sen. ep. 88, 32 admits that a man
ignorant of *studia liberalia* may become
sapiens, but not one *qui litteras nescit.*

ab aratro...de pagis: 1, 14, 17 *n.* The
MS. reading *plagis* is a poetical word not
found in Cic. It occurs in Liv. 9, 41, 15.

15. **illos quidem...sed:** 4, 43 *n.*

pereruditos: a rare word; cf. Att.
4, 15, 2.

16. **ego non intellego:** in sentences of

scias me intellegere, primum idem esse dico voluptatem, quod
ille ἡδονήν. Et quidem saepe quaerimus verbum Latinum par
Graeco, et quod idem valeat; hic nihil fuit quod quaereremus.
Nullum inveniri verbum potest quod magis idem declaret Latine
5 quod Graece, quam declarat voluptas. Huic verbo omnes,

1 esse: *ego* coni. Madvig.   2 ἡδονήν: *hedonem* AB.   2 et quidem: *equidem* B.
2 quaerimus: *quaeremus* A¹.   5 quod: *quam* B.

this kind Cicero generally repeats the
verb, as here, or substitutes *item* for it;
rarely does *non* end the sentence without a verb and without *item*. In the
colloquial style this may be tolerated,
as in Att. 14, 12, 2 Octavius, quem
quidem sui Caesarem salutabant, Philip-
pus non (as *itaque* follows, many edd.
think *item* has fallen out); ib. 16, 9
Varroni quidem displicet consilium
pueri, mihi non; Att. 6, 1, 6 quod si
cuiquam, huic tamen non (where the
verb is left to be understood in the first
clause); Sen. Rh. contr. 10, 5, 16 ille
servos alii emptori potest esse, Atheni-
ensi non. *Non* rarely ends a clause or
sentence in other connexions, excepting
where it means 'no' in answer to a
question; see Draeger § 84; add to his
exx. Fam. 4, 9, 3; Verr. act. pr. 20
and 2, 2, 106; S. Rosc. 54; Q. Rosc. 41;
Ad Herenn. 4, 33; Hor. s. 2, 3, 264;
Virg. Ecl. 3, 2; Sen. Rh. 7, 4, 5; ib.
7, 8, 2. A curious passage is Brut. 255
hanc gloriam testimoniumque Caesaris
tuae quidem supplicationi non, sed
triumphis multorum antepono; the *non*
there has been changed by Weidner and
others to *minus*, but is no stranger than
e.g. *non* in Att. 8, 3, 5 eam (fugam) si
nunc sequor, quonam? cum illo non;
Ad Herenn. 3, 33 aegrotum in lecto
cubantem faciemus ipsum illum de quo
agetur, si formam eius detinebimus; si
eum non, at aliquem aegrotum non de
minimo loco sumemus; Varro r. r. 1, 9, 7
quae sit idonea terra ad colendum aut
non; ib. 3, 11, 1 locum eligere oportet
palustrem; si id non....

1. **primum**: no *deinde* follows; so in
1, §§ 17, 29 and often.

idem esse dico voluptatem: Madvig
condemns *esse*: 'neque enim de re (*esse*)
agitur, quid sit et in quo posita voluptas,
sed de nomine, disputaturusque Cicero
de vi ac notione rei primum dicit, pro
Graeco Epicuri nomine se Latinum sub-
stituere, quod idem significet: "Quam
rem ille ἡδονήν appellat, eandem ego
voluptatem."' But Cicero undoubtedly

did sometimes insert *esse* even in passages where there was only a question
of *naming* something; so Acad. 1, 28 illa
vis quam qualitatem esse diximus;
below, 2, 77 voluptas...quam in motu
esse dicitis; 3, 22 illa quae officia esse
dixi; 5, 18; N.D. 2, 105 dicitur esse
polus (translation from Aratus) also
altera (sc. stella) dicitur esse Helice; ib.
109 Arctophylax, volgo qui dicitur esse
Bootes; Tusc. 2, 44 non satis intellego
quid dicas summum esse, quid breve
(compared with § 45 quid summum dicat
in dolore, quid breve in tempore).
C. F. W. Müller compares ὀνομάζεται
εἶναι. As to many other passages there
may be doubt, as 4, 31 and 5, 20 rebus
eis quas primas secundum naturam esse
diximus. This may mean 'those objects
which we have asserted to be the first
that accord with nature' and not 'those
objects which we have described as the
first that accord with nature'; but when
we compare 5, 18 eis quae prima secundum naturam nominant, the second
meaning becomes probable [*in motu ut
sit* in 2, 75 is comparable with *esse* here;
cf. definiebas esse, above, 2, 5].

2. **et quidem**: 1, 15; 1, 35.
par...valeat: for the tautology cf. 1, 55
praesens et quod adest (with note there);
Acad. 2, 32 quod sit eorum consilium aut
quid velint; ib. 2, 66 errem et vager.

4. **nullum...Graece**: 'aperta sententia est, nullum esse Latinum nomen,
quod Graecum sibi respondens magis
exprimat quam voluptas exprimat (id,
quod ei respondeat). Sed confusa
notione nominis, quod duplex est,
Graecum et Latinum, et rei, quae una
est, neglegentius et brevius sic dixit,
tamquam unum esset eiusdem rei nomen
Graecum et Latinum, retinuitque idem
subiectum in utraque parte sententiae
(*idem declaret Latine quod Graece*), cum
alterum substitui deberet (*quod Graece
Graecum*)' (Madvig). There is a somewhat
similar incompleteness of expression in
Orat. 34 quid enim tam distans quam a
severitate comitas?

qui ubique sunt, qui Latine sciunt, duas res subiciunt, laetitiam in animo, commotionem suavem iucunditatis in corpore. Nam et ille apud Trabeam 'voluptatem animi nimiam' laetitiam dicit eandem, quam ille Caecilianus, qui 'omnibus laetitiis laetum' esse se narrat. Sed hoc interest, quod voluptas dicitur etiam in 5 animo (vitiosa res, ut Stoici putant, qui eam sic definiunt: sublationem animi sine ratione opinantis se magno bono frui), non 14 dicitur laetitia nec gaudium in corpore. In eo autem voluptas omnium Latine loquentium more ponitur, cum percipitur ea quae sensum aliquem moveat iucunditas. Hanc quoque iucundi- 10 tatem, si vis, transfer in animum; iuvare enim in utroque dicitur, ex eoque iucundum, modo intellegas inter illum, qui dicat:

Tanta laetitia auctus sum, ut nihil constet,

1 qui...sciunt: *qui latine sciunt qui ubique sunt* B.   2 suavem iucunditatis: ita A; *iucunditatis suavem* B.   6 sic: om. B.   12 iucundum: *interdum* B.   13 ut: *et* B. 13 constet: *constetur* B.

1. qui...qui: for the two successive relative clauses (*not coordinate*) cf. 1, 22; and Draeger § 480, 2. The usage is especially common in official documents. Cf. qui patres qui conscripti.

2. commotionem: the word is elsewhere in the philosophical writings of Cicero a rendering of πάθος, mental agitation. **nam et:** for the slight anacoluthon see 1, 40 *n*.

3. ille apud Trabeam: the same phrase (Kühner on Tusc. 1 § 31) prefaces another quotation in Tusc. 4, 67. So *ille apud Terentium*, below, 5, 28; *i. a. Euripidem*, Tusc. 3, 67; for *ille Caecilianus* cf. *Hector Naevianus* in Fam. 5, 12, 7. **voluptatem animi**, etc.: Cicero links these two quotations together in Fam. 2, 9, 2. That from Trabea is given more fully in Tusc. 4, 35 ut ille qui 'voluptatem animi nimiam summum esse errorem' arbitratur; whence Bentley conjectured the line to be 'ego voluptatem animi nimiam summum esse errorem arbitror.' Ribbeck suggests *autumo* for *arbitror*. With *laetitiis laetum* cf. 1, 67 laetamur laetitia.

6. eam sic definiunt: sublationem: cf. Off. 1, 142 ordinem sic definiunt, compositionem rerum; so Tusc. 4, 18; and ib. 3, 11 sic...definitur iracundia, ulciscendi libido; but ib. 4, 12 quam (voluntatem) sic definiunt: voluntas est etc. (see C. F. W. Müller on Acad. 2, 113). So *ita* is sometimes succeeded by a similar defining clause, as in Acad. 2, 77; Tusc. 4, 26 and 4, 13 (referring to the same Stoic definition) quam ita definiunt, sine ratione animi elationem.

Compare also Acad. 2, 113 ita iudico, politissimum omnium philosophorum. **sublationem,** etc.: for this Stoic definition see 3, 35 *n*.

7. non dicitur, etc.: the general usage of prose writers confirms Cicero's statement; but cf. § 98; Tusc. 5, 96 corpus gaudere (an Epicurean passage); Or. in sen. 14 in omni parte corporis semper oportere aliquod gaudium versari (also with reference to Epicureanism); Sall. Jug. 2, 4 corporis gaudiis; Liv. 37, 37, 7 salubre corpori gaudium. Sen. ep. 46, 1 gavisus stronger than delectatus.

8. in eo...ponitur, cum, etc.: the temporal clause with *cum* is often, as here, explanatory of a preceding clause or words in a preceding clause which have not a strict but only an indirect temporal reference; so 1, 55 in eis rebus peccant, cum; below, § 16; often in definitions, see Draeger, II², p. 547. In such cases the verb of the *cum*-clause is almost always indicative. [Madvig refers *in eo* to *corpore*, and he appears to take *in eo* as 'in connexion with this,' an unnatural sense for *in* to bear when linked with *ponere*. He objects to the interpretation given above, because (1) it detaches this sentence from the one which precedes, (2) it introduces a definition of *voluptas* as though none had been given before. But these irregularities are in themselves slight, and of a kind quite common in Cicero's philosophical writings; indeed they could be paralleled in almost any writer.]

12. illum...eum: 1, 32.

13. tanta, etc.: the author is unknown.

et eum qui:

Nunc demum mihi animus ardet,

quorum alter laetitia gestiat, alter dolore crucietur, esse illum medium:

5   Quamquam haec inter nos nuper notitia admodum est, qui nec laetetur nec angatur, itemque inter eum qui potiatur corporis expetitis voluptatibus, et eum qui excrucietur summis doloribus, esse eum qui utroque careat.

V. Satisne igitur videor vim verborum tenere, an sum etiam **15** 10 nunc vel Graece loqui vel Latine docendus? Et tamen vide ne, si ego non intellegam quid Epicurus loquatur, cum Graece, ut videor, luculenter sciam, sit aliqua culpa eius, qui ita loquatur, ut non intellegatur. Quod duobus modis sine reprehensione fit, si aut de industria facias, ut Heraclitus, 'cognomento qui

1 et eum: *et* om. B.   3 esse: *ē* A[1].   7 voluptatibus: *voluptatis* B.
7 excrucietur: ita B; *crucietur* A.   9 vim: *viam* B.   11 loquatur: *loquitur* B.
14 cognomento: *cognomenta* B.

As Bentley first suggested, there is an allusion to this line in Tusc. 4, 35 (where the passage of Trabea is quoted) tum (libido) efferetur alacritate, ut nihil ei constet quod agat.

2. **nuncdemum**: Cael. 37 dubito quem patrem potissimum sumam: Caecilia-numne aliquem vehementem atque durum? 'Nunc enim demum mi animus ardet, nunc meum cor cumulatur ira.'

3. **crucietur...excrucietur**: so in § 53 excrucietur...cruciet.

5. **quamquam**, etc.: the words of Chremes to Menedemus at the outset of the 'Hautontimorumenos.' The three persons are three fathers exhibited on the comic stage (cf. Cael. quoted above); the father who is delighted with his son, the father who treats his son ill, and the tolerant, indifferent, father.

8. **utroque**: for the neuter singular substantival pronoun referring to more than one preceding subject cf. § 18.

9. **satisne**: Cicero seems always to give *satis* in this phrase its full force, whereas *satin* or *satine* in comedy is often merely equivalent to *nonne* (Brix on Plaut. Trin. 925).

etiam nunc: i.e. at my age.

10. **et tamen**: note on 1, 14.

11. **ut videor**:=*ut mihi videor*, as often.

12. **luculenter**: this form is somewhat questionable, as it only has good MSS. support here, in Cicero's writings, and is not quoted elsewhere excepting from Apuleius, whereas Cicero used *luculente*

a good many times, and the form is Plautine. The most recent editors still allow *turbulenter* to stand in Fam. 2, 16, 7, though it is equally open to suspicion. These two words (*luculenter*, *turbulenter*) are the only adverbs in *-ter* connected with adjectives in *-entus*, which are presented to us by the Cicero-nian MSS.; Cicero even avoided *violenter*. On this subject see Neue-Wagener, II, p. 734 sq.

qui ita loquatur: as against *loqui-tur* (Davies) Madvig urges that the verb is 'necessaria pars sententiae pendentis, in qua a certo subiecto (Epicuro) trans-itur ad generis notionem (*eius hominis qui, ut hinc efficitur, sic loquatur*), et causali etiam nexu implicata. Neque enim raro in huiusmodi notatione subiecti simul significatur causa iudicii, quod de eo fiat, aut omnino eius qualitas, et ob eam rem coniunctivus ponitur.' There are two exx. of this below, § 102. Madvig notes that the indicative is unusual in N.D. 1, 117 quid est autem quod deos venere-mur propter admirationem eius naturae, in qua egregium nihil videmus? [It is hardly possible to say that the sub-junctive is a *necessity* here. Cicero often chooses to write the indicative in a relative clause where subj. would seem to us more natural. See C. F. W. Müller on Deiot. 21 (*habebat*).]

14. **si aut...aut cum**: the change in the position of *aut* is not uncommon; so *ut aut...aut ut*, Orat. 149, Liv. 2, 27, 2;

σκοτεινός perhibetur, quia de natura nimis obscure memoravit,'
aut cum rerum obscuritas, non verborum, facit ut non intellegatur oratio qualis est in Timaeo Platonis. Epicurus autem,
ut opinor, nec non volt, si possit, plane et aperte loqui, nec de
re obscura, ut physici, aut artificiosa, ut mathematici, sed de 5

1 σκοτεινός: scotinus AB.   3 Platonis: platone A.

ne aut...aut ne, Fam. 11, 28, 8 (Matius),
S. Rosc. 82, Varro r.r. 2, 7, 10; *qui aut...
aut cui*, Liv. 7, 39, 10. So *et* is often
displaced, as in Acad. 2, 12; 2, 69 (where
see my n.); Att. 3, 23, 3: see C. F. W.
Müller; imp. Pomp. 49; cf. also De Or.
2, 264 ea quae videantur et veri similia
...et quae sint subturpia; Orat. 70 de
quo praeclare et multa praecipiuntur et
res est cognitione dignissima; Fam.
4, 5, 3 (Sulpicius); Varro r.r. 3, 7, 5
aquam esse oportet unde et bibere et
ubi lavari possint; Ad Herenn. 2, 48
quom ostendimus et consulto factum et
dicimus; Sen. ep. 114, 10 (verba) modo
fingit et ignota ac deflectit (remarkable
if correct); Plin. n. h. 18, 127 quadri-
pedes et fronde eorum gaudent et
homini....Less simple distortions of
order also occur, as in Liv. 36, 16, 10 ut,
sive victus esset...sive vinceret, ut...;
Cic. De Or. 3, 14 sed quoniam haec iam
neque in integro nobis esse possunt et
summi labores nostri...mitigantur; Liv.
44, 22, 2 cum aut...aut quo die. For
similar dislocations in Lucretius see
Munro's note on 6, 105. The interchange
of *si* and *cum* is far from uncommon;
see Rep. 3, 23; Hor. ep. 1, 7, 10; Ad
Herenn. 4, 3 hoc si industria solum fieri
posset, tamen essemus laudandi cum
talem laborem non fugissemus; also my
note on Acad. 2, 64.

cognomento, etc.: this was recognised by Muretus as a quotation, probably from Lucilius. The word *cognomentum*, as Madvig says, 'comicorum
est et eorum scriptorum qui antiqua
aut obsolescentia retinuerunt, aut obso-
leta revocarunt, Sallustii, Messallae,
Taciti.' *Perhibere* is poetical, and is not
the equivalent of *dicere* but means *cum
laude narrare et commemorare* (Madvig,
Opusc. 1, 200); Cicero (in prose and
apart from quotations) only has the
word thrice, viz. Rep. 2, 4; Tusc. 1, 28;
Fam. 5, 12, 7. *Memoro* for *commemoro*
is very rare in Cicero, occurring once
only in the speeches, viz. Verr. 2, 4, 107;
twice in the philosophical works, viz.
Tim. 39; Leg. 2, 62, and I think nowhere
else; considering the ease with which the

compound verbs dropped the preposition in our MSS. the word is not above
suspicion in these passages. The poet
apparently made the first syllable of
σκοτεινὸς long, perhaps writing it *scottinus*
(cf. *cottidie* and *Brittanni*, unique in
Lucr. 6, 1106; bassis, bassilica, for
which see Lindsay, Latin Language,
p. 115, ed. 1894). If the consonant was
left single, we may compare prōpola in
Lucil. and prōpino in Martial, prōlogus
in comedy; also Hectōris Nestōris (once
universal at Rome, Varro l. l. 10, 70, and
rhetōrica (Enn.)); Non. p. 515 gives in
a quotation from Cassius Hemina,
'prudens perplexim scottinos (so MSS.)
scribit,' where Madvig (followed by Luc.
Müller) supposes *scottinos* to be a gloss
added by a scribe. In Liv. 23, 39, 2, an
envoy sent by Philip to Hannibal is
called 'Heraclitus, cui Scotino cognomen
erat,' wherein many scholars have
seen a gloss. Acc. to Busolt, II, p. 10,
the name σκοτεινὸς first occurs in Ps.
Ar. de Mundo c. 5. This passage of
Lucilius or some old Latin versifier is
the earliest extant in which the name
ὁ σκοτεινὸς is given to Heraclitus,
though Diog. L. 9. 6 quotes 'κοκκυστὴς
ὀχλολοίδορος Ἡράκλειτος αἰνικτής' from
Timon the Sillograph; cf. Lucr. 1, 639
clarus ob obscuram linguam magis inter
inanis (i.e. Stoics) | quamde gravis inter
Graios qui vera requirunt (i.e. Epicureans), Aetna 537 obscuri verissima dicta
libelli, Heraclite, tui; Hieron. Chron. ad
Olymp. 69, 4 Heraclitus cognomento
tenebrosus. Cic. describes his obscurity
as purposed, N.D. 1, 74; 3, 35; so
Diog. l.l.

1. **perhibetur**: five out of seven exx.
in Merg. are in quotations: in the other
two in pass. = *dicitur* (both in philosophical writings). An extraordinary ex.
is Att. 1, 1, 4, but *perhiberet* is for
adhiberet. Fam. 5, 12, 7 perhibendus.

3. **Timaeo**: a large fragment of
Cicero's rendering (a youthful work) is
preserved.

5. **ut physici**: though above, 1, 19
and below, § 102, and often elsewhere,
Cicero gives Epicurus the title of

illustri et facili et iam in volgus pervagata loquitur. Quamquam
non negatis nos intellegere quid sit voluptas, sed quid ille dicat;
e quo efficitur, non ut nos non intellegamus quae vis sit istius
verbi, sed ut ille suo more loquatur, nostrum neglegat. Si enim **16**
5 idem dicit quod Hieronymus, qui censet summum bonum esse
sine ulla molestia vivere, cur mavolt dicere voluptatem quam
vacuitatem doloris, ut ille facit qui quid dicat intellegit? sin
autem voluptatem putat adiungendam eam, quae sit in motu
(sic enim appellat hanc dulcem: 'in motu,' illam nihil dolentis
10 'in stabilitate'), quid tendit? cum efficere non possit ut cuiquam
qui ipse sibi notus sit, hoc est qui suam naturam sensumque
perspexerit, vacuitas doloris et voluptas idem esse videatur. Hoc

1 et iam: *etiam* AB; corr. Goerenz.   1 loquitur: *loquatur* B.   2 nos: *non* E.
3 efficitur: *efficiatur* B.   3 nos non: *non* om. B.   8 putat: ita B; *putat
dicat* A.   10 cum: *eum* B.   12 perspexerit: *prospexerit* A[1].   12 videatur:
videtur B.

physicus, he excludes him from the band
of φυσικοί, a name currently restricted
to pre-Socratic writers, who touched on
little outside physics. Epicurus seems
to have called himself φυσιόλογος rather
than φυσικός. He is here treated as
ἠθικός.
    artificiosa: 'technical.' This adjective
covers the senses both of *ars* and *arti-
ficium.*
    1. **et iam:** rare, and often obviously
avoided from fear of ambiguity; but
found here and there, as Mur. 85 (in some
MSS.); Cael. 20: 'Qui calumniari volet,
quaeret, quid ad Epicurum pertinuerit
quod *iam,* id est, post Epicurum illa
pervagata in vulgus essent' (Madvig).
    in volgus: this expression (with the
sense of *volgo*) is widely spread in Latin;
occasionally (but not in Cicero) *ad volgus*
takes its place, as in Liv. 1, 26, 5. In
Cicero and early writers the phrase *in
volgus* is connected with verbs or participles; later also with adjectives.
    pervagata: 3, 5 rebus non pervagatis
(where inferior MSS. give *pervulgatis,* as
here *pervulgata*); so often. In many
applications, *pervolgatus, pervagatus* are
of identical sense, and it may be doubted
whether Madvig was right in his note
here in recommending the adoption of
an old conjecture *pervolgetur* in Inv.
2, 113 ne is honos nimium pervagetur
(so all MSS.). In speaking of a false
reading, *promulgata* for *pervolgata* in
Verr. 2, 104, Madvig writes 'nisi de lege
et rogatione proponenda numquam aut

Cicero aut alii in prosa oratione ponunt
ante Plinium; nam pro Murena 30
proeliis promulgatis poetae sunt verba.'
    3. **e quo:** before all gutturals Cicero
uses predominantly *ex* rather than *e*; see
the elaborate lists in Neue-Wagener
II, p. 875 sq.
    non ut...non: note on § 24.
    5. **idem dicit:** sc. *summum bonum
esse.*
    7. **quid dicat intellegit:** § 21 dicit
quod intellegit.
    8. **in motu,** etc.: note on § 31.
    9. **nihil dolentis:** elsewhere always
(*voluptas*) *nihil dolendi,* which may be
the right reading here.
    10. **quid tendit?** Cf. quid pugnas? in
Quinct. 43; Acad. 2, 54. *Tendere* for
contendere is found nowhere else in
Cicero; the usage is early (Ter. Eun. 626)
and late (Virgil, Hor. *quid ultra tendis?*
etc.). Scaliger's em. *tundit* is amusing.
    11. **ipse sibi notus:** cf. Petron. 58 aut
ego non me novi aut, and sensus sui in
3, 16.
    12. **hoc est...afferre...extorquere:** the
form is a common one, as Ter. Ad. 132;
Acad. 2, 80; Div. 2, 83; Lucr. 6, 379 sq.;
also often, *quid aliud est,* followed by
infinitive clause, then *nisi* followed by
another infinitive clause; so Cato m. 5;
Phil. 3, 21; Div. 2, 78. Sometimes *nisi
hoc* or *nisi hoc est* or *si hoc non est*
stands for *nisi,* as in Verr. 2, 1, 128; 2, 3,
71; Off. 3, 55; S. Rosc. 54 quid est aliud
iudicio ac legibus ac maiestate vestra
abuti ad quaestum ac libidinem, nisi

est vim afferre, Torquate, sensibus, extorquere ex animis cognitiones verborum quibus imbuti sumus. Quis enim est qui non
videat haec esse in natura rerum tria? unum, cum in voluptate
sumus, alterum, cum in dolore, tertium hoc in quo nunc equidem
sum, credo item vos, nec in dolore nec in voluptate; ut in volup- 5
tate sit qui epuletur, in dolore qui torqueatur. Tu autem inter
haec tantam multitudinem hominum interiectam non vides nec
17 laetantium nec dolentium? Non prorsus, inquit, omnisque qui
sine dolore sint, in voluptate, et ea quidem summa, esse dico.—
Ergo in eadem voluptate eum, qui alteri misceat mulsum ipse 1
non sitiens, et eum, qui illud sitiens bibat?

1 cognitiones: *cogitationes* A.   2 enim est: ita A; *est enim* B.   4 equidem
sum: *quidem sumus* A; *sumus* B.   5 item: *idem* AB al.; corr. Ernesti.   7 interiectam: om. B.   9 quidem: *quam* B.   9 esse dico. Ergo: *esse. Dico ergo* AB.

hoc modo accusare (where Landgraf
strangely takes *modo* as 'only'). In
later Latin *quam* often takes the place
of *nisi* (as it does in other relations) as in
Sen. dial. 10, 16, 5 and N.Q. 7, 14, 1;
Val. Max. 3, 7, 6. Sometimes the clause
with *nisi* is omitted as below, § 54;
Phil. 1, 22; 5, 5; 10, 5; Liv. 6, 40 §§ 8, 19.
A noun may replace the infinitive as
Catull. 29, 15 quid est alid sinistra
liberalitas? with which cf. Phil. 2, 5.
As Madvig remarks (note on 5, 31) in
Phil. 2, 7 quid est aliud tollere ex vita
vitae societatem, tollere amicorum col-
loquia absentium, we have not an ex.
of *nisi* omitted between two compared
or contrasted clauses, but the two
clauses are parallel, as in Ovid, Her.
18, 181 velle quid est aliud fugientia
prendere poma | spemque suo refugi
fluminis ore sequi?

1. **cognitiones verborum:** = τὰς εἰω-
θυίας ἀξιώσεις τῶν ὀνομάτων, Thuc.
3, 82. Madvig and other scholars have
found the use of *cognitiones* strange; but
cognitio is 'knowledge' and the plural
'bits of knowledge'; see note on 3, 17.
For *extorquere* cf. N.D. 1, 32 Speusippus
...evellere ex animis conatur cognitionem deorum; ib. 1, 36 (Zeno) tollit
omnino usitatas perceptasque cognitiones deorum.

2. **imbuti:** 1, 60 *n.*

5. **sum:** Cicero would hardly have
spoilt the contrast with *vos* by writing
sumus.

credo item vos: cf. Lael. 7 quaerunt
ex me, credo ex hoc item Scaevola; ib.
16 pergratum mihi feceris, spero item
Scaevolae; below, 5, 76 mihi vero ista

valde probata sunt, quod item fratri
puto; Phil. 12, 2 auxerat...meam spem,
credo item vestram. Madvig quotes a
similar parenthesis from Plat. Prot.
314 c οἶμαι δὲ καὶ Πρόδικον.

6. **tu autem:** to be symmetrical, the
sentence should have gone on *nec in
voluptate nec in dolore, qui,* etc. There
is anacoluthon of a not uncommon kind.
See note on 1, 24 et vetuit.

inter haec: not *hos*; see § 67.

8. **non prorsus:** = οὐ πάνυ, 'not so at
all.' The other order, *prorsus non,* occurs
in Verr. 2, 2, 162; Tusc. 4, 8. So *nullo
modo prorsus,* Plaut. Trin. 729; N.D. 3,
21; but *nullo prorsus modo,* ib. 1, 74; Lael.
57 nulli prorsus assentior. As C. F. W.
Müller in Philologus XII, 692, pointed
out, *nil prorsus* (or *prorsum*) in Ter.
Andr. 435 and Haut. 894 is the equivalent of *prorsum nil* in Haut. 776.
Apparently whenever *prorsus* is combined with a negative, it strengthens
the negative, and is not itself affected
by the negative, so that *non prorsus* has
not the sense of *non omnino.*

10. **ergo:** *inquam* is omitted, rather
harshly; see 1, 28 *n.* Doubtless in some
of the passages where *inquam* or *inquit*
is left out the MSS. are at fault; these
words were much subject to contraction
and would be easily lost. Thus in Lael.
37 all the better MSS. except P give
'tum ego: etiamne si vellet...?' whereas
in the next sentence the conditions are
exactly reversed, P giving *inquit* and
the other MSS. omitting it. Cf. also
below, 3, 14 and 4, 2. In De Or. 2, 225
the excited nature of the passage justifies the omission of *inquit.*

VI. Tum ille: Finem, inquit, interrogandi, si videtur, quod quidem ego a principio ita me malle dixeram hoc ipsum providens, dialecticas captiones. Rhetorice igitur, inquam, nos mavis quam dialectice disputare? Quasi vero, inquit, perpetua oratio rhetorum solum, non etiam philosophorum sit. Zenonis est, inquam, hoc Stoici. Omnem vim loquendi, ut iam ante Aristoteles, in duas tributam esse partes, rhetoricam palmae, dialecticam pugni similem esse dicebat, quod latius loquerentur rhetores, dialectici autem compressius. Obsequar igitur voluntati tuae dicamque, si potero, rhetorice, sed hac rhetorica philosophorum, non nostra illa forensi, quam necesse est, cum populariter loquatur, esse interdum paulo hebetiorem. Sed dum dialecticam, **18** Torquate, contemnit Epicurus, quae una continet omnem et perspiciendi quid in quaque re sit, scientiam et iudicandi quale

1 interrogandi si: *interrogantis si* A[1]; *interrogandi fac si* A[2].   2 malle: *male* A[1].
3 captiones: om. B.   3 inquam: *inquit* A[1].   7 Aristoteles: *aristotiles*
AB, ut in § 19.   8 pugni: ita E; *pugnis* AB al.   9 compressius: *comprensius* A[1].

1. **finem**: so below 4, 1 finem ille (sc. *fecit*); N.D. 3, 94; Madvig compares the ellipses in Greek of verbs in the imperative after μή, μή μοι. The omission of *facio* is common in other circumstances; see Dräger 1, p. 199.
   quod: sc. that there should be a truce to questions.
2. **ita**: slightly pleonastic, as often; so above, 1, 26 quod tibi ita videri necesse est; 3, 11; 5, 77 quod nisi ita efficitur; Madvig gives a list of exx. which might be largely extended.
   hoc ipsum...captiones: *hoc* is generic, 'this kind of thing,' as in Acad. 2, 49 soritas hoc vocant; and *id* below § 24; also *istud* in Tac. an. 2, 38 non preces sunt istud sed efflagitatio, and *haec* below § 18 and in Quint. 9, 3, 70 Cornificius haec traductionem vocat; cf. Ovid, Tr. 2, 501; Vell. Pat. 2, 83 § 1 haec. For the generic use of *id, quod* in Varro see Keil on r. r. 2, 3, 6. The same use attaches to neuter pronouns in Greek, e.g. τοῦτο in Dem. Leoch. § 63. It is quite likely that *hac*, the reading of nearly all mss., is correct in Ovid, Tristia 2, 285 cum quaedam spatientur in hac ('this kind of place') ut amator eodem conveniat, quare porticus ulla patet? (Owen, *in hoc*, with Bentl. Madv.). For the connexion between singular and plural, in addition to the passages quoted above, cf. Ovid, Am. 2, 4, 12 in-

sidiae sunt pudor ille meae; ib. 1, 7, 60 sanguis erat lacrimae, and Luc. 9, 811 sanguis erant lacrimae; Ovid, Her. 15 (16), 294 et tua sim quaeso crimina solus ego; (many other exx. in the poets).
3. **dialecticas captiones**: cf. ὀνομάτων θηρεύσεις in Plat. Theaet. 166 c.
   rhetorice...dialectice: cf. 5, 10.
5. **non etiam philosophorum**: 'non satis ad id, quod hic obicitur, respondet Cicero, sed, quidquid continua oratione dicatur, rhetorice dici statuit' (Madvig).
6. **vim loquendi**: so § 30; 5, 30 vis diligendi; 5, 76 v. percipiendi; Part. Or. 82 v. laudandi.
   ut...Aristoteles: for the parenthesis see note on 4, 6.
7. **rhetoricam palmae**, etc.: the same account is given of this illustration of Zeno's in Orat. 113; Quint. 2, 20, 7; Sext. A.M. 2, 7; Isid. orig. 2, 23. But in Acad. 2, 145 another application of the illustration is quoted.
9. **compressius**: cf. Brut. 29; Part. Or. 79.
10. **rhetorice, sed hac rhetorica**: Boeckel quotes Lael. 100 sapientium...de hac dico sapientia; Brut. 38 suavis, sed suavitate ea....
11. **populariter l.**: so Leg. 1, 19; below, 5, 12 genus librorum...populariter scriptum.
14. **quid...sit**: the essence (τί); quale ...sit, the qualities (ποῖόν τι).

sit quidque, et ratione ac via disputandi, ruit in dicendo, ut mihi
quidem videtur, nec ea quae docere volt, ulla arte distinguit, ut
haec ipsa, quae modo loquebamur. Summum a vobis bonum
voluptas dicitur. Aperiendum est igitur quid sit voluptas; aliter
enim explicari, quod quaeritur, non potest. Quam si explica- 5
visset, non tam haesitaret. Aut enim eam voluptatem tueretur,
quam Aristippus, id est, qua sensus dulciter ac iucunde movetur,
quam etiam pecudes, si loqui possent, appellarent voluptatem,
aut, si magis placeret suo more loqui, quam ut

> Omnes Danai atque Mycenenses,   1
> Attica pubes

reliquique Graeci qui hoc anapaesto citantur, hoc non dolere
solum voluptatis nomine appellaret, illud Aristippeum contemneret, aut, si utrumque probaret, ut probat, coniungeret doloris

1 sit quidque: ita A; *quidque sit* B.   1 dicendo: *docendo* coni. Bake.   2 ulla:
illa B.   4 dicitur: om. B.   10 atque: *aut* AB; corr. Lambinus.   11 Attica:
aut artica B; *ut artica* E.   13 appellaret: *appellant* B.   14 ut: *aut* AB.

1. **ruit**: cf. 1, 18 Epicuri propriae
ruinae (with note); pro dom. 141 in
agendo ruere.
2. **ut haec ipsa**: sc. *nulla arte distinguit.*
6. **haesitaret**: note on 1, 20 haeret;
but *haesitare* is always used by Cicero in
a metaphorical sense; see my note on
Acad. 2, 52.
8. **pecudes**: often brought into connexion with hedonism, as Acad. 1, 6;
2, 139; Lael. 20; see passages quoted by
Usener, p. 274 *n.*; below § 109 voluptatem bestiis concedamus; § 40; § 111
pecudis bonum; Sen. ben. 3, 31, 4
muscarum ac vermium bonum (but see
context).
si loqui possent: in fanciful supposi-
tions of this kind Cicero often employs
the present subjunctive, as in 3, 1 and
5, 39 vites si loqui possint; 4, 61 si
reviviscant.
10. **omnes Danai**, etc.: from an unknown tragedy. '*Citantur* ne hic quidem
est ut in lexicis explicari video, *nominantur*, sed fuit in illo cantico vocatio quaedam et citatio, ut adessent.' Apart
from the meaning 'to rouse rapid movement' this is the only sense the word
citare bears in Cicero; for even in De Or.
1, 251, where all mss. give *Paeanem*...
citarimus (edd. mostly *recitarimus*), it
is quite possible that this is the sense;
for *Paean* is the name of a god, as well
as the name of a hymn in honour of the
god. The singer who sings a hymn in

which the god is summoned may well be
spoken of as summoning the god. The
same remarks apply exactly to the disputed passage of Hor. s. 1, 3, 7 si colli-
buisset, ab ovo | usque ad mala citaret
'io Bacche (or Bacchae)'; and it is
noticeable that 'io Paian' (Ov. ars 2, 1)
was the beginning of the one class of
hymn, as 'io Bacche' was of the other.
Wilkins on De Or. l. l. quotes and condemns an explanation given of *citare
paeanem* by Lachmann on Lucr. 2, 70
as equivalent to *celeri* ἀγωγῇ peragere;
but the word *celeri* there is erroneous,
for *citare* implies not *rapid*, but *loud*
utterance, like that of a κῆρυξ or *praeco.*
In the passage of the De Or. the mss.
give generally after *Paeanem* the words
aut munionem, for which the favourite
correction has been *hymnum*. I urged
in a note in Wilkins' edition that not a
general term like *hymnum* was needed
but a word as special in its sense as
Paeanem; the explanation I have given
above of *citarimus* strengthens the case
for the name of some divinity (such as
Munychiam, which I suggested, based
on the πότνια Μουνυχίη λιμενοσκόπος
of Callimachus, Dian. 259).
12. **anapaesto**: sc. *carmine*; so in
Tusc. 3, 57; in Gell. pr. § 20 *anapaestum*
means one anapaestic verse. So *iambus*
as in N.D. 3, 91 quem Hipponactis
iambus laeserat; Hor. A.P. 79.
hoc non dolere: note on 1, 1.
14. **utrumque**: note on § 20.

vacuitatem cum voluptate et duobus ultimis uteretur. Multi **19**
enim et magni philosophi haec ultima bonorum iuncta fecerunt,
ut Aristoteles virtutis usum cum vitae perfectae prosperitate
coniunxit, Callipho adiunxit ad honestatem voluptatem, Diodorus ad eandem honestatem addidit vacuitatem doloris. Idem
fecisset Epicurus, si sententiam hanc, quae nunc Hieronymi est,
coniunxisset cum Aristippi vetere sententia. Illi enim inter se
dissentiunt. Propterea singulis finibus utuntur et, cum uterque
Graece egregie loquatur, nec Aristippus, qui voluptatem sum-

2 enim et: *autem* B.   3 usum: *summi* BE.   4 adiunxit: *adiungit* B.   9 nec: *hec* B.

1. **duobus ultimis:** so 3, 22 duo
ultima; the opposite is *singulis finibus*
below; cf. Sen. ep. 66, 45 apud Epicurum duo bona sunt (but they are not the
same as here).

2. **haec:** 'such as these'; cf. note on
§ 17 hoc ipsum.

3. **virtutis,** etc.: so Cicero represents
Aristotle's (1098 *a* 16) ἐνέργεια κατ' ἀρετὴν
ἐν βίῳ τελείῳ. Cf. § 38 vitae perfectione.

4. **Callipho:** in Cicero's time, Greek
words in -ων with stem -οντ or -ωντ
retained the *n* in the nom. case, when
transliterated; while most of those with
stem -ον dropped the *n*. But in earlier
days the rule did not hold; both these
classes of words were treated alike, being
assimilated to Latin words of the type
of *sermo*; thus λέων, λέοντος became
leo, leonis. Later on Latin followed more
closely Greek usage, retaining the τ of
the stems. In some Greek proper names
which became familiar at Rome at an
early period, Cicero seems to follow, at
least in the nominative case, the older
usage; *Callipho* is given by the mss. here
and below, 2, 34; 4, 50; 5, 73; Acad.
2, 131; Tusc. 5, 85. Madvig says:
'*Antipho* non Ciceronis est, sed comici
alicuius (II de Orat. 242)'; but there is
evidence for it in Div 2, 144. In the
other cases Cicero seems usually to have
preserved the τ; so *Antiphontem* in Div.
2, 144 (close by *Antipho*); cf. ib. 1, 39;
Calliphontem Acad. 2, 139. Below, 2, 35,
the mss. give *Calliphonis* but as *Polemonis* immediately precedes this may be due
to assimilation; but in 5, 21 *Calliphoni*
and in Off. 3, 119 *Calliphonem* stands
apart from any disturbing cause. In
Div. 1, 116 the word *Antiphonis* is not
above suspicion (bracketed by C. F. W.
Müller). In one word Latin was curiously perverse, writing *Charonta* for
Χάρωνα. As to *Polemon* and the like see
note on 4, 14.

adiunxit...voluptatem: according to

Clem. Strom. II, 496 Pott. the school
of Callipho said that ἀρετή is first
embraced for the pleasure it brings and
then is placed on a level with pleasure:
'κατὰ δὲ τοὺς περὶ Καλλιφῶντα ἕνεκα μὲν
τῆς ἡδονῆς παρεισῆλθεν ἡ ἡδονή, χρόνῳ
δὲ ὕστερον, τὸ περὶ αὐτὴν κάλλος κατ-
ιδοῦσα, ἰσότιμον ἑαυτὴν τῇ ἀρχῇ, τοῦτ'
ἐστι τῇ ἡδονῇ παρέσχεν.' Cicero says
in Tusc. 5, 87 eadem Calliphontis
erit Diodorique sententia, quorum uterque honestatem sic amplectitur ut
omnia quae sine ea sint longe retro
ponenda censeat. The meaning of this
is somewhat doubtful; it is either (1)
that in the combination of virtue with
pleasure, virtue was considered by far
the predominant element, or (2) that
those views of the *summum bonum*
which excluded ἀρετή were held vastly
inferior to those in which it was an
element. Nothing further is known of
Callipho and Diodorus, excepting that
the latter, like Hieronymus, was
nominally a Peripatetic, and having been
a pupil of Critolaus, succeeded him in
the headship of the School (5, 14 and 73
and Clem. Strom. II, 496 Pott.). As to
the combination of virtue with pleasure
cf. Aresas ap. Stob. 1, 846 (Mullach,
II, p. 52) δοκέει μοι καὶ ὁ βίος ὁ κατ'
ἀνθρώπων ἄριστος ἦμεν, ὅκα τὸ ἁδὺ τῷ
σπουδαίῳ συγκατακραθῇ καὶ ἁ ἁδονὰ τᾷ
ἀρετᾷ.

5. **honestatem:** cf. n. on 2, 45.

6. **sententiam...sententia:** note on
1, 3.

nunc: Hieronymus was of course later
than Epicurus.

8. **propterea:** this word shows that
dissentiunt is used in a strong sense of
absolute opposition, not partial dis-
agreement. Some adverb like *plane*
might have been expected before *dissentiunt*.

9. **Graece egregie:** note on 1, 8 Latine
deterius.

mum bonum dicit, in voluptate ponit non dolere, neque Hieronymus qui summum bonum statuit non dolere, voluptatis nomine
umquam utitur pro illa indolentia, quippe qui ne in expetendis
20 quidem rebus numeret voluptatem. VII. Duae sunt enim res
quoque, ne tu verba solum putes. Vnum est sine dolore esse, 5
alterum cum voluptate. Vos ex his tam dissimilibus rebus non
modo nomen unum (nam id facilius paterer), sed etiam rem unam
ex duabus facere conamini, quod fieri nullo modo potest. Hic,
qui utrumque probat, ambobus debuit uti, sicut facit re, neque
tamen dividit verbis. Cum enim eam ipsam voluptatem quam 1
eodem nomine omnes appellamus, laudat locis plurimis, audet
dicere ne suspicari quidem se ullum bonum seiunctum ab illo
Aristippeo genere voluptatis, atque ibi hoc dicit ubi omnis eius
est oratio de summo bono. In alio vero libro, in quo breviter

3 umquam: *inquam* A[1]; *numquam* B. 　4 quidem rebus: *rebus quidem* E.
5 quoque: *quarum* B. 　8 conamini: *conamur* B. 　8 fieri nullo modo: *nullo
modo fieri* B. 　9 re: om. B. 　11 appellamus: *appellant* A. 　12 seiunctum: *se
victum* A. 　13 eius est oratio: ita A; *oratio eius est* B.

1. in voluptate: note on § 26 partem in genere.

5. ne...putes: the same slight ellipse (of *hoc dico* or the like) occurs below, § 77 and 4, 36, and often elsewhere (1, 43).

unum...alterum: neuters, spite of *duae res* before; cf. 1, 21.

6. rebus...nomen: slightly illogical; the confusion of the *names* and the confusion of the *things* should, strictly speaking, have been kept quite separate.

8. fieri: *ferri*, on the necessity of which Davies insisted (because of *paterer* above), is needless, the expression *quod...potest* is fixed and of common occurrence; cf. Acad. 2, 54 conceditur similis esse, quo contentus esse potueras; tu autem vis eosdem plane esse; quod fieri nullo modo potest.

9. utrumque: 'the combination,' τὸ σύνολον: see my notes on Acad. 1, 24 and 2, 60; cf. Acad. 2, 138 aut...honestatem esse finem, aut voluptatem aut utrumque; below, 3, 44; 4, 39; above § 18. As against the reading *utramque* here Madvig remarks: 'hic quidem paene necessarium neutrum genus, quo obscuratur separata notio singularum rerum (Drakenb. ad Liv. XLIV, 36, 2); nam *rem* nimis infinite repeteretur in hac sententia; in superiore recte *verbo* contrarium erat.'

10. cum enim, etc.: Madvig points out that the course of the exposition is rather disorderly. Cicero starts to

prove that Epicurus fuses two things, viz. ἡδονή and ἀπονία, which should have been kept distinct. He treats at considerable length of the Aristippean ἡδονή, and when in § 28 he turns to the other element (*deinde ubi erubuit*, etc.) the transition is very indistinct.

11. omnes appellamus: so below, § 28 eam voluptatem, quam omnes gentes hoc nomine appellant, videtur amplexari vehementius: also § 41.

12. ne suspicari quidem, etc.: note on § 7.

14. alio libro: Usener, Epicurea, praef. XLIV sq. has acutely criticized the collection of κύριαι δόξαι which has come down to us, and has found the strongest reasons in its disorder, omissions, and structure generally, for supposing that it did not come from the hand of Epicurus himself, but is an anthology put together from his works by a careless pupil. Or perhaps it grew by accretions. There is an interesting reference in the Herculanean Vol. coll. II, tom. VII, f. 14 (Gomperz, Zeitschr. f. d. oesterr. gymn. 1866, p. 708) to a variety of reading in κυρ. δ. 2. Usener makes too much of this. There is little evidence in the numerous quotations that different versions of the collection were in circulation. In all probability the collection as preserved by Diogenes Laertius is the same as that used by Cicero. The δόξα which Cic. in N.D.

comprehensis gravissimis sententiis quasi oracula edidisse
sapientiae dicitur, scribit his verbis, quae nota tibi profecto,
Torquate, sunt (quis enim vestrum non edidicit Epicuri κυρίας
δόξας, id est quasi maxime ratas, quia gravissimae sint ad beate
5 vivendum breviter enuntiatae sententiae?). Animadverte igitur
rectene hanc sententiam interpreter: 'Si ea, quae sunt luxuriosis 21
efficientia voluptatum, liberarent eos deorum et mortis et doloris

1 edidisse: *edisse* A¹.   3 κυρίας δόξας: *cyrias doxas* AB.   4 ratas: *tutas* E.
5 enuntiatae: *enunciatae* AB.   5 animadverte: *animaverte* A¹.   7 efficientia:
efficienciam B.   7 voluptatum: ita A; *voluptatem* A²B.

1, 85 and Plut. Col. 1125 *e* quotes as first
stands first in Diogenes. The title,
κύριαι δόξαι, is exceedingly well attested. In N.D. 1, 85 Cicero describes
the book as giving 'selectae brevesque
sententiae.' An alternative title seems
to have been Ἐπικούρου φωναί: see
a scholion on Clem. Al. given by Usener,
p. 342. Cf. Epic. ap. Diog. L. 10, 35 τῶν
ὀλοσχερεστάτων δοξῶν.
  1. **quasi oracula**: so § 102 quasi oraculum; cf. 1, 63 de caelo delapsa regula.
Epicurus used χρησμωδεῖν of his own
utterances; see Vat. γνῶμαι § 29; and
the *quasi* shows that Cicero is translating
some such word from the Greek. Cf.
Lucr. 5, 110 fundere fata | sanctius et
multo certa ratione magis quam |
Pythia quae tripode a Phoebi lauroque
profatur (also 1, 738); also a couplet in
the epitaph of Epic. given by Diog. L.
10, 12 τοῦτο Νεοκλῆος πινυτὸν τέκος ἢ
παρὰ Μουσέων | ἔκλυεν ἢ Πυθοῦς ἐξ ἱερῶν
τριπόδων. The Epicureans even called
their founder a god; so Lucr. 5, 8; Tusc.
1, 48. So Timon says of Pyrrho, comparing him with the sun-god, 'μοῦνος δ'
ἀνθρώποισι θεοῦ τρόπον ἡγεμονεύεις.'
  3. **edidicit**: there is abundant evidence that Epicurus and his successors
insisted on brief statements of doctrine
being committed to memory. At the
beginning and end of his epistle to
Herodotus, Epicurus indicates that the
letter was intended to be learned by
heart (Diog. L. 10, 35 and 83); and the
same is the case with the epistle to
Pythocles (ib. 84, 116). Cf. what Diocles
ap. Diog. L. 10, 12 says of Epicurus,
'ἐγύμναζε δὲ τοὺς γνωρίμους καὶ διὰ
μνήμης ἔχειν τὰ ἑαυτοῦ συγγράμματα.'
His last words were an injunction to his
friends, 'τῶν δογμάτων μεμνῆσθαι' (ib.
16). The obligation 'iurare in verba
magistri' was always stronger in the
Epicurean school than in any other; and
the 'schoolboy lessons' inculcated in the

Garden were often made matter for
reproach; see note on 2, 95.
  4. **id est quasi...sententiae**: these
words have been suspected of forming
a gloss; but Madvig well defends them;
as he says, the passage gives no mere
elucidation of the phrase κυρίας δόξας,
but explains its application to these
particular maxims: 'librarius nemo
talem explicationem nominis addidisset.
Ceterum cum Cicero iam dixisset:
*breviter comprehensis gravissimis sen-
tentiis*, non nimis eleganter in idem
eum rursus incidere, non nego.' He notes
that *ad beate vivendum* is to be taken
with *gravissimae* rather than with
enuntiatae. As to clauses with *id est*, see
1, 72 *n.*: 2, 6 *n.*; as to *quasi* § 5 *n.*
  6. **si ea**, etc.: this is the tenth κυρία
δόξα (Diog. L. 10, 142): 'εἰ τὰ ποιητικὰ
τῶν περὶ τοὺς ἀσώτους ἡδονῶν ἔλυε τοὺς
φόβους τῆς διανοίας τούς τε περὶ μετεώρων
καὶ θανάτου καὶ ἀλγηδόνων, ἔτι τε τὸ
πέρας τῶν ἐπιθυμιῶν ἐδίδασκεν, οὐκ ἂν
ποτε εἴχομεν ὅ, τι ἐμεμψάμεθα αὐτοῖς,
πανταχόθεν ἐκπληρουμένοις τῶν ἡδονῶν
καὶ οὐθαμόθεν οὔτε τὸ ἀλγοῦν οὔτε τὸ
λυπούμενον ἔχουσιν, ὅπερ ἐστὶ τὸ κακόν.'
Cf. Athen. 7, 278 *f* οἴεται γὰρ οὗτος ὁ
σοφὸς καὶ τὸν ἀσώτων βίον ἀνεπίληπτον
εἶναι adding, however, from above
εἴπερ αὐτῷ προσγένοιτο τὸ ἀδεὲς καὶ
ἴλεων. 'Pro μετεώροις deos Cicero posuit,
a re non aberrans; minus expressit
discrimen τοῦ ἀλγοῦντος et τοῦ λυπου-
μένου, quorum illud ad corpus, hoc ad
animum pertinet' (Madvig). This δόξα
is a defiant version of the doctrine that
virtue owes its value to the pleasure
to which it gives birth; but it does
nothing to impair the other doctrine
that the two are fundamentally inseparable. (See 1 §§ 32 sq.)
  7. **efficientia voluptatum**: Cicero applies extensively the native Latin use
of the present participle with dependent
genitive to represent the Greek adjec-

metu docerentque qui essent fines cupiditatum, nihil haberemus,
quod reprehenderemus, cum undique complerentur voluptatibus
nec haberent ulla ex parte aliquid aut dolens aut aegrum, id est
autem malum.'
Hoc loco tenere se Triarius non potuit. Obsecro, inquit, 5
Torquate, haec dicit Epicurus? (quod mihi quidem visus est,
cum sciret, velle tamen confitentem audire Torquatum). At ille
non pertimuit saneque fidenter: Istis quidem ipsis verbis, inquit;
sed quid sentiat non videtis. Si alia sentit, inquam, alia loquitur,
numquam intellegam quid sentiat; sed plane dicit quod intellegit. 1
Idque si ita dicit, non esse reprehendendos luxuriosos, si sapientes
sint, dicit absurde, similiter et si dicat non reprehendendos

2 quod reprehenderemus: om. codd.; corr. Davies.   3 id est: *idem* E.   7 velle:
vellē A². 　　8 pertimuit: *pertinuit* B. 　　8 que: om. B. 　　9 videtis: *videt* B.
10 intellegit AB: *intellegam* codd. dett.; cf. 1 § 15. 　　11 reprehendendos: *repen-
dendos* A¹, ut est l. 12. 　　11 luxuriosos si: *luxuriosi* A¹.

tives in -κός with the same construction.
Cf. 3, 55 (bona) efficientia, quae Graeci
ποιητικά: 5, 81 eorum (bonorum) con-
ficientia; but Fat. 33 causas id efficientis.
See Draeger, 11², § 207.

2. **complerentur**: the genitive construction with *complere* and similar
verbs was probably in Cicero's time
archaic and colloquial. One ex. only
occurs in the speeches, viz. Verr. 5, 147
cum completus iam mercatorum carcer
esset; here perhaps *turba* has fallen out
after *mercatorum*. Only one ex. is
quoted from the philosophical writings,
i.e. Cato m. 46, but here it is an error
to suppose that the genitive depends
on *compleo*; see my note on the passage.

3. **dolens aut aegrum**: Tusc. 1, 79
nihil est quod doleat, quin id aegrum
quoque esse possit.

id est autem: 'non memini alibi sic
poni *id est autem*, quia continuativa
huius particulae significatio ab hac
brevi adiunctione alienior videtur;
saepius sic dicitur *id est*, et alia sententiae forma *id est enim*' (Madvig). If
the objection is solely to the 'brevis
adiunctio,' it hardly holds good; cf. e.g.
4, 72 dicam Graece προηγμένα, Latine
autem producta. *Autem* is common in
small explanatory parentheses as Acad.
2, 61 and often in Livy.

5. **tenere se**: Madvig calls the order
se tenere 'less good'; but it is found in
Acad. 2, 12 (where M. sees a difference
which I cannot trace); Sest. 117 vix se
populus Romanus tenuit (but ib. 134
tenere se non potuit); Pis. 49; Deiot. 11;

Phil. 7, 1 and 13, 46; Petron. 64 and often
elsewhere: *tenere se* as in Phil. 5, 48;
Juv. 1, 31. So 'te teneo' and 'teneo te.'
No doubt the choice of order in such
cases depends on a feeling for emphasis
and euphony, which is sometimes too
subtle to be caught by us.

8. **saneque fidenter**: N.D. 1, 18 tum
Velleius fidenter sane, ut solent isti (sc.
Epicurei).

9. **aliud sentit**: Cael. ap. Fam. 8, 1, 3
aliud sentire et loqui (of Pompeius);
Acad. 2, 15 aliud diceret ac sentiret
(of Socrates' irony); Att. 7, 6, 2 dices:
'quid tu igitur sensurus es?' Non idem
quod dicturus.

10. **plane dicit quod intellegit**: 'it is
his custom to express clearly what he
clearly understands.' The inference is
that he does not in this case know what
he is talking about; hence *dicit absurde*,
not *plane*. The whole run of the argument shows that *intellegit* is the right
reading. And it is supported by T. D.
2, 44 Epicurus...tantum monet quantum intellegit. Cf. Sen. ben. 1, 3, 8
Chrysippus verbis non ultra quam ad
intellectum satis est utitur.

12. **similiter et si dicat**: *et* substituted
for *ac* where the sense is truly comparative, not copulative (see note on 1, 67
aeque et); so 4, 31 similem habeat
voltum et si; *aliter et* (with following
vowel) in Att. 10, 11, 1 and 11, 23, 1;
alius et, Sall. Cat. 52, 2. Lucretius once
writes (3, 1092) *minus et* for *quam* (with
a vowel following). [Cicero and prose
writers generally do not employ *ac* or

parricidas, si nec cupidi sint nec deos metuant nec mortem nec dolorem.

Et tamen quid attinet luxuriosi ullam exceptionem dari aut fingere aliquos qui, cum luxuriose viverent, a summo

atque after comparatives, for *minus ac* in older editions of Att. 5, 11, 2 is an error, *ac* not being in the MSS.; and recent edd. of Att. 13, 2, 3 rightly interpose a stop between *diutius* and *ac nollem*. The only other exx. quoted from prose for *ac* after comparative are Liv. 22, 10, 6 (in a quotation from an old document) and Suet. Iul. 14. Yet *atque* follows the superlative sometimes, as in Fam. 9, 13, 2 non possum ego non aut proxime atque ille aut etiam aeque laborare; and in Leg. agr. 1, 13 simillime atque, *simillime* takes the construction of *similiter*.] Lamb. read *similiter ut si*, which Cicero has in three places, Off. 1, 87; Cato m. 17; Tusc. 4, 41. See note on § 33 simul et; also on 4, 31 similem...et; and on 4, 64 aeque et.

non reprehendendos, etc.: Madvig criticizes Cicero's exposition for want of lucidity, but his own remarks are hard to follow. 'Comparatio parricidarum quam absurditatem ostendat, non apparet, nisi hoc dicit, inaniter totum hoc ab Epicuro poni, quod adiungat condicionem, quae numquam effici possit. Atqui Epicurus non docebat asotos aliquando non reprehendendos *esse*, sed non *fore* reprehendendos, nisi iis necessario adiuncta pravitas aliqua esset. Et ipse Cicero statim ostendit non esse illam necessario adiunctam, posseque esse tales luxuriosos. Nec Epicurus de asotis dixit, quos Cicero negat finitas cupiditates habere posse sed de genere illo voluptatis quo uterentur.' But (1) the object of the introduction of *parricidae* is surely clear enough; Cicero wishes to cast odium on the doctrine of Epicurus by showing that it would apply to all sinners and criminals alike; and this the philosopher himself could not have denied. (2) What is meant by the distinction drawn between 'reprehendendos *esse*' and '*fore*' is hard to see; Epicurus wrote οὐκ ἄν ποτε εἴχομεν, not οὐκ ἄν ποτε ἔχοιμεν, and this proposition Cicero's words are perfectly well suited to represent. (3) It is again difficult to understand the point of the remark *et ipse...luxuriosos*. What Epicurus averred in the tenth κυρία δόξα was that *luxuria* left the four great ills of life, passion, dread of gods, dread of death, pain, uncured. Naturally Cicero tries to show that the *luxuriosi* can

escape these ills. (4) The criticism that Epicurus wrote not of the ἄσωτοι but of the kind of pleasure which they pursue, is most unsubstantial. Madvig proceeds: 'Deinde, si in coniunctione rerum prorsus separatarum absurdum illud esse vult, minime, ut parricidium et doloris mortisve metus plane seiuncta sunt, sic in Epicuri sententia luxuriosa voluptas et reliqua illa. Cum enim in voluptate summum bonum ponat, ostendit cur in corporis et luxuriosa voluptate non ponat beatam vitam eosque reprehendat qui in illa voluptatem et reliqua illa. Cum enim in voluptate summum bonum ponat, ostendit cur in corporis et luxuriosa voluptate non ponat beatam vitam eosque reprehendat qui in illa volutentur.' These sayings are again dark. The first sentence seems to imply that the parallel Cicero draws between parricide and *luxuria* will not hold. But surely both are alike in what is the sole point of importance for Cicero's argument, viz. that they do not bring peace. How the latter of the two sentences is connected in meaning with the former I have failed to divine. In the remainder of his note, Madvig insists that Cicero ought to have been content at this point (*hoc loco in praeparatione disputationis*) with indicating that *luxuriosi* can exist free from dread; 'cetera de ipsa luxuriosae voluptatis reprehensione hoc loco declamatorie adiunguntur et turbant legentem.'

1. **si nec cupidi sint**, etc.: the four κύριαι δόξαι which stand first in the collection are directed against these four principal evils of life. Attention is drawn to this fact by an unknown Epicurean writer in one of the Herculanean fragments quoted by Usener, p. 68; cf. also another fragment (ib. p. 69) παρέστω μόνον ἡ τετραφάρμακος· ἄφοβον ὁ θεός, ἀναίσθητον ὁ θάνατος, καὶ τἀγαθὸν μὲν εὔκτητον (hence no need for *cupiditates inanes*), τὸ δὲ δεινὸν (pain) εὐεκκαρτέρητον.

2. **exceptionem:** the conditional clauses in the δόξα are compared to the modifying clauses (technically *exceptiones*) in the legal *formula*. See Acad. 2, 97.

3. **dari aut fingere:** Madvig illustrates the change from the passive to the active infinitive dependent on an impersonal expression, from Fat. 23 and 46; Brut. 196; De Or. 2, 177; Leg. 1, 56; Inv. 2, 36 and 117; Phil. 5, 39; Lig. 14 (where the reading has been

philosopho non reprehenderentur eo nomine dumtaxat, cetera
22 caverent? Sed tamen nonne reprehenderes, Epicure, luxuriosos

needlessly altered by edd.); Sen. de
prov. 1, 1; add Liv. 5, 39, 11 (*placuit*);
5, 20, 8 (*satius esse*); 5, 30, 3 (*nefas*);
24, 11, 2 (*placuit*); Luc. 10, 347.
Madvig expresses a doubt whether
Cicero intended to use this freedom
in Div. 1, 77 signa convelli ac se
sequi iussit, because the standards
themselves might be said *sequi ducem*;
though Virgil did use it in Aen. 5, 773
and perhaps in Ecl. 6, 85; so Liv. 21, 38, 6
(after *miror*). Since verbs of wishing
tend, like impersonal verbs, to take the
passive infinitive (see note on 1, 30)
there is nothing surprising in the transition after *volo*, as in Att. 9, 6, 7 (where
Boot changes the reading without the
least necessity) and Cael. 79 and Liv. 31,
10, 7; or *malo* as in Liv. 21, 38, 6; 35,
4, 2; cf. Virg. Aen. 3, 61 (*idem animus*).

1. eo nomine: Usener, p. 73 κυρ. δόξ. 10.
dumtaxat: 'merely'; cf. the words
below 'ob eam ipsam causam quod ita
viverent.' *Dumtaxat* in its earliest uses
(in legal formulae) was applied to the
limitation of sums of money or things
of other kinds. Philologists continue to
connect *taxat* (which was separable from
the *dum* in early Latin) in one way or
another with *tangere*. Bréal calls it a
subj. of an *s*-aorist of *tango*, 'donec
tetigerit, jusqu'à ce qu'il *ait* atteint,'
then 'jusqu'à et non plus loin.' The
explanation is probably in substance as
old as Aelius Stilo. See Festus, p. 356.
Varro has preserved *taxis*=*tetigeris*.
Lindsay (Latin Language, p. 565) calls
taxat a present subj. of a by-form of
tango as *viso* of *video* and *quaeso* of
quaero. But in the earliest passages
taxat has the precise meaning of *aestimet*,
so much so that the genitive of value is
attached to it, as e.g. in C.I.L. 1, 197, 12
sei quis magistratus multam inrogare
volet [quei volet dum minoris] partus
familias taxsat, liceto; the abl. of value
also occurs. The process by which this
original sense is arrived at, starting from
the fundamental idea of *tango*, is very
forced. I am still inclined (as I wrote
in commenting on Lael. 53) to connect
taxat with Oscan *tanginom* (*sententia*, τὸ
δόξαν) and with *tongēre*, about which
there is this curious statement in Festus,
p. 356 M.: Aelius Stilo ait noscere esse,
quod Praenestini tongitionem dicant
pro notionem. Significat et latius dominari. Ennius: alii rhetorica tongent. Et
vincere etiam quandoque videtur significare. The text is thus restored with

fair certainty by K. O. Müller. The ex-
cerpt of Paulus is: 'tongere nosse est,
nam Praenestini tongitionem dicunt
notionem. Ennius: alii rhetorica tongent.' If, as appears, Festus understood
tongere in the passage of Ennius to mean
latius dominari, he has blundered
strangely; so, too, about the meaning
vincere, of which, however, he speaks
doubtfully. [The gloss often quoted for
tongere, as e.g. by Forc. De Vit s.v., is a
forgery; see Luc. Müller's Lucilius,
p. 244.] In post-Augustan Latin writers
a verb *taxare* appears with a wider range
of usage: it is applied to estimating
or valuing anything (whether concrete
or not) with the constructions of value.
Then it comes to mean 'to punish' as
in Sen. ben. 4, 36, 3. In Gellius and the
Gromatici (see Lexica, s.v.) stones are
said *taxari* when they are wrought by the
mason. The sense is usually explained
(rather ineptly) by the stone having
been 'saepius tactus' by the mason;
rather the notion of diminishing property by mulcts is extended to other
modes of diminishing. A somewhat
similar change explains the sense 'to
taunt' a person or 'depreciate' a thing.
There are analogies in the uses of
multare. *Taxatio*=*aestimatio* occurs once
in Cicero (pro Tull. 7), and often later.
Festus l.l. explains *taxator*: 'scenici
taxatores dicuntur, quod alter alterum
maledictis tangit'; this he gives as
evidence that *taxare* is connected with
tangere. The gloss is suspicious; if trustworthy, the use of *taxator* may belong
to a late time, when *taxare*=*male dicere*
was common. *Tangere*='abuse,' 'cheat'
is of course found at all periods, and is
like our vulgar phrase 'to touch up.' The
construction in *tangere aliquem triginta
minis* (Pl. Epid. 705) and the like phrases
is best explained as one of value, 'to
touch a man up to the tune of 30
minae.' If *taxare* were really connected
with *tangere*, expressions of this kind
would afford the nearest analogy to the
use of *taxat* in the old laws.
cetera: i.e. the dread of the gods, etc.
2. caverent: Madvig justifies the
asyndeton, saying that the direct statement would be *hoc saltem nomine non
reprehenduntur, cetera cavent*. It must be
confessed, however, that the proposal of
Lambinus to insert *si* before *cetera* has
in its favour the εἰ-clause in the δόξα
of Epicurus, the *si*-clause which Cicero
twice uses in this section, and the word

ob eam ipsam causam, quod ita viverent, ut persequerentur cuiusque modi voluptates, cum esset praesertim, ut ais tu, summa voluptas nihil dolere? Atqui reperiemus asotos primum ita non religiosos, ut 'edint de patella,' deinde ita mortem non timentes, 5 ut illud in ore habeant ex Hymnide:

Mihi sex menses satis sunt vitae, septimum Orco spondeo.

1 ut: *quod* B.　　2 ut: om. B.　　3 nihil: *michi* B.　　4 edint: *edient* A¹; *edent* A²; om. B. corr. Madv.; *edant* alii.　　4 ita mortem: *mortem ita* B.

exceptionem. Madvig argues (I cannot think soundly) that *fingere* proves the MSS. to be correct: 'nam fingebantur animo qui illam condicionem implerent, quod cetera illa, quae reprehendi possent, caverent.' He rightly condemns Goerenz for making *caverent* depend on *dumtaxat*, which is, all through Latin, an adverb and not a conjunction. There is much confusion in commentaries and works on scholarship, touching the use of this word; E. Wölfflin truly says (Archiv 4, 325): 'die Partikel dumtaxat macht den Philologen wie den Juristen viel zu schaffen.' Yet all its applications are easily derived from its original use in the statutes, as given above. There it indicates a *superior* limit, 'at most,' thence it is easily diverted to the notion of an *inferior* limit, 'at least,' or 'at all events.' Ad Brut. 1, 3, 4 consules... bonos quidem, sed dumtaxat bonos. Sometimes again, the notion of a limit, purely and simply, is present in the word and it then means 'merely.' Practically these senses will be found to cover all the occurrences of the phrase. Wichert in his 'Stillehre,' p. 322, has taken exception to its use in a concessive clause in De opt. gen. or. 8, where Cicero speaks of certain faults which, he says, are avoided by all speakers who deserve the name of *Attici*: 'sed qui ea tenus valuerunt (i.e. so far as to get rid of these faults) sani et sicci dumtaxat habeantur ('sound and wiry at all events, if nothing else'), sed ita ut palaestritae, non ut Olympiis coronam petant' (i.e. for the highest excellence more is needed than to shun error). There is nothing strange in the use of *dumtaxat* here, and there is no reason why the word should not be attached to a concessive subjunctive. In all the instances where *dumtaxat* means 'at least' it may be regarded as indicating a concession (as *sane* often does) which the hearer or reader is expected to make. Apart from statutes, *dumtaxat* presents itself in only one

place in the remains of pre-Ciceronian Latin, viz. in a line of the prosaic Lucilius. Catullus avoided the word; Lucretius used it twice, as he did some other legal phrases (*de plano* for example), and he was followed by Horace and Ovid, but scarcely by any other poet. Cicero rather favoured the word; Caesar patronised it once; his continuators twice; Livy twice. After that most of the prominent writers employ it occasionally. It lingered on to a late time, probably becoming more and more of a literary curiosity (once in Gregory of Tours, according to Bonnet).

　1. viverent: see note on 2, 34 (evenirent).

　2. cuiusque modi: § 3 *n.*

　3. asotos: so N.D. 3, 77; Macrob. 6, 4, 22 attributes the use of *asotia* to the 'veteres.' Arist. Eth. Nic. 4, c. 1 comments on the extension of the original sense of ἄσωτος, i.e. 'spendthrift,' to include profligacy in general.

　ita non: cf. § 63; adeo non, Liv. 8, 5, 7; tam nil, Pers. 1, 122; tam tota, Varro r.r. 1, 2, 3; non minus non, Plin. ep. 1, 20, 20; my note on Acad. 2, 55. For the participle with acc. cf. Madv. Gr. §289 *a* who says the acc. is due to *adverb* (but not always, e.g. De Or. 2, 364 tam sui despiciens).

　4. edint de patella: doubtless this is either a proverb or a quotation from the old drama, otherwise the form *edint* would scarcely occur here (on this and similar forms see Neue II², 441 sq.). For a similar brief quotation cf. 3, 16 sed fortuna fortis. These *luxuriosi* evidently eat from the sacrificial *patera* in pure defiance. We are reminded of the club of young men mentioned by Demosthenes in his 'Conon,' who dubbed themselves Τρίβαλλοι and went about τὰ ἑκάταια κατεσθίοντες: also of βωμολόχος (possibly 'altar-licker' rather than 'altar-besetter' as it was explained in ancient times) and *sacrilegus*, 'the picker-up of things consecrated.'

　5. Hymnide: a play of Caecilius,

Iam doloris medicamenta illa Epicurea tamquam de narthecio
proment: 'Si gravis, brevis; si longus, levis.' Vnum nescio, quo
modo possit, si luxuriosus sit, finitas cupiditates habere.

23   VIII.   Quid ergo attinet dicere: 'Nihil haberem quod reprehenderem, si finitas cupiditates haberent'? Hoc est dicere: 5
'Non reprehenderem asotos, si non essent asoti.' Isto modo ne
improbos quidem, si essent boni viri. Hic homo severus luxuriam
ipsam per se reprehendendam non putat. Et hercule, Torquate,
ut verum loquamur, si summum bonum voluptas est, rectissime
non putat. Nolim enim mihi fingere asotos, ut soletis, qui in 10
mensam vomant, et qui de conviviis auferantur crudique pos-

---

1 narthecio: *narthetio* A.   4 quid ergo: *quod ergo* B.   4 haberem: *habere* A.
7 quidem: *quam* B.   7 hic homo: *hoc homini* B.   8 Torquate: *o* torquate A
(*o* superscr. m. 2).   11 postridie: *posteri die* A¹; *postero die* A² al.

'conveyed' from Menander; this line
was again conveyed by Lucilius ap.
Non. 526 M.: 'qui sex mensis vitam
ducunt, Orco spondent septimum.' An
ancient version of 'a short life and a
merry one.' Ritschl, Opusc. 2, 506,
supposes that the readings here of some
MSS., *exenemide, exonemide*, point to a
form *Huminis* (doubtless a *meretrix*, the
ἄσωτος being her lover).

1. **medicamenta**: φάρμακα: cf. τετραφάρμακος in the passage quoted in note
on § 21 si nec cupidi sint.
narthecio: a rare word: Mart. 14,
78; so νάρθηξ, a casket.
2. **brevis**...**levis**: a not uncommon
jingle; Parad. 26 breviora, leviora; cf.
94, 95; see also some passages in note
on *levis*...*brevis* in 1, 40; also note on 1,
49 maximos morte finiri; cf. also N.D. 1,
70. [As to *brevis*...*levis* see Wölfflin in
Archiv 1, 382.] Sen. ep. 24, 2 aut non
magnum aut non longum esse quod
metuis; ib. 24, 14; 78, 7.
unum nescio: cf. the elliptic *nisi
unum* in Plaut., as Mil. Gl. 24, where
see Tyrrell's note.
3. **possit**: a sudden transition from
plural to singular, not uncommon in
Cicero, as N.D. 1 §§ 50, 101, 102, 114;
De Or. 1, 160 (where see Wilkins' note);
in his note on N.D. 1, 50 Davies quotes
Greek parallels. The opposite change,
from singular to plural, sometimes
occurs, as in N.D. 1, 106, Acad. 2, 32, 140.
Madv. is unduly severe with Goerenz,
who suggested that the indefinite subject was omitted, as in Greek. M. says:
'quid id ad Ciceronem?' Goerenz
doubtless had in mind passages like

De Or. 1, 30 impellere voluntates quo
velit; see my note on Acad. 1, 2.
6. **isto modo**: so § 103; cf. the elliptic
use of *isto modo* in answer to questions,
Tusc. 1, 11; 4, 9.
7. **hic**: 'hereupon.'
9. **ut verum loquamur**: Tusc. 1, 112
verum si loqui volumus.
10. **nolim mihi**...**ut soletis**: cf. N.D. 2,
47 (also addressed to an Epicurean) noli,
quaeso, prae te ferre vos plane expertis
esse doctrinae. As to the change of
number see above, note on 'possit,' and
for the ethical dative cf. In Cat. 2, 10
qui mihi...vino languidi eructant cae-
dem; Draeger § 191; Kühner, Gram.
§ 76, 8 c. The sense of the passage is
'I should be sorry to imagine to myself' (cf. Acad. 2, 51 mens...sibi fingit
aliquid). These pictures of debauchery
were no doubt proposed by the Epicureans by way of horrible examples,
a fact which is often left out by
their critics; cf. § 68. To these moral
lessons belonged mention of moral
storms (χειμῶνες καὶ καταιγισμοί) and
ἐπεντρώματα and νύγματα and other
phrases ridiculed by Plutarch, Cleomedes, Athenaeus, Philo and others
(see Usener, Epicurea, § 413).
11. **vomant**: cf. the reproaches addressed to Antonius, Phil. 2, 76.
crudi: Cluent. 168 cum ad illud
prandium crudior venisset; cf. Sen. d.
1, 3, 2; 4, 10; Hor. ep. 1, 6, 61 crudi tumi-
dique lavemur; Sen. ep. 89, 22 dominus
crudus ac nauseans; 24, 16 ipsae voluptates in tormenta vertuntur, epulae
cruditatem adferunt; Sen. d. 12, 10, 3
vomunt ut edant, edunt ut voment;

tridie se rursus ingurgitent, qui solem, ut aiunt, nec occidentem
umquam viderint nec orientem, qui consumptis patrimoniis
egeant. Nemo nostrum istius generis asotos iucunde putat
vivere. Mundos, elegantis, optimis cocis, pistoribus, piscatu,
5 aucupio, venatione, his omnibus exquisitis, vitantes cruditatem,
'quibus vinum defusum e pleno sit,† hirsizon,' ut ait Lucilius,

1 occidentem: *hoc cadentem* A¹.   3 istius...venatione: affert Nonius, p. 217.
6 hirsizon: ita A; *hrysizon* B; *hirsiphon* al.

Mart. 12, 76, 2 ebrius et crudus nil habet
agricola; ib. 3, 13, 4. Sen. d. 5, 13, 5 qui
vinum male ferunt et ebrietatis suae
temeritatem ac petulantiam metuunt,
mandant suis ut e convivio auferantur.

1. **ingurgitent:** Cicero twice has *in-gurgitare se in aliquam rem* (in a metaphorical sense), Pis. 42 and Phil. 2, 65;
cf. Plaut. Curc. 1, 2, 33 (126) merum
ingurgitare in se; Petron. 79 anus...
ingurgitata.

solem, etc.: Athen. 6, 273 c quotes
the instance of a Sybarite who boasted
that he had not seen the sun rise or set
for 20 years, and in 12, 520 a he says the
peculiar climate of Sybaris made this
way of living healthy, whence it was a
saying 'ὅτι τὸν βουλόμενον ἐν Συβάρει μὴ
πρὸ μοίρας ἀποθανεῖν, οὔτε δυόμενον οὔτε
ἀνίσχοντα τὸν ἥλιον ὁρᾶν δεῖ.' Cf.
Sen. ep. 77, 17 (to a glutton) solem
quoque, si posses, extorqueres; 122, 2
sunt qui officia lucis noctisque perver-
terint nec ante diducant oculos hesterna
graves crapula quam adpetere nox
coepit. Seneca goes on to compare these
men with the 'antipodes' and to quote
a saying of M. Cato, the censor, to the
effect that in the same city with ourselves these 'antipodes' may be found,
'qui nec orientem umquam solem viderunt nec occidentem.' Also Liv. 31,
41, 10 per somnum et vinum dies
noctibus aequare; Plin. n. h. 14, 141
interea, ut optime cedat, solem orientem
non vident, ac minus diu vivont; Colum.
1, pr. § 16; Mayor on Juven. 8, 11 si
dormire incipis ortu Luciferi.

3. **istius generis:** Cicero has *eius
generis, eiusdem g.* and the like, but not
omnis g. (which Caes. and his continuators avoid, but Livy and later writers
use freely) nor *cuiusque g.* (which Caes.
has); see Wölfflin in Archiv 5, 395.
Often the phrase *in omni genere* stands
where later writers would put *omnis
generis.* [Pis. 96 omnes mortales omnium generum ordinum aetatum is of
course different; so is dom. 75 splendore
omnis generis hominum.]

4. **piscatu...venatione:** cf. Cels. 2, 26
minima inflatio fit ex venatione aucupio
piscibus pomis. The lexica give exx. of
the concrete use of *inflatio* and *venatio,*
piscatus and *venatus.*

5. **his omnibus:** Draeger § 363 erroneously denies to Cicero the summative
use of *omnia, cetera* and the like at the
end of an enumeration, with asyndeton;
haec omnia occurs in Tusc. 3, 7 and Verr.
2, 1, 74; also doubtless in Verr. 2, 4, 46
haec omnia is the right reading, for the
varying position of *autem* in the mss.
shows it to be an interpolation; cf. too
Acad. 2, 85 (but reading doubtful).
Many parallels are to be found in Livy,
Tac. and other writers. Early exx. of
haec omnia (not in Draeger) are in Cat.
agr. 51; 73; 133. [See note on 1, 6
multos alios, and on 4, 35 cetera.] The
ablatives are of course comitative and
not instrumental, dependent on *vitantes,*
as Kühner, in his German translation,
and others have supposed.

6. **vinum,** etc.: Cicero in quoting has
perturbed the metre and there are no
means of restoring the lines with certainty. Munro, in his able discussion of
the passage (Journal of Phil.VIII, 217 sq.),
complains that Luc. Müller (in his
Lucilius) returned to errors exploded
by Madvig. Munro's χρυσίζον is so
obviously right that it is useless to
discuss previous suggestions, some of
which were very grotesque, such as the
proposal to read *hir-siphon,* 'a hand-
siphon' (*hir* = χείρ). For χρυσίζον M.
quotes Athen. 27 b ὁ Σπωλητῖνος δὲ
οἶνος καὶ πινόμενος ἡδὺς καὶ τῷ χρώματι
χρυσίζει. Somewhat similar is Milton,
Sams. Ag. 543, 'the dancing ruby
sparkling outpoured,' and Parad. L.
5, 633, 'rubied nectar.' M. gives, as
the only other example in Latin of
defundere vinum ('to decant,' while
diffundere is 'to rack off') Hor. s.
2, 2, 58 ac, nisi mutatum, parcit defundere vinum; but a parallel from
Columella is given by Forc. and others
from Gratius Faliscus and Palladius by

'cui nihildum sit vis et sacculus abstulerit,' adhibentis ludos et

1 dum sit: ita ABE Crat.; *dempsit* vett.   1 vis: *nix* Lambinus.

Georges. Doubtless Horace l.l. had in mind the passage of Lucilius; so, too, I think, had Petronius when he wrote (§ 5) sic flumine largo | plenus Pierio defundes pectore verba; for he mentions Lucilius just before and other phrases in the same piece of verse have a Lucilian tinge.

e pleno: this probably means 'from a full cask,' i.e. there is no stint. The phrase may have been proverbial; cf. Theocr. 10, 13 ἐκ πίθου ἀντλεῖς: Cic. Brut. 288 de dolio hauriendum; Sen. dial. 7, 24, 3 ut...(liberalitas) quasi ex pleno fluat (cf. too ib. 10, 3, 4): and also Ov. Tr. 5, 1, 37 pleno de fonte ministrat. But it is noticeable that *plenum vinum* meant sometimes a 'full-bodied' wine, as in Cels. 1, 6; see the next note.

1. nihildum: if this word be right, the general drift of the line as written by Lucilius must have been that the wine had not yet lost anything of its strength by straining. Perhaps L. wrote *cui nildum pix vis* (gen. sing.) *et sacculus abstulit*, for *pix* was used to render wine milder, as Plin. n. h. 14, 120 says. That this emendation is in the right direction seems to be shown by Varro's imitation, 'vinum cui nihil sacculus abstulit' (Gramm. Latini, ed. Keil, 5, p. 590). The restoration of Baehrens, 'cui nil dum situs et sacculus abstulerit' is thus better than that of L. Müller, 'cui nil | durist [*duri* Madv.] cum nix et sacculus abstulerit' and that of Munro, 'cui nihilum est viri set sacculus abstulit omne.' But the indicative *abstulit* is more probable than *abstulerit* and hence the hexameter form is more likely than the elegiac. [Cicero himself uses *nihildum* a few times, as Verr. 2, 4, 9; In Cat. 3, 6; Fam. 12, 7, 2; Att. 7, 12, 4; 9, 2; 15, 4, 5, also *neque dum* a few times, but not *nullus dum* (of which Livy is fond) nor other similar forms which occur in early and late Latin.] Munro appears to think that the *clearness* produced by straining is necessarily implied by χρυσίζον, but that is hardly so. Madvig protests against *dempsit* being taken as equivalent to *dempserit*, because it is identical in form with the perf. indic.; but there certainly are analogies for this; see Neue II², 539 sq.; *nihildum* a few times in Epp. (Fam. 10, 12, 2).

sacculus: Petron. 73 vinum in conspectu sacco defluens. The straining of the wine did not always (as Madvig assumes) improve its flavour; Hor. s. 2, 4, 53 at illa | integrum perdunt lino vitiata saporem. In pro Scaur. 42 Cicero speaks of the Sardinians as having a bad pedigree. The Phoenicians, a most treacherous race, founded Carthage, where the inhabitants, after mingling with the Africans and pursuing a career of turbulence and faithlessness, banished certain of their number who colonised Sardinia. 'Quare cum integri nihil fuerit in hac gente plena, quam valde eam putamus tot transfusionibus coacuisse?' The word *plena* is used in allusion to the sense it has in the passage of Celsus, quoted above. For *diffundere vina* see Mayor and Friedländer on Juven. 5, 30; and cf. the lexica under *capulare, capulator*.

adhibentis ludos: cf. § 64 cetera illa adhibebat, etc. *Ludos:* Gaditanarum and the like. The word is often used alone in reference to banquets, Hor. ep. 2, 2, 56 iocos Venerem convivia ludum with the bad significance which Cicero conveys here by *et quae secuntur*. 'Es, bibe, lude' occurs commonly on tombstones; see Bücheler, Carmina Epigraphica, 935, 19 and 1500 with his notes; cf. too note on § 106 Sardanapalli. *Ludi* in Lucr. 4, 1131 (wrongly questioned by Lachmann) has a similar connotation, as the context shows. The word *ludus* lies concealed, I believe, in a passage quoted twice by Nonius (70 and 353) from Varro's 'Modius,' where V. alludes (as often) to Epicurus. The MSS. of Nonius (353) give 'asse vinum, asse pulmentarium, secundas quo natura aurigatur, non necessitudo.' L. Müller (note on Non. 70) writes *quoi*, interpreting *secundas* as *s. mensas* and remarking 'hominis divitis eiusdemque sobrii mores describi apparet.' Riese, in his edition of the fragments of the Menippean satires, writes *quom* for *quo*. But Varro is alluding to the classification of the desires by Epicurus and the words *natura aurigatur non necessitudo* indicate a desire which is natural but not necessary (see above 1, 45 with notes). *Quo*, therefore, is right, 'in the direction of which,' but *secundas* is corrupt; I would read *asse ludus*. There is abundant evidence to show that Epicurus placed the amatory *ludus* among things natural but not

quae secuntur, illa, quibus detractis clamat Epicurus se nescire
quid sit bonum; adsint etiam formosi pueri qui ministrent,
respondeat his vestis, argentum, Corinthium, locus ipse, aedifi-
cium—hos ergo asotos bene quidem vivere aut beate numquam
dixerim. Ex quo efficitur, non ut voluptas ne sit voluptas, sed **24**
ut voluptas non sit summum bonum. Nec ille qui Diogenem
Stoicum adulescens, post autem Panaetium audierat, Laelius,
eo dictus est sapiens, quod non intellegeret quid suavissimum

2 adsint: *adsit* A¹.   4 aut: *at* B.

necessary. Martial 1, 103, 9, had the
passage of Varro in mind; 'et Veientani
bibitur faex crassa rubelli, asse cicer
tepidum constat et asse venus.' There
are other fragments of the 'Modius' in
which V. quotes Epicurus' recommen-
dations of an uncostly life; see note on
§ 24 o lapathe.

1. **quae secuntur:** similarly N.D. 1, 95
quid sequatur videtis; Dio Cass. 45, 26
(a speech of Cicero) τοὺς κώμους, τὰς
μέθας, τἆλλα πάντα τὰ τούτοις ἑπόμενα;
V. Hugo, Notre-Dame, Liv. 7, c. 1 la
taverne lui plaisait et ce qui s'ensuit;
Cleomedes, ed. Ziegler, p. 166, l. 27
ἀσχήμονι μέθῃ καταυλούμενος καὶ λοιπὸν
τὰ τούτοις ἑπόμενα πράσσων (in the
course of a long passage abusing Epicurus).

clamat: note on 1, 57.

2. **formosi:** for the spelling *formonsi*
see Schönwerth-Weyman in Archiv 5,
195, 196.

3. **Corinthium:** this is used sub-
stantively in Tusc. 2, 32 and by later
writers.

4. **ergo:** this resumptive use is common both in Cicero (above 1, 72;
Draeger § 354 g) and elsewhere, cf. Tac.
Dial. 34 init.; resumptive uses attach
to *igitur* (Draeger § 355, 9); *sed* (Draeger
§ 333, 5); *tamen, sed tamen* (my note on
Acad. 2, 17), *verum tamen.*

bene vivere: Hor. ep. 1, 6, 56 si bene
qui cenat bene vivit.

5. **ne sit…non sit:** Madvig (note on
§ 15) thus states the use of *ut ne* and *ut
non:* 'ea verba quae voluntatem et
studium efficiendi significant, ut paene
notio finis et consilii insit, velut *oro,
peto, praecipio, curo* cett., propterea
semper habent aut *ne* aut *ut ne,* etiam
caveo, Lael. 99, ad Qu. Fr. 1, 1, 38;
Liv. xxxiv, 17, 8, ut dicitur etiam *caveo
ut,* id est *operam do* [et *interdico* De Or.
1, 215]; ea contra verba in quibus
generalis inest significatio rei effectae et
consequentis, quod magis inclinant in

sententiarum effectivarum naturam,
fere *ut non* habent, raro, nec tamen
numquam, *ut ne,* accedente levi signifi-
catione studii et voluntatis; (*non efficitur,
ut ne,* hoc est, *non efficitur,* quod vultis,
ut ne).' Cf. Att. 11, 9, 3 (Boot) utinam
susceptus non essem aut ne quid…
The combination *ut ne* is very common
in Cicero; Merguet's Lexica, s.v. *ne,* give
over 100 instances, and there are many
in the other writings. In many cases
I cannot trace even the *levis significatio
studii et voluntatis* which Madvig supposes. It would be idle to assume that
in the present passage Cicero changed
his point of view in passing from *ut ne*
to *ut non.* One might suspect that
Cicero wrote *non ut ne* for euphony, were
it not that *non ut non* occurs elsewhere,
as above § 15 and Fam. 13, 29, 4. The
clause *ita ut ne* frequently occurs (De
Or. 3, 171, 172; Ad Herenn. 3, 24; Varro,
r. r. 2, 10, 3; ib. 3, 16, §§ 16, 27, 34; cf.
sic…uti ne, Cato agr. 1, 1); the notion is
in such circumstances, so far as I can
see, as purely consecutive as it is when
ita ut non is written. Many traces are
left of the time when *ne* and *non* had not
been differentiated in use, and the instances in which *ut ne* is indistinguishable in sense from *ut non* may be sur-
vivals. After Cicero's time *ut ne* is
comparatively rare. Caesar and Sallust
avoid it altogether; Livy has it only
in one or two passages; Tacitus once.
To Draeger's list of later exx. (§§ 411;
542, 2; 562 c) add Plin. n. h. 16, 12; Apul.
de deo Socr. 110 ed. Goldb.

6. **Diogenem:** he came with Carneades
and Critolaus on the famous embassy to
Rome in 155 B.C.

7. **adulescens:** Madvig points out that
L. was older than Scipio Africanus, who
was 31 or 32 in 155. The intimacy of
Panaetius with the Scipionic circle is
well known.

Laelius…sapiens: see Lael. § 7 and
p. 15 of the Introduction to my ed.

esset (nec enim sequitur ut, cui cor sapiat, ei non sapiat palatus),
sed quia parvi id duceret.

O lapathe, ut iactare, nec es sati' cognitu' qui sis!

1 enim sequitur ut cui: *ergo sequer et* B.   3 ut: *et* E.   3 nec es sati': *ne*
cessatis AB; *necesse est* al.   3 cognitu' qui: sic AB; *cognitu quis* E.

1. **cor sapiat**: apart from the phrase
cordi est, cor is hardly found in ordinary
prose excepting when the bodily heart
is meant. Cicero had in mind here
doubtless some passage of an old writer,
possibly a jest of Lucilius on the two
senses of *sapere*. [There seems to be a
gross jest on *sapiat* in Mart. 11, 90
where probably the same book of
Lucilius is quoted from which Cicero
quotes hereabouts.] In archaic Latin
cor was the seat of the understanding;
in Tusc. 1, 18 Cicero quotes *Corculum*
(name of a Nasica) and 'egregie cordatus
homo.' So all through popular Latin; see
Rebling, 'Charakteristik der römischen
Umgangssprache,' ed. 2, p. 20. Petronius 75 uses *corcillum* for 'one's wits,'
corcillum est quod homines facit. In Plaut.
Cas. 837 *corculum* is a term of endear-
ment; cf. our 'sweetheart' and 'dear
heart' in old letters. Cf. § 91 hoc est
non modo non cor habere sed ne palatum quidem, with which cf. Petron. 59
cor non habebas.

2. **parvi duceret**: Draeger, § 201, 4
says that no parallel is quoted from
elsewhere for this expression; he mentions *pensi ducere* in Val. M. 2, 9, 3. But
cf. Att. 7, 3, 8 pluris ea duxit quam
omnem pecuniam; Sall. Iug. 32, 5
minoris d. A curious ex. of *ducere* is in
Ad Herenn. 4, 28 neminem prae se
ducit hominem. [Cf. 4, 57 minoris aesti-
manda ducebat.]

id: here generic, 'that kind of thing';
see note on § 17 hoc ipsum.

3. **o lapathe**, etc.: probably from the
fourth book of Lucilius' satires, which, as
the scholiast on Pers. 3, 1 says, chastised
the luxury and vices of the wealthy.

ut iactare: Munro in Journal of
Philology, VII, 299, rightly condemns L.
Müller's interpretation 'laudaris' (an
error to be found generally in the
commentaries and translations); the
sense is 'thou art flouted,' 'tossed
aside'; so Plaut. Rud. 374; Cic. Att. 4,
9; 11, 16, 3; Fam. 1, 5 *b*, 1; div. in Caec.
45. Doubtless Lucilius (who borrows
much from Greek philosophy which has
not been recognised by his interpreters)
was stirred to praise the *lapathus* by
Epicurus, who frequently preached the

lesson that a dinner of herbs with peace
is better than a stalled ox with strife.
Cf. Hieron. adv. Jovin. 11, 11, t. 11, p.
340 c Vall. Epicurus voluptatis assertor
omnes libros suos replevit oleribus et
pomis; Porphyr. de abstin. 1, 48 τῶν
γὰρ Ἐπικουρείων οἱ πλείους ἀπ' αὐτοῦ τοῦ
κορυφαίου ἀρξάμενοι μάζῃ καὶ τοῖς ἀκρο-
δρύοις ἀρκούμενοι φαίνονται: Plut. n. p. s.
vivi p. 1097 d ἐν μάζῃ καὶ φακῇ τὸ
ἥδιστον (from Epic.); Aelian, var. hist.
4, 13 (Ἐπίκουρος) ἔλεγεν ἑτοίμως ἔχειν
καὶ τῷ Διὶ ὑπὲρ εὐδαιμονίας διαγωνίζεσθαι
μᾶζαν ἔχων καὶ ὕδωρ: Lactant. 3, 17, 5
discit (ab Epicuro) aqua et polenta
vitam posse tolerari. The Stoics were
bound to rival the Epicureans in these
injunctions. Sen. ep. 110, 18 puts the
very words of Epic. into the mouth of
a Stoic: 'habemus aquam, habemus
polentam, Jovi ipsi controversiam de.
felicitate faciamus'; cf. too what
Philemon ap. Meineke Com. 4, p. 29
says of Zeno: 'πεινῆν διδάσκει καὶ
μαθητὰς λαμβάνει· εἷς ἄρτος, ὄψον ἰσχάς,
ἐπιπιεῖν ὕδωρ': and Ζηνώνειον φακῆν,
Timon in Bergk's Anth. Lyr. p. 138.
Varro in his 'Modius' undoubtedly had
both Epicurus and Lucilius in mind
when he wrote (ed. Bücheler, § 318):
'hanc eandem voluptatem tacitulus
taxim consequi lapathio et ptisana
possim' [*tacitulus taxim*, a slang phrase
'mum and easily,' also in § 187 and
tacitus taxim in Pomp. ap. Ribbeck 23].
In the same 'Modius' there is (§ 315)
a passage insisting on the difference
between Epicurus and the gluttons
(*ganeones*), and Epicurus' views about
λιτότης βίου are obvious in other
fragments of the satire, and probably
coloured the whole of it. [§ 317 begins
with *putat* which most likely had Epicurus for its subject.] With the passage
from the 'Modius' just quoted we may
compare another from the 'σκιαμαχία,'
viz. 'hoc dico, compendiaria sine ulla
sollicitudine ac molestia ducundi (gen.
of gerund) ad eandem voluptatem posse
perveniri'; here the 'short cut' to
pleasure is doubtless that indicated by
Epicurus. It may be noted that this
'σκιαμαχία' contains a quotation from
Lucilius; cf. § 508 with § 417. The praise

In quo Laeliu' clamores σοφὸς ille solebat
Edere compellans gumias ex ordine nostros.
Praeclare Laelius, et recte σοφός, illudque vere:
O Publi, o gurges, Galloni! es homo miser, inquit.
5   Cenasti in vita numquam bene, cum omnia in ista
Consumis squilla atque acupensere cum decimano.

Is haec loquitur qui in voluptate nihil ponens negat eum bene
cenare, qui omnia ponat in voluptate, et tamen *non* negat

1 Laeliu': *cognitu laelius* AB.   1 σοφὸς: *sophos* AB, ut infra.   2 gumias:
ita A; *guimas* BE.   3 illudque vere: *illud vere* B.   4 miser: ita A²; *miseri* A¹B.
5 cenasti: *cenastis* B.   5 ista: *isto* A.   6 consumis: *cū sumis* A¹.   6 acupensere:
accubans aere AB; *accubant aere* E.   6 decimano: ita A; *decimacio* B.   7 haec:
hic B.   8 qui: *quia* B.   8 ponat: *ponit* B.   8 non: om. AB.

of the simple vegetable is widespread.
Erasmus in his Adagia quotes Rodolphus
Agricola as attributing to the Greeks a
proverb: 'egregia de lente,' which
Erasmus thinks was in Greek δεινὰ
περὶ φακῆς: cf. Hudibras 1, 1 mira de
lente, as 'tis in th' adage, | id est to
make a leek a cabbage; but this interpretation is more like another proverb
given by Crates ap. Bergk., Anth. Lyr.
p. 128 μὴ πρὸ φακῆς λοπάδ᾽ αὔξων |
εἰς στάσιν ἄμμε βάλῃς. The whole of
Horace's ep. 1, 12, where he recommends living on herbs and nettle, has
an Epicurean ring; in epod. 2, 57 he
praises *lapathus* and *malvae*; cf. Cat.
agr. 157, 1 on the 'brassica pytha-
gorea.'
  nec es sati' cognitu': cf. Crates (or
Teles) ap. Bergk., Anth. Lyr. p. 129
οὐκ οἶσθα πήρα δύναμιν ἡλίκην ἔχει
θέρμων τε χοίνιξ καὶ τὸ μηδενὸς μέλειν:
Fabianus Papirius ap. Sen. Rh. contr. 2,
1, 13 o pauperies quam ignotum bonum
es! and Virgil's sua si bona norint.
  1. σοφὸς: at a much earlier time a
Sempronius received the title. Possibly
ut has fallen out before this word.
  2. gumias: ἀπὸ τοῦ γέμειν, says L.
Müller (from Scaliger). Paul. ex F. p.
112, connects it with *gula*, absurdly;
Stowasser in Archiv 8, 444, makes it
a word borrowed from Semitic, but his
reasons are not plausible. Non. 117
quotes another passage from Lucilius
(30, 45 Müller) for *gemiae* (so the codd.),
which Müller changes to *gomiae*. Cf.
Apul. apol. 57 gumiae cuiusdam et de-
sperati lurconis (*lurco* is a Lucilian
word).
  4. Publi...Galloni: Hor. s. 2, 2, 46
refers to this passage of Lucilius: 'haud
ita pridem | Galloni praeconis erat aci-
pensere mensa | infamis'; cf. pro Quint.

94. Possibly, like the more celebrated
praeco Granius, this Gallonius was
tolerated in the aristocratic society of
the satirist's time.
  gurges: the word attached itself as
a nickname to Q. Fabius Maximus,
consul in 292 and 276 B.C.
  5. cum...consumis: Draeger § 570
says that after the time of Plaut. and
Ter. the adversative clause with *cum*
('though') always has the subjunctive;
but see Hale, 'Cum-constructions,' p.
216 sq. where exx. of *cum tamen* are
given, even from Cicero, with the
indic., which is found in most poets
(particularly Lucret. from whom Hale
only quotes 4, 1204). L. Müller illustrates *cum...atque cum* from Lucilius;
there are a good many parallels in
Lucretius.
  6. squilla: Mayor and Friedländer
on Juven. 5, 81.
  acupensere: for this and other
spellings (*acipenser, aquipenser*) see
authorities in Georges, Lexikon d. lat.
Wortformen, s. v.; add *aquipenser* in
Corp. Gloss. Lat. 2, p. 18, l. 44. Cf. Fat.
fr. 5 (acupenser) est piscis, ut ferunt, in
primis nobilis; a fragment of Plaut.
Bacaria ap. Macrob. 3, 16, 1 quis est
mortalis tanta fortuna affectus umquam
| qua ego nunc sum? quoius haec ventri
portatur pompa: | vel nunc, qui mihi
in mari acipenser latuit antehac, |
quoius ego latus in latebras reddam
meis dentibus et manibus.
  decimano: the sense here has no
reference to the tithe-gatherer (as has
often been erroneously thought) but is
related to the *decimus* or *decumanus
fluctus*; Paul. ex F. 71 also gives *decu-
mana ova*, 'quia sunt magna, nam et
decimum ovum maius nascitur et
fluctus decimus fieri maximus dicitur.'

libenter umquam cenasse Gallonium (mentiretur enim), sed bene.
Ita graviter et severe voluptatem secernit a bono. Ex quo illud
efficitur, qui bene cenent, omnis libenter cenare, qui libenter,
25 non continuo bene. Semper Laelius bene. Quid bene? Dicet
Lucilius: 5

                    cocto,
    Condito,
sed cedo caput cenae:

        sermone bono,
quid ex eo?   10

        si quaeris, libenter;

veniebat enim ad cenam, ut animo quieto satiaret desideria
naturae. Recte ergo is negat umquam bene cenasse Gallonium,
recte miserum, cum praesertim in eo omne studium consumeret.

1 umquam cenasse: *cenasse umquam* B.   1 sed bene: ita A¹B; *si bene* A².
4 dicet: *dicit* B.   12 enim: *autem* E.   12 ut animo: *ut in animo* B.   13 is negat
umquam: *his negatum quam* A¹B.   14 in eo: om. B.   14 studium: om. E.

2. **secernit:** Epict. fr. 27 τὸ καλῶς ζῆν
τοῦ πολυτελῶς διαφέρει.
4. **non continuo:** not uncommon; so
below, 4 §§ 30, 75. Cicero has not *non
statim* (Ad Herenn. 4, 6, followed in § 7
by *non continuo*). See Landgraf on S.
Rosc. 94.
6. **cocto:** Lucilius wrote *bene* before
cocto; cf. Att. 13, 52, 1 (of the dinner
Cicero gave to Caesar after Pharsalia)
edit et bibit ἀδεῶς et iucunde, opipare
sane et apparate, nec id solum, sed 'bene
cocto, condito, sermone bono et, si
quaeri' libenter.' L. Müller insists that
Cicero misunderstands the words, and
that the poet meant *sermone* to depend
on *condito* ('seasoned with'). In that
case cf. Cato m. 10 comitate condita
gravitas.
8. **caput cenae:** Tusc. 5, 98 (of Spartans) iure nigro quod caput cenae erat.
12. **veniebat…naturae:** exactly what
Epicurus would praise; the very phrase
desideria naturae is Epicurean (§ 27); for
the phrase cf. 3, 37 studia naturae; also
Sen. d. 7, 20, 5; 9, 9, 2 d. naturalibus.
14. **recte miserum:** 'durissime hoc
loco ex *negat* auditur *dicit*, non solum
ob propinquitatem, sed quod idem
adverbium repetitur, ut eadem verbi
notio ipsa anaphorae figura servari
videatur, et quod variatur paulum significatio, ut sit *appellat*' (Madvig). After
quoting as somewhat harsh the exx. in
1, 61; 2, 68; 4, 22, 69; 5, 88, he says:
'nullus tamen locus hoc, de quo agimus,

durior, ut excusetur Lambinus qui *recte
dicit* scripsit; probari non debet.'
cum praesertim: this combination
of particles has caused more trouble
than was necessary to grammarians and
commentators. In reality each particle
preserves its force in the combination,
and is unaffected in its meaning by the
other. The function of *praesertim* is
merely to draw special attention to the
clause with which it goes. Madvig
quotes Orat. 32 nec vero si historiam
non scripsisset nomen eius exstaret,
cum praesertim fuisset honoratus et
nobilis, calling it a 'locus mire ab inter-
pretibus vexatus'; Orelli, he says, would
have seen the drift of it 'si non *cum* sed
cum praesertim pro *quamvis* accepisset.'
But the sense is 'although (mark this
well), etc.' It is not unnatural, therefore, that *praesertim* should be attached
to *cum*-clauses of opposite kinds, the
causal-confirmative kind and the adver-
sative-negative kind; in the first case
the combination comes to be equivalent
to 'and particularly as,' in the second
to 'and that although.' In the same way
praesertim may attach itself to the adversative, as well as to the causal *qui*-
clause. It is not always easy to determine
from a context which of these two forces
qui or *cum* has when used alone; and
the ambiguity naturally remains sometimes when *praesertim* is added. Either
sense will suit the passage before us
perfectly well. Madvig, indeed, protests

Quem libenter cenasse nemo negat. Cur igitur non bene? Quia,
quod bene, id recte, frugaliter, honeste; ille porro prave, nequiter,
turpiter cenabat; non igitur *bene*. Nec lapathi suavitatem
acupenseri Galloni Laelius anteponebat, sed suavitatem ipsam
5 neglegebat; quod non faceret si in voluptate summum bonum
poneret.

IX. Semovenda est igitur voluptas, non solum ut recta
sequamini, sed etiam ut loqui liceat frugaliter. Possumusne ergo 26
in vita summum bonum dicere, cum id ne in cena quidem posse
10 videamur? Quo modo autem philosophus loquitur? 'Tria genera
cupiditatum, naturales et necessariae, naturales et non necessariae, nec naturales nec necessariae.' Primum divisit ineleganter;

2 quod: *quid* A¹.   2 frugaliter: *fugaliter* A¹: 2 prave: *male prave* codd.;
corr. Wesenberg.   3 cenabat; non igitur *bene*. Nec: *cenabat. Non igitur nec* codd.;
corr. Madvig.   3 lapathi: *lapithi* A; *laphatis* B.   4 acupenseri: *accubans ere*
A; *accŭbans ere* B. ─ 4 Galloni: ita A; *Gallony* B.   11 et necessariae: *et neces-*
sarias A¹B; *et necessariarum* A² (per compendium non satis certum).   11 et non
necessariae A²; *non* om. A¹; *et in necessarias* B.   12 nec naturales nec necessariae: om. B.

against the causal meaning here: 'mihi
hoc parum ad rem pertinere videtur, non
fuisse tantum studium in eo ponendum,
nec video cur eo miserior fuerit.' But
the whole passage is to this very effect
'non fuisse tantum studium in eo ponendum,' and it is not irrelevant to intimate
that the more a man sets his heart on a
thing, the more wretched he is likely
to be or to appear to others in the event
of failure. Wichert is quite right in
asserting (against Madvig) that where
a clause with *cum praesertim* is followed
by one with *tamen*, the two are not
strictly correspondent. Thus in S. Rosc.
66 videtisne quos nobis poetae tradi-
derint patris ulciscendi causa supplicium
de matre sumpsisse, cum praesertim
deorum immortalium iussis atque
oraculis id fecisse dicantur, tamen... the
tamen is not conditioned by *cum prae-*
sertim and would have been needed just
as much if the whole clause *cum...*
fecisse had been omitted. Nor is Madvig
quite justified in writing 'transitus ad
significandam rem eo memorabilem
quod aliud expectetur, fit iam in sim-
plici particula, ut II de Div. 142: *nec*
tam multum dormiens ullo somnio sum
admonitus, tantis praesertim de rebus;
for the opposition would be there without *praesertim*, which only emphasises
it. As Madvig notes, there is no distinction between *cum praesertim* and
praesertim cum. In the sentence follow-

ing our passage there is opposition,
which might similarly have been made
clearer by writing *quem tamen*. [The
sense 'and that although' is in 4, 36.]

2. **porro**: the word is in Cicero generally continuative as above, 1, 32 and
64; below, 2, 61, also 4, 21 and 75 (perge
porro). But sometimes, as here, it takes
on an adversative tinge; thus in S. Rosc.
39 it is combined with *autem*. The
adversative sense became commoner
and more pronounced in later Latin,
until *porro* acquired entirely the uses of
sed. A somewhat similar change affects
rursus; see note on 3, 34.

4. **acupenseri**: *comparatio compendi-*
aria, common both in Greek and Latin,
see Kühner-Stegmann, § 241, 10. Tusc.
5, 73.

8. **ut...liceat**: see note on § 90.

possumusne ergo, etc.: 'dure omitti-
tur prior accusativus, cum etiam in eo
ipsa vis sententiae sit (Lambinus: *igitur*
voluptatem)....Itaque non improbabilis
est Th. Bentleii suspicio *quod ne*'
(Madvig).

10. **tria genera**: so 1, 45 with notes.

12. **divisit ineleganter**: *elegantia* is
often used of neatness and precision in
logical processes, as below § 27 e. disserendi, and in Tusc. 2, 6; so of legal
formulae which are at once clear and
compact. Cf. Tusc. 5, 93 vides ut Epicurus cupiditatum genera diviserit, non
nimis fortasse subtiliter, utiliter tamen.

duo enim genera quae erant, fecit tria. Hoc est non dividere, sed
frangere. Qui haec didicerunt quae ille contemnit, sic solent:
'Duo genera cupiditatum, naturales et inanes, naturalium duo,
necessariae et non necessariae.' Confecta res esset. Vitiosum est
27 enim in dividendo partem in genere numerare. Sed hoc sane
concedamus; contemnit enim disserendi elegantiam. Confuse
loquitur; gerendus est mos, modo recte sentiat. Equidem illud
ipsum non nimium probo et tantum patior, philosophum loqui
de cupiditatibus finiendis. An potest cupiditas finiri? Tollenda
est atque extrahenda radicitus. Quis est enim in quo sit cupiditas, 1
quin recte cupidus dici possit? Ergo et avarus erit, sed finite,
et adulter, verum habebit modum, et luxuriosus eodem modo.
Qualis ista philosophia est quae non interitum afferat pravitatis,

1 erant: *erat* A[1].   1 fecit: om. B.   2 qui haec...solent: haec verba in multis
codd. desunt.   3 inanes: *inane* B.   4 esset: *essent* B.   5 numerare: *nominare* B.
6 enim: om. B.   7 equidem: ita B; *et quidem* A.   8 tantum: *tm̄* A; *tñ (tamen)* B.
8 loqui: om. B.   11 quin: *qui non* B.

1. **duo genera**: curiously, Epicurus
does go to work exactly in this fashion
in his letter to Menoeceus ap. Diog. L.
10, 127.

    dividere...frangere: Sen. ep. 89, 2
philosophiam in partes, non in frusta
dividam.

4. **vitiosum**: often of logical faults;
so 4, 50; Acad. 2, 93.

5. **partem in genere**: cf. Herc. pap.
19–698, col. 2, l. 9 (Scott, p. 258):
τὸ εἶδος εἶναι φάσκοντες γένος: the
same fault as is criticised here.

    in genere: for *in* as connecting two
things assumed to be equivalent see
Draeger § 170, 3 *c*. But he does not
clearly distinguish the exx. where the
two matters connected by *in* are related
as part to whole, and those in which
the two are on a level. Cf. Rep. 4, 10
artem ludicram in probro ducerent;
Plin. n. h. 6, 35 in probro existimatur.

6. **confuse**: the word and its cognates
often indicate want of logical precision,
especially as regards subdivision, par-
tition and definition; see my note on
Acad. 2, 47, and add to the illustrations
there quoted, Off. 1, 95; Verr. 2, 4, 87
disposite accusare, as opposed to Sest. 5
confusa atque universa defensio; Fin.
5, 67 confusio virtutum...distinguitur;
Corp. Gl. Lat. 5, p. 663, l. 58 perplexe
loquitur.

9. **an...finiri**: this is Stoic doctrine,
which even the Stoicising Antiochus can
hardly have accepted; see 3, 35 *n.*;

cf. Us. § 471. In what follows there
is a good deal of quibbling. It appears
below that Cicero would not have objected to the substance of Epicurus'
doctrine, had he used some other word
than ἐπιθυμία.

    10. **quis est**, etc.: cf. Tusc. 4, 57 quis
enim potest in quo libido cupiditasve
sit, non libidinosus et cupidus esse?
The whole context there is like the
present passage.

    11. **quin**: as to the difference between
qui non and *quin* Madvig says: 'mihi et
multo saepius *quin* a scribis dissolutum
videtur, quam *qui non* contractum, et
ubi non simpliciter praecedat *quis est*,
nemo est, sed, ut h. l., definitio quaedam
(*in quo sit cupiditas*) ex qua aliquid
necessario sequatur, fere semper dici
quin.' But in Cicero *nemo est quin*,
quis est quin are far commoner than
nemo est, quis est qui non. See note on
5, 32.

    12. **habebit modum**: I know of no
instance of such a phrase as *aliquis habet
modum*, though impersonal subjects are
found (below, 3, 45; Cato m. 85).
Possibly *habebit* has an indefinite subject, τὸ πρᾶγμα, or it is a corruption of
adhibebit. Cf. Clu. 191 mulieris modus,
'moderation.'

    13. **qualis**, etc.: cf. 4, 22 quae est
igitur ista philosophia quae communi
more in foro loquitur, in libellis suo?

    int. aff. pravitatis: for the gen. cf.
§ 118 voluptatis aditus intercludat. In

sed sit contenta mediocritate vitiorum? Quamquam in hac
divisione rem ipsam prorsus probo, elegantiam desidero. Appellet
haec desideria naturae, cupiditatis nomen servet alio, ut eam,
cum de avaritia, cum de intemperantia, cum de maximis vitiis
loquetur, tamquam capitis accuset. Sed haec quidem liberius **28**
ab eo dicuntur et saepius. Quod equidem non reprehendo; est
enim tanti philosophi tamque nobilis audacter sua decreta
defendere. Sed tamen ex eo quod eam voluptatem, quam omnes
gentes hoc nomine appellant, videtur amplexari saepe vehementius, in magnis interdum versatur angustiis, ut hominum

2 rem ipsam: *remissionem* A; *remissam* B.   2 probo: ita B; *probam* A¹;
reprobo A².   2 appellet: *appellat* B.   5 quidem: *quae* A.   7 tamque: *tantique* B.
7 audacter: *audaciter* B.   9 hoc: om. B.   9 saepe vehementius: *vehem. sepe* B.

a note on Acad. 2, 19, fidem faciat sui
iudici, I have discussed some genitives
of this kind, especially those with *fidem
facere, modum f., finem f.*, and have
pointed out that in the best writers the
genitive more commonly follows such
expressions than the dative. The dative
of the gerund hardly occurs. In Pl. Asin.
882 (ed. Leo) nearly all edd. read
(against the mss.) quidmodi amplexando
facies? Many make a similar change in
167 qui modus dandi; these changes are
groundless. It is much more likely that
the dative is corrupt in Mil. 1311 quid
modi flendo quaeso hodie facies? Madvig suspects the reading of De Or. 3, 104
locis quos ad fidem orationis faciendam
adhiberi dixit Antonius; but the reason
he gives 'quia *fides orationis* vix sic
absolute dicitur,' is surely untenable;
the passage is in no way distinguishable
from many others. He condemns also
Liv. 3, 59, 1 inhibito modo nimiae
potestatis (so codd.), but the passage
may well be sound; *modus n. potestatis*
would stand by itself (see my note on
Acad. 2, 27), and there is no apparent
reason why *modum n. p.* should not be
object to *inhibere* as well as *imperium,
supplicia*, etc.

1. mediocritate: the Aristotelian
μεσότης.

quamquam...desidero: note on *an
...finiri* above. For *rem ipsam probo* cf.
Tusc. 5, 93 qu. in note on § 26 *divisit
ineleganter*.

3. alio: 'for another purpose'; perhaps here only in Cicero with this sense;
Livy has *alio relinqui, nasci*, 4, 54, 7 and
7, 18, 7; somewhat of the same sense
attaches to *alio spectare, respicere*.

7. nobilis: 'famed'; a common

enough sense of the word but one which
has sometimes caused misunderstand-
ings. Thus some editors inferred from
a jest of Cicero's on the *nobilitas* of
Democritus in Acad. 2, 125, that he
regarded D. as noble by birth (see my
note there) and a similar mistake has
been made about the *nobilitas* of
Pythagoras, mentioned in Tusc. 4, 2.
Cf. Qu. Cicero pet. cons. 12 qui nequa-
quam sunt tam genere insignes quam
vitiis nobiles; pro Quinct. 69 (of a demo-
crat) ut nobili ne gladiatori quidem
faveret; Phaedr. 1, 14, 12 stupore vulgi
factum nobilem. The application to
philosophers is very frequent.

audacter: the spelling *audaciter* in B
may well be right, in spite of the fact
that Quintilian and Charisius reject it;
see the evidence in Neue-Wagener,
II, 684.

decreta:= δόγματα, as often; see my
note on Acad. 2, 27. The word *dogma*
is treated as Latin below, § 105, and in
Acad. 2, 106, 133 and occasionally elsewhere (even in Juvenal and Martial) but
never became thoroughly acclimatized
until a very late period, though Labe-
rius, in Cicero's time, had ventured on
an accusative *dogmam*.

9. amplexari: 2, 43; 4, 36.

10. hominum conscientia: cf. §§ 53–60
and 3, 38 tenebras et solitudinem nacti
(in a passage directed against the Epicureans). Plut. Col. c. 34, 1127 d quotes
from the 'διαπορίαι' of Epicurus: 'εἰ
πράξει τινὰ ὁ σοφὸς ὧν οἱ νόμοι ἀπαγο-
ρεύουσιν, εἰδὼς ὅτι λήσει;' καὶ ἀποκρίνεται
'οὐκ εὔοδον τὸ ἁπλοῦν (? οὔτε ἁπλοῦν) ἐστι
κατηγόρημα,' and remarks τοῦτ' ἐστι,
πράξω μὲν οὐ βούλομαι δὲ ὁμολογεῖν. Cf.
Leg. 1, 41; Off. 3, 77.

conscientia remota nihil tam turpe sit quod voluptatis causa non videatur esse facturus. Deinde, ubi erubuit (vis enim est permagna naturae) confugit illuc ut neget accedere quicquam posse ad voluptatem nihil dolentis. At iste non dolendi status non vocatur voluptas. Non laboro, inquit, de nomine.—Quid quod res alia tota est?—Reperiam multos, vel innumerabilis potius, non tam curiosos nec tam molestos quam vos estis, quibus quicquid velim facile persuadeam.—Quid ergo dubitamus quin, si non dolere voluptas sit summa, non esse in voluptate dolor sit maximus? cur non id ita fit?—Quia dolori non voluptas contraria est, sed doloris privatio.

29 X. Hoc vero non videre, maximo argumento esse voluptatem illam qua sublata neget se intellegere omnino, quid sit bonum! (eam autem ita persequitur: quae palato percipiatur, quae auribus; cetera addit, quae si appelles, honos praefandus sit) hoc igitur quod solum bonum severus et gravis philosophus

---

1 quod: *quid* B.   1 causa non videatur: *videatur causa* B.   2 deinde: *deinde enim* B.   2 enim est: *est* (om. *enim*) BE.   4 nihil: *nichi* E.   10 maximus: *maximis* A¹.   10 non id: *id non* B.   15 honos: *bonos* BE.   15 praefandus: *prefraudus* E; *perfraudus* B.

---

2. **erubuit:** N.D. 1, 111 (voluptates) non erubescens persequitur omnis nominatim.
vis...naturae: a similar parenthesis in S. Rosc. 63 magna est enim vis humanitatis; cf. below § 58 and 5, 32 maxime in hoc quidem genere perspicua est vis naturae. Mil. 61 (conscientiae); Cat. 3, 27 (id.); Cael. 63 (veritatis). Epict. d. 2, 20, 15 ascribes the inconsistencies of Epicurus to φύσις: cf. fr. 52 (Schw.) καίτοι δέδωκέ μοι ἡ φύσις αἰδῶ καὶ πολλὰ ὑπερυθριῶ ὅταν τι ὑπολάβω αἰσχρὸν λέγειν. τοῦτό με τὸ κίνημα οὐκ ἐᾷ τὴν ἡδονὴν θέσθαι ἀγαθὸν καὶ τέλος τοῦ βίου. See note on § 49 natura victus. [I think that Cicero wrote in De Or. 1, 196 patria... cuius rei tanta est vis et tanta naturae (MSS. natura) ut.... *Tanta natura* is hardly Latin, but cf. Div. 2, 29.]
4. **non dolendi status:** so § 32.
5. **non laboro:** Tusc. 2, 29 concludunt ratiunculas Stoici cur non sit (dolor) malum; quasi de verbo non de re laboretur.
6. **innumerabilis:** the *rustici*.
7. **molestos:** cf. Acad. 2, 75.
9. **dolor sit maximus:** see Plut. qu. in note on 1, 37 doloris privatio.
12. **hoc vero non videre:** exactly the same exclamatory infinitive occurs

below, 4, 76 hoc non videre. The usage is very common in the old drama and in Cicero; and becomes much less frequent afterwards. By many authors it was avoided altogether (among them Caesar and Tacitus); Livy has only one example. Draeger § 154, 3 can find only two instances to quote from classical poets, Hor. s. 1, 9, 72 and Virg. Aen. 1, 37, but many others exist, as Hor. epod. 8, 1; 11, 11; sat. 2, 4, 83; 2, 8, 67; Virg. Aen. 1, 97. I have no doubt that in the much disputed passage of Lucr. 2, 16 the MSS. reading 'nonne videre nil aliud sibi naturam latrare,' is correct, though it gives the only example of this infin. in Lucr.
14. **persequitur:** cf. N.D. qu. above, note on § 28 erubuit.
15. **appelles:** 'mention'; below § 51 verborum, quae appellantur; for this sense cf. my note on Acad. 1, 25 and De Or. 2, 65; 3, 167.
honos praefandus: so Fam. 9, 22, 4; Plin. n. h. 7, 171 praefandi humoris e corpore effluvium; Quintil. 8, 3, 45 in praefanda videmur incidere. Cf. below § 68.
16. **igitur:** note on 1, 4.
severus et gravis: above, § 24 graviter et severe.

novit, idem non videt ne expetendum quidem esse, quod eam voluptatem hoc eodem auctore non desideremus cum dolore careamus. Quam haec sunt contraria! Hic si definire, si dividere **30** didicisset, si loquendi vim, si denique consuetudinem verborum 5 teneret, numquam in tantas salebras incidisset. Nunc vides quid faciat. Quam nemo umquam voluptatem appellavit, appellat; quae duo sunt, unum facit. Hanc in motu voluptatem (sic enim has suavis et quasi dulcis voluptates appellat) interdum ita extenuat ut M'. Curium putes loqui, interdum ita laudat ut quid το praeterea sit bonum neget se posse ne suspicari quidem. Quae iam oratio non a philosopho aliquo sed a censore opprimenda est.

---

1 videt: *vidit* B.   3 hic…incidisset: affert Nonius, p. *177*.   3 si dividere: ita B et Nonius; *individere* A¹; *vel dividere* A². 4 didicisset: *potuisset* Nonius. 8 has suavis: *suaves has* B.   9 M': *Marcum* AB; *M.* codd. ceteri.   9 putes: *potes* A¹.   10 ne: *nec* E.   11 est: om. B.

---

1. **novit:** §§ 7, 8.
quod…**eodem auctore,** etc.: as Madvig remarks, the sense of this is *quod is nos moneat et hortetur ne desideremus,* not *tradat nos non desiderare.* The abl. abs. *auctore aliquo* is not used merely to indicate that a fact is *stated* on the authority of someone other than the speaker or writer. The word *auctor* carries with it the notion of influence exerted and modifying action or belief. Such a sentence as the following is late and exceptional: Plin. n. h. 4, 9 Peloponnesus circuitu DLXIII. M. passuum colligit, auctore Isidoro.
3. **quam**…**contraria:** for the separation see my note on Acad. 2, 83.
4. **loquendi vim:** § 17 consuetudinem verborum: § 16 cognitiones verborum.
5. **salebra:** 5, 84 haeret (oratio) in salebra; Orat. 39; cf. too div. in Caec. 36 intellego quam scopuloso difficilique in loco verser.
6. **appellavit, appellat:** a common trick of style; so Sull. 32 res publica, quae domesticos hostis ne ab eis ipsa necaretur necavit; Phil. 2, 114 quod nemo fecerat, fecerunt; Planc. 91; Off. 2, 79; Tusc. 3, 14. See note on § 68.
8. **suavis et quasi d.:** n. on 1, 39; 1, 47; perhaps προσηνεῖς was the Greek word (Plut. 1122 *e*, cf. 786 *c*).
interdum…**interdum:** according to Wölfflin, Archiv 2, 243, there is only one passage in Latin of earlier date than this (Fam. 7, 17, 1) where one *interdum* corresponds with another, as here. Cicero

too introduced *tum…tum*; Lucretius *nunc…nunc*; Virgil *iam…iam*; Ovid *saepe…saepe*. *Interim…interim* is not older than Seneca. The use of *interim* for *interdum*, though given by MSS. in Rosc. Am. 80, is later than Cicero.
9. **extenuat:** 'refines away'; Tusc. 5, 94 multa ab Epicureis disputantur, eaeque voluptates singillatim extenuantur.
10. **neget:** cf. my note on Acad. 1, 7.
11. **non a philosopho,** etc.: cf. 1, 51.
a censore: 'non *philosopho—censori* hoc quidem loco Cicero dixit, quod non ad cuius officium hoc pertineat sed cuius opera ad eam rem utendum sit, significat.…Nec tamen id ad omnes locos, in quibus *ab* cum gerundivo coniungitur, pertinet' (Madvig). The construction is especially common in Cicero, but this, I think, is the only ex. in the philosophical writings. In a note on Caec. 33 Jordan has well classified the Ciceronian exx.: (*a*) those in which the motive is desire for clearness, as where a verb such as *consulere* already takes a dat. (e.g. pro imp. Cn. P. 6), or the dat. with the gerundive might easily be mistaken for a dat. of another class, as e.g. Phil. 14, 11 supplicatio ab eo, qui ante dixit, decernenda non fuit; (*b*) instances where desire for symmetry has prevailed, as in Mur. 54 locus perpurgatus ab eis qui ante me dixerunt, a me, quoniam ita Murena voluit, retractandus; (*c*) exx. in which (as here) stress is laid on the idea of agency. In De Or. 2, 86 nam neque is qui optime potest,

Non est enim vitium in oratione solum sed etiam in moribus. Luxuriam non reprehendit, modo sit vacua infinita cupiditate et timore. Hoc loco discipulos quaerere videtur, ut qui asoti 31 esse velint philosophi ante fiant. A primo, ut opinor, animantium ortu petitur origo summi boni. Simul atque natum animal est, 5 gaudet voluptate et eam appetit ut bonum, aspernatur dolorem ut malum. De malis autem et bonis ab eis animalibus, quae nondum depravata sint, ait optime iudicari. Haec et tu ita posuisti, et verba vestra sunt. Quam multa vitiosa! Summum enim bonum et malum vagiens puer utra voluptate diiudicabit, 1(stante an movente? quoniam, si dis placet, ab Epicuro loqui

2 sit: *si* B.   5 animal: *animale* AB.   7 ut malum: *et malum* A[1].   8 sint: *sunt* A.   8 iudicari: *iudicare* A[1].   11 an: *ante* AB; in A syllaba *te* est extra versum, fortasse a sec. m.   11 dis placet: *displicet* B.   11 loqui discimus: *discimus loqui* B.

deserendus ullo modo est a cohortatione nostra, neque is qui aliquid potest deterrendus, the abstract phrase *coh. nostra* seems to stand for *nobis cohortantibus*; it is possible (with Wilkins, *ad loc.*) to regard *a* as meaning 'in respect of,' but less likely. The constr. in question first appears in the treatise ad Herenn., and is rare outside Cicero's writings; Brut. ap. Fam. 11, 20, 3; Liv. 9, 40, 16; 44, 22, 12; Sen. ep. 65, 3; Lactant. (ap. Draeger § 189, 1).

3. **hoc loco**: like *hic*.

disc. quaerere: 'to be making a bid for converts'; cf. the half-slang phrase *opus quaerere*, 'to be on the lookout for a job'; Liv. 5, 3, 6 tamquam artifices improbi, opus quaerunt; Tusc. 3, 81 haec Graeci in singulas scholas et in singulos libros dispertiunt; opus enim quaerunt. Cicero's phrase reminds us of the title of a comedy by Alexis, 'ἀσωτο-διδάσκαλος,' in which reference was undoubtedly made to Epicurus. The structure of the word *discipulus* is strange; Stowasser in Archiv 5, 289 disconnects it from *discere* and tries to connect it with *dis-capio*, on the strength of *capulus, concipilare, decipula, excipulum, muscipula, disceptare*. Bréal, ib. 579 assumes *discipulus* to have been constructed by false analogy from *manipulus*, to mean in the first instance 'a band of learners.'

5. **petitur**: 1, 30 *n*.

animal: in spite of *animantium* just before, cf. N.D. 2, 42 in ea parte quae sit ad gignenda animantia aptissima, animal gigni nullum. Cicero does not, I

think, use *animans* in the nom. sing.; on the other hand, the plural of *animal* rarely occurs in his writings. Out of fourteen exx. quoted by Merguet from the philosophical works, eight come from the De Finibus, viz. here, § 31; 5, 25 (*bis*); 5, 26 (*ter*); 5, 33 (*bis*). [Neue, I[2], 186, and Georges, Wortf. s. v. *animal*, qu. Lucr. 3, 635 for *animale* as a form of the noun, but the ex. is not sound. In N.D. 3, 36 the codd. give *animal* where *animale* would be natural. See Havet's ed. of Phaedrus, p. 180.]

8. **tu...vestra**: for the sudden change from the individual to the school cf. De Or. 1, 160 tum Scaevola, 'quid est, Cotta,' inquit, 'quid tacetis?' with Wilkins' note.

10. **vagiens puer**: cf. 1, 71 infantes pueri.

11. **stante an movente**: see note on 1, 37 (solam). The words that follow are curious. In Cicero's original there must have been κατασταστηματική to which the writer objected as an outlandish phrase. The other terms used by Epic. like ἡδονὴ ἐν στάσει would not afford ground for the objection. Cicero preserves the colouring of the original by employing somewhat unusual Latin. Cf. Tusc. 4, 30 vitia adfectiones sunt manentes, perturbationes autem moventes. For the quasi-deponent use of *movens* see Neue-Wagener III, 12; Riemann, Études, ed. 1, p. 156; cf. the juridical expression *res moventes*, once used by Liv. 5, 25, 6.

si dis placet: the expression occurs at all periods of Latin, rarely without irony, as in Plaut. Capt. 454.

discimus. Si stante, hoc natura videlicet volt, salvam esse se,
quod concedimus; si movente, quod tamen dicitis, nulla turpis
voluptas erit quae praetermittenda sit, et simul non proficiscitur
animal illud modo natum a summa voluptate, quae est a te
5 posita in non dolendo. Nec tamen argumentum hoc Epicurus a **32**
parvis petivit aut etiam a bestiis, quae putat esse specula naturae,
ut diceret ab eis duce natura hanc voluptatem expeti nihil
dolendi. Neque enim haec movere potest appetitum animi, nec
ullum habet ictum quo pellat animum status hic non dolendi.
10 Itaque in hoc eodem peccat Hieronymus. At ille pellit, qui
permulcet sensum voluptate. Itaque Epicurus semper hoc utitur
ut probet voluptatem natura expeti, quod ea voluptas quae in
motu sit et parvos ad se alliciat et bestias, non illa stabilis in qua
tantum inest nihil dolere. Qui igitur convenit ab alia voluptate
15 dicere naturam proficisci, in alia summum bonum ponere?
   XI. Bestiarum vero nullum iudicium puto. Quamvis enim **33**

---

6 aut etiam: *ante et* B.   6 specula: *spicula* B.   9 ictum: *ritum* E.
animum status: *animi statum* codd.; corr. Victorius.   11 utitur: ita (superscr.
a sec. m. *nititur*) A; *utatur* B.   12 voluptas: *vobis* A¹.   14 nihil: *non* B.   14 qui:
quid codd.; corr. Lambinus.

1. **salvam esse se**: again we have a
Stoic view represented.
   2. **tamen**: here, as often, *tamen* does
not merely indicate opposition to what
has just been expressed, but takes a
wider range; it is not 'nevertheless,' i.e.
'in spite of what has just been said,'
but 'after all,' i.e. 'in spite of anything
that can be said.'
   nulla...sit: it is not usual for two
clauses, one being categorical, and one
causal, as here, to stand side by side
without some connecting link. Either
aut before *quae* might have been expected or *tam* before *turpis*.
   5. **argumentum**: always 'proof' in
good Latin, not 'argument'; but proof
not embodied in anything external, such
as circumstantial evidence, or tangible,
as a legal instrument.
   6. **parvis**: *parvi* is often thus substan-
tivally used for *pueri*; so below 3 §§ 16,
17; 5 §§ 31, 42, 43; see other exx. of this
and *parvuli* (once in Caes. and common
later) in an article by A. Funck in Archiv
7, 94.
   quae putat, etc.: 'lenis est irrisio
Epicuri a bestiis argumenta ducentis.
Nam de pueris similiter alii philosophi
loquebantur, apud ipsum Ciceronem
Peripateticus Piso v, 61 et maxime 55'

(Madvig). But Cicero or his authority
so far forgets the contention hereabouts
as in § 109 to appeal to the testimony
of the beasts against Epicurus; and
there is a similar appeal both in the
Stoic portion of the treatise (3 §§ 62, 3)
and in the Peripatetic (5 § 38).
   specula naturae: so 5, 61 in quibus
(pueris) ut in speculis natura cernitur;
cf. Pis. 71 tamquam in speculo.
   8. **appetitum**: a common rendering
of ὁρμή (cf. Off. 1, 101); but all the other
passages in the De Finibus, where it is
used, occur in the Peripatetic portion
(the fifth book). Still commoner is
appetitio, which we find twice in book 3
(§ 23, where see note, and § 49) and many
times in book 4. Cf. *appetere*, above
§ 31, and 1, 30; *appetendi initia* 1, 42.
Expeti above is αἱρεῖσθαι.
   9. **habet ictum**: i.e. 'does not come
within range, so as to strike.' The nearest
parallels to this use of *ictus* are in phrases
like *sub ictu esse*, and *extra ictum positus*.
   14. **ab alia...in alia**: very similar
criticisms are passed in book 4 on the
Stoic scheme; cf. esp. §§ 26, 38, 39, 42,
43, 48.
   16. **bestiarum...puto**: after assigning
the fifth place in the scale of ἀγαθά to
ἡδονή Socrates says in the Phileb. 67 B

depravatae non sint, pravae tamen esse possunt. Vt bacillum
aliud est inflexum et incurvatum de industria, aliud ita natum,
sic ferarum natura non est illa quidem depravata mala disciplina,
sed natura sua. Nec vero ut voluptatem expetat natura movet
infantem, sed tantum ut se ipse diligat, ut integrum se salvumque 5
velit. Omne enim animal, simul et est ortum, et se ipsum et omnes
partis suas diligit duasque quae maximae sunt in primis amplec-

1 sint: *sunt* A.   1 ut bacillum...ita natum: affert Nonius, p. 78 (om. *de
industria*).   1 bacillum: *baccillum* A¹ et Nonius.   5 se: *si* A¹.   6 simul et:
ita AB; *simul ut* edd. nonnulli.   6 est: om. AB.

πρῶτον δέ γε (sc. οὐ γίγνοιτ' ἂν) οὐδ' ἂν οἱ
πάντες βόες τε καὶ ἵπποι καὶ τἆλλα σύμ-
παντα θηρία φῶσι τῷ τὸ χαίρειν διώκειν·
οἷς πιστεύοντες, ὥσπερ μάντεις ὄρνισιν, οἱ
πολλοὶ κρίνουσι τὰς ἡδονὰς εἰς τὸ ζῆν ἡμῖν
εὖ κρατίστας εἶναι κ.τ.λ. On the other
hand, Arist. Eth. N. 10, 2, 4 ἴσως δὲ καὶ
ἐν τοῖς φαύλοις ἔστι τι φυσικὸν ἀγαθὸν
κρεῖττον ἢ καθ' αὑτά, ὃ ἐφίεται τοῦ οἰκείου
ἀγαθοῦ (the word ἀγαθόν is probably a
gloss). Cf. Sen. ep. 124, 1 (argument
against Ep.) in mutis animalibus et
infantibus non esse (bonum).

iudicium: as often = κριτήριον.

2. **incurvatum:** the verb *incurvare* is
found only in poets (beginning with
Catullus), and later prose writers; here
incurvatum has probably come (by assimilation to *inflexum*) out of *incurvom*;
cf. Div. 1, 30 incurvom et leviter a
summo inflexum bacillum; *incurvos* also
is found in Verr. 2, 2, 87; and Ad
Herenn. 4, 63; Varro r.r. 1, 50, 2. On
the use of *curvos* and its cognates see a
careful article by Ad. Müller in Archiv
3, 117 sq. and 236 sq. He shows that the
simple *curvos* is avoided by the prose
authors of the best and even of the
silver age, excepting the technical
writers.

3. **natura...natura sua:** careless writing; cf. nn. on 1 §§ 3, 56.

4. **nec vero...infantem:** Chalcid. in
Tim. 204 admits that children tend to
pleasure and gives a physical explanation.

5. **ut...velit:** this is the doctrine both of
the Stoics, and of the later Peripatetics;
cf. 3, 16 and 5, 24 and see notes there.

integrum se...velit: this omission of
esse is common at all times in Latin; so
3, 57 liberis consultum volumus; see
note on § 102.

6. **simul et est ortum:** the mss. give
simul et here and in 5, 24; and the Med.
ms. of the letters to Atticus gives four

exx., viz. 2, 20, 2; 10, 4, 12; 10, 16, 4;
16, 11, 6; while in Q.F. 2, 6, 3 the first
hand of Med. gives *et*, the second *ut*
(adopted by C. F. W. Müller). Madvig
condemns as not Latin both *simul et*
and *simul ut*, which latter has good mss.
authority in Acad. 2, 51; Tusc. 4, 5;
De Or. 2, 21; Planc. 14 (Erfurt ms. has
simul ut et); Phil. 3, 2; Verr. 2, 1, 67;
Att. 9, 9, 1; Ad Herenn. 4, 65. [In
Lucan 6, 129 for *simul e campis* Hein-
sius read *simul ut*, Bentley *simul ac; s. et*
would have been better.] It is important
to notice that in eleven out of fifteen
Ciceronian exx. (with that from Ad
Herenn.) of *simul et* and *simul ut*, a
guttural or a vowel immediately follows,
so that *ac* was impossible for Cicero (see
my note on Acad. 2, 34). Madvig thinks
that all the instances are due to the
insertion of *at* or *et* by copyists in
passages where *simul* stood for *simul ac*.
If so why did not the copyists insert *ac*
or *atque*? We have seen instances in
which ancient writers used *et* for *ac*
where a vowel followed (note on 1, 67)
and we have an analogy in *similiter et*,
similis et (note on § 21). For *simul et*
there are many analogies, such as *idem
ut si* below, 4, 15; *eadem ut si* in Off. 1, 42
in eadem sunt iniustitia ut si; *eodem
modo ut* Ad Herenn. 1, 10; Lucret. 2, 72
nec similest ut cum (where *ut* was probably written for the sake of avoiding *ac*
before the guttural); *proinde ut* for
proinde ac (always in Plaut. according
to Brix on Capt. 304); *perinde ut*,
varying in Cicero with *p. atque* and *ac*;
pro eo ut; for *similiter ut si* see note on
§ 21. [Simul et = Simul etiam: Thomas
on Verr. 5, § 3; Riemann, p. 529.]

7. **duasque quae...sunt:** the expression is loose, as though these were
merely two among others. The argument here has a general resemblance
to that in 5, 24 sq.; also 5, 37. Cf.

titur, animum et corpus, deinde utriusque partes. Nam sunt et
in animo praecipua quaedam et in corpore, quae cum leviter
agnovit, tunc discernere incipit, ut ea, quae prima data sint
natura, appetat asperneturque contraria. In his primis naturali- **34**
5 bus voluptas insit necne magna quaestio est. Nihil vero putare
esse praeter voluptatem, non membra, non sensus, non ingeni
motum, non integritatem corporis, non valetudinem, summae
mihi videtur inscitiae. Atque ab isto capite fluere necesse est
omnem rationem bonorum et malorum. Polemoni et iam ante

3 agnovit: *novit* B.   3 tunc: ita A; *tum* B.   3 prima: *primo* B.   4 asperneturque: *aspernaturque* A¹.   4 primis: *primas* A¹.   7 corporis: hoc verbum
post v. *valetudinem* habent AB; *non valetudinem* om. E.

Plut. n. p. s. vivi, c. 14 § 3 (1096 *d*) καίτοι
τί γένοιτ᾽ ἂν ἀλογώτερον ἢ δυοῖν ὄντοιν ἐξ
ὧν ὁ ἄνθρωπος πέφυκε, σώματος καὶ ψυχῆς,
ψυχῆς δὲ τάξιν ἡγεμονικωτέραν ἐχούσης,
σώματος μὲν ἴδιόν τι κατὰ φύσιν καὶ
οἰκεῖον ἀγαθὸν εἶναι, ψυχῆς δὲ μηθὲν κ.τ.λ.
Cf. also Stob. Ecl. 2, 248 (from a Peripatetic source) φίλον εἶναι ἡμῖν τὸ σῶμα,
φίλην δὲ τὴν ψυχήν, φίλον δὲ τὰ τούτων
μέρη καὶ τὰς δυνάμεις καὶ τὰς ἐνεργείας,
ὧν κατὰ τὴν πρόνοιαν τῆς σωτηρίας τὴν
ἀρχὴν γίγνεσθαι τῆς ὁρμῆς καὶ τοῦ
καθήκοντος καὶ τῆς ἀρετῆς.
2. **praecipua**: Tusc. 4, 30 sunt in corpore praecipua...vires valetudo...sunt
item in animo; cf. below, § 110 *n*.
leviter agnovit: cf. 5, 24 perspicere
coepit (*in re simili*).
3. **prima**...**natura**: a rendering of τὰ
πρῶτα κατὰ φύσιν, a phrase widely used,
with varying sense, in the post-Aristotelian schools, which has been treated
by Madvig in Appendix IV (pp. 815–
25, ed. 3).
data natura: in a note on Acad. 1, 15
I have given many exx. of *natura* and
a natura after passive verbs. The difference is that the simple abl. is adverbial
like *φύσει*, while with the other form
there is personification. Thus there is a
comic personification in Fam. 7, 26, 2
a beta et a malva deceptus sum,
'Mr Beet and Mr Mallow.' In the poets
(esp. Ovid) as in the laxer prose authors,
the preposition is of course often inserted where strict writers would leave
it out; so Varro r.r. 1, 59, 2 datur ab
arte (followed by *natura datum*); Plin.
n. h. 16, 40 a visu discerni; ib. 17, 4 ab
ipsa mea censura notandus.
5. **voluptas insit necne**: this the
Stoics denied (3, 17 *n*.); see also 5, 45 (a
passage closely corresponding with this);
and cf. Madvig's Appendix.

nihil vero, etc.: the criticism is repeated in § 114.
6. **membra**: 'debuit addere *integra*;
nam bonitas et integritas harum rerum
in primis numerabantur, non ipsae. Cfr.
v, 18' (Madvig).
ingeni motum: so 4, 35; *ingenio
moveri*, Leg. 2, 46; *motu mentis* Acad.
2, 48; so sometimes *animi motus*,
though that phrase is generally applied
to emotion rather than thought. Cf.
my notes on Acad. 1, 35; 2, 34.
8. **inscitiae**: always in Cicero blame-
ful ignorance, while *inscientia* is ignorance pure and simple; later the distinction tends to disappear. See Krebs-
Schmalz s. v. *inscientia*.
atque: here *atqui* might have been
expected; see 1, 58. Cf. 85 *n*. (ac tamen).
capite: 'fountain-head.'
9. **Polemoni**, etc.: on the relation of
Polemo to Antiochus see on Acad. 1, 19:
2, 131. The statement about the 'old
Academics and Peripatetics,' which immediately follows is thoroughly characteristic of Antiochus of Ascalon; see note
on 4, 14 and the discussion of Polemo's
τέλος in my note on Acad. 2, 131. As to
the drift of the whole argument, down
to the end of § 35, Madvig seems to me
to have seriously misunderstood it.
Cicero's purpose, he says, is to show that
while other philosophers made their
summum bonum harmonize with their
πρῶτα κατὰ φύσιν, Epicurus failed to do
so. But, says Madvig, some of these
thinkers (Aristippus, Hieronymus, Carneades) did not distinguish at all
between the πρῶτα κατὰ φύσιν and the
summum bonum, while others (as the
Stoics) excluded from their *τέλος* the
prima naturae commoda altogether, and
others again gave them only a subordi-
nate position in their *summum bonum*.

Aristoteli ea prima visa sunt, quae paulo ante dixi. Ergo nata est sententia veterum Academicorum et Peripateticorum, ut finem bonorum dicerent secundum naturam vivere, id est virtute adhibita frui primis a natura datis. Callipho ad virtutem nihil adiunxit nisi voluptatem, Diodorus vacuitatem doloris.... His 5 omnibus quos dixi, consequentes sunt fines bonorum, Aristippo simplex voluptas, Stoicis consentire naturae, quod esse volunt e virtute, id est honeste, vivere, quod ita interpretantur: vivere

5 doloris: post hoc lacunam primus indicavit Madvig.   6 sunt fines: *fines* sunt B.   7 Stoicis: *stoici* AB.

Hence Madvig condemns Cicero for carelessness, which his editors have rivalled, 'difficillima silentio transmittentes aut nihil distincte expedientes. But the facts which Madvig supposes Cicero to have overlooked were notorious and (as can be abundantly proved) perfectly familiar to him. Neither he nor his authority here can have dreamed of starting with so flagrantly erroneous an assumption as that all the ethical schemes mentioned contained a list of πρῶτα κατὰ φύσιν which might be compared with the τέλος. Cicero's idea rather is that in all the schools excepting that of Epicurus the development of the ethical scheme proceeds uniformly from the elements with which it starts to the highest stage of moral wisdom. This is the case even in the Stoic school, where the child is regarded as being born with every aptitude, which is brought to perfection by the sage through a long course of προκοπή: and even the perfectly virtuous man is engaged in the selection of τὰ κατὰ φύσιν: the only difference between him and the beginner being that he constantly succeeds in attaining the τέλος. In the school of Aristippus the first attraction and the last is to ἡδονὴ ἐν κινήσει and so on. The Stoics themselves did not allow that there was any breach of continuity in their moral fabric; see 3, 22 *n.* The same holds good of the other schools here mentioned. The face of the disciple is turned in the same direction all through his moral training. But among the Epicureans the child first embraces ἡδονὴ ἐν κινήσει and is required later to make jettison of this and put the ἡδονὴ ἐν στάσει in its place. Doubtless the criticism of Cicero (or Antiochus) is forced and unfair, but it has not the gross inconsistency which Madvig ascribes to it. It should be noticed that

in § 35 very vague terms are used: *extrema,* 'goal,' *initiis,* 'starting-point.' Alcinous' ['rectius Albinus' (Diels in Index)] ἐπιτομὴ τῶν Πλάτωνος δογμάτων shows the Antiochean confusion of Platonism, Peripateticism, Stoicism; see Diels, p. 76. Eudorus, contemporary of Arius Didymus and *possibly* pupil of Antiochus, is 'Stoicus germanus' while calling himself an Academic, Diels 81.

4. **Callipho:** see § 19 *n.* an allusion to his doctrine in Cael. 41 alii cum voluptate dignitatem coniungendam putaverunt.

5. **vacuitatem:** *nihil nisi* must be carried on. Perhaps *tantum* (tātū) has fallen out after *vacui-tatem.*

his omnibus quos dixi: it is obvious from what follows that words have dropped out before *his.* Aristippus and the Stoics must have been mentioned; probably also Hieronymus and Carneades and Epicurus. But I think Madvig is wrong in supposing that there was any definite mention of πρῶτα κατὰ φύσιν. The word *consequentes* does not necessitate the supposition (see above); doubtless Madvig is right in contending that the word cannot mean 'consistent with themselves' or 'coherent'; but the context makes it easy to understand that the consistency indicated is that between *initia* and *extrema.* The form of the exposition shows there is no room for a mention of the πρῶτα κατὰ φύσιν: as the statement about Callipho and Diodorus indicates, the whole catalogue here had reference to the *finis* only.

7. **simplex voluptas:** as opposed to the combinations of Callipho and Diodorus.

8. **e virtute:** κατ᾽ ἀρετήν; so 4, 26; 4, 35 ex virtute agere; 3, 29 cum virtute vivere; Sen. clem. 1, 19, 9 qui se ex deorum natura gerit; Tacitus, Germ. 7 duces ex virtute sumunt.

cum intellegentia rerum earum quae natura evenirent, eligentem
ea quae essent secundum naturam, reicientemque contraria. Ita **35**
tres sunt fines expertes honestatis, unus Aristippi vel Epicuri,
alter Hieronymi, Carneadi tertius, tres, in quibus honestas cum
5 aliqua accessione, Polemonis, Calliphontis, Diodori, una simplex,
cuius Zeno auctor, posita in decore tota, id est in honestate. Nam
Pyrrho Aristo Erillus iam diu abiecti. Reliqui sibi constiterunt,
ut extrema cum initiis convenirent, ut Aristippo voluptas,
Hieronymo doloris vacuitas, Carneadi frui principiis naturalibus
10 esset extremum. XII. Epicurus autem cum in prima commendatione voluptatem dixisset, si eam, quam Aristippus, idem
tenere debuit ultimum bonorum, quod ille; sin eam quam
Hieronymus, fecisset idem, ut voluptatem illam [Aristippi] in
prima commendatione poneret.

15 Nam quod ait sensibus ipsis iudicari voluptatem bonum esse, **36**
dolorem malum, plus tribuit sensibus quam nobis leges permittunt, *cum* privatarum litium iudices sumus. Nihil enim

---

1 evenirent: *evenerint* B.   2 reicientemque: *reficientemque* A¹B.   4 Carneadi:
ita A¹B; *Carneadis* A².   6 in (ante *honestate*): om. B.   7 Pyrrho: *parirho* A;
pyrro B.   11 si: *sed* B.   11 et 13 idem: *id est* A¹.   12 tenere...fecisset idem: om. B.
13 Aristippi A: *aristippo* BE: secl. P. Marsus Madv.   17 *cum*: om. codd.; hic
inseruit Th. Bentley, post *litium* Lambinus.   17 privatarum: *privarium* A¹.

vivere cum intelleg.: for this definition see note on 3, 31.

1. **evenirent**: Cicero, as Madvig says,
suddenly changes his point of view
from the Stoics of his own time (*volunt*)
to those of old. Similar changes are not
uncommon; see 2, 21; 3, 67 and 71;
4 §§ 14, 20, 56, 59.

4. **Carneadi**: note on § 38.

6. **cuius Zeno auctor**: for the omission
of *erat* cf. 5, 7 Peripatetici veteres quorum princeps Aristoteles, where Madvig
objects, but has overlooked 2, 35 and
Acad. 2, 129 Megaricorum disciplina
cuius princeps Xenophanes, and ib.
§ 131 quorum princeps Aristippus; also
Tusc. 3, 18 frugalitas ut opinor a fruge,
qua nihil melius e terra; Leg. 3, 35 leges,
quarum prima de mandandis magistra-
tibus. In some of these places editors
have erroneously inserted the verb.
[Madvig on 5, 7 qu. Liv. 22, 53, 5
iuvenes quosdam, quorum principem
L. Metellum, mare ac navis spectare.]

decore: a rendering of the Stoic τὸ
καλόν.

7. **Pyrrho Aristo Erillus**: see § 43;
5, 23.

reliqui...Epicurus autem: this pro-

leptic use of *reliqui* and *ceteri* is common;
see my notes on Lael. 7; Cato m. 3.

10. **in prima commendatione**: 'as the
thing which nature first recommends.'
For *commendatio*=οἰκείωσις see 3, 16,
23; 5, 41. The context gives *commendatione* a concrete sense. For *in* see note
on § 26 and cf. Tusc. 3, 14 in vitio ponitur.

11. **si eam**: for the carrying on of the
construction of the verb cf. Balb. 13
utrum inscientem voltis contra foedera
fecisse an scientem? si scientem...;
Verr. 2, 2, 155; Phil. 12, 16 idcircone
...arma cepimus...ut legati ad pacem
mitterentur? si accipiendam, cur
non rogamur? si postulandam, quid
timemus? Div. 2, 51 deum dicam an
hominem? si deum... Off. 1, 134.

13. **Aristippi**: is a gloss. It is the
'pleasure' of Hieronymus that he would
have commended.

15. **nam quod ait**: a common form of
transition; fifteen exx. similar to this
will be found in Merguet's Lexicon to
the philosophical writings, vol. II, p. 627.

sensibus iudicari: so *sensu iudicari* in
1, 31.

17. **iudices**: here in the wide sense,
including *arbitri*; just as the phrase

possumus iudicare nisi quod est nostri iudici. In quo frustra
iudices solent, cum sententiam pronuntiant, addere: 'si quid mei
iudici est.' Si enim non fuit eorum iudici, nihilo magis hoc non
addito illud est iudicatum. Quid iudicant sensus? Dulce amarum,
leve asperum, prope longe, stare movere, quadratum rotundum. 5
37 Aequam igitur pronuntiabit sententiam ratio adhibita primum
divinarum humanarumque rerum scientia, quae potest appellari
rite sapientia, deinde adiunctis virtutibus, quas ratio rerum
omnium dominas, tu voluptatum satellites et ministras esse

2 iudices solent: *solent iudices* B.   2 si quid: *si quod* B.   4 quid iudicant:
quid iudicat A; *quod iudicant* B.   5 leve: ita A; *lene* B.   5 stare movere: *movere*
stare B.   6 aequam: ita ed. Ascensiana; *quam* codd.   6 primum: *primo* B.
7 potest appellari rite: *rite potest appellari* B.

iudicia privata often includes all private
trials, even those which were technically
distinguishable from *iudicia*, as *arbi-
tria*.

1. **in quo frustra**, etc.: the object of
these *iudices* would seem to have been
to escape responsibility for a decision
given *ultra vires*. Law-books give one no
inkling of what this responsibility
amounted to. Parallels to the expression *si quid mei iudici est*, 'if it falls
within my jurisdiction,' occur only outside the sphere of law, excepting in
Liv. 3, 36, 6 cum priores decemviri
appellatione collegae corrigi reddita ab
se iura tulissent, et quaedam, quae sui
iudici videri possent, ad populum reie-
cissent; Caes. B.C. 1, 13, 1 dicens sui
iudici rem non esse; ib. 1, 35, 3. Sometimes *iudicium sit aliorum* is used, as
in Off. 1, 3; both this form and the other
are combined in Cic. ad Brut. 1, 4, 2
quod scribis quid ego sentiam mei iudici
esse, statuo...senatus aut populi Romani iudicium esse; cf. Sen. Clem.
1, 1, 2 iurisdictio mea est. Cf. too Caes.
B.C. 3, 12, 2 neque sibi iudicium sump-
turos, 'would not assume the right to
decide'; Nep. Att. 9, 7 ille, sui iudici,
potius quid se facere par esset intue-
batur quam quid alii laudaturi forent;
where *sui iudici* used as an appositional
phrase is curious. The phrase *hoc mei
consili est*, 'this is for me to determine,'
is also found.

3. **nihilo magis...iudicatum:** 'the decision was not a whit the sounder when
the clause was left out.' With *nihilo m.
est iudicatum* cf. *iudicatum negare* of a
decision pronounced, but alleged to be
invalid, Flacc. 49.

hoc non addito: Fam. 13, 10, 4

sed tamen nihilo infirmius illud hoc
addito.

5. **leve asperum:** in Tusc. 5, 73 (where
Epicureanism is discussed) the words
indicate *pleasantness* and *unpleasant-
ness*; of sound in N.D. 2, 146. On all
the points here mentioned the judgment
of the senses was questioned by the
Sceptics; see Acad. 2 § 79 ff.

movere: the use of *movens* as depo-
nent (above, § 31 *n.*) does not justify the
intransitive use of *movere*, to which
there is no parallel in Cicero or any
writer near his time; even *movere* for
m. castra and the like in the historical
writers and *terra movit* of earthquakes
(twice in Livy) do not go as far as
this.

6. **ratio,** etc.: the passage has a Stoic
tinge. The phrase *pronuntiabit sententiam* carries on the judicial metaphor:
σοφία and ἀρεταί form the *consilium* of
the judge; cf. *adhibere consilium* of the
judge in Verr. 2, 2, 81.

7. **divinarum humanarumque rerum
scientia:** a definition of philosophy
which was widespread in ancient times
(see references to Cicero and Seneca, in n.
on Acad. 1, 9; add Off. 1, 153); Varro
imitated it in the title of his great work
'antiquitates rerum divinarum atque
humanarum.' The definition is often
treated as specially Stoic; see Bonhöffer, Epictetus, vol. 1, p. 2; Sen. ep.
31, 8 rerum scientia...et ars per quam
humana ac divina noscantur; ep. 74, 29
scientia divinorum humanorumque;
dial. 12, 9, 3.

quae...sapientia: this seems to be a
protest against the use of *sapientia* to
denote φρόνησις in 1, 43.

9. **satellites:** note on § 69 ancillulas.

voluisti; quarum adeo omnium sententia pronuntiabit primum
de voluptate, nihil esse ei loci non modo ut sola ponatur in summi
boni sede, quod quaerimus, sed ne illo quidem modo ut ad
honestatem applicetur. De vacuitate doloris eadem sententia
5 erit. Reicietur etiam Carneades, nec ulla de summo bono ratio 38

3 quod: *quam* codd.   5 erit: *est* codd.; corr. Th. Bentley.   5 etiam: *autem* B.
Carneades: *carniades* A[1].   5 summo bono ratio: *summa honoracio* B.

1. **sententia:** this is abl.,
the subject of *pronuntiabit*
being *ratio*; cf. 1, 29
omnium philosophorum sententia; not
different from *mea sententia* and *sententiis* in Tusc. 1, 24. But the text is
suspicious; the judge is usually said to
deliver judgment *de consili sententia*.
Perhaps *de* has been corrupted into *adeo*
here or has fallen out after that word.

3. **quod quaerimus:** I have, without
hesitation, changed the mss. reading,
because I cannot conceive Cicero to
have used the phrase *quaerere sedem
summi boni*. Cf. 5, 41 hoc, quod quaerimus, summum; 2, 4 quaerimus finem
bonorum; § 69 voluptatem in solio sedentem; also Lactant. inst. 3, 11 miror
nullum omnino philosophum exstitisse,
qui sedem ac domicilium summi boni
reperiret.

4. **eadem sententia:** possibly *est* of
the mss. is an insertion; cf. 4, 36 eorum
enim omnium multa praetermittentium,
dum eligant aliquid quod sequantur,
quasi curta sententia (sc. est); Verr.
2, 1, 100 hinc ratio cum; Tim. 9 causa;
Acad. 2, 132 eadem dicenda.

5. **Carneades:** his τέλος is here and
in many other places described as not
including virtue. So above § 35; below
3, 30; 5, 22; 4, 49; but in 5, 18 the *prima
secundum naturam* are made to include
the 'quasi virtutum igniculi et semina.'
In another passage, Tusc. 5, 84, there is
a somewhat different statement, for
which see note on Fin. 4, 15. Cicero
repeatedly declares that this view of
Carneades was put forward with little
seriousness, as a weapon for use in his
controversy with the Stoics; so Acad.
2, 131; Fin. 5, 20; Tusc. 5, 84. At any
rate this Carneadean opinion found few
supporters; cf. Tusc. 5, 87 si qui sunt
qui desertum illud Carneadeum curent
defendere; and Fin. 4, 49 si qui Carneadeum finem tueri voluerunt. Indeed
Clitomachus, the most famous pupil of
Carneades, declared that he had never
been able to discover what the opinion
of his master was concerning the *summum bonum*; see Acad. 2, 139, where it

is also stated (but not definitely on the
authority of Clitomachus) that Carneades sometimes championed the τέλος
of Callipho with such zeal, that he was
believed to accept it. Doubtless, like the
rest of the Sceptics, of whatever shade,
he was ready on occasion to speak for
or against any definite scheme (see Leg.
1, 39). In the general tradition about
the ethical views of Carneades, no account was taken of his defence of the
combination of pleasure and morality
put forward by Callipho. In two curious
fragments of the 'Menippean Satires'
Varro (an adherent of Antiochus) makes
mention of Carneades in relation to
ethics. [With the Carneadia divisio cf.
a passage of Aug. ep. 118.] They bear
in part on the 'Carneadia divisio' which
I shall discuss in an appendix; I mention them here for the light they throw
on the nature of the τέλος of Carneades.
The first is from the 'Sesquiulixes'
(frag. 483 in Bücheler's ed.): unam
viam Zenona munisse duce virtute,
hanc esse nobilem: alteram Carneadem
desubulasse bona corporis secutum. The
proposal (Roeper and others) to substitute the name of Epicurus here for
that of Carneades is violent. The phrase
bona corporis forms part of the τριλογία
τῶν ἀγαθῶν (see note on Acad. 1, 19) and
occurs often in Cicero's writings, but
only in those portions of them where he
was especially influenced by Antiochus
(Acad. 1, 21; Fin. 3–5; Tusc. Disp.). The
phrase would be entirely unsuitable for
describing the scheme of Epicurus (above
§ 34). On its relation to πρῶτα κατὰ φ.
see App. A. This passage therefore shows
that Varro believed Carneades to have
excluded ἀρετή from his τέλος. The
other passage is from the same satire
(Bücheler § 484): alteram viam defor-
masse virtutis se cupis acris aceti. The
last four words (*se* is doubtless an error
for *e*) have all the appearance of being
a quotation from Lucilius and may well
in him have referred to Carneades, whom
he doubtless mentioned often (see Lact.
ap. Müller 1, 12) but cannot have met in

aut voluptatis non dolendive particeps aut honestatis expers
probabitur. Ita relinquet duas de quibus etiam atque etiam
consideret. Aut enim statuet nihil esse bonum nisi honestum,
nihil malum nisi turpe, cetera aut omnino nihil habere momenti
aut tantum ut nec expetenda nec fugienda, sed eligenda modo 5
aut reicienda sint, aut anteponet eam, quam cum honestate
ornatissimam, tum etiam ipsis initiis naturae et totius perfectione vitae locupletatam videbit. Quod eo liquidius faciet,
si perspexerit rerum inter eas verborumne sit controversia.

39 XIII. Huius ego nunc auctoritatem sequens idem faciam. 10
Quantum enim potero, minuam contentiones omnesque sententias simplices eorum in quibus nulla inest virtutis adiunctio

1 expers probabitur: ita A²; *exprobabitur* A¹; *expers probatur* B.   2 relinquet:
relinquunt B.   7 ipsis: om. B.   8 locupletatam: *locupletam* B.   11 sent.
simplices: ita A; *simplices sent.* B.   12 inest: ita A; *est* B.   12 adiunctio
omnino: ita A; *omnino adiunctio* E; *omnis adiunccio* B.

155 as Müller supposed. Clitomachus
(Acad. 2, 102) dedicated a book to
Lucilius; Varro incorporated in his
satires many fragments of the older
writers, especially Lucilius; in the 'Sexa-
gessis' is a tag from Ennius. The words
in question remind us of 'Italo perfusus
aceto' and the like. The other words
mean that C. drew an unflattering
picture of the 'other road,' the Stoic path
leading to virtue, as they conceived it;
deformare is often thus used by Cicero.
It is thus clear that in the actual
statement of his τέλος C. found no room
for virtue. But it does not therefore
follow that virtue had no place in his
whole moral scheme. We have seen that
virtue was one of the corner-stones of
Epicurean Ethics, as an indispensable
means for the attainment of the τέλος:
the same is doubtless true of Hieronymus, and of Carneades. In all these
schemes virtue was a means, not an end,
in itself; herein lay the chief opposition
to the Stoic doctrine.
1. parti-ceps...ex-pers: note the contrast and cf. *im-pert-ire.*
2. relinquet: sc. *ratio*; duas sc.
rationes; careless writing.
3. nihil esse...reicienda sint: for
these Stoic expressions see book 3.
6. anteponet eam, etc.: by a similar
method of exhaustion Chrysippus used
to assign the palm to the Stoic scheme
(Acad. 2, 138). The prize system here is
the 'Old Academic,' for which see book 5.
7. perfectione: note on § 19 vitae perfectae prosperitate.

11. minuam contentiones: a legal
phrase, in harmony with the legal
references in § 37. Cf. Acad. 2, 83 and
the references to Seneca Rhetor and
Caesar in my note there.
12. in quibus: for *in quorum scriptis*, in
accordance with the very common
identification of an author with his
works cf. my note on Acad. 2, 101. *Stoicus*
is generally masc. in Cicero but cf. Fam.
9, 22, 5. In Acad. 2, 85 *Stoicum* may be
for *Stoicorum*, and in N.D. 1, 15 Balbus,
qui tantos progressus habebat in Stoicis,
doubtless *Stoicis* is masculine, not neuter
(as the lexica say s. v.). The passage, as
I understand it, is unlike those which
Madvig quotes, where there is careless
incoherence between antecedent and
relative, as Balb. 32 quaedam foedera
extant, ut Cenomanorum...quorum in
foederibus; ib. 48 num quis eorum, qui
de foederatis civitatibus esset civitate
donatus, in iudicium est vocatus?
C.I.L. 1, 198, l. 83. De Or. 3, 16 is
erit ex eis, qui aut illos non audierit
aut iudicare non possit (so MSS. but
edd. generally *audierint, possint*); I
may add Fam. 13, 15, 1 en hic ille
est de illis maxime qui inridere atque
obiurgare me solitus est. The other exx.
quoted are less strange, as De Or. 3, 184
illud assentior Theophrasto, qui putat
(for *quod putat*); so ib. 2, 313; Cato m. 85;
Fam. 1, 9, 13; prov. cons. 36. A large
number of more or less similar irregularities occur in MSS. and have been
generally questioned, but probably
wrongly, as Cael. ap. Fam. 8, 3, 1; id.

omnino a philosophia semovendas putabo, primum Aristippi
Cyrenaicorumque omnium, quos non est veritum in ea voluptate,
quae maxime dulcedine sensum moveret, summum bonum ponere,
contemnentis istam vacuitatem doloris. Hi non viderunt, ut ad 40
5 cursum ecum, ad arandum bovem, ad indagandum canem, sic
hominem ad duas res, ut ait Aristoteles, ad intellegendum et

1 semovendas: *semovenda* B.   1 primum...ponere: affert Gellius, 15, 13.
6 ad (ante *duas*): om. E.

8, 4, 2; Qu. Fr. 1, 1, 43; Verr. 5, 111;
Rep. 6, 15; C. F. W. Müller refers to
Petron. 83 ex hac nota litteratorum,
quos odisse divites solent; Enn. ap. Gell.
6, 17, 10 ea libertas est, qui purum pectus
gestitat. In the latter ex. and some
others we have not so much an irregularity in the correspondence of antecedent and relative, as an irregular
epexegetic relative clause. [In Q. Fr.
1, 1, 43 non est tibi his solis utendum
existimationibus ac iudiciis qui nunc
sunt hominum, sed eis etiam qui futuri
sunt, Tyrrell keeps the MSS. reading, but
the text is altered by Tyrrell and Purser
(after Becher) in the very similar
passage of Cael. Fam. 8, 4, 2 in evitandis
consiliis eis qui se intenderant adver-
sarios.] 1, 55, referred to here by
Madvig, is hardly an ex. but ex eo genere
qui and the like (see note on 3, 70) are
parallel.

1. **putabo**: the tense assimilated to
minuam.

2. **Cyrenaicorumque omnium**: Cicero
doubtless has in mind here the followers
of Theodorus, Hegesias and Anniceris,
all of Cyrene, for whom see Zeller, II, 1,
ed. 3, pp. 294, 326 sq.

non est veritum: this impersonal
use is found only in two or three fragments of the older drama, and one of
Varro sat. Men.; and there the constr.
is *veretur* or *reveretur me alicuius*, not
with the infin. Gellius, 15, 13, 9 and
Macrobius Gram. Lat. (Keil) 5, 648, 6,
quote this passage as a rarity. Cicero has
puditum est (Flacc. 52) and *pertaesum est*
(Qu. Fr. 1, 2, 4), expressions found in a
good many other writers, as are *miseri-
tum est* and *pigitum est*. See Neue-
Wagener, vol. III, pp. 655 sq.

4. **ut ad cursum**, etc.: the argument
closely corresponds with 4, 37 sq.; cf.
esp. in omni animante est summum
aliquid atque optimum, ut in equis, in
canibus. In the language there is
striking agreement with a passage of

the N.D. 2, 37 scite enim Chrysippus:
ut clipei causa involucrum, vaginam
autem gladii, sic praeter mundum cetera
omnia aliorum causa esse generata, ut
eas fruges atque fructus quos terra
gignit, animantium causa, animantes
autem hominum, ut equom vehendi
causa, arandi bovem, venandi et custo-
diendi canem: ipse autem homo ortus
est ad mundum contemplandum et
imitandum, nullo modo perfectus, sed
est quaedam particula perfecti. Bywater, in Journal of Philology, VII, 85,
supposes that both these passages are
ultimately derived from Aristotle's lost
dialogue περὶ φιλοσοφίας: V. Rose
assigns the passage here to another
dialogue, the προτρεπτικός. The doctrine in Fin. accords well with all that
Aristotle says of the ἠθικαί and δια-
νοητικαὶ ἀρεταί, but the passage in N.D.
has acquired a thoroughly Stoic cast;
see Mayor on the passage and my note
on 3, 21. Madvig refers to [Plut.] Plac.
Phil. p. 874 *f* (Diels p. 274) ἀναγκαῖον
τὸν τέλειον ἄνδρα καὶ θεωρητικὸν εἶναι
τῶν ὄντων καὶ πρακτικὸν τῶν δεόντων
(attributed to Aristotle and Theophrastus). Sen. ep. 124, esp. §§ 11, 12.

6. **ad intellegendum et agendum**:
'numquam apud Ciceronem (nisi forte
hic 1, 36 ubi tamen ablativus per se poni
poterat) gerundium substantivo a praepositione pendenti praepositione non
repetita apponitur.' So Madv. who quotes
for the omission in such circumstances
Liv. 21, 4, 3; 22, 8, 5; Hor. ep. 2, 1, 19. The
reference to Hor. seems to be an error;
that passage bears no resemblance to
the others. C. F. W. Müller hesitates,
but the exx. to which he refers in a note
on Acad. 1, 20 are simpler; and the
question of the omission of the preposition between *intellegendum* and
agendum is different from that of the
attachment of the gerund epexegeti-
cally without it. Madvig's exx. from
Livy touch *only* the latter point.

agendum, esse natum quasi mortalem deum, contraque ut tardam
aliquam et languidam pecudem ad pastum et ad procreandi
voluptatem hoc divinum animal ortum esse voluerunt, quo nihil
41 mihi videtur absurdius. Atque haec contra Aristippum, qui eam
voluptatem non modo summam, sed solam etiam ducit, quam
omnes unam appellamus voluptatem. Aliter autem vobis placet.
Sed ille, ut dixi, vitiose. Nec enim figura corporis nec ratio
excellens ingeni humani significat ad unam hanc rem natum
hominem ut frueretur voluptatibus. Nec vero audiendus Hieronymus, cui summum bonum est idem, quod vos interdum vel potius
nimium saepe dicitis, nihil dolere. Non enim, si malum est dolor,

1 agendum: ante hoc verbum *ad* inseruit Ernesti; om. ABE.   3 quo nihil:
quod nichil B.   4 Aristippum: *astippum* A.   5 ducit: *dicit* B.   7 ille: om. B.
10 potius: om. B.   11 nimium saepe: *sepe minimum* B.

1. **quasi mortalem deum**: the phrases
θεοὶ θνητοὶ for men, and ἀθάνατοι
ἄνθρωποι for gods were attributed to
Heraclitus; see Bywater on frag. 67;
cf. too note on § 88 dempta aeternitate,
and for the context Acad. 2, 139 virtus
...pecudum illos motus esse dicit, hominem iungit deo. As to *pecudem* see note
on § 18 above.

3. **quo...absurdius**: 4, 40 quo nihil
potest esse perversius.

4. **atque haec...Aristippum**: in brief
summative clauses like this the verb is
often omitted, as below, 2, 113 ergo
haec in animis; Acad. 1, 20 ergo haec
animorum; in my note there I have
quoted illustrations to which add Off.
1, 46 atque haec in moribus; Fam. 9,
18, 2 ergo hoc primum; Aug. ep. 118
§ 17 et hoc in moralibus.

contra Aristippum: Epicurus is post-
poned to c. 14.

6. **omnes appellamus**: § 20 *n*.

7. **sed ille vitiose**: in short clauses
like this, containing an emphatic adverb, the verb is very frequently
omitted, both by Cicero and other
writers; so above, 1, 63. I have quoted
many illustrations in my note on Acad.
2, 94, to which I now add Ter. Ad. 156,
266, 426, 566, 653, 703, 752, 943 (there
are many exx. in his other plays);
Plaut. Ps. 249; Att. 5, 11, 2; 13, 22,
4; 13, 26, 1; Cael. ap. Fam. 8, 6, 1;
Cat. agr. 110 si demptus erit odor
deterior, id optime. In Fam. 9, 15, 3
quod autem altera epistula purgas te
non dissuasorem mihi emptionis Neapo-
litanae fuisse sed auctorem modera-

tionis, urbane, neque ego aliter accepi,
the MSS. have *urbanae*, and the reading
was cleverly corrected by Madvig, Fin.
p. 806, after vain attempts by others.
(Cf. Petron. 48 where *urbane* occurs
exactly in the same way.) Lucan 3, 111
melius (sc. Caesar fecit), quod plura
iubere puduit quam Roma pati, has
been misunderstood by Francken and
others. There is often omission when
emphasis is thrown on an adjective.
Cf. Lael. 14 veriora.

figura corporis, etc.: the line of argument is Stoic; see 3, 23 *n*.

9. **nec vero audiendus**: the omission
also of *est* with the gerundive nearly always occurs in Cicero in short emphatic
clauses at the beginning of a sentence;
so Off. 1, 88 nec vero audiendi qui; Att.
12, 11, 1 sed omnia humana tolerabilia
ducenda; 15, 20, 3 sed humana ferenda.
N.D. 1, 35 nec audiendus eius auditor
Strato; Lael. 73 tantum autem cuique
tribuendum; ib. 78 cavendum vero;
Off. 3, 92; Cato m. 35, 36; Qu. 10, 3, 22
non tamen protinus audiendi qui cre-
dunt. The ellipse of the verb is common
in both of two brief correlated clauses
of various kinds, and one of these may
contain a gerundive; as Fam. 12, 2, 2
sed haec tolerabilia, illud non ferendum;
Off. 3, 113 ut laudandus Regulus, sic illi
...vituperandi; cf. Acad. 2, 132; Off. 1,
150; also on § 35, above. In Mil. 65
Clark leaves out a past tense of the verb
'to be,' the MSS. giving *Quin etiam audiendus fuerit* where *fuit* is needed. The
omission of the past tense is improbable
and the slight change to *fuit* far better.

carere eo malo satis est ad bene vivendum. Hoc dixerit potius
Ennius:

    Nimium boni est, cui nihil est...mali.

Nos beatam vitam non depulsione mali, sed adeptione boni
iudicemus, nec eam cessando, sive gaudentem, ut Aristippus,
sive non dolentem, ut hic, sed agendo aliquid considerandove
quaeramus. Quae possunt eadem contra Carneadeum illud **42**
summum bonum dici, quod is non tam ut probaret protulit,
quam ut Stoicis, quibuscum bellum gerebat, opponeret. Id
autem eius modi est, ut additum ad virtutem auctoritatem
videatur habiturum et expleturum cumulate vitam beatam, de
quo omnis haec quaestio est. Nam qui ad virtutem adiungunt
vel voluptatem, quam unam virtus minimi facit, vel vacuitatem
doloris, quae etiam si malo caret, tamen non est summum bonum,
accessione utuntur non ita probabili, nec tamen cur id tam parce

---

5 iudicemus: *dicemus* B.   9 opponeret: ita A; *apponerent* B.

2. Ennius: who represents Eurip.
Hec. 627 κεῖνος ὀλβιώτατος | ὅτῳ κατ'
ἧμαρ τυγχάνει μηδὲν κακόν. Cicero's
quotation is probably not exact; see
Ribbeck, Enn. v. 354 *n*. Cf. Publilius
Syrus 467 (ed. Bickford-Smith) nimium
boni est in morte cui nil sit mali, which
probably means that if a man arrives
at death without disaster he is all too
happy.
    5. gaudentem: indefinite subject like
eligentem in § 34.
    6. agendo aliquid: Cicero rarely uses
agere without an object; when it is
omitted there is generally a contrast, as
above § 40 ad intellegendum et agendum;
Acad. 2, 22 faciendo...agendo. See my
note on Acad. 1, 23.
    considerandove: θεωρίᾳ. In a note-
worthy passage of Off. 1, 153 Cicero uses
actio as covering θεωρία as well as practical life.
    8. non tam ut probaret: 'not so much
from a desire to accept the view himself.' In Acad. 2, 131 (speaking of the
same matter) Cicero writes: 'non quo
probaret, sed ut opponeret Stoicis,'
meaning, 'not that he held the view
himself' (*non quo* as above, 1, 29, below,
4, 63 and often). Madvig rightly condemns the view of Davies that *non ut*
and *non quo* in these two passages are
identical in sense. Nor is *probaret=p.
aliis*, as Goerenz supposed; for Carneades must have desired the approval of
his audience at least, and always secured

it, according to De Or. 2, 161 Carneades
nullam umquam rem defendit quam
non probarit ('did not render accept-
able'). Madvig quotes Att. 14, 17, 4
earum exempla tibi misi non ut delibe-
rarem, reddendaene essent...sed quod
..., saying, 'consilium simul causam rei
continet'; but *ut* there seems to be
purely of purpose, 'from no desire to
debate the matter'; cf. Hor. A.P.
257. Davies cited Fat. 35 for *non
ut=non quo* and Madvig explains in
such a way as to admit an approxi-
mation to that sense, but the passage
is probably corrupt; see C. F. W.
Müller *ad loc.*
    11. expleturum cumulate: the Greek
text here doubtless had the verb
συμπληροῦν, similarly translated elsewhere.
    de quo: the words *de quo omnis
haec quaestio est* occur in § 5; and in
Acad. 2, 115, etc.
    14. non est summum bonum: the word
summum must be due to the copyists
here. The argument requires that
vacuitas doloris should be treated as
mere nothingness, and as neither evil
nor good. Moreover, the fact that it is
not *summum bonum* is no reason why
it should not be added to *virtus*.
    15. non ita: 'not very.'
    tamen: 'even if that were not so';
note on 1 § 14 and on 2 § 31.
    id: the process of adding other *bona*
to virtue.

tamque restricte faciant intellego. Quasi enim emendum eis sit quod addant ad virtutem, primum vilissimas res addunt, dein singulas potius, quam omnia, quae prima natura approbavisset, **43** ea cum honestate coniungerent. Quae quod Aristoni et Pyrrhoni omnino visa sunt pro nihilo, ut inter optime valere et gravissime

1 intellego...eis: *intellegunt cum enim dandum eis* B.   2 dein: ita A; *deinde* B. 4 honestate: ita AB; *voluptate* alii codd.; verba *ea...coniungerent* om. Marsus et Lambinus.   4 quod: *cum* codd.; corr. Madvig.   4 Pyrrhoni: *pirroni* A; *pyrroni* B.   5 visa sunt: *sunt visa* B.

2. addant ad: this is by far the commonest construction of *addo* in Cicero. Others are dat., but nearly confined to persons as below, 4, 61; Mur. 47; *summae*, Verr. 3, 116; adverbs like *eo, huc*; and rarely *in*; also rarely *ut*; acc. and inf. (fairly common). *Adde quod* (conj.) is not Ciceronian, for N.D. 3, 68 is a quotation.

dein: this has good MSS. authority below, 4, 50, and in seventeen or eighteen other passages given in Merguet's lexica as against not far from 700 exx. of *deinde*. Seeing how easily *deinde* by contraction passes into *dein*, and looking to the probabilities, *dein* can hardly be called certain. (A similar contraction of *ante* to *an̄* gave rise to the reading *antestaretur* in Mil. 68.) Merguet gives no instance of *proin* excepting in a quotation; the lexicon to the phil. writings gives eight instances of *exin*, five in poetical or otherwise archaic passages; two others (both in Div. 1, 55) come in the course of a story transcribed from Caelius Antipater; the remaining one is in N.D. 2, 101. The MSS. of Caesar give one ex. of *dein* against nine of *deinde*. Later prose writers, who were averse to no form which was archaic or poetical, doubtless used *dein*.

4. coniungerent: the tense is accommodated to that of *approbavisset*, at which point the change is made from historic present to actual past. The change is still more awkward below, 4, 39 cum autem ad summum bonum volunt pervenire, transiliunt omnia et duo nobis opera pro uno relinquunt, ut alia sumamus, alia expetamus, potius quam uno fine utrumque concluderent. In these two passages and in 2, 66 (where the subjects of the verbs are different) the passage from the indicative before *potius quam* to the subjunctive after it indicates a decided preference on the part of the subject to the principal verb for one kind of action

rather than another. And this meaning very often exists even when *potius quam* stands between two words or phrases of exactly similar construction, for example, above 1, 4 Synephebos ego potius Caecili aut Andriam Terenti quam utramque Menandri legam? Also below 5, 91.

quae quod, etc.: the line of argument here is very similar to that in 4, 40. As to the reading I have followed Madvig but not without hesitation. He interprets 'nam quod ad Pyrrhonis et Aristonis sententiam attinet, quibus haec, etc.' Madvig has here inserted *nam*; had Cicero written this there could have been no doubt as to the nature of *quod*. But as it stands, it may be more naturally taken as giving the cause for *recte*. And if the notion of cause is once admitted, it becomes a question whether *quoniam* (Otto) is not at least as good a correction. As to the opinions of Aristo and Erillus and Pyrrho see note on 4, 43.

5. inter optime valere: on prepositions with the inf. see Wölfflin in Archiv 3, 71. He says that *inter* is found so used only here and Sen. ben. 5, 10, 2 nihil interest inter dare et accipere, and then in Christian writers; but he overlooks a passage of Nigidius Figulus, quoted by Gell. 11, 11, 1: inter mendacium dicere et mentiri distat. Horace, Ovid and later poets use *praeter* with following infin., but there is a doubt whether in such instances *praeter* is not adverbial. Wölfflin indeed calls this idea a 'grammatisches Kunststück'; but seeing how often *praeter* is used as an adverb in close connexion with nouns, adjectives and participles, and occasionally even with finite verbs, the usage cannot have been impossible with the infinitive. [Madvig says 'aliud futurum erat *inter aegrotandum*'; but *inter* with gerund is poetical and post-classical; for exx. from Livy see Stacey in Archiv 10, 75.]

aegrotare nihil prorsus dicerent interesse, recte iam pridem contra eos desitum est disputari. Dum enim in una virtute sic omnia esse voluerunt ut eam rerum selectione exspoliarent nec ei quicquam, aut unde oriretur, darent, aut ubi niteretur, virtutem ipsam quam amplexabantur sustulerunt. Erillus autem ad scientiam omnia revocans unum quoddam bonum vidit, sed nec optimum, nec quo vita gubernari possit. Itaque hic ipse iam pridem est reiectus; post enim Chrysippum non sane est disputatum.

XIV. Restatis igitur vos; nam cum Academicis incerta luctatio est, qui nihil affirmant et quasi desperata cognitione certi id sequi volunt, quodcumque veri simile videatur. Cum Epicuro **44** autem hoc plus est negoti quod e duplici genere voluptatis coniunctus est, quodque et ipse et amici eius et multi postea defensores eius sententiae fuerunt, et nescio quo modo is qui auctoritatem minimam habet maximam vim, populus cum illis

---

1 contra eos: post *desitum* habet B.   3 selectione: *electione* B.   3 exspoliarent: *expoliaverunt* A; *spoliaverunt* B.   4 oriretur, darent: *ore retunderet* B.   8 reiectus: parvo spatio relicto om. B.   8 Chrysippum: *crisippum* AB, ut infra.   10 incerta: *uncta* A; *iuncta* B.   10 luctatio: *locucio* B.   15 is: *his* A.   16 habet: ita A¹B; *habent* A².   16 populus cum illis: *cum illis populus* B.

2. **desitum est disputari**: Cicero never used *coepi, desii* with passive inf. The one passage in which the MSS. give anything of the kind, Tusc. 1, 29 sed qui nondum ea quae multis post annis tractari coepissent physica didicissent, has been corrected, because *coepissent* is syntactically difficult, and the neighbourhood of *didicissent* accounts for the corruption. See Draeger § 92, 1 A; and Riemann, Études sur Tite-Live, p. 161 sq.

dum...voluerunt: *dum* here has a slightly causal or adversative sense; see exx. in Draeger § 507 c. *Dum* with perf. is fairly common in Cicero and older writers, but not later; Caesar avoids it and Livy has it only once.

3. **rerum selectione**: this has a Stoic tinge.

4. **ubi niteretur**: so N.D. 2, 125; above 1, 41 nec habet ubi consistat.

8. **post enim**: Lamb. wished to read *p. Chr. enim*, and this is the usual collocation; but Madvig shows that Cicero, like other writers, does sometimes place *enim, autem, vero* between preposition and case; below 3, 36.

11. **certi**: cf. Acad. 2, 103 veri et certi nota.

id...quodcumque: § 12 omnes quicumque.

14. **coniunctus ex**: Inv. 2, 158 iuncta ex duplici genere (altered by Friedrich); ib. 157 ex horum partibus iunctum; Tusc. 1, 43 iunctis ex anima tenui et ex ardore solis ignibus; Att. 4, 15, 1 ut est ex me et ex te iunctus Dionysius M. Pomponius (of a freedman who took his names partly from Cicero, partly from Atticus); *iunctus ex* is also found in Acad. 1, 40, and possibly Tim. 27. 'Sed durius Cicero ad ipsum Epicurum transtulit quod de summo eius bono proprie diceretur' (Madv.). But all through here the philosophers are identified with their views about the τέλος; so § 38 reicietur Carneades, etc.

16. **populus cum illis facit**: this hardly means that the Epicurean philosophy had penetrated among the people (see note on 1, 25) nor even that any large proportion of professed philosophers were Epicureans; in the time of Lucian at any rate the great majority of these were Stoics (Hermot. c. 16). The sense merely is that the multitude are votaries of pleasure. Sen. ep. 29, 10 quotes as from Epic. (Us. § 187): 'numquam volui populo placere; nam quae ego scio, non

facit. Quos nisi redarguimus, omnis virtus, omne decus, omnis
vera laus deserenda est. Ita ceterorum sententiis semotis relinquitur non mihi cum Torquato, sed virtuti cum voluptate
certatio. Quam quidem certationem homo et acutus et diligens,
Chrysippus, non contemnit totumque discrimen summi boni in
earum comparatione positum putat. Ego autem existimo, si
honestum esse aliquid ostendero, quod sit ipsum sua vi propter
seque expetendum, iacere vestra omnia. Itaque eo, quale sit,
breviter, ut tempus postulat, constituto accedam ad omnia tua,
Torquate, nisi memoria forte defecerit.

3 non mihi: *enim michi* B.   4 homo...putat: affert Nonius, p. 282.   4 et
diligens: *sed diligens* A; om. B.   6 earum: *ea rerum* vel *eam rem rerum* codd.
Nonii.   6 existimo: om. B.   7 esse aliquid: *aliquid esse* B.   7 sua vi: ita
A; *in sua* B.   9 tua: ita AB; *via* E.   10 forte: om. B.

probat populus, quae probat populus,
ego nescio.' Letters of Epic. and Metrod.
showed that they had little repute in
their lifetime; cf. Sen. ep. 79, 15, 16.
  1. **virtus...decus...laus:** Stoic remi-
niscences again: *decus* is τὸ καλὸν and
the Stoic virtue is the only thing
which is truly ἐπαινετόν, as is set forth in
book 3. In § 47 *laudes=virtutes*; and cf.
Off. 3, 101 nusquam possumus nisi in
laude, decore, honestate utilia reperire;
Tusc. 2, 16 officium...laus...decus.
  4. **acutus et d.:** 'homo sine dubio
versutus et callidus,' N.D. 3, 25;
'acerrimo vir ingenio,' Div. 1, 6; 'quem
acutissimum ferunt,' De Or. 1, 50; 'homo
acutissimus,' Varro L.L. 9, 1—all of
Chrysippus.
  5. **non contemnit:** this implies that
other Stoics did make light of the debate. Cf. Acad. 2, 140 unum igitur par
quod depugnet relicum est, voluptas
cum honestate. De quo Chrysippo fuit,
quantum ego sentio, non magna contentio.
  6. **comparatione:** Madvig points out
that the edd. were wrong in supposing
that the word contained a reference to
the matching of gladiators with each
other, for the *noun* has no such use.
  si...ostendero...iacere: see C. F. W.
Müller on S. Rosc. 123.
  7. **propter seque:** *que* can attach itself
in classic Latin to the disyllabic prepositions (excepting *apud*); but when a
pronoun follows (as here) *que* sometimes is tacked on to it. The union of
que with the prepositions ending in *b* is
avoided, also with *ad*, and Cicero rejects
aque. With other monosyllabic prepositions *que* may go, but in Cicero (apart
from one or two official formulae) *exque*,

inque only appear before demonstra-
tives (Landgraf's ed. of S. Rosc. p. 411).
  8. **eo quale sit...constituto:** =*cum
constituero quale id sit.* Cf. Lael. 56
constituendi sunt qui sint in amicitia
fines diligendi; with my note; also note
on 3, 23 and on 5, 58 below.
  9. **ut tempus ... defecerit:** Cicero
keeps up the illusion of the dialogue;
cf. § 51.
  accedam ad omnia tua: cf. ἀπαντᾶν
πρός, often used of argument. The reading
of E and some other mss. is pronounced
by Madvig to be impossible. It is true that
tua is needed; but the saying that *via*
would not make sense is somewhat hard.
Via is sometimes used κατ' ἐξοχήν for
'the right path,' just as *locus* often is
'the right spot'; so in *decedere de via*,
and the like phrases; and in Att. 2, 19, 2
utor via, 'I keep to the high road'
(wrongly suspected by many edd.). It
is true that in N.D. 2, 57 ignem...ad
gignendum progredientem via, Cicero
is (as Madvig says) translating closely a
Greek text in which ὁδῷ occurred. But
he has the same phrase, ib. 2, 81, where
he does not appear to be translating
literally, and there is no inherent reason
why *via* should not have the same application as ὁδῷ. Cf. Quint. 2, 17, 41 viam
id est ordinem. As to Ter. Andr. 442
etenim ipsus secum eam rem recta
reputavit via, Madv. says, 'incerta est
scriptura etsi editur nunc (1874): *rem
reputavit via*,' but Fleckeisen (ed. 1898)
keeps *recta* of the mss. Cf. too Cic.,
Rep. 1, 33 deinde alia quaeremus,
quibus cognitis spero nos ad haec ipsa
via perventuros; Brut. 46 neminem
solitum via nec arte dicere; Virg. G.
2, 22 sunt alii quos ipse via sibi repperit

Honestum igitur id intellegimus, quod tale est ut detracta **45**
omni utilitate sine ullis praemiis fructibusve per se ipsum possit
iure laudari. Quod quale sit non tam definitione qua sum usus
intellegi potest, quamquam aliquantum potest, quam communi
omnium iudicio et optimi cuiusque studiis atque factis, qui
permulta ob eam unam causam faciunt, quia decet, quia rectum,
quia honestum est, etsi nullum consecuturum emolumentum
vident. Homines enim, etsi aliis multis, tamen hoc uno plurimum
a bestiis differunt quod rationem habent a natura datam men-
temque acrem et vigentem celerrimeque multa simul agitantem
et, ut ita dicam, sagacem, quae et causas rerum et consecutiones
videat et similitudines transferat et disiuncta coniungat et cum
praesentibus futura copulet omnemque complectatur vitae consequentis statum. Eademque ratio fecit hominem hominum ap-
petentem cumque eis natura et sermone et usu congruentem, ut
profectus a caritate domesticorum ac suorum serpat longius et
se implicet primum civium, deinde omnium mortalium societate
atque, ut ad Archytam scripsit Plato, non sibi se soli natum

1 est ut: om. B. 2 fructibusve per se: *fructibus vespere* B. 5 atque: *et* B.
6 unam causam: *causam unam* B. 9 habent: *habeant* AB. 10 acrem et: *et*
om. B. 10 multa simul: *simul multa* B. 13 consequentis: *presentis* B.
14 fecit hominem: *hominem fecit* B. 14 hominum: post hoc *amicicias* inserendum
esse indicat A². 16 a: om. B. 17 omnium mortalium: *mort. omn.* B.
18 soli: *solo* B.

usus. Madvig's idea that *via* is impossible for *ratione et via* appears untenable.
1. **honestum**, etc.: on the definition
of *honestum* see above, § 5 *n*. The whole
passage, §§ 45–7, bears a striking resemblance to Off. 1, §§ 11–14, which de-
serves perusal. In both passages a description seems to be given of the origin
of the four cardinal virtues in *reason*;
but the details in both are very obscure.
2. **possit iure laudari**: Stoic phraseology.
8. **aliis multis**: this collocation is
much commoner than the other, *multis
aliis*; so ordinarily *alia omnia* not *omnia
alia.*
10. **celerrime...agitantem**: rapidity of
movement is constantly in ancient
writings put forward as the leading
characteristic of mind.
11. **sagacem**: the word first meant
'keen-scented'; Enn. 235 (Baehr.) nare
sagaci; N.D. 2, 158 canum sagacitas
narium; cf. De Or. 2, 186 ut odorer
quam sagacissime possim; Att. 6, 4, 3
tu sagacius odorabere; hence the apo-

logetic phrase here, *ut ita dicam*. The
conjecture of Markland (on Stat. s. 3,
3, 98), *satagacem*, is curious.
12. **similitudines transferat**: cf. note
on 3, 33.
14. **hominem hominum**: this kind of
collocation is very common; below
3 §§ 63, 68; N.D. 1, 77 homini homine
pulchrius nihil videbatur; ib. 3, 11;
Rep. 3, 23; Off. 2 §§ 12, 17, 21; 3 §§ 21,
27; Mil. 68; Ter. Eun. 232; cf. below
3, 63 hominum inter homines. A vast
number of parallels will be found in an
article by Landgraf on 'Substantivische
Parataxen' in Archiv 5, 161 sq.
15. **natura**: adverbial = φύσει: but
Cicero mixes up *natura* and *ratio* in the
passage; cf. *rationem a natura datam*
and *eadem ratio* just above with *eadem
natura* just below, followed by *eadem
ratio* again a little farther on.
16. **profectus a caritate**, etc.: the context closely resembles 5, 65; cf. esp.
'caritas generis humani quae...serpit
sensim foras, cognationibus primum...
deinde totius complexu gentis humanae.'
18. **Plato**: Ep. 9, p. 358 *a* ἕκαστος
ἡμῶν οὐχ αὑτῷ μόνον γέγονεν, ἀλλὰ τῆς

meminerit, sed patriae, sed suis, ut perexigua pars ipsi relin-
46 quatur. Et quoniam eadem natura cupiditatem ingenuit homini
veri videndi, quod facillimé apparet cum vacui curis etiam quid
in caelo fiat scire avemus, his initiis inducti omnia vera diligimus,
id est fidelia, simplicia, constantia, tum vana, falsa, fallentia
odimus, ut fraudem, periurium, malitiam, iniuriam. Eadem ratio
habet in se quiddam amplum atque magnificum, ad imperandum
magis quam ad parendum accommodatum, omnia humana non
tolerabilia solum, sed etiam levia ducens, altum quiddam et
47 excelsum, nihil timens, nemini cedens, semper invictum. Atque
his tribus generibus honestorum notatis quartum sequitur et in
eadem pulcritudine et aptum ex illis tribus, in quo inest ordo et

2 eadem: *eam* B.   3 etiam quid: *et quid iam* B.   4 avemus: *habemus* AB.
6 malitiam: om. B.   6 eadem: post hoc *enim* inserit B.   9 quiddam:
quoddam B.   10 nemini: *nulli* B.

γενέσεως ἡμῶν τὸ μέν τι ἡ πατρὶς μερί-
ζεται, τὸ δέ τι οἱ γεννήσαντες, τὸ δὲ
οἱ λοιποὶ φίλοι. The same passage is
copied more closely in Off. 1, 12 and less
closely ib. § 22; there is an echo of it in
Mur. 83 M. Cato qui mihi non tibi sed
patriae natus esse videris, which passage
is again echoed by Lucan, 2, 383 nec sibi
sed toti genitum se credere mundo. The
sentiment is of course a commonplace
in Latin literature, but is especially
characteristic of Stoicism. See Sen. ep.
95, 51 ff. Cicero quotes another of the
letters of Plato (so called) below, § 92.

1. **sed...sed**: the anaphora is common; Draeger, § 333, 1 *a*.

ut perexigua pars, etc.: so Rep.
1, 8 tantumque nobis in nostrum privatum usum, quantum ipsi superesse
posset, remitteret (sc. res publica).

2. **cupiditatem...veri videndi**: the
same expression in Tusc. 1, 44; Off. 1, 13.
The context is in both places like the
present passage. The passage in Tusc.
esp. illustrates the words *quid in caelo
fiat* here.

4. **avemus**: this word was probably
somewhat archaic and colloquial in
Cicero's day. He has the verb only twice
in his speeches; ten times in the philosophical writings, and a few times in the
letters. Varro employed it; Livy has
it only twice; Caes., Sall., Nep., Mart.,
Juven., Quint., Suet., Curt. avoided it; in
Seneca's writings it rests on an emendation of Madvig's in one place; Tacitus
has it thrice; in the text of Petron. 88
it rests on an emendation (not accepted
by Büch.) for *audemus*.

7. **ad imperandum**, etc.: this resembles Off. 1, 13 closely.

8. **omnia...ducens**, etc.: the picture is
that of the ideal sage, for whom all
these characteristics were claimed in
every system, but especially in the
Stoic. Similar language will be found
in 5, 73 and in Acad. 2, 127; in my note
there I have given illustrations from
Cicero and others.

9. **altum...et excelsum**: cf. Parad. 41
animo excelso et alto et virtutibus
exaggerato. But it must be confessed
that the words look suspiciously like a
gloss here. So perhaps in Mur. 60 finxit
te ipsa natura ad honestatem gravita-
tem temperantiam magnitudinem animi
iustitiam, ad omnes denique virtutes
magnum hominem et excelsum, the
words *magnum hominem et excelsum*
come from a marginal exclamation with
which a copyist relieved his feelings. For
finxit ad cf. Hor. A.P. 366 voce paterna
fingeris ad rectum.

10. **nihil timens**, etc.: Cicero was here
rendering words like ἀτάρβητος in the
Greek text.

invictum: see 3, 76.

11. **in eadem pulcritudine**: Madvig
qu. Tusc. 3, 42 quae secuntur, in eadem
sententia sunt; ib. 1, 94 in eadem brevitate reperiemur; N.D. 1, 31 in eisdem
sunt erratis fere; *in eo genere sunt* is, as
he says, an ordinary phrase, below 3, 69;
Verr. 2, 3, 92; Div. 1, 89; Top. 76;
harder, however, is 4, 36 (below) animus
est in quodam genere corporis (where *in*
denotes equivalence, as not seldom);
and Rep. 1, 44 quae genera sunt in eis

moderatio. Cuius similitudine perspecta in formarum specie ac
dignitate transitum est ad honestatem dictorum atque factorum.
Nam ex his tribus laudibus, quas ante dixi, et temeritatem
reformidat et non audet cuiquam aut dicto protervo aut facto
5 nocere vereturque quicquam aut facere aut eloqui, quod parum
virile videatur.

XV. Habes undique expletam et perfectam, Torquate, formam **48**
honestatis, quae tota quattuor his virtutibus, quae a te quoque
commemoratae sunt, continetur. Hanc se tuus Epicurus omnino
10 ignorare dicit quam aut qualem esse velint, qui honestate summum bonum metiantur. Si ad honestatem enim omnia referantur,
neque in ea voluptatem dicant inesse, ait eos voce inani sonare
(his enim ipsis verbis utitur) neque intellegere nec videre, sub

---

1 specie: *spē* E.   1 ac dignitate: *adignitate* AB.   4 audet: *audi* B.   5 nocere:
nuere A¹.   5 aut (post *facere*) om. B.   8 quattuor his: ita A; *his quattuor* B.
9 se: *si* B.   10 qui: ita A; *hy qui* B.   11 si ad honestatem enim: ita A; *si
enim ad hon.* B.   12 dicant: *dicunt* B.   13 intellegere: *intelligitur* E.

---

singula vitiis quae ante dixi; Tusc. 4, 42
aegritudines susceptae continuo in
magna pestis parte versantur. Add
Fin. 4, 65 illud in eadem causa est; Att.
1, 18, 1 illae ambitiosae nostrae fuco-
saeque amicitiae sunt in quodam
splendore forensi; De Or. 2, 243 ut...
in aliquo insigni ad irridendum vitio
reperiantur; Ad Herenn. 3, 12 quoniam
in eodem virtutis studio sint; Varro r.r.
1, 6, 1 quo in genere terrae (sit fundus);
Plin. n. h. 16 § 2 diximus et in oriente
quidem iuxta oceanum compluris in
eadem necessitate gentis. *Esse in spe, in
timore*, etc. often of things. Reminiscence in Aug. ep. 118, § 15, cf. below,
2 § 115.

1. **formarum**: in § 115 the same parallel is drawn between beauty of external
shapes and beauty of moral action. Cf.
also Off. 1, 14, which closely corresponds.

4. **reformidat**: the subject is probably σωφροσύνη, involved in *quartum*
above: 'annotanda singularis orationis
brevitas in hac forma: *ex his tribus
laudibus et temeritatem reformidat*, etc.
Videtur Cicero significare voluisse, quid
ex singulis illis haec quarta haberet et
traheret, ut haec fere sententia sit: Ex
his laudibus oritur partim temeritatis
reformidatio, partim protervitatis cet.'
(Madvig).

7. **habes...formam**: so 4, 19 habes...
formam eorum de quibus loquor philo-

sophorum; Tusc. 3, 38 habes formam
Epicuri vitae beatae.

8. **quae tota**: see my note on Acad.
1, 27.

10. **aut qualem**: *aut* is due to the
negative; cf. 2, 7; but in 1, 29 quid et
quale; 37 quae qualisque.

11. **referantur...dicant**: Madvig calls
this 'durissimus transitus,' and says it
is not justified by the change from
active to passive infinitive which sometimes occurs (§ 21 *n.*) nor by anything
that is quoted by editors.

12. **voce inani sonare**: Cicero has in
mind a passage of Epicurus περὶ τέλους
which he renders in Tusc. 3, 42 saepe
quaesivi ex eis qui appellabantur sapientes, quid haberent, quod in bonis relinquerent si illa detraxissent, nisi si vellent
voces inanis fundere; nihil ab eis potui
cognoscere, qui si virtutes ebullire solent
et sapientias, nihil aliud dicent nisi eam
viam qua efficiantur eae voluptates quas
supra dixi. Phrases like these were
often used by Epicurus. The Epicureans
argued that whatever opponents might
say, *all* virtuous actions were done for
pleasure, see Sen. d. 7. 9, 1. Cf. too Tusc. 5,
119 philosophi quorum ea sententia est,
ut virtus per se ipsa nihil valeat, omneque
quod honestum nos et laudabile esse dicimus, id illi cassum quiddam et inani vocis
sono decoratum. Sen. ep. 123, 10; Acad. 2,
71; Hor. ep. 1, 17, 41 virtus inane nomen.

13. **sub hanc**: Madvig shows that the

hanc vocem honestatis quae sit subicienda sententia. Vt enim consuetudo loquitur, id solum dicitur honestum, quod est populari fama gloriosum. 'Quod,' inquit, 'quamquam voluptatibus quibusdam est saepe iucundius, tamen expetitur propter 49 voluptatem.' Videsne quam sit magna dissensio? Philosophus 5 nobilis, a quo non solum Graecia et Italia, sed etiam omnis barbaria commota est, honestum quid sit, si id non sit in voluptate, negat se intellegere, nisi forte illud, quod multitudinis rumore laudetur. Ego autem hoc etiam turpe esse saepe iudico et, si quando turpe non sit, tum esse non turpe, cum id a multi- 1 tudine laudetur, quod sit ipsum per se rectum atque laudabile; non ob eam causam tamen illud dici esse honestum, quia laudetur a multis, sed quia tale sit ut, vel si ignorarent id homines, vel si obmutuissent, sua tamen pulcritudine esset specieque laudabile. Itaque idem natura victus, cui obsisti non potest, dicit alio 1 loco id, quod a te etiam paulo ante dictum est, non posse iucunde

1 hanc vocem: *hac voce* codd.; corr. Wesenberg.   6 nobilis: *nobis hys* B.
7 quid sit: *quod sit* B.   7 non sit: *non est* codd.; corr. Madvig.   10 esse: om. B.
12 non ob eam causam tamen: *tamen non ob eam causam* B.   12 esse honestum:
honestum esse B.   12 laudetur: *laudatur* B.   15 itaque idem: *ita idemque* E.
16 quod: *quid* B.   16 a te etiam paulo: *ante paulo* E; *ante populo* B.

constr. of *subicere* is with dat. (above, 2, 6 *vis subiecta vocibus*; 2, 13 *huic verbo subiciunt*; 5, 36, and Acad. 1, 31) or *sub* and acc., and that the exx. quoted with the abl. break down on examination. In all instances where he mentions *sub* with abl. as occurring in editions, recent edd. give the acc. As he says, in Virg. Georg. 2, 19 laurus parva sub ingenti matris se subicit umbra, the words *se subicit* are equivalent to *crescit*.

2. consuetudo loquitur: cf. Ac. 1, 25 quibus (verbis) consuetudo utitur pro Latinis; for the change from or. obl. to recta see 1, 30 *n*.

3. populari f. gloriosum: see note on 1, 42; and cf. 1, 61 illam umbram quod appellant honestum, non tam solido quam splendido nomine; cf. notes on 3 §§ 11, 28; also Epict. d. 2, 22, 21 ὁ Ἐπικούρου λόγος ἀποφαίνων ἢ μηδὲν εἶναι τὸ καλὸν ἤ, εἰ ἄρα, τὸ ἔνδοξον: Acad. 2, 140 illos qui nomen honestatis a se ne intellegi quidem dicant nisi forte, quod gloriosum sit in volgus, id honestum velimus dicere. Cf. too Philodemi rhet. ed. Sudhaus, p. 217, where it is said that the sophistical rhetoricians, when they chance to praise a good man and blame a bad (instead of *vice versa*),

take a *popular* and not a *natural* view of virtue: κἂν ἄρα ποτὲ τῶν ἀγαθῶν τινας ἐνκωμιάζωσι καὶ τῶν ἀτόπων κατηγορῶσιν, οὐ τῶν κατ' ἀλήθειαν ὄντων ἀλλὰ τῶν τοῖς πολλοῖς νομιζομένων καὶ καθόλου τῶν τὰς δημώδεις ἀρετὰς καὶ κακίας ἐχόντων· εἰ γὰρ αὖ τῶν ὄντων ὡς ἀληθῶς, κἂν τὰς κατὰ φύσιν ἀρετὰς καὶ κακίας ᾔδεσαν κ.τ.λ.

6. a quo...commota est: Sen. ep. 79, 15 quotes from a letter of Epicurus, who says that he and Metrodorus passed their lives unknown to and almost unheard of by Greece.

7. barbaria: the form *barbaries* seems to be of doubtful authority not only in Cicero, but everywhere else. Friedrich retains it in Brut. 258, but *barbaria* is nearer to the MSS. and is rightly read by Martha.

9. saepe: goes with *turpe esse*, as is shown by *si quando*; but the collocation is awkward.

12. illud...id: note on 1 § 2.

14. obmutuissent: so that there could be no *multitudinis rumor*.

15. natura victus: cf. § 28 vis magna naturae, with note; see also the argument in § 58; and Off. 1, 5 si non... naturae bonitate vincatur (of the Epicureans).

vivi nisi etiam honeste. Quid nunc 'honeste' dicit? idemne, quod **50**
iucunde? Ergo ita: non posse honeste vivi, nisi honeste vivatur?
An nisi populari fama? Sine ea igitur iucunde negat posse *se*

2 ergo: *ego* B. 3 posse se vivere: *posse vivere* codd.; corr. Baiter; *posse vivi* Lambinus.

1. **quid nunc**, etc.: Madvig seems to
have somewhat misunderstood the argument (such as it is) when he says that
to be consistent Cicero should have
written *non posse iucunde vivi nisi
iucunde vivatur.* The other substitution
was made in order to lead up to *nisi
populari fama*, which Epicurus had
allowed to be the equivalent of *honeste.*
Unless *nisi honeste vivatur* had preceded
nisi populari fama there would have
been absolutely no relevance in the
latter phrase. (See below.) The criticism is in the nature of a quibble, but
it is not so perverse as Madvig supposes.
When the great scholar writes 'recte
Cicero negat honesti notionem in Epicuri disciplina ullam certam et suam
vim habere,' he seems to me unfair to
Epicurus; at all events the statement
would be equally true of all moral
systems based on utility.

3. **populari fama**: sc. *vivatur.* The
abl. is somewhat strange, and *in* may
have fallen out after *nisi*; but cf. Phil.
13, 7 si non spiritu at virtutis laude
vivemus, where Halm reads *cum laude*
because cod. V has *claude.* Madvig
thinks that Cicero should have written
an populari fama, as an alternative to
idemne quod iucunde? but assimilated
the alternative in form to the words
immediately preceding. In my view the
alternative expressed by *an nisi populari fama* is an alternative merely to the
last words of the previous sentence, *nisi
honeste vivatur.*
Cf. also Aug. ep. 118, 3 dic mihi...quis
eorum (philosophorum) finem actionum
suarum constituerit in fama vulgi aut in
lingua hominum vel bonorum atque
sapientium?

posse se vivere: in a great number of
passages of Cicero all the MSS. or the best
omit the pronominal subject of the infinitive, where, as in the codd. here, it is
the same as that of the principal verb,
and the principal verb is one of speaking
or thinking. Considering how carelessly,
in a vast number of places, the *codices*
omit pronouns where they are obviously
needed (for which see C. F. W. Müller's
critical notes on S. Rosc. 61; Caec. 25;
Cael. ap. Fam. 8, 3, 1), it is quite conceivable that all the examples are due to
error. Müller has adopted correction in

nearly all the instances in his text of
Cicero; but even he is not quite consistent; thus in Acad. 2, 81 non tu
verum testem habere, sed eum non sine
causa falsum testimonium dicere osten-
deris, he inserts *te* before *testem*, but in
S. Rosc. 61 confitere huc ea spe venisse,
he does not import *te* into the text. nor
in N.D. 1, 84 quam bellum erat confiteri
potius nescire; ib. 109 puderet me dicere
non intellegere; Acad. 2, 64 ut respondere
posse diffiderem; Leg. 2, 7 at ego effugisse
arbitrabar. And he leaves untouched
Verr. act. pr. 23 hic alios negasse audere,
alios respondisse non putare id perfici
posse; Acad. 2,104 alterum (sc. *ei*) placere
(dicit) alterum (sc. *eum*) tenere; although
in other similar passages the pronoun is
supplied. It is not logically possible to
separate the passages just mentioned
from the following; Mur. 7 qui gravissime ferre dixit; Verr. 2, 4, 147 hoc
memini dicere (sc. *me*); Leg. 3, 43 est
boni auguris meminisse...praesto esse
debere; Orat. 23 ego idem...recordor
longe omnibus unum anteferre Demos-
thenen; ib. 38 fatetur; Leg. 3, 45 de
quo servi et latrones scivisse aliquid
dicerent; Tusc. 2, 40 ferre non posse
clamabit; Fam. 4, 13, 6 omnes vias per-
sequar quibus putabo ad id quod
volumus pervenire posse (so Tyrr.).
Flacc. 85 ...non debuisse (sc. *eum*) but
Flacc. is in prec. sent. When the pronominal accusative which would go
with the infinitive already stands in the
same case in a preceding clause it is very
natural that it should be left out. So
div. in Caec. 59 dicturum te esse audio,
quaestorem illius fuisse; De Or. 3, 147
vel me licet existimes desperare ista
posse perdiscere; ib. 18 an me tam im-
pudentem esse existimatis ut vobis hoc
praesertim munus putem diutius posse
debere? (Here Wilkins reads *putem me,*
other recent edd. keep to the MSS.) Tusc.
1, 60 and Fam. 3, 8, 2. In all these exx. (so
far as they come within his volumes of
the Teubner text) Müller has inserted
the pronoun, or otherwise changed, exc.
Tusc. 1, 60. The number of places in
Cicero's letters to Atticus in which the
MSS. omit the pronoun, while the edd.
generally give it, is considerable: Att.
1, 7; 11, 24, 5 (P. inserts *te*, though it is
just like 1, 7); 2, 16, 2 (*se* Boot) and T.

vivere? Quid turpius quam sapientis vitam ex insipientium
sermone pendere? Quid ergo hoc loco intellegit honestum? Certe
nihil nisi quod possit ipsum propter se iure laudari. Nam si
propter voluptatem, quae est ista laus, quae possit e macello
peti? Non is vir est, ut, cum honestatem eo loco habeat, ut sine 5
ea iucunde neget posse vivi, illud honestum, quod populare sit,
sentiat et sine eo neget iucunde vivi posse, aut quicquam aliud
honestum intellegat, nisi quod sit rectum ipsumque per se, sua
vi, sua sponte, sua natura laudabile.

51 XVI. Itaque, Torquate, cum diceres clamare Epicurum non 10
posse iucunde vivi, nisi honeste et sapienter et iuste viveretur,
tu ipse mihi gloriari videbare. Tanta vis inerat in verbis propter
earum rerum, quae significabantur his verbis, dignitatem, ut
altior fieres, ut interdum insisteres, ut nos intuens quasi testificarere laudari honestatem et iustitiam aliquando ab Epicuro. 15
Quam te decebat eis verbis uti quibus si philosophi non uterentur,
philosophia omnino non egeremus! Istorum enim verborum

1 ex: *et* B.　　　2 sermone pendere: *pendere sermone* B.　　　3 nam si: *non si* B.
5 peti: *petitur* B.　　　5 ut, cum: *et cum* B.　　　6 quod populare sit: *propter*
populare sic B.　　　7 iucunde: *iocunde* AB.　　　9 sua sponte, sua natura: *sua*
natura, suā sponte B.　　　14 testificarere: ita A²; *testificare* A¹; *testificari* B.
16 decebat: ita A²; *dicebat* A¹B.　　　16 eis: *his* AB; corr. Baiter.　　　16 non:
om. B.

in a sentence where the reflexive occurs
several times in the same sentence. There
is good reason to suppose that Cicero
sometimes omitted the pronominal subject before the fut. inf.; for this see note
on 5, 31. This fact renders the mss.
lections more tolerable in some passages
where at first sight they are strange, as
Har. resp. 7 cogitet esse consecratum
Miloni (M esse se); Quinct. 59 inferiorem
esse patitur; but cannot be said to
remove doubt.

1. **quid turpius:** sc. *est.*

4. **macello:** Div. 2, 59 si Epicuri liber
de voluptate rosus esset, putarem anno-
nam in macello cariorem fore. The
fauces macelli was the haunt of fast men:
Verr. 2, 3, 145; Quinct. 25.

5. **non is vir est,** etc.: an argumentum
ad hominem from his character.

ut...ut: the same repetition in 3, 43.

10. **clamare:** cf. § 65 and *vociferari,*
as used by Lucret. 1, 733.

12. **videbare:** in the 2nd pers. sing.
pass. and dep. *-ris* predominates so
greatly in our mss. as to lead to the
probability that Cicero employed it
exclusively; in the pres. subj. and im-

perf. indic. and subj. and in fut. ind. *-re*
is the commoner ending of the two. See
Neue-Wagener, III, 202 sq.

13. **dignitatem:** cf. 3, 1.

14. **altior:** cf. Liv. 30, 32, 11 celsus
haec corpore voltuque ita laeto ut
vicisse iam crederes dicebat; 7, 16, 5
celsi et spe haud dubia feroces; Val. F.
2, 547 celsior armis taurus (after a
victory); Stat. s. 1, 2, 7 Elegea...celsior
assueto; V. Aen. 6, 49 maiorque videri
(of the Sibyl possessed by inspiration).
[Altiores is a false reading in Acad. 2,
127; see my note there.]

interdum insisteres: a sign of excite-
ment, as in Sil. 10, 154 at fessus mae-
rore simul cursuque metuque | et tamen
haud irae vacuus non certa per aequor |
interdum insistens Perusinus membra
ferebat; cf. Leg. 1, 15 crebro insistens;
Div. 2, 128 numquam animus insistens;
also § 119 finem fecimus et ambulandi et
disputandi (with note).

17. **verborum:** for the stress laid on
names cf. note on 2, 13; below § 67; De
Or. 1, 120 impudentiae nomen effugere
(wrongly suspected by some edd.); Off.
3, 57 vitiorum nomina subire.

amore, quae perraro appellantur ab Epicuro, sapientiae, fortitudinis, iustitiae, temperantiae, praestantissimis ingeniis homines
se ad philosophiae studium contulerunt. 'Oculorum,' inquit 52
Plato, 'est in nobis sensus acerrimus, quibus sapientiam non
5 cernimus. Quam illa ardentis amores excitaret sui!' Cur
tandem? an quod ita callida est, ut optime possit architectari
voluptates? Cur iustitia laudatur aut unde est hoc contritum
vetustate proverbium: 'quicum in tenebris'? Hoc dictum in
una re latissime patet, ut in omnibus factis re, non teste move-
10 amur. Sunt enim levia et perinfirma quae dicebantur a te, animi 53
conscientia improbos excruciari, tum etiam poenae timore, qua
aut afficiantur aut semper sint in metu ne afficiantur aliquando.
Non oportet timidum aut imbecillo animo fingi non bonum illum
virum, qui, quicquid fecerit, ipse se cruciet omniaque formidet,
15 sed omnia callide referentem ad utilitatem, acutum, versutum,

4 acerrimus: *acerrimis* A¹.   5 *si videretur* add. dett. post *sui*.   6 an quod...volup-
tates: affert Nonius, p. 70.   6 callida est: *classidas* Nonius.   11 etiam: *enim* B.
11 qua aut: ita A²; *qua ut* A¹B.   13 oportet: *omnem* E. Fort. in archetypo vel ō
vel *ōtet* scriptum erat, ut in codice Veronensi Gai, quod E male interpretatus est.
13 imbecillo: *inbecilli* B.   14 quicquid: ita A; *quicquam* B.   15 versutum:
versatum E.

1. **quae perraro**, etc.: this is probably
a libel on Epicurus. See De Nat. D.
1 §§ 115, 123.
appellantur: § 29 *n*.
sapientiae: =φρονήσεως, note on 1, 42,
sapientia quae ars vivendi...est.
4. **Plato**: Phaedr. 250 D ὄψις γὰρ
ἡμῖν ὀξυτάτη τῶν διὰ σώματος ἔρχεται
αἰσθήσεων, ᾗ φρόνησις οὐχ ὁρᾶται· δεινοὺς
γὰρ ἂν παρείχεν ἔρωτας εἴ τι τοιοῦτον
ἑαυτῆς ἐναργὲς εἴδωλον παρείχετο εἰς
ὄψιν ἰόν. Translated also, a little
more carelessly, in Off. 1, 15: formam ipsam et tamquam faciem honesti
vides, quae si oculis cerneretur, mira-
biles amores, ut ait Plato, excitaret
sapientiae; Sen. ep. 115, 3; 89, 1
utinam, quemadmodum universa mundi
facies in conspectum venit, ita philosophia tota nobis possit occurrere, simil-
limum mundo spectaculum. profecto
enim omnes mortales in admirationem
sui raperet relictis eis, quae nunc magna
magnorum ignoratio credimus.
sensus acerrimus: see illustrations
of this from Aristotle and others in my
note on Acad. 2, 20 and add Hor. A. P.
180 (sight keener than hearing); Sen.
ep. 6, 5 (the same); id. 124, 5 refers to
Epic. subtilior adhuc acies nulla quam
oculorum et intentior; Chalcid. in Tim.

c. 226 mentions Stoics who called God
vision (deum visum vocantes). Sen.
N.Q. 2, 12, 6 qu. from Aristotle applies
this to explain the fact that the eye
sees lightning before the ear perceives
thunder.
6. **architectari**: note on 1, 32: 1, 42
(artifex).
7. **contritum v. proverbium**: the
same phrase in Off. 3, 77, applied to
same proverb, *quicum in tenebris*; for
which cf. Petr. 44 cum quo audacter
posses in tenebris micare; Fronto, p. 13,
Nab. aliud scurrarum proverbium: en
cum quo in tenebris mices; Aug. de trin.
8, 5. *Micare* was sometimes an alternative for drawing lots; Off. 3, 90;
Suet. Aug. 13. Cf. 3 § 38 and Sen. ben.
2, 10, 3.
9. **re, non teste**: note on § 28 hominum conscientia.
11. **tum etiam**: 'nec memini, *tum* sic
posito, non praecedente *cum*, addi
etiam' (Madvig ed. 1869). In ed. 1876
he gives Leg. 1, 35, and N D. 1, 43 (the
latter due to Allen).
qua...afficiantur: cf. *possit* in 2, 43.
13. **non bonum**: so Acad. 2, 50; in
De Or. 1, 118 the *mali* and the *non boni*
are compared; cf. § 11 non dolendo.
15. **callide...versutum**: Cicero, N.D.

vēteratorem, facile ut excogitet, quo modo occulte, sine teste,
54 sine ullo conscio fallat. An tu me de L. Tubulo putas dicere?
Qui cum praetor quaestionem inter sicarios exercuisset, ita aperte
cepit pecunias ob rem iudicandam, ut anno proximo P. Scaevola

1 excogitet: *excogitare* B.   2 L.: *lucio* ABP.   3 ita: *itaque* B.

3, 25 versutos eos appello quorum
celeriter mens versatur; callidos autem
quorum, tamquam manus opere, sic
animus usu concalluit.

2. de L. Tubulo: the story is obscure.
L. Hostilius Tubulus was praetor in
142 B.C., seven years after the Calpur-
nian law had established the first per-
manent criminal court, the *quaestio
repetundarum*. Cicero speaks as if by
142 the *quaestio inter sicarios* had been
established, with a magistrate as president for the year. There is no proof of
this elsewhere; and, indeed, a passage
of Ascon. in Mil. § 32 (p. 46) makes it
probable that some years later, even if
such a court had been organised, it had
no regular magistrate or even substitute allotted to it. It is known that
under the law of Sulla a judge who took
a bribe in a case of murder became
liable to the same punishment as a
murderer (Clu. 90; Dig. 48, 8, 1 pr.).
Under the *lex repetundarum* the bribed
judge was liable. But in this case
Tubulus is punished by a *quaestio extra
ordinem*; the process by which this
quaestio was started closely resembles
that by which a court was set up in 172
to try M. Popillius (Liv. 42, 21, 2) and,
indeed, seems to have been the usual proceeding. See Madvig. As to the course
of the trial and its issue Ascon. p. 23 has
a story obviously unknown to Cicero.
The comment (which is on a passage of
pro Scaur. 5, in which T. is called 'unum
ex omni memoria sceleratissimum et
audacissimum') runs thus: 'L. hic
Tubulus praetorius fuit aetate patrum
Ciceronis. Is propter multa flagitia cum
de exilio accersitus esset, ne in carcere
necaretur, venenum bibit.' The special
quaestio over rode *provocatio* according to
Mommsen Staatsr. II, p. 110, but he says
this is not exemplified in the case of
Tubulus because he was treated as *exul*.
Mommsen seems to have misunderstood
Ascon. who means 'summoned in a case
involving the penalty of exile.' Mommsen takes it to mean 'called back from
exile,' cf. Strafrecht, p. 71 *n.*; de le-
gatione revocatus in Att. 4, 15, 9. The
other passages of Cicero where Tubulus
is mentioned are below, 4, 77 and 5, 62;

N.D. 1, 63 'Tubulus si Lucius umquam,
si Lupus aut Carbo, Neptuni filius,' ut
ait Lucilius, putasset esse deos, tam
periurus aut tam impurus fuisset; ib. 3,
74; Scaur. 5; Gell. 2, 7, 20 classes
Catiline, Clodius and Tubulus together.
Asconius seems to have confused Tubulus with Carbo the friend of the Gracchi,
who is mentioned along with him by
Lucilius. See Brut. 103; Fam. 9, 21, 3.
The references to Tubulus in Cicero
show that his story was well known at
the time and no error could have been
made about his death. The Scaevola
who proposed the bill for the *quaestio*
was the one afterwards known as
pontifex.

3. cum...exercuisset...cepit: the
plup. is hard to explain. Madvig refers to
Cato m. 41 haec cum C. Pontio...locu-
tum Archytam, Nearchus Tarentinus
se a maioribus natu accepisse dicebat,
cum quidem ei sermoni interfuisset
Plato. But the tense is accommodated
(as Madvig himself indicates) not to
locutum but to *dicebat*; a similar explanation applies to Verr. act. pr. 13 and to
Liv. 38, 58, 9 (in or. obl.) forte ita inci-
disse ut, quo die ad Magnesiam L. Scipio
Antiochum devicisset, aeger P. Scipio...
abesset; and to 42, 33, 3 id tantum
deprecari ne inferiores eis ordines quam
quos, cum militassent, habuissent. The
other passage given by M. is Liv. 32, 26, 2
cum duos exercitus in provincia hab-
uisset...totum prope annum...consump-
sit, is as hard as ours. It seems most
likely that Cicero wrote *ceperat*. If
ceperat had been written *exercuisset*
would have been intelligible. Possibly
one bribe received by Tub. was in
question and he may have received it,
to save appearances, after the decision
[but Cicero credits him with no desire
to save appearances].

4. ob rem iudicandam: apart from
ob eam rem, quam ob rem (rarely *quas
ob res*), *quam ob causam*, and the like,
Cicero rarely uses *ob* of purpose excepting in legal phrases. Mur. 1 ob
consulatum obtinendum, is a rare exception; cf. too Font. 17. I doubt
whether *ob hoc* in Caec. 73 is sound;
after the time of Cicero and Caes. such

tribunus plebis ferret ad plebem, vellentne de ea re quaeri. Quo
plebiscito decreta a senatu est consuli quaestio Cn.
Caepioni; profectus in exsilium Tubulus statim nec respondere ausus; erat
enim res aperta.

5 XVII. Non igitur de improbo, sed *de* callido improbo quaerimus, qualis Q. Pompeius in foedere Numantino infitiando fuit,
nec vero omnia timente, sed primum qui animi conscientiam
non curet, quam scilicet comprimere nihil est negoti. Is enim qui
occultus et tectus dicitur, tantum abest ut se indicet, perficiet
10 etiam, ut dolere alterius improbe facto videatur. Quid est enim

1 tribunus plebis: *TR. PL.* AB.   1 ferret: *ferrent* B.   2 Caepioni: ita
A et cod. Morelianus; *scipioni* B; *C. N. Scipioni* P.   3 ausus: ita codd.; *ausus
est* ed. Romana, Baiter.   5 sed de callido: *sed callido* AB; *de* om. codd.
exceptis Lincolniensi et dett. nonnullis.   6 foedere: *fodere* A; *federe* B.
7 timente: *timentē* A; *timentem* B; corr. Lambinus.   9 tectus: *rectus* B.
10 etiam: ita A; *et* B.   10 improbe: ita B; *improbo* A et Crat.

expressions (*ob id, ob quod,* etc.) became
common, and *ob hoc* might easily have
been inserted in Caec. l.l.

1. **quo pleb.**: 'in consequence of'; so
1, 63 *ea scientia*; below § 66 hic dolor =
d. hinc ortus.

3. **profectus**: for the omission of *est*
cf. § 55 contraque....

5. **sed de**: *de* only given by inferior codd.
callido improbo: the attachment of
an adj. to a nominalised adj. or part.
is not uncommon in Cicero; so Att.
12, 21, 5 fortis aegroti; Ad Herenn.
2, 32 paupere improbo; Verr. 2, 4, 89
improbi praesentis; Lael. 54 insipiente
fortunato; Q. Fr. 1, 3, 1 spirantis
mortui; Phil. 11, 20 nihil agenti pri-
vato; cf. too Publil. 103 (ed. Bickford-
Smith) intemperans aeger; Liv. 4, 48, 13
privatum inopem; Sen. ben. 4, 10, 5
pauperi viro bono (ib. ep. 66, 21);
Sen. Rh. contr. 2, 1, 28 novicio divite;
Pers. 3, 83 aegroti veteris. Phrases such
as malum publicum, bonum publicum,
pessimum publicum, nonnulli nostri
iniqui, etc. are common. Planc. ap.
Fam. 10, 8, 4 boni civis imparati.

6. **Q. Pompeius**: the story, as Madvig remarks, testifies to *impudentia*
rather than *calliditas*. As Cicero is
moralising here, he might have stated
that nine years afterwards this man
was entrusted with the care of Roman
morals, being appointed censor.
infitiando: the connexion with *fateri*
is sometimes emphasised, as Part. or. 50
multi...mori maluerint falsum fatendo
quam verum infitiando dolere; Sest. 40
infitiando confiteri. The spelling found in

old edd., *inficiae, inficiari,* is of course
erroneous.

7. **omnia timente**: a common end-
phrase (seven exx. in speeches) but
omnia timuimus is pronounced 'uner-
träglich' by O. E. Schmidt in Att. 11,
23, 3 (N.J. 1897 and Rh. M. 1898).

primum: *deinde* should follow; the
anacoluthon is picked up § 57 deprehensus omnem poenam contemnet. Erit
enim....

9. **tantum abest ut...perficiet**: excepting in a few passages, confined to
Cicero, *tantum abest ut* is followed by a
second *ut*; there is another ex. of the
independent clause below, 5, 57; cf. also
Brut. 278; Att. 13, 21, 5. A rare (and
older) form is *tantum abest ab eo ut...ut*;
Tusc. 1, 76; Liv. 25, 6, 11. With *ab eo*,
abest still remains impersonal, but if a
noun with *ab* follows, it becomes personal as in Brut. 156; Off. 1, 43; Marc.
25, and then, of course, no second *ut*
succeeds. A rare form is *tantum abest ne
...ut*, found in Or. 229 (MSS. but edd.
mostly write *ut*).

10. **improbe facto**: as Madvig says, it
is unlikely that copyists would substitute this for *improbo f.*; cf. too 57
improbe fecit. A few expressions like
recte factum, male factum, bene parta
(*male admissa,* Tac. dial. 12) are common; apart from these the combination
of an adverb with a nominalised passive
participle, though rare, is well attested.
Editors have sometimes erred in oblit-
erating the usage; thus the MSS. reading
in Lucr. 5, 1224 nequod ob admissum
foede dictumve superbe is, I believe,

55 aliud esse versutum? Memini me adesse P. Sextilio Rufo, cum is rem ad amicos ita deferret, se esse heredem Q. Fadio Gallo, cuius in testamento scriptum esset se ab eo rogatum, ut omnis

1 Rufo: *fuso* A.   2 Fadio: *fabio* ABP (AE tamen recte habent *fadiae* in § 55 et *fadius* in § 58).

sound; *admissum* is a noun, even in Cicero, Part. Or. 120, and so *ne quod* can agree with it, but it retains so much of its verbal character as to justify the attachment of the adverb. It may be doubted whether Lucretius would have employed the construction: ob *plus* nominal acc. *plus* passive participle. The first certain example of the usage seems to be in Sall. Jug. 79, 7 ob rem corruptam domi. With the Lucretian line cf. Cic. Sull. 72 ecquod est huius factum aut commissum, non dicam audacius, sed quod cuiquam paulo minus consideratum videretur? Lael. 6 multa eius...vel provisa prudenter, vel acta constanter, vel responsa acute ferebantur; Nep. Timoth. 1, 2 multa sunt huius praeclare facta.

quid est aliud, etc.: note on § 16.

1. **memini me adesse:** in my note on Lael. 2 I wrote: 'if the person who recalls an event was a witness of it, he may either (*a*) vividly picture to himself the event and its attendant circumstances so that it becomes really present to his mind's eye for the moment, in which case he uses the present infinitive, or (*b*) he may simply recall the *fact* that the event *did* take place, in which case the perfect infinitive is used. If he was not a witness he evidently can conceive the event only in the latter of these two ways.' In colloquial English, the difference is the same between 'I remember going' and 'I remember that I went.' The perf. inf. of personal experiences grows commoner, I think, in the later Latin; so Sen. clem. 2, 1, 1; 5, 24, 1; ep. 11, 4; 75, 9; 95, 26; Quint. 9, 4, 90; 10, 3, 12; Plin. ep. 2, 14, 10. There is the same distinction between *vidi* with pres. and perf. inf. (Cael. 28 vidi...emersisse).

2. **rem...deferret:** Madvig notes that the expression *res defertur* is commonly employed of something already mentioned. But he quotes Verr. 2, 1, 64 is ad eum rem istam defert, Philodamum esse quendam, etc.; C. F. W. Müller compares *rem temptare* in Liv. 1, 57, 3; 2, 35, 4; Hor. ep. 2, 1, 164; for referre, deferre rem, cf. Verr. 2. 4 § 85.

Fadio: the dat. with *heres* was re-tained, when similar datives, common in old Latin, had been replaced by genitives. The parallels in Cicero are nearly all in legal or official phrases like *tutor liberis, legatus consuli.* Thus Cat. 2, 11 huic ego me bello ducem profiteor, is a rarity. After Cicero's time, the older usage was revived by the archaists; see Landgraf in Archiv 8, 66 sq. [The phrase *accusatorem filio suo* occurs thrice in Clu. 190–2; but I take it to be an error induced, as often, by the ignorance of the scribes about the true form of the gen. *fili.*]

3. **omnis hereditas:** Fadius was intended by the testator to be merely nominal *heres*, bound privately to hand over the property to the daughter who, by the Voconian statute, could not be instituted *heres*. Scholars have usually inferred from this passage that the courts at the time did not enforce, as they did at a later time, an agreement between the testator and the *heres* to defeat the statute. In this case the agreement was not provable by independent evidence so that the inference is not quite certain. The words indicate that such agreements were usual (*quod debuisset rogare*) and that if definite proof had existed, custom if not law was strong enough to compel Sextilius to surrender the property (*hunc mentiri cuius interesset*). The passage also shows that the statute aimed at preventing a woman from succeeding to more than a certain proportion of an estate; this proportion is stated by Ps. Quint. decl. 264 to have been half. As Cicero says *omnis hereditas* and not *hereditas* merely, it is natural to suppose that the will mentioned the daughter and bestowed on her as much as the statute permitted. But many scholars have assumed that she stood to get either all or nothing. Whether the lex Voconia restricted a woman's right of succession when there was no will, is a much disputed question. It is natural to suppose that in the present case Fadia was an only daughter. Unless the statute prevented it, Fadius might simply have refrained from making a will, in which circumstances his

hereditas ad filiam perveniret.   Id Sextilius factum negabat.
Poterat autem impune; quis enim redargueret? Nemo nostrum
credebat, eratque veri similius hunc mentiri, cuius interesset,
quam illum, qui id se rogasse scripsisset, quod debuisset rogare.
5 Addebat etiam se in legem Voconiam iuratum contra eam facere
non audere, nisi aliter amicis videretur. Aderamus nos quidem
adulescentes, sed multi amplissimi viri, quorum nemo censuit
plus Fadiae dandum, quam posset ad eam lege Voconia pervenire.
Tenuit permagnam Sextilius hereditatem, unde, si secutus esset
10 eorum sententiam, qui honesta et recta emolumentis omnibus
et commodis anteponerent, nummum nullum attigisset. Num
igitur eum postea censes anxio animo aut sollicito fuisse? Nihil
minus, contraque illa hereditate dives ob eamque rem laetus.
Magni enim aestimabat pecuniam non modo non contra leges,
5 sed etiam legibus partam; quae quidem vel cum periculo est
quaerenda vobis. Est enim effectrix multarum et magnarum
voluptatum. Vt igitur illis qui, recta et honesta quae sunt, ea **56**
statuunt per se expetenda, adeunda sunt quaevis pericula decoris
honestatisque causa, sic vestris, qui omnia voluptate metiuntur,
20 pericula adeunda sunt, ut adipiscantur magnas voluptates. Si
magna res, magna hereditas agetur, cum pecunia voluptates
pariantur plurimae, idem erit Epicuro vestro faciendum, si suum
finem bonorum sequi volet, quod Scipioni magna gloria proposita,
si Hannibalem in Africam retraxisset. Itaque quantum adiit

1 Sextilius factum: *factum Sextilius* B.   2 redargueret: *redarguet* A¹.   3 hunc:
hanc B.   4 id: om. B.   13 eamque: *eam* B.   18 quaevis: ita codd. aliquot;
ceu A (correctum, ut videtur, ex *seu*); *sepe* B.   22 pariantur: *periantur* A¹.
22 idem: ita codd. aliquot; *idemque* AB.   22 vestro: *nescio* E.

object would have been accomplished. Perhaps the will contained other provisions
which the *heres* was to carry out before
handing over the estate to the daughter.
The case mentioned in § 58 should be
taken into account. The lady there was
surprised that S. Peduc. handed over to
her what he had a right to keep. This cannot surely have been the *whole* property?

5. **se in legem iuratum:** Madvig says
that this can only mean that Sextilius
had been a magistrate and had taken
the customary oath to obey the whole
body of statutes. But it is possible that,
when trying some case under the Voconian law, S. had taken an oath to
observe it. Cicero several times speaks
as if the taking of oaths to observe
particular statutes were not uncommon;
so Clu. 91–6, esp. 92 si in aliquam legem

aliquando non iuraverat; Sest. 61 quasi
vero ille non in alias quoque leges iam
ante iuraverit.

6. **nisi aliter:** see n. to 1, 28 nisi molestum est.

7. **sed multi:** after *nos quidem, etiam*
is not needed.

11. **attigisset:** Qu. Rosc. 35 si quid
communi nomine tetigit (of money).

13. **dives:** for the omission of *erat* see
n. on 1, 3. But the construction of the
abl. *illa* hereditate is strange. Has *factus*
fallen out after *dives*?

16. **est enim,** etc.: Epict. d. 3, 7, 15
ὁ πλοῦτος δὲ ἀγαθόν, καὶ οἱονανεὶ τὸ ποιη-
τικώτατόν γε τῶν ἡδονῶν· διὰ τί μὴ περι-
ποιήσῃ αὐτόν;

17. **quae sunt:** for the postponement of
the relative in the clause cf. 2, 86; 4, 45?

24. **itaque:** i.e. gloria proposita.

periculum! ad honestatem enim illum omnem conatum suum re-
ferebat, non ad voluptatem. Sic vester sapiens magno aliquo emolumento commotus pecuniae cum causa, si opus erit, dimicabit
57 Occultum facinus esse potuerit, gaudebit; deprehensus omnem
poenam contemnet. Erit enim instructus ad mortem contem- 5
nendam, ad exsilium, ad ipsum etiam dolorem. Quem quidem
vos, cum improbis poenam proponitis, impetibilem facitis, cum
sapientem semper boni plus habere voltis, tolerabilem.
XVIII. Sed finge non solum callidum eum, qui aliquid im-

3 cum causa, si: ita AB; vid. comm.; *animi causa* codd. nonnulli.   3 erit: ita
ABE; *fuerit* Madv.   6 quem: *quam* B.

3. cum causa...dimicabit: 'cum ipsa
causa indicata sit (*magno aliquo emolumento commotus*) universe dicere *cum
causa*, hoc est, non sine causa (II De
Orat. 247, in Verr. 2, 1, 21) dimicaturum
sapientem Epicureum, perversum est;
nec, cum causa an sine causa, sed quid
omnino paratus sit facere, quaeritur.'
These objections of Madvig seem to
have been accepted by all succeeding
scholars who have dealt with the
passage; but I venture to think that
they are unsound. In the first place,
there seems to be a fallacy in the
phrase *universe*; it is true that *cum causa*
refers to the general principle that one
must have reason to fight, but this
general principle is introduced in the
closest connexion with the special
statement. One cannot see why Cicero
should not say that the hope of great
gain is good reason for fighting. It is
true that the words *cum causa* might
have been dispensed with, but there is
nothing unnatural in their addition:
'excited by the hope of some great gain,
he will fight with good reason.' Again,
the assertion that the question here is
not whether the *sapiens* will fight with
or without reason, but whether he will
fight at all, seems to be most arbitrary.
This argument, if pressed, would tell
just as much against the words *magno...
commotus* and *si opus erit* as against
cum causa. For *cum causa* De Or. 2, 247;
Q. Fr. 1, 2, 6; Verr. 2, 1, 21; Cael. 68;
Varro r.r. 1, 17, 4; 3, 16, 7; Ad Herenn.
2, 45; ib. 2, 2, 5; Tac. an. 13, 37 uses
causā alone; Ovid, Her. 19 (20), 140
per causam, 'having a good excuse'; so
also *cum ratione facere aliquid* (Cic.;
Ad Herenn., and others). [Of the
numerous emendations Moritz Haupt's
cum Medusa is the most curious.]

4. potuerit, gaudebit: this seems to
be on the same pattern as Graeculus
esuriens in caelum, iusseris, ibit (Juven.
3, 78). For exx. from Cicero and others
see Kühner, Gram. 2, p. 760.
5. instructus ad: so De Or. 3, 31;
Verr. 2, 4, 41; Pl. Bacch. 373 omnis ad
perniciem instructa domus; Ter. Haut.
450 quam ea nunc instructa pulchre ad
perniciem siet; etc.
7. impetibilem: *passibilis* and *im-
passibilis* belong to the Ecclesiastical
writers; *impetibilis* and *patibilis* ('en-
durable' in Tusc. 4, 51, but in N.D.
3, 29 *natura patibilis*=παθητικὴ οὐσία)
were probably invented by Cicero. In
early Latin the termination -*bilis* was
attached to the stem of the verb, not to
that of the participle; so *ascendibilis*
(Pomp.) while *ascensibilis* is late; *odibilis*
(Accius, Varro); *conducibile* is given in
Plaut. Trin. 25 by *ABCD*; in 36 rightly
by *A* where *BCD* have *conductibile*. Ad
Herenn. 2, 21 *conducibile*. In Cic. Acad.
1, 41 *comprehendibile* is the right reading; *comprehensibilis* does not occur till
Sen. n. q. 6, 24, 1; *incomprehensibilis* is
in Colum. Plin. Sen. The only two words
in Cicero formed differently are *flexi-
bilis*, *plausibilis*; the latter only in Div.
in Caec. 8 and Tusc. 3, 51. Varro has
alibilis, *restibilis*. Some curious words
of the kind appear in late Latin, as
docibilis, *dicibile*=ῥητόν, C. Gl. Lat. 2,
p. 48, l. 41; *discernibilis* (Aug.). The
termination -*ilis* was attached to the
participial stem quite early (*altilis*, *sen-
silis*, *missilis*).
8. semper boni plus: see 5, 93.
9. callidum: Tyrrell says on Att.
1, 16, 5 that Crassus is here put forward
as the type of the *callidus*; but Crassus
here illustrates *praepotentem* not *callidum*
and is on the same plane as Pompeius.

probe faciat, verum etiam praepotentem, ut M. Crassus fuit, qui tamen solebat uti suo bono, ut hodie est noster Pompeius, cui recte facienti gratia est habenda; esse enim quam vellet inicus poterat impune. Quam multa vero iniuste fieri possunt quae nemo possit reprehendere! Si te amicus tuus moriens rogaverit **58** ut hereditatem reddas suae filiae, nec usquam id scripserit, ut scripsit Fadius, nec cuiquam dixerit, quid facies? Tu quidem reddes; ipse Epicurus fortasse redderet, ut Sex. Peducaeus, Sexti filius, is qui hunc nostrum reliquit effigiem et humanitatis et

1 qui tamen: ins. *non* Cobet. (Mnemosyne, 1880, p. 191).   2 noster: *vester* B. 3 inicus: *iniquus iustus* A.   6 suae filiae: ita A; *filiae suae* B.   7 ut scripsit: om. cod. Morel.   7 Fadius: *foedus* cod. Morel.   7 quid: *quod* B.

2. **uti**:=give rein to, indulge, cf. Vell. 2, 52, 2 usus impetu suo='indulging his natural impetuosity.' Att. 2, 1, 8 optimo animo utens. Fam. 2, 16, 6 utor aetatis vitio. **suo bono**: what is this? As Madvig says, it cannot be *potentia*, because of *tamen*; for this reason, doubtless, Cobet in Mnemosyne (1880) added *non* after *tamen*. Madvig makes *bono=pecunia*; but this is far from satisfactory; the *potentia* rested on the money and Cicero could hardly say that Crassus used the one, not the other; nor can he have intended to assert either of Crassus or of Pompey, that he did not make use of his *potentia* at all. Moreover, Cicero does not intend to be uncomplimentary here to Crassus, any more than to Pompeius (who is *bonitatis eximiae*, Sen. dial. 10, 13, 6). Cf. Vell. P. 2, 46, 2 Crasso,...qui vir cetera sanctissimus immunisque voluptatibus neque in pecunia neque in gloria concupiscenda aut modum norat aut capiebat terminum. The word *bono* must be used for *bonum animi* as in Marc. 19 gaude tuo tam excellenti bono; Fam. 6, 5, 3 ne punctum quidem temporis in ista fortuna fuisses nisi eo ipso bono tuo, quo delectatur, se violatum putasset (see the context); Cael. 11 qui se...naturali quodam bono defenderet; Sen. ep. 13 § 15; Nep. Thras. 1, 3 quae ille universa naturali quodam bono fecit lucri; Cicero, Off. 1, 114 suum quisque igitur noscat ingenium, acremque se et bonorum et vitiorum suorum iudicem praebeat; Liv. 7, 6, 3; 35, 43, 1; C.I.L. 3, 1759 eximiumque bonum corporis atque animi; Hieron. ep. 1, 5 (Migne) conscientiae bono fruitur. [Ov.] Her. 21, 37 nunc laudata gemo, nunc me certamine vestro perditis, et proprio vulneror ipsa bono. Here, therefore,

suo bono is not like *sua bona* in 'o fortunati nimium sua si bona norint,' and bonis suis obsessus. Sen. ep. 19, 11; 7, 12 bona tua; 13, 15; 26, 2 bono suo utatur; 71, 8; 75, 9; 76, 10; 93, 2. *Bonum* and *bona* may indicate blessings of any kind, bodily, mental, or external, or a combination of these; cf. N.D. 1, 103 utatur suis bonis oportet qui beatus futurus est; Fam. 15, 14, 3 bono litterarum utemur; Cato m. 33; Tusc. 5, 27; naturae bono (Sen. d. 4, 15, 2); utuntur natura sua (bad), Sen. ben. 1, 1, 9; ex bono suo ortis, Sen. d. 7, 4, 5; C.I.L. 6, 1779 (Bücheler, c. ep. 111, 22) disciplinarum bono; Petron. 75 (Büch.) bonum tuum concoquas; Phaedr. 1, 2, 30 qui noluistis vestrum ferre, inquit, bonum malum perferte; Tac. dial.41 bono saeculi sui. For the opposite phrase cf. Vell. P. 1, 6, 2 Sardanapalum...nimium felicem malo suo; Hieron. ep. 22 § 24 naturali ducimur malo; Brut. 130 naturale quoddam stirpis bonum; ib. 234; Persius 2, 63 et bona dis ex hac scelerata ducere pulpa.

noster Pompeius: the illusion of the dialogue is kept up; see Vell. P. 2, 29, 4 potentia sua numquam aut raro ad impotentiam usus (of P.).

3. **quam vellet**: for the so-called 'potential subjunctive' see n. on velit in 3, 65.

8. **Peducaeus**: the elder was the praetor to whom Cicero was attached as quaestor in Sicily; the younger was a close friend of Cicero and Atticus.

9. **effigiem**: so Phil. 9, 12 nullum monumentum clarius Ser. Sulpicius relinquere potuit quam effigiem morum suorum, virtutis constantiae pietatis ingeni filium; Fam. 6, 6, 13; Liv. 5, 18, 5; 26, 41, 24.

probitatis suae filium, cum doctus, tum omnium vir optimus et
iustissimus, cum sciret nemo eum rogatum a C. Plotio, equite
Romano splendido, Nursino, ultro ad mulierem venit eique nihil
opinanti viri mandatum exposuit hereditatemque reddidit. Sed
ego ex te quaero, quoniam idem tu certe fecisses, nonne intellegas
eo maiorem vim esse naturae, quod ipsi vos qui omnia ad vestrum
commodum et, ut ipsi dicitis, ad voluptatem referatis, tamen ea
faciatis, e quibus appareat non voluptatem vos, sed officium
sequi, plusque rectam naturam quam rationem pravam valere.

59 Si scieris, inquit Carneades, aspidem occulte latere uspiam, et
velle aliquem imprudentem super eam assidere, cuius mors tibi
emolumentum futura sit, improbe feceris, nisi monueris ne
assidat; sed impunite tamen; scisse enim te quis coarguere
possit? Sed nimis multa. Perspicuom est enim, nisi aequitas,

---

2 cum sciret: *tum sciret* E.   2 C.: *Gaio* AB.   3 Nursino: *mirsino* A¹.
7 et, ut ipsi: *et ipsi ut* B.   9 plusque rectam: *plus quam rectam* B.   12 emolumentum futura: ita AB Crat. cod. Morel.; *emolumentum factura* Orelli cum cod.
Glogavensi; *emolumento futura* duo codd. Oxonienses.   12 ne: *eum ne* B.
13 assidat: ita AB.   13 impunite: ita AB; *impune* Orelli.

---

2. **Plotio**: unknown.

3. **Romano...Nursino**: all *equites* were
Romani; sometimes the phrase *munici-*
palis eques, of one whose domicile is in a
municipium, is disparaging. Mayor on
Juven. 8, 238; Mommsen, Staatsr. III,
562 ff.

splendido: a mere social epithet,
since there were no technical distinctions of rank among the *equites* in
Cicero's time; on the evolution of distinctions under the Empire, and the use
of *splendidus, illustris*, etc., as applied
to the *eques*, see Mommsen, l.l.

nihil op.: a variant for *necop.*

4. **mandatum**: on the technical legal
use of the word see Roby in Dict. Ant.

5. **nonne intellegas**: Merguet's lexica
give five exx. of *nonne* in indirect question (dependent on *quaerere* in every
instance, so below, 3, 13); add Or. 214;
said by Draeger, § 467 e, not to occur
outside Cicero. In direct interrogation
nonne seems to be avoided by some
writers; Caes., Sall. and Tac. have it
once only; Sen. Rh. not at all.

6. **vim naturae**: § 28 n.

7. **commodum...voluptatem**: so § 61
utilitates...voluptates.

9. **plusque rectam naturam...valere**:
rather pleonastic after maiorem vim
naturae above.

10. **si scieris...feceris**: there can be no

reason for assuming (with Draeger 2,
p. 717, ed. 2) that *scieris* is perf. subj.

12. **emolumentum**: Roby [add *orna-*
mentum (several times in Cicero)], Gram.
2, p. xxix, gives exx. of nouns used in
nom. where predicative dat. is also
common; add to his list adiumentum,
Att. 12, 29, 2; exemplum, Liv. 8, 7, 17;
Ter. Ad. 771 (in MSS.); honos, Plin. n. h.
21, 11; religio, Liv. 6, 27, 4 and Plin.
n. h. 18 § 8, 19 § 133, 25 § 30. [There is
little authority for *veneno esse*; the text
of Varro, r.r. 1, 2, 18, gives it; but this
place is rendered suspicious by the fact
that we have *venenum* in other passages
of the r.r., viz. 1, 2, 20; 1, 45, 2; 1,
51, 1; and Plin. in two passages, viz.
16, 79 and 22, 78, couples *venenum est*
with a predicative dat. as though
veneno est did not exist; and in 24, 2
praesentaneo veneno is governed by *in*
to be supplied from the preceding clause.
It is therefore rash to write *veneno*
rather than *venenum* at the end of
Lucr. 1, 759 where MSS. have *vene* only
esp. as Lucr. has *venenum est* in 6, 97:
and 4, 637.]

13. **impunite**: 'miror cur hoc uno loco
Cicero hac forma usus sit, qua praete-
eum unus, qui supersit, Matius (ad Fam
xi, 28, 3)' (Madvig). It is perhaps more
likely that the copyists introduced *im-*
punite for *impune*, which one of Mendels

fides, iustitia proficiscantur a natura, et si omnia haec ad
utilitatem referantur, virum bonum non posse reperiri; deque
his rebus satis multa in nostris de re publica libris sunt dicta a
Laelio.

XIX. Transfer idem ad modestiam vel temperantiam, quae **60**
est moderatio cupiditatum rationi oboediens. Satisne ergo
pudori consulat, si quis sine teste libidini pareat? an est aliquid
per se ipsum flagitiosum, etiam si nulla comitetur infamia? Quid?
fortes viri voluptatumne calculis subductis proelium ineunt,
sanguinem pro patria profundunt, an quodam animi ardore
atque impetu concitati? Vtrum tandem censes, Torquate, Imperiosum illum, si nostra verba audiret, tuamne de se orationem
libentius auditurum fuisse an meam, cum ego dicerem nihil eum
fecisse sua causa omniaque rei publicae, tu contra nihil nisi sua?
Si vero id etiam explanare velles apertiusque diceres nihil eum
fecisse nisi voluptatis causa, quo modo eum tandem laturum fuisse
existimas? Esto, fecerit, si ita vis, Torquatus propter suas uti- **61**
litates (malo enim dicere quam voluptates, in tanto praesertim
viro); num etiam eius collega P. Decius, princeps in ea familia
consulatus, cum se devoverat et equo admisso in mediam aciem

---

5 vel...rationi: *vel cupiditatum temperantiam quae est moderatio rationi* B.
18 post *enim* addit *ita* Bremi; *sic* Klotz.   19 etiam: *et* B.   19 eius collega:
ita A; *collega eius* B.   20 devoverat; *devoveret* codd. et edd. nonnulli.

sohn's MSS. gives in the passage of Matius.

3. **dicta a Laelio:** in Rep. 3 he refutes
Philus who had rendered the argument
of Carneades to the effect that justice
is based on expediency.

5. **transfer idem:** cf. Lucr. 1, 870
transfer item; above § 14 transfer in
animum.

7. **consulat, si quis:** for *si quis* equivalent to ὅστις cf. n. on pro Sull. 31.

9. **voluptatum calculis:** cf. Lael. 58
exigue et exiliter amicitiam ad calculos
vocare; below, § 78.

11. **Imperiosum:** Cicero refers to the
T. Manlius who slew his son (see 1, 23)
and evidently attributed the cognomen
Imperiosus to that incident; and so
Liv. 4, 29, 6 and Front. Strat. 4, 1, 40;
also Claudius Quadrigarius ap. Gell.
9, 13, 20. But in 7, 4, 5 Livy says that
the father of this Manlius, viz. L. Manlius, earned the title by his cruelty to
this very T. Manlius. And the name
Imperiosus (or rather *Imperiossus*) is
attached to the father in the Fasti
Capitolini, under the years 391, 395
a. u. c., whereas the grandfather is
called Capitolinus. 'Accidisse idem in
Capitolinorum vetusto cognomine, notum est, ut eius origo a re illustri falso
repeteretur' (Madvig). The expression
Manliana imperia was proverbial;
below, § 105; Liv. 4, 29, 6; 8, 7, 22;
8, 34, 2. Gell. 1, 13, 7 makes a curious
mistake: Liv. 4, 29, 6, arguing against a
story to the effect that a Postumius had
been guilty of cruelty to his son, argues
that if it had been true, the proverb
would have been *Postumiana imperia*
not *Manliana*. But Gellius joins the
two as though both had been in vogue.
He quotes *Manlia imperia* from Claudius Quadrigarius (9, 13, 20). Sen. ben.
3, 37, 4.

18. **malo enim dicere quam:** so Fam. 3,
10, 1, but in Att. 13, 42, 1 malo ita d. q.

19. **princeps...consulatus:** often the
gen. of gerund or gerundive follows
princeps used in this sense; so in many
writers. Sometimes *ad* and acc. Pr.
philosophiae wrongly questioned by
Boot in Mnem. XXIII on Tusc. 4, 44. For
princeps 'founder' see n. on Acad. 2, 129.

20. **devoverat:** as to the reading *devo-*

Latinorum irruebat, aliquid de voluptatibus suis cogitabat? Vbi
ut eam caperet aut quando, cum sciret confestim esse moriendum
eamque mortem ardentiore studio peteret, quam Epicurus voluptatem petendam putat? Quod quidem eius factum nisi esset iure
laudatum, non esset imitatus quarto consulatu suo filius, neque
porro ex eo natus cum Pyrrho bellum gerens consul cecidisset
in proelio seque e continenti genere tertiam victimam rei publicae
62 praebuisset. Contineo me ab exemplis. Graecis hoc modicum

1 ubi ut: ita A¹B; *ubi aut* A².   4 esset iure: *iure esset* B.   5 consulatu:
consolatu A.   6 Pyrrho: *pirro* AP; *pyrro* B.   7 e: om. B.   8 modicum:
modo cum A¹.

veret Madvig says 'quaeritur num duo
verba copulative coniuncta eidem con-
iunctioni, quae propter ipsam copulatio-
nem necessario eandem principalem vim
retineat, diverso modo subici possint.'
He allows this to Propertius, 'poeta
oratione durissimus,' but denies it to
prose writers. In the present passage
there is 'una et simplex temporis significatio.' In S. Rosc. 81 edd. generally
have followed Madvig in correcting the
MSS. Occasionally something is interposed which compels a change of mood;
or there may be a change of point of
view; M. quotes Quinct. 60 quod neque
pecunia debebatur et, si maxime debe-
retur, commissum nihil esset; Liv. 38,
36, 4 (*quod* with ind. followed by *quod*
with subj., the statement in the second
place being presented as the view of
others than the writer). Cf. 1, 24 n.
on et vetuit, 4, 43 *n.* In other circumstances, where the verbs dependent
on *cum* are not 'copulative coniuncta'
and the *cum* is repeated, a change of
mood is common enough; so Fam.
9, 16, 7; Liv. 44, 39, 7; 30, 44, 10.
In Verr. 4, 77 there is some distance
between the two *cum* clauses and slight
or. obl. intervenes. In Quintil. 5, 6,
4 cum faciat et...liberat is still kept
by Meister. Cf. Leg. agr. 2, 64 tum
cum haberet et tum cum erant; Fam.
9, 2, 4 noteworthy change with (repeated) *dum*; cf. Varro r.r. 1, 2, 12
dum videatis et venit aeditumus
(cf. 1, 5, 4); Liv. 29, 37, 8 cum ad
tribum Polliam ventum est et praeco
cunctaretur, in spite of Madvig. Madvig thinks the *tense* of devoveret necessarily wrong, because as Dav. pointed
out the *devotio* consisted in the religious
ceremony which was over when D.
dashed on the foe (Liv. 8, 9, 9). But not
much stress is to be laid on this argument. Yet see Div. 1, 51; Liv. 9, 4, 10;

ad Herenn. 4, 57; Sen. ep. 67, 9 D. se
pro re p. devovit [et]...irruit.

1. **irruebat:** the *devotio* in battle
was not peculiar to the Romans;
Liv. 10, 38 records it among the
Samnites, and something of the kind
happened among the Gauls. On *devotio* generally see Bouché-Leclercq ap.
Daremberg and Saglio s.v.

ubi ut eam caperet: Madvig copiously
illustrates by exx. from different authors
of *quid ut, ut quo,* and even *ut qualiter,
ut quam multi* (the last two in Pliny) at
the beginning of questions. He points
out that Cic. Att. 7, 7, 7 rendered ἵνα
τί; by *ut quid?* Also Mart. 3, 77, 10;
add Cic. Quinct. 44, and see Wölfflin in
Archiv 4, 617, 8.

2. **eam:** spite of *voluptatibus*: the
transition from plural to singular is
much rarer than that from singular to
plural. Madvig quotes Acad. 2, 22, but
I have shown in my note there that the
passage should be differently inter-
preted. The same may be said of
Div. 1, 72 ea genera divinandi non
naturalia sed artificiosa dicuntur; in
quo haruspices...numerantur. It is not
necessary to supply *genere* with *quo*
as Madvig does; *in quo=in qua re* is
a fixed phrase referable to an antecedent in any gender or number. I have
illustrated the passage from the general
singular to the plural in my note on
Acad. 1, 38 (perturbationem).

4. **iure:** =*suo iure; per se.*

6. **cum Pyrrho:** so Tusc. 1, 89; but
elsewhere, as Off. 1, 61 and 3, 16; Cato
m. 75; Parad. 12; Sest. 48, Cicero
speaks of *two* Decii as having sacrificed
themselves. There is no warrant in history for the story of the *devotio* of the
third Decius, or for his death in battle.

7. **e continenti genere:** like *terra continens, natura c.* 'from the same family
in unbroken succession.'

est: Leonidas, Epaminondas, tres aliqui aut quattuor; ego si
nostros colligere coepero, perficiam illud quidem ut se virtuti
tradat constringendam voluptas; sed dies me deficiet, et, ut A.
Varius, qui est habitus iudex durior, dicere consessori solebat,
5 cum datis testibus alii tamen citarentur: 'Aut hoc testium satis
est, aut nescio quid satis sit,' sic a me satis datum est testium.
Quid enim? te ipsum, dignissimum maioribus tuis, voluptasne
induxit ut adulescentulus eriperes P. Sullae consulatum? Quem
cum ad patrem tuom rettulisses, fortissimum virum, qualis ille
10 vel consul vel civis cum semper, tum post consulatum fuit! Quo
quidem auctore nos ipsi ea gessimus ut omnibus potius quam
ipsis nobis consuluerimus. At quam pulcre dicere videbare, cum **63**
ex altera parte ponebas cumulatum aliquem plurimis et maximis
voluptatibus nullo nec praesenti nec futuro dolore, ex altera
15 autem cruciatibus maximis toto corpore nulla nec adiuncta nec
sperata voluptate, et quaerebas, quis aut hoc miserior aut
superiore illo beatior; deinde concludebas summum malum esse
dolorem, summum bonum voluptatem!

XX. L. Thorius Balbus fuit, Lanuvinus quem meminisse tu
20 non potes. Is ita vivebat ut nulla tam exquisita posset inveniri
voluptas, qua non abundaret. Erat et cupidus voluptatum et

2 quidem: *quid est* B.   3 et: om. B.   3 A.: *aulus* ABP.   4 habitus:
habitus est B.   4 consessori: *confessori* BP.   6 sit: om. B.   9 rettulisses:
retulisses ABP.   10 cum semper, tum: *eum semper cum* B.   13 cumulatum
aliquem: *aliquem cumulatum* B.   15 adiuncta: *adiuncto* A[1].   16 miserior:
miseriorum B.   17 beatior: *beatiorum* B; *beatior foret* dett.   19 L.: *lucius* AB.
20 posset inveniri voluptas: *voluptas posset inveniri* B.

1. **tres aliqui:** 'numerus non definitus
significatur' (Madvig). See Reisig-
Haase, ed. Schmalz and Landgraf, n. 354.
1 Hen. IV, Act 2, Sc. 4, l. 114: 'I am not
yet of Percy's mind, the Hotspur of the
north; he that kills me *some* six or seven
dozen of Scots at a breakfast, washes
his hands, and says to his wife, "Fie
upon this quiet life! I want work." "O
my sweet Harry," says she, "how many
hast thou killed to-day?" "Give my
roan horse a drench," says he, and
answers "*some* fourteen" an hour after.'
tres aut qu.: in Greek τρία καὶ τέτταρα,
cf. Xen. An. 4, 7, 10 δύο καὶ τρία βήματα.

2. **colligere:** 'quote,' as in 1, 34.

3. **tradat constringendam:** 1, 47.

11. **ea gessimus:** i.e. the suppression of
the conspiracy of Catiline.

14. **futuro:** adjectival, not participial;
as the abl. abs. with the fut. part. is
post-Ciceronian; Draeger, § 580.

17. **beatior:** as to the reading *foret*
given after this in some MSS., Madvig
says that it occurs only once in Cicero,
viz. in Att. 7, 21, 2; but Rep. 2, 24 must
be added. Caes. has the word only once;
in the well-known epigram on Terence.
In the older and later Latin exx. abound;
early *forem* has the force of *futurus
essem*; later it becomes a substitute for
essem. According to Kunze, Sallustiana,
Leipzig, 1893, *forem* occurs (unattached
to a participle) thirty-four times in
Sallust and retains its future force in all
but seven of these places.

19. **L. Thorius Balbus:** the name appears on a common coin, bearing the
head of the Juno of Lanuvium with an
inscription referring to her; Mommsen,
Münzw. p. 569. Mommsen thinks the
Thorius mentioned here was one who
commanded under Metellus in Spain in
the war against Sertorius and was killed

eius generis intellegens et copiosus, ita non superstitiosus ut illa
plurima in sua patria sacrificia et fana contemneret, ita non
timidus ad mortem, ut in acie sit ob rem publicam interfectus.
64 Cupiditates non Epicuri divisione finiebat, sed sua satietate.
Habebat tamen rationem valetudinis: utebatur eis exercita- 5
tionibus ut ad cenam et sitiens et esuriens veniret, eo cibo qui
et suavissimus esset et idem facillimus ad concoquendum, vino
et ad voluptatem, et ne noceret. Cetera illa adhibebat, quibus
demptis negat se Epicurus intellegere quid sit bonum. Aberat
omnis dolor, qui si adesset, nec molliter ferret et tamen medicis 1
plus quam philosophis uteretur. Color egregius, integra valetudo,
summa gratia, vita denique conferta voluptatum omnium varie-
65 tate. Hunc vos beatum; ratio quidem vestra sic cogit. At ego
quem huic anteponam non audeo dicere; dicet pro me ipsa virtus

---

5 habebat...valetudinis: *habebat. tamen ratione valetudinis* codd.　　　5 valetudinis: *valitudinis* AP.　　　5 eis: *his* A; *hys* B.　　　6 cenam; *cẹnam* A; *scenam* B;
coenam P.　　　7 concoquendum: *coquendum* B.　　　12 vita: *una* B.　　　12 conferta
voluptatum: *voluptatum conferta* B.　　　　　12 omnium: *omni* E et cod. Morel.
13 cogit. At ego: *cogitat ego* codd.; corr. Th. Bentleius.

in battle there (Florus, 2, 10; Plut. Sert.
12, where, however, the name is Θω-
ράνιος). A Thoria appears on a Lanuvine
inscr.; C.I.L. XIV, 2108.
　1. **eius generis:** 'that line'; N.D. 1, 43
in eodem genere.
　ita non s.: note on 2, 22.
　2. **patria:** used here of the *municipium*. In Leg. 2, 5 Cicero applies the
word to Arpinum, and on Atticus
questioning the usage, says 'omnibus
municipibus duas esse censeo patrias,
unam naturae, alteram civitatis,' and
'alteram loci patriam, alteram iuris.' In
Roman law, no one could be at once a
Roman citizen and a citizen of a non-
Roman community; Balb. 28; Caec. 100.
　contemneret...sit interfectus: this is
a good instance of the fact that 'sequence of tenses' is no mechanical
operation in Latin, but that the tenses
have their individual force. The imperfect carries with it at all times a
notion of the *continuance* to some extent of the action of the verb, but it
would be absurd to insist on this notion
in the case of *interficio* by writing *inter-
ficeretur*.
　3. **timidus ad:** so often in Cicero but
Fam. 7, 17, 1 t. in with abl.
　7. **concoquendum:** cf. N.D. 2, 24.
　8. **ne noceret:** = *ita ut ne*. Cicero in
these expressions sometimes drops *ita*,

as in Fat. 29, but nowhere else allows
ne to stand alone, as here, nor does
he use *ita ne* (in Livy, Hor., Quint.,
etc.); *ne* alone is found in Livy and
Tacitus.
　10. **molliter ferret:** i.e. *molli animo*; cf.
Off. 1, 71 in dolore mollis; but Cato m.
5 gerundum est molliter sapienti=aequo
animo. Madvig has an interesting note
on similar ambiguities in Latin; so
soluta somno of the mind asleep, Div. 1,
128, 129, but *solutus somno* in Rep. 6, 29,
'awakened from sleep'; *ponere barbam*
often for *deponere*, but in Ovid *capillos
ponere* often of arranging the hair; *gratiam facere alicuius rei* in the double sense
of releasing a person from a duty, and
of permitting to him a privilege; *fugam
facere* in Liv. 8, 9, 12, of the fugitives,
but 21, 5, 16, of those who put them
to flight. Many other illustrations might
be given; e.g. Lucr. uses *motus dare* both
of a thing which exhibits movement,
being set in motion by something
else, and of that which causes motion.
Sometimes the same phrase may have
exactly opposite senses, as emancipatus,
see n. on Cato M. 38.
　13. **hunc vos beatum:** a noteworthy
instance of ellipse. But possibly *vos* is
an error for *vis*; cf. § 75; also § 109.
　sic: like *ita*, commonly for a pronominal accus.

nec dubitabit isti vestro beato M. Regulum anteponere, quem
quidem, cum sua voluntate, nulla vi coactus praeter fidem, quam
dederat hosti, ex patria Carthaginem revertisset, tum ipsum,
cum vigiliis et fame cruciaretur, clamat virtus beatiorem fuisse
5 quam potantem in rosa Thorium. Bella magna gesserat, bis
consul fuerat, triumpharat nec tamen sua illa superiora tam
magna neque tam praeclara ducebat quam illum ultimum casum,
quem propter fidem constantiamque susceperat, qui nobis
miserabilis videtur audientibus, illi perpetienti erat voluptarius.
10 Non enim hilaritate nec lascivia nec risu aut ioco, comite levitatis,
saepe etiam tristes firmitate et constantia sunt beati. Stuprata **66**
per vim Lucretia a regis filio testata civis se ipsa interemit. Hic
dolor populi Romani duce et auctore Bruto causa civitati
libertatis fuit, ob eiusque mulieris memoriam primo anno et vir
5 et pater eius consul est factus. Tenuis L. Verginius unusque de
multis sexagesimo anno post libertatem receptam virginem

---

2 voluntate: *voluptate* BE. 3 Carthaginem: *cartaginem* A; *Kartaginem* B.
3 tum: *eum* AB cod. Morel. 4 fuisse: *esse* B. 5 rosa Thorium: *rosa. Thorius* AB.
6 sua illa superiora: ita A; *illa sua superiora* B. 8 propter: ita B; *praeter*
A Crat. 9 voluptarius: *voluntarius* codd.; corr. P. Marsus. 10 hilaritate:
in largitate A[1]. 10 nec lascivia: ita A; *et lascivia* B. 11 saepe: ita AB; *et*
saepe E; *sed saepe* Madv. 12 ipsa: ita A; *ipsam* B. 12 interemit: *interfecit* B.
15 est factus: *factus est* B. 15 L.: *lucius* AB. 15 Verginius: ita AB.

---

1. **M. Regulum:** the story of Regulus' embassy and murder is incredible;
see an excellent analysis of the evidence
in Pauly-Wissowa, s. v. Atilius, No. 51.

3. **ex patria revertisset:** in the best
prose, the dep. *revertor* is used in pres.
and tenses connected; while in perf. and
connected tenses the active is in use;
but *reversus* occurs once in Cicero (Phil.
6, 10) and once in Caesar (B.G. 6, 42, 1).
See Neue-Wagener III, 126 sq. After
reverti, ex is commoner than *ab*.

4. **clamat:** § 51.

5. **rosa:** the collective sense is common; Tusc. 5, 73; Sen. ep. 36, 9; 122, 8;
de ira 2, 25, 2; Prop. 1, 17, 22. So flos
often, Prop. 5, 3, 57; tegula, Ov. A. A. 2,
622; porco haedo gallina, Cato m. 56.

9. **voluptarius:** 1, 37; 3, 35; 4, 31.

11. **saepe**, etc.: there is an *inconcinnitas* here which led Ernesti to conjecture *hilares hilaritate*, and Davies
tristi firmitate. The words *saepe etiam
tristes* are practically parenthetic; 'men
are not made happy by merriment or
wantonness, nor yet by laughter or jest;
on the contrary (*sed*) they are made
happy by staunchness and firmness,

and that oftentimes though they be in
gloom.' For *firmitas* and *constantia* see
note on 3, 50.

12. **testata:** i.e. through those to whom
she told her story.

se ipsa: §§ 33, 53.

hic dolor: i.e. dolor huius rei: cf. 1,
63 ea scientia.

13. **duce et auctore:** the words are
often combined, as in Mil. 39; Sest. 61
dux auctor actor illarum rerum.

14. **et...et...est:** Draeger § 101.

15. **L. Verginius:** but Decimus in Rep.
2, 63; see Pais, Storia di Roma, I, 451.

unus de multis: so Off. 1, 109; but
Tusc. 1, 17 and Brut. 274 non fuit orator
unus e multis; cf. Plin. ep. 1, 3, 2.

16. **receptam:** Key in his Dict. s. v.
recipio asks what is the justification for
the *re* here, and in Flor. 1, 44 (3, 9).
Much the same justification as that for
the use of *reddere* meaning not 'to give
back' but 'to give what is due'; and in
countless instances the *re-* in compound
verbs has lost its original force. In Phil.
4, 7 est datum rei publicae Brutorum
genus et nomen ad libertatem populi
Romani vel constituendam vel reci-

filiam sua manu occidit potius quam ea Ap. Claudii libidini, qui
tum erat *cum* summo imperio, dederetur.

67 XXI. Aut haec tibi, Torquate, sunt vituperanda, aut patrocinium voluptatis repudiandum. Quod autem patrocinium aut
quae ista causa est voluptatis, quae nec testes ullos e claris viris 5
nec laudatores poterit adhibere? Vt enim nos ex annalium
monumentis testes excitamus eos quorum omnis vita consumpta
est in laboribus gloriosis, qui voluptatis nomen audire non possent,
sic in vestris disputationibus historia muta est. Numquam audivi
in Epicuri schola Lycurgum, Solonem, Miltiadem, Themistoclem, 10
Epaminondam nominari, qui in ore sunt ceterorum omnium
philosophorum. Nunc vero, quoniam haec nos etiam tractare

1 sua: *suam* AB.　　　1 potius: *post* A¹.　　　1 Ap.: *P.* AB.　　　2 tum: *tamen* B.
2 *cum* add. Iwan Müller: *in* add. Orell.　　　6 annalium: *animalium* BE.　　　7 monumentis: *monimentis* AB.　　8 qui: om. E.　　　10 Lycurgum: *ligurcum* A; *lygurgum* B.
10 Miltiadem: *miliciadem* A.　　　11 ceterorum omnium philosophorum: ita A; *philosophorum ceterorum omnium* B; *ceterorum philosophorum omnium* E.　　　12 etiam: *et* B.

piendam, Cicero gives the verb its literal
force. In the historical writers *recipere*
often merely means 'to acquire' or 'to
conquer.' Cf. Sen. ep. 50, 9 virtutes receptae ('when once acquired') exire non
possunt; cf. Anton. ap. Cic. Att. 14, 13a,
2 repositum in optima spe puerum.

　2. **erat cum summo imperio:** both *in
imperio esse* and *cum imp. esse* are common, but *esse summo imperio* is more
than dubious. In Fam. 8, 2, 1 (Caelius)
the MSS. give *esse maiore periculo*; in
Fam. 4, 15, 2 proprio periculo esse;
6, 4, 4 quanto fuerim dolore; Att. 1, 12, 3
rem esse insigni infamia; Qu. Fr. 3, 2, 2,
to which M. refers, is not parallel; Att.
5, 14, 2 e. magno timore; in Fam.
9, 21, 2 fuerunt sella curuli; Qu. Fr.
3, 4, 1 est tam gravi fama hoc iudicium.
[C. F. W. Müller, Fam. p. xxix qu. Nipp.
Opusc. p. 173 and Andresen; Madv.
Adv. 2, 237 refers to Phil. 8, 18 esse
magno alicuius beneficio and Fam. 7, 30,
3; esse odio magno in Verr. act. pr. 42.
Madvig is commenting on Att. 9, 1, 4.
His objection against *in summo imp.* is
nothing, as we have in magno, tanto, etc.]

　3. **haec:** generic, see note on 2, 17.
Cf. 16.

　4. **quod...aut quae:** see n. on Acad.
2, 32 for *aut* when a question is slightly
changed.

　6. **laudatores:** 'a iudiciorum consuetudine hoc nomen traductum est...
excitantur testes proprie cum surgere
iubentur et prodire' (Madvig).

　8. **non possent:** i.e. si (nomen voluptatis) ad eos perveniret; as Madvig ex-

plains. For *nomen rei audire non posse*
he cites Rep. 2, 52; Liv. 33, 35, 3 (add
ubi nec Pelopidarum nomen nec facta
audiam, qu. in Fam. 7, 30, 1, and *videre
non posse* in Pis. 64; Liv. 1, 26, 10; Sen.
ad Helv. 9, 6; Plin. ep. 6, 8, 7). [For
voluptatis nomen cf. Acad. 2, 138 invidiosum nomen voluptatis fugere; Acad.
fr. 20, p. 89, 17 (ed. Müller)].

　9. **historia muta est:** Acad. 2, 5 historiae loquantur; see illustrations in my
note there, and add Off. 2, 3 litterae
conticuerunt.

　10. **schola:** not uncommonly used of a
'school' of philosophy: De Orat. 1, 56.

　11. **nominari:** as Usener says, p. 329 *n.*
Cicero, in order to be quite correct,
should have used *laudari.* Cf. Plut.
n. p. s. vivi, c. 15, p. 1097 *c* ἀλλὰ τὴν
ἀτοπίαν οὐδὲ βουλόμενόν ἐστι τοῦ ἀνθρώπου παρελθεῖν, τὰς μὲν Θεμιστοκλέους καὶ
Μιλτιάδου πράξεις ὑπὸ πόδας τιθεμένου
καὶ κατευτελίζοντος: id. Colot. c. 33,
p. 1127 *a* τοὺς δὲ πολιτικοὺς ἄνδρας ἐπὶ
γέλωτι καὶ καταλύσει τῆς δόξης ὀνομάζουσι
μόνον (followed by contemptuous references to Epaminondas); ib. p. 1127 *d*
τοὺς δὲ πρώτους καὶ σοφωτάτους τῶν
νομοθετῶν κακῶς λέγοντες. Inscr. of
Oinoanda (Heberdey and Kalinka in
Bull. de Corr. XXI, p. 374) condemns
στρατεία as χαλεπόν, and ῥητορεύειν as full
of σφυγμός and ταραχή. As to the attitude
of Epicurus to public life see Diog. L. 10,
119; Cic. Sest. 23.

　12. **haec:** sc. philosophical writing;
nos not Cicero but *Romani,* as is shown
by *etiam.*

coepimus, suppeditabit nobis Atticus noster e thesauris suis
quos et quantos viros! Nonne melius est de his aliquid quam **68**
tantis voluminibus de Themista loqui? Sint ista Graecorum;
quamquam ab eis philosophiam et omnes ingenuas disciplinas
5 habemus; sed tamen est aliquid quod nobis non liceat,
liceat illis. Pugnant Stoici cum Peripateticis. Alteri negant
quicquam esse bonum nisi quod honestum sit, alteri plurimum se
et longe longeque plurimum tribuere honestati, sed tamen et in
corpore et extra esse quaedam bona. Et certamen honestum et
o disputatio splendida! Omnis est enim de virtutis dignitate
contentio. At cum tuis cum disseras, multa sunt audienda etiam

1 suppeditabit: *suppeditabat* B.   1 e: ita AB: *et* E.   3 loqui? *loquitur* B.
4 eis: *his* AB.   10 est: om. B.   11 tuis: *tu vis* B.   11 cum: ita A¹; *tu* A².
11 disseras: *desideras* B.

1. **thesauris**: here 'stores of learning'
but in Att. 15, 27, 2 excudam Ἡρακλεί-
δειον quod lateat in thesauris tuis,
merely 'stores of books.' There are many
allusions in Cicero's letters to the knowledge Atticus possessed of history and
biography; cf. esp. Att. 16, 13 c, 2 ardeo
studio historiae...quae nec institui nec
effici potest sine tua ope (followed by a
request for some historical details).
Madvig (see also Boot on Att.) thinks
that Cicero may be hinting at the history written by Atticus; but the word
thesauri would hardly be applied to it.

2. **quos et quantos viros**: Madvig
illustrates from Leg. 3, 20; Div. 1, 52;
Plin. ep. 5, 15, 5.

3. **tantis vol.**: cf. τηλικαῦτα βιβλία
in Epict. qu. in note on 1, 25. For Epicurus, as a voluminous writer, compared
with Livy cf. Sen. ep. 46, 1; Verr. 2, 1, 97
volumen eius rerum gestarum maximum.
But Madvig truly remarks '*tanta illa
volumina* nonnihil habent ex oratoria
superlatione.' One would have expected
either the common *tot et tantis* or *totis*
as in N.D. 1, 93 Timocraten totis voluminibus conciderit (sc. Epicurus, about
whom the context is), or *tot* as in Acad.
fr. 1 quid Antipater digladiatur cum
Carneade tot voluminibus? Themista
was wife of Leonteus of Lampsacus, one
of the intimates of Epicurus. For information about her see Usener's index
s. v. Apart from the present passage,
tradition has preserved mention of only
one book addressed to her by Epicurus,
and of some letters from him to her.
Lactant. 3, 25, 15 makes a strangely
erroneous remark about her: 'nullas
umquam mulieres philosophari docue-

runt praeter unam ex omni memoria
Themisten.'
sint ista Graecorum: cf. § 80 sit ista
in Graecorum levitate perversitas.

5. **non liceat, liceat**: the artifice of
style much as in § 30, where see note (appellavit). Cf. also below 5, 95 (possit).

8. **longe longeque**: Wölfflin, in his
paper on 'Gemination' in Latin (in the
Sitzungsb. of the Kön. Bayr. Acad. for
1882, pp. 422–91), quotes this passage
as the earliest ex. of the doubling of an
adverb, which became pretty common
afterwards (without *que*) as *vero vero*,
Petron. 75; *modo modo*, ib. 42, 46.
Hor. s. 1, 6, 18 has *longe longeque*,
for which Cicero writes below (§ 111)
longe multumque. Lungo lungo in Italian.
Wölfflin gives as the only classical exx.
of the doubling of adjectives Plaut. Cas.
621 tota tota occidi; and Hor. s. 2, 7,
92 liber liber sum. [Cf. Enn. 341 Baehr.
atque atque accedit muros Romana
iuventus, qu. by Gell. 10, 29, 1 with the
caution 'nisi memoria in hoc versu
labor'; Non. 530, 3 gets it from Gell.]

11. **cum disseras**: from the time of
Ursinus the subj. has been found to be
difficult. 'Vereor ne mendum hic hae-
reat; neque enim coniunctivi ulla videtur ratio esse, quoniam post *tuis* secunda
persona de incerto subiecto accipi nequit, nisi forte in certo subiecto eadem
tamen significatio est rei tantum fictae
et cogitatae, sed tum *sint* sequi debebat'
(Madvig). On the other hand, C. F. W.
Müller declares that if the indicative
had occurred in the mss. he would have
regarded it with as much suspicion as
Madvig did the subjunctive. If Madvig
argues that *tuis* makes the indefinite

de obscenis voluptatibus, de quibus ab Epicuro saepissime
69 dicitur. Non potes ergo ista tueri, Torquate, mihi crede, si te
ipse et tuas cogitationes et studia perspexeris; pudebit te, inquam, illius tabulae, quam Cleanthes sane commode verbis
depingere solebat. Iubebat eos, qui audiebant, secum ipsos 5
cogitare pictam in tabula Voluptatem pulcerrimo vestitu et
ornatu regali in solio sedentem, praesto esse Virtutes ut ancillulas
quae nihil aliud agerent, nullum suum officium ducerent nisi ut
Voluptati ministrarent et eam tantum ad aurem admonerent,
si modo id pictura intellegi posset, ut caveret ne quid faceret 1
imprudens, quod offenderet animos hominum, aut quicquam e
quo oriretur aliquis dolor. 'Nos quidem Virtutes sic natae sumus,
ut tibi serviremus, aliud negoti nihil habemus.'

1 de (ante *quibus*): om. AB. 2 dicitur: *dici* E. 2 ergo: *igitur* B. 5 depingere:
ita codd. meliores: *pingere* dett. (ita P). 7 ut: *ac* B. 9 ministrarent: *ministraret*
BE. 11 quicquam: *quicquid* B. 12 dolor: *dolorum* BE. 13 negoti nihil:
negotium nihil A; *negocium non* BE.

subject to *disseras* impossible, Müller
contends that no other subject could be
imagined: 'an a Torquato potissimum
vel potius solo putamus disseri cum suis
velle Ciceronem? Immo quisquis dis-
serat cum Epicureis, ei audienda esse
multa de obscenis voluptatibus.' Müller
seems to be right and the subj. is of
the type (specially common in Cicero)
which we find, e.g. below 4, 74 cum...ac-
cesseris. In *cum*-clauses of this kind particularly when, as here, they precede the
correlated clause, the idea has come to be
practically iterative (as Hale, 'Cum-constructions,' p. 240, seems to feel), though
it may not have been so originally. See
e.g. Brut. 143; Riem. Synt. p. 331 n. 2.

1. **obscenis:** see notes on §§ 23, 29;
and cf. N.D. 1, 111 obscenis voluptatibus quas quidem non erubescens persequitur (Epicurus) omnis nominatim;
Tusc. 5, 94 obscenas voluptates, de
quibus multa ab illis habetur oratio.

2. **non potes...si perspexeris:** Draeger, II², p. 713.

mihi crede: Schmalz has shown
(Zeitschrift für d. Gymnasialwesen,
1881, p. 115) that in the language of
every-day life *crede mihi* was the usual
phrase, while in the more formal de-
partments of literature *mihi crede* was
preferred. In Cicero's speeches and
philosophical writings the latter is alone
used; the former occurs once in the
letters Ad Fam.; and several times in
those to Atticus. [According to Georges
the passages from Cicero are all collected
in Mahne's Miscellen, 1, 41.] But *credite*

hoc mihi in Verr. 4. 133 seems to show
that *crede mihi* was avoided because of
dactylic rhythm.

4. **tabulae:** this occurred in a treatise
περὶ ἡδονῆς, and was famous in ancient
times. See Off. 3, 117; Aug. c. d. 5, 20.
Another such picture, possibly from the
same source, is found in Tusc. 5, 13, 14.
The *tabula* of Cebes is an imitation.

5. **depingere:** *pingere* has poor authority (see cr. n.) but would not in itself be
impossible here, as Madvig supposes;
the mention of the picture would justify
it. The lexica give exx. of the simple
verb so used.

7. **ancillulas:** above, § 37; Athen. 12,
546 f σαφῶς ὑπουργὸν ποιῶν ('Επίκουρος)
ἐν τούτοις τὴν ἀρετὴν τῆς ἡδονῆς καὶ θερα-
παίνης τάξιν ἐπέχουσαν: Sen. dial. 7, 13, 5
virtus antecedat, comitetur voluptas et
circa corpus ut umbra versetur: virtutem quidem excelsissimam omnium,
voluptati tradere ancillam nihil magnum animo capientis est; d. 7, 11, 2;
7, 13, 5; id. ben. 4, 2, 1 Epicureorum...
apud quos virtus voluptatum ministra
est: illis paret, illis deservit, illas supra
se videt; Ad Herenn. 4, 20 si voles
divitias cum virtute comparare, vix
satis idoneae tibi videbuntur divitiae
quae virtutis pedisequae sint; Sen. ep.
90, 35 illa philosophia quae virtutem
donavit voluptati; dial. 3, 10, 2 virtutes
in clientelam vitiorum demittere.

9. **ad aurem admonere:** also often
in. For *ad* cf. Ter. Phorm. 1030; Virg.
Aen. 5, 527; Sen. ben. 2, 23, 2.

10. **si modo...posset:** 'Cleanthis hanc

XXII. At negat Epicurus (hoc enim vestrum lumen est) **70**
quemquam, qui honeste non vivat, iucunde posse vivere; quasi
ego id curem quid ille aiat aut neget. Illud quaero, quid ei, qui
in voluptate summum bonum ponat, consentaneum sit dicere.
5 Quid affers, cur Thorius, cur †Chius Postumius, cur omnium
horum magister, Orata, non iucundissime vixerit? Ipse negat,
ut ante dixi, luxuriosorum vitam reprehendendam nisi plane
fatui sint, id est nisi aut cupiant aut metuant. Quarum ambarum
rerum cum medicinam pollicetur, luxuriae licentiam pollicetur.
10 His enim rebus detractis negat se reperire in asotorum vita quod
reprehendat. Non igitur potestis voluptate omnia dirigentes aut **71**
tueri aut retinere virtutem. Nam nec vir bonus ac iustus haberi
debet, qui, ne malum habeat, abstinet se ab iniuria. Nosti, credo,
illud:

15   Nemo pius est, qui pietatem—;

cave putes quicquam esse verius. Nec enim, dum metuit, iustus
est, et certe, si metuere destiterit, non erit; non metuet autem,
sive celare potuerit, sive opibus magnis, quicquid fecerit, obtinere,

---

1 negat Epicurus: *epicurus negat* B.   2 quasi...neget: affert Nonius, p. 70.
3 quid: *quod* Nonius.   3 aiat: *alat* ABE.   3 qui in voluptate: *qui voluptatē* B.
4 ponat: ita ABE; *putat* codd. multi.   5 cur Chius: *cur chius* A Crat. cod. Morel.
E; *curehius* B; *cur C. Hirrius* Scaliger.   5 Postumius: *postumus* BE.   8 id est:
idē B; *idem* E.   9 cum medicinam: *medicinam cum* E; *cum* om. B.   12 nec:
nisi B.   15 pietatem: *pietate* E.   17 destiterit: *desistit* A; *destitere* B.   18 potuerit: ita B; *poterit* A. Cf. n. ad 1, 70.

esse cautionem, satis verbi modus et
tempus admonet' (Madvig).
  1. **lumen**: 'strong point'; so Acad.
2, 107 illa sunt lumina duo, quae
causam continent; see my n. there.
The application to persons ('shining
light') is akin, as in Qu. fr. 2, 8, 3 illorum
praediorum scito mihi vicinum Marium
lumen esse; Mil. 21; Phil. 5, 39. Vell.
Pat. 2, 52, 3 collisa inter se duo rei
publicae capita effossumque alterum
Romani imperi lumen.
  4. **ponat**: for the reading *putat* see
5, 20 *n.*
  consentaneum, etc.: so below, §§ 80,
84, 98; 5, 80; Off. 3, 117 non id
spectandum est, quid dicat (Epicurus)
sed quid consentaneum sit ei dicere qui
bona voluptate terminaverit, mala
dolore.
  5. **quid affers, cur...vixerit**: for the
brevity here cf. 1, 14 *n.*
  Chius Postumius: many older scho-

lars from Scaliger onwards read here
C. Hirrius Postumius or (C. Hirrus P.),
regarding the man as the same with C.
Hirrius mentioned by Varro r. r. 3, 17, 3
and Plin. n. h. 9, 171, as the first to use
fishponds for breeding *muraenae*. But
Varro and Pliny give no *cognomen*, and
Postumius is *nomen* not *cognomen*;
moreover, *omnium horum*, which (as M.
notes) can hardly be generic here, requires the mention of more than two
persons. C. Sergius Orata (contemporary with L. Crassus the orator) is often
mentioned for his luxury.
  7. **nisi plane fatui sint**: somewhat
of a perversion of Epicurus; see § 21.
  12. **tueri...retinere**: cf. n. on 1, 6 and
cf. 2, 11.
  nec...: for the slight anacoluthon see
n. on 1, 23 and Madv. Fin. p. 792 f. (ed. 3).
  15. **nemo**, etc.: the passage is quoted
only here.
  18. **opibus magnis**: see 1, 52 *n.*

certeque malet existimari bonus vir, ut non sit, quam esse, ut non putetur. Ita, quod certissimum est, pro vera certaque iustitia simulationem nobis iustitiae traditis praecipitisque quodam modo ut nostram stabilem conscientiam contemnamus, aliorum errantem 72 opinionem aucupemur. Quae dici eadem de ceteris virtutibus 5 possunt, quarum omnium fundamenta vos in voluptate tamquam in aqua ponitis. Quid enim? Fortemne possumus dicere eundem illum Torquatum?—delector enim, quamquam te non possum, ut ais, corrumpere, delector, inquam, et familia vestra et nomine. Et hercule mihi vir optimus nostrique amantissimus, A. Torquatus, i◦ versatur ante oculos, cuius quantum studium et quam insigne fuerit erga me temporibus illis, quae nota sunt omnibus, scire necesse est utrumque vestrum; quae mihi ipsi, qui volo et esse et haberi gratus, grata non essent, nisi eum perspicerem mea causa mihi amicum fuisse, non sua, nisi hoc dicis sua, quod i⸵ interest omnium recte facere. Si id dicis, vicimus. Id enim

---

1 malet: *mallet* ABE cod. Morel.; *malle* Crat.   1 bonus vir: ita A et cod. Morel.; *vir bonus* B.   2 certissimum: *turpissimum* Th. Bentleius; alii multa alia coniecerunt.   7 fortemne: *fortem non* E.   10 nostrique: *nostri* Q (sic) E 10 A.: *aulius* A; *aulus* B.   11 et quam: *et tam* B; *fuerit et tam* E.

---

1. bonus vir: a distinction of meaning has been drawn between *vir bonus* and *bonus vir* (as by Kühner, Gram. 2, p. 1070), but an examination of a sufficient number of passages shows that none such exists. See Wilkins on De Or. 2, 85.

ut non: Draeger, II², p. 761.

2. certissimum: *cerritissimum* (Haupt) is not Ciceronian; Att. 8, 5, 1, and 15, 21, 2 are conjectures. *Turpissimum* (Th. Bentl.) is a possible correction, for our MSS. confuse *p* and *t* in places, and this confusion would be helped out by the similarity in many MSS. between *t* and *c*.

iustitia...iustitiae: see n. on 1, 56; germana iustitia Off. 3, 69.

3. quodam modo: a slight apology for the strength of the expressions; see 3, 48.

5. opinionem: this by way of turning the tables on the Epicureans, who blamed the lovers of τὸ καλὸν for hunting after what is *populari fama gloriosum* (2, 48).

aucupemur: Leg. 3, 35 homine... omnis rumusculos populari ratione aucupante; Pis. 57 levitatis est inanem aucupari rumorem et omnis umbras etiam falsae gloriae consectari.

quae dici eadem: cf. § 106 and 3, 12; 3, 50 haec eadem; 4, 19 ea quae tributa est tanta praestantia.

7. in aqua: 'to write in water' was a

common proverb even in ancient times; see Otto in Archiv 4, 22; Sprichwörter, p. 31.

10. A. Torquatus: probably the A. Torquatus named in Att. 9, 8, 1 de L. Torquato quod quaeris, non modo Lucius sed etiam Aulus profectus est † alter multos (read *ante multo*). He was very likely the *quaesitor* in the case of Milo and praetor in 52 B.C. After the defeat of Pompeius he lived in exile at Athens, where Cicero addressed to him the letters in Fam. 6, 1–4. His relationship with the Torquatus of the dialogue cannot be made out. Had he been *frater* or even *frater patruelis* (as has been supposed) or indeed any near relative, Cicero could hardly have avoided mentioning the fact here.

12. temporibus illis: in Fam. 6, 1, 7 Cicero says to him 'ego habeo cui plus quam tibi debeam neminem.'

13. qui volo: for the ind. where subj. might have been expected see 1, 10.

14. gratus, grata: for the double sense cf. Fam. 5, 11, 1.

15. hoc dicis sua; exactly the converse of the ground taken by Torquatus.

16. interest...facere: 'that right action rewards everybody.' The argument would have been clearer if *sua vi*, or something of the kind, had been inserted.

volumus, id contendimus, ut offici fructus sit ipsum officium. Hoc **73**
ille tuus non volt omnibusque ex rebus voluptatem quasi
mercedem exigit. Sed ad illum redeo. Si voluptatis causa cum
Gallo apud Anienem depugnavit provocatus et ex eius spoliis
5 sibi et torquem et cognomen induit ullam aliam ob causam, nisi
quod ei talia facta digna viro videbantur, fortem non puto. Iam
si pudor, si modestia, si pudicitia, si uno verbo temperantia
poenae aut infamiae metu coërcebuntur, non sanctitate sua se
tuebuntur, quod adulterium, quod stuprum, quae libido non se
10 proripiet ac proiciet aut occultatione proposita aut impunitate
aut licentia? Quid? illud, Torquate, quale tandem videtur, te **74**

---

2 voluptatem: om. B.   4 eius: om. A¹.   5 ullam: ita ed. Veneta a. 1480;
nullam codd.   7 pudor: ita AB; *pudor est* E.   8 poenae: om. B.   11 aut
licentia: *ac licentia* Lambinus, fort. recte.   11 quid: *quod* B.

---

1. ut...sit: brief for *ut doceamus esse*;
see 1, 14 *n.*

   ipsum officium: cf. Fam. 3, 13, 2
mihi propono fructum amicitiae nostrae
ipsam amicitiam. There is practically
little difference between this position
and that of the Epicureans. Both
positions assume that the virtuous act
is rewarded by the peace of mind which
it brings. Rep. 6, 8 sapientibus conscientia ipsa factorum egregiorum am-
plissimum virtutis est praemium.

3. sed...redeo: similar resumptive
clauses in Tusc. 1, 38 sed redeo ad an-
tiquos; De Or. 2, 62 sed illuc redeo;
Lael. §§ 1, 75, 96; Cato m. 32, etc.

5. sibi...induit: 1, 23 *n.*; cf. Liv. 9,
18, 2 novi...ingenii, quod sibi victor
(Alexander) induerat; ib. 6, 18, 14 me
patronum profiteor plebis quod mihi
cura mea et fides cognomen induit.

7. si...coërcebuntur: here what would
naturally be said of the virtuous man,
that he is restrained from evil, is said of
the virtues themselves; though as soon
as the person is lost sight of, it should
have been said of the vices. In Friedländer's edition of Juven. 2, 39 is an
admirable note contributed by C. F. W.
Müller, illustrating irregularity of the
kind, for which he uses the old, but not
altogether suitable name, 'res pro rei defectu'; so artes reprehenduntur, Planc.
62; Att. 1, 5, 3 de litterarum missione ac-
cusor (where some have wished to read
intermissione); Plaut. Curc. 215 and Liv. 27, 47, 9;
Fam. 2, 1, 1 officium accusatur. Cael.
6 quod obiectum est de pudicitia.
Pudor and *pudicitia* often occur together, as in Leg. 1, 50; Verr. 2, 5, 34;

Phil. 2, 15. *Modestia* is properly 'order-
liness,' the 'law-abiding' spirit mani-
fested by a man towards others in
public or private affairs; Off. 1, 142 the
word is used to render εὐταξία. *Temperantia* is wider, and the nearest
equivalent to σωφροσύνη: cf. Tusc. 3, 16
σωφροσύνην...quam soleo tum temperantiam, tum moderationem appellare,
non numquam etiam modestiam; the
wording shows that *modestia* is regarded
as the least satisfactory rendering of
the three. As to *coercebuntur* Madvig
says: 'annotandum verbum plurale non
solum post anaphoram coniunctionis in
subiectis sed etiam post subiecta aper-
tissime (*uno verbo*) in unam postremam
notionem collecta et conflata.' Even
subjects separated by *nec...nec, vel...
vel* (Mil. 13), *aut...aut*, occasionally take
a plural verb; Draeger, § 105.

9. quod ad.: as Madvig notes, the
change to *quo* is not needed; *se proicere*
and the like often occur absolutely used
(of persons).

11. aut lic.: as reasons favourable to
ac l. Madvig notes (1) the fact that the
last two words are more akin to one
another than they are to *occultatione*;
(2) that in § 71 there were two things
(*celare* and *magnis opibus obtinere*) not
three—a rather weak argument; (3)
that the second *aut* could not in the case
of three substantives be employed to
indicate a new subdivision, as in Sest. 24
si parvo puero aut si imbecillo seni aut
debili; and often; (4) that if that were
possible, it would not be lucid here. But
in the case of repeated *et* Cicero often
puts things on a level when he might
have grouped some together, over

isto nomine, ingenio, gloria, quae facis, quae cogitas, quae
contendis, quo referas, cuius rei causa perficere quae conaris,
velis, quid optimum denique in vita iudices, non audere in conventu dicere? Quid enim mereri velis, iam cum magistratum
inieris et in contionem ascenderis (est enim tibi edicendum quae 5
sis observaturus in iure dicendo, et fortasse etiam, si tibi erit
visum, aliquid de maioribus tuis et de te ipso dices more maiorum),
quid merearis igitur, ut dicas te in eo magistratu omnia voluptatis
causa facturum esse, teque nihil fecisse in vita nisi voluptatis
causa? An me, inquis, tam amentem putas, ut apud imperitos 10
isto modo loquar? At tu eadem ista dic in iudicio aut, si coronam
times, dic in senatu. Numquam facies. Cur, nisi quod turpis
oratio est? Mene ergo et Triarium dignos existimas apud quos
turpiter loquare?

4 mereri: *merere* B.   5 contionem: *contencionem* B.   7 dices: *dicas te* AB.
12 quod: om. B.   13 existimas: ita B; *existimes* A.   13 quos: *quod* B.
14 loquare. Verum esto: *loquare verum. esto* A; *loquere verum esto* BE.

against one of them; thus, e.g. Acad.
2, 53 interesse inter vigilantium visa
et sanorum et sobriorum et eorum qui
essent aliter affecti; where grouping
might be (and is elsewhere in similar
passages) effected by leaving out *et* in
the two first places; cf. Off. 2, 22 and
1, 139; so Cael. 45 inerat...ratio et bonis
artibus instituta et cura et vigiliis
elaborata (ac vig. Klotz); Sest. 31 ne
quis...miretur, quid haec mea oratio
tam longa aut tam alte repetita aut
quid ad P. Sesti causam...delicta pertineant; ib. 100 viam aut asperam atque
arduam aut plenam esse periculorum
aut insidiarum; Pis. 22 quasi aliquod
Lapitharum aut Centaurorum convi-
vium; Phil. 3, 6 quam potuit urbem
eligere aut opportuniorem ad res gerun-
das aut fideliorem aut fortiorum virorum aut amiciorum rei publicae civium?
Leg. agr. 2, 67 quod solum tam exile aut
macrum est...? Flacc. 24 utrum hic
tandem disceptationem et cognitionem
veritatis an innocentiae labem aliquam
aut ruinam fore putatis? Har. resp. 54
aut universus interitus aut victoris
dominatus aut regnum.

illud...quale v.: so below § 104;
Acad. 2, 115 hoc...quale est; etc.

3. in conventu: cf. 4, 22; 5, 85 and
Acad. 2, 144 with my note.

4. mereri: N.D. 1, 67 quid mereas ut
Epicureus esse desinas? The use is not
uncommon elsewhere.

5. in contionem ascenderis: = *in*

rostra in cont. asc.; cf. Macrob. 2, 3, 6
Caninius quoque Rebilus...rostra cum
ascendisset, pariter honorem iniit consulatus et eieravit. The assumed date
of the dialogue is at the time when
Torquatus had reached the praetorship
(urban) but had not yet entered on
office.

edicendum: the new praetor would
explain in his speech any points in his
intended administration of the law
which were novel, and embodied in his
edition of the 'edict.' Publication was
usually first made from the *rostra*; cf.
Sctum de Bacchanalibus, *utei in
conventionid exdeicatis* (but ne minus
trinum nundinum there seems to indicate written publication); cf. Off.
3, 80.

6. et...etiam: Acad. 1, 5 with my n.

7. de maioribus: Suet. Tib. 32 praetorem conlaudavit quod honore inito
consuetudinem antiquam retulisset de
maioribus suis memorandi. Madvig
curiously writes 'non memini alibi
tradi praetorem in contione edixisse et
edicto orationem addidisse.'

8. igitur: n. on 1, 4; cf. 2, 23.

12. nisi quod: 'aut sic quaeritur:
Quam aliam causam habes nisi hanc? id
est: *nisi quod*, aut sic: *Quam causam
(omnino) habes, si hanc non habes?* id
est: *si turpis oratio non est*; tertium
illud: *Quam causam habes, nisi—est?*
interrogationi ad negationem inclinanti
exceptionem similem adiungere vide-

XXIII. Verum esto: verbum ipsum voluptatis non habet **75**
dignitatem, nec nos fortasse intellegimus. Hoc enim identidem
dicitis, non intellegere nos quam dicatis voluptatem. Rem
videlicet difficilem et obscuram! 'Individua' cum dicitis et
5 'intermundia,' quae nec sunt ulla nec possunt esse, intellegimus;
voluptas, quae passeribus nota est omnibus, a nobis intellegi
non potest? Quid si efficio ut fateare me non modo quid sit
voluptas scire (est enim iucundus motus in sensu), sed etiam
quid eam tu velis esse? Tum enim eam ipsam vis, quam modo
10 ego dixi, et nomen imponis, in motu ut sit et faciat aliquam

---

3 voluptatem: *voluptatis* B.   4 videlicet: *vides* codd.; corr. Manutius.   4 cum
dicitis: om. cod. Morel.   6 nota est omnibus: ita A; *omnibus nota est* B.
7 ut: om. B.   7 me: *ne* BE.   8 scire: *sciretur* B.   9 eam tu velis: ita A;
velis tu eam B.   10 ego dixi: *dixi ego* BE.   10 imponis: *iam ponis* B.

---

tur, ac si dicas *nisi forte*, quod hinc
alienum est' (Madvig). Cf. § 102.

   1. verum esto: so § 92 and often;
verum is conjunction, not adjective;
hence correct my n. on Acad. 2, 10. *esto*
is sometimes followed by concessive
subjunctive, as there, sometimes by
indicative, as here.

   verbum ipsum: i.e. without the gloss
which the Epicureans put upon it.

   3. rem … obscuram: appositional
phrases (where the apposition is to a
whole sentence and clause, and not to
a single word) in Cicero usually present
a substantive in the nominative case,
as above, § 1 audax negotium. Fam.
3, 12, 1 (negotium). Madvig thinks the
accus. occurs only here and De Or. 2, 79;
Orat. 52; Tusc. 1, 102 (all with *rem*).
But Phil. 2, 85 almost certainly supplies
another example: 'unde diadema? non
enim abiectum sustuleras sed attuleras
domo, meditatum et cogitatum scelus.'
Here the alternatives, to take *attuleras
domo scelus* together, or to put a full
stop at *domo*, are both unsatisfactory;
cf. Att. 13, 22, 2, where *rem* is probably
appositional, the MSS. evidence for *o*
being weak. Probably also Tusc. 3, 49
negat Epicurus…negat…negat…: omnia philosopho digna, sed cum voluptate
pugnantia. The connexion of the accusative in the appositional phrase with
that in the main part of the sentence
appears to be a matter of form, and not
one of meaning. Most wrongly Thomas
on Verr. 2, 2, 5 les appositions à toute
une proposition sont mises plus ordi-
nairement à l'accusatif (Draeger, § 309).
Dr. says the exact opposite. It is hard

to draw the line between apposition
and exclamation: Sen. d. 5, 19, 2
magnam rem at beginning of sentence
might be either. Here one might say,
with Madvig, that the sense is *rem
videlicet difficilem nos non intellegere
dicitis*; but in other passages, in order
to establish a connexion of meaning,
some editors have made the forced supposition that a verb *general in sense* is
to be supplied from the context to
govern the appositional accus. (Wilkins on De Or. 2, 79, Nipperdey on
Tac. Ann. 1, 27); Pro Clu. § 117 and Att.
13, 40, 1. Sallust and writers after him
use appositional phrases almost as
freely as the Greeks; see Draeger,
§ 309. [Cf. Quint. 1, 1, 10 cogitet ora-
torem institui, rem arduam; Vell. P.
2, 69, 6 Rhodum ceperat, rem immanis
operis; and on the other hand, Fam.
6, 4, 3 relicum est ut te angat quod absis
a tuis tam diu. Res molesta, etc.; Att. 14,
13, 2 res odiosa.] Ov. Her. 12, 99 donec
terrigenae, facinus mirabile, fratres |
inter se strictas conseruere manus.

   4. individua: n. on 1, 17.

   5. intermundia: 'the lucid inter-
space 'twixt world and world'=μετα-
κόσμια in Epic. The same rendering in
N.D. 1, 18.

   nec possunt esse: only the Epicureans believed in *innumerabiles mundi*;
see above, 1, 21.

   6. passeribus: quoted here like 'the
small gilded fly' in King Lear (4, 6, 114);
see Otto in Archiv 3, 393 (Sprichw.
p. 267); Erasmus, Adagia 1065 (Wytt.).

   10. nomen…in motu ut sit: the periphrasis is necessary as a single word is

varietatem, tum aliam quandam summam voluptatem, quo addi
nihil possit; eam tum adesse, cum dolor omnis absit; eam
76 stabilem appellas. Sit sane ista voluptas. Dic in quovis conventu
te omnia facere, ne doleas. Si ne hoc quidem satis ample, satis
honeste dici putas, dic te omnia et in isto magistratu et in omni 5
vita utilitatis tuae causa facturum, nihil nisi quod expediat,
nihil denique nisi tua causa, quem clamorem contionis aut quam
spem consulatus eius, qui tibi paratissimus est, futuram putas?
Eamne rationem igitur sequere, qua tecum ipse et cum tuis utare,

1 quo: ita A; *qua* BE.   2 absit: *assit* B.   3 in quovis conventu: *in quo conventu vis* B.   4 si ne: *sum* E.   4 quidem: ita A; *quid est* BE.   7 tua: ita A; *tui* B.   8 putas: ita cod. Monacensis Madvigii; *putes* AB.   9 sequere: ita A; *sequare* B.

wanting to express the meaning. For *ut sit* after *nomen* cf. n. on 1, 14 fin. and on 2, 13.

faciat...varietatem: 1, 38.

1. quo addi: *quo* with *addere* also in Mur. 28.

3. stabilem appellas: *stabilis* does not actually occur in the exposition of Torquatus; see 2 § 32; § 16 in stabilitate.

sit...ista voluptas: pronominal attraction; 'be it granted that that state is really pleasure'; see 1, 39.

4. ample: this and *amplissime*, also *amplus* and *amplissimus*, convey always in Cicero an idea of distinction, not merely that of extent; cf. Off. 2, 37 ampla et honesta res; Rep. 5, 8 vita opibus firma, gloria ampla, virtute honesta. The comparatives usually refer to extent, as *amplior metus*, Clu. 128; *numerus*, Verr. 2, 2, 124; but not quite always, as Marc. 26. There is a curious passage in Verr. 2, 2, 61 iste amplam occasionem calumniae nactus, where the good MSS. authority is in favour of omitting the words *occasionem calumniae*; though C. F. W. Müller remarks 'vocab. *ampla* iam Ciceronis aetate in usu fuisse mirum videtur' (on *ampla* 'handle' see R. Schöll in Archiv 1, 534 sq.). Cicero's usage is against the correctness of the reading of the inferior MSS.; but probably *amplam* is a gloss on *ansam* which it has displaced. So Planc. 84 reprehensionis ansam; Caec. 17 controversiarum; I do not see why the MSS. reading in Sest. 22 sermonis ansas dabat, should be wrong, though the gen. there is subjective.

7. tua causa: Publil. Syr. 350 (ed. B. Smith) malus est vocandus qui sua causa est bonus. It is doubtful whether *tui causa*, etc. for *tua c.* etc. were used in Latin before the time of Apuleius. The exx. have almost disappeared with growing knowledge of the better class of MSS. Wölfflin, in the course of an excellent paper in Archiv 1, 172, quotes Plaut. Most. 597, having failed to notice that Studemund's earliest examination of the palimpsest (1868) had already disposed of the phrase *causa tui* by revealing the word *fenoris* in front of causa. Cicero probably no more said *nostri causa* than he said *sponte dei* or the like. C. F. W. Müller reads *sua causa* in Verr. 2, 3, 121, removing the last trace of the usage from the text of Cicero. But a few expressions such as *vestrum frequentia* in Leg. agr. 2, 55 seem to be sound; see Draeger, § 204. This usage most likely traces back to fixed phrases *omnium nostrum, vestrum*, the genitive being retained when *omnium* was dropped. Madvig says the passage from possessive pronoun to objective genitive was only made in Cicero in the case of nouns denoting an agent, as *accusator mei*; and he condemns as unsound the one passage in Cicero where a gen. now stands merely for a possessive, viz. Fam. 2, 6, 5 tui unius studio; the first hand of the Med. indeed has there *tuo*, in accordance with Cicero's practice elsewhere: 'nostrum' inquit 'peditum illud, milites, est opus,' Liv. 7, 33, 10.

7. quem...putas: 5, 61 *n*. The subjunctive *putes* is without reason here, as in Verr. 1, 1, 40 *putetis* and Clu. 194 *putet*, given by all MSS. and changed by editors.

9. sequere: fut.; cf. Acad. 2, 61 tune ...eam philosophiam sequere quae confundit vera cum falsis?

profiteri et in medium proferre non audeas? At vero illa, quae
Peripatetici, quae Stoici dicunt, semper tibi in ore sunt in iudiciis,
in senatu. Officium, aequitatem, dignitatem, fidem, recta,
honesta, digna imperio, digna populo Romano, omnia pericula
5 pro re publica, mori pro patria, haec cum loqueris, nos barones

3. **officium**, etc.: the accusatives all
depend on *loqueris* and the phrases
'digna imperio,' 'digna populo Romano,' 'omnia pericula pro republica'
and 'mori pro patria' are imagined as
quotations. For *loqui aliquid*, 'to prate,'
cf. 4, 7; Tusc. 5, 31; Cael. 75.

5. **barones**: this strange word occurs
in Div. 2, 144 (addressed to an athlete
by a seer to whom he had gone for the
interpretation of a dream); Att. 5, 11, 6
apud Patronem (Epicurean philosopher!) et reliquos barones te in maxima
gratia posui; Fam. 9, 26, 3 an tu id
melius, qui etiam philosophum in-
riseris, cum ille, si quis quid quaereret
(see n. on 1, 55), dixisset, cenam te
quaerere a mane dixeris? Ille baro te
putabat quaesiturum, unum caelum
esset an innumerabilia. In more than
one of these passages, older edd. have
oddly misinterpreted the word, but in
all it has the same meaning, 'dolt,'
'dullard,' 'gobemouche,' 'heavy fellow.'
Cic. ap. Gramm., de dubiis nomin. 5,
572, 17 ed. Keil (letter to Pansa), 4, 3,
p. 298 ed. Müller. Festus twice quotes
(328, 9) a line of Lucilius, 'varonum ac
rupicum squarrosa incondita rostra,'
where probably *baronum* should be
written; and the same line is quoted by
Tert. de an. 6 quid autem facient tot ac
tantae animae rupicum et barbarorum,
quibus alimenta sapientiae desunt? The
change to *baronum* proposed by Pithou,
is undoubtedly right. It is noteworthy
that Lucilius is quoted by Lact. *à propos*
of the stupidity of philosophers, and it
may well be that the line had a similar
reference in Lucilius. The word next
occurs in Petronius 53 and 63 (*bis*); in
the former place a rope-dancer is called
baro insulsissimus and in the latter the
name attaches to 'hominem Cappado-
cem, longum, valde audaculum, et qui
valebat bovem iratum tollere.' And I
have no doubt Petron. used the diminutive *barunculus* in 67, where Trimalchio
draws attention to his wife's heavy
jewellery and says 'videtis mulieris
compedes: sic nos barunculi spoliamur'
(edd. *barcalae*, for which no sensible
explanation has ever been forthcoming).
Cf. Corp. Gl. 4, p. 313, l. 17 baruo

barunculus; *latrunculus*, etc. Pers.
5, 138 has it in an address, meaning
'dolt'; on which passage a scholion
runs, 'barones dicuntur servi militum,
qui utique stultissimi sunt,' and Isid.
orig. 9, 4, 31 gives a similar explanation:
'mercennarii sunt qui serviunt accepta
mercede. Iidem et barones Graeco nomine quod sint fortes in laboribus; βαρὺς
enim dicitur gravis, quod est fortis.'
Hence Stowasser in Archiv 2, 319, corrects Gloss. Ampl.³ 77 baramercemiarius,
into baro. mercenarius. [The word
berones which occurs in Bell. Al. 53
applied to soldiers of a body-guard,
and, formerly taken to be a variety of
barones, is now derived from the name
of a Spanish tribe.] *Baro* occurs in
other glosses, sometimes being explained
by *fortis* or *mercennarius*, sometimes by
such words as βάκηλος. Also there is a
word *barosus*, apparently a derivative,
equated with σοβαρός, βάναυσος, βάκηλος
(Funck in Archiv 8, 372). Sometimes
baro is glossed by ἀνήρ, and throughout
the Middle Ages this was the ordinary
meaning. That the word was a camp-
word originally there can be little
doubt; like *latro*, *calo*, *volo*, *quaternio*,
and other words of like formation. Many
ideas have been held of its derivation;
Nettleship on Pers. l.l. connects it with
barrus, an elephant (Hor. ep. 12, 1).
Celtic and Germanic analogues have also
been discovered; but the occurrence of
baro in Lucilius makes these conjectures
improbable. It is not unlikely, I think,
that Isidore is right in connecting *baro*
and βαρύς: the word, like *latro*, may have
originated among the Greek merce-
naries [cf. Fisch's derivation of *mirmillo*
from μορμώ, Arch. 5, 78]. For the quantity (*bāro*) we have practically only the
testimony of Lucilius (whom Persius
doubtless copied), and he may have
made free with the quantity; see n. on
2, 15. The connexion of *baro* and modern *baron* has been disputed; but the
whole history of the word makes the
connexion probable; this origin has no
more indignity about it than that of
'marshal' or 'constable.' Fisch in
Archiv 5, 56 sq. has an important
article on personal substantives in -*o*;

77 stupemus, tu videlicet tecum ipse rides. Nam inter ista tam
magnifica verba tamque praeclara non habet ullum voluptas
locum, non modo illa, quam in motu esse dicitis, quam omnes
urbani, rustici, omnes, inquam, qui Latine locuntur, voluptatem
vocant, sed ne haec quidem stabilis, quam praeter vos nemo 5
appellat voluptatem.

XXIV. Vide igitur ne non debeas verbis nostris uti, sententiis
tuis. Quod si voltum tibi, si incessum fingeres, quo gravior
viderere, non esses tui similis; verba tu fingas et ea dicas, quae
non sentias? aut etiam, ut vestitum, sic sententiam habeas aliam 1
domesticam, aliam forensem, ut in fronte ostentatio sit, intus
veritas occultetur? Vide, quaeso, rectumne sit. Mihi quidem
eae verae videntur opiniones, quae honestae, quae laudabiles,
quae gloriosae, quae in senatu, quae apud populum, quae in
omni coetu concilioque profitendae sint, ne id non pudeat sentire 1
78 quod pudeat dicere. Amicitiae vero locus ubi esse potest aut quis

2 magnifica: *magnificata* B.   7 debeas: *dubites* cod. Morel.   8 fingeres:
fringeres A.   9 esses: *esse* B.   10 ut: *sic* B; *sit* E.   12 quidem: *quid* BE.
13 eae: *hae* A; *et* BE.   15 non pudeat sentire: *pudeat non sentire* B; *pudeat ne
sentire* E.

in his lists many camp-words are to be
found. He inclines to *varo* as the
original form and (comparing *Varro*)
makes the first application to be to a
man who from crookedness of leg or
back was unfit for military service (but
Meyer (ib. 5, 226) justly remarks that if
baro comes from *varus* it cannot have
arisen among Latin-speakers). This ignores a good deal of the information
which we possess concerning actual
usage. [F. strangely says, 'Ciceros
Eitelkeit, auch von militärischen Din-
gen etwas verstehen zu wollen, spiegelt
sich wieder im Gebrauche dieses Wortes';
where does this 'Eitelkeit' appear elsewhere?] Wölfflin has written about *baro*
in Archiv 9, 14, also in Sitzungsb. d. k.
bayr. Acad. 105 sq.; this last I have not
seen. In Archiv 9, 466 there is notice
of a paper by Riccoboni, 'Barone e
vocaboli affini' in Atti del R. Instituto
Veneto di Scienze, 1894–5. Carl Wagener in Bursian, 1903, says Settegast, in
Roman. Forschungen von Vollmöller,
I, 240, has made clear the connexion
with 'baron.' He also refers to Wölfflin
in Aufgaben des Thesaurus linguae
Latinae, p. 105, and Heraeus, Die
Sprache des Petronius u. die Glossen,
pp. 11 sq.
3. **omnes urbani**: 2, 28. Cf. Sen. ep.

52, 12 impudicum incessus ostendit;
ep. 66, 5 modestus incessus.
8. **incessum fingeres**: Off. 2, 43 ficto
non modo sermone sed voltu; the actor
is said in Leg. 3, 40 fingere voltus, of the
audience; Clu. 72; Ter. haut. 5, 1, 14 (887)
voltus quoque hominum fingit scelus;
Sen. d. 9, 15, 5 frontem suam fingere;
from another point of view De Or. 1, 127
ea quae nobis non possumus fingere,
facies voltus sonus. There is much in
ancient literature attesting the importance laid upon comeliness of movement;
see especially Sen. ep. 66, 5, ib. 36 prudenter ambulare, composite sedere. Cf.
Dio Chrys. 31, 162 and see φρονίμη
περιπάτησις in passage quoted on 3, 55;
prudens ambulatio, Sen. ep. 113, 22,
where see reference to Chrysippus, etc.;
Lucian, Herm. c. 18, gives as a reason
for joining the Stoics: 'ἑώρων αὐτοὺς
κοσμίως βαδίζοντας, ἀναβεβλημένους
εὐσταλῶς.' Cf. C.I.L. 1, 1007 sermone
lepido tum autem incessu commodo.
See n. on 3, 55.
9. **tu fingas**: 'are you the man to...';
Acad. 2, 125 tune inane quicquam putes
esse? Phil. 7, 5 (a string of such subjunctives).
11. **fronte**: Att. 4, 15, 7 fronte an
mente.
13. **quae...sint**: § 15.

amicus esse cuiquam quem non ipsum amet propter ipsum?
Quid autem est amare, e quo nomen ductum amicitiae est, nisi
velle bonis aliquem affici quam maximis, etiam si ad se ex eis
nihil redundet? Prodest, inquit, mihi eo esse animo. Immo
5 videri fortasse. Esse enim, nisi eris, non potes. Qui autem esse
poteris nisi te amor ipse ceperit? quod non subducta utilitatis
ratione effici solet, sed ipsum a se oritur et sua sponte nascitur.
'At enim sequor utilitatem.' Manebit ergo amicitia tam diu
quam diu sequetur utilitas, et, si utilitas constituet amicitiam,
10 tollet eadem. Sed quid ages tandem, si utilitas ab amicitia, ut **79**
fit saepe, defecerit? Relinquesne? quae ista amicitia est? Re-

3 ex eis nihil: *ex his nihil* A.   4 redunet Madv.: *redeunt et* ABE.   5 nisi
eris, non potes: ita codd.: *nisi videris, non prodest* Graserus.   5 qui autem...
solet: affert Nonius, p. 399.   6 poteris: *potes* Nonius.   6 subducta: ita
Nonius; *subdubia* codd. Tulliani.   7 a: ita AB; *ad* E.   8 sequor utilitatem:
sequitur utilitas coni. Graserus.   9 quam diu: om. A[1]B.   9 constituet amicitiam: ita A; *amicitiam constituet* B.   10 ages: *agis* B.   11 relinquesne? quae
ista: *relinques neque ista* A.

1. **ipsum...propter ipsum:** *propter se*
avoided because of ambiguity.

2. **amare...amicitiae est:** so N.D.
1, 122 (also against the Epicureans).

3. **ad se:** 1, 67 n. sibi.

4. **inquit:** for this use ('quoth he!')
without any definite subject, see my note
on *dicit* in Acad. 2, 79. Cf. 1, 4 and
below, § 93. The usage is widespread;
it is particularly common in some
Ecclesiastical writers, as Tertullian and
Arnobius, who often add *inquit* to a
quotation from Scripture (so sometimes
'saith he' in the N.T.). Cicero attaches
inquit to a citation from a poet in Att.
14, 12, 2, where it has been unjustly
questioned by many editors (including
Tyrrell and Purser).

5. **esse enim, nisi eris:** this careless
phrase seems to have actually fallen
from Cicero's pen. The words *nisi eris*
are protected by *qui autem esse poteris*;
so that a correction like that of Graser
(adopted by Baiter), *esse enim, nisi
videris, non prodest,* is out of court; to
say nothing of the poor sense which the
emendation supplies. And there is no
reasonable correction of the words *esse
enim...non potes* which will make the
sentence logical; moreover *esse enim*
clearly refers to *videri* immediately preceding. E. Thomas, in Revue de Philologie vii, 169, proposed *prodesse...potest*;
he should at least have gone a step
further and changed *enim.*

6. **subducta:** n. on § 60.

7. **solet:** 'Cicero infirmavit nonnihil
(conclusionem argumenti) in illis: *quod
non solet* cet. Neque enim ex eo quod
fieri solet, sed ex ipsa rei natura et
repugnantia ducitur' (Madvig). Surely
this criticism *nimis exigue atque exiliter
ad calculos vocat* (Lael. 58) not only the
writer but the Latin language.

a se oritur: *a se* and *ex se* are both
possible; Tusc. 3, 37 (virtus) oriatur a
se; Planc. 67 ego huc a me ortus et per
me nixus ascendi; Cael. 19 si ipse orietur
et nascetur ex sese; Verr. 2, 5, 180 (of
Cato) ipse sui generis initium ac nominis
ab se gigni et propagari volebat; Phil.
6, 17 quem (Cicero himself) a se ortum
hominibus nobilissimis praetulistis;
Brut. 96 (of Pompey) homo per se
cognitus, and so Cat. 1, 28; see other
parallels in my note on Acad. 2, 23. The
epitaph of a self-made man in C.I.L.
14, 173 qui in primis annis a se petens
omnia ornamenta...; in Quint. 10, 3, 1
et haec quidem auxilia extrinsecus ad-
hibentur; in eis autem quae nobis ipsis
paranda sunt, the emendation of Gertz,
e nobis, is very probable.

8. **at...utilitatem:** this adds nothing
to *prodest* above. This use of *sequor,* 'I
take as my guide'; 'I make my aim';
'I am attracted by' is common, esp.
in the letters; see Acad. 2, 70 with my n.

10. **tollet:** Lael. 32 si utilitas congluti-
naret amicitias, eadem mutata dissol-
veret; Arist. Eth. N. 8, 4, 2 οἱ δὲ διὰ τὸ
χρήσιμον ὄντες φίλοι ἅμα τῷ συμφέροντι

tinebis? qui convenit? quid enim de amicitia statueris utilitatis
causa expetenda, vides. ' Ne in odium veniam, si amicum destitero
tueri.' Primum cur ista res digna odio est, nisi quod est turpis?
Quod si, ne quo incommodo afficiare, non relinques amicum,
tamen, ne sine fructu alligatus sis, ut moriatur optabis. Quid, 5
si non modo utilitatem tibi nullam afferet, sed iacturae rei
familiaris erunt faciundae, labores suscipiendi, adeundum vitae
periculum? ne tum quidem te respicies et cogitabis sibi quemque
natum esse et suis voluptatibus? Vadem te ad mortem tyranno
dabis pro amico, ut Pythagoreus ille Siculo fecit tyranno? aut, 10
Pylades cum sis, dices te esse Oresten, ut moriare pro amico?
aut, si esses Orestes, Pyladem refelleres, te indicares et, si id
non probares, quo minus ambo una necaremini, non precarere?

2 veniam: *veniantur* B.   4 si, ne quo: *si ne quo* B, *si ne tuo* A Crat.   5 quid,
si: *quod si* A.   7 erunt: *erit* E.   8 quidem: *quid est* B.   9 et: om. BE.
9 vadem te: *vadente* B.   11 Oresten: ita A; *Orestem* B.   12 si: om. E.

διαλύονται· οὐ γὰρ ἀλλήλων ἦσαν φίλοι,
ἀλλὰ τοῦ λυσιτελοῦς.

2. ne...tueri: sc. *retinebis ne*; *odium*,
sc. *civium*.

in odium veniam: substitute for
passive; so too deponents: in opinionem,
suspicionem venire.

3. primum: no *deinde* follows. Cf. 1, 17.

5. alligatus: here merely adjectival.
Cf. *amissus*, Fam. 5, 16, 4.

7. faciundae: see Neue-Wagener III,
333.

8. te respicies: Fam. 10, 24, 8
(Planc.); Ter. haut. 1, 1, 18 (70).

9. vadem ad mortem: these words
give support to *vadem mortis*, which
phrase has been suspected in Tusc. 5, 63,
where the story of Damon and Phintias
is also told; see below, 5, 63 (Orestes
and Pylades).

10. Pythagoreus: Off. 3, 45 Damonem
et Phintiam Pythagoreos; for information concerning the story see Holden's
note there.

tyranno: for *facere aliquid alicui*
Madvig quotes Rosc. Com. 18; Verr. 2, 4,
49; dom. 124; Div. 2, 126; Sall. Cat. 55, 2;
Jug. 85, 17; Nep. Paus. 3, 5; Ter. Andr.
1, 1, 85; Justin 22, 5, 3. [There is a
much debated passage in Att. 7, 3, 2
si ista nobis cogitatio de triumpho in-
iecta non esset, quam tu quoque appro-
bas, ne tu haud multum requireres illum
virum qui in sexto libro informatus est;
quid enim tibi faciam, qui illos libros
devorasti? The allusion is to the sketch
of the ideal statesman in the sixth book

of Cicero's De Republica. The words
quid tibi faciam? have been often
wrongly suspected, and often wrongly
explained. They comically express the
idea that Atticus, having studied closely
the ideal statesman drawn by Cicero,
must be expected to be a severe critic
of Cicero's political conduct. The sense
is 'there is no escape from you'; 'I am
powerless against you,' literally, 'what
line of action is open to me in reference
to you?' The sense is the same in all
other passages where *quid faciam* occurs
with the dative or indeed with the
ablative. Acad. 2, 96 quid faceret huic
conclusioni? 'How was he to escape
from this argument?' Caec. 30 quid
huic tu homini facias? 'There's no way
of dealing with this fellow.' Hor. s.
1, 1, 63 quid facias illi? Also Phil. 13, 37;
Plaut. Pseud. 78 [see my n. on Acad. l.l.].
Sen. n. q. 7, 30, 3 neque enim omnia
deus homini fecit (for benefit of man).

13. precarere: the change to *depreca-
rere* (ed. Ven.) seems needless. Cicero
has *quo minus* after verbs which do not
express definitely an idea of hindrance
not only when these verbs are negatived,
or virtually negatived, as after *quid dici
poterit* (below, 3, 38), *illud non perficies*
(Fam. 3, 7, 6), *non pugnabo* (div. in Caec.
58), *nihil desideramus* (Att. 2, 4, 5), *ne con-
sulerent* (Verr. 2, 3, 16)—but when there
is no negative, as in *factum est* (Fam. 1,
4, 2), *praestare debebit* (Off. 1, 121). So in
Caes. and other writers after *per me stat,
movebatur*, etc.; see Draeger, § 542, 4. The

XXV. Faceres tu quidem, Torquate, haec omnia; nihil enim **80**
arbitror esse magna laude dignum quod te praetermissurum
credam aut mortis aut doloris metu. Non quaeritur autem quid
naturae tuae consentaneum sit sed quid disciplinae. Ratio ista
5 quam defendis, praecepta quae didicisti, quae probas, funditus
evertunt amicitiam, quamvis eam Epicurus, ut facit, in caelum
efferat laudibus. At coluit ipse amicitias. Quis, quaeso, illum
negat et bonum virum et comem et humanum fuisse? De ingenio eius in his disputationibus, non de moribus quaeritur. Sit
0 ista in Graecorum levitate perversitas, qui maledictis insectantur
eos, a quibus de veritate dissentiunt. Sed quamvis comis in
amicis tuendis fuerit, tamen, si haec vera sunt (nihil enim
affirmo), non satis acutus fuit. At multis se probavit. Et quidem **81**
iure fortasse, sed tamen non gravissimum est testimonium multi-

---

2 esse magna laude dignum: *magna laude dignum esse* B; *magna laude dignum
esset* E.   3 quid: ita A; *quod* B.   4 quid: *quod* AB.   7 quaeso: *quasi* codd.:
corr. Davies.   11 in amicis tuendis fuerit: ita A; *fuerit in amicis tuendis* B.

---

idea of hindrance or prevention on
which *quo minus* depends, is often not
present in the main verb of the principal
clause but is to be gathered from the
whole context. That *deprecari* was not
a verb to which the notion of hindering
closely attached itself is shown by the fact
that neither in Cicero nor in any other
writer of so early a date does it take the
construction with *quo minus*, which is
found in Liv. 3, 9, 10; Sen. ben. 3, 25.

2. **arbitror...credam:** slightly pleonastic. Cf. Verr. 2, 5, 22; Imp. P. 46;
Ter. Ad. 236.

6. **ut facit:** similarly 4, 66 ut omnes
insipientes sint miseri, quod profecto
sunt. Many exx. of such parenthetic
phrases in Antibarbarus (Krebs and
Schmalz), s. v. *ut*.

8. **comem:** some of the secondary
MSS. have *commune* for *comem*, which
was taken to be contracted; hence
Madvig supposes that *comem* should be
written for *communem* in Cato m. 59
Cyrum...communem erga Lysandrum
atque humanum fuisse. Madvig says:
'alia est *communitas* quae in Laelio 65
postulatur, tum quae apud Suetonium
in imperantibus cum se ceteris aequant
laudatur.' This is somewhat hyper-
critical: cf. Lael. l.l. simplicem et communem et consentientem (amicum)
eligi par est; Mur. 66 quemquamne
existimas Catone proavo tuo commodi-
orem communiorem moderatiorem fuisse

ad omnem rationem humanitatis? Fam.
4, 9, 2; Suet. Claud. 21, 5.

10. **maledictis:** though *male dicere
alicui* is not uncommon in Cicero, and
elsewhere, *bene dicere alicui* is rare in
classical Latin. In Antibarbarus s.v. it
is said to be only classical with the
meaning 'to speak well *of*' a person (as
in Ovid, Tr. 5, 9, 9); for *dicere aliquid
alicui*, 'to say something with reference
to a person,' cf. n. on 1, 7 Tarentinis
scribere. The only ex. of *bene dicere*
with dat. in Cicero is Sest. 110 cui bene
dixit umquam bono? *Bene dicta*, where
it occurs, corresponds to *bene dicere*
used absolutely, not to *bene dicere alicui.*
Cicero perhaps did not use *bene facere
alicui*; for in Inv. 1, 109 the best MSS.
have *benigne*; and probably *male facere
alicui* occurs only in Fam. 11, 21, 1;
bene facta corresponds to *bene facere*
without the dative; *male facta* is probably only found in a quotation from
Ennius ap. Off. 2, 62, for in Inv. 2, 108
the word rests on doubtful authority
(in Deiot. 36 the correct reading is
benigne).

12. **haec:** 'my view.'

nihil...affirmo: 'parum apte, cum
omnia hactenus δογματικῶς disputarit,
subito intericit Academicae dubitationis
significationem' (Madvig). The words
are indeed little in accord with § 43.

13. **et quidem:** 1, 35 *n.*

14. **non gravissimum:** § 44.

tudinis. In omni enim arte vel studio vel quavis scientia vel in
ipsa virtute optimum quidque rarissimum est. Ac mihi quidem,
quod et ipse bonus vir fuit et multi Epicurei et fuerunt et hodie
sunt et in amicitiis fideles et in omni vita constantes et graves
nec voluptate sed officio consilia moderantes, hoc videtur maior 5
vis honestatis et minor voluptatis. Ita enim vivunt quidam ut
eorum vita refellatur oratio. Atque ut ceteri dicere existimantur
melius quam facere, sic hi mihi videntur facere melius quam
dicere.

82   XXVI.   Sed haec nihil sane ad rem; illa videamus, quae a te 1
de amicitia dicta sunt.   E quibus unum mihi videbar ab ipso
Epicuro dictum cognoscere, amicitiam a voluptate non posse
divelli ob eamque rem colendam esse quod, *cum* sine ea tuto et

---

2 quidque: *quodque* B.   2 rarissimum: *carissimum* B.   3 et multi Epicurei:
et multi et epicurei A.   3 et fuerunt: *sunt fuerunt* B; *fuerunt* A; corr. Lambinus.
4 amicitiis: *amicicia* BE.   5 sed: *se* BE.   6 quidam: ita A¹B; *quidem* A².
10 a te: *ad te* A.   11 de amicitia: *de amiciciis* A.   11 videbar: ita A²B; *vide-batur* A¹.   13 cum: om. codd.; addidit Madv.

1. **in omni**, etc.: Madvig's explanation of the omission of *vel* before *arte*
and the introduction of *quavis* is somewhat obscure and unsatisfactory: 'nunc
video *vel* hic cum correctione aliqua
poni, ut ante primum nomen poni non
debuerit. Nam cum *artem* dixisset, non
artem nominandam fuisse significat,
quod maius videatur, sed studium,
etiamsi artis formam et dignitatem non
attingat, vel omnino quamvis cuiusvis
rei scientiam; tum in tertio *vel*, ubi
addita praepositio significat hoc seiungi
ab illa serie, ascendit oratio vel potius
transfertur ad aliud, ut sit: *etiam in
ipsa virtute.*' The drift of the sentence,
in connexion with the preceding, is to
show that competent judges are rare
everywhere. The *vel* before *studio* merely
dissociates it from *arte*, the words *in
omni arte vel studio* going close together.
Then *quavis scientia* widens and gene-
ralizes the preceding clause, for every
ars and *studium* has its own form of
scientia; 5, 26 omnium artium recte dici
potest commune esse ut in aliqua
scientia versentur; the *vel* before *in*
means as Madvig says *etiam*, but there
is no *translatio ad aliud*, *virtute* being
connected with *scientia* as closely as are
arte and *studio*. There is, of course, no
reference to the specially Stoic doctrine
whereby ἀρετή, ἐπιστήμη, τέχνη were
equated.

2. **optimum...rarissimum**: so 'omnia

praeclara rara,' Lael. 79; χαλεπὰ τὰ
καλά, etc.

ac mihi quidem: § 34 *n.*, 85 *n.*

4. **et graves**: the *et* here would have
been *ac* but for the guttural following;
see my note on Acad. 2, 34.

6. **ita vivunt**, etc.: Arist. Eth. N.
10, 2, 1 (of Eudoxus) ἐπιστεύοντο δ' οἱ
λόγοι διὰ τὴν τοῦ ἤθους ἀρετὴν μᾶλλον ἢ
δι' αὐτούς: Greg. Naz. c. 10 (qu. by
Mayor on Juven. 14, 319) ὡς ἂν δὲ μὴ
δόξειεν ἡδονῇ τινὶ | ταύτην ἐπαινεῖν, κοσ-
μίως καὶ σωφρόνως | ἔξη ('Επίκουρος)
βοηθῶν ἐκ τρόπου τῷ δόγματι. Sen. ep.
20 § 2; 21.

10. **nihil...ad rem**: cf. 4, 73.

12. **cognoscere**: 'to recognize'; a not
uncommon sense, which Madvig illustrates from Att. 12, 22, 1; 14, 19, 4;
Non. p. 276; Verr. 2, 1, 59 and 5, 72.
Cf. *cognitio* in § 110 below.

13. **cum sine**: 'minus recte *si* interpo-
suit (Manutius); neque enim cum condi-
cione argumentum concluserat Torquatus, sed ita esse posuerat' (Madvig).
About this note C. F. W. Müller says:
'paene incredibile esset quantum erret
Madvigius.' What the error is, I do not
know, unless it lies in the dogmatism
of the note; the notion of cause rather
than condition seems to me to be much
more suitable to the passage. *Cum*
(*quom*) has often fallen out in MSS. when
close to *quod*; so below, § 101 (in B and
the Erlangen MS.).

sine metu vivi non posset, ne iucunde quidem posset. Satis est
ad hoc responsum. Attulisti aliud humanius horum recentiorum,
numquam dictum ab ipso illo, quod sciam, primo utilitatis causa
amicum expeti, cum autem usus accessisset, tum ipsum amari
5 per se etiam omissa spe voluptatis. Hoc etsi multis modis reprehendi potest, tamen accipio quod dant. Mihi enim satis est, ipsis
non satis. Nam aliquando posse recte fieri dicunt nulla exspectata
nec quaesita voluptate. Posuisti etiam dicere alios foedus quod- 83
dam inter se facere sapientis ut, quem ad modum sint in se ipsos
10 animati, eodem modo sint erga amicos; id et fieri posse et saepe
esse factum et ad voluptates percipiendas maxime pertinere.
Hoc foedus facere si potuerunt, faciant etiam illud, ut aequitatem, modestiam, virtutes omnis per se ipsas gratis diligant.
An vero, si fructibus et emolumentis et utilitatibus amicitias
15 colemus, si nulla caritas erit quae faciat amicitiam ipsam sua

1 ne: *nec* codd.; corr. Madv.   1 ne iucunde quidem posset: om. B.
1 quidem: *quid* E.   1 est ad: *est enim ad* B.   2 horum...sciam:
affert Nonius, p. 167.   3 ipso illo: ita A; *illo ipso* B; *ipso* om. Nonius.
3 quod: *qui* B.   5 voluptatis: A² in marg. addit *vel utilitatis.*   5 etsi:
ita A; *etiamsi* B.   5 multis modis; ita codd. nonnulli et Madv. coll. Oratore § 153;
multimodis codd. optimi.   7 recte: *non recte* B.   7 exspectata: *expecta* E;
expectacione B.   8 quaesita: ita A; *exquisita* B.   10 modo: om. B.
11 percipiendas: *perspiciendas* AB. An: ita B; *at* A.

1. **ne iucunde quidem**: Epic. went so
far as to say that in friendship it is
more blessed to give than to receive;
see Usener, fragm. 544.

2. **ad hoc**: Cicero avoids the substantival dat. *huic*; below, § 85 cui loco...
responsum.

humanius: in Lael. 45, 46 different
shades of view held in the Epicurean
school touching friendship are compared and the opinion of the founder
himself is said to be 'multo *inhumanius.*'

3. **numquam d.**: cf. Usener § 398 note
to p. 275, l. 25.

4. **expeti...accessisset**: see n. on 2,54.

5. **multis modis**: it is highly improbable that Cicero wrote *multimodis*; the
form is treated as obsolete in Orat. 153;
cf. too Tusc. 5, 111 multis modis variis-
que. It is somewhat surprising that
Cicero should use *multis modis* so rarely;
there are no other exx. in Merguet, except in quotation.

6. **accipio quod dant**: a proverbial
phrase corresponding to τὰ διδόμενα
δέχεσθαι, 'not to look a gift-horse in
the mouth'; Plat. Gorg. 499 c; Att.
15, 17, 1 quid tu autem? τὰ μὲν διδόμενα: meque obiurgavit vetere pro-
verbio, τὰ μὲν διδόμενα: Fam. 1, 1, 2

quod dat accipimus. Acad. 2, 68 quod
tu mihi das, accepero; Verr. 2, 2, 150
quod mihi abs te datur, id accipio.
There is a slight variation in the form
in Att. 1, 14, 4 aperte tecte quidquid est
datum libenter accepi; the connexion
of the phrasing with the proverb as
quoted above makes strongly in favour
of rendering *aperte tecte* 'whether
openly or secretly.' If the reading
accipe quod do in Juven. 7, 165 be
correct, the context separates the
passages from those I have given above.
In De Or. 2, 74 tantum quantum ipsi
patiebantur accepimus, Boot, Mnem.
XXIII, p. 203, following Ernesti, reads
impertiebant or *-bantur*; but the context
justifies *patiebantur.*

ipsis non satis: *satis* repeated so
as not to end the sentence with *non*;
see n. on 2, 95; Acad. 1, 10.

8. **quaesita**: the sense of *exquirere
voluptatem* is hardly suitable here.

12. **foedus**: cf. 1, 70.

14. **an vero**: the interrogative form of
the sentence (as Madvig says) demands
an; there is no confusion in MSS. commoner than that of *at* and *an.*

utilitatibus...colemus: n. on 1, 42.

15. **sua sponte**, etc.: cf. 5, 44.

RDF

sponte, vi sua, ex se et propter se expetendam, dubium est quin
84 fundos et insulas amicis anteponamus? Licet hic rursus ea
commemores, quae optimis verbis ab Epicuro de laude amicitiae
dicta sunt. Non quaero quid dicat sed quid convenienter possit
rationi et sententiae suae dicere. 'Vtilitatis causa amicitia est 5
quaesita.' Num igitur utiliorem tibi hunc Triarium putas esse
posse quam si tua sint Puteolis granaria? Collige omnia quae
soletis: 'Praesidium amicorum.' Satis est tibi in te, satis in
legibus, satis in mediocribus amicitiis praesidi; iam contemni non
poteris; odium autem et invidiam facile vitabis; ad eas enim 1
res ab Epicuro praecepta dantur. Et tamen tantis vectigalibus

4 sed quid: *sed quod* BE.   5 est quaesita: ita A; *quaesita est* B.   7 granaria:
gramana A; *graviana* B; *gramina* codd. dett.   9 praesidi: *praesidii* Crat.;
praesidium AB.   10 enim res: *res enim* BE.

1. **dubium est quin**: 'have we any
doubt about...?' Cf. 5, 91.

3. **de laude am.**: 'in praise of...,'
dom. 27 praedicatio de mea laude; Leg.
2, 63.

4. **non quaero**, etc.: n. on 2, 70.

7. **quam si tua sint**: cf. J. Lebreton
in Rev. de Phil. XXII, p. 274 on tenses
in these comparative cond. sent. After
a principal clause with pres. or fut.
(1) *quam si* with present or perfect
occurs 3 times (here: Off. 1, 23; Fam.
16, 5, 1): with imperf. or pluperf. 26
times (e.g. Fin. 3, 44; 5, 56); (2) *quasi*
with pres. or perf. 42 times (e.g. Fin. 2,
42): with imperf. or plupf. 3 times (Lael.
14; Leg. 2, 51, 53).

granaria: these grain stores are nowhere else mentioned; but a very large
proportion of the whole Mediterranean
trade with Italy passed through Puteoli;
and doubtless much of the imported
corn was stored there. The granaries were
private, not public, as the context shows.
Granaria Puteolis = g. qu. sunt P. Puteoli
was afterwards supplanted by Ostia;
see Waltzing, vol. II, especially 64–89,
on *horrea*.

8. **praesidium**: so 1, 68; Lael. 46
praesidi adiumentique causa (Epicurus'
view of friendship); Quint. 5, 11, 41 ubi
amici, ibi opes. Sen. (ep. 9, 8) qu.
Epicurus' letter: 'ut habeat qui sibi
aegro adsideat, succurrat in vincula
coniecto vel inopi.' Usener, § 175.

9. **mediocribus**: the Greek original
contrasted the ideal with the everyday
type of friendship; the contrast runs
through the Laelius; cf. Lael. 22.

praesidi: the *praesidium* of the MSS.
is a correction caused by the Ciceronian
form of the genitive, which was not

understood; so in § 69 and Liv. 22, 14, 15,
quoted by Madvig: 'Rutili...nunc animum induxi scribere inveteratum errorem non amplius sustineri posse ratus.'
C. F. W. Müller on Off. 2, 47 (p. 72, 23).
Quite likely Lamb. was right in writing
Antoni in Brut. 1, 12, 1. Corruptions
traceable to this cause abound in MSS.;
so Ad Herenn. 3, 27 (*brachio*); 4, 16.
Madvig quotes from the poets exx. of
satis plus substantive (nom. or accus.)
referred to verb; as Virg. Aen. 11, 366;
Ovid, Met. 3, 149; Lucr. 1, 241 (where
*tactus satis esset causa leti = t. letum satis
efficeret*); also Cic. Inv. 2, 113 num iam
satis pro eo quod fecerit honos habitus
sit, where *satis* qualifies the whole
phrase *honos habitus sit*, not *honos* alone.
Madvig hesitates about two passages,
(1) Att. 12, 50 si satis consilium quadam
de re haberem; and indeed expressions
like *satis animi, consili habere* are so
common as to raise suspicion of the
passage; but on the other hand there
is no apparent reason why *satis* should
not qualify *consilium habere*, as well as
honorem habere; (2) the same applies to
the other ex. Ad Herenn. 1, 1 vix satis
otium studio suppeditare possumus.
Madvig justly condemns the misinter-
pretation by edd. of passages like
Liv. 6, 18, 10 vobis auxilium satis
est, 'you are content with your
auxilium,' i.e. 'you want nothing beyond
it.'

contemni: n. on 1, 67 despicationes.
Sen. dial. 4, 11, 1 utilis...ira quia con-
temptum effugit; 12, 13, 8 (and Lucr.);
clem. 1, 7, 3; ep. 105, 5, 6; dial. 6,
19, 2.

11. **et tamen**: n. on 1, 15.

vectigalibus: often of private re-

ad liberalitatem utens etiam sine hac Pyladea amicitia multorum
te benivolentia praeclare et tuebere et munies. At quicum ioca 85
seria, ut dicitur, quicum arcana, quicum occulta omnia?
Tecum optime, deinde etiam cum mediocri amico. Sed fac
5 ista esse non importuna; quid ad utilitatem tantae pecuniae?
Vides igitur, si amicitiam sua caritate metiare, nihil esse praestantius, sin emolumento, summas familiaritates praediorum
fructuosorum mercede superari. Me igitur ipsum ames oportet,
non mea, si veri amici futuri sumus.

10 XXVII. Sed in rebus apertissimis nimium longi sumus. Perfecto enim et concluso neque virtutibus neque amicitiis usquam

---

1 liberalitatem: *libertatem* AB cod. Morel.   1 etiam: *eam* AB cod. Morel.;
corr. Manutius.   2 benivolentia: ita AB; *benevolentia* vulg.   2 et tuebere A cod.
Morel.; *tuebare* BE: *tuebere* Madv.   2 ioca seria: *ioca et seria* A.   4 cum:
qui E.   4 fac: *facta* B.   5 importuna: *inportuna* A¹B; *inoportuna* A (corr. fort.
prima manu).   7 sin: *suo* B.   8 fructuosorum: *preciosorum* Crat.   10 sed: *si* B.
10 sumus: *fuimus* E.   10 perfecto: *profecto* A¹.   11 concluso: *concludo* A¹.

venues; cf. magnum vectigal est parsi-
monia, Parad. 49.

1. **Pyladea:** § 79. For similar adjectives cf. De Orat. 3, 71.

2. **et tuebere et:** the ejection of the
first *et* here is no more necessary than
that of the second *quicum* below; *tuebere* and *munies* are no more similar in
meaning than *arcana* and *occulta*.

munies: Ovid, P. 2, 3, 25 en ego non
paucis quondam munitus amicis.

at, etc.: a supposed objection of Torquatus. The Epicureans doubtless
argued that *ioca seria* (anything and
everything) can only be shared with the
verus amicus; cf. Ad Herenn. 2, 37
utile est veros amicos habere: habeas
enim quicum iocari possis. The word
utile points to an Epicurean maxim,
and the treatise Ad Herennium is
largely tinged by Epicureanism.

ioca seria, etc.: Lael. 22 quid dul-
cius quam habere quicum omnia audeas
sic loqui ut tecum? In the Laelius
Cicero attacks Epicurus for his doctrine
of friendship, but this is altogether in
his vein. Att. 1, 18, 1 nihil mihi scito
tam deesse quam hominem eum quocum omnia, quae me cura aliqua
afficiunt, una communicem, qui me
amet, qui sapiat, quicum ex animo
loquar, nihil fingam, nihil dissimulem,
nihil obtegam. [In the foregoing
passage many edd. drop *una*, partly
because it is far separated from *quocum*, partly as superfluous with *communicem*; neither reason is sound; cf.
una consentire in Sest. 109. The grounds

on which *qui me amet qui sapiat* are
supposed to be a quotation in verse,
are very slight. The change from *quocum*
to *quicum* is incredible.] For *ioca seria*
cf. Sall. Jug. 96 ioca atque seria cum
humillimis agere; Liv. 1, 4, 9 seria ac iocos
celebrare; Tac. an. 2, 13 per seria, per
iocos eundem animum; 6, 2 ludibria
seriis permiscere solitus; Fronto, Ad
Am. 1, 1 iocum seriumque permittavi-
mus; Curt. 9, 29 per seria ac ludum;
more quoted by Sonny in Archiv 9, 65.

3. **arcana:** Virg. Aen. 4, 421 solam
nam perfidus ille | te colere, arcanos
etiam tibi credere sensus; *arcanus* not
in speeches, here only in philosophical
works.

5. **importuna:** the word *inopportunus*
belongs to a late period; improved
knowledge of MSS. has ejected it from
De Or. 2, 20 and 3, 18. *Non imp.* here
=οὐκ ἀνεπιτήδεια: this weaker sense
is rare in Cicero, but occurs in the two
passages of De Or. and in other writers,
as Sall. Jug. 92, 7; Tac. an. 12, 12, 5;
Sil. 3, 540; Gell. 3, 7, 5.

quid ad: always elliptical, n. on Acad.
2, 94: cf. above 1, 39 nihil ad.

9. **si...sumus:** 'de proprietate formae
eius: *si—futuri sumus* (εἰ—μέλλομεν)
qua significamus ad quid consequendum
aliquid necessarium sit (ubi nunc fere
dicunt: *si nos amicos fieri oportet*), dixi
in Opusc. Acad. 11, p. 281' (Madvig).

10. **longi:** so μακρός of persons in
Plato.

perfecto: the abl. abs. neut. with
subject unexpressed, occurs in all

locum esse, si ad voluptatem omnia referantur, nihil praeterea est magno opere dicendum. Ac tamen, ne cui loco non videatur esse responsum, pauca etiam nunc dicam ad reliquam orationem 86 tuam. Quoniam igitur omnis summa philosophiae ad beate vivendum refertur, idque unum expetentes homines se ad hoc 5 studium contulerunt, beate autem vivere alii in alio, vos in voluptate ponitis, item contra miseriam omnem in dolore, id primum videamus, beate vivere vestrum quale sit. Atque hoc dabitis, ut opinor, si modo sit aliquid esse beatum, id oportere totum poni in potestate sapientis. Nam si amitti vita beata 1 potest, beata esse non potest. Quis enim confidit semper sibi illud stabile et firmum permansurum quod fragile et caducum sit? Qui autem diffidet perpetuitati bonorum suorum, timeat necesse est ne aliquando amissis illis sit miser. Beatus autem esse in 87 maximarum rerum timore nemo potest. Nemo igitur esse beatus 1 potest. Neque enim in aliqua parte, sed in perpetuitate temporis

2 magno opere: *magnopere* AB.   4 omnis summa: ita A; *summa omnis* B. 7 in dolore: *indole* E.   11 beata: om. B.   11 quis: *quid* BE. 11 semper sibi: ita A; *sibi semper* B.   12 illud: ita AB; *id* E.   13 diffidet: ita A; *diffidit* BE.   15 esse beatus: ita AB; *beatus esse* E.

periods of Latin without dependent clause; with such clause it appears first in Cicero and is rare outside his writings in the best period, but common in Livy, Tacitus and some other writers. See Draeger, § 584. A dependent *ut*-clause is found in Off. 2, 42; *cum matre* depends on *compecto* in Scaur. 8; later, the dependent constructions take a wider range.

2. **magno opere:** Cic. rather more frequently uses this form than *magnopere*. Caesar almost always *magnopere*.

ac tamen: Madvig lays down the rule that Cicero in introducing some consideration opposed to what precedes, uses *et tamen* or *ac tamen* not *at tamen*, which is only in place 'in descensu ad minus post *si, si non, etsi,* interposito saepe vocabulo' (add *quamvis*); Att. 3, 19, 2; 16, 11, 2; Fam. 12, 15, 2 (Lentulus). Cf. 5 §§ 14, 94. Sometimes *ac* or *atque* without *tamen* as 2, 34. Tyrrell and Purser read *ac tamen* in F. 16, 8, 1 (Quintus Cic.) with Wesenberg.

4. **omnis:** goes with *summa* not *ph.*; 5, 38 in homine summa omnis animi est. For the context cf. 1, 62; 5 §§ 12, 16, 86; Madvig refers to Varro ap. Aug. c. d. 19, 1 nulla est homini causa philosophandi nisi ut beatus sit.

6. **beate vivere...ponitis:** n. on 1, 1.

7. **item...in dolore:** n. on 1, 41.

8. **quale:** attached to infin. below, § 104; in Brut. 294; Virg. ecl. 5, 46; cf. Lucr. 2, 122; cf. ipsum Latine loqui in Brut. 140 and Martha there. Sen. d. 11, 16, 2 hoc fuit eius lugere...parentare.

atque, etc.: the Stoic colouring of the passage is obvious; see 3, 45.

9. **esse beatum:** τὸ εἶναί τινα εὐδαίμονα; a substitute for εὐδαιμονίαν.

10. **in potestate:** see Sen. ep. 16, 6 quid sit iuris nostri.

13. **diffidet:** for the form of the sentence cf. Off. 2, 24 qui se metui volent, a quibus metuentur, eosdem metuant ipsi necesse est. *Diffidat,* given by some of the older edd., would supply a sufficiently usual form; in that case the shadow of the coming subj. in the second clause is cast upon the verb in the first; see my n. on Cato m. 2; also n. on 3, 73 and Madvig's n. [The reading can hardly be right in Sen. dial. 9, 11, 6 (Haase) qui mortem timebit, nihil umquam pro homine et viro faciet: at qui sciat hoc sibi cum conciperetur statim condictum, vivet ad formulam.] The change of tense in passing from *confidit* to *diffidet* has many parallels; as § 88 qui ponit... qui putabit; see C. F. W. Müller on Cicero, Orat. 1, p. 76, l. 4.

15. **m. rerum timore:** 'when in alarm about very important matters.'

16. **in perpetuitate:** in the context

vita beata dici solet, nec appellatur omnino vita, nisi confecta
atque absoluta, nec potest quisquam alias beatus esse, alias
miser; qui enim existimabit posse se miserum esse, beatus non
erit. Nam cum suscepta semel est beata vita, tam permanet
5 quam ipsa illa effectrix beatae vitae sapientia neque exspectat
ultimum tempus aetatis, quod Croeso scribit Herodotus prae-
ceptum a Solone. At enim, quem ad modum tute dicebas, negat
Epicurus ne diuturnitatem quidem temporis ad beate vivendum
aliquid afferre, nec minorem voluptatem percipi in brevitate
:o temporis, quam si illa sit sempiterna. Haec dicuntur incon- **88**
stantissime. Cum enim summum bonum in voluptate ponat,
negat infinito tempore aetatis voluptatem fieri maiorem quam
finito atque modico. Qui bonum omne in virtute ponit, is potest
dicere perfici beatam vitam perfectione virtutis; negat enim
15 summo bono afferre incrementum diem. Qui autem effici voluptate beatam vitam putabit, qui sibi is conveniet, si negabit
voluptatem crescere longinquitate? Igitur ne dolorem quidem.

1 dici: *duci* AB.   1 vita: ita AB; *vita beata* codd. dett. Forte verba *nisi* et *vita*
sunt transponenda.   4 semel est: *est semel* B.   7 at enim: *etenim* codd.; corr.
Manutius.   7 dicebas: *ducebas* BE.   8 diuturnitatem: ita A et cod. Glogauensis;
nec diuturnitate BE.   8 quidem: om. cod. Glogauensis et Lambinus; *ne
diuturnitatem quidem* Madv.   10 haec: *nec* B.   14 perfici: ita AB; *perspici* E·
15 effici voluptate beatam vitam: ita A; *voluptate vitam effici beatam* B.   16 is:
om. B.   16 conveniet: *conveniret* B.   16 negabit: ita AB[1]; *negabat* B[2]E.

there seems a reminiscence of Aristotle's arguments about βίος τέλειος:
cf. Eth. N. 1, 7, 16.
  1. **vita nisi:** see adn. crit. The old
readings give miserable sense; *beata vita*
only affords a tautology; but *vita* alone is
nonsensical; 'a life is not called a life at
all unless when it is finished.' Madvig's
subtleties do not get over the difficulty.
  2. **alias...alias:** see Wölfflin in Archiv
2, 233 sq. The double *alias* appears in
Plaut., Varro, Cic., Caes. and is rare
afterwards.
  4. **suscepta,** etc.: cf. Sen. ep. 50, 9
virtutes receptae exire non possunt.
  6. **Croeso:** Arist. Eth. N. 1, 11, 1 ff.;
Herod. 1, 32; Mayor on Juven. 10, 274.
  7. **at enim:** 'recte, quod in codicibus
est, mutavit Davisius Manutii coniec-
turam sequens. nam neque proximorum
ratio redditur neque Ciceronis disputatio
continuatur, sed interponitur a diversa
parte Epicuri sententia, qua is se expedire conabatur' (Madvig).
  8. **ne...quidem:** Madvig shows the
necessity of this reading; *nec quidem...
nec* is not Latin.

  10. **inconstantissime:** cf. Acad. 2, 69
inconstantia levatur auctoritas.
  12. **negat,** etc.: see 1, 63 *n.*
  13. **is potest dicere:** for the Stoics see
3, 47 *n.*
  14. **perfectione virtutis:** this phrase is
a little loose, because, although virtue,
in the Stoic scheme, is the outcome
of gradual advancement (προκοπή) of
natural endowments towards perfection
(τελείωσις), yet it is itself incapable of
degree.
  17. **ne dolorem quidem:** the grammatical form of the preceding sentence
is continued without regard to the construction which the sense would strictly
require. Madvig qu. N.D. 1, 82 quid
igitur censes? Apim illum nonne deum
videri Aegyptiis? Tam hercle quam tibi
illam vestram Sospitam; Ter. Hec. 278
ita animum induxerunt, socrus omnis
esse iniquas: haud pol me quidem (distinctly for *haud pol ego sum iniqua*);
Leg. 1, 52 postremo, si propter alias res
virtus expetitur, melius esse aliquid
quam virtutem necesse est. Pecuniam-
ne igitur, an honores, an formam, an

An dolor longissimus quisque miserrimus, voluptatem non optabiliorem diuturnitas facit? Quid est igitur cur ita semper deum appellet Epicurus beatum et aeternum? Dempta enim aeternitate nihilo beatior Iuppiter quam Epicurus; uterque enim summo bono fruitur, id est voluptate. 'At enim hic etiam dolore.' : At eum nihili facit. Ait enim se, si uratur, 'Quam hoc suave!'

2 optabiliorem: *optabilem* A¹.   3 appellet Epicurus beatum: ita A; *epicurus appellet beatum* B; Epicurus beatum appellet E.   4 Iuppiter: *iupiter* AB.   6 nihili: *nihil* AB.   6 se: supra versum A (fort. prima manu); om. BE.

valetudinem? Liv. 5, 35, 3 hanc gentem Romam venisse comperio; id parum certum est solamne an adiutam? See similar irregularities in note on 1, 14.

2. **ita:** Madvig points out that this does not go with *semper*, but means *ita ut facit*: '*semper* respuit adverbium gradum notans'; although such an adverb is sometimes applied to negatives and words like *par*.

4. **nihilo beatior:** so Inscr. of Oinoanda: text of Heberdey and Kalinka, Bulletin de Correspondance Hellénique, XXI, p. 369 ὄντα δ' οἷα τὴν διάθεσιν ἡμῶν ἰσόθεον ποιεῖ, καὶ οὐδὲ διὰ τὴν θνητότητα τῆς ἀφθάρτου καὶ μακαρίας φύσεως λειπομένους δείκνυσιν· ὅτε μὲν γὰρ ζῶμεν ὁμοίως τοῖς θεοῖς, χαίρομεν (lacuna). There is an allusion to a famous saying of Epicurus: Ael. var. h. 4, 13 ὁ αὐτὸς ἔλεγεν ἑτοίμως ἔχειν καὶ τῷ Διὶ ὑπὲρ εὐδαιμονίας ἀγωνίζεσθαι μᾶζαν ἔχων καὶ ὕδωρ: cf. too Diog. L. 10, 135 ζήσῃ ὡς θεὸς ἐν ἀνθρώποις. To this boast there are many allusions elsewhere; see Usener p. 339 sq. In the Herculanean roll 152 (Scott p. 148 sq.) the doctrine of the equal happiness of σοφοί and θεοί is laid down. But at times Epic. admitted a difference of degree between the happiness of gods and sages; Diog. L. 10, 121. Of course on his principle that the element of time is unessential to the degree of happiness, the importance here attributed to *aeternitas* is irrelevant; cf. the quotations from Sextus in Sen. ep. 73, also 74 § 13; Plut. n. p. suaviter vivi, c. 7, p. 1091 *d* ἀφθάρτους καὶ ἰσοθέους ἀποκαλοῦντες ἑαυτούς: also 1, 40 with the nn. there. Of course Stoic θεοί as opposed to ὁ θεός are not aeterni. The doctrine of Epic. is again the same as that of the Stoics: Sen. d. 1, 1, 5 bonus tempore tantum a deo differt; ib. 2, 8, 2; also ep. 53, 11 non multo te di antecedent... diutius erunt, at mehercules magni artificis est clusisse totum in exiguo. Tantum sapienti sua quantum deo omnis

aetas patet. Est aliquid quo sapiens antecedat deum: ille beneficio naturae non timet, suo sapiens. Ecce res magna habere imbecillitatem hominis, securitatem dei

Iuppiter: for *est* omitted see 1, 3, 72.

5. **fruitur...dolore:** Davies quoted in illustration of the zeugma Att. 10, 4, 4 fortuna qua illi florentissima, nos duriore conflictati videmur. 'Durissime Livius in comparatione post *quam* ex praecedente *obesse* audiri voluit *prodesse* XLV, 20, 9 et 24, 8' (Madvig). A strong zeugma occurs in Cat. 3, 24 omnis hic locus acervis corporum et civium sanguine redundavit; cf. De Or. 3, 216 (sonant).

6. **si uratur:** i.e. in the bull of Phalaris; the same saying is quoted in Tusc. 2, 17; 5, 31; Pis. 42; Sen. ep. 67, 15; 66, 18; Lact. 3, 27, 5; 3, 17, 5; 3, 17, 42. Cf. also below, 5, 80 and 85; Tusc. 2, 18; 5, 75; and especially 5, 87 sequetur igitur horum ratione vel ad supplicium beata vita virtutem cumque ea descendet in taurum Aristotele Xenocrate Speusippo Polemone auctoribus...eadem Calliphontis erit Diodorique sententia. ...Reliqui habere se videntur angustius, enatant tamen, Epicurus, Hieronymus et si qui sunt qui desertum illud Carneadeum curent defendere. Nemo est eorum quin bonorum animum putet esse iudicem eumque condocefaciat ut ea quae bona malave videantur, possit contemnere. Cicero then goes on to praise all the utterances of Epicurus which he condemns here. Diog. L. 10, 118 (Epicurus says) κἂν στρεβλωθῇ δ' ὁ σοφός, εἶναι αὐτὸν εὐδαίμονα. The idea that the perfect man must be happy even on the rack is older than Epicurus; see Plat. rep. 361 E and Arist. Eth. Nic. 7, 13, 3 οἱ δὲ τὸν τροχιζόμενον καὶ τὸν δυστυχίαις μεγάλαις περιπίπτοντα εὐδαίμονα φάσκοντες εἶναι, ἐὰν ᾖ ἀγαθός, ἢ ἑκόντες ἢ ἄκοντες οὐδὲν λέγουσιν (an allusion to the Cynics).

dicturum. Qua igitur re ab deo vincitur, si aeternitate non **89**
vincitur? In qua quid est boni praeter summam voluptatem,
et eam sempiternam? Quid ergo attinet gloriose loqui, nisi
constanter loquare? In voluptate corporis (addam, si vis, 'animi,'
5 dum ea ipsa, ut voltis, sit ex corpore) situm est vivere beate.
Quid? istam voluptatem perpetuam quis potest praestare
sapienti? Nam quibus rebus efficiuntur voluptates, eae non sunt
in potestate sapientis. Non enim in ipsa sapientia positum est
beatum esse, sed in eis rebus quas sapientia comparat ad volup-
10 tatem. Totum autem id externum est, et quod externum, id in
casu est. Ita fit beatae vitae domina fortuna, quam Epicurus ait
exiguam intervenire sapienti.

XXVIII. Age, inquies, ista parva sunt. Sapientem locupletat **90**
ipsa natura, cuius divitias Epicurus parabilis esse docuit. Haec
15 bene dicuntur nec ego repugno, sed inter sese ipsa pugnant.
Negat enim tenuissimo victu, id est contemptissimis escis et
potionibus, minorem voluptatem percipi quam rebus exquisitissi-
mis ad epulandum. Huic ego, si negaret quicquam interesse ad
beate vivendum, quali uteretur victu, concederem, laudarem
20 etiam; verum enim diceret, idque Socratem, qui voluptatem
nullo loco numerat, audio dicentem, cibi condimentum esse
famem, potionis sitim. Sed qui ad voluptatem omnia referens

1 ab: ita A; *a* B.   4 loquare: *loqui* B.   5 ut: *aut* BE.   5 ex: *et* A; *e* B;
corr. Baiter.   7 eae: *hę* A; *hee* B.   7 sunt in potestate: ita A; *in potestate*
sunt BE. (*In* om. A¹.)   9 quas: *qua* BE.   10 externum: *extremum* B (bis).
14 haec: *nec* B.   15 pugnant: *repugnant* B.   16 id est: *idem* B.   21 nullo:
inillo A.

1. **ab deo:** *a* is far commoner in
Cicero before *d* than *ab*; Wagener in the
new ed. of Neue II, p. 834, says he has
reckoned 84 exx. of *a deo* or *a dis* against
14 of *ab* (of which this is one).
2. **summam v.**, etc.: for *perpetuitatem*
summae voluptatis.
3. **gloriose:** a retort upon Torquatus;
as in § 77; see 1, 42: cf. 2, 48.
10. **totum id:** after *rebus*; cf. 1, 20; 2, 6.
12. **exiguam interv.:** n. on 1, 63.
14. **ipsa natura:** cf. n. on 1, 45.
16. **negat,** etc.: Diog. L. 10, 130 οἱ γὰρ
λιτοὶ χυλοὶ ἴσην πολυτελεῖ διαίτῃ τὴν
ἡδονὴν ἐπιφέρουσιν, ὅταν ἅπαν τὸ ἀλγοῦν
κατὰ τὴν ἔνδειαν ἐξαιρεθῇ. καὶ μᾶζα καὶ
ὕδωρ τὴν ἀκροτάτην ἀποδίδωσιν ἡδονήν,
ἐπειδὰν ἐνδέων τις αὐτὰ προσενέγκηται.
Epic. wrote much in praise of bread and
water. [Usener reads ἀηδίαν in the first
of the two places where ἡδονήν occurs;

correction.] Cf. Usener, fr. 463. Solon,
p. 19 (Bergk's Anth. Lyr.) enlarges on
the theme that the poor may be as
wealthy in the true sense, as the rich.
id est: n. on 2, 6 and Acad. 1, 8.
19. **uteretur:** the doctrine might have
been expected to be put more generally
(*uteremur* or *quali quis uteretur*). The
German translators take the subject of
uteretur to be indefinite 'man'; but if
the text be right the subject must be
the same as that of *negaret*; cf. below,
consequatur (§ 92).
20. **Socratem:** in Xen. Mem. 1, 3, 5;
1, 6, 5. Hor. s. 2, 2, 20 tu pulmentaria
quaere sudando; Tusc. 5, 90 pulpa-
mentum fames (of Anacharsis); Sen. ep.
119, 4 nihil contemnit esuriens.
21. **nullo loco numerat:** 2, 50.
audio: 'I listen readily.'

vivit ut Gallonius, loquitur ut Frugi ille Piso, non audio nec eum
91 quod sentiat dicere existimo. Naturalis divitias dixit parabilis
esse, quod parvo esset natura contenta. Certe, nisi voluptatem
tanti aestimaretis. Non minor, inquit, voluptas percipitur ex
vilissimis rebus quam ex pretiosissimis. Hoc est non modo cor 5
non habere sed ne palatum quidem. Qui enim voluptatem ipsam
contemnunt, eis licet dicere se acupenserem maenae non anteponere; cui vero in voluptate summum bonum est, huic omnia
sensu, non ratione sunt iudicanda, eaque dicenda optima, quae
92 sint suavissima. Verum esto; consequatur summas voluptates 10
non modo parvo, sed per me nihilo, si potest; sit voluptas non
minor in nasturcio illo, quo vesci Persas esse solitos scribit
Xenophon, quam in Syracusanis mensis, quae a Platone graviter
vituperantur; sit, inquam, tam facilis, quam voltis, comparatio
voluptatis, quid de dolore dicemus? cuius tanta tormenta sunt, 15
ut in eis beata vita, si modo dolor summum malum est, esse non
possit. Ipse enim Metrodorus, paene alter Epicurus, beatum esse
describit his fere verbis: 'cum corpus bene constitutum sit et
sit exploratum ita futurum.' An id exploratum cuiquam potest

1 Frugi ille Piso: *frui ille ipso* BE.   1 nec eum: ita AB; *nec enim* codd. dett.
2 quod: om. E.   6 ne: om. B.   6 qui enim...anteponere: affert Nonius, p. 530.
6 voluptatem ipsam: *voluptates ipsas* Nonius.   7 eis: ita Nonius; *is* A¹; *his* BE.
7 acupenserem: *accupem se rē me* A; *accupenserem mene* BE.   10 sint: ita A;
sunt B.   10 suavissima: *firmissima* B.   16 eis: *hys* B; *his* E.   17 alter:
ita A²B Crat.; *aliter* A¹ et cod. Morel.

1. **vivit ut Gallonius:** an extravagant
statement, after all that has been admitted about the frugality of Epicurus.
Cf. Gnom. Vat. § 36 ὁ Ἐπικούρου βίος
τοῖς τῶν ἄλλων συγκρινόμενος ἕνεκεν
ἡμερότητος καὶ αὐταρκείας μῦθος ἂν νο-
μισθείη. Gallonius, a Lucilian character. See Corp. Gloss. s. v. pila where
there are references to Gundermann,
Rh. M. XLI, p. 632; Lejay, Revue Criti-
que, p. 426 (no vol. given); F. Marx,
Stud. Vindob. XVIII, p. 309; above,
2, 25, 70; see Epict. 3, 24, 38.
Piso: Madvig quotes a parallel to
the corruption *ipso* in Ascon. p. 15 (ed.
Clark); there is another in the text of
Fam. 14, 1, 3. For *loquitur ut Piso*
cf. Sen. dial. 7, 18, 1 'aliter,' inquit,
'loqueris, aliter vivis.'
5. **cor:** see n. on § 24. Plutarch, de
aud. poetis, 14 D (Wytt.).
12. **scribit:** Cyrop. 1, 2, 8 (κάρδαμον);
Cicero quotes the passage again, Tusc.
5, 99.
13. **Syracusanis** m.: Plat. rep. 404 D

Συρακοσίαν...τράπεζαν καὶ Σικελικὴν ποι-
κιλίαν ὄψου: Gorg. 518 B Μίθαικος ὁ τὴν
ὀψοποιίαν συγγεγραφὼς τὴν Σικελικήν;
Tusc. 5, 100 Italicarum Syracusiarum-
que mensarum (quoted from Plat. ep. 7,
p. 326 B); Hor. od. 3, 1, 18 Siculae
dapes.
16. **est, esse:** see my n. on Acad. 2, 22.
17. **beatum esse:** n. on § 86.
18. **his fere verbis:** ap. Clem. strom. 2,
21, p. 179 ἀγαθὸν ψυχῆς τί ἄλλο ἢ τὸ σαρκὸς
εὐσταθὲς κατάστημα καὶ τὸ περὶ ταύτης
πιστὸν ἔλπισμα; The words are quoted
again as from Metrodorus in Tusc. 2, 17
and (in a paraphrased form) 5, 27. They
became almost proverbial and were often
attributed to the Epicurean school
generally. So Cleomed. 2, 1, 87 (p. 158,
12, ed. Ziegler), and ib. 2, 1, 91 (p. 166, 3);
in the latter passage this and other
Epicurean utterances are compared to
the frenzied deliverances of the women-
votaries of Demeter, and of the Jews.
19. **potest esse:** see my n. on Acad.
2, 22.

esse quo modo se hoc habiturum sit corpus, non dico ad annum,
sed ad vesperum? Dolor igitur, id est summum malum, metuetur
semper, etiam si non aderit; iam enim adesse poterit. Qui potest
igitur habitare in beata vita summi mali metus? Traditur, in- **93**
5 quit, ab Epicuro ratio neglegendi doloris. Iam id ipsum absurdum,
maximum malum neglegi. Sed quae tandem ista ratio est?
Maximus dolor, inquit, brevis est. Primum quid tu dicis breve?
deinde dolorem quem maximum? Quid enim? summus dolor
pluris dies manere non potest? Vide ne etiam mensis! nisi forte
10 eum dicis qui, simul atque arripuit, interficit. Quis istum dolorem

1 se hoc: ita AE; *se hic* B.   2 id: om. B.   4 inquit: *enim* B.   5 id: *ad* B;
om. A; corr. Ernestius.   9 nisi: *ne* E.   10 qui: *qui si* B.   10 interficit:
interfecit B.

1. **ad annum**: here, 'in a year's time';
but the sense sometimes is 'next year,'
'when next year comes'; as in De Or.
3, 92 apparatu nobis est et rebus exquisitis...ut tibi, Caesar, faciendum est
ad annum; Caesar was aedile elect, and
it cannot be intended that his aedilician
games were to be exhibited in just a year
from the moment of speaking. Cf. too
Att. 5, 2, 1 Furnium nostrum quem ad
annum tribunum plebis videbam fore;
5, 18, 1 ad ver, 'when next spring
comes.' Although expressions like *ad
D annos* are not infrequent, yet *ad
annum* alone is rare. This is the only
passage in Merguet's Lexica; Lucil.
9, 55 (Müller) has the phrase; also
Varro, Pappus, ap. Non. 26 de eo
questum ad annum veniam ad novum
magistratum. In Cael. ap. Fam. 8, 14, 2
where *ad annum* used to be read,
C. F. W. Müller now has *in annum*; the
preposition is absent from the mss.

2. **ad vesperum**: Cato m. 67 cui sit
exploratum se ad vesperum esse victu-
rum. The fem. *vespera* is found in good
texts now in only two passages of Cicero,
viz. Phil. 2, 77 (where Gell. and some
existing mss. give *vesperum*); and In
Cat. 2, 6; in Caes. there is no instance.
The abl. in Cicero and the best writers
is *vespere* only. [Sen. dial. 6, 10, 4 nihil
de hodierna nocte promittitur.]
4. **habitare**: cf. Att. 2, 9, 2 video quo
invidia transeat et ubi sit habitatura;
other exx. of *habitare* with abstract
subjects are given in the lexica.
5. **id ipsum**: for *est* omitted see 1, 3.
Madvig in a note here draws the limits
within which *ipse* may stand for *is ipse*.
He first removes from the question
passages in which *ipse* denotes a person

so clearly by contrast that the demonstrative is not needed; so *ipse dixit*
("non pro eo alius"); *quaeram ex ipso*
("non ex alio de eo"); so Fin. 2, 82
ipsis non satis; also 5, 2 and 5, 39. In
such cases it is the addition of the
demonstrative rather than its omission,
which is notable; indeed in some instances (as in 5, 39) it could not be
added without materially changing the
sense. A numerous class of examples in
which the demonstrative is sometimes
inserted and sometimes omitted is that
in which *ipse* is followed by a relative,
as above, 1, 13 ab ipsis qui eam disciplinam probant. Madvig doubts *ipsum*
for *id ipsum* in Leg. 2, 12 estne ob
ipsum habenda nullo loco; Fam. 6, 19, 2
si modo ipsum sciet; Att. 10, 14, 3;
12, 14, 3; Div. 2, 119. In all these places
(to which Att. 12, 39, 2 may be added)
edd. now generally give *id ipsum*: Sen.
d. 4, 11, 2 ipso quo timentur. [In
similar circumstances in Greek αὐτό
might stand alone in all.] With regard
to Fam. 4, 13, 2 ut ipsum quod maneam
in vita, peccare me existimem, Madvig
says 'videri potest ita defendendum
esse, ut *quod maneam* relativae sententiae vicem expleat. Cf. Sen. Cons. ad
Marc. 12, 2 ipsum quod habuisti
fructus est?' Of Leg. 2, 34 he remarks
that the sense forbids *et ipsa* to stand
for *et ea ipsa* and further, that the
'codices antiqui' of Livy give *ipse* for
is ipse in only three places, viz. 5, 43, 4;
21, 55, 11; 22, 4, 2. [There is often
variation in even good mss. touching
is ipse; so Quinct. 69; Verr. 2, 3, 123.
And in edd. the demonstrative has
often been wrongly added, as in Acad.
1, 39; Verr. 2, 4, 20.]

timet? Illum mallem levares, quo optimum atque humanis-
simum virum, Cn. Octavium, Marci filium, familiarem meum,
confici vidi, nec vero semel nec ad breve tempus, sed et saepe
et plane diu. Quos ille, di immortales! cum omnes artus ardere
viderentur, cruciatus perferebat! Nec tamen miser esse, quia 5
summum id malum non erat, tantum modo laboriosus videbatur;
at miser, si in flagitiosa atque vitiosa vita afflueret voluptatibus.

94 XXIX. Quod autem magnum dolorem brevem, longinquom
levem esse dicitis, id non intellego quale sit. Video enim et
magnos et eosdem bene longinquos dolores, quorum alia toleratio 10
est verior, qua uti vos non potestis, qui honestatem ipsam per
se non amatis. Fortitudinis quaedam praecepta sunt ac paene
leges, quae effeminari virum vetant in dolore. Quam ob rem
turpe putandum est, non dico dolere (nam id quidem interdum est
necesse), sed saxum illud Lemnium clamore Philocteteo funestare, 15

> Quod eiulatu, questu, gemitu, fremitibus
> Resonando mutum flebilis voces refert.

Huic Epicurus praecentet, si potest, cum

> E viperino morsu venae viscerum
> Veneno imbutae taetros cruciatus cient!   20

Sic Epicurus: 'Philocteta, st! brevis dolor.' At iam decimum

3 et saepe: *etiam saepe* B.   4 et plane diu: *et* om. AB; addidit Halm.; *plane
et diu* Madv.   4 di: *dii* A; *dy* B.   8 quod: *quid* BE.   9 levem: *lenem* A.
9 esse: om. B.   10 quorum: ita AB Crat.; *quae non* cod. Morel.; *quaenam* codd.
dett.   14 dolere: *dolore* B.   14 interdum est: ita A; *est interdum* B.   15 Philocteteo: ita A; *philoctere* BE.   16 eiulatu: *heiulatu* A.   17 mutum: *mutu* E.
18 praecentet: ita B; *et* A.   18 si: *si qui* Crat.   18 potest, cum E viperino:
potest cui viperino AB; corr. Baiter.   21 st: ita Madv.; *si* codd.   21 brevis dolor:
ita Madv.; *brevis dolor levis* AB.

2. **Cn. Octavium**: consul in 76 B.C.

7. **miser, si**: for the omission of *esset*
cf. Tusc. I, 90 odiosum, si id esset
carere.

10. **bene long.**: Lucil. 30, 54 (Müller)
bene longincum morbum.

longinquos: Nettleship in Journal of
Philology xx, 176, truly states that
longinquus in the sense of *longus* 'is
confined to time, action, or condition,
and is never apparently extended to
physical length.'
  alia toleratio: cf. Acad. 2, 51
inanium visorum una depulsio est; and
the passages quoted in my note there;
also my n. on Acad. 2, 45 cognitionem.

15. **saxum**, etc.: the verses quoted are
from the Philoctetes of Attius. In
Tusc. 2, 33 Cicero quotes the end of the
line which precedes *quod eiulatu*, etc.

viz. *in lecto umido*. Madvig approves
the correction *tecto* for *lecto*, and supposes *saxum* here to refer to the cave
in which Philoctetes lived. Cf. Soph.
Ph. 1262 ἔξελθ' ἀμείψας τάσδε πετρήρεις
στέγας.

18. **praecentet**: the reference is to the
use of incantation for the purpose of
healing (ἐπάδειν, ἐπῳδαί). The pro-
fessional *praecantatrix* was known to
Plautus (Mil. 692); so *praecantrix* in
Varro ap. Non. 494, and *praecanere,
praecantator, praecantamen, praecantatio*
are all used in connexion with medical
sorcery. For *praecento* cf. *occentare* and
accentus; though *praecanto, occanto* are
found; as are *praecano, occano*, for
praecino, occino.

21. **Philocteta**: Madvig points out that
in the *nom.* case, Greek -ης is not repre-

annum in spelunca iacet. 'Si longus, levis; dat enim intervalla
et relaxat.' Primum non saepe, deinde quae est ista relaxatio, **95**
cum et praeteriti doloris memoria recens est et futuri atque
impendentis torquet timor? 'Moriatur,' inquit. Fortasse id opti-
5 mum, sed ubi illud: 'Plus semper voluptatis'? Si enim ita est,
vide ne facinus facias, cum mori suadeas. Potius ergo illa
dicantur: turpe esse, viri non esse debilitari dolore, frangi,
succumbere. Nam ista vestra: 'Si gravis, brevis; si longus, levis'
dictata sunt. Virtutis, magnitudinis animi, patientiae, forti-
10 tudinis fomentis dolor mitigari solet.

1 levis: *lenis* A. 3 cum: *quae* B. 3 est et: *sit et* A. 6 facinus facias:
facias facinus B. 6 mori suadeas: *mori si videas* BE.

sented by -*a* in Cicero, except in words
introduced early, as *pirata*, *Persa* (name
of a dog in a story going back to old
times in Div. 1, 103; *Perses* elsewhere).
The abl. in Cicero often ends in a -*a*
and the accus. sometimes in -*am*. See
Neue, 1², 31–40.
st!: I have followed Madvig with
some hesitation. Wherever *st!* is given
in current texts of Cicero (unless in
quotations) it is due to conjecture. So
Rep. 6, 12; Fam. 16, 24, 2; Att. 2, 1, 10.
In the last of these passages the conjecture seems to be particularly doubtful. [It would be as simple a correction
of the mss. here to read 'si durus brevis,'
leaving out *dolor*.]
  1. **dat intervalla**: Scott, Herc. pap.
26, p. 212, col. 13 (in re simili) ἀναπνοάς
γε λαμβάνει. Sen. ep. 78, 17 utrum vis
longum esse morbum an concitatum et
brevem? si longus est habet intercape-
dinem, dat refectioni locum (see the
context); also 78, 8. Cf. n. on 1, 49.
  2. **non saepe**: the sense 'it is not
often so' is inferior to 'it is often not
so.' This latter sense is perhaps possible.
Just as *non prorsus* stands for *prorsus
non* in circumstances where *non* would
otherwise have a stop after it (n. on
§ 17), so perhaps here *non saepe* took
the place of *saepe non* to avoid ending
the clause with *non*; cf. n. on Acad. 1, 10.
  3. **et futuri**, etc.: for the form et A et
B atque C, where C begins with a vowel
see n. on Acad. 1, 23; cf. ib. 2, 34.
  4. **id optimum**: for omission of *est*
see 1, 3.
  5. **ubi**: 'what becomes of...?'; so
often as Acad. 2 §§ 39, 82, 95.
  plus...voluptatis: 1, 62 *n*.
  6. **facinus facias**: so Ennius 305
(Müller); Liv. 1, 41; 24, 22; for the
'figura etymologica' generally see

Draeger, § 171, 1; and excellent articles
by Schmalz in Act. Erlang. 2, pp. 1–69
and 509–13.
  cum...suadeas: causal clause. Merguet's lexica give 25 quotations for
suadeo; the acc. and inf. constr. occurs
in Caec. 15; Arch. 14; but there is no
other instance of the simple infin.,
which, however, is found in De Or. 1,
251. But Draeger's statement (11², p. 324)
that this is the earliest occurrence of the
infinitive construction, is incorrect;
see Ad Herenn. 3, 5 (dissuadere). Draeger gives exx. from Virg. and later
authors, among them (p. 402) Aen. 12,
813 (add Phaedr. 1, 15, 6); and p. 409 instances of *suadeo* with accus. of person
(instead of dat.) and inf. Of course an
object clause with acc. and inf. is not uncommon; so Arch. 14; in Caec. 15 we
have *id* as object followed by explanatory clause. Cicero once (Phil. 13, 35)
uses *persuasum est* with simple inf.
[Caes. avoided the simple verb *suadere*.]
Prov. cons. 42 postea me ut sibi essem
legatus non solum suasit verum etiam
rogavit, is peculiar; either *me* is due to
the consciousness that *rogavit* is coming;
or it is a corruption of $\overset{i}{m}$ for *mihi*, or
perhaps an insertion.
  9. **dictata**: 'a schoolboy's lesson,'
something given out to be copied down
or committed to memory; so below,
4, 10 quasi dictata decantare; Tusc.
2, 26; N.D. 1, 72; Qu. fr. 3, 1, 11; Hor.
ep. 1, 1, 55 and 1, 18, 13 and 2, 1, 71;
Pers. 1, 29; Juven. 5, 122 (see Mayor's
n.). For the reproach here against Epic.
cf. 2, 20 and Sen. ep. 12 § 11 perseverabo
Epicurum tibi ingerere, etc.
  10. **fomentis**: only the plur. of this
word occurs in good Latin. The primary
sense is that of a bandage or poultice

96 XXX. Audi, ne longe abeam, moriens quid dicat Epicurus, ut intellegas facta eius cum dictis discrepare: 'Epicurus Hermarcho S. Cum ageremus,' inquit, 'vitae beatum et eundem supremum diem, scribebamus haec. Tanti aderant vesicae et

4 haec. Tanti: *ne tanti* B.   4 tanti aderant: ita A; *tanti autem* B; *tanti autem aderant* cod. Morel.

to keep down pain or inflammation; and in metaphorical uses the application is always to something that soothes mental pain or uneasiness; so Tusc. 2, 59 haec sunt solacia, haec fomenta dolorum. In the much-debated passage of Horace, **ep.** 1, 3, 25 quod si | frigida curarum fomenta relinquere posses | quo te caelestis sapientia duceret, ires, the interpretation which makes *curarum* a defining genitive, so that the *fomenta* consist of the *curae* (see Wilkins, ad loc.), seems to be excluded by usage. Even if *fomenta* could be applied to anything bad, like *curae*, it would still be necessary that the *curae*, if treated as equivalent to *fomenta*, should be regarded as *soothing* or *healing* appliances, which is manifestly impossible; cf. also Sen. ep. 51, 5 fomenta Campaniae (of Hannibal), where see context.

1. **ne longe abeam**: so Sex. Rosc. 47 ne longius abeam; cf. below, 5, 80 *n.* and Rep. 3, 28 nec vero longius abibo; Verr. 4, 109 non obtundam diutius.

2. **discrepare cum**: on the analogy of *pugnare cum*, etc.

Hermarcho: Sen. ep. 92, 25; Diog. L. 10, 22 quotes as from a letter to Idomeneus: 'τὴν μακαρίαν ἄγοντες καὶ ἅμα τελευτῶντες (Madvig τελευταίαν, after Davies) ἡμέραν τοῦ βίου ἐγράφομεν ὑμῖν ταυτί· στραγγουρικά τε παρηκολούθει καὶ δυσεντερικὰ πάθη ὑπερβολὴν οὐκ ἀπολείποντα τοῦ ἐν ἑαυτοῖς μεγέθους· ἀντιπαρετάττετο δὲ πᾶσι τούτοις τὸ κατὰ ψυχὴν χαῖρον ἐπὶ τῇ τῶν γεγονότων ἡμῖν διαλογισμῶν (Cicero inserts *inventorumque*) μνήμῃ. σὺ δὲ ἀξίως τῆς ἐκ μειρακίου παραστάσεως πρὸς ἐμὲ καὶ φιλοσοφίαν ἐπιμελοῦ τῶν παίδων Διοδώρου.' It will be observed that *ὑμῖν* is first used, then *σύ*. Apparently part of the extract is addressed to a number of friends (not to Hermarchus solely, nor to Idomeneus solely) and the last sentence to Hermarchus alone. Cicero takes no notice of *ὑμῖν*: either his copy did not contain the word, or knowing that Hermarchus was alone addressed in the last sentence, wrongly concluded that the whole letter belonged to him, and dropped *ὑμῖν* as inconsistent. In the will

of Epicurus (see further down), it is stated that the children of Metrodorus were living with Hermarchus. On the authority of Apollodorus in his 'Χρονικά,' Diog. L. 10, 15, gives this account of the death of Epic.: 'τελευτῆσαι δὲ αὐτὸν λίθῳ τῶν οὔρων ἐπισχεθέντων, ὡς φησὶ καὶ Ἕρμαρχος ἐν ἐπιστολαῖς, ἡμέρας νοσήσαντα τεσσαρεσκαίδεκα. ὅτε καὶ φησὶν Ἕρμιππος ἐμβάντα αὐτὸν ἐς πύελον χαλκῆν κεκραμένην ὕδατι θερμῷ καὶ αἰτήσαντα ἄκρατον ῥοφῆσαι· τοῖς δὲ φίλοις παραγγείλαντα τῶν δογμάτων μεμνῆσθαι, οὕτω τελευτῆσαι. Cicero alludes to the letter of Epic. in Tusc. 2, 45; 5 §§ 26, 74, 88; so Sen. ep. 66, 47; 92, 25; Epict. diss. 2, 23, 21. Marc. Aur. 9, 41, alludes to other utterances of Epic. about his illness. Cic. Fam. 7, 26, 1 mentions that the Stoics attributed the last illness of Epic. to a vicious life. Diog. L. 10, 7, quotes Timocrates to the effect that for many years Epic. was so ill as to be unable to rise from his couch. If Diog. L. 10, 24 may be trusted, Metrodorus, who died before Epicurus, wrote περὶ τῆς Ἐπικούρου ἀρρωστίας. A fragment of Philodemus V.H.² 1, 128, professes to give words written by him when at his last gasp: ἐκπνέων· 'ἑβδόμῃ γὰρ ἡμέρᾳ ὅτε ταῦτ' ἔγραφον, οὐχὶ ἀποκεχωρήκεν δὴ κατὰ τὴν οὔρησιν ἐμοὶ οὐθὲν καὶ ἀλγηδόνες ἐνῆσαν τῶν ἐπὶ τὴν τελευταίαν ἡμέραν ἀγουσῶν. σὺ οὖν, ἂν τι γένηται, τὰ παιδία τὰ Μητροδώρου διοίκησον τέτταρα ἢ πέντ' ἔτη μηθὲν πλεῖον δαπανῶν ἤ περ νῦν εἰς ἐμὲ δαπανᾷς κατ' ἐνιαυτόν.' καὶ προβάς· 'ὑπὲρ τῶν υἱῶν οἶδα καὶ Αἰγέα καὶ Διόδωρον καὶ τῆς σῆς φρενὸς ὄντας οὐκ ἀρέσκευμά μόνον'... This looks like a free version of the letter quoted by Cicero and Diog. L. but carried beyond the point at which they stop. Apparently the sons of Metrodorus are commended to Aegeus and Diodorus, as well as Hermarchus. In the will there is also a recommendation to Amynomachus and Timocrates. As to the letters of Epicurus, of which numerous traces exist, information will be found in Usener, pp. 131–64.

4. **vesicae et torminum**: Plin. n. h. 20, 36, mentions together *tormina* and

torminum morbi, ut nihil ad eorum magnitudinem posset
accedere.' Miserum hominem! Si dolor summum malum est,
dici aliter non potest. Sed audiamus ipsum: 'Compensabatur,'
inquit, 'tamen cum his omnibus animi laetitia, quam capiebam
5 memoria rationum inventorumque nostrorum. Sed tu, ut dignum
est tua erga me et philosophiam voluntate ab adulescentulo
suscepta, fac ut Metrodori tueare liberos.' Non ego iam Epa- 97
minondae, non Leonidae mortem huius morti antepono, quorum
alter cum vicisset Lacedaemonios apud Mantineam atque ipse
10 gravi volnere exanimari se videret, ut primum dispexit, quaesivit,

1 torminum: AB Crat. cod. Morel.; *viscerum* codd. dett.   2 miserum: ita AB;
en miserum cod. Glogauensis; *ecce miserum* codd. dett.   3 compensabatur: *com-
pensabat* B.   6 et philosophiam: ita A; *et erga philosophiam* B.   10 exanimari:
exanimati BE.   10 dispexit: ita A; *despexit* codd. cett.

stranguria; cf. 32, 24 t. ac vesicae ac cal-
culorum mala. Plut. n. p. suaviter vivi,
p. 1097 *e* ['Επίκουρος] *νόσῳ νοσῶν ἀσκίτῃ
τινὰς ἑστιάσεις φίλων συνῆγε καὶ οὐκ
ἐφθόνει τῆς προσαγωγῆς τοῦ ὑγροῦ τῷ
ὕδρωπι, καὶ τῶν ἐσχάτων Νεοκλέους λόγων
μεμνημένος ἐτήκετο τῇ μετὰ δακρύων
ἰδιοτρόπῳ ἡδονῇ* (a quotation from a
letter of Epic.); ib. 1089 E *οὐδὲ γὰρ ἂν
προσέπιπτεν ἀνδράσι νοῦν ἔχουσι στραγ-
γουρικὰ πάθη καὶ δυσεντερικὰ καὶ φθίσεις
καὶ ὕδρωπες, ὧν τοῖς μὲν αὐτὸς Ἐπίκουρος
συνηνέχθη, τοῖς δὲ Πολύαινος, τὰ δὲ Νεο-
κλέα καὶ Ἀγαθίβουλον ἐξήγαγε*; strophus
glossed by *dolor ventris* and *torcinem* (for
which see *torquimina* in Corp. Gloss.).
The word *tormina* (cf. *tormen-tum*) is
used by Cato 126; 156,5;157, 9; Lucret.
5, 997 has *vermina* (Sen. ep. 78, 9
verminatio, and 95, 17 of the brain);
in connexion with which may be mentioned an altar discovered at Rome in
recent times, dedicated to a god *Ver-
minus*. Cic. Tusc. 4, 27 has *torminosus*.
Non. 32 M. seems to quote *tormines*,
but the reading is not quite sure.
Stories are told of the death of Antisthenes resembling those about Epic.;
see Mullach, Fragm. II, p. 267.
2. **miserum hominem:** on *o* see my
nn. on Att. 13, 6, 4 (in Hermathena, 25
(1899), p. 333); cf. 2, 12, 1 *o suaves
epistulas tuas*; add 15, 13, 3, where *o*
is added by edd. to hominem nequam
but not to succeeding cautum. The
ecce of the inferior MSS. is intolerable, because Cicero nowhere uses *ecce*
with acc. [Madvig's reason for condemning the punctuation of preceding
edd. (*ecce miserum, si*, etc.), viz. 'con-
dicio non exclamationi, sed iudicio

adiungenda erat,' is not sound; see, e.g.
Phil. 2, 54 and 13, 34.] Cicero makes
but little use of *en* (not at all in the
philosophical writings), and generally
with indirect constructions or whole
clauses (like 'en hic ille est'); but the
accus. must apparently be allowed to
him; see Verr. 2, 1, 93; 2, 5, 55; Phil.
5, 15 (hence correct Draeger, § 179 B).
Köhler in Archiv 6, 38, says *en* takes
nom. first in Virg. and not in prose before
Tac.; he does not notice Cic. Deiot. 17
en causa cur regem fugitivos accuset;
perhaps *causa* (*cā*) was added there by
copyists who did not understand the construction *en cur*.... The nom. with *o* is of
course common in Cicero as elsewhere.
5. **rationum inventorumque:** in the
Greek there is only τῶν γεγονότων ἡμῖν
διαλογισμῶν. Cicero often gives
double renderings, and this trick in
rendering from the Greek is common
in Latin literature; thus Ennius represents ποῖ νῦν τρέπωμαι; (Eur. Med.) by
*quo nunc me vertam? quod iter incipiam
ingredi?* See n. on 1, 38 fin.
8. **huius morti:** for repetition cf. 1,
3 *n.*; 2, 19.
10. **ut primum dispexit:** the verb *dispicere* primarily meant to catch a
glimpse of something through a narrow
opening, then to see in circumstances of
difficulty; below, 4 §§ 64, 65 and 5 § 41;
see other exx. in my n. on Acad. 2, 61.
The rare verb διαβλέπειν in Plat.
Phaed. 86 D has, I think, a similar
sense; Socrates there knits his brow and
looks through narrowed eyelids. Cf.
διόψις (Plutarch and Plato, Tim. 40 D,
whence, however, Archer-Hind has
ejected the word). There is a slight

salvosne esset clipeus. Cum salvom esse flentes sui respondissent, rogavit essentne fusi hostes. Cum id quoque, ut cupiebat, audivisset, evelli iussit eam, qua erat transfixus, hastam. Ita multo sanguine profuso in laetitia et victoria est mortuus. Leonidas autem, rex Lacedaemoniorum, se in Thermopylis 5 trecentosque eos, quos eduxerat Sparta, cum esset proposita aut fuga turpis aut gloriosa mors, opposuit hostibus. Praeclarae mortes sunt imperatoriae; philosophi autem in suis lectulis plerumque moriuntur. Refert tamen quo modo. *Beatus* sibi videtur esse moriens. Magna laus. 'Compensabatur,' inquit, 10 **98** 'cum summis doloribus laetitia.' Audio equidem philosophi vocem, Epicure. Sed quid tibi dicendum sit oblitus es. Primum enim, si vera sunt ea, quorum recordatione te gaudere dicis, hoc est, si vera sunt tua scripta et inventa, gaudere non potes. Nihil enim iam habes quod ad corpus referas; est autem a te 15 semper dictum nec gaudere quemquam nisi propter corpus nec dolere. 'Praeteritis,' inquit, 'gaudeo.' Quibusnam praeteritis? si ad corpus pertinentibus, rationes tuas te video compensare cum istis doloribus, non memoriam corpore perceptarum voluptatum; sin autem ad animum, falsum est, quod negas animi 20 ullum esse gaudium quod non referatur ad corpus. Cur deinde Metrodori liberos commendas? quid *in* isto egregio tuo officio et tanta fide (sic enim existimo) ad corpus refers?

99   XXXI. Huc et illuc, Torquate, vos versetis licet, nihil in hac praeclara epistula scriptum a̱b Epicuro congruens et con- 25

5 rex: *rex si* B.   9 quo modo. *Beatus* sibi videtur: *quo modo sibi videtur* A; *quo modo sibi videbatur* B; corr. Madv.   16 nec gaudere: *ne gaudere* BE. 22 *in* isto: *in* supplevit Madv.; *ex* Manutius; om. codd.   25 epistula scriptum: *scriptum epistola* B.

logical inconsistency in the sentence; *cum...videret* implies full consciousness, after which it is strange to have the words *ut primum dispexit*, 'as soon as he returned to consciousness,' which words obviously go with what follows.

3. **evelli:** cf. Fam. 5, 12, 5 in which passage mss. read *avelli* (corrected by Kayser from this passage). He is followed by edd. gen. incl. Mend. and C. F. W. Müller; Mend. qu. Wölfflin in Herm. xxii, 593.

7. **gloriosa:** 1, 37; de Div. 1, 51.
9. **quo modo:** for the ellipse cf. Tusc. 2, 43 utendum est igitur his. Quaeres fortasse quo modo. Abundant illustrations are given by Gutsche 'de interrogationibus obliquis apud Ciceronem.'

Halle, 1885. Madvig exposes the old reading *refert tamen quod sibi videtur esse morienti magna laus*. There is no connexion with context; and the words themselves are incapable of explanation. The older edd. had often explained *réfert* as *dicit* or *exponit*, but as M. indicates that use is not older than Hor. and Livy.

11. **audio:** often, as here, of *willing* listening.
12. **quid...sit:** n. on § 70.
14. **inventa:** philosophical discoveries (see § 96: De Orat. 1, 84 inventa philosophorum: Sen. ep. 64, 7 and Lucr. 5, 9).
17. **praeteritis:** a reference to γεγονό-των in the letter of Epic. (Diog. L. 10, 22).
20. **quod negas:** 'your denial that....'
24. **vos versetis:** so 5, 86.

veniens decretis eius reperietis. Ita redarguitur ipse a se,
convincunturque scripta eius probitate ipsius ac moribus. Nam
ista commendatio puerorum, memoria et caritas amicitiae,
summorum officiorum in extremo spiritu conservatio indicat
5 innatam esse homini probitatem gratuitam, non invitatam
voluptatibus nec praemiorum mercedibus evocatam. Quod enim
testimonium maius quaerimus, quae honesta et recta sint, ipsa
esse optabilia per sese, cum videamus tanta officia morientis?
Sed ut epistulam laudandam arbitror eam quam modo totidem 100
10 fere verbis interpretatus sum, quamquam ea cum summa eius
philosophia nullo modo congruebat, sic eiusdem testamentum
non solum *a* philosophi gravitate, sed etiam ab ipsius sententia
iudico discrepare. Scripsit enim et multis saepe verbis et breviter
aperteque in eo libro, quem modo nominavi, mortem nihil ad
15 nos pertinere. Quod enim dissolutum sit, id esse sine sensu,
quod autem sine sensu sit, id nihil ad nos pertinere omnino. Hoc

---

1 redarguitur: *redarguetur* AB. 1 se: ita A; *sese* B. 10 ea: *ei* B.
11 philosophia: ita B; *philosophi* A. 12 *a*: om. codd.; supplevit Manutius.
13 et multis: *multis et* E. 13 breviter: *licenter* B. 14 aperteque: *apteque* A.
15 quod enim: *quid enim* B.

---

1. redarguitur: this word and *refellatur* in the similar passage, § 81, are in
favour of reading *convincuntur*, though
I do not regard (with Madvig) the
phrase *scripta vincuntur probitate,* 'his
writings are overborne by his principles,' as impossible.

5. innatam: n. on 1, 31; cf. 4, 4.

invitatam: cf. Cicero's word *invitamentum*; he does not use the similar
words *incitamentum, inritamentum.*

6. praemiorum: defining gen.

mercedibus: Ovid, Pont. 2, 3, 12 non
facile invenias multis e milibus unum |
virtutem pretium qui putet esse sui: |
ipse decor recte facti, si praemia desint |
non movet et gratis paenitet esse pro-
bum; cf. ib. 35 sq. Sen. d. 7, 9, 4
[virtus] ipsa pretium sui; ben. 4, 1, 2
virtus gratuita (cf. in mercedem colant
there); also 4, 1, 3.

7. testimonium...ipsa esse: cf. Du
M. on Flacc. 30.

10. interpretatus: the verb often
means 'to translate,' as below, 3, 35;
Acad. 1, 8 Menippum imitati non inter-
pretati.

summa philosophia: like *summa res
publica*; cf. Rep. 2, 39 quae (centuria)
ad summum usum urbis tignariis est
data. In Cat. 4, 24 de summa salute
vestra populique Romani decernite

diligenter. *Summa philosophiae* (§ 86)
would hardly be in place here.

13. et multis, etc.: for the form *et* A *et*
BC*que* see § 20.

14. modo: this word, like *nuper*, may
cover considerable spaces of time; cf.
e.g. Lael. §§ 6, 13, with my nn., also
below, 5, 4; Off. 2, 75; Cato m. §§ 27, 61;
Verr. 2, 4, 6; Liv. praef. 12 *nuper*
divitiae avaritiam invexere; Sen. Rh.
contr. 2, 4, 3, where *modo* covers the
time between birth and maturity; Sen.
de ira 2, 5, 5 nuper sub divo Augusto;
id. ben. 4, 30, 2 (of Cinna); n. q. 7, 3, 2
and 7, 25, 3 and 5; ep. 49, 4; Lucr.
5, 334, 336.

mortem: see note on *mors* in 1, 40.
The reference here is to κυρ. δ. 2 ὁ θάνατος οὐδὲν πρὸς ἡμᾶς· τὸ γὰρ διαλυθὲν
ἀναισθητεῖ· τὸ δ᾿ ἀναισθητοῦν οὐδὲν πρὸς
ἡμᾶς. Usener gives on p. 395 a mass of
references to passages where this doctrine is mentioned, and refers for others
to Ménage on Diog. L. 10, 124 and
Fabricius on Sextus, p. 185. Lucretius
enlarges on the text at great length.

16. hoc ipsum, etc.: the criticism which
Cicero makes here was also made by
Plutarch (possibly drawing on the same
Greek source) in a passage quoted by
Gell. 2, 8: Plutarchus secundo librorum
quos de Homero composuit, imperfecte

ipsum elegantius poni meliusque potuit. Nam quod ita positum
est, quod dissolutum sit, id esse sine sensu, id eius modi est ut
101 non satis plane dicat, quid sit dissolutum. Sed tamen intellego
quid velit. Quaero autem quid sit quod, cum dissolutione, id
est morte, sensus omnis exstinguatur, et cum reliqui nihil sit 5
omnino, quod pertineat ad nos, tam accurate tamque diligenter
caveat et sanciat, ut Amynomachus et Timocrates, heredes sui,
de Hermarchi sententia dent quod satis sit ad diem agendum
natalem suum quotannis mense Gamelione, itemque omnibus
mensibus vicesimo die lunae dent ad eorum epulas qui una 10
secum philosophati sint, ut et sui et Metrodori memoria colatur.
102 Haec ego non possum dicere non esse hominis quamvis et belli
et humani, sapientis vero nullo modo, physici praesertim, quem

1 nam quod: *nam quid* B.   4 cum: om. BE.   7 sanciat: *sanciat* A; *sanctitat* B.
7 Amynomachus: ita B et Crat.; *aminomachus* A et cod. Morel.; *antinomachus*
codd. dett.   8 de: *ad* B.   11 sint: ita AB; *sunt* E.   11 ut et: *et ut* A.

atque praepostere atque inscite syllo-
gismo esse usum Epicurum dicit verba-
que ipsa Epicuri ponit (then follows
κυρ. δ. 2); nam praetermisit, inquit, quod
in prima parte sumere debuit τὸν
θάνατον εἶναι ψυχῆς καὶ σώματος διά-
λυσιν, tum deinde eodem ipso [un-
classical combination of *idem* and *ipse*!]
quod omiserat, quasi posito, concesso-
que ad confirmandum aliud utitur.
Progredi autem hic, inquit, syllogismus
nisi illo prius posito non potest. Gellius
naturally treats the criticism as trivial,
seeing that the severance of mind and
body in death is obvious. But Madvig
and other scholars before him have
pointed out from a passage of Alex.
Aphrod. on Arist. Top. 1, 7, that the
criticism as it appeared in the Greek
original was misunderstood by Cicero
and Plutarch both; the objection
brought was that Epicurus argued from
the διαλυθέν which is ἀναισθητοῦν to
the διάλυσις or process of dying. At
one point Cicero and Plut. ap. Gell. are
not in agreement; Cicero says that Epic.
should have explained *quid sit dissolutum*, i.e. what he meant by the word
διαλυθέν: whereas Plut. blames him
for not defining θάνατος. Perhaps the
Greek critic called for definitions both
of θάνατος and of διαλυθέν or διάλυσις.

2. id est: see n. on 1, 72; 2, 6.
7. caveat: in his will, preserved by
Diog. L. 10, 16 sq. (Usener, fragm. 217).
Cicero has here abbreviated the passage.
Aelian and Plutarch ap. Us. fr. § 218,
quote as from the will provisions not
contained in the copy given by Diog. L.;

and criticise Epic. for inconsistency as
Cicero does here. According to Diog. L.
10, 118, Epic. held that the σοφός will
not bestow a thought on his burial. See
a singular comment qu. by Us. fr. § 578
from V.H.
   8. de...sententia: *de* or *ex* senatus s.;
but only *ex* senatus consulto; *ex* auctoritate sen. (not *de*, I think).
   11. sui...memoria: it is quite possible
that the MSS. have changed here
original *sua*, by assimilation with *Metrodori*; cf. n. on § 76.
   12. quamvis: 'as nice as you please':
Lael. 17.
   13. physici: the title is often applied
to Epic. by Cicero as above, 1, 19; Tusc.
1, 48; N.D. 1, 77 and 83; 2, 48. For
references to other writers see Usener's
index, s. v. φυσικός.
   praesertim: cf. Lael. 15: a later
writer would probably have used *nedum*
here.
   quem se ille esse volt: this use of
velle, 'to claim' or 'to pretend,' is
common; but *esse* is usually omitted,
as in 5, 13 Strato physicum se voluit;
Div. 2, 118; Off. 2, 78; De Or. 2, 246;
Top. 78; de opt. gen. or. 6 and 15; Phil.
2, 14 and 4, 6; Lucr. 5, 1120. Madvig
gives these exx. and Phil. 2, 19 cupio
me audacem; also Tusc. 5, 66 qui se
hunc mathematicum malit, but *malit*
there bears its usual sense, like *velit*
above, Fin. 2, 33 integrum se salvomque
velit. Cf. further Catull. 97, 9 se facit
esse venustum; Cato, orig. 7 § 2 (Jordan) me nunc volo ius pontificium optime
scire; Nep. Dion 1, 3 etsi Dionysi cru-

se ille·esse volt, putare ullum esse cuiusquam diem natalem.
Quid? idemne potest esse dies saepius, qui semel fuit? Certe
non potest. An eiusdem modi? Ne id quidem, nisi multa annorum
intercesserint milia, ut omnium siderum eodem unde profecta
5 sint fiat ad unum tempus reversio. Nullus est igitur cuiusquam
dies natalis. 'At habetur!' Et ego id scilicet nesciebam! Sed
ut sit, etiamne post mortem coletur? idque testamento cavebit
is, qui nobis quasi oraculum ediderit nihil ad nos pertinere post
mortem? Haec non erant eius, qui innumerabilis mundos in-
10 finitasque regiones, quarum nulla esset ora, nulla extremitas,
mente peragravisset. Num quid tale Democritus? Vt alios
omittam, hunc appello, quem ille unum secutus est. Quod si dies **103**
notandus fuit, eumne potius, quo natus, an eum, quo sapiens

1 putare: *putari* AB.   5 Nullus: *Nullius* E.   6 at habetur: *et habet* BE.
6 scilicet: om. A¹.   8 nobis: *vobis* E.   8 ad nos pertinere post mortem: ita A;
post mortem ad nos pertinere B.   10 ora: *hora* AB.   11 num quid: *num
quod* B.   11 ut: om. B.   12 quod si: *quid si* B.   13 eumne: *eumque* BE.

delitas ei displicebat, tamen salvom...
studebat; Plaut. Curc. 335; and for the
omission of *esse* such phrases as *integ-
ram (causam) servatam oportuit* in Acad.
2, 10, where see my n.
2. **certe non potest**: sc. *esse* cf. 4, 48.
5. **reversio**: Cicero is alluding to the
old theory of the *magnus annus* or
astronomical cycle, which appears in
several dialogues of Plato, and was
especially propounded by the Stoics;
see Munro on Lucr. 1, 1029.
6. **habetur**: 'is deemed to exist.' I
think that the simple phrase *habere
natalem*, 'to keep a birthday,' for *agere*
(§ 101) was not in use; though *habere
diem* with an epithet attached (sense
'regard as') is found, as Virg. Aen. 5, 49
dies...quem semper acerbum | semper
honoratum, sic di voluistis, habebo;
Suet. Aug. 23 ut...diem cladis quotannis
maestum habuerit ac lugubrem; Nep.
Tim. 5, 1 diem natalem festum habere.
et ego: for *et* in retorts cf. Draeger,
§ 311, 13.
8. **quasi oraculum**: § 20 *n.*
9. **haec...peragravisset**: so strikingly
like what Lucr. 1, 74, says of Epic.:
'extra | processit longe flammantia
moenia mundi | atque omne immensum
peragravit mente animoque,' that it is
natural to suppose an imitation here.
But the assertion about Epicurus may
have been a commonplace in his school,
and doubtless there were similar com-
monplaces in other schools: cf. Timon
to Pyrrho ap. Sext. A.M. 1, 305 μοῦνος

δ'ἀνθρώποισι θεοῦ τρόπον ἡγεμονεύεις | ὃς
περὶ πᾶσαν ἑλὼν (?ἀλεὶς) γαῖαν ἀναστρέ-
φεται | δεικνὺς εὐτόρνου σφαίρας περικαύ-
τορα κύκλον (Mullach 1, p. 97): Sen. dial.
8, 5, 6 cogitatio nostra caeli munimenta
perrumpit, and Horace's (od. 1, 28, 5)
animoque rotundum percurrisse polum.
10. **nulla extremitas**: 1, 17 *n.*; Acad.
2, 116, with my note.
11. **Democritus**: for the ellipse cf. 2,
17.
12. **quem...unum**: 1, 21 *n.*
13. **eumne**: a rare instance of a verb
like *oportuit* being supplied from the
gerundive; so Lael. 74 omnino amicitiae
corroborati iam confirmatisque et ingeniis et aetatibus iudicandae sunt, nec
si qui ineunte aetate venandi aut pilae
studiosi fuerunt, eos habere necessarios,
quos tum eodem studio praeditos dilex-
erunt. Madvig also qu. Quint. 4, 5, 20
quaedam interim nos et invitis litiga-
toribus simulandum est dicere...non
numquam quasi interpellemur ab eis
subsistere; saepe avertenda ad ipsos
oratio est ('nam *subsistere nos* non simulamus, sed vere subsistentes simulamus
nos interpellari'); Cic. Inv. 2, 130, where
after *erit dicendum* comes *deinde inducere* (sc. *oportebit*, which many edd.
needlessly inserted); Varro r. r. 3, 9, 8
in cubilibus, cum parturient, acus sub-
sternendum; cum pepererunt, tollere
substramen; Cels. 3, 7, 1. Madvig also
notes that after the verbal in -τέον the
infin. sometimes follows as though δεῖ
had been written. [Liv. 26, 32, 2 qu. by

RDF

14

factus est? Non potuit, inquies, fieri sapiens nisi natus esset. Isto modo, ne si avia quidem eius nata non esset. Res tota, Torquate, non doctorum hominum, velle post mortem epulis celebrari memoriam sui nominis. Quos quidem dies quem ad modum agatis et in quantam hominum facetorum urbanitatem 5 incurratis, non dico (nihil opus est litibus); tantum dico, magis fuisse vestrum agere Epicuri diem natalem, quam illius testamento cavere ut ageretur.

104 XXXII. Sed ut ad propositum (de dolore enim cum diceremus, ad istam epistulam delati sumus), nunc totum illud concludi sic 10 licet: Qui in summo malo est, is tum, cum in eo est, non est beatus; sapiens autem semper beatus est et est aliquando in dolore; non est igitur summum malum dolor. Iam illud quale tandem est, bona praeterita non effluere sapienti, mala meminisse non oportere? Primum in nostrane est potestate quid meminerimus? 15 Themistocles quidem, cum ei Simonides an quis alius artem memoriae polliceretur, 'Oblivionis,' inquit, 'mallem. Nam **105** memini etiam quae nolo, oblivisci non possum quae volo.' Magno hic ingenio, sed res se tamen sic habet, ut nimis imperiosi philosophi sit vetare meminisse. Vide ne ista sint Manliana vestra 20 aut maiora etiam, si imperes, quod facere non possim. Quid,

---

1 esset. Isto: *esset, et isto* codd.; corr. Manutius.   6 incurratis: *incurrat* E.
9 Post *propositum* add. *revertamur* codd. dett.   *revertamur*: om. AB.   10 delati: *dilati* E.   11 is tum: *istum* A¹; *iste* A²B.   15 est potestate: ita A; *potestate est* B.
15 quid: *quod* B.   21 possim: *possum* BE.

M. is not to the point; *gerendum fuisse* is dependent on *censerent*, and is followed by *urbem recipi* only because *censeo* takes both these constructions; see Weissenborn *ad loc.*]
2. **isto modo:** so § 23; Sen. d. 3, 13, 3 bis; ib. 14, 1; ben. 6, 15, 1; ib. 3, 30, 1. **res tota:** *est* omitted 1, 3 *n.*
3. **velle...celebrari:** cf. 2, 86 esse beatum.
5. **facetorum urbanitatem:** 1, 39 facete et urbane; for *urbanitas*, polished wit ('πεπαιδευμένη ΰβρις'), see 1, 7.
9. **ut ad propositum:** sc. *revertamur*; the ellipse falls quite within the boundaries of Cicero's usage; Madv. in addenda to ed. 3, qu. Att. 2, 6, 2 sed ut ad rem; Sen. ben. 4, 40, 5 et ut breviter; C. F. W. Müller adds Val. M. 3, 1 ext., 1 et ut a Graecis aliquid; a subj. which should follow *ut* is sometimes omitted in other circumstances, as Att. 6, 2, 8.
13. **quale:** n. on 2, 86.

14. **non effluere:** 1, 1; *effluere=effl. e memoria*, 1, 41 and elsewhere. So *excidere* often.
15. **quid mem.:** for the indirect constr. see 1, 16.
16. **an quis alius:** as Madvig says, this form has come out of a parenthetic direct question (*an quis alius?*). He condemns *uno an altero* for *un. aut alt.* in Rep. 1, 18; also ib. 2, 28 an certe Pythagoreum (because *certe* is incompatible with this form of doubtful suggestion); in both places edd. now read *aut*, but perhaps in the former *et* is right. **artem memoriae:** cf. 5, 2 memoriae disciplina: and my nn. on Acad. 2, 2.
18. **magno hic ingenio:** sc. either *erat* or *hoc dixit*; for the ellipse see 1, 3; 1, 18 and often.
19. **sed...tamen:** 'but apart from that'; 2, 42; 3, 31.
20. **Manliana:** n. on § 60.

si etiam iucunda memoria est praeteritorum malorum? ut pro-
verbia non nulla veriora sint quam vestra dogmata. Volgo enim
dicitur: 'Iucundi acti labores,' nec male Euripides (concludam,
si potero, Latine; Graecum enim hunc versum nostis omnes):

5   Suavis laborum est praeteritorum memoria.

Sed ad bona praeterita redeamus. Quae si a vobis talia dice-
rentur, qualibus C. Marius uti poterat, ut expulsus, egens, in
palude demersus, tropaeorum recordatione levaret dolorem suum,
audirem et plane probarem. Nec enim absolvi beáta vita
10 sapientis neque ad exitum perduci poterit, si prima quaeque
bene ab eo consulta atque facta ipsius oblivione obruentur. Sed **106**
vobis voluptatum perceptarum recordatio vitam beatam facit,
et quidem corpore perceptarum. Nam si quae sunt aliae, falsum
est omnis animi voluptates esse e corporis societate. Corporis
15 autem voluptas si etiam praeterita delectat, non intellego cur
Aristoteles Sardanapalli epigramma tanto opere derideat, in

3 iucundi: *iucunde* A; *iocunde* B.   4 nostis: om. BE.   5 est praeteritorum
memoria: *memoria est praeteritorum* B.   7 C.; *gaius* A; *graius* B.   8 demersus: *dimersus* A.   11 obruentur: *obruerentur* ABE.   14 animi voluptates:
voluptas animi BE.   14 e: om. B.   16 tanto opere: ita B; *tantopere* AE.

2. **dogmata:** n. on 2, 28.

3. **iucundi acti labores:** for the omission of the verb in proverbial phrases
cf. 1, 15 quot homines, tot sententiae;
2, 52 quicum in tenebris; 3, 16 fortuna
fortis.

Euripides: Andromeda ἀλλ' ἡδύ τοι
σωθέντα μεμνῆσθαι πόνων. Nauck, p. 399.

concludam: 'numeris, ut Horatius
concludere versum dixit' (Madvig). Cicero
uses *conficere* of verse in Acad. 2, 22;
but *concludere* is freely applied to
'rounding off' other things, as arguments and periods. Hor. s. 1, 10, 59
pedibus quid claudere senis; Quint.
9, 4, 123 sensus numeris conclusus.

4. **si potero, Latine:** so Tusc. 1, 15
dicam, si potero, Latine; Rep. 1, 65.

nostis omnes: as only Torquatus and
Triarius are present (1, 13), *omnes* is
strange; and moreover elsewhere Cicero
addresses Torquatus alone. It is highly
probable that *nosti* should be read.

5. **suavis...memoria:** V. Aen. 1, 203
forsan et haec olim meminisse iuvabit;
Cic. fam. 5, 12, 4 habet enim praeteriti
doloris secura recordatione delectationem;
Sidon. Ap. 5, 582 post gaudia...delectat
meminisse mali.

7. **egens:** on the strength of this and
similar passages Landgraf in Archiv

7, 275, ingeniously but improbably
argues that there was a word *ĕgens*
(*exgens* like *extorris*, etc.), as well as
ēgens. Why did the poets avoid so
convenient a word? Cf. Landgr. on
Rosc. § 23.

10. **prima quaeque...consulta:** 'all his
good purposes in succession.' This use
of *primus quisque* is widely spread in
Latin; Lucret. has *primum quidquid*.

14. **animi...societate:** see 1, 55.

16. **Aristoteles:** in Tusc. 5, 101 A. is
quoted as saying that the epitaph be-
fitted an ox rather than a king. There
is reference to Sardanapallus in the extant writings of Arist. (Eth. N. 1, 5, 3)
but nothing corresponding with Cicero's
quotation. Athen. p. 335 *f* also refers to
Aristotle's saying, but somewhat differently; he does not quote Aristotle
directly, but at second hand through
Chrysippus.

Sardanapalli: for the references in
ancient literature generally to this
mythical Assyrian (or Persian) monarch
see Pauly, Realenc. s. v. Sardanapallus
(name given to Elagabalus Dio Cass. 80,
2 and 78, 22). Two stories were current
about the inscription on his tomb:

(A) A fragment of Aristobulus ap.
Athen. 12, 530 *f*, mentions a tomb at

quo ille rex Syriae glorietur omnis se secum libidinum voluptates
abstulisse. Quod enim ne vivos quidem, inquit, diutius sentire

1 omnis se: *omnis* A; *se omnes* B; corr. Baiter.
abstulisse: ita A; *abstulisse libidinum voluptates* B.
poterat: 'haec verba in A vix legi possunt' (Baiter).

1 libidinum voluptates
2 inquit, diutius sentire

the town of Anchiala near Tarsus, with the figure of the King upon it making a gesture of contempt with the fingers; and the inscription ran: 'Σαρδανάπαλλος ὁ Ἀνακυνδαραξέω παῖς Ἀγχιάλην καὶ Τάρσον ἔδειμεν ἡμερῇ μίῃ. ἔσθιε πῖνε παῖζε. ὡς τἆλλα τούτου οὐκ ἄξια τοῦ ἀποκροτήματος.' Niese in a Marburg progr. (1880) makes it clear, (1) that Arrian, Anab. 2, 5, copied Aristobulus with variations, (2) that Aristobulus drew his information from Callisthenes, (3) that the story must be traced back to an Ionic writer older still, possibly Hellanicus. Plut. de virt. Al. 2, c. 3 substitutes ἀφροδισίαζε for παῖζε, and Apollodorus, quoted by Schol. on Arist. Aves 1021, gives ὄχευε. The words ἔσθιε πῖνε παῖζε became proverbial; cf. *es bibe lude* qu. in n. on 2, 23 adhibentes ludos, and St Paul in Cor. 1, 15, 32.

(B) Another tale was that the tomb of S. was at Nineveh and that an oriental inscription was on it which was rendered into Greek verse by Choerilus of Samos. The fullest report of the version is given by Athen. p. 336 from Chrysippus: 'εὖ εἰδὼς ὅτι θνητὸς ἔφυς σὸν θυμὸν ἄεξε | τερπόμενος θαλίῃσι· θανόντι τοι οὔτις ὄνησις. | καὶ γὰρ ἐγὼ σποδός εἰμι Νίνου μεγάλης βασιλεύσας. | κεῖν' ἔχω ὅσσ' ἔφαγον καὶ ἐφύβρισα καὶ σὺν ἔρωτι | τέρπν' ἔπαθον· τὰ δὲ πολλὰ καὶ ὄλβια πάντα λέλυνται (some other authorities give λέλειπται) | ἥδε σοφή βιότοιο παραίνεσις, οὐδέ ποτ' αὐτῆς | λήσεαι. ἐκτήσθω δ' ὁ θέλων τὸν ἀπείρονα χρυσόν.' | Ll. 3, 4 are quoted and imitated in scores of extant passages. [The two tales were sometimes confused, as by Strabo 14, 5, 9 (Mein.). Phoenix of Colophon ap. Athen. p. 530 refers the metrical inscription to Ninus; see the curious fragment. He must have had a version in some respects different.] Cicero renders these two lines thus in Tusc. 5, 101: haec habeo quae edi quaeque exsaturata libido | hausit: at illa iacent multa et praeclara relicta. Compare a curious passage in Sen. ben. 6, 3, 1 egregie mihi videtur M. Antonius apud Rabirium poetam, cum fortunam transeuntem alio videat et sibi nihil relictum praeter ius mortis, id quoque si cito occupaverit, exclamare 'hoc

habeo quodcumque dedi,' clearly an imitation of the form of the Sardanapallus epitaph. [The context in Seneca seems to show that *dedi* is right.] Diog. L. 6, 86 quotes an imitation of the epitaph by Crates: 'τοῦτ' ἔχω ὅσσ' ἔμαθον καὶ ἐφρόντισα καὶ μετὰ Μουσῶν | σέμν' ἐδάην· τὰ δὲ πολλὰ καὶ ὄλβια τῦφος ἐμάρψε': cf. Plut. quomodo quis, etc. c. 17, 546 A; also the fragment of Alexis' Ἀσωτοδιδάσκαλος qu. by Athen. 336 f from Chrysippus: 'ἕξεις δ' ὅσ' ἂν φάγῃς τε καὶ πίῃς μόνα.' Echoes are found on Roman tombstones; so C.I.L. 6, 18131 quod edi bibi mecum habeo, quod reliqui perdidi; ib. 9, 2114 dum vixi, vixi quo modo decet ingenuom, quod comedi et ebibi, tantum mea est (Bücheler, Carm. ep. n. 187). Allusions to Sardanapallus are innumerable; he is often mentioned in criticisms of Epicurus; see e.g. Usener, fragm. 414, 443*; and Vol. Herc. ap. Scott, p. 91. Many references in Mayor on Juven. 10, 362; Sonny in Archiv, 8, 491. It is quite possible that Lucilius had S. in mind when he wrote (30, 3 Müll.) 'et sua perciperet retro rellicta iacere'; *sua* (cf. *mea* qu. just above) the things that properly belong to a man. Cf. C.I.L. 9, 4756 spes et fortuna valete nil iam plus in me vobis per saecla licebit quod fuerat vestrum amisi, quod erat meum, hic est. Cicero alludes in Att. 10, 8, 7 Sardanapalli vicem mori, to the legends about the last debauch of S.; and in Rep. 3, fragm. 4 S. ille vitiis multo quam nomine ipso deformior, 4 compares the name with σαρδανόφαλλοι, a title for buffoons.

2. **abstulisse**: the dead were spoken of as having carried away with them the things of life; Petron. 43 (of a man just dead) quot putas illum annos secum tulisse? C.I.L. 6, 12845 (Bücheler, 387) quadraginta duo mecum fero flebilis annos; ib. 5254 (B. 86) nullum dolorem ad inferos mecum tuli; cf. B. 420; Luc. 10, 43 qui secum invidia qua totum ceperat orbem | abstulit imperium (of Alexander); Suet. Aug. 28 moriens ut spem feram mecum. C.I.L. 14, 3945 (B. 366) si quid mortui habent hoc meum erit, cetera liqui. See the Epitaph qu. in Gibbon, ed. Bury, 6, 452. In Parker's ABC of Gothic Arch. there

poterat, quam dum fruebatur, quo modo id potuit mortuo per-
manere? Fluit igitur voluptas corporis et prima quaeque avolat
saepiusque relinquit causam paenitendi quam recordandi. Itaque
beatior Africanus cum patria illo modo loquens:

5   Desine, Roma, tuos hostis....

reliquaque praeclare:

        Nam tibi moenimenta mei peperere labores.

Laboribus hic praeteritis gaudet, tu iubes voluptatibus, et hic
se ad ea revocat, e quibus nihil umquam rettulerit ad corpus,
10 tu totus haeres in corpore.

XXXIII. Illud autem ipsum qui obtineri potest, quod dicitis, **107**
omnis animi et voluptates et dolores ad corporis voluptates ac
dolores pertinere? Nihilne te delectat umquam (video quicum
loquar), te igitur, Torquate, ipsum per se nihil delectat? Omitto
15 dignitatem, honestatem, speciem ipsam virtutum, de quibus
ante dictum est, haec leviora ponam: poema, orationem cum
aut scribis aut legis, cum omnium factorum, cum regionum

---

1 poterat: *potuit* B.   1 potuit mortuo: ita A; *mortuo potuit* B.   2 fluit:
om. BE.   3 paenitendi: *penitendi* BE.   7 nam: ita E; *namque* AB.
7 moenimenta: *monimenta* AE; *monumenta* B; corr. Klotz.   7 peperere:
repperere A.   9 nihil: om. B.   9 rettulerit: *retulerit* AB.   12 ad corporis
voluptates ac dolores: om. B.   13 nihilne te: ita A; *nihil tene* B.   16 ante:
antea B.   16 ponam: poema: *poema ponam* AB.   16 cum aut: *aut cum* B.
17 cum regionum: *aut regionum* B.

is a quotation from Anthony à Wood
describing the gateway tower of the
Schools at Oxford, in which is the effigy
of King James I on the throne giving
with his right hand to *Fame* a book,
with the inscription on the cover: *haec
habeo quae scripsi*; while with his left he
hands a vol. to the effigy of the University
with the inscription on the cover: *haec
habeo quae dedi.*

inquit: sc. *Aristoteles*; cf. Tusc. 5, 101
(quoted from A.) haec habere se mor-
tuom dicit, quae ne vivos quidem
diutius habebat quam fruebatur.

3. paenitendi: Tusc. 4, 79; Acad.
fragm. 16. Cic. does not use *paenitentia.*

5. desine, Roma: almost certainly
from Ennius; quoted also in De Or.
3, 167 with another small fragment
'testes sunt Campi magni.' His poem
entitled 'Scipio' was probably written
in trochaic tetrameters. Madvig refers
desine etc. to the Annales along with the
complete hexameter which follows;
Vahlen considers all three quotations
to belong to the Satirae.

6. reliquaque: 1, 12 *n.*

9. rettulerit: Madvig explains the
subjunctive by attributing adversative
force to *quibus*. 'Rarius hoc est in eius-
modi sententia relativa, quae simul
generis definitionem contineat (*ea, e
quibus*); sed tamen similiter, § 102:
*cavebit is qui nobis quasi oraculum edi-
derit* cet.; Act. I in Verr. 11 *eum, cui
legatus fuisset, in invidiam adduxit.*
The class-definition would however be
by itself sufficient reason here for the
subjunctive, and the adversative notion
is not very appropriate to the circumstances. Another explanation is possible, that there is or. obl. 'of which, as
he reminds himself.'

14. igitur: resumptive: n. on 2, 23.

15. speciem...: 'the mere fair aspect
of the virtues'; Lucr. 1, 148 naturae
species ratioque; above § 49 honestum
...specie laudabile.

16. leviora: cf. Brut. 3 leviorum artium and 70 minora; Cato m. 50; De
Or. 1, 212.

poema, etc.: there is anacoluthon,

conquiris historiam, signum, tabula, locus amoenus, ludi, venatio,
villa Luculli (nam si 'tuam' dicerem, latebram haberes; ad corpus
diceres pertinere), sed ea quae dixi, ad corpusne refers? an est
aliquid, quod te sua sponte delectet? Aut pertinacissimus fueris,
si perstiteris ad corpus ea quae dixi referre, aut deserueris totam 5
108 Epicuri voluptatem, si negaveris. Quod vero a te disputatum est
maiores esse voluptates et dolores animi quam corporis, quia
trium temporum particeps animus sit, corpore autem praesentia
solum sentiantur, qui id probari potest ut is, qui propter me
aliquid gaudeat, plus quam ego ipse gaudeat? [Animo voluptas 10
oritur propter voluptatem corporis, et maior est animi voluptas
quam corporis. Ita fit, ut gratulator laetior sit quam is, cui
gratulatur.] Sed, dum efficere voltis beatum sapientem, cum
maximas animo voluptates percipiat omnibusque partibus
maiores quam corpore, quid occurrat non videtis. Animi enim 15

1 amoenus: *amenus* AB.   1 venatio: *venaciones* B.   2 Luculli: *lucilli* ABE.
3 diceres: *dicere* E.   5 si perstiteris...referre: ita B; *si hi* (vel *in*) *perstiteris...*
referre A.   5 quae: om. B.   6 vero: om. E.   9 qui id: ita B; *quid* A; *quid*
id E.   10 plus quam ego ipse gaudeat: om. AB.   10 [animo...gratulatur]: haec
verba spuria esse vidit Bremius.   15 maiores: *maioris* ABE.   15 quid: *quod* B.

caused by the interposition of the
parenthesis *nam si...pertinere*; the sentence takes a fresh start with the words
sed ea (n. on Acad. 1, 41). Cf. below, 3,
11 *n.*; Madvig qu. Tusc. 2, 16; 3, 16 and
Att. 15, 3, 1. *Poema* like *orationem*
depends on *scribis, legis*. Cf. the inscr. of
Oinoanda, that we should do good to
future generations by teaching them
Epicureanism (Bull. de Corr. Hell. xxi,
pp. 402–4).

1. **historiam**: 1, 25.

venatio: 'wild beast fights,' 1, 69 *n.*:
Off. 2, 55. In 2, 23 above it means 'game.'

4. **pertinacissimus**: cf. 3, 1.

5. **perstiteris...referre**: in the four
other exx. of *persto* given by Merguet, it
is followed by *in* and abl.; the infin. is
found elsewhere only in verse and later
prose. The infin. with *insto* or *insisto* is
found in Verr. 2, 3, 136; Fam. 10, 16, 1;
and in poetry and later prose.

6. **quod vero**, etc.: Cicero here refers
to two distinct portions of the speech
of Torquatus (§§ 55 and 66 sq.). Torquatus nowhere contended that friendship would lead a man to take more joy
in his friends' delight than the friend
himself would feel. The contention of T.
merely was that 'laetamur amicorum
laetitia aeque atque nostra' (§ 67).
Moreover T. did not connect his doc-

trine of friendship with his statement
about mental pleasure; Cicero here
makes the doctrine about friendship a
direct consequence of the view about
mental pleasure. The authority for the
words *plus...gaudeat* is not strong, and
Cicero may have written *aeque atque*,
not *plus quam*. [Cf. Tusc. 3, 72 quasi
fieri ullo modo possit quod in amatorio
sermone dici solet, ut quisquam plus
alterum diligat quam se.] Perhaps *aut*
has fallen out before *ut is*; for the clause
ut cf. 2, 6.

10. **animo...gratulatur**: the words are
so obviously a figment, that they are
not worth discussion. Madvig gives
other exx. of this kind of addition to
the text of Cicero.

14. **omnibus partibus**: an intensifica-
tion of *multis partibus*; so 5, 93; Inv.
1, 58; Caes. B.G. 5, 15, 1. The phrase
means 'infinitely,' as *multis partibus* is
'many times over.' The renderings
sometimes given, 'in all respects,' 'in
many respects' are erroneous; see
C. F. W. Müller's n. on Seyffert's ed. of
Lael. § 47. Madvig qu. Off. 3, 35 omni
pondere gravior.

15. **quid occurrat**: 'what cuts across
your path'; cf. Acad. 2, 44 occurretur,
sicut occursum est; Fin. 1, 19 *n.*

animi enim dolores quoque: Madvig

dolores quoque percipiet omnibus partibus maiores quam corporis. Ita miser sit aliquando necesse est is, quem vos
beatum semper voltis esse, nec vero id, dum omnia ad voluptatem doloremque referetis, efficietis umquam. Quare aliud **109**
5 aliquod, Torquate, hominis summum bonum reperiendum est,
voluptatem bestiis concedamus, quibus vos de summo bono
testibus uti soletis. Quid si etiam bestiae multa faciunt duce sua

1 dolores quoque: *quoque dolores* codd.; corr. Madv.   4 referetis: *refertis* BE.

5 aliquod: *aliquid* codd.; corr. Lambinus.

brings three objections against the reading of the mss., (1) the contrast is between *voluptates* and *dolores*, therefore *quoque* should go with the latter word; (2) *quoque* adheres so closely to the word which it emphasises that it cannot be sundered from that word by a particle like *enim*; thus at least *animi quoque enim* should have been written; (3) he cannot recall a passage in Cicero where *quoque* and *enim* are in juxta-position, though there are many exx. in Livy, and he gives two from Varro L. L. 5, p. 30 Bip. and 9, p. 130; to which C. F. W. Müller adds r. r. 1, 23, 2 and 2, pr. 5; also Gell. 10, 7, 2 (from Varro); also his own text of Acad. 1, 26 (but this is doubtful, see the nn. in my ed.). Müller combats the idea that *quoque* must of necessity in Cicero bear on the word immediately preceding, citing Fin. 3, 15 si enim Zenoni licuit, cum rem aliquam invenisset inusitatam, inauditum quoque ei rei nomen imponere, cur non liceat Catoni; *quoque* constantly between epithet and noun—here the advent of the noun is delayed; for the contrast is between *rem* and *nomen*, but *inauditum* is forced to the head of the clause in order to bring it close to *inusitatam*, and *quoque* tends likewise to the beginning of clauses. Also the very similar passage, Tusc. 4, 31 viribus corporis et nervis et efficacitati similes similibus quoque verbis animi vires nominantur (so edd. generally with Manut. for *similibusque*); and div. Caec. 8. Müller adds that the prominence of *animi* and *corporis* here would easily mislead Cicero into emphasising *animi* by the attachment of *quoque*. Madvig truly says that the copyists have some-times shifted *quoque* (and he might have added, other particles) into intolerable positions; and he refers to his own Opusc. 1, 181 and Wesenberg Em. p. 36. A difficult *quoque* in S. Rosc. 40, where Landgr. and Luterb. assume *brevity*; ib. 93, on which cf. Madv. l.c.

(no note in Landgr.). Tusc. 1, 79 nihil esse quod doleat quod non aegrum esse quoque possit (where *aegrum esse* form one notion). Fam. 9, 17, 1 seems to give an ex. of *quoque* not belonging to any particular word. *Quoque* seems to precede where it ought to follow, Liv. 10, 14, 9. Draeg. Synt. Tac. 229. Madv. Adv. 11, 508 corrects Sen. ep. 109, 4 malus malo nocet; facit quoque peiorem, iram, metus incitando ('prave ponitur *quoque* et loco et quod nihil novi additur'—but these reasons seem questionable; *nocere* and *peiorem facere* are certainly not identical notions). Also Curt. 5, 2, 19 (ib. p. 532). Verr. 4, 29 cum abs te appellatus esset, negasse habere sese: apud alium quoque eas habuisse depositas ne qua invenirentur. Thomas remarks, '*quoque* contre l'ordinaire tombe ici sur toute la proposition, *apud...habuisse depositas*, qui correspond à *negasse*,' but quotes no parallels. [Exx. of *quoque* elliptic in Ad Her. 1, 14 ante quoque; 2, 6; a curious irregular ex. in 2, 1, 1; also 2, 21, 33; in 3, 14, 25 there is a strange opposition between adaucto sono vocis and verbis continuandis vocem *quoque* augere. *Quoque* refers to a whole proposition in Verr. act. pr. 21; 2, 171; Div. Caec. 8 (qu. by M.); 2, 100 (practically); Leg. agr. 2, 67 hoc quoque (Quirites); see C. F. W. Müller.] Quinct. 14 summus honos quoque where s. q. h. would be natural. Nep. Ages. 6, 2 se id quoque for *se quoque id* (altered in Nipperdey-Lupus). In Tusc. 5, 3 *quoque* contrasts *animos* with *corpora*.

3. **voltis esse:** cf. 1, 29; 2, 65, 75.

nec vero, etc.: 1, 19 eripuit...nec tamen assecutus est.

4. **aliud aliquod:** see Madv. on 1, 18; the apposition between *aliquid* and *summum bonum* here would be strange; so in Clu. 184.

6. **bestiis...testibus:** see n. on 2, 32.

7. **quid si etiam**, etc.: the difficulties of this passage have been much discussed

quaeque natura partim diligenter vel cum labore, ut in gignendo, in educando, perfacile appareat aliud quiddam eis propositum, non voluptatem? partim cursu et peragratione laetantur, congregatione aliae coetum quodam modo civitatis

110 imitantur; videmus in quodam volucrium genere non nulla 5 indicia pietatis, cognitionem, memoriam, in multis etiam desideria videmus. Ergo in bestiis erunt secreta a voluptate humanarum quaedam simulacra virtutum, in ipsis hominibus virtus nisi voluptatis causa nulla erit? et homini, qui ceteris animantibus plurimum praestat, praecipui a natura nihil datum esse dicemus? 10

1 quaeque: *quaque* AB.　1 diligenter: ego conieci; *indulgenter* codd.; vide comm. 4 coetum: *cetum* A; *tecum* BE.　5 volucrium, Charisius (146, 28); *volucrum* A; *voluerunt* B.　6 indicia: *iudicia* BE.　7 ergo: *erunt* E.　10 praecipui: *praecipue* AB; *praecipuum* alii codd.; corr. Manutius.　10 datum esse dicemus: *esse dicemus datum* B.

from early times. The sense would have been clearer had Cicero written after *natura* words such as *quae ostendunt eas non suam voluptatem sequi*; there closing the sentence, and introducing in a fresh sentence the subdivision of the *multa* into classes. Then the words *partim cursu et peragratione laetantur* are wholly out of keeping with the argument; they really play into Torquatus' hands. Although I do not venture confidently to condemn this clause as due to marginal annotation, I think it highly suspicious. Cicero often substitutes *partim...alii* for *partim, partim* (as Div. 1, 93; Rep. 4, 3; Lael. 45 and elsewhere), and the questionable clause may be due to some copyist who thought that a second *partim* was needed. The extraordinary readings *cicures et*, *turtures et* in some inferior MSS. indicate that the whole clause may have been suggested by Tusc. 5, 38 earum ipsarum (bestiarum) partim solivagas, partim congregatas, immanis alias, quasdam autem cicures, and that the insertion has survived only in corrupted forms, different corruptions appearing in different types of MSS.; *turtures* I take to be a correction of *cicures*. Madvig supposes it to have been suggested by *volucrium*. Then *indulgenter* can hardly be right. For the point of the argument mention is not needed of the *indulgence* shown by creatures to their offspring; the word would only express remotely and indirectly the *disinterestedness* of the affection. Moreover, the *toil* expended as opposed to *pleasure* should be brought to the front. I therefore read *diligenter*; *in* has come from *-im*; *vel cum labore* is a strengthening of

diligenter, 'with close application or rather toil.' [The em. of C. F. W. Müller adding *ut* before *appareat* is not worth making.]

1. **ut in gignendo**, etc.: cf. Ar. Eth. N. 8, 1, 3 (1155 *a*, 20) and Lael. 27, 81.

3. **peragratione**: a rare word occurring in Cicero only here and Phil. 2, 57 *p. itinerum*. As Madvig says, *peragrare* regularly takes acc. and one would expect with the subst. a definition of the places traversed; but *peragrare* is used absolutely in Mil. 98, and *lustratio* is similarly employed in Tusc. 5, 79; N.D. 1, 87. Madvig is right in saying that the reference here is not to the transmigration of animals, but to their dispersion 'sine coetu.'

5 **volucrium**: see Neue-Wagener 1, 398. It is strange that birds should be here mentioned rather than animals, in which these indications are more clearly seen. With the mention of birds *etiam* was to be expected; cf. Plin. n. h. 10, 207 quid? non et adfectus indicia sunt etiam in serpentibus? That *genere* should be put where *generibus* would be more accurate, is comparatively unimportant.

6. **cognitionem, memoriam**: these two words seem to go closely together; the reference is to the power animals have of remembering and recognising again after a lapse of time, those of their own race with whom they have had to do. The parallel passages in Tusc. 5, 38 and Lael. 81 show that there is no reference to the recognition of human beings, as Madvig supposed. For *cognitionem* cf. § 82 *cognoscere* with note.

7. **erunt...nulla erit?** n. to 2, 13.

10. **praecipui**: cf. Tusc. 5, 38 ut bestiis aliud alii praecipui a natura datum est,

XXXIV.   Nos vero, siquidem in voluptate sunt omnia, longe **111**
multumque superamur a bestiis, quibus ipsa terra fundit ex sese
pastus varios atque abundantes nihil laborantibus, nobis autem
aut vix aut ne vix quidem suppetunt multo labore quaerentibus.
5 Nec tamen ullo modo summum pecudis bonum et hominis idem
mihi videri potest. Quid enim tanto opus est instrumento in
optimis artibus comparandis? quid tanto concursu honestissi-
morum studiorum, tanto virtutum comitatu, si ea nullam ad
aliam rem nisi ad voluptatem conquiruntur? Vt, si Xerxes, cum **112**
0 tantis classibus tantisque equestribus et pedestribus copiis
Hellesponto iuncto, Athone perfosso maria ambulavisset, terram

2 superamur: *separamur* E.   2 fundit ex sese: *ex sese fundit* BE.   3 abundantes: *habundantibus* B.   4 multo labore: *labore multo* E; *labores multo* B.
7 quid: *qui* B.   8 si: *sed* E.   8 nullam: *iam non* B.   9 si Xerxes: *si
exerses* BE.   11 Athone: ita B; *atthone* A.

quod suum quaeque retinet, nec dis-
cedit ab eo, sic homini multo quiddam
praestantius; Div. 2, 121 non video
quid praecipui somnus habeat; above,
§ 33 sunt et in animo praecipua quaedam et in corpore.

1. **longe multumque**: § 68 longe longeque.

2. **ipsa**: 'unbidden,' αὐτομάτη.

3. **abundantes**: the abl. accompanies
this word in Cicero far oftener than not;
Stöcklein in Archiv, 7, 418.

4. **vix aut ne v. qu.**: so 4, 32; Amm.
M. 17, 4, 15; Cic. N.D. 2, 20 aut vix aut
nullo modo; Fam. 9, 8, 2 cum his ipsis
vix, his autem detractis ne vix quidem;
Att. 3, 23, 2 Clodium sanxisse ut vix aut
omnino non posset...infirmari sua lex.

5. **nec tamen**, etc.: see 4, 2; 4, 51.
pecudis bonum: 2 § 18 *n.*

9. **nisi ad**: cf. 4, 47 nisi in.
si, etc.: the main sentence *si Xerxes...*
diceret...*videretur*, is complicated by
the addition to its protasis of the *cum*-
clauses, and the addition of a second
protasis *si...quaereret*, also extended by
the attachment of a *cum*-clause. For
the two protases cf. 1, 7 *n.* Was Cicero
thinking here of the symbolic gifts
which were an acknowledgment of
conquest? See herbam do in Corp.
Gloss. 6, 517 and reff.; and Archiv 6,
398.

11. **maria ambulavisset, terram navigasset**: cf. Isocr. Pan. § 89 ὥστε τῷ
στρατοπέδῳ πλεῦσαι μὲν διὰ τῆς ἠπείρου,
πεζεῦσαι δὲ διὰ τῆς θαλάττης, τὸν μὲν
Ἑλλήσποντον ζεύξας, τὸν δ' Ἄθω διορύξας
(qu. by Ar. Rh. 3, 9 as a specimen of
antithetic style); [Lys.] Epitaph. § 29 ὁδὸν

μὲν διὰ τῆς θαλάσσης ἐποιήσατο, πλοῦν
δὲ διὰ τῆς γῆς. Iwan Müller in an
Erlangen progr. (1870) quotes Lucian,
Rhet. praec. § 18 ἀεὶ ὁ Ἄθως πλείσθω
καὶ ὁ Ἑλλήσποντος πεζενέσθω καὶ ὁ ἥλιος
ὑπὸ τῶν Μηδικῶν βελῶν σκεπέσθω: Dio
Chrys. 3 §§ 30, 31 εἰ βούλοιτο πεζεύεσθαι
μὲν τὴν θάλασσαν, πλεῖσθαι δὲ τὰ ὄρη,
τοὺς δὲ ποταμοὺς ἐκλείπειν ὑπὸ ἀνθρώπων
πινομένους: Philost. Imag. 1, 8 (of Posei-
don) πεζεύοντι τὴν θάλασσαν : Himerius
Or. 2, 25 τῆς δὲ (sc. γῆς) πλέων τὴν
φύσιν ἤμειβε, τῆς δὲ (θαλάσσης) πεζεύων
τὴν χρείαν ἤλεγχε : Greg. Naz. Or. 18,
p. 279 c Χριστὸν...ὃς πεζεύει πέλαγος:
Lycophr. Cass. 1414 ἀλλ' ἀντὶ πάντων
Περσέως ἕνα σπορᾶς | στελεῖ γίγαντα
τῷ θάλασσα μὲν βατὴ | πεζῷ ποτ' ἔσται,
γῆ δὲ ναυσθλωθήσεται | ῥήσσοντι πηδοῖς
χέρσον : Julian Or. 1, p. 28 B ἐπειρᾶτο
πλεῖν καὶ πεζεύειν ἀπεναντίον τῇ φύσει
μαχόμενος. Cicero is obviously here rendering a rhetorical commonplace, which
accounts for the syntax in *maria ambulavisset, terras navigasset*. Quint. 1, 5, 38
cites *ambulo viam* as a solecism; in Ovid,
Fast. 1, 122 libera perpetuas ambulat
illa vias, the reading is not quite certain :
for *perpetuas* some mss. give *per tutas*.
Quint. 1, 4, 28 notes *campus curritur*
and *mare navigatur* as good Latin; exx.
of *navigare* and *natare* with acc. in
Draeger, § 165; Off. 3, 42 stadium currit.
Among passages in Latin writers similar
to this concerning Xerxes are Sen. suas.
2, 21 si iam X. ad nos suo mari navigat,
fugiamus antequam nobis terra subri-
piatur; Amm. M. 22, 8, 4 unde...X.
maria pedibus peragravit; 17, 13, 27
peragrans pedibus flumina; Anth. Lat.

navigasset, si, cum tanto impetu in Graeciam venisset, causam
quis ex eo quaereret tantarum copiarum tantique belli, mel se
auferre ex Hymetto voluisse diceret, certe sine causa videretur
tanta conatus, sic nos sapientem plurimis et gravissimis artibus
atque virtutibus instructum et ornatum non, ut illum, maria 5
pedibus peragrantem, classibus montes, sed omne caelum
totamque cum universo mari terram mente complexum, voluptatem petere si dicemus, mellis causa dicemus tanta molitum.
113 Ad altiora quaedam et magnificentiora, mihi crede, Torquate,
nati sumus, nec id ex animi solum partibus, in quibus inest 10
memoria rerum innumerabilium, in te quidem infinita, inest
coniectura consequentium non multum a divinatione differens,
inest moderator cupiditatis pudor, inest ad humanam societatem
iustitiae fida custodia, inest in perpetiendis laboribus adeun-
disque periculis firma et stabilis doloris mortisque contemptio— 15
ergo haec in animis, tu autem etiam membra ipsa sensusque
considera, qui tibi, ut reliquae corporis partes, non comites
114 solum virtutum, sed ministri etiam videbuntur. Quod si in ipso
corpore multa voluptati praeponenda sunt, ut vires, valetudo,
velocitas, pulcritudo, quid tandem in animis censes? in quibus 20

---

1 navigasset: *navigavisset* ABE.   10 inest: om. B.   11 in te: ita A; *inde* BE;
vite codd. cett.   12 consequentium: *consequencia* E.   17 corporis: om. B.
18 quod: ita B; *quid* A.

Riese 442 X. magnus adest...calcatur
pontus, fluctuat altus Athos; ib. 239
novus hic dominus terramque diemque
fretumque permutat (*diemque* referring
to the cloud of arrows); Arnob. adv.
g. 2, 5 ut ille immanis X. mare terris
immitteret et gressibus maria transiret;
cf. too Sall. Cat. 13, 1 a privatis compluribus subvorsos montes, maria con-
strata esse. Sen. d. 3, 21, 1 terras
transferre maria concludere (of marine
villas).
6. omne caelum...complexum: Plat.
Theaet. 173 E.
8. petere: *expetere* might have been
expected here, and may have been
written by Cicero; see my n. on Cato m.
43. *Peti* below, 4, 47 is different.
9. ad altiora...nati sumus: 5, 21 ad
maiora quaedam...nati sumus.
mihi crede: n. on 2, 69.
11. rerum inn.: Acad. 2, 30 eo cum
accessit rerum innumerabilium multitudo, where see my n.; cf. too Lact. 7, 8
artium rerumque innumerabilium scien-

tia (of the mind). The *divina memoria*
of Torquatus is mentioned in Brut. 265.
13. ad...societatem: but for the awkwardness of the double genitive, *societa-
tis* would have been written. But to
suppose that *tuendam* (Leid.) or some
such word has dropped out is not
unreasonable. Cicero here gives δια-
νοητικαὶ ἀρεταί followed by three out
of the four cardinal virtues, φρόνησις
being omitted.
16. ergo haec in animis: n. on § 41
atque haec...Aristippum.
membra...partes: 3, 18 membrorum,
id est partium corporis.
18. ministri: cf. § 41 and 3, 23 ut
membra nobis ita data sunt ut ad quandam rationem vivendi data esse appa-
reant, where see n.
quod si, etc.: it is assumed that these
endowments would be desirable, even
if productive of no gratification or
pleasure. Cf. 3, 17, 51.
19. vires...pulcritudo: see Acad. 1, 19,
with my n.

doctissimi illi veteres inesse quiddam caeleste et divinum putaverunt. Quod si esset in voluptate summum bonum, ut dicitis,
optabile esset maxima in voluptate nullo intervallo interiecto
dies noctesque versari, cum omnes sensus dulcedine omni quasi
5 perfusi moverentur. Quis est autem dignus nomine hominis,
qui unum diem totum velit esse in genere isto voluptatis?
Cyrenaici quidem non recusant; vestri haec verecundius, illi
fortasse constantius. Sed lustremus animo non has maximas 115
artis, quibus qui carebant, inertes a maioribus nominabantur,
0 sed quaero num existimes, non dico Homerum, Archilochum,
Pindarum, sed Phidian, Polyclitum, Zeuxim ad˙ voluptatem
artis suas direxisse. Ergo opifex plus sibi proponet ad formarum
quam civis excellens ad factorum pulcritudinem? Quae autem
est alia causa erroris tanti, tam longe lateque diffusi, nisi quod
5 is qui voluptatem summum bonum esse decernit, non cum ea
parte animi, *in* qua inest ratio atque consilium, sed cum cupiditate, id est cum animi levissima parte, deliberat? Quaero enim
de te, si sunt di, ut vos etiam putatis, qui possint esse beati,

3 esset: *esse* BE.   3 maxima in voluptate: ita A; *in maxima voluptate* B.
3 intervallo: *vallo* B.   7 haec: *hic* B.   9 qui: om. A.   9 a maioribus:
ita E; *amoribus* AB.   11 Polyclitum: ita E; *policlitum* A; *piloclitum* B.
11 Zeuxim: *zeuxim* A; *ceurim* BE.   14 alia: *illa* A.   15 esse: om. B.   15 decernit:
decerit B; *dicerint* E.   15 non: om. B.   16 *in*: om. AB.   17 deliberat? Quaero:
deliberatur quaero B.   18 di: *dii* AB.   18 possint: *possunt* codd.; corr. Lambinus.

1. **veteres:** Plato, Aristotle and followers.
3. **nullo...interiecto:** cf. § 40 which
Cicero seems to have forgotten here.
4. **dies noctesque:** 1, 51 and n. to
Cat. m. 1.
quasi perfusi: cf. 2, 6.
5. **dignus nomine hominis:** n. to 1, 4.
7. **verecundius:** for the ellipse see n.
on 3, 63.
8. **constantius:** 1, 23 quod quamquam
Aristippi est a Cyrenaicisque melius
liberiusque defenditur.
maximas artis: i.e. *virtutes*; there is a
Stoic touch here; see 4, 4.
9. **quibus qui:** n. on 1, 26.
inertes: cf. Lucil. 13, l. 16 (L. Müller),
quoted by Servius on Virg. Aen. 4, 158:
ut perhibetur iners, ars in quo non erit
ulla; Cic. part. or. 35 animi...quem ad
modum affecti sint, virtutibus vitiis,
artibus inertiis.
10. **sed quaero:** in contrast with *non
has* above, with a slight change of construction. As to the inconstancy of
moods in this sentence see C. F. W.

Müller and also on Acad. p. 71, 21;
Tusc. p. 283, 28; Rep. p. 273, 37; Orat.
Vol. 1, p. 86, l. 1.
11. **Phidian...Zeuxim:** the same artists
are mentioned together in Acad. 2, 146.
Modern writers about ancient art have
often wrongly assumed that Cicero here
and there also intended to convey that
these three names were the greatest in
the annals of Greek art. See my n. on
Acad. l. l.
12. **direxisse:** cf. § 71.
opifex: see 3 § 4, a similar passage.
The word applies to all craftsmen,
whether artists or mere mechanics.
13. **factorum pulcritudinem:** cf. Aug.
Ep. 118, 16 p. factorum atque dictorum.
15. **ea parte**, etc.: on the Platonic aspect of this see Hirzel p. 653.
16. **cum cupiditate...deliberat:** Sen.
ep. 13, 6 ut...cum tua patientia deliberes.
18. **si sunt di...si...beati sint:** the
change of mood in parallel *si*-clauses is
common; so Att. 7, 10; 16, 14, 1; De
Or. 2, 176; Liv. 21, 13, 5; 37, 7, 9; Ad
Herenn. 2, 43; 4, 2.

cum voluptates corpore percipere non possint, aut, si sine eo
genere voluptatis beati sint, cur similem animi usum in sapiente
esse nolitis.

116 XXXV. Lege laudationes, Torquate, non eorum, qui sunt ab
Homero laudati, non Cyri, non Agesilai, non Aristidi aut Themis- 5
tocli, non Philippi aut Alexandri, lege nostrorum hominum, lege
vestrae familiae; neminem videbis ita laudatum ut artifex
callidus comparandarum voluptatum diceretur. Non elogia
monumentorum id significant, velut hoc ad portam : ʻHunc unum
plurimae consentiunt gentes populi primarium fuisse virum.ʼ 1
117 Idne consensisse de Calatino plurimas gentis arbitramur, primarium fuisse populi, quod praestantissimus fuisset in con-
ficiendis voluptatibus? Ergo in eis adulescentibus bonam spem
esse dicemus et magnam indolem, quos suis commodis inservi-
turos et, quicquid ipsis expediat, facturos arbitrabimur? Nonne 1
videmus quanta perturbatio rerum omnium consequatur, quanta
confusio? Tollitur beneficium, tollitur gratia, quae sunt vincla
concordiae. Nec enim, cum tua causa cui commodes, beneficium

1 percipere: *percipe* A; *percipi* B.   4 sunt: *sint* AB.   5 Agesilai: *hagesi.*
lai ABE.   8 voluptatum: *utilitatum* AB.   8 elogia: *eulogia* AB.
9 hunc unum: *uno cum* AB; *uno cui* codd. alii; *unum hunc* Orellius: corr. Madv.
10 populi: om. B.   11 idne: *et due* B.   12 fuisse populi: ita A; *populi fuisse* B.
15 arbitrabimur: ita A cod. Morel.; *arbitramur* B.   15 nonne: *nomine* A.
17 vincla: ita A; *vincula* B.   18 tua causa: ita cod. Glogauensis; *tuā causā* A;
tuam causam B.   18 cui: ita AB; *cuiquam* codd. cett.; *cuipiam* Madv.

1. cum...non possint: it is not quite
certain whether the Epicurean gods
were incapable of bodily pleasure.

7. artifex...voluptatum: 1, 42 *n.* A
different construction in Verr. 2, 5, 183
artifices ad corrumpendum iudicium.

8. elogia:=ἐλεγεῖα. The change of *e*
to *o* is in some instances in Latin due
to the neighbourhood of *l*; cf. *oliva,*
lopadas, soluo=*se-luo* (Stolz). The
word always indicates a brief inscription on a tombstone or other
memorial, or a short clause in a will
(Clu. 135); or (in late writers) an entry
of a plaint against a debtor or male-
factor; it never has the sense of *laudatio.*

9. hunc unum, etc.: the same two
lines are given in Cato m. 61, but the
inscription probably contained more;
see my n. there. The resemblance to the
elogium of L. Scipio, son of Barbatus
(C.I.L. 1, 32) is striking: hunc oino
ploirume cosentiont R(omai) | duonoro
optumo fuise viro. The tomb was outside the porta Capena, close to that of

the Scipiones, Servilii, Metelli (Tusc. 1,
13).

11. idne consensisse: Livy pushes the
accusative construction beyond Cicero's
usage, as in 8, 6, 8 consensit et senatus
bellum; 1, 32, 12.

plurimas gentis: referring to the
peoples with whom Calatinus came in
contact on his public service, in the
course of which, as consul in 258 and
254, he fought in Sicily. Cicero often
eulogises him as an old Roman hero.

primarium...populi: Cicero would
hardly have omitted *virum* here had it
not been expressed above.

15. quicquid ipsis expediat: cf. 2, 76.

arbitrabimur: the deliberative subj.
is not common with verbs of thinking;
see C. F. W. Müller on Orat. 1, 196, 32.

16. perturbatio...confusio: so N.D.
1, 3 perturbatio vitae sequitur et magna
confusio (the results of Epicureanism).

17. vincla: cf. Off. 1, 50.

18. cum...commodes: ʻif at any time
(whenever) you lendʼ: cf. n. to Acad. 2, 14.

illud habendum est, sed feneratio, nec gratia deberi videtur ei
qui sua causa commodaverit. Maximas vero virtutes iacere
omnis necesse est voluptate dominante. Sunt etiam turpitudines
plurimae quae, nisi honestas natura plurimum valeat, cur non
5 cadant in sapientem non est facile defendere. Ac ne plura com- **118**
plectar (sunt enim innumerabilia), bene laudata virtus voluptatis
aditus intercludat necesse est. Quod iam a me exspectare noli.
Tute introspice in mentem tuam ipse eamque omni cogitatione
pertractans percontare ipse te, perpetuisne malis voluptatibus
10 perfruens in ea, quam saepe usurpabas, tranquillitate degere
omnem aetatem sine dolore, assumpto etiam illo, quod vos
quidem adiungere soletis, sed fieri non potest, sine doloris metu,
an, cum de omnibus gentibus optime mererere, cum opem in-
digentibus salutemque ferres, vel Herculis perpeti aerumnas.
15 Sic enim maiores nostri labores non fugiendos tristissimo tamen
verbo aerumnas etiam in deo nominaverunt. Elicerem ex te **119**

1 feneratio: ita B; *veneratio* A.   2 sua causa commodaverit: *suā causā commodaverit* A; *suam commodaverit causam* B; corr. Baiter.   3 necesse: *nec
esse* BE.   4 honestas: Crat.; *honesta* AB.   5 in sapientem: *insipientem* E.
5 ac: *at* BE.   7 aditus: *bene aditus* B.   10 quam: *quem* A.   13 gentibus
om. B.   13 mererere: *merere* ABE.   15 nostri: *vestri* B.   15 fugiendos:
figiendos A; *fingendo* BE.   16 elicerem coni. Gruter et Baiter: *eligerem* ABE;
exigerem vulg.

1. feneratio: Lael. 31 beneficium
feneramur; Sen. ben. 1, 2, 3 turpis
feneratio est beneficium acceptum ferre;
Plin. ep. 1, 13, 6 ne videar quorum reci-
tationibus adfui, non auditor fuisse sed
creditor; Mart. 7, 86, 9 non est sportula
quae negotiatur: | pascis munera, Sexte,
non amicos; Sen. ben. 6, 12, 2 multum,
ut ait Cleanthes, a beneficio distat
negotiatio; ep. 9 § 10 negotiatio non
amicitia; ben. 1, 1, 9; 2, 10, 2; 2, 21, 2;
2, 31, 2; 3, 15, 4; 4, 3, 3.
5. cadant in sapientem: 3, 68.
6. bene laudata, etc.: if the text is
sound the sense must be that if teachers
show forth aright the merits of virtue,
then the approach of pleasure will be
barred. But possibly *laudata* is erroneous for *fundata*. [But perhaps *quod
iam* shows *laudata* to be right.]
voluptatis: see n. on § 27. In Tusc.
5, 27 fortunae aditus interclusisti, the
context shows *fortunae* to be genitive.
10. usurpabas: =*nominabas*, as below,
3, 33 and often.
13. mererere: see 1, 7. Madvig notes
the imperfect subj. in spite of *malis*.
14. aerumnas: Cicero himself here in-

dicates that the word was archaic; but
there are several passages to show that
it was not entirely out of use. Quint.
8, 3, 26 pronounces it obsolete. But
Cicero used it occasionally (as below,
5, 95) as he used some other words of
poetical and archaic character, though
he would have condemned the mania
for such terms which Sallust first exhibited in prose. Both Sall. and Livy
employed *aerumna*. The expression is
often connected with Hercules, as in
Plaut. Pers. 2; Epid. 178; Juven. 10,
361. Cicero also has *aerumnosus*.
15. tamen: here proleptic, referring to
etiam in deo.
16. elicerem: the reading *eligerem ex
te* is not to be justified by Tusc. 3, 83
stirpes eligendae sunt; nor by the
passages which C. F. W. Müller mar-
shals in his n. there in support of the
MSS. reading *eligendae*. The sense 'I
would pick this out of you' is utterly unsuitable here. [The construction *exigere
ex aliquo* is hardly possible in Cicero; he
has *ex rebus* above, 2, 73, and even that
is a rarity. The ordinary construction is
ab aliquo, as below, 4, 80.]

cogeremque ut responderes, nisi vererer, ne Herculem ipsum ea,
quae pro salute gentium summo labore gessisset, voluptatis causa
gessisse diceres.

Quae cum dixissem, Habeo, inquit Torquatus, ad quos ista
referam, et, quamquam aliquid ipse poteram, tamen invenire 5
malo paratiores—familiaris nostros, credo, Sironem dicis et
Philodemum, cum optimos viros, tum homines doctissimos.
Recte, inquit, intellegis. Age sane, inquam. Sed erat aequius
Triarium aliquid de dissensione nostra iudicare. Eiuro, inquit
arridens, inicum, hac quidem de re; tu enim ista lenius, hic 1
Stoicorum more nos vexat. Tum Triarius: Posthac quidem,
inquit, audacius. Nam haec ipsa mihi erunt in promptu, quae
modo audivi, nec ante aggrediar quam te ab istis, quos dicis,
instructum videro. Quae cum essent dicta, finem fecimus et
ambulandi et disputandi.   1

3 diceres: *dicere* BE.   4 quae cum: *que dum* B.   6 credo: *credo, inquam* cod.
Glogauensis.   6 Sironem: ita ABE; *Scyronem* ed. Rom. (1471).   8 sane: om. BE.
9 aliquid: *aliquod* B.   9 eiuro: *iuro* codd.; corr. Goerenz.   10 lenius:
levius BE.   subscriptiones: incipit liber tertius de finibus bonorum et malorum
A; explicit liber secundus de finibus bonorum et malorum marci tuly ciceronis.
Marci tuly Ciceronis de finibus bonorum et malorum liber tertius incipit B.

2. **gessisset**: n. on 1, 25 (referatur).
6. **Sironem**: Acad. 2, 106.
7. **viros...homines**: here, as often,
the change from *vir* to *homo* is merely
for change's sake; but it often has a
purpose; see Tusc. 2, 53: Sest. 82, and
n. to Arch. 16.
8. **age sane**: 'well, well'; a *formula
concedentis*, as in Pl. Ps. 1326.
erat aequius: see my n. on Lael.
15.
9. **eiuro...inicum**: cf. Verr. 2, 3, 137
id forum sibi inicum eierare; Phil.
12, 18 me inicum eierabant; De Or.
2, 285 (quoting Scipio Nasica Serapio)
eiero, inicus est...non ego mihi illum
inicum eiero, verum omnibus. Tusc.
4, 73 Venerem unam excludit ut inicam.
The legal oath would be tendered when
the *reus* argued 'aut accusatorem mu-
tandum aut iudices mutandos' (Ad
Herenn. 1, 22) and there might be an
appeal to a tribune: cf. Asc. 84 appellavit tribunos Antonius iuravitque se id
eiurare quod aequo iure non posset uti.

Plut. Cat. Min. 48 ἀπολέγειν ('reject')
opp. to ἀπολείπειν. For the omission of
ut in the passages quoted above cf. Arch.
19 Chii (Homerum) suum vindicant,
and the passages given in the Addenda
to my edition; add Ter. Haut. 204 illum
insimulat durum; Cic. Mil. 66 non
poteram Cn. Pompeium...timidum suspicari; Plin. n. h. 20, 119 ocimum
Chrysippus graviter increpuit inutile
stomacho; ib. 107.
10. **lenius...audacius**: n. on 1, 3 and
Cat. M. 3.
14. **finem...disputandi**: Apul. met.
1, 21, p. 19 (ed. Helm) is finis nobis
et sermonis et itineris communis fuit.
Madvig says 'nullam ambulationem
Cicero initio libri I commemoravit.' But
the *ambulatio* is implied in the word
insisteres above, § 51. In most of Cicero's
dialogues it is pointed out that the interlocutors are seated during the discussion; see my note on Acad. 1, 14
adsidamus. On the other hand Tusc.
1, 7 and 2, 10; Leg. 1, 15 with 2, 1.

INDEX

a and ab before d, II 89
a + abl. with gerundive, II 30
a with abl. after pass. inf., I 30
a, ex, de, with audire, I 39
  with quaerere, I 39
a se oriri, II 78
ab aliquo esse, I 21
ab, ex, with reverti, II 65
abeo (ne longe abeam), II 96
ablative, abs. without subject, II 85
  causal, strong, I 33, 36, 42; II 83
  instrumental, I 23; II 36
  qualitative, I 1
  separative (alienus), I 11
  sociative (ratione), I 32, 62; (sen-
    tentia), II 37
abundantes, II 111
ac, after neg., I 22
  and aut, II 73
  and pariter, I 67
  not before guttural, II 81
ac mihi quidem, II 81
ac tamen ‖ at tamen, II 85
Academics, I 13, 18, 27; II 34, 80
accedere ‖ accidere, I 41
accedere ad, II 44
accessio ad minuendas, I 51
accipere voluptatem, II 6
accipio quod dant, II 82
accusative, after pres. part., II 22
  with ambulare, II 112
  with consentire, II 117
  with ecce not found in Cic., II 96
acupenser, II 24
ad = secundum, I 30
ad altiora nasci, II 113
ad annum, II 92
'ad Herennium' (Epicurean), II 85
ad se redundare, II 78
ad with timidus, II 63
adamare, I 69
adde quod (is not Ciceronian), II 42
addere ad, II 42
addito (hoc addito), II 36
adducere, II 12
adhibere, II 23
adjectives, as subst. (cetero), I 26
  in -bilis and -ilis, II 57
  two together, one treated as subst.,
    II 54
adlevatio, I 40
admissum, I 2
admittere, metaph., I 2
adscendere in contionem, II 74
adverb, attached to passive part.
  regarded as subst., II 54

adverb (cont.)
  instead of object, I 4; II 65
  with esse, I 62
aegritudo, I 56
aeque with et, ac, ut, quam, I 67
aequius erat, II 119
aerumna, aerumnosus, II 118
affluere ‖ afluere, I 39
Afranius and Greeks, I 7
age sane, II 119
Albucius, I 8
alia omitted after multa, I 18
alias contrasted with nunc, I 28
alias ‖ alia, I 7
alias...alias, II 87
aliena = ἀλλότρια, I 26
alienus, constr., I 11
  = 'plagiarist,' I 17
alio, adv., II 27
alio genere, modo, II 9
aliqui, II 62
aliud, aliquid, aliquod, II 109
alius, proleptic, I 25
altior fieri, II 51
altiora (ad altiora nati), II 113
amare and amicitia, II 78
ambigere, II 4
ambigua, I 22
ambiguity, cases of, II 64
ambulare with accus., II 112
ambulatio, II 119
amor = amicitia, I 69
amotio, II 9
ample, II 76
amplexari, II 28, 43
amputatus circumcisusque, I 44
an and at, I 5, 28, 34; II 83
an quis alius, II 104
anacoluthon: alii once only, I 66
  others, I 40; II 13, 16, 107, 115
  primum without deinde, I 17;
    II 13, 54, 79
  with nec, neque, I 23; II 71
anapaestum, II 18
ancillulae, I 69
angustus, I 61
animadversio, I 30
animal ‖ animans, II 31
animal, animale, II 31
animals, arguments from, I 30; II 32,
  33, 109
animi, pl., I 47
animo...sensibus, I 64
Annicerii, I 37
annus (in (ad) annum), II 92
anticlimax, II 12

Antiochus, I 30, 42; II 34
antiqui, I 6
Antisthenes, I 38; II 96
ἅπαξ εἰρημένα, I 21, 25, 27, 66; II 5, 9
Apollodorus, II 96
appellare, 'mention,' II 29
appetendum, I 42
appetere, I 30; II 32
appetitus, II 32
appositional phrases, II 1, 72, 75, 103
apprehendere, II 3
aqua (in aqua ponere fundamenta),
    II 72
arbitratu meo, I 72
arcana, II 85
Arcesilas, II 2
Archilochus, II 115
architectari, II 52
architectus beatae vitae, I 32
ardor, I 43
argumentari, I 31
argumenti conclusio, I 30
argumentum, II 32
Aristippus, I 20, 23, 26, 30, 37, 50,
    57; II 34
Aristotle, does not supply material
    for De Fin., I 7
  happiness, II 19
  περὶ φιλοσοφίας, II 39
  pleasure and virtue, I 42
  sense knowledge, I 30
ars memoriae, II 104
ars vivendi, I 42, 72
artes, I 26
artifex, I 42; II 116
artificiosus, II 15
asciscere, I 23
asoti, II 22
aspernari, I 30
assonance (brevis, levis), II 22; (im-
    pediente, impendente), I 40;
    (inesse, necesse), ib.; (labore,
    dolore), I 32
asyndeton, II 31
at, *see* an
at etiam, I 39
Atilius, I 5
Atilius Calatinus, II 117
atoms, and free will, I 19
  and thought, I 21
atomus, I 17
atque ‖ atqui, I 58; II 34
atque, and aut, I 9
  explanatory, I 34
attingere, II 55
attraction, cases in parenthetic
    clause, I 14
  cases in relative clause, I 14, 29
  moods, I 40
  otherwise, I 54; II 8
  pronominal, I 39; II 75
auctor, II 29

aucupari, II 71
audacter, audaciter, II 28
audio, II 98
audire, a, ex, de, I 39
aut, I 55; II 108
  and atque, I 9
  and et (quem aut qualem), II 48,
    73
  collocation, II 15
  for et, I 4
  for neque, I 25
  in parallel clauses, I 36
  tres aut quattuor, II 62
  see ac, atque
aut ‖ ac, II 73
aut aut for et et, I 47
autem etiam juxtaposed, I 61
author and works identified, I 7;
    II 39, 44
avere, II 46

barbaria -es, II 49
barones, II 76
beatum esse, II 92
bene with adj., I 52, 71; II 94
bene beateque vivendum, I 5
bene, male facta, II 80
bene vivere, I 11; II 23
benevolentia, I 52
bestiae, *see* animal
bimembral questions, I 5, 12, 72;
    II 110
blanditiae voluptatis, I 33
bona corporis, II 38
bonum (suo bono), II 57
brevity, I 14
  in quibus=in eis in qu., I 18; II 3
  omission of that on which indirect
    question depends, I 20
  other exx., II 8, 10, 70, 72
Brutus, I 8

cadere in, I 41; II 117
Caecilius, II 22
Caesar's Latin, I 28, 35, 39 (bis), 61,
    62; II 1, 6, 29
calculus of pleasure and pain, I 33;
    II 60
callido improbo (de), II 54
callidus and versutus, II 53
Callipho, II 19, 34
captiones, II 17
captiosa, I 22
caput, 'fountain-head,' II 34
caritas humani generis, II 45
Carneades, I 50; II 35, 38, 59
Carneiscus, I 65
Catiline, conspiracy of, II 63
Catullus, I 28
causa, and gratia, I 36
  in eadem causa, I 49
  causa tua, tui, etc., II 76

celeritas, 'short duration,' I 40
censere and sentire, II 6
centurions, I 9
cerritus, II 71
change, act. and pass., II 21, 48
  mood, I 32; II 61
  number (verb), I 1, 22; II 23;
    (nouns), I 5; II 22, 31, 61
  or. rect. and or. obl., I 30
  point of view, II 34
  tense, I 35; II 4, 42, 118
  see prepositions, pronouns
chiasmus, I 28, 31
  avoided, I 4
chorus, of a school of philosophers,
  I 26
chronology disregarded, I 6
Chrysippus, I 39; II 38
cibus et potio, II 7
Cicero and Epicureanism, I 16
citare, II 18
clamare, I 57; II 23, 51, 65
claudicare, I 66, 69
clause, resumptive, II 73
Cleanthes' tabula, II 69
clemens, II 12
clinamen, I 19
coepi with inf., II 43
coercendi, I 51
cognitio, 'legal investigation,' I 24;
  'recognition,' II 110; cf. 82
cognitio rerum, I 25
cognitio verborum, II 16
cognomentum, II 15
cognoscere, I 24; II 82
cognosci et percipi, I 64
cohors, I 9
colligere, 'quote,' I 34; II 62
collocation, adj. before noun, II 1
  emphatic word at end, I 32
  aliis multis ‖ multis aliis, II 45
  aut, II 15
  esse, I 40; II 75
  est, II 98
  possit, I 44
  quam, II 29
  saepe, II 49
  si ita se res (res se) habeat, I 25
  see pronouns
Colotes, I 65
comis ‖ communis, II 80
commendatio, II 35
commenticius, I 19
commota est barbaria, II 49
commotio, II 13
comparatio, II 44
comparatio compendiaria, II 25
complexio, I 19
comprehendere firme, II 6
comprobare, I 65
concedere ut, II 6; cf. v 78
concludere (numeris), II 105

concludere rationem, I 22
concludere sententiam argumenti,
  I 30
conclusio, I 22, 30
concursio and concursus, I 17
concursio, turbulenta, I 20
conditional sentence, double protasis, I 7; II 112
  fut. ind. in protasis and apodosis,
    I 20
  fut. perf. and pres. ind., II 69
  perf. subj. in protasis, I 22, 56
conditus (from condire), II 25
confirmare, I 23
conformare, I 23
Congus, I 7
coniunctus ex, II 44
consentaneum, II 70
consentire, with acc., II 117
consentire naturae, II 34
consequentes fines, II 34
consequentium repugnantiumve
  ratio, I 63
consequitur aliquid aliquis, I 32
consilium, eo consilio ut, I 72; II 6
consistere, I 41
constantius, II 114
constringendus, I 47
construction incorrectly carried on
  from sentence to sentence, II 88
consuetudo loquitur, II 48
contemni non poteris, II 84
conterere se in, I 72
continens, 'temperate,' I 37
continere, constr. with and without
  in, I 35
continere vitam omnem, I 12
continuo, II 24
contracted verb forms, *see* decesse,
  dixti
controversia verborum, II 38
convenit, impersonal, I 17
conventu, in, II 74
convicia, I 69
cor, II 24, 91
Corinthium, II 23
corpora solida, 'heavy bodies,' I 18
corpusculum, I 17
Crassus, II 57
crede mihi, mihi crede, II 69, 113
credo parenthetical, not ironical, I 39
critics of Latin literature, I 1, 4
Croesus, II 87
cruciare and excruciare, II 14
crudus, II 23
cuiusquemodi, II 3, 22
cum, and abl. of circumstance, I 9
  and subj., II 117
  causal, II 95; with ind., I 10
  explanatory clause with, II 5, 14
  in eo cum, II 14
  in 'qualitative time clause,' I 1

cum (*cont.*)
  mixed up with protasis, II 112
  repeated with subj., II 24
  with change of mood, II 61
  with discrepare, II 96
  with fut. and fut. perf., I 7
cum || quom fallen out when close to
  quod, II 82, 101
cum...tum, I 34
cum causa, II 56
cum praesertim, II 25
cupiditates, I 43
curiosi, I 3
cursus, I 37
curvos, II 33
Cynics, I 32; II 88
Cyrenaics, I 23, 55, 57; II 39

dative, ethic, II 23
  of agent, I 11
  with alienus, I 11
  with bene dicere etc., II 80
  with facere, II 79
  with nouns (heres etc.), II 55
  with prospicere, I 35
  with scribere (dat. comm.), I 7
de, short introd. clause with, I 26
  with migrare, I 62
  see preposition
death, Epicurean view, I 40, 49, 62;
  II 100
decesse, II 10
Decii, II 61
decimanus, II 24
declinatio, I 19
decreta, II 28
dedocendi, I 51
deferre rem, II 55
defetigatio, I 3
definire with acc. and inf., II 5
definition, II 5
defundere, diffundere, II 23
dein, I 50; II 42
deinde ibidem, I 19
delabi de caelo, I 63
delectari with abl. with and without
  ab, I 14
delectari in, I 39
delectus, dilectus, I 33
delicatus, I 5
Democritea dicere, I 17
Democritus and atoms, I 19
  and death, I 49
  and fortune, I 63
  and παιδεία, I 26
  and the first impulses of nature,
    I 30
  and the needs of nature, I 45
Democritus eruditus, I 20
dempsit || dempserit, II 23
denique, I 3
deorsum, deorsus, I 18

depellere, repellere, I 33
depravatum, I 30
depulsio, II 41
deripere, I 43
desitum est with inf., II 43
desperantes omnia, I 61
despicationes, I 66
devotio, II 61
di (si dis placet), II 31
dialectica, I 20; II 17, 18
dialogue, I 29
dicere res, I 8
dici aut fingi, I 41
dictata, II 95
dictum sit, I 37
dies noctesque, II 114
difficile est, I 3
difficilis, 'morose,' I 61
dignus nomine hominis, II 114
dilabi (sc. ex memoria), I 41
diminutive, contemptuous, I 4
Diodorus, II 34
Diogenes, I 6, 72; II 24
dirigere ad, I 54; II 115
discidium, dissidium, I 44
discipulus, II 30
discordare, I 44, 58
discrepare, constr. with cum, II 96
dislocations in MSS., I 55
dispicere, II 97
dissentiunt, II 19
distinctio, I 33
dividere, frangere, II 26
dixti, II 10
docere, 'prove,' I 29
dogmata, II 105
Dogmatists, I 64
dolor, I 49
domus, dominus, I 58
  una in domo, I 65
dormitator, I 61
double readings, putat dicat, II 16
double rendering, I 38, 64; II 2, 96
Drausus, Drusus, I 23
dubium est quin, II 83
dulcis motus, II 10
dum with perf., II 43
dumtaxat, II 21
durus dolor, I 43
dux et auctor, II 66

e = secundum, II 34
  see also ex
e quo, II 15
e regione, I 19
ecce and acc., II 96
ecce autem, etc., I 61
edict of praetor, II 74
edint, II 22
ediscere, II 20
effectrix, I 67
efficere rationem, I 22

efficiens, II 10, 21
effigies, II 58
efflorescere, I 69
effluere, I 41; II 104
ĕgens, ēgens, II 105
eiurare, II 119
elaboro and laboro, I 10
elegans, I 10
elegantia, II 26
elicere, II 2
  and eligere, II 119
eligendi optio, I 33
ellipse after quo modo, II 97
  after ut, II 104
  in introducing apod., I 6
  of esse with gerundive, I 6, 43;
    II 41; with part., I 13, 35, 39;
    II 54
  of homine, I 35
  of inf. with velle, nolle, I 21, 28;
    II 33
  of inquam, I 28; II 9, 17
  of parts of esse, I 17, 59 (bis), 72;
    II 2, 6, 88, 93, 95, 103, 106
  of pred. in brief emphatic clause:
    ut...(sic), I 3; II 35, 37, 41, 50,
    105; (proverbs), ib.
  of preposition, I 32
  of protasis, II 67
  of si, II 57
  of subject to infin., II 50
  of verb: (possibly to be supplied
    from following neg.), I 2; (sint
    to be supplied with dicta from
    following complete verb), I 6
  of verb of duty from gerundive,
    II 103
  other instances, I 7, 9, 14, 30, 63,
    69; II 5, 17, 25
  sundry, I 8, 18, 31, 32; II 3, 26,
    65, 102
  with ne, I 43; II 20, 77
elogium, II 116
eloquentia, of style, I 15
emancipare, I 24
en, II 96
enim, in introd. clause, I 18
enim est, I 43
enim, 'why,' I 25
Ennius, I 7; II 41, 106
eoque, I 56
epexegetic phrase, I 72
Epicurean doctrine, refuted by lives,
  II 81
  and public life, II 67
Epicureans, I 6, 28
  and suicide, I 49
  consider man and beasts have the
    same good, I 23
  heretics, I 55
  ignorant, I 26
  late, I 31, 69

Epicureans (cont.)
  system easy, I 13
  why numerous, I 25
  writers, I 8
Epicurus, a plagiarist, I 17
  allows no middle state, I 55
  alone saw truth, I 14
  and Democritus, I 21, 28
  and force, I 18
  and free will, I 19
  and logic, I 63
  and mathematics, I 20
  and pleasure, I 28
  and science, I 63
  boasts himself self-taught, I 32
  definitions, I 22, 29
  education, I 26
  eulogised, I 32
  letters, II 96
  on ἔρως, I 61; II 7, 33
  on friendship, I 65
  on happiness of gods, I 61
  on justice, I 50
  περὶ τέλους, II 7
  senses, I 22
  serene, I 37
  simple life (λιτότης), II 90
  σοφός, II 7
  style, I 14
  virtue and pleasure inseparable,
    I 42
epigramma, II 106
ergo resumptive, II 23
erigi, I 57
Erillus, II 35, 43
errores, I 14
erubescere, II 28
eruditi, I 26
esse, and fieri, I 69; see ut
  dico esse, II 13
  with adv., I 62
esse in sententia, II 2
est, esse, II 92
  see collocation, ellipse
est ut, II 6
esto: verum esto, II 75, 92
et, see aeque, aut, autem, similiter,
  simul
et ‖ etiam, I 55
et, in retort, II 102
et...et, II 84
et...et...ac, I 57
et A et B atque C, II 95
et A et BCque, II 100
et iam, II 15
et...neque, I 6
et quidem, I 35; II 9, 81
et tamen, I 11, 15; II 84
etiam, see et, autem
Eudoxus, I 30
evolutio, I 25, 72
ex, ab with reverti, II 65

ex aliquo transferre aliquid, I 7
ex eo quod, I 8
ex se oriri, II 78
exaggeration, I 32; II 108
exaudire, I 71
exceptio, II 21
excidere, I 41
exedere, I 51, 59
exigere ex, II 119
existimare =iudicare, I 12
exitum (ad exitum pervenire), II 3
exitum reperire, I 54
expedire se, I 66
expetendum, I 11
expetere, II 32
expleri, II 42
explicare, I 55
extenuare, II 30
extorquere, II 16
extremitas, II 102
extremum (τέλος), I 11, 41
  ad extremum, I 26
  of space, I 17
exultare, I 54

fabella, I 4
fac ut, II 96
facete, I 7
facete et urbane, I 39
fastidium, I 5
fatui, II 70
feneratio, II 117
ferae, I 34
fere, I 18
ferre || facere, I 3
ferreus scriptor, I 5
ferri ('carried along'), I 17
fictae fabulae, I 65
fidem facere, etc., II 27
fieri || ferri, II 20
figura etymologica, II 95
finem = extremum = ultimum, II 5, 6
fines malorum (=dolor), I 55
fingere incessum, II 77
finire, def., II 5
finita, infinita oratio, Madvig's use
  of the terms, I 23
finitae cupiditates, I 62
foedus, II 83
foedus amicitiae, I 70
fomenta, II 95
forem (=futurus essem), II 63
forma, 'sketch,' II 48
formosi, formonsi, II 23
formula, II 3
fortitudo, I 49
free will, I 19
frequenter, I 16
friend=alter ego, I 67
friendship, I 65 sq. (II 78 sq.)
frons, II 77
Fronto, I 8

fructus (in fructu), I 12
fruor, fruendus, I 3
fugiendum, I 11
fut. perf., *see* verb
futurus, adjectival, II 63

Gallonius, II 24, 90
gaudere, application, I 37
  quod gaudeat, I 62
gaudere in, I 39
gaudium, of body, II 13
gemination, II 68
genitive, *see* noun
genus, II 63
  alio genere, alio modo, II 9
  e continenti genere, II 61
  ex eo genere qui, II 39
  istius generis, II 23
genus hoc, I 1
geometrica, I 20
gloria =gloriae studium, I 51
gloriari in, I 39
gloriose, II 89
gloriosus, I 37; II 97
gods, Epicurean, I 62; II 115
  and the σοφός, II 88
Gorgias, II 1
Graece egregie, II 19
granaria, II 84
gratia and causa, I 36
gratis, adv., II 83
gratus, II 72
gumia, II 24
gurges, II 24
gustare, I 58
gymnasia, I 69

habere, II 9
  'brings,' I 42
  with part. pass., II 6
habere natalem, II 102
habitare, II 92
haec, generic, II 19, *and see* pronoun
haerere, I 20
haesitare, II 18
halo, I 61
happiness: Aristotle, II 19
  ideal Epicurean, I 40
Heraclitus and πολυμάθεια, I 26; also
  II 15
Herillus, *see* Erillus
Hermarchus, II 96
hic, adv., II 23
hic dolor, II 66
Hieronymus, II 8, 35
historia, I 25; II 67, 107
hoc, referring forward, I 40
hoc est, followed by two infinitive
  clauses, II 16
Homerus, I 7; II 115
homines optimi, I 25
homo juxtaposed with hominum, II 45

honestas, II 19
honestum, II 45
  used by Epicureans, II 50, cf. I 42
honorem praefari, II 29
Hortensius, I 2
humanius, II 82

iactari, II 24
iam...etiam, II 2
iam...iam, II 30
iambus, II 18
ictus, II 32
id est, I 33, 71, 72; II 1, 6, 21, 90,
  101
id totum, I 36; II 11
idcirco, I 39
igitur, at beginning of a sentence,
  I 61
  continuation, I 4
  position after and before est, I 28
  resumptive, II 23, 29, 107
ignavi, I 61
ignoratio,...ignorantia, I 43
ille, see pronoun
ille apud Trabeam, II 13
ille Caecilianus, II 13
illogicality, in quod...arguerent, I
  24
  in use of inter, I 30
  in use of subj., I 23
  slight, I 4, 15, 16, 20, 40, 42;
    II 20, 21, 33, 97, 109
illusion of dialogue, II 44
imago, I 21
imbui, I 60; II 16
impediente. impendente, I 40
imperio (in summo imperio esse), II
  66
imperiosus, II 60
imperiti, I 37
impetibilis, II 57
importare, I 51
importunus ‖ inopportunus, II 85
impotens, I 52
impunite, II 59
in, see ponere, prepositions
in annum, II 92
in eadem pulchritudine, II 47
in eo cum, II 14
in fructu, I 12
in summo imperio esse, II 66
in volgus, II 15
inania, I 46
inanis ‖ immanis, I 59
inanitas, I 44
incessus, II 77
inciderit, I 7
incommoda, I 53
inconcinnitas, II 65
inconsistency in Epicurean school,
  I 55 f.
inconstantissime, II 88

incurvare, II 33
index ‖ iudex, I 50
indicare se, I 50; II 79
indicari ‖ iudicari, I 30
indicative, see verb
indicens (=non dicens), etc., II 10
individua, I 17; II 75
indolentia, II 11
indoloria, II 11
induci, I 62
induere cognomen, II 73
indulgenter ‖ diligenter, II 109
industria, I 49
ineleganter, II 26
inermis, I 22
iners, II 115
inertissimae segnitiae, I 5
infans, ‘child,’ II 33
  ‘incapable of speaking,’ I 52
infinitio, I 21
infinitive, see verb
infinitum inane, I 17
infitiari, II 54
ingeni motus, II 34
ingurgitare, II 23
inicus, II 119
iniectus animi, I 31 n.
initia, I 72; II 46
  rerum gerendarum initia, I 42
innasci, I 31
innumerabiles mundi, I 21; II 102
innumerabiles res, II 113
inquit, see ellipse
  with indef. subj., II 78, 106
inquit ille ‖ ille in., II 11
inscientia, inscitia, I 46; II 34
insistere, II 3, 51
insitus, I 31
institutio, I 70
instructus ad, II 57
integrum est ut, II 6
inter, see preposition
intercapedo, I 61
interdum...interdum, II 30
interim...interim, II 30
intermundia, II 75
interpres, I 6
interpretari, I 34; II 100
interrogare aut interrogari, I 29
intervalla, I 49; II 94
inventor veritatis, I 32
invidi, I 61
invidia verbi, I 43
invidiosum nomen, II 12
invitamentum etc., II 99
ioca seria, II 85
ipsa, I 49, 63; =αὐτομάτη, II 111
ipse, ‘even,’ I 46
ipse, ‘unmittelbar,’ I 37
ipsi propter se ipsos, I 69; II 78
ipsum sua vi propter seque, II 44
iracundiae (plur.), I 27

irregular syntax, I 66; exposition, II 20
ita followed by defining clause, II 13
  hoc ita dicere, I 25
  not with semper, II 88
  (quod ita), I 26; II 17
ita non, II 22, 63, 88
itaque, apodotic, I 19
itaque = et ita, I 34
item, in abbreviating parenthesis, II 16
  replaces verb after noun, II 13
  (cf. III 51)
iucunde ac suaviter, I 57
iucundi acti labores, II 105
iucunditas, I 37, 53, 67; II 6, 13, 14
iudicare, in absolute sense, I 2
iudicatum est, II 36
iudices, II 36
iudicia rerum, I 22
iudicia sensuum, I 64
iudicii est, II 36
iudicium ('power of judging'), II 33
iudicium, 'literary taste,' I 6
  'criticism,' I 7
iurare in leges, II 55
iure, II 61
ius loquendi, II 17
iustitia, I 50

labi, I 18
labor hic noster, I 1
laboro (non laboro), II 28
Laelius, II 24, 25, 59
Laelius Decumus, I 7
laetari in, I 39
laetitiis laetum, II 13
lapathus, II 24
late patere, I 36
Latin and Greek, I 10
Latina (Latine) scripta, I 4
Latine deterius, I 8
laudabilis, I 42
laudator, II 67
laudes = virtutes, II 47
laus amicitiae, II 84
legere aliquem de aliqua re, I 6
lenius...audacius, II 119
leviter agnoscere, II 33
levius fore, I 41
libera voluptas, I 58
liberalitas, I 52
liberi, I 34
libet (quod liberet), II 5
libidines, I 46
Licinus, I 5
linea (ad lineam), I 18
liquida voluptas, I 58
'literal translation,' I 4
litterae || libri, I 12
litterae = μαθήματα, II 12; = writings, I 1

litterae utraeque, I 10
Livy, I 24; II 29
loci, loca, I 6
locus, 'the right place,' I 29, cf. I 37
  hoc loco, II 30
  nullo loco numero, II 90
longe multumque, II 111
longinquos, II 94
longus, 'prolix' (of persons), II 85
loqui, with accus., II 76
  si loqui possent, II 18
  ut verum loquamur, II 23
Lucan (uses tunc, not tum), I 28
lucifugus, lucifuga, I 61
Lucilius, I 7, 9; II 15, 23, 24
Lucretius introduces nunc...nunc, II 30
luculenter, luculente, II 15
ludicra, I 69
ludus, I 69; II 23, 107
ludus est with inf., I 27
lumen, 'strong point,' II 70
lurco, II 24 n.
lusos || elusos, II 2
lustratio, II 109
lustro, I 61
luxuria, luxuriosi, II 21

macellum, II 50
magistra, I 71
magno opere, II 85
magnus annus, II 102
Mago, I 24
maiestas atque imperium, I 23
maledicere, a compound verb, I 15
maledicta, II 80
malefacta, II 80
male Graecus, I 8
malo dicere || ita dicere, II 61
maluisti, scansion, I 9
mandatum, II 58
Manilius, I 7
Manliana imperia, II 60, 105
Manlius Torquatus (consul 347), I 23; (consul 165), I 24
materia, I 18
mathematics and the atom, I 20
medicamenta, II 22
mediocres amicitiae, II 84
mediocritas, II 27
medium between pleasure and pain, I 38
Megarians, I 63
membra || partes, II 113
memini, constr., II 55
memoriter, I 34
memoro for commemoro, II 15
mereri, II 74
Metrodorus, I 25, 63; II 7, 96
micare, II 52
migrare de, I 62
mimus vitae, I 49

mind, and body, I 56
  and movement, II 45
minuere contentiones, II 39
minutus, I 60
mirari satis non queo, I 10
mittere librum, I 8
moderatio, II 73
modestia, II 73
modo, I 60; isto modo, II 23, 103
modo (temporal), II 100
modum habere, II 27; prope modo, I 2
modus, with genitive, I 3
  cuiusque modi, II 3, 22
  multis modis, II 82
modus, 'the right manner,' I 29
molesti, II 28
molestia, I 37
molliter ferre, II 64
mollitia animi, I 33
monet, I 47
monstrosus, monstruosus, I 61
montuosus, I 61
mood, see verb
morbus animi, I 59
morosus, I 61
mors, Epicurus on, II 100 (cf. I 40)
mortales (omnes), II 6
mortalis deus, II 40
motus ingeni, II 34; in motu voluptas, II 16
movens voluptas, I 37; II 31
movere, intrans., II 36
moveri ingenio, II 34 n.
multis modis, II 82
multum = valde and saepe, I 5
mundi innumerabiles, I 21; II 102
municipalis eques, II 58
munire se, II 84
munus vitae, I 11
musica, I 20
mutae bestiae, I 71

nam, 'indeed,' I 19
nam in 'occupatio,' I 6
nam quod ait, II 36
name and thing, II 13, 51, 67
narthecium, II 22
nasci ad altiora, II 113
  ad maiora, I 23
natura = φύσει, II 45
natura: a natura with pass. inf.,
  I 30; II 33
  physical frame, I 37
  quid n. postulet, I 42
natura orationis, I 63
natura victus, II 49
naturae consentire, II 34
naturae fines, I 44
naturales cupiditates, I 45
navigare with acc., II 112
ně = nonne, I 57
  position, I 6

ně and nec continuing modo or ut,
  I 10
ně for ita ut ně, II 64
ně non for ut after verbs of fearing,
  I 34
ně...quidem, I 20, 39
nebulo, I 61
nec + perf. subj. in prohibitions,
  I 25
nec...nec, I 50
nec..quidem, II 87
nec tamen, II 111
nedum, II 102
neque and aut, I 25
  after neg., I 30
neque and nec, I 51
nequedum, II 23
nequeo, non queo, I 10
nescius, I 1
nihil ad, I 39; II 82
nihil dolens, II 16
nihil dolere, II 11
nihil opinans, II 58
nihil timens, II 46
nihil ut, ut nihil, I 34
nihildum, II 23
nimio etiam, II 7
nisi aliter, II 55
nisi molestum est, I 28; II 5
nisi quod in questions, II 74
nivem esse albam, I 30
nobilis (philosophus), II 28
noctes diesque, I 51
nomen audire non posse, II 67
nomen Romanum, I 4
nominare, II 67
non at end of clause, II 13
  coalescing, I 1, 31, 38; II 53
non dicente, II 10
non dolendi status, II 28, cf. II 31
non minus non, II 22
non quaero quid, II 84
non saepe, II 95
non ut and quo, II 42
nondum quaero, II 11
nonne, position of, II 10
  in indirect question, II 58
nos, II 67
nosse vim voluptatis, II 7; cf. 29
nostri (sc. Academics), II 1
nostrum = hominum, I 32
notio insita in animis, I 31
notus sibi, II 16
noun, collective noun linked with
  plur., I 25
  collective sense attached to sing.,
  II 65
  diminutive (vincla), II 117
  Greek, in -ων, II 19; in -ης, II 94
  in -tio, I 21
  plur. abstract, I 47, 66
  see change

noun (*cont.*)
 ablative
  ratione, I 29, 32, 62
  cf. sententia, II 37
 accusative
  with consentire, II 117
  with loqui, II 76
  with navigare, II 112
 dative
  pred. dat. and nom. interchanging,
   II 59
  with scribere, I 7
 genitive
  and dat., II 27
  definitive, with causa, I 18
  double, avoided, II 113
  double (Theophrasti orationis ornamenta), I 14
  explanatory, I 33, 52
  in -i causes confusion, II 55,
   84
  of Greek nouns in -ης, I 14
  of person dep. on multa, I 18; cf.
   23, 26, 27; II 68
  of price (parvi ducere), II 24
  plur. in -um, -ium, II 110
  with alienus, I 11
  with compleri, II 21
  with efficiens, II 21
  with fidem facere, etc., II 27
  with modus, I 3
 novus vicinus, I 3
 nubilo, I 61
 nulla, 'not at all,' I 56, 65
 nulla vi praeter, II 65
 nullusdum (not Ciceronian), II 23
 number, *see* change
  sing. for plur., II 110
 numerus (e quorum numero), II 1
 numquidnam, I 39
 nunc...nunc, II 30
 nuper, II 100
 nutare, II 6
 nutus, I 20

o with accusative, II 96 n.
ob, use in Cic., II 54
obscenae voluptates, II 68
occaecati, I 33
occultae res, I 64
occurrere, I 19; II 108
Octavius, II 93
officia deserere, I 33
omittere dolores, I 56
omnes, applied to two, II 105
omnes qui ubique sunt, II 6
omnes urbani, II 77
omnino...sed, I 10
omnis, summative use (his omnibus),
 II 23
omnis summa, II 86
opifex, II 115

opinio =οἴησις, I 43; opinionem aucupari, II 71
optimum (hoc vero optimum), II 6
optimum quidque rarissimum, II 81
opus esse, II 5
oracula of Epicurus, II 20
oratio =λέξις, I 10
oratio obliqua, levelling effect on
 moods, I 23; change to or. rect.
 and or. obl., I 30
oratio perpetua, I 29; II 2
oriri a (ex) se, II 78
ornatus, I 10
ornatus =κόσμος, I 20
ostendere, 'promise,' I 29
Ovid, his usage of tunc, I 28
 introduced saepe...saepe, II 30

Paeanem citare, II 18
paene, ref. to preceding words, I 4
paenitendum, II 106
pain, consolations for, I 40
pairs of friends, I 65
Panaetius, I 6; II 24
parabilis, I 46
parens philosophiae (Socrates), II 1
parenthesis (ut facit), II 80
pariter ac, etc., I 67
pars ‖ genus, II 26
partes mundi, I 19
partibus omnibus, II 108
particeps, II 38
participle, *see* verb
partim, II 109
partitio cupiditatum, I 45
partus ancillae, I 12
parum (non parum), II 12
parvi =pueri, II 32
passeres, II 75
patefactio, II 5
patella, II 22
patientia, I 49
patria, II 63
pecudes and Epicureans, II 18
pecunia =pecuniae cupiditas, I 51
pecunias capere, I 24
Peducaeus, II 58
pendere, I 62
per se, II 50
peragrare animo, II 102
peragratio, II 109
percipere =καταλαμβάνεσθαι, I 30
percipere corpore voluptatem, I 23
pereruditi, II 12
perfect, *see* verb
perfectio virtutis, II 88
perfectio vitae, II 38
perfunctio, I 49
perfundi iucunditate, II 6
perhibere, II 15
pericula, I 10
perinde, I 72

Peripatetics, II 33, 34
periphrasis, II 75
perpetua oratio, I 29; II 2
perpetuitas, II 87
persequi, I 12
Persius, I 7
perspicuom, I 42, 56
persto, II 107
pertinacia, I 28
pertinax, II 9, 107
pervagata, II 15
petere, expetere, II 112
petulans, I 61
Phaedrus, I 16
Phidias, Zeuxis, II 115
Philoctetes, II 94
Philodemus, I 16, 72
  de ira, I 28
  περὶ θεῶν διαγωγῆς, I 30
Philus, II 59
physica, fem. and neut. pl., I 20
physicus, I 19; II 102
Pindarus, II 115
pingere, depingere, II 69
Piso ‖ ipso, II 90
Plato, I 5, 7
  and pleasure, I 37
  Epistles, II 45
  middle state, I 38
  Phaedrus, II 4
  Philebus, I 56
  Platonic view of the seat of
    pleasure, II 115
  Timaeus, II 15
pleasure, and σάρξ, I 55
  and virtue, I 42; II 21
  mental and bodily, I 55
  not ἀγαθόν, I 31
  passive, the greatest, I 37
  unarguable, I 30
  weighed against pain, I 32
plenum (e pleno), II 23
plenus voluptatum, I 53
pleonasm, slight, I 21, 42; II 58
  altum et excelsum, II 47
  consequens ac posterus, I 67; II 13
  iusto odio dignissimus, I 33
  praesens et quod adest, I 55
  with ita, II 17
Plotius, II 58
pluperfect, see verb
plural, see noun
poema, II 107
poena legum, I 51
poetry, Epicurean disregard for, I 72
Polemo, II 34
Polyaenus, I 20
Polyclitus, II 115
Pompeius, II 54
ponat ‖ putat, II 70
pondera, I 18, 19
pondere suo, I 18

ponere in voluptate non dolere, II 19
ponere quaestionem alicui, II 1
Pontius, I 9
populari fama gloriosum, II 48
populariter, II 17
populus cum illis facit, II 44
porro, I 32; II 25
Posidonius, I 6
Postumius, II 70
potest esse, II 92
potestas (in potestate), II 86
potiri voluptate, I 62
potius quam, II 42
potiusque, I 51
potus (subst.), I 37
potus, cibus et, I 37
praecentare, II 94
praeceptrix, I 43
praecipua, II 33
praecipuom, II 110
praescribere, praescriptio, II 3
praesertim, II 102
praesidia vitae, I 35
praesidium, I 10; II 84
praeterea, continuative, I 41, 42
Praxiphanes, I 65
precari, deprecari, II 79
predicate, see verb
prepositions:
  ab, ex, I 17
  ad after nisi, II 111
  ad me, I 14
  'as,' II 26
  changed, I 14, 17; II 12
  contineri, in aliqua re, I 35
  de, 'after pattern of,' I 8
  e and de of translations from, I 4
  erga and in, I 68
  gaudere, gloriari in, I 39
  in longinquitate, I 40
  in quaerendo, II 3
  in quibus = in eis in quibus, I 18
  not repeated with rel., I 49
  omitted, I 32
  repeated (inter), I 30; (in), I 4, 34
  repeated with gerund, II 40
present, see verb
prima naturā data, II 33
primi (subst.), I 9
primo, primum, I 50
primum...principio, I 17
  without deinde, I 17; II 79
primum...secundum 'premisses,'
    I 39
primus quisque, II 105
princeps, constr., II 61
probare, 'quote,' I 6
probare voluptatem et dolorem, I 23
prodesse (quod prodesset), II 5
profecto, I 41
prohibere, constr., I 27
prolepsis, of alius, I 25

promulgare, II 15
pronouns, antec. and rel. do not
    correspond, II 39
    changed, II 7
    generic id, II 24
    generic uses, hoc, haec, I 30; II 17,
    19
    hoc...id, I 2
    id, II 42
    id repeats illud, II 49
    ille is, II 14
    ipse, I 53
    ipse without is, I 13
    is ipse, I 32; II 93
    is qui with adversative force, I 14
    juxtaposed, II 115
    neut. acc. subst., I 14; II 18
    neut. sing. ref. to masc. or fem.
    or plur., I 20, 31, 56; II 6, 20, 42
    plur. referring to una res, II 9
    position, II 27
    postponed in clause, II 56
    quae...ea, I 1
    quo neut. abl. in comparisons
    along with quam, I 19
    quod...ad id not ad quod, I 42
    quodcumque with antecedent id,
    II 43
    referred to substantive contained
    in adj. (Democritus contained
    in Democritea), I 17
    rel. =ut, 'as,' I 17
    rel. at head of successive clauses,
    I 13, 22
    rels. drawn together, I 26, 52
    repetition of pronoun, I 11, 29;
    II 13, 43
    se ipsa, II 66
    substantival (id) not referring to
    a definite subject in context, I 3
    te ipse || ipse te, II 69
    see se, suus, sibi
pronuntiare, II 37
prorsus (ita prorsus), I 23
prorsus non, non prorsus, II 16
prosperum, I 71
provincias dare, I 20
provocare, 'draw out,' I 26
putas || putes, II 76
Pyladea, II 84
Pyrrho, II 35, 43
Pythagoreans, I 17, 38

quae...eadem, II 72; cf. quae...
    talia, II 105
quae qualisque, I 37; cf. 29
quae tota, II 48
quaerere (discipulos quaerere), II 30
quaerere (audire) with ex, de, ab, I 39
quaerere opus, II 30
quaerere sedem summi boni, II 37
quaesita voluptas, II 82

quaeso, I 34
quaestio, II 1
quale, attached to infin., II 86
qualis, in question, II 27, 74
quam, along with abl. of comparison
    after comparative, I 19
quam nihil, tam nihil, I 57
quamvis =quantumvis, II 102
quanti maximi, I 41
quantity of words, abnormal, II 15
quantum potuimus, I 12
quantus in exclamation after quod
    si, I 59
quapropter, I 71
quasi, I 30, 39, 47; II 5, 7, 20, 30
    (suaves et quasi dulces), 102, 114
que, after neg., I 41
    attached to prep., I 13, 43; II 44
    attached to reliqua, II 106
    corresponds with nec, I 48
    et...et...que, I 12
quemadmodum...sic, I 39
questions, bimembral, I 5, 12, 72;
    II 110
questions, rhetorical, answered, II
    102
qui, quis, quid, I 11; *see also* pro-
    nouns
qui et quanti, II 68
qui non and quin, II 27
quicum in tenebris (mices), II 52
quid? I 6; *see also* pronouns
quid ad, II 85
quid ergo, II 7
quid est aliud, II 54
quid et quale, I 29; II 6
quid igitur est? I 17
quo, abl. neut. pron., I 30, 41, 57
quo+magis, II 6
quo circa, I 68
quo loco=ubi, II 3; cf. I 66
quo minus, I 58
quo minus necaremini deprecari,
    II 79
quod, followed by epexegetic clause,
    II 12
quod || quo, II 73
quod || quoniam, II 43
quod...aut...quae, II 67
quod...dicat, I 4
quod...idem, I 55
quod minime volt, I 25
quod quia, I 67
quodam modo, apologetic, II 71
quodcumque, *see* pronouns
quoniam || cum, I 10
quoque, force and position, II 108
quorum || quarum, I 21
quot homines, etc., I 15

ratio || oratio, I 30
ratione, I 62

ratione et via, I 29
ratione facere, I 32
-rĕ and -rĭs, II 51; *see* verb
recipere, II 66
recte of Epicureanism, I 42
recusare, I 33
redarguitur, II 99
referre, I 11, 23, 42; II 5
rĕfert, II 97
regio (e regione), I 19
regula =κανών, I 63
Regulus, II 65
reliqui, proleptic, II 35 (cf. alii)
repetition: accedit, accedere, I 41
  iustitia, iustitiae, II 71
  natura, II 33
  of noun in rel. clause, I 39
  of sounds (qu), II 6
  of statement, II 6
  of verb with non, II 13
  of words, I 56
  saepe, II 30
  sapientia, I 3
  sed, II 45
  sententia, II 19
  si, I 69
  ut, I 34, 69; II 50, 73
  voluptatem at end of two successive clauses, I 23
reprehendere, II 3
reprehensa, I 28
reprobare, I 23
rerum ignoratio, I 63
rerum verborumne controversia, II 38
res pro rei defectu, II 73
restinctio, II 9
reversio, II 102
revertor, II 65
rhetoric and palm of hand, II 17
robustus animus, I 49
rogatiuncula, I 39
ruere, II 18

s silent, I 9
sacculus, II 23
sacrilegus, II 22
saepe, collocation, II 49
saepe...saepe, II 30; saepe etiam, I 47
saepti et muniti, I 51
sagax, II 45
salebra, II 30
Sallust, II 1, 6
  avoids et quidem, I 35; and idcirco, I 39
  uses appositional phrases, II 75
sancire, I 35
sane, II 21
  age sane, 'well, well,' II 119
sanguis, 'flesh and blood,' I 34
sapere, I 25

sapiens, I 40
sapiens Epicureus, I 40, 61
sapiens semper beatus, I 62
sapientia, I 43
sapientia =φρόνησις, I 42; II 51
Sardanapallus, II 106
sat, satis, I 47
satis praesidi, II 84
satis sit (erit) dictum, I 37
satisfacere, one word, I 15
satisne, II 15
Scaevola, I 8
Sceptics, I 64
schola, II 1 (thesis), 67 (school)
Schopenhauer, I 37
scientia divinarum rerum, II 37
sciscere, I 23
scotinus, II 15
scribere ad aliquem (alicui), I 8
se, suus, sibi with indef. reference, I 67; II 78
sed ecce, I 61
sed...(et) autem, I 10
sed resumptive, II 107
sedatio animi, I 64
selectio, II 43
semper boni plus, II 57; cf. semper plus voluptatis, II 95
Seneca on Epicurus, I 37; II 11
senses, foundation of everything, I 30, 64
  contrasted with mind, I 63
sententia, II 37
sentire, I 31
sentire =censere, II 6
seorsum (deorsum), I 18
separation of grammatically connected words (non tam id reprehendunt), I 1
septem, II 7
sequĕre, II 76
  quae secuntur, II 23
sequi, 'to make one's aim,' II 78
sequitur aliquid aliquem, I 32
sequitur ut, II 6
sero sentire, I 60
Sextilius, II 55
si, and cum, II 15 [cp. Orat. 170 (Abrincensis)]
si repeated, I 69
si...sive; si...sin, I 20
si maxime, I 2
si quis quid quaereret, II 76
si quod ‖ aliquod, I 55
sic, followed by defining clause, II 13
sic definiunt with accusative, II 13
sic quemadmodum, I 39
sic ut, I 11
sicine, I 34
sicut alia, I 7
signiferi, I 9

Silanus, I 24
similiter et (ac), II 21
similitudines transferre, II 45
simul et (ut), II 33
simulacrum, I 21
sine causa, I 34
singular, see number
situm est in nobis, I 57
Socrates, II 1, 90
sole illustriora, I 71
solem...nec orientem, etc., II 23
soliditas, of atoms, I 17; I 18 (solidus)
sollicitare aut angere, I 41
solus (sapiens solus), I 44
solutus, adj., I 33
sonare, II 6
Sophists, I 50; II 1
sorites, I 37
species, II 107
speculum, II 32
splendidus eques, II 58
splendor nominis, I 42
sponte sua, II 83
squilla, II 24
st!, II 94
stabilis sententia, I 55
stabilitas, II 9, 16
stans (stabilis) voluptas, I 37; II 31,
    75
statue (=constitue), I 41
Stoicism, I 18
    ἀρετή, I 42, 61 (Stoici); II 34
    logic, I 63
    on cupiditas, II 27
    rejects Scepticism, I 64
    Stoical views, II 43, 44, 45, 86,
        115
    τὸ καλόν, I 42; II 45
    view of pleasure, II 31, 33, 34, 37
study v. pleasure, I 25
stulti, I 57
stultus and sapiens, I 59
suadeo, constr., II 95
suavitas, I 37
subducere, II 78
subicere, constr., II 48
subici (vis vocibus), II 6
subirasci, II 12
subject to verb thrown into next
    clause, II 60
sublatio animi, II 13
successio, I 37
sui memoria, II 101
suicide, I 49
    Epicurean views on, I 62
summa philosophia, II 100
summa voluptas, II 89
summative clauses, II 41, 113
sun's apparent size, I 20
suscipere vitam, II 87
suus, 'original,' I 17
Syracusanae mensae, II 92

tabula of Cleanthes, II 69
tacitulus taxim, II 24 n. on ut iactare
Tacitus, I 27, 39 (bis), 62; II 6, 29
tam (non tam), I 1
tam multus ‖ tantus, I 1
tam nil, II 22
tamen, I 15
    after quodsi, I 51
    proleptic, II 118
    resumptive, II 23 n.
    sed tamen, II 105
tamen, 'after all,' II 31
tamquam, I 13
    in tentative rendering, I 42
tangere locum, I 9
tanta natura (-ae), II 28
tanta tot, I 25
tanta volumina, II 68
Tantalus, I 60
tanto opere, elliptic, I 10
tantum=tanto opere, I 5
tantum abest ut, followed by cate-
    goric clause, II 54
tantum patior, II 27
tantum satis esse, I 30
Tarentini bilingual, I 7
tautology, I 5; II 78; see also repeti-
    tion
tegere se, I 35
temperantia, II 73
tempora=καιροί, I 32, 33
tendere (quid tendit?), II 16
tenebrio, I 61 n.
tenere...tueri, I 67; II 11
tenere se, II 21
tense, see verb
terminare, I 38
theatrum and life, I 49
Themista, II 68
thesauri, II 67
Thorius Balbus, II 63
time in relation to happiness, I 63
timere, constr., I 34
timidus ad, II 63
timor maximarum rerum, II 86
titillare, titillatio, I 39
tollere sensus, I 64
tongere, tongitio, II 21
tormina, II 96
Torquatus, A., II 72
torques, I 23
torrens, of speech, II 3
tot et tanta, II 68
totum id, id totum, II 89
tradere se constringendum, II 62
tranquillitas, I 43
tranquillus joined with quietus, I 71
transfer idem, II 60
transferre=μεταφέρειν, I 7; II 10
Tritanus, I 9
tua (causa tua (tui)), II 76
Tubulus, II 54

tueri, I 6
tueri aut retinere, II 71
tum ‖ tunc, I 28; II 33
tum etiam without cum preceding,
   II 53
tum...tum, II 30
turbulenter, II 15
turma, I 9

u dropt in scansion, I 9
ubi 'what becomes of,' II 95
ubi aut quod, II 7
ubi niteretur, II 43
ultima duo, II 18
ultimum, extremum, etc., I 17
unum, emphatic, II 22
unus de multis, II 66
urbanitas, I 7; II 103
uri, II 88
usurpare = nominare, II 118
ususfructus, I 12
ut, aeque ut, I 67
   change of construction affecting,
     I 24, 45
   clause, II 6
   concedere ut, II 6
   concessive, I 55
   elaborare ut, I 10
   eodem modo ut, etc., II 33
   est ut, II 6
   fore ut, futurum ut, I 1
   in confirming clauses (si probaret,
     ut probat), II 18
   in questions with ubi? quid? etc.,
     II 61
   integrum est ut, II 6
   is ut, II 64
   ne non for, after a verb of fearing,
     I 34
   nihil ut, ut nihil, I 34
   non ut and quo, II 42
   simul ut, II 33
   parenthetic, II 15, 17, 41, 109
   position, I 72
   repeated, I 34, 69
   ut...sic, not corresponding, I 3
ut ad minima veniam, I 32
ut aut, aut ut, I 33
ut ita dicam, II 11, 45
ut ne, I 70; II 24
ut non, II 71
ut omittam, I 24
uti, 'find to be,' I 2
utinam ne in nemore, I 5
utrumque, II 18; τὸ σύνολον, II 20

vacillare, I 66
vacuitas doloris, II 8
vagiens puer, II 31
valde, II 9
Valerius Corvinus, I 23
vapio, I 61

variari, I 38; II 10
varietatem facere, II 10, 75
Varro πολυγραφώτατος, I 11
   and Lucilius, II 38
vas ad mortem (mortis), II 79
ve (non faciendumve), I 47
vectigalia, II 84
vel dicam, I 10
velle (se velle esse sapientem), 'to
   claim to be a philosopher,' II 102
venatio, II 23, 107
vendibilis, I 12
veneno est, II 59
vera ratio, I 43, 52
Verbs, carried on from sentence to
   sentence, II 35
   juxtaposed, II 33, 68
   see change
concord
   indef. subject, II 90
   plural with disjoined subjects,
     II 73
   singular with two subjects con-
     nected by et...et, I 25, 53;
     II 66
   subject thrown into following
     clause, II 60
forms
   decesse, II 10
   dixti, II 10
gerund
   quarum potiendi spe, I 60
   venandi = venationis, I 69
gerundive
   from verb not governing acc., I 3
   with a, ab, II 30
   with notion of possibility, I 6
   without esse, I 43
mood
   change with quia, I 32
   see change, conditional sentence
   indicative
   aequius erat, II 119
   among subjunctives, I 10
   and subj., II 12
   for subj. (et vetuit), I 24
   in causal clause, I 10; and subj.,
     ib.
   with si, II 44
   infinitive
   acc. and inf. with definire, II 5
   act. and pass. joined, II 21
   after desitum est, II 43
   after est and noun (ludus est), I 27
   as noun, I 1; II 9
   as noun in acc., II 18, 86; with
     prep., II 43
   exclamatory, II 29
   inf. act. and pass. after impers.,
     I 30
   inf. clause and ut clause inter-
     changing, II 6

Verbs, **mood**, *infinitive (cont.)*
inf. clause dep. on noun, II 99
inf. pass. with velle, II 103; other
  verbs of desire, II 21
inf. with persto, insto, II 107
with epithet (quale), II 86
subjunctive
after sunt qui, I 31
and indic. in rel. clauses, I 6, 10,
  11, 14, 17, 23, 27, 30 (or. obl.),
  37, 38, 43, 66, 68; II 15, 72, 77,
  106, 119
by assimilation, I 52
causal, I 52
concessive (dictum sit), I 37
delib. not common with verbs of
  thinking, II 117
in or. obl., I 19
in quod clauses (n. on percussit),123
iterative, II 68
jussive, I 35
potential (quam vellet), II 57
pres. in appeal, II 77
quod arguerent, I 24
quod dicat..., I 4
with cum, II 68; with cum (ind.
  and subj.), I 23
with quia, I 53; cf. I 32
with quidquid, II 117
participle
nominalized part. or adj. with
  another adj., II 54
fut. as adj., II 63
pass. with temporal force, II 1
perf. pass. as adj., II 79
pres. =adjective in -κός, II 21
pres. +obj. (desperantes omnia),
  I 61
pres. as abbreviated clause, I 17
tense
assimilation, II 39
change, I 63; II 86, 88; *see* change,
  conditional sentence
fut. and fut. perf., I 69
fut. and fut. perf. in cum clause,
  I 7
fut. perf. ind. (potuerit), I 69
fut. perf. ind. followed by perf.
  subj., II 4
perf. of repeated action, I 16
perf., with dum slightly causal,
  II 43
plup. subj. for imperf., II 54
plup. subj. in cum-clause after
  pres. infin. (expeti cum accessisset), II 82
pres., continuous, I 29
sequence of tenses not mechanical,
  II 63
verbal nouns
=possibility, I 33, 70; II 94

Verbs, **verbal nouns** *(cont.)*
tend to concinnitas, I 37
with passive sense, I 37
verecundius, II 114
vereor, constr., I 34
impers., II 39
verisimile est, constr., II 6
vero, II 10
versare, II 99
verus amicus, II 85
vesci =frui, II 10
Vescia, Veseris, I 23
vesper, vespera, vespere, II 92 n.
vespero, vespillo, I 61 n.
veteres, II 114
via, 'the right way,' I 29; II 44
via ad aliquid, I 63
via vitae, I 71
viam ‖ vim, I 63
victi et debilitati, I 47
video, 'read,' II 2
videor =mihi videor, II 15
videre non posse, II 67
videro, I 35; II 9
vir bonus, bonus vir, II 71
vir =homo, II 119
Virgil, II 30
and Epicureanism, I 20
virtus =decus =laus, II 44
  =ars, II 115
vis loquendi, II 30
vis naturae, II 28, 58
vituperatores philosophiae, I 2
vivere cum voluptate, I 41
vivitur populari fama, II 50
vix aut ne vix quidem, II 111
voce inani sonare, II 48
vocet ad se, I 54
vociferari, II 51
volgus (in), II 15
volo esse, II 108
voluptarius, II 65
voluptas, implies utilitas, I 34, 42;
  II 61
in motu voluptas, II 16
not among prima naturae, II 34
voluptas =commodum, II 58
voluptas animi, I 40, 55
voluptas movens, I 37; II 31
voluptatem accipere, II 6
vox naturae, I 71

words in different senses coming
  close together, I 35

Xerxes, II 112

Zeno, Epicurean, I 16
Stoic, II 17
zeugma, II 88
Zeuxis, II 115

ἀβλεψία, I 33
αἱρετόν, I 11, 23
ἀκρισία, I 61
ἀληθινὴ φιλοσοφία, I 40, 43
ἀλλοτριοῦσθαι, I 30
ἀλλόφυλον, I 30
ἀμφίβολα, I 22
ἀνεμπόδιστος, I 40
ἀνοχλησία, ἀοχλησία, I 37; II 8, 11
ἀνταπόδοσις, I 53
ἀντικοπή, I 17
ἀπάθεια, I 37; II, 11
ἀπειρία, I 21
ἀπονία, I 37; II 11
ἀποφυγὴ λυπῶν, I 37
ἀρεταὶ διανοητικαί, II 113
ἀρετή as τέχνη, I 42
ἀρχαί, I 30, 42, 72
ἀρχιτέκτων, I 42
ἀσωτοδιδάσκαλος, II 30
ἀταραξία, I 50, 64
αὐτάρκεια, I 62
ἀφορμή, I 42
ἀχαριστία, I 57

βίος τέλειος, II 87
βωμόλοχος, II 22

γαλήνη, γαληνίζειν, I 43
γαργαλίζειν, -σμός, I 39
γαστήρ, I 55

δείκελα, I 21
δέχεσθαι τὰ διδόμενα, II 82
διαβλέπειν, II 97
διαλεκτική, I 22
δίνη, I 20
δίοψις, II 97
δόγμα, II 28

εἴδωλα, I 21
ἔκδετος, ἔκδοτος, I 47
ἔμφυτος, ἐμφύεσθαι, I 31
ἐναργές, I 42; II 6
ἐπαίρεσθαι, I 57
ἐπαναφέρειν τι εἴς τι, I 11, 23
ἐπιχαιρεκακία, I 61
ἐρώτημα, I 39
εὐαρεστεῖσθαι, I 30
εὐδαιμονία, I 11; II 86
εὐκαιρία, I 32
εὐπόριστος, I 46
εὐστάθεια, I 40, 61
εὐσταθὲς σαρκὸς κατάστημα, II 9
εὐταξία, II 73

ἥδεσθαι, ἡδονή, I 55
ἡδονὴ ἐν κινήσει, στάσει, I 37
ἡμερόκοιτος, I 61
ἡσυχία, I 43

θηριώδης, I 59, 61

καλόν, τό, I 61; II 35

κανονικόν, I 63
καταλαμβάνεσθαι, I 30
καταστηματικὴ ἡδονή, I 37; II 9
κορυφαῖος, I 26
κριτήριον, I 22=pleasure+pain, I 30

λεκτόν, I 63; II 6
λέξις, I 10
λογική, I 22

μαθήματα, I 71
μεσότης, II 27
μεταφέρειν, II 10

οἴησις, I 43
οἰκειοῦσθαι, I 30; οἰκείωσις, II 35
ὁμόφυλον, I 30
ὁρμή, I 42; II 32
ὅρος, I 38

πάθος, I 30; II 13
παρέγκλισις, I 19
πέρας, I 38
περιπλοκή, I 19
πληγή, I 18
ποικίλλεσθαι, I 38
πόνος, I 56
προδιδάσκειν, I 69
πρόληψις, I 30, 31; II 6
προσκρούειν, I 30
πρῶτα κατὰ φύσιν, II 33

σάρξ, I 55
σκοτεινός (Heraclitus), II 15
σοφίσματα, I 22
σοφός, Epicurean, I 62; Laelius, σοφός, II 24, 46
στάσις (inner), I 58
συλλογίζεσθαι, συλλογισμός, I 22, 30
συμπεραίνειν, συμπέρασμα, I 30
σχέσεις, I 17
σωφροσύνη, II 73

ταραχή, I 37
τερατολόγος, I 61
τετραφάρμακος, II 21
τέχνη τοῦ βίου, I 42
τρόπος, I 29
τύχη, I 63

ὕλη, I 18

φεύγειν, I 30
φευκτά, I 11, 23, 30
φρόνησις=sapientia, I 42
φύσει δίκαιον, φύσεως δίκαιον, I 50
φυσιολογία, I 64, 71
φυσιόλογος, II 15

χαρά, χαίρειν, I 55
χάρις, I 57
χορός, I 26
χρυσίζον, II 23

CAMBRIDGE
Printed by W. LEWIS
at the University Press